Rebecca Sudworth. 1987.

D0667701

FILM GENRE READER

FILM GENRE READER

edited by BARRY KEITH GRANT

University of Texas Press, Austin

Copyright © 1986 by the University of Texas Press
All rights reserved
Printed in the United States of America

First edition, 1986

Requests for permission to reproduce material from this work should be sent to:
  Permissions
  University of Texas Press
  Box 7819
  Austin, Texas 78713-7819

LIBRARY OF CONGRESS CATALOGING-IN-PUBLICATION DATA

Film genre reader.
  Chiefly reprints of articles originally published
1970–1984.
  Bibliography: p.
  Includes index.
  1. Film genres. 2. Moving-picture plays—History and
criticism. I. Grant, Barry Keith, 1947–   .
PN1995.F4579 1986   791.43'01'5   86-11228
ISBN 0-292-72436-5
ISBN 0-292-72455-1 (pbk.)

Since this page cannot legibly accommodate all the copyright notices, the following pages constitute an extension of the copyright page.

Chapters 1, 4, 5, 9, 12, 17, and 19 previously appeared in *Film Genre: Theory and Criticism,* edited by Barry K. Grant (Metuchen, N.J.: Scarecrow Press, 1977) and are republished here by permission of Scarecrow Press.

PN
1995
.F4579
1986

ACKNOWLEDGMENTS

ANDREW TUDOR. "Genre," from *Theories of Film* (New York: Viking Press, 1973), 131–150. Copyright © 1973 by Andrew Tudor. Reprinted by permission of the Viking Press and Martin Secker & Warburg Ltd.

EDWARD BUSCOMBE. "The Idea of Genre in the American Cinema," from *Screen* 11, no. 2 (March–April 1970): 33–45. Copyright © 1970 by *Screen*. Reprinted by permission.

RICK ALTMAN. "A Semantic/Syntactic Approach to Film Genre," appeared originally in a slightly different form in *Cinema Journal* 23, no. 3 (Spring 1984): 6–18. Copyright © 1984 by *Cinema Journal*. Reprinted by permission.

JUDITH HESS WRIGHT. "Genre Films and the Status Quo," from *Jump Cut*, no. 1 (May–June 1974): 1, 16, 18. Copyright © 1974 by *Jump Cut*. Reprinted by permission of *Jump Cut* and the author.

JEAN-LOUP BOURGET. "Social Implications in the Hollywood Genres," from *Journal of Modern Literature* 3, no. 2 (April 1973): 191–200. Copyright © 1973 by *Journal of Modern Literature*. Reprinted by permission of *Journal of Modern Literature*.

ROBIN WOOD. "Ideology, Genre, Auteur," from *Film Comment* 13, no. 1 (January–February 1977): 46–51. Copyright © 1977 by Robin Wood. Reprinted by permission of the author.

BARBARA KLINGER. "'Cinema/Ideology/Criticism' Revisited: The Progressive Genre," appeared originally in a slightly different form as "'Cinema/Ideology/Criticism'—The Progressive Text," in *Screen* 25, no. 1 (January–February 1984): 30–44. Copyright © 1984 by *Screen*. Reprinted by permission of *Screen* and the author.

THOMAS SCHATZ. "The Structural Influence: New Directions in Film Genre Study," from *Quarterly Review of Film Studies* 2, no. 3 (August 1977): 302–312. Copyright © Redgrave Publishing Company, Bedford Hills, New York. Reprinted by permission of Redgrave Publishing Company.

THOMAS SOBCHACK. "Genre Films: A Classical Experience," from *Litera-ture/Film Quarterly* 3, no. 3 (Summer 1975): 196–204. Copyright © 1975 by *Literature/Film Quarterly*. Reprinted by permission.

DOUGLAS PYE. From "Genre and Movies," from *Movie*, no. 20 (Spring 1975): 29–43. Copyright © 1975 by *Movie*. Reprinted by permission of *Movie* and the author.

EDWARD MITCHELL. "Apes and Essences: Some Sources of Significance in American Gangster Films," from *Wide Angle* 1, no. 1 (1976): 18–23. Copyright © 1976 by Johns Hopkins University Press. Reprinted by permission of Johns Hopkins University Press and the author.

PAUL SCHRADER. "Notes on Film Noir," from *Film Comment* 8, no. 1 (Spring 1972): 8–13. Copyright © 1972 by Film Comment Publishing Corp. Reprinted by permission of The Film Society of Lincoln Center.

JOHN G. CAWELTI. "*Chinatown* and Generic Transformation in Recent Ameri-can Films," from *Film Theory and Criticism*, 2d ed., edited by Gerald Mast and Marshall Cohen (New York: Oxford University Press, 1979), 559–579. Copy-right © 1979 by John G. Cawelti. Reprinted by permission of the author.

MAURICE YACOWAR. "The Bug in the Rug: Notes on the Disaster Genre," from *Film Genre: Theory and Criticism*, edited by Barry K. Grant (Metuchen, N.J.: Scarecrow Press, 1977), 90–107. Copyright © 1976 by Maurice Yacowar. Re-printed by permission of Scarecrow Press and the author.

MARGARET TARRATT. "Monsters from the Id," from *Films and Filming* 17, no. 3 (December 1970): 38–42, and no. 4 (January 1971): 40–42. Copyright © 1970 by Margaret Tarratt. Reprinted by permission.

THOMAS ELSAESSER. "Tales of Sound and Fury: Observations on the Family Melodrama," from *Monogram*, no. 4 (1973): 2–15. Copyright © 1985 by the British Film Institute. Reprinted by permission of the author and the British Film Institute.

BRIAN HENDERSON. "Romantic Comedy Today: Semi-Tough or Impossible?" appeared originally in a slightly different form in *Film Quarterly* 31, no. 4 (Sum-mer 1978): 11–23. Copyright © 1978 by The Regents of the University of Cali-fornia. Reprinted by permission of The Regents and the author.

JANE FEUER. "The Self-Reflexive Musical and the Myth of Entertainment," from *Quarterly Review of Film Studies* 2, no. 3 (August 1977): 313–326. Copy-right © Redgrave Publishing Company, Bedford Hills, New York. Reprinted by permission of Redgrave Publishing Company.

Stills courtesy of Cinemabilia, New York City; George Eastman House, Rochester, N.Y.; Museum of Modern Art Film Stills Archive, New York City; and the Cana-dian National Film, TV and Sound Archives, Ottawa, Ontario.

For Genevieve, with love

Contents

Introduction   xi

Part One: Theory

1. Genre   ANDREW TUDOR   3
2. The Idea of Genre in the American Cinema
   EDWARD BUSCOMBE   11
3. A Semantic/Syntactic Approach to Film Genre
   RICK ALTMAN   26
4. Genre Films and the Status Quo   JUDITH HESS WRIGHT   41
5. Social Implications in the Hollywood Genres
   JEAN-LOUP BOURGET   50
6. Ideology, Genre, Auteur   ROBIN WOOD   59
7. "Cinema/Ideology/Criticism" Revisited: The Progressive
   Genre   BARBARA KLINGER   74
8. The Structural Influence: New Directions in Film Genre
   Study   THOMAS SCHATZ   91
9. Genre Film: A Classical Experience   THOMAS SOBCHACK   102
10. Experience and Meaning in Genre Films
    BARRY KEITH GRANT   114
11. Genre and Performance: An Overview
    RICHARD DE CORDOVA   129

Part Two: Selected Genre Criticism

12. The Western (Genre and Movies)   DOUGLAS PYE   143
13. Apes and Essences: Some Sources of Significance in the American
    Gangster Film   EDWARD MITCHELL   159
14. Notes on Film Noir   PAUL SCHRADER   169
15. *Chinatown* and Generic Transformation in Recent American
    Films   JOHN G. CAWELTI   183
16. Shoot-Out at the Genre Corral: Problems in the "Evolution" of the
    Western   TAG GALLAGHER   202
17. The Bug in the Rug: Notes on the Disaster Genre
    MAURICE YACOWAR   217
18. Children of the Light   BRUCE F. KAWIN   236
19. Monsters from the Id   MARGARET TARRATT   258

20. Tales of Sound and Fury: Observations on the Family
    Melodrama   THOMAS ELSAESSER   278
21. Romantic Comedy Today: Semi-Tough or Impossible?
    BRIAN HENDERSON   309
22. The Self-Reflexive Musical and the Myth of Entertainment
    JANE FEUER   329
23. Footnote to Fact: The Docudrama   SETH FELDMAN   344
24. The Body Snatchers: Genre and Canadian Cinema
    JIM LEACH   357

Bibliography   371

Notes on Contributors   405

Index   409

Introduction

Stated simply, genre movies are those commercial feature films which, through repetition and variation, tell familiar stories with familiar characters in familiar situations. They also encourage expectations and experiences similar to those of similar films we have already seen. Genre movies have comprised the bulk of film practice, the iceberg of film history beneath the visible tip that in the past has commonly been understood as film art. They have been exceptionally significant as well in establishing the popular sense of cinema as a cultural and economic institution, particularly in the United States, where Hollywood studios early on adopted an industrial model based on mass production. Traditionally, Hollywood movies have been produced in a profit-motivated studio system which, as the result of sound business practice, has sought to guarantee acceptance at the box office by the exploitation and variation of commercially successful formulas. In this system, praised for the "genius" of its efficiency by André Bazin, genre movies are the Model T's or the Colt revolvers with interchangeable parts.

Yet despite this central place of genre in the cinema, critical recognition of its importance is a relatively recent development. The first significant essays of film genre criticism, Robert Warshow's articles on the gangster film and the western (originally published in the *Partisan Review* in 1948 and 1954, respectively) and Bazin's two pieces on the western from the early fifties, were all written within a few years of each other. Chronologically, genre criticism thus narrowly predates the early work of auteurism, but it developed more slowly because it failed to enjoy the popularization that heralded the arrival of director-oriented "theory," first in Great Britain and then North America through the writings of Andrew Sarris. Valorizing the artist responsible for the dubious art of film, auteur criticism proved at the time more amenable to the serious discussion of cinema.

It is not surprising that Warshow and Bazin focused on westerns and gangster films, since these have been perhaps the two most durable of American film genres, beginning with *The Great Train Robbery* (Edwin S.

Porter, 1903) and *The Musketeers of Pig Alley* (D. W. Griffith, 1912). To-day it seems clear that these essays suffer from an impressionism and pre-scriptiveness that, while unfortunate, is also not uncharacteristic of later genre criticism. Yet the flaws in these first essays are readily understand-able, given that they were unprecedented and written at a time when genres were undergoing radical change after a period of relative stability. Indeed, despite their problems, they have also pointed the way for many of the concerns of later critics. For example, Warshow was extremely per-ceptive in the essay on gangster films about the essential dynamics of the genre and the satisfactions it typically provides the viewer; thus he antici-pated one of the central topics of more sophisticated contemporary film theory—the "positioning" or "construction" of the spectating subject. His cogent observation that "the real city . . . produces only criminals; the imaginary city produces the gangster" reveals that in some way he understood genre as a system of conventions structured according to cul-tural values, an idea not dissimilar to what structuralists would more re-cently call the "deep structure" of myth. Warshow's distinction initiated the now generally accepted separation of historical verisimilitude (but not history) from the analysis of genre, which is the way it had most often been discussed before. In addition, this acknowledgment of a difference between actual social restraints ("the real city") and the structures of the imaginative escape from it ("the imaginary city") adumbrates the project of later leftist critics in deconstructing the processes, what Roland Barthes would call the mythologies, by which ideology contains and reinforces itself.

While the work of these two critics may be seen as crucial to the devel-opment of a more rigorous genre criticism, however, in another sense they were only attempts at articulating concepts already implicitly under-stood by filmmakers and viewers alike. Well before their articles were first published, the idea of genre circulated in public thinking, if not in critical discourse. Films were loosely typed by producers, audiences, and even re-viewers: a movie was a "western" or a "war movie" or a "musical," and such descriptive labels came to signal information to prospective consum-ers about the story and kind of pleasure it was likely to offer. Only after this economic relation was firmly established was it possible for critics to realize that if those handy descriptive tags actually referred to true tradi-tions of film practice, then they might be worth identifying and analyz-ing. *Genre* thus became a critical term as well as a collection of popular categories, and it has since proven a useful conceptual tool for under-standing popular film as both art and artifact.

As film study developed in the seventies, interest in the narrative film, nurtured a decade earlier by auteurism's enthusiasm for popular Ameri-can movies, began to wane in favor of more formal concerns. Critical interest shifted from the signified of films to the practice of signification, from what a film "means" to how it produces meaning. Accordingly, both nonnarrative, experimental films and those that somehow broke with the seamless, "classical" construction of Hollywood narrative (what Noel Burch has called the "institutional mode of representation"), received an increasing degree of critical attention. At the same time, a heightened concern with the operation of ideology in art, stimulated by the importation to film of theoretical work by John Berger, Louis Althusser, Brecht, Freud, and others, shattered the operating assumption that an understanding of a film's director and his or her *oeuvre* would provide the key to interpretation. Rather, meaning was now seen to arise from the conjunction of various discursive codes at work in the film text, of which the directorial code was only one. Fuller, Hawks, and Hitchcock became, in the famous formulation by Peter Wollen in the revised edition of *Signs and Meaning in the Cinema* (1972), "Fuller," "Hawks," and "Hitchcock"—that is, filmic structures designated by the name appearing on the director's credit. As Barthes had shown, writing degree zero, a discourse that exists outside ideology, is impossible.

Eventually, this emphasis on signification and ideology brought about a renewed interest in the classical narrative film, and genre films in particular became an important site of inquiry. The general view of popular film now was that it was little more than bourgeois illusionism, essentially conservative in both style and theme. Genres therefore existed primarily as mythic edifices to be deconstructed. They were valuable for study because generic analysis could easily involve the consideration of economic and historical contexts (conditions of production and consumption), conventions and mythic functions (semiotic codes and structural patterns), and the place of particular filmmakers within genres (tradition and the individual auteur). Thus genre criticism has been able to accommodate the interests of the newer approaches to film, and in fact may be seen as a locus of the overlapping but often separate concerns of auteurism, Marxism, semiology, and structuralism. At this point in genre criticism, though, it would seem that genre films are not viewed solely with suspicion as mythic embodiments of the dominant ideology. In the last few years, for example, leftist critics have made a convincing case for reading many contemporary horror films as critiques of American society rather than as endorsements of its fears and repressions. While it is true that genre movies tell familiar stories with familiar characters in familiar situations, it by no means follows that they do so in ways that are completely familiar.

The intention of *Film Genre Reader* is to gather together some of the best work on genre produced in recent years. The book is divided into two sections, the first concentrating on theory and the second on criticism. As the essays in Part One were generally written earlier than those in the second section, it is recommended that this part be read first. However, at the same time it should be noted that the anthology was not conceived as a definitive history of genre criticism. A number of important essays, such as those by Warshow and Bazin as well as Susan Sontag's important 1965 article on science fiction movies, have not been included for the practical reason that they are all readily available elsewhere. Nor are the essays here presented in a strict chronological arrangement; rather, they proceed in a manner that should help the reader to achieve a progressive understanding of film genre. (One further stylistic note: the first mention in each essay of a film is followed parenthetically by the name of the director and the year of release. This is not meant to suggest an auteurist bias but to provide the reader with information necessary for further research and for locating the films in distributors' catalogues.)

Part One begins with Andrew Tudor's consideration of some of the problems arising in the very attempt to delineate individual genres. Edward Buscombe next offers a partial solution to Tudor's dilemma by theorizing a distinction, adapted from literary criticism, between a film's "outer forms" (iconography) and "inner forms" (themes) and by discussing their relationship. Rick Altman then suggests a way to approach the range of works within individual genres by introducing concepts borrowed from linguistics. The social and political implications of genres and of individual genre films are discussed by both Judith Hess Wright and Jean-Loup Bourget; yet they present almost diametrically opposed arguments. For Wright, genre films act as conservative reaffirmations of dominant values because they are grounded in the predictability of conventions, while Bourget sees them as possessing the ability to become subversive statements for precisely this reason. Robin Wood then considers this issue in relation to the place of the auteur by contrasting some of the genre work of Alfred Hitchcock and Frank Capra. The political issues raised by Wright, Bourget, and Wood are then placed by Barbara Klinger within the influential theoretical framework for categorizing the relation of all narrative films to ideology originally proposed by Jean-Louis Comolli and Jean Narboni. Next, Thomas Schatz offers an overview of the ways in which structuralism has been applied to film genre. The special kind of experience engendered by genre films is discussed in Thomas Sobchack's essay as well as my own. Part One concludes with Richard de Cordova's discussion of performance, a largely ignored area of genre study, and its function in a number of different genres. Thus the essays in this part introduce a range of approaches to film genre, many of them critically applied in the second section.

Each of the selections of Part Two treats a particular genre from a somewhat different perspective, and together they provide a comprehensive overview of applied genre criticism. Since the western is perhaps the wellspring of film genre and since it has been subjected to the most sustained analyses, this section begins with a discussion of this genre by Douglas Pye, employing the concept of modes as outlined in the work of Northrop Frye. The history and social myths that contributed to the development of the gangster film, a genre that shares many elements with the western, are then examined by Edward Mitchell. Paul Schrader discusses film noir primarily from a stylistic perspective, and although he begins by asserting that film noir is actually not a genre, it would seem that his analysis, and the work of later critics, has demonstrated that it may indeed be considered as one. John G. Cawelti and Tag Gallagher both address the question of generic alteration or "evolution," and once again there is a marked difference of opinion. While Cawelti identifies distinct modes of change in recent genre films, Gallagher seriously challenges the accuracy of the commonly held evolutionary view. Maurice Yacowar's essay on the disaster film seeks to define a typology of that genre, while Bruce Kawin offers a useful distinction between horror and science fiction, a matter that has proven more difficult for film than for literature. Margaret Tarratt next discusses the narratives of science fiction films from a Freudian perspective, an approach also found in the stylistic analysis of melodrama by Thomas Elsaesser. Romantic comedy as a specific genre within the comic mode is examined by Brian Henderson, and his acknowledgment of audience reception as an important element of genre analysis is seen in the next two essays, Jane Feuer's analysis of the musical's mythic functions and Seth Feldman's discussion of the relatively new genre of docudrama. As one might expect, genre criticism has concentrated on the American cinema, and the essays collected in this volume are no exception. But such questions as the relation of genre to ideology have ramifications beyond Hollywood. From Japanese samurai films to Italian westerns to French gangster films, almost all national cinemas have been influenced to some degree by American genre movies. Feldman's essay begins to explore genre and national contexts, and this approach is considered in greater detail by Jim Leach's discussion of the relation between Hollywood genres and the Canadian feature film industry. This essay, which concludes Part Two, may serve as a vivid example of how genres work across national boundaries.

This collection may of course be read in the order presented, or in groups concerned with similar issues. For example, an examination of genre and ideology would include, among others, the essays by Wright, Bourget, Wood, Klinger, Leach, Elsaesser, and Feuer. The relation between genre and auteur is examined in the selections by Bourget, Wood, Cawelti, and Gallagher. Or the complexities of genre and the viewing experience would connect the essays by Sobchack, Kawin, Henderson, Feldman, and myself. Other groupings are certainly possible, and however one chooses to use the book, it should provide both the general reader and the student of film with a comprehensive view of film genre. And the clear difference of opinion among many of these essays should make for interesting reading and lively debate.

B.K.G.

FILM GENRE READER

Part One: THEORY

1. Genre

ANDREW TUDOR

Auteur originated in film criticism of the recent past; *genre* had a lengthy pedigree in literary criticism long before the advent of the cinema. Hence the meaning and uses of the latter term vary considerably, and it is very difficult to identify even a tenuous school of thought on the subject. For years it provided a crudely useful way of delineating the American cinema. The literature abounds with references to the western, the gangster movie, or the horror film, all of which are loosely thought of as genres. On occasion it becomes almost the end point of the critical process to fit a film into such a category, much as it once made a film "intelligible" to fit it into, say, the French "nouvelle vague." To call a film a western is thought of as somehow saying something interesting or important about it. To fit it into a class of films suggests we presumably have some general knowledge about it. To say a film is a western is immediately to say that it shares some indefinable "X" with other films we call westerns. In addition, it provides us with a body of films to which our film can be usefully compared—sometimes the only body of films. The most extreme, and clearly ridiculous, application might be to argue that it is necessarily more illuminating to compare, say, *The Man Who Shot Liberty Valance* (John Ford, 1962) with a Roy Rogers short than with *The Last Hurrah* (Ford, 1958). It is not that the first comparison might not be instructive; merely that it is not necessarily the case. Extreme genre imperialism leads in this direction.

Now almost everyone uses terms like "western," the neurotic critic as much as the undisturbed cinemagoer. The difference, and the source of difficulty, lies in how the critic seeks to use the term. What is normally a thumbnail classification for everyday purposes is now being asked to carry rather more weight. The fact that there is a special term, *genre*, for these categories suggests that the critic's conception of "western" is more complex than is the case in everyday discourse; if not, why the special term? But in what way critical usage is more complex is not entirely clear.

Note: This chapter is excerpted from a longer essay published previously.

In some cases it involves the idea that if a film is a western it somehow draws on a tradition—in particular, on a set of conventions. That is, westerns have in common certain themes, certain typical actions, certain characteristic mannerisms; to experience a western is to operate within this previously defined world. Jim Kitses tries to isolate characteristics in this way by defining *genre* in terms of such attributes: ". . . a varied and flexible structure, a thematically fertile and ambiguous world of historical material shot through with archetypal elements which are themselves ever in flux." [1] But other usages, such as "horror" films, might also mean films displaying certain themes, actions, and so on, or, just as often, films that have in common the *intention* to horrify. Instead of defining the genre by attributes, it is defined by intentions. Likewise with the distinction between "gangster" movies and "thrillers."

Both these uses display serious problems. The second (and for all practical purposes least important) suffers from the notorious difficulties of isolating intentions. In the first and more common case the special genre term is frequently entirely redundant. Imagine a definition of a western as a film set in the western United States between 1860 and 1900 and involving as its central theme the contrast between garden and desert. Any film fulfilling these requirements is a western, and a western is only a film fulfilling these requirements. By multiplying such categories it is possible to divide all films into groups, though not necessarily mutually exclusive groups. The usefulness of this (and classification can only be justified by its use) depends on what it is meant to achieve. But what is certain is that just as the critic determines the criteria on which the classification is based, so he or she also determines the name given to the resultant groups of films. Our group might just as well be called "type 1482/9a" as "westerns."

Evidently there are areas in which such individually defined categories might be of some use: a sort of bibliographic classification of the history of film, for instance, or even an abstract exploration of the cyclical recurrence of certain themes. The films would be simply defined in terms of the presence or absence of the themes in question. But this is not the way in which the term is usually employed. On the contrary, most writers tend to assume that there is some body of films we can safely call the western and then move on to the real work—the analysis of the crucial characteristics of the already recognized genre. Hence Kitses' set of thematic antinomies and four sorts of genre conventions. Or Bazin's distinction between classic and "sur-western," assuming, as it does, that there is some independently established essence of the western that is distilled into *Stagecoach* (Ford, 1939).[2] These writers, and almost all writers using the term *genre*, are caught in a dilemma. They are defining a western on the basis of analyzing a body of films that cannot possibly be said to be westerns until after the analysis. If Kitses' themes and conventions are the defining characteristic of the western, then this is the previously discussed case of arbitrary definition—the category becomes redundant. But these themes and conventions are arrived at by analyzing films *already distinguished from other films by virtue of being "westerns."* To take a genre such as a western, analyze it, and list its principal characteristics is to beg the question that we must first isolate the body of films that are westerns. But they can only be isolated on the basis of the "principal characteristics," which can only be discovered from the films themselves after they have been isolated. That is, we are caught in a circle that first requires that the films be isolated, for which purposes a criterion is necessary, but the criterion is, in turn, meant to emerge from the empirically established common characteristics of the films. This "empiricist dilemma" has two solutions. One is to classify films according to a priori criteria depending on the critical purpose. This leads back to the earlier position in which the special genre term is redundant. The second is to lean on a common cultural consensus as to what constitutes a western and then go on to analyze it in detail.

This latter is clearly the root of most uses of genre. It is this usage that leads to, for example, the notion of conventions in a genre. The western, it is said, has certain crucial established conventions—ritualistic gunfights, black and white clothing corresponding to good and bad distinctions, revenge themes, typed villains, and many, many more. The best evidence for the widespread recognition of these conventions is to be found in those films that pointedly set out to invoke them. *Shane* (George Stevens, 1953), for example, plays very much on the stereotyped imagery, contrasting the stooping, black-clad, sallow, gloved Palance with the tall (by dint of careful camera angles), straight, white-buckskinned, fair, white-horsed Ladd. The power of this imagery is such that the sequence in which Shane rides to the showdown elevates him to a classically heroic posture. The point is reinforced by comparing Stevens's visualization of his characters with the very different descriptions offered in Schaefer's novel. The film "converts" the images to its own conventional language. Other obvious examples are provided by the series of Italian westerns. The use of Lee Van Cleef in leading roles depends very much on the image he has acquired over two decades of bit-part villains. Actors in the series—Van Cleef, Clint Eastwood, Eli Wallach, Jack Elam, Woody Strode, Henry Fonda, Charles Bronson—perpetually verge on self-parody. The most peculiar of the films, *Once upon a Time in the West* (Sergio Leone, 1969), is a fairy-tale collection of western conventions, verging on self-parody and culminating in what must be the most extended face-off ever filmed. Indeed, the most telling suggestions as to the importance of conventions are to be found in the gentle parodies *Cat Ballou* (Elliott Silverstein, 1965), *Support Your Local Sheriff* (Burt Kennedy, 1969), and *The Good Guys and the Bad Guys* (Kennedy, 1969). Without clear, shared

1. *Shane:* The classically heroic posture of Shane (Alan Ladd).

conceptions of what is to be expected from a western, such humor is not possible. One of the best sequences in *Cat Ballou* encapsulates the importance of the imagery, the sequence in which Lee Marvin is changed from drunken wreck to classic gunfighter. Starting very humorously with Marvin struggling into a corset, the transformation not only alters him but brings out a response in us as piece by piece the stereotyped image appears.

In short, to talk about the western is (arbitrary definitions apart) to appeal to a common set of meanings in our culture. From a very early age most of us have built up a picture of a western. We feel that we know a western when we see one, though the edges may be rather blurred. Thus in calling a film a western the critic is implying more than the simple statement "This film is a member of a class of films (westerns) having in common *x*, *y*, and *z*." The critic is also suggesting that such a film would be universally recognized as such in our culture. In other words, the crucial factors that distinguish a genre are not only characteristics inherent in the films themselves; they also depend on the particular culture within

2. *Cat Ballou:* Lee Marvin as the drunken ex-gunfighter.

which we are operating. And unless there is world consensus on the subject (which is an empirical question), there is no basis for assuming that a western will be conceived in the same way in every culture. The way in which the genre term is applied can quite conceivably vary from case to case. Genre notions—except the special case of arbitrary definition—are not critics' classifications made for special purposes; they are sets of cultural conventions. Genre is what we collectively believe it to be.

It is for precisely this reason that notions about genre are potentially so interesting—but more for the exploration of the psychological and sociological interplay between filmmaker, film, and audience than for the immediate purposes of film criticism. (Given that it is not entirely possible to draw a clear line between the two, this is really an argument for using a concept in one area rather than another.) Until we have a clear, if speculative, notion of the connotations of a genre class, it is difficult to see how critics, already besieged by imponderables, could usefully apply the term, certainly not as a special term at the root of their analyses. To use the concept in any stronger sense it becomes necessary to establish clearly what filmmakers mean when they conceive themselves as making a western; what limits such a choice may impose on them; in effect, what relationship exists between *auteur* and *genre*. But specific answers to such questions must tap the conceptions held by particular filmmakers and industries. To methodically analyze the way in which a filmmaker utilizes a genre for his or her own purposes (at present a popular critical pursuit) requires that we clearly establish the principal components of that filmmaker's conception of the genre. But this is not all. The notion that someone utilizes a genre suggests something about audience response. It implies that any given film works in a particular way because the audience has certain expectations of the genre. We can meaningfully talk of, for instance, an auteur breaking the rules of a genre only if we know what these rules are. And, of course, such rule-breaking has no consequence unless the audience knows as well. Now, as I have suggested, *Shane* may well take on its almost "epic" quality because Stevens for the most part sticks to the rules. In a similar way, *Two Rode Together* (Ford, 1961) and *Cheyenne Autumn* (Ford, 1964) are slightly disconcerting because they break the rules, particularly vis-à-vis the relation between Indian and white man. And, most obviously in recent years, Peckinpah's westerns use such elements to disturb the conventional universe of this genre—the much-remarked opening scene of *Ride the High Country* (1962) with its policeman and motor cars; the cavalry charging the French army in *Major Dundee* (1965); the car in *The Wild Bunch* (1969). Now you, the reader, may agree that these are cases of deliberate rule-breaking, and such agreement reflects that there is, in America and in Europe as well, some considerable consensus of what constitutes the characteristic "language" of a western. But this could well be a special case. To infer from it that all genre terms are thus easily employed is hardly justified.

This is not to suggest that genre terms are totally useless but merely that to employ them requires a much more methodical understanding of the working of film. And this in turn requires that we specify a set of sociological and psychological context assumptions and construct explicit genre models within them. If we imagine a general model of the workings of film language, genre directs our attention to sublanguages within it. Less centrally, however, the genre concept is indispensable in more strictly social and psychological terms as a way of formulating the interplay between culture, audience, films, and filmmakers. For example, there is a class of films thought of by a relatively highly educated middle-class group of filmgoers as "art movies." Now for present purposes genre is a conception existing in the culture of any particular group or society; it is not a way in which a critic classifies films for methodological purposes, but the much looser way in which an audience classifies its films. According to this meaning of the term, "art movies" is a genre. If a culture includes such notions of genre, then over a period of time and in a complicated way certain conventions become established as to what can be expected from an "art movie" as compared to some other category. The critics (the "posh" critics, in this case) are mediating factors in such developments. But once such conventions develop, they can in turn affect a filmmaker's conception of what he or she is doing. Hence the "art movie" category is commercially played up.

Let me take an impressionistic example, bearing in mind that much more extensive work would be needed to establish this in anything more than an intuitive way. At the beginning of the 1960s the general conception of an art movie revolved around the films of a group of European directors. Bergman was already established with, in particular, *The Seventh Seal* (1956) and *Wild Strawberries* (1957). The first year of the new decade had seen Antonioni's *L'Avventura* (1960), Resnais' *Hiroshima Mon Amour* (1959), and Fellini's *La Dolce Vita* (1959). These four directors—though perhaps Resnais less than the others—served to define the "conventions" of the developing art movie genre: deliberately and obviously intellectual (there is nothing more deliberate than the final scene of *La Dolce Vita*), with extremely visible individual stylistic characteristics. Bergman's silhouettes, puritan obsessiveness, and grunting Dark Age meals; Antonioni's minimal dialogue, grey photography, and carefully bleak compositions; and Fellini's self-indulgent surrealistic imagery, partly in *La Dolce Vita* but much more clearly in *8½* (1962), circumscribed what was expected of an art movie. Increasingly, European films, whether "deliberate" copies (a sub-Antonioni example is Giuseppe Patroni Griffi's 1963 film *Il Mare*) or later films made by the original directors, were based on the conventions that the earlier films had established. Antonioni's *Il Deserto Rosso* (1964), Fellini's *Juliet of the Spirits* (1965), and Bergman's *Winter Light* (1963) and *The Silence* (1963) are almost stylistic parodies of each director's earlier films. *Juliet of the Spirits* becomes the ultimate in color-supplement art movies, a combination of the earlier films and the newly established conventions of the genre.

This should serve to illustrate the way in which notions of genre might constructively be used in tapping the sociopsychological dynamics of film, although it is not designed to convince anyone of the particular case of "art movies." To properly establish such an argument would require detailed research on the changing expectations of art-movie audiences (perhaps via analysis of the "posh" critics), on the genre conceptions (and self-conceptions) held by individuals and groups in various film industries, and on the films themselves. Now there does not seem to me to be any crucial difference between the most commonly employed genre term—

the western—and the art-movie category that I have been discussing. They are both conceptions held by certain groups about certain films. Many of the theoretical problems of using genre terms have, however, been overlooked in the case of the western. It has become so much a part of our cultural patterning that film criticism has tended to use it as if it were possible to assume common agreement in all the respects on which research would be necessary in the art-movie case. It may be that there is such common agreement on the western; but it does not follow that this would be true of all genre categories. Anyway, it is not at all clear that there is that much consensus on the western. It seems likely that for many people the most western of westerns (certainly the most popular, if revivals are any indicator) is John Sturges's *The Magnificent Seven* (1960). On the other hand, in the 1940s the same position might be filled by *My Darling Clementine* (Ford, 1946), in the 1950s by *High Noon* (Fred Zinneman, 1952). Conventions change, often for reasons entirely out of the control of filmmakers and film critics.

In sum, then, genre terms seem best employed in the analysis of the relation between groups of films, the cultures in which they are made, and the cultures in which they are exhibited. That is, it is a term that can be usefully employed in relation to a body of knowledge and theory about the social and psychological context of film. Any assertion we might make about a director's use of genre conventions—Peckinpah uses the contrast between our expectations and actual images to reinforce the "end of an era" element in *Ride the High Country* and *The Wild Bunch*—assumes, wrongly, the existence of this body of knowledge. To labor the point, it assumes (1) we know what Peckinpah thinks; (2) we know what the audience thinks about the films in question and about westerns; (3) Peckinpah knows what the audience thinks; and so on. Most uses of genre effectively invent answers to such questions by implicitly claiming to tap some archetypal characteristic of the genre, some universal human response. This depends on the particular context of the assumptions employed and on a more general notion of film language. To leap in with genre immediately is to put the cart before the horse.

Notes

1. Jim Kitses, *Horizons West* (Bloomington and London: Indiana University Press, 1970), p. 19.

2. André Bazin, "Evolution du Western," *Cahiers du Cinéma* 9, no. 54 (December 1955), reprinted in André Bazin, *Cinéma et sociologie*, vol. 3 of *Qu'est-ce que le cinéma?* (Paris: Editions du Cerf, 1961). This essay is available in English in André Bazin, *What Is Cinema?* edited and translated by Hugh Gray (Berkeley: University of California Press, 1971), 2: 149–157.

2. The Idea of Genre in the American Cinema

EDWARD BUSCOMBE

Genre is a term much employed in film criticism at the moment, yet there is little agreement on what exactly it means or whether the term has any use at all. There appear to be three sorts of questions one could profitably ask: first, do genres in the cinema really exist, and if so, can they be defined? second, what are the functions they fulfill? and third, how do specific genres originate or what causes them?

It seems sensible to start with a brief review of the history of genre criticism in literature, since it is in this context that certain problems first arise. The notion that there are different kinds of literature, with different techniques and subjects, was first developed by Aristotle; in his *Poetics* he tried to separate what he called poetry—what we simply call literature— into a number of categories such as tragedy, epic, lyric, and so forth. His purpose was to decide what were the particular qualities of each distinctive kind, and what each kind could be expected to do and not do. He then tried to establish their relative importance, and after much debate concluded that tragedy was the highest kind of poetry.

During the Renaissance Aristotle's ideas were taken up and erected into a rigid system of rules so that certain precise styles and forms were prescribed for each kind (the three dramatic unities are the most notorious example). Such codification was extended in the neoclassical period of the seventeenth and eighteenth centuries, when literature was divided into more and more categories, or "species," as they were called, each with its own proper tone, form, and subject matter. As a result of this rather mechanical and dictatorial approach, the theory of literary kinds gradually became discredited. Even the classical Dr. Johnson was moved to exclaim: "There is therefore scarcely any species of writing, of which we can tell what is its essence, and what are its constituents; every new genius produces some new innovation, which, when invented and approved subverts the rules which the practice of foregoing authors had established." [1]

Under the impact of the romantic revolt against rules and traditions of all kinds, the idea of literary species, or genres, as they later came to be called, suffered greatly. Artists were to be free to write in any manner to which the spirit moved them. It was not until the rise in the late 1930s and early 1940s of a Chicago-based school of criticism known as the neo-Aristotelians that much attention was paid to the influence on the artist of already existing forms and conventions. The neo-Aristotelians were consciously reacting against the so-called New Criticism, which had expressly repudiated any kind of historical approach to literature. The famous catch phrase "a poem is a poem is a poem" sums up their attitude: that a work of literature exists by itself and relies upon no reference to any external reality, whether contemporary or historical.

The neo-Aristotelians were concerned with rescuing literature from such self-imposed isolation, and in attempting to do so they partially resurrected the theory of genres. But they did not always avoid what has often been a source of confusion; Aristotle had spoken of literary kinds in two senses: first, as a number of different groups of conventions that had grown up historically and developed into particular forms such as satire, lyric, and tragedy; and second, as a more fundamental division of literature, into drama, epic, and lyric, corresponding to major differences in the relation between artist, subject matter, and audience.

More time, in fact, was spent in assessing the natures and possibilities of these three modes of literature than in exploring the historical genres. As a result, not much of the work is relevant to the cinema, for these three modes (which correspond approximately to drama, fiction, and poetry) appear to be equally present in the cinema. And, on the other hand, such work as has been done on the development of particular genres like the Gothic novel or Victorian melodrama has not ventured far beyond the mere recording of lists of examples.

Nevertheless, some profit is to be gained from the literary critics, even if only a warning. Many people wish to avoid the whole question of genre because it is held that it will lead to the laying down of rules and regulations that will arbitrarily restrict the freedom of artists to create what they like, or the freedom of critics to talk about anything they want to. But if the theory of genres in literature has usually been restrictive and normative, it need not necessarily be so. One does not have to set up a Platonic ideal, to which all particular examples try vainly to aspire, nor even to say that the closer any individual film comes to incorporating all the different elements of the definition, the more fully it will be a western, or gangster picture, or musical. Aristotle's original intention was descriptive, not prescriptive.

Some positive assistance is afforded by Wellek and Warren in their *Theory of Literature*. They neatly state the crux of the problem: "The dilemma of genre history is the dilemma of all history: i.e., in order to discover the scheme of reference (in this case, the genre) we must study the history; but we cannot study the history without having in mind some scheme of selection."[2]

As they recognize, the problem is only another aspect of the wider philosophical problem of universals. With regard to the cinema, we may state it thus: if we want to know what a western is, we must look at certain kinds of films. But how do we know which films to look at until we know what a western is?

For some people the futility of many of the arguments that arise out of this dilemma—such as whether a film like, say, *Lonely Are the Brave* (David Miller, 1962) is a western or not—is so obvious that they give up in despair. But having posed the problem in such apparently insoluble terms, Wellek and Warren offer a way out. To begin with, common sense suggests that it is possible to draw up a list of elements found in films that, for the purposes of the argument, are called westerns and to say that any film with one or more of these elements is thereby held to be a western, though not therefore necessarily identical to other examples of the form. Wellek and Warren go further, however: "Genre should be conceived, we think, as a grouping of literary works based, theoretically, upon both outer form (specific metre or structure) and also upon inner form (attitude, tone, purpose—more crudely, subject and audience). The ostensible basis may be one or the other (e.g., 'pastoral' and 'satire' for the inner form: dipodic verse and Pindaric ode for the outer); but the critical problem will then be to find the *other* dimension, to complete the diagram."[3]

This idea of both inner and outer form seems essential, for if we require only the former, in terms of subject matter, then our concept will be too loose to be of much value; and if only the latter, then the genre will be ultimately meaningless, since devoid of any content.

What, then, are the cinematic equivalents of, first, outer form? Not rhythm, clearly. To the extent to which a film can be said to have rhythm, this depends not upon the conventions of the genre within which it is made, but upon the artistic personalities of the director and editor (except perhaps the rapid montage sequences of many gangster films). Nor does the notion of structure open up many possibilities. It seems extremely difficult to argue that there is any significant similarity between the plots of different westerns, for example. There are, of course, a number of plot structures that reappear in film after film. There is the one in which a bigoted and usually disciplinarian cavalry officer is narrowly prevented from starting a "full-scale Indian war." Or, again, there is the one in which a reformed gunfighter (or ex-marshal) is reluctantly persuaded to accept responsibility for cleaning up the town. But to use such structures as a basis for defining the genre would mean ending up not with one genre called "the western," but an almost infinite number of subgenres.

Some may wish to argue that this is the best that can be done. Yet it does seem that these films have something more in common, something that makes the two kinds of story mentioned above part of the same genre.

Since we are dealing with a visual medium we ought surely to look for our defining criteria in what we actually see on the screen. It is immediately apparent that there before our eyes is a whole range of "outer forms." There is, first of all, the setting, the chief glory of many of the films. Often it is outdoors, in very particular kinds of country: deserts, mountains, plains, woods. Or it is indoors—but again, special kinds of indoors: saloons, jails, courtrooms, ranch houses, hotels, riverboats, brothels—all places frequented by those who live an outdoor and/or wandering kind of life.

Then there are the clothes: wide-brimmed hats, open-neck shirts with scarves, tight jeans (which have become steadily tighter as the years have gone by), sometimes worn with leather chaps and almost always with spurs and high-heeled boots; or, alternatively, army uniforms or the wide but carefully distinguished variety of Indian costume. There are also certain clothes for specialist occupations. There are bootlace ties for gamblers and black gloves for psychopathic hired guns; a man who wears a watch chain is often a judge; and a black hat can denote a preacher; a bowler, a newspaperman. For women there are usually only two sorts of clothes: wide, full skirts and tight bodices or the more tomboyish jeans and shirt. (There is a third costume usually reserved for the Mexican girl or prostitute—often synonymous—in which the bodice is looser and the neckline appreciably lower.)

Third, there are the various tools of the trade, principally weapons, and of these, principally guns. They are usually specifically identified: Colt 45's, Winchester and Springfield rifles, shotguns for certain situations (such as robbing banks or facing a numerically superior enemy), and, in westerns of an earlier period, single-shot, muzzle-loading muskets. Such care in the choice of weapons is not mere pedantry nor dictated purely by considerations of historical accuracy, for an incredible variety of arms were in use. The weapons employed in the films are there for largely stylistic reasons; consider, for example, the significant difference in the style of movement required to cock a Winchester and a Lee-Enfield 303. Other weapons have their place: knives, often the murderous looking Bowie type, whips (used by women or bullies), sometimes cannon for the military, and assorted Indian hardware, notably the bow and arrow. Again, there are specialist weapons. The man who wears a bootlace tie should be watched carefully in case he produces a Derringer.

Next in importance come horses, also used in formally differentiated ways. Indians ride barebacked or with only a blanket, a sign perhaps of their closeness to the animal world. White and black horses have frequently a symbolic function, and if a woman does not ride sidesaddle she is no lady, though not always the worse for that. Doctors and judges ride in a buggy, unless, like Doc Holliday, they have ceased to practice. We know, too, what kind of people travel in stagecoaches: in descending order of their entitlement to respect, women, gamblers, corset salesmen, and Easterners.

Fourth, there is a large group of miscellaneous physical objects that recur and thereby take on a formal function. Trains are invariably of the same kind, with cowcatchers in front of the engine, carriages with a railed open platform at the back (useful for fights), and seats either side of a central aisle. Mines, general stores, and forts also feature largely, representing the corruption of money, the virtue of honest industry, and an oasis of strength in a hostile land. Indians, too, in spite of the more liberal attitudes of the last few years, are still primarily important not as people in their own right but as part of the setting.

All these things operate as formal elements. That is to say, the films are not "about" them any more than a sonnet is about fourteen lines in a certain meter. For example, *Winchester 73* (Anthony Mann, 1950) is not about the gun, which is a mere connecting device to hold the story together. The film, like all films, is about people. Obviously the formal structure is looser than that of a sonnet; not all the elements need be present. But if we say that a western is a film that includes at least one of them (and of course the list is by no means exhaustive), then we are saying something both intelligible and useful. The visual conventions provide a framework within which the story can be told.

But what is more important is that they also affect what kind of story it will be. Just as the nature of the sonnet makes it more likely you will be successful in writing a love poem of a very personal kind rather than something else, and has so grown up as a genre with both outer and inner form, so too what kind of film a western is, is largely determined by the nature of its conventions. One can put this more forcefully in a negative way: it is unlikely you will produce a good poem on a large-scale historical theme such as the Trojan War if you choose the sonnet form. So, too, if you are going to make a western, you will tend not to consider certain themes or subjects (unless, as in *High Noon* [Fred Zinneman, 1952], you are consciously trying to adapt the form to your purpose in an arbitrary way).

In trying to be more specific here, one is inevitably on dangerous ground, for unless one has seen all the westerns ever made (or, to be absolutely logical, all the westerns that ever could be made), there cannot be any certainty that generalizations will hold. Since the object is to stimulate discussion, not end it, however, a start can be made by saying that because of the physical setting, a western is likely to deal successfully with stories about the opposition between man and nature and about the establishment of civilization. As Jim Kitses points out in his book *Horizons West,* such oppositions are seen from two points of view: for nature or for civilization. If, on the other hand, you want to deal with the sense of fear, isolation, and excitement engendered by great cities, you won't do it very well within the framework of the western.

This much perhaps is obvious. But it is possible to go further. The men in westerns wear clothes that are aggressively masculine, sexy in a virile sort of way. (As if to underline this, the gambler, whose clothes are flashier, is invariably a ladies' man.) This in turn determines the character of the hero—taciturn, tough, uncomplicated, self-sufficient. It is surely no accident that the most famous western heroes are not, by conventional standards, good-looking. John Wayne, Randolph Scott, James Stewart, Gary Cooper, and Kirk Douglas all have their attractions, but they are not, like Cary Grant, at home in a drawing room. Likewise, the clothes of the women determine that they will be either very feminine or very masculine. Part of the interest comes from feminine clothes hiding a masculine character—Angie Dickinson in *Rio Bravo* (Howard Hawks, 1959)—or vice versa, as with characters like Calamity Jane, who usually turn out to be pining for a home and children.

But either way, because the men are so aggressively masculine and lead wandering lives and the women are forced either to stay at home or become the equivalents of men, few westerns have a strong love interest. The formal elements of the genre make it hard to deal with subjects that presuppose in the characters an interest in, and a time for, the heart's affections.

It is also likely that, given the arsenal of weapons on view in the films, violence will play a crucial part in the stories. This is not to say that there could not be pacifist westerns, though they are significantly less common than pacifist war films, because the kind of weapons used makes the violence less immediate and unpleasant. But it is hard to think of a western in which there is at least no threat of violence. Thus the world of the West is different from that of a Henry James novel, where no hand is ever raised in anger. Because the guns are there as part of the formal structure, there will be, characteristically, a dilemma that either can only be resolved by violence or in which the violence would be a solution, though a wrong one. The characters will be of a kind whose virtue resides not so much in subtlety of intellect, or sensitivity, or imagination, as in their willingness and ability to stand up for themselves, to be in some sense, not necessarily physical, strong.

One could go on. But it might already be objected that it is the subject matter that determines the outer form, not the other way round; that the things a director wants to say will decide the form he or she uses. Not

3. Femininity and masculinity in *Rio Bravo* (John Wayne and Angie Dickinson).

enough is known about how most westerns are conceived in the minds of directors and writers to say whether this is the actual process of creation. One may be forgiven for suspecting, however, that the worst way to make a western is to think of a theme and then try to transpose it into western form.

If one looks at a cinematic genre in this way, as being composed of an outer form consisting of a certain number of visual conventions that are, in a sense, arbitrary (in the same way that a tragedy has five acts), then certain problems are on the way to being solved. First, we are not bound to make any very close connections between the western genre and historical reality. Of course there are connections. But too many discussions of these problems fall down over this point because it is usually assumed that the relationship must be a direct one; that since in fact there was a West, westerns must be essentially concerned with it. Kitses, for instance, states that "the basic convention of the genre is that films in Western guise are about America's past."[4] This is simply not true of many of the films, including several of the ones he discusses, for only Peckinpah of his three directors is at all preoccupied with historical themes. In some of his films Mann includes such material, though that is not where the central interest lies; and Boetticher appears quite oblivious to any such considerations. To be fair, Kitses is aware of other elements in the genre. He summarizes what he calls "interrelated aspects of the genre" under the headings of "history," "themes," "archetypes," and "icons" (which are equivalent to what I have called visual conventions).[5] But he fails to show in what their interrelation consists; nor, ultimately, does this first chapter have much to do with his discussion of particular directors, and for the reason I have suggested, that history, to which Kitses devotes most of his attention, is a relatively unimportant part of many westerns.

There are several reasons why it is necessary to resist the temptation to talk about westerns largely in terms of history. First, one usually ends up by talking about Ford, who is, clearly, more concerned with it than most. But Ford is not the western. Second, if this is what westerns chiefly present, it is hard to see why half the world's population should spend its time watching them. Third and most serious, to define westerns as films about a certain period of America's past is to misunderstand the nature and meaning of genres and how they work.

Before going on to deal with this, however, two more points should be made. Although the western seems to me the most important of the genres, the one in which the largest body of good work has been done, there are obviously others. The same approach could be applied to them; namely, to inquire into the outer form, the visual and other conventions, and to see whether there is the same relation between form and content, whether it could be shown that the subject matter dealt with is determined by a series of formal and given patterns. The gangster movie[6] is an obvious subject of inquiry, though one problem is that it shades off into the thriller, so that at one end of the spectrum we have, say, *White Heat* (Raoul Walsh, 1949) and at the other, Hitchcock. Musicals, too, would repay attention. Nor need visual elements be the only defining ones, for film is not only a visual art. For example, it is (or used to be) understood that in Hollywood's romantic comedies people do not sleep together unless they are married. Clearly this is a convention—it never was actually true. And it cannot be explained merely by referring to the Hays Code, for that would make it simply a restriction. Although it does limit the kind of subject that can be dealt with, in the same way that it does in the Victorian novel, a lot of mileage can be got out of it. The famous scene in *It Happened One Night* (Frank Capra, 1934) where Clark Gable and

Claudette Colbert share a room together uses the convention as the basis of its humor. All the same, the major defining characteristics of genre will be visual: guns, cars, clothes in the gangster film; clothes and dancing in the musical (apart from the music, of course!); castles, coffins, and teeth in horror movies.

The second point is that while it is possible to talk of themes and archetypes in genres, as Kitses does in his book, it doesn't in the end help very much. He cites archetypes such as "the journey and the quest, the ceremonies of love and marriage, food and drink, the rhythms of waking and sleeping, life and death."[7] Not only do these appear in other genres besides the western; they exist in films that can scarcely be classified into any genres, and what is more, they occur in other forms of art besides the cinema. What we need is a way of looking at a genre that can make clear what is distinctive about it and how its outer and inner forms relate.

But what functions does genre perform? Or, in other words, why bother to talk about it at all? Can't we get along just as well with our present director-oriented theories, while admitting that some films are like others? The trouble is that our present theories are so extreme. They assume that the auteur (who need not necessarily be the director, of course) is personally responsible for everything that appears in the film—or that *someone* is responsible, if only a heavy-handed producer. This form of overcompensation, a reaction to the critical Dark Ages when American cinema was dismissed as repetitive rubbish, mass-produced to a formula (unfortunately all too successful) in the factories of Hollywood, has led to a situation in which American films are held to be wholly the expressions of the artistic personalities of their highly original creators.

There may well be several reasons for this, apart from the swing of the pendulum. There is a kind of critical snobbery which assumes that you cannot really appreciate a film unless you have seen all its director's other films and which leads to the more bizarre forms of auteur-hunting.[8] For if an individual film is good, then it must have an auteur behind it, and if he or she is an auteur, it follows that this person's other works will be good—or at least interesting. And yet there are films which are totally successful and which derive their power from the traditions of a genre rather than from any distinctive directorial contribution. *Casablanca* (Michael Curtiz, 1942) is such a one, as Andrew Sarris recognizes in *The American Cinema*. It doesn't help much to have seen other Curtiz films, but one's enjoyment is enormously enriched by having seen Humphrey Bogart and the rest in other films of the period. It may be objected that strictly speaking this has nothing to do with genre, since the qualities that actors can bring to a film cut across genres. Yet is it not a fact that Bogart's battered face instantly communicates a blend of cynicism and

honesty, weariness and generosity, that is genuinely part of a tradition of
the American film noir? What he represents in the film owes little to
Michael Curtiz, much to the other films he played in.

But the chief justification of the genre is not that it allows merely com-
petent directors to produce good films (though one is grateful enough for
that). Rather, it is that it allows good directors to be better. And the main
reason why this has not been more generally recognized is that the auteur
theory is not very well equipped to deal with popular art. Even in its less
extreme forms, it cannot really make room for the contribution of the
tradition in which a film was made. Thus in order to appreciate *Casablanca,* we must do more than simply accept Curtiz as an auteur (which is
what Higham and Greenberg want us to do in *Hollywood in the Forties*).[9] When we are faced with genuinely distinctive artists, we too often
consider them apart from the genre background they work in. Robin
Wood's book on Hitchcock is an excellent piece of criticism. But in his
discussion of *Psycho* (1960) he says nothing of the film's obvious relation
to the horror genre. Surely our sense of fear depends at least in part on
our built-in response to certain stock symbols that Hitchcock employs.
People rarely take Hitchcock seriously when he talks about his pictures;
yet at the head of the section on *Psycho* Wood has this quotation: "The
process through which we take the audience [is it not significant that he
so often says 'we,' not 'I'?], you see, it's rather like taking them through
the haunted house at the fairground. . . ."[10] The house itself, with its
vague suggestion of Victorian Gothic, is straight out of any number of
horror films. And when at the end Vera Miles goes down to the cellar, we
are terrified, not just because we have heard Norman say he is taking
his mother down there (we don't know yet that his mother is a corpse,
though of course we suspect all is not well); our certainty that something
unpleasant will be found comes from our knowledge that nasty things
come out of cellars in this kind of film. This is not to deny Wood's ascrip-
tion of Freudian overtones to the cellar; but the trouble with Freudian
overtones is that you aren't supposed to be aware of them. It seems more
likely that our conscious reaction to the scene owes more to our having
assimilated them through an exposure to the tradition of the genre.

Most people see films this way. No one would suggest that we must be
bound by the aesthetic criteria of the man in the street. Yet anyone who is
at all concerned with education must be worried at the distance between
much of the criticism now written and the way the average audience reacts to a film. For them it is not a new Hawks or Ford or Peckinpah; it is a
new western. And to sympathize with this view is not to deny the claims
of these directors to be artists. Popular art does not condemn its creators
to a subsidiary role. Instead it emphasizes the relation between the artist
and the material, on the one hand, and the material and the audience on

4. *Psycho:* Obvious relations to the horror genre.

the other. The artist brings to the genre his or her own concerns, techniques, and capacities—in the widest sense, a style—but receives from the genre a formal pattern that directs and disciplines the work. In a sense this imposes limitations, as I have suggested. Certain themes and treatments are, if not ruled out, unlikely to be successful if they work too hard against the genre. But the benefits are considerable. Constant exposure to a previous succession of films has led the audience to recognize certain formal elements as charged with an accretion of meaning. Some of these I have tried to isolate, and in some cases their meaning has been suggested. Some critics like to refer to them as "icons."

All too often, however, discussion has ceased there. But it is vital to see not how icons relate to the cinema in general but to genres in particular, and how in the popular cinema they may be reconciled to our natural desire to see films as the expression of an artistic personality.

This can best be done through the notion that a genre film depends on a combination of novelty and familiarity. The conventions of the genre are known and recognized by the audience, and such recognition is in itself a pleasure. Popular art, in fact, has always depended on this; one might argue that the modern idea of novelty (or "originality") as a major, even *the* major, quality to be desired in a work of art dates from the romantic period. And, as Raymond Williams shows in *Culture and Society,* it is during this period that art began to move away from its contact with a large, roughly homogeneous audience. We have there the beginnings of the present-day division between "mass" and "highbrow" culture. All too easily this originality degenerates into eccentricity, and communication is sacrificed in the interests of self-expression. It is one of the chief merits of the American cinema that this has, on the whole, not yet happened; and because this is so, the popular cinema (which is almost, though not quite, synonymous with the American cinema) offers one of the richest sources of material for those teaching liberal studies to the culturally unsophisticated. Those who are unconvinced by this might wish to argue that the opposite of eccentricity is the cliché. It is true that if a director slavishly copies the conventions rather than uses them, then we get a film which is just what Hollywood is so often, even now, held to have produced exclusively: a thoroughly predictable string of stock situations and images. However, this article is not primarily intended as propaganda for Hollywood. That battle, if not won, is at least being fought by increasing numbers of people on ever widening fronts. Rather, the intention is to argue that it is a mistake to base the argument for popular cinema exclusively on a case for the auteur.

One of the best examples of the way in which genre actually works is in Peckinpah's *Guns in the Afternoon* [in the United States released as *Ride the High Country,* 1962—Ed.]. Knowing the period and location, we expect at the beginning to find a familiar western town. In fact, the first minutes of the film brilliantly disturb our expectations. As the camera roves around the town we discover a policeman in uniform, a car, a camel, and Randolph Scott dressed up as Buffalo Bill. Each of these images performs a function. The figure of the policeman conveys that the law has become institutionalized; the rough and ready frontier days are over. The car suggests, as in *The Wild Bunch* (Peckinpah, 1969), that the West is no longer isolated from modern technology and its implications. Significantly, the camel is racing against a horse; such a grotesque juxtaposition is painful. A horse in a western is not just an animal but a symbol of dignity, grace, and power. These qualities are mocked by having it compete with a camel; and to add insult to injury, the camel wins.

Randolph Scott is not just an actor. It is enough to have seen two or three of his films to know that he represents a quiet, cheerful kind of integrity. Peckinpah uses this screen image by having him play against it all through the film; but the initial shock of seeing him in a wig, running a crooked booth at the fair, does more than upset our expectations about his role in the film. It calls into question our whole attitude to the heroes

5. The opening race in *Ride the High Country*.

of western legend. Scott dressed up as Buffalo Bill is an image that relies not only on Scott's screen personality, but also on the audience's stock response to Buffalo Bill, for he too is debased by this grotesque impersonation. This, Peckinpah is saying, is the state that things have come to, that heroes are exploited for money.

Clearly, then, although Peckinpah is working against the conventions, he could not do this unless he and the audience had a tradition in common. He needs the outer form, though in many ways he is making an antiwestern. What is especially interesting is the relation between this and the inner form. Here I am obliged to take issue again with Jim Kitses. He believes that Peckinpah's films are essentially about a search for personal identity. While not wishing to deny that some such concern may be traced in the pictures, one must protest that this rather tends to ignore the most obvious fact about them: that they are westerns. Personal identity can be sought for anywhere, anytime. But the essential theme of *Guns in the Afternoon* is one that, while it could be put into other forms, is ideally suited to the one chosen. The film describes the situation of men who have outlived their time. Used to a world where issues were decided simply, on a test of strength, they now find this way of life threatened by complications and developments they do not understand. Since they cannot, or will not, adapt, all that remains to them is a tragic and bitter heroism.

The cluster of images and conventions that we call the western genre is used by Peckinpah to define and embody this situation, in such a way that we know what the West was and what it has become. The first is communicated through images that are familiar, the second through those that are strange. And together they condition his subject matter. Most obviously, because the film is a western, the theme is worked out in terms of violent action. If it were a musical, the theme might be similar in some ways, but because the conventions would be different, it would probably not involve violence (or if it did, the violence might well be highly stylized and so quite different in effect). And if it were a gangster picture, it seems unlikely that the effect of the film's ending, its beautifully elegiac background of autumn leaves, would be reproduced, suggesting as it does that the dead Judd is at one with nature, that nature which seems at the beginning of the film to have been overtaken by "civilization."

Much of what has been said has been expressed in other ways by recent writers, occasionally more esoterically. What needs to be done now is to put to work our increasing understanding of how important semiology is, to explore the precise relation between the artist and his or her given material, in order to explain our intuitive feeling that a genre is not a mere collection of dead images waiting for a director to animate it, but a tradition with a life of its own. We return to the third question asked at the beginning of this article. Genres predate great directors. The western was going along happily under its own steam well before John Ford, or even James Cruze, came upon it. We need much more work on the early history of these various forms if we are to fully comprehend their strange power and the exact process by which they grew rich enough to attract the talents they did. Last, the question of the relation between the western and history, which I have argued is by no means simple, and not always central, can only be answered with certainty when we know how the form began. It's usually assumed that it sprang, fully armed, from pulp fiction, and yet so much of it is visual that it is hard to believe this is quite true. And if the western originates in history and is a response to it, what about the musical? Or the horror film? Can we possibly evolve a theory to fit them all?

Notes

1. Samuel Johnson, *The Rambler*, no. 125, in *The Yale Edition of the Works of Samuel Johnson* (New Haven and London: Yale University Press, 1969), 4:300.

2. René Wellek and Austin Warren, *Theory of Literature,* 3d ed. (New York: Harcourt, Brace & World, 1956), p. 260.

3. Ibid., p. 231.

4. Jim Kitses, *Horizons West* (Bloomington and London: Indiana University Press, 1970), p. 24.

5. Ibid., pp. 24–25.

6. See Colin McArthur, "Genre and Iconography," paper delivered at a British Film Institute seminar.

7. Kitses, *Horizons West,* p. 20.

8. I use the term loosely, to mean the artist awarded credit for a film's succession: the distinction between *auteur* and *metteur-en-scène* has no importance here.

9. Charles Higham and Joel Greenberg, *Hollywood in the Forties* (London: A. Zwemmer; New York: A. S. Barnes, 1968), p. 19.

10. Robin Wood, *Hitchcock's Films* (London: Zwemmer; New York: Barnes, 1965).

3. A Semantic/Syntactic Approach to Film Genre

RICK ALTMAN

What is a genre? Which films are genre films? How do we know to which genre they belong? As fundamental as these questions may seem, they are almost never asked—let alone answered—in the field of cinema studies. Most comfortable in the seemingly uncomplicated world of Hollywood classics, genre critics have felt little need to reflect openly on the assumptions underlying their work. Everything seems so clear. Why bother to theorize, American pragmatism asks, when there are no problems to solve? We all know a genre when we see one. Scratch only where it itches. According to this view, genre theory would be called for only in the unlikely event that knowledgeable genre critics disagreed on basic issues. The task of the theorist is then to adjudicate among conflicting approaches, not so much by dismissing unsatisfactory positions but by constructing a model that reveals the relationship between differing critical claims and their function within a broader cultural context. Whereas the French clearly view theory as a first principle, we Americans tend to see it as a last resort, something to turn to when all else fails.

Even in this limited, pragmatic view, whereby theory is to be avoided at all costs, the time for theory is nevertheless upon us. The clock has struck thirteen; we had best call in the theoreticians. The more genre criticism I read, the more uncertainty I note in the choice or extent of essential critical terms. Often what appears as hesitation in the terminology of a single critic will turn into a clear contradiction when studies by two or more critics are compared. Now, it would be one thing if these contradictions were simply a matter of fact. On the contrary, however, I suggest that these are not temporary problems, bound to disappear as soon as we have more information or better analysts. Instead, these uncertainties reflect constitutive weaknesses of current notions of genre. Three contradictions in particular seem worthy of a good scratch.

When we establish the corpus of a genre we generally tend to do two things at once, and thus establish two alternate groups of texts, each corresponding to a different notion of corpus. On the one hand, we have an unwieldy list of texts corresponding to a simple, tautological definition of the genre (e.g., western = film that takes place in the American West, or musical = film with diegetic music). This *inclusive* list is the kind that gets consecrated by generic encyclopedias or checklists. On the other hand, we find critics, theoreticians, and other arbiters of taste sticking to a familiar canon that has little to do with the broad, tautological definition. Here the same films are mentioned again and again, not only because they are well known or particularly well made, but because they somehow seem to represent the genre more fully and faithfully than other apparently more tangential films. This *exclusive* list of films generally occurs not in a dictionary context, but instead in connection with attempts to arrive at the overall meaning or structure of a genre. The relative status of these alternate approaches to the constitution of a generic corpus may easily be sensed from the following typical conversation:

> "I mean, what do you do with Elvis Presley films? You can hardly call them musicals."
>
> "Why not? They're loaded with songs and they've got a narrative that ties the numbers together, don't they?"
>
> "Yeah, I suppose. I guess you'd have to call *Fun in Acapulco* a musical, but it's sure no *Singin' in the Rain*. Now there's a real musical."

When is a musical not a musical? When it has Elvis Presley in it. What may at first have seemed no more than an uncertainty on the part of the critical community now clearly appears as a contradiction. Because there are two competing notions of generic corpus on our critical scene, it is perfectly possible for a film to be simultaneously included in a particular generic corpus and excluded from that same corpus.

A second uncertainty is associated with the relative status of theory and history in genre studies. Before semiotics came along, generic titles and definitions were largely borrowed from the industry itself; what little generic theory there was tended therefore to be confused with historical analysis. With the heavy influence of semiotics on generic theory over the last two decades, self-conscious *critical* vocabulary came to be systematically preferred to the now-suspect *user* vocabulary. The contributions of Propp, Lévi-Strauss, Frye, and Todorov to genre studies have not been uniformly productive, however, because of the special place reserved for genre study within the semiotic project. If structuralist critics systematically chose as the object of their analysis large groups of popular texts, it was in order to cover a basic flaw in the semiotic understanding of textual analysis. Now, one of the most striking aspects of Saussure's theory of language is his emphasis on the inability of any single individual to effect change within that language.[1] The fixity of the linguistic community thus serves as justification for Saussure's fundamentally synchronic approach to language. When literary semioticians applied this linguistic model to problems of textual analysis, they never fully addressed the notion of interpretive community implied by Saussure's linguistic community. Preferring narrative to narration, system to process, and *histoire* to *discours*, the first semiotics ran headlong into a set of restrictions and contradictions that eventually spawned the more process-oriented second semiotics. It is in this context that we must see the resolutely synchronic attempts of Propp, Lévi-Strauss, Todorov, and many another influential genre analyst.[2] Unwilling to compromise their systems by the historical notion of linguistic community, these theoreticians instead substituted the generic context for the linguistic community, as if the weight of numerous "similar" texts were sufficient to locate the meaning of a text independently of a specific audience. Far from being sensitive to concerns of history, semiotic genre analysis was by definition and from the start devoted to bypassing history. Treating genres as neutral constructs, semioticians of the sixties and early seventies blinded us to the discursive power of generic formations. Because they treated genres as the interpretive community, they were unable to perceive the important role of genres in exercising influence on the interpretive community. Instead of reflecting openly on the way in which Hollywood uses its genres to short-circuit the normal interpretive process, structuralist critics plunged headlong into the trap, taking Hollywood's ideological effect for a natural ahistorical cause.

Genres were always—and continue to be—treated as if they spring full-blown from the head of Zeus. It is thus not surprising to find that even the most advanced of current genre theories, those that see generic texts as negotiating a relationship between a specific production system and a given audience, still hold to a notion of genre that is fundamentally ahistorical in nature.[3] More and more, however, as scholars come to know the full range of individual Hollywood genres, we are finding that genres are far from exhibiting the homogeneity that this synchronic approach posits. Whereas one Hollywood genre may be borrowed with little change from another medium, a second genre may develop slowly, change constantly, and surge recognizably before settling into a familiar pattern, while a third may go through an extended series of paradigms, none of which may be claimed as dominant. As long as Hollywood genres are conceived as Platonic categories, existing outside the flow of time, it will be impossible to reconcile *genre theory*, which has always accepted as given the timelessness of a characteristic structure, and *genre history*, which has concentrated on chronicling the development, deployment, and disappearance of this same structure.

A third contradiction looms larger still, for it involves the two general directions taken by genre criticism as a whole over the last decade or two. Following Lévi-Strauss, a growing number of critics throughout the seventies dwelled on the mythical qualities of Hollywood genres and thus on the audience's ritual relationship to genre film. The film industry's desire to please and its need to attract consumers were viewed as the mechanism whereby spectators were actually able to designate the kind of films they wanted to see. By choosing the films it would patronize, the audience revealed its preferences and its beliefs, thus inducing Hollywood studios to produce films reflecting its desires. Participation in the genre film experience thus reinforces spectator expectations and desires. Far from being limited to mere entertainment, filmgoing offers a satisfaction more akin to that associated with established religion. Most openly championed by John Cawelti, this ritual approach appears as well in books by Leo Braudy, Frank McConnell, Michael Wood, Will Wright, and Tom Schatz.[4] It has the merit not only of accounting for the intensity of identification typical of American genre film audiences, but it also encourages the placing of genre film narratives into an appropriately wider context of narrative analysis.

Curiously, however, while the ritual approach was attributing ultimate authorship to the audience, with the studios simply serving, for a price, the national will, a parallel ideological approach was demonstrating how audiences are manipulated by the business and political interests of Hollywood. Starting with *Cahiers du Cinéma* and moving rapidly to *Screen*, *Jump Cut*, and a growing number of journals, this view has recently joined hands with a more general critique of the mass media offered by the Frankfurt school.[5] Looked at in this way, genres are simply the generalized, identifiable structures through which Hollywood's rhetoric flows. Far more attentive to discursive concerns than the ritual approach, which remains faithful to Lévi-Strauss in emphasizing narrative systems, the ideological approach stresses questions of representation and identification previously left aside. Simplifying a bit, we might say that it characterizes each individual genre as a specific type of lie, an untruth whose most characteristic feature is its ability to masquerade as truth. Whereas the ritual approach sees Hollywood as responding to societal pressure and thus expressing audience desires, the ideological approach claims that Hollywood takes advantage of spectator energy and psychic investment in order to lure the audience into Hollywood's own positions. The two are irreducibly opposed, yet these irreconcilable arguments continue to represent the most interesting and well defended of recent approaches to Hollywood genre film.

Here we have three problems that I take to be not limited to a single school of criticism or of a single genre but implicit in every major field of current genre analysis. In nearly every argument about the limits of a generic corpus, the opposition of an inclusive list to an exclusive canon surfaces. Wherever genres are discussed, the divergent concerns of theorists and historians are increasingly obvious. And even when the topic is limited to genre theory alone, no agreement can be found between those who propose a ritual function for film genres and those who champion an ideological purpose. We find ourselves desperately in need of a theory which, without dismissing any of these widely held positions, would explain the circumstances underlying their existence, thus paving the way for a critical methodology that encompasses and indeed thrives on their inherent contradictions. If we have learned anything from poststructuralist criticism, we have learned not to fear logical contradictions but instead to respect the extraordinary energy generated by the play of contradictory forces within a field. What we need now is a new critical strategy enabling us simultaneously to understand and to capitalize on the tensions existing in current generic criticism.

In assessing theories of genre, critics have often labeled them according to a particular theory's most salient features or the type of activity to which it devotes its most concentrated attention. Paul Hernadi, for example, recognizes four general classes of genre theory: expressive, pragmatic, structural, and mimetic.[6] In his extremely influential introduction to *The Fantastic,* Tzvetan Todorov opposes historical to theoretical genres, as well as elementary genres to their complex counterparts.[7] Others, like Frederic Jameson, have followed Todorov and other French semioticians in distinguishing between semantic and syntactic approaches to genre.[8] While there is anything but general agreement on the exact frontier separating semantic from syntactic views, we can as a whole distinguish between generic definitions that depend on a list of common traits, attitudes, characters, shots, locations, sets, and the like—thus stressing the semantic elements that make up the genre—and definitions that play up instead certain constitutive relationships between undesignated and variable placeholders—relationships that might be called the genre's fundamental syntax. The semantic approach thus stresses the genre's building blocks, while the syntactic view privileges the structures into which they are arranged.

The difference between semantic and syntactic definitions is perhaps most apparent in familiar approaches to the western. Jean Mitry provides us with a clear example of the most common definition. The western, Mitry proposes, is a "film whose action, situated in the American West, is consistent with the atmosphere, the values, and the conditions of existence in the Far West between 1840 and 1900."[9] Based on the presence or absence of easily identifiable elements, Mitry's nearly tautological definition implies a broad, undifferentiated generic corpus. Marc Vernet's more detailed list is more sensitive to cinematic concerns, yet overall it follows the same semantic model. Vernet outlines general atmosphere ("emphasis on basic elements, such as earth, dust, water, and leather"), stock characters ("the tough/soft cowboy, the lonely sheriff, the faithful or treacherous Indian, and the strong but tender woman"), as well as technical elements ("use of fast tracking and crane shots").[10] An entirely different solution is suggested by Jim Kitses, who emphasizes not the vocabulary of the western but the relationships linking lexical elements. For Kitses the western grows out of a dialectic between the West as garden and as desert (between culture and nature, community and individual, future and past).[11] The western's vocabulary is thus generated by this syntactic relationship, and not vice-versa. John Cawelti attempts to systematize the western in a similar fashion: the western is always set on or near a frontier, where man encounters his uncivilized double. The western thus takes place on the border between two lands, between two eras, and with a hero who remains divided between two value systems (for he combines the town's morals with the outlaw's skills).[12]

In passing we might well note the divergent qualities associated with these two approaches. While the semantic approach has little explanatory power, it is applicable to a larger number of films. Conversely, the syntactic approach surrenders broad applicability in return for the ability to isolate a genre's specific meaning-bearing structures. This alternative seemingly leaves the genre analyst in a quandary: choose the semantic view and you give up *explanatory power*; choose the syntactic approach and you do without *broad applicability*. In terms of the western, the problem of the so-called "Pennsylvania western" is instructive here. To most observers it seems quite clear that films like *High, Wide and Handsome* (Rouben Mamoulian, 1937), *Drums along the Mohawk* (John Ford, 1939), and *Unconquered* (Cecil B. DeMille, 1947) have definite affinities with the western. Employing familiar characters set in relationships similar to their counterparts west of the Mississippi, these films construct plots and develop a frontier structure clearly derived from decades of western novels and films. But they do it in Pennsylvania, and in the wrong century. Are these films westerns because they share the syntax of hundreds of films we call westerns? Or are they not westerns, because they don't fit Mitry's definition?

In fact, the "Pennsylvania western" (like the urban, spaghetti, and sci-fi varieties) represents a quandary only because critics have insisted on dismissing one type of definition and approach in favor of another. As a rule, semantic and syntactic approaches to genre have been proposed, analyzed, evaluated, and disseminated separately, in spite of the complementarity implied by their names. Indeed, many arguments centering on generic problems have arisen only when semantic and syntactic theoreticians have simply talked past each other, each unaware of the other's divergent orientation. I maintain that these two categories of generic analy-

6. *Red River:* The Texas western.

sis are complementary, that they can be combined, and in fact that some of the most important questions of genre study can be asked only when they *are* combined. In short, I propose a semantic/syntactic approach to genre study.

Now, in order to discover whether the proposed semantic/syntactic approach provides any new understanding, let us return to the three contradictions delineated earlier. First, there is the split corpus that characterizes current genre study—on the one side an inclusive list, on the other an exclusive pantheon. It should now be quite clear that each corpus corresponds to a different approach to generic analysis and definition. Tautological semantic definitions, with their goal of broad applicability, outline a large genre of semantically similar texts, while syntactic definitions, intent as they are on explaining the genre, stress a narrow range of texts that privilege specific syntactic relationships. To insist on one of these approaches to the exclusion of the other is to turn a blind eye on the necessarily dual nature of any generic corpus. For every film that participates actively in the elaboration of a genre's syntax there are numerous others content to deploy in no particular relationship the elements traditionally

7. *Drums along the Mohawk:* The "Pennsylvania" western.

associated with the genre. We need to recognize that not all genre films relate to their genre in the same way or to the same extent. By simultaneously accepting semantic and syntactic notions of genre we avail ourselves of a possible way to deal critically with differing levels of "genericity." In addition, a dual approach permits a far more accurate description of the numerous intergeneric connections typically suppressed by single-minded approaches. It is simply not possible to describe Hollywood cinema accurately without the ability to account for the numerous films that innovate by combining the syntax of one genre with the semantics of another. In fact, it is only when we begin to take up problems of genre history that the full value of the semantic/syntactic approach becomes obvious.

As I pointed out earlier, most genre theoreticians have followed the semiotic model and steered clear of historical considerations. Even in the relatively few cases where problems of generic history have been addressed, as in the attempts of Metz and Wright to periodize the western, history has been conceptualized as nothing more than a discontinuous succession of discrete moments, each characterized by a different basic version of the genre—that is, by a different syntactic pattern that the genre adopts.[13] In short, genre theory has up to now aimed almost exclusively at the elaboration of a synchronic model approximating the syntactic operation of a specific genre. Now, quite obviously, no major genre remains unchanged over the many decades of its existence. In order to mask the scandal of applying synchronic analysis to an evolving form, critics have been extremely clever in their creation of categories designed to negate the notion of change and to imply the perpetual self-identity of each genre. Westerns and horror films are often referred to as "classic," the musical is defined in terms of the so-called "Platonic ideal" of integration, the critical corpus of the melodrama has largely been restricted to the postwar efforts of Sirk and Minnelli, and so on. Lacking a workable hypothesis regarding the historical dimension of generic syntax, we have insulated that syntax, along with the genre theory that studies it, from the flow of time.

As a working hypothesis, I suggest that genres arise in one of two fundamental ways: either a relatively stable set of semantic givens is developed through syntactic experimentation into a coherent and durable syntax, or an already existing syntax adopts a new set of semantic elements. In the first case, the genre's characteristic semantic configuration is identifiable long before a syntactic pattern has become stabilized, thus justifying the previously mentioned duality of the generic corpus. In cases of this first type, description of the way in which a set of semantic givens develops into a henceforth relatively stable syntax constitutes the history of the genre while at the same time identifying the structures on which genre theory depends. In dealing with the early development of the musical, for example, we might well follow the attempts during the 1927–1930 period to build a backstage or night-club semantics into a melodramatic syntax, with music regularly reflecting the sorrow of death or parting. After the slack years of 1931–1932, however, the musical began to grow in a new direction; while maintaining substantially the same semantic materials, the genre increasingly related the energy of music-making to the joy of coupling, the strength of the community, and the pleasures of entertainment. Far from being exiled from history, the musical's characteristic syntax can be shown by the generic historian to grow out of the linking of specific semantic elements at identifiable points. A measure of continuity is thus developed between the task of the historian and that of the theoretician, for the tasks of both are now redefined as the study of the interrelationships between semantic elements and syntactic bonds.

This continuity between history and theory is operative as well in the second type of generic development posited earlier. When we analyze the large variety of wartime films that portray the Japanese or Germans as villains, we tend to have recourse to extrafilmic events in order to explain particular characterizations. We thus miss the extent to which films like *All through the Night* (Vincent Sherman, 1942), *Sherlock Holmes and the Voice of Terror* (John Rawlins, 1942), or the serial *The Winslow Boy* (Anthony Asquith, 1948) simply transfer to a new set of semantic elements the righteous cops-punish-criminals syntax that the gangster genre of the early thirties had turned to starting with *G-Men* (William Keighley, 1935). Again, it is the interplay of syntax and semantics that provides grist for both the historical and the theoretical mill. Or take the development of the science fiction film. At first defined only by a relatively stable science fiction semantics, the genre first began borrowing the syntactic relationships previously established by the horror film, only to move in recent years increasingly toward the syntax of the western. By maintaining simultaneous descriptions according to both parameters, we are not likely to fall into the trap of equating *Star Wars* (George Lucas, 1977) with the western (as numerous recent critics have done), even though it shares certain syntactic patterns with that genre. In short, by taking seriously the multiple connections between semantics and syntax, we establish a new continuity, relating film analysis, genre theory, and genre history.

But what is it that energizes the transformation of a borrowed semantics into a uniquely Hollywood syntax? Or what is it that justifies the intrusion of a new semantics into a well-defined syntactic situation? Far from postulating a uniquely internal, formal progression, I would propose that the relationship between the semantic and the syntactic constitutes the very site of negotiation between Hollywood and its audience, and thus between ritual and ideological uses of genre. Often, when critics of opposing persuasions disagree over a major issue, it is because they have established within the same general corpus two separate and opposed canons, each supporting one point of view. Thus, when Catholics and Protestants or liberals and conservatives quote the Bible, they are rarely quoting the same passages. The striking fact about ritual and ideological genre theoreticians, however, is that they regularly stress the same canon, that small group of texts most clearly reflecting a genre's stable syntax. The films of John Ford, for example, have played a major role in the development of ritual and ideological approaches alike. From Sarris and Bogdanovich to Schatz and Wright, champions of Ford's understanding and transparent expression of American values have stressed the communitarian side of his films, while others, starting with the influential *Cahiers du Cinéma* study of *Young Mr. Lincoln* (1939), have shown how a call to community can be used to lure spectators into a carefully chosen, ideologically determined subject position. A similar situation obtains in the musical, where a growing body of ritual analyses of the Astaire-Rogers and postwar MGM Freed unit films is matched by an increasing number of studies demonstrating the ideological investment of those very same films.[14] The corpus of nearly every major genre has developed in the same way, with critics of both camps gravitating toward and eventually basing their arguments on the same narrow range of films. Just as Minnelli and Sirk dominate the criticism of melodrama, Hitchcock has become nearly synonymous with the thriller. Of all major genres, only the film noir has failed to attract critics of both sides to a shared corpus of major texts—no doubt because of the general inability of ritual critics to accommodate the genre's anticommunitarian stance.

This general agreement on a canon stems, I would claim, from the fundamentally bivalent nature of any relatively stable generic syntax. If it takes a long time to establish a generic syntax and if many seemingly promising formulas or successful films never spawn a genre, it is because only certain types of structure, within a particular semantic environment, are suited to the special bilingualism required of a durable genre. The structures of Hollywood cinema, like those of American popular mythology as a whole, serve to mask the very distinction between ritual and ideological functions. Hollywood does not simply lend its voice to the public's desires, nor does it simply manipulate the audience. On the contrary, most genres go through a period of accommodation during which the public's desires are fitted to Hollywood's priorities (and vice-versa). Because the public doesn't want to know that it is being manipulated, the successful ritual/ideological "fit" is almost always one that disguises Hollywood's potential for manipulation while playing up its capacity for entertainment.

Whenever a lasting fit is obtained—which it is whenever a semantic genre becomes a syntactic one—it is because a common ground has been found, a region where the audience's ritual values coincide with Hollywood's ideological ones. The development of a specific syntax within a given semantic context thus serves a double function: it binds element to element in a logical order, at the same time accommodating audience desires to studio concerns. The successful genre owes its success not alone to its reflection of an audience ideal, nor solely to its status as apology for the Hollywood enterprise, but to its ability to carry out both functions simultaneously. It is this sleight of hand, this strategic overdetermination, that most clearly characterizes American film production during the studio years.

The approach to genre sketched out in this article of course raises some questions of its own. Just where, for example, do we locate the exact border between the semantic and the syntactic? And how are these two categories related? Each of these questions constitutes an essential area of inquiry, one that is far too complex to permit full treatment here. Nevertheless, a few remarks may be in order. A reasonable observer might well ask why my approach attributes such importance to the seemingly banal distinction between a text's materials and the structures into which they are arranged. Why this distinction rather than, for example, the more cinematic division between diegetic elements and the technical means deployed in representing them? The answer to these questions lies in a general theory of textual signification that I have expounded elsewhere.[15] Briefly, that theory distinguishes between the primary, linguistic meaning of a text's component parts and the secondary or textual meaning that those parts acquire through a structuring process internal to the text or to the genre. Within a single text, therefore, the same phenomenon may have more than one meaning depending on whether we consider it at the linguistic or textual level. In the western, for example, the horse is an animal that serves as a method of locomotion. This primary level of meaning, corresponding to the normal extent of the concept "horse" within the language, is matched by a series of other meanings derived from the structures into which the western sets the horse. Opposition of the horse to the automobile or locomotive ("iron horse") reinforces the organic, nonmechanical sense of the term "horse" already implicit in the language, thus transferring that concept from the paradigm "method of locomotion" to the paradigm "soon-to-be-outmoded preindustrial carry-over."

In the same way, horror films borrow from a nineteenth-century literary tradition their dependence on the presence of a monster. In doing so, they clearly perpetuate the linguistic meaning of the monster as "threatening inhuman being," but at the same time, by developing new syntactic ties, they generate an important new set of textual meanings. For the nineteenth century, the appearance of the monster is invariably tied to a romantic overreaching, the attempt of some human scientist to tamper with the divine order. In texts like Mary Shelley's *Frankenstein*, Balzac's *La Recherche de l'absolu,* or Stevenson's *Dr. Jekyll and Mr. Hyde,* a studied syntax equates man and monster, attributing to both the monstrosity of being outside nature as defined by established religion and science. With the horror film, a different syntax rapidly equates monstrosity not with the overactive nineteenth-century mind, but with an equally overactive twentieth-century body. Again and again, the monster is identified with his human counterpart's unsatisfied sexual appetite, thus establishing with the same primary "linguistic" materials (the monster, fear, the chase, death) entirely new textual meanings, phallic rather than scientific in nature.

The distinction between the semantic and the syntactic, in the way I have defined it here, thus corresponds to a distinction between the primary, linguistic elements of which all texts are made and the secondary, textual meanings that are sometimes constructed by virtue of the syntactic bonds established between primary elements. This distinction is

stressed in the approach to genre presented here not because it is convenient nor because it corresponds to a modish theory of the relation between language and narrative, but because the semantic/syntactic distinction is fundamental to a theory of how meaning of one kind contributes
to and eventually establishes meaning of another. Just as individual texts
establish new meanings for familiar terms only by subjecting well-known
semantic units to a syntactic redetermination, so generic meaning comes
into being only through the repeated deployment of substantially the
same syntactic strategies. It is in this way, for example, that making music—at the linguistic level primarily a way of making a living—becomes
in the musical a figure for making love—a textual meaning essential to
the constitution of that syntactic genre.

We must of course remember that, while each individual text clearly
has a syntax of its own, the syntax implied here is that of the genre, which
does not appear as *generic* syntax unless it is reinforced numerous times
by the syntactic patterns of individual texts. The Hollywood genres that
have proven the most durable are precisely those that have established the
most coherent syntax (the western, the musical); those that disappear the
quickest depend entirely on recurring semantic elements, never developing a stable syntax (reporter, catastrophe, and big-caper films, to name
but a few). If I locate the border between the semantic and the syntactic at
the dividing line between the linguistic and the textual, it is thus in response not just to the theoretical but also to the historical dimension of
generic functioning.

In proposing such a model, however, I may leave too much room for
one particular type of misunderstanding. It has been a cliché of the last
two decades to insist that structure carries meaning, while the choice of
structured elements is largely negligible in the process of signification.
This position, most openly championed by Lévi-Strauss in his cross-
cultural methodology for studying myth, may seem to be implied by my
model, but is in fact not borne out by my research.[16] Spectator response, I
believe, is heavily conditioned by the choice of semantic elements and atmosphere, because a given semantics used in a specific cultural situation
will recall to an actual interpretive community the particular syntax with
which that semantics has traditionally been associated in other texts. This
syntactic expectation, set up by a *semantic signal,* is matched by a parallel tendency to expect specific syntactic signals to lead to predetermined
semantic fields (e.g., in western texts, regular alternation between male
and female characters creates expectation of the semantic elements implied by romance, while alternation between two males throughout a text
has implied—at least until recently—confrontation and the semantics of
the duel). This interpenetration of the semantic and the syntactic through

the agency of the spectator clearly deserves further study. Suffice it to say for the present that linguistic meanings (and thus the import of semantic elements) are in large part derived from the textual meanings of previous texts. There is thus a constant circulation in both directions between the semantic and the syntactic, between the linguistic and the textual.

Still other questions, such as the general problem of the "evolution" of genres through semantic or syntactic shifts, deserve far more attention than I have given them here. In time, I believe, this new model for the understanding of genre will provide answers for many of the questions traditional to genre study. Perhaps more important still, the semantic/syntactic approach to genre raises numerous questions for which other theories have created no space.

Notes

1. Ferdinand de Saussure, *Course in General Linguistics*, edited by Charles Bally and Albert Sechehaye, translated by Wade Baskin (New York: McGraw-Hill, 1959), pp. 14–17.

2. Especially in Vladimir Propp, *Morphology of the Folktale* (Bloomington: Indiana Research Center in Anthropology, 1958); Claude Lévi-Strauss, "The Structural Study of Myths," in *Structural Anthropology,* trans. Claire Jacobson and Brooke Grundfest Schoepf (New York: Basic Books, 1963), pp. 206–231; Tzvetan Todorov, *Grammaire du Décaméron* (The Hague: Mouton, 1969); and Tzvetan Todorov, *The Fantastic,* translated by Richard Howard (Ithaca: Cornell University Press, 1975).

3. Even Stephen Neale's recent discursively oriented study falls prey to this problem. See *Genre* (London: British Film Institute, 1980).

4. John Cawelti, *The Six-Gun Mystique* (Bowling Green: Bowling Green University Popular Press, [1970]), and John Cawelti, *Adventure, Mystery and Romance* (Chicago: University of Chicago Press, 1976); Leo Braudy, *The World in a Frame: What We See in Films* (Garden City: Anchor Books, 1977); Frank McConnell, *The Spoken Seen: Films and the Romantic Imagination* (Baltimore: Johns Hopkins University Press, 1975); Michael Wood, *America in the Movies, or Santa Maria, It Had Slipped My Mind* (New York: Delta, 1975); Will Wright, *Sixguns and Society: A Structural Study of the Western* (Berkeley: University of California Press, 1975); Thomas Schatz, *Hollywood Genres: Formulas, Filmmaking, and the Studio System* (New York: Random House, 1981).

5. See especially the collective text "*Young Mr. Lincoln* de John Ford," *Cahiers du Cinéma,* no. 223 (August 1970): 29–47, translated in *Screen* 14, no. 3 (Autumn 1973): 29–43; and Jean-Louis Comolli's six-part article "Technique et ideologie," *Cahiers du Cinéma,* nos. 229–241 (1971–1972). The entire *Screen* project has been usefully summarized, with extensive bibliographical notes, by Philip Rosen, "*Screen* and the Marxist Project in Film Criticism," *Quarterly Review of Film Studies* 2, no. 3 (August 1977): 273–287; on *Screen*'s approach to

ideology, see also Stephen Heath, "On Screen, in Frame: Film and Ideology," *Quarterly Review of Film Studies* 1, no. 3 (August 1976): 251–265. The most important influence on all these positions is Louis Althusser, "Ideology and Ideological State Apparatuses," in *Lenin and Philosophy and Other Essays,* translated by Ben Brewster (New York: Monthly Review Press, 1971), pp. 127–186.

6. Paul Hernadi, *Beyond Genre: New Directions in Literary Classification* (Ithaca: Cornell University Press, 1972).

7. Todorov, *The Fantastic.*

8. Fredric Jameson, "Magical Narratives: Romance as Genre," *New Literary History* 7 (1975): 135–163. It should be noted here that my use of the term "semantic" differs from Jameson's. Whereas he stresses the overall semantic input of a text, I am dealing with the individual semantic units of the text. His term thus approximates the sense of "global meaning," while mine is closer to "lexical choices."

9. Jean Mitry, *Dictionnaire du cinéma* (Paris: Larousse, 1963), p. 276.

10. Marc Vernet, *Lectures du film* (Paris: Albatros, 1976), pp. 111–112.

11. Jim Kitses, *Horizons West* (Bloomington: Indiana University Press, 1969), pp. 10–14.

12. Cawelti, *The Six-Gun Mystique.*

13. See, for example, Christian Metz, *Language and Cinema* (The Hague: Mouton, 1974), pp. 148–161; and Wright, *Sixguns and Society,* passim.

14. This relationship is especially interesting in the work of Richard Dyer and Jane Feuer, both of whom attempt to confront the interdependence of ritual and ideological components. See in particular Richard Dyer, "Entertainment and Utopia," in *Genre: The Musical,* edited by Rick Altman (London and Boston: Routledge and Kegan Paul, 1981), pp. 175–189; and Jane Feuer, *The Hollywood Musical* (Bloomington: Indiana University Press, 1982).

15. Charles F. Altman, "Intratextual Rewriting: Textuality as Language Formation," in *The Sign in Music and Literature,* edited by Wendy Steiner (Austin: University of Texas Press, 1981), pp. 39–51.

16. The most straightforward statement of Lévi-Strauss's position is in "The Structural Study of Myths." For a useful elucidation of that position, see Edmund Leach, *Claude Lévi-Strauss* (New York: Viking Press, 1970).

4. Genre Films and the Status Quo

JUDITH HESS WRIGHT

The ideas of order that [the culture industry] inculcates are always those of the status quo. . . . Pretending to be the guide for the helpless and deceitfully presenting to them conflicts that they must perforce confuse with their own, the culture industry does not resolve these conflicts except in appearance—its "solutions" would be impossible for them to use to resolve their conflicts in their own lives. —T. W. ADORNO, The Culture Industry [1]

American genre films—the western, the science fiction film, the horror film, the gangster film—have been the most popular (and thus the most lucrative) products ever to emerge from the machinery of the American film industry. Critics have long pondered the genre film's success and have attempted to ferret out the reasons for the public's appreciation of even the most undistinguished "singing cowboy" westerns. In general, critics have examined these films as isolated phenomena—as found objects— instead of considering genre films in relation to the society that created them. Genre films have been defined as pure myth, as well-made plays, and as psychodramas bearing within themselves the working out of un- conscious anxieties inherent in the psychological makeup of us all. Cer- tainly any and all of these explanations contain some truth; however, none of them explains why American genre films grew to become our most numerous, if not most artistically significant, film productions.

I think that we may see what genre films are by examining what they do. These films came into being and were financially successful because they temporarily relieved the fears aroused by a recognition of social and political conflicts; they helped to discourage any action that might other- wise follow upon the pressure generated by living with these conflicts. Genre films produce satisfaction rather than action, pity and fear rather than revolt. They serve the interests of the ruling class by assisting in the maintenance of the status quo, and they throw a sop to oppressed groups who, because they are unorganized and therefore afraid to act, eagerly accept the genre film's absurd solutions to economic and social conflicts. When we return to the complexities of the society in which we live, the same conflicts assert themselves, so we return to genre films for easy com- fort and solace—hence their popularity.

Genre films address these conflicts and resolve them in a simplistic and reactionary way. Genre films have three significant characteristics that make such resolutions seem possible and even logical. First, these films never deal directly with present social and political problems; second, all of them are set in the nonpresent. Westerns and horror films take place in the past; science fiction films, by definition, take place in a future time. The gangster film takes place in a social structure so separate from the contemporary structure in which it appears to be taking place that its actual time and place become irrelevant. Third, the society in which the action takes place is very simple and does not function as a dramatic force in the films—it exists as a backdrop against which the few actors work out the central problem the film presents. As Robert Warshow points out in *The Immediate Experience*,[2] the westerner exists in isolation. We have no idea where he gets his money or where he washes. His trials and confrontations take place in utter isolation (the desert or mountains) or in the setting of a tiny, uncomplicated western town. Horror films present an isolated group of people who live in a tiny village or meet in a castle or island that they do not leave until the end of the movie, if at all. Many science fiction films show professionals moving away from society—to an island, an experimental station of some sort, the South Pole, outer space—to cope with alien intruders. Although some science fiction films are set in modern cities, the cities are weirdly empty and serve as labyrinths through which the protagonists thread their ways. The gangster lives in a very limited world populated by a few other gangsters and their molls.

All of these genre films, science fiction included, present a greatly simplified social structure. However frequently this kind of very limited social structure may have existed in the past, it no longer exists in the present. Thus, genre films are nostalgic; their social structure posits some sort of movement backward to a simpler world. And in this simple structure, problems that haunt us because of our inability to resolve them are solved in ways not possible today. Genre films reject the present and ignore any likely future.

The genre films focus on four major conflicts. The western centers on the violent act and ascertains when, if ever, it becomes morally right. The horror film attempts to resolve the disparities between two contradictory ways of problem solving—one based on rationality, the other based on faith, an irrational commitment to certain traditional beliefs. The science fiction film provides a solution to the problems presented by intrusion— that is, they tell us how to deal with what may be called "the other." Gangster films resolve the contradictory feelings of fear and desire that are aroused by attempts to achieve financial and social success.

The problems posed by these contradictions are solved simply. The western decrees that the violent act can become morally right when it occurs within the confines of a code that allows for executions, revenge killings, and killings in defense of one's life and property. In the microcosmic western society everyone's code is the same; thus absolute guilt and innocence are possible because social and moral goodness are the same. Horror films present human beings as fallen, prey to uncontrollable evil impulses. Only by reliance on traditional beliefs and the domination of a well-defined upper class can we be saved from doom and perdition. The science fiction film's answer to the problem of the intruder is sheerest isolationism. No possible advance in knowledge gained from communication could possibly outweigh the dangers it presents—the only sane response is to eradicate it. The gangster film, by implication, opts for happy anonymity. To be successful is to become vulnerable; the successful ones become the foes of all who wish to take their place. Gangster films show the fearful results of attempting to rise within a hierarchical society and thus defend class lines. These simplistic solutions—the adherence to a well-defined, unchanging code, the advocacy of methods of problem solving based on tradition and faith, the advocacy of isolationism, and the warning to stay within one's station to survive—all militate against progressive social change.

In order to flesh out these assertions it is necessary to examine each of the genres in some detail. The western male is dominated by a code of honor that prescribes his every action; violence by lynching or shooting, amorous advances, or friendships are determined by some fixed rule. One lynches cattle rustlers but not petty thieves—one runs them out of town. One sleeps only with bar girls, not eastern schoolteachers. One never shoots a man in the back; one is utterly loyal to one's friends, defending them physically and verbally at every possible opportunity. At a certain mystical point in the interaction between two opposing forces, the western version of the duel becomes morally acceptable; both the villain and the hero know immediately when this point comes, as they do not exist as psychological entities apart from the code—rather, they embody the code. The earliest westerns afford the clearest expression of the workings of this code. In these movies the heroes and villains are like chess pieces moved about to depict the code's intricacies. In a great many westerns we can note the eerie occurrence of two phrases that are as far as these movies go toward positing motivation: "I have to . . ." and "All I know is . . ." These phrases express how the code provides motivation, not the persons themselves. Westerners act together in absolute, unthinking accord. Westerns examine those aspects of the code that determine the westerner's response to situations demanding violence. The compartmentalizations of the code—one treats bank robbers one way and friends another—allow for situations involving contradictory responses. What happens, for example, in *The Virginian* (Victor Fleming, 1929), a movie that Robert Warshow calls "archetypal," when a captured rustler is at the same time a friend? Gary Cooper, a chess-piece representation of the code, is caught on the horns of a moral and social dilemma. Although he must bow to the will of the other members of the posse, for whom the situation is not complicated (the rustler is not their friend), and assist in the lynching and see his friend exonerate him, Cooper must work within the code to redeem himself—to rid himself of guilt by balancing the books.

And there is a single, simple solution. His friend has been drawn into rustling by the film's real villain, Trampas. Cooper must wipe him out, at the same time showing the restraint demanded of the westerner. He must wait for that mystical point in time at which the showdown becomes morally and socially right. And Trampas, because he is a villain and thus cannot act in any other way, provides Cooper with sufficient injury and insult, and is thus shot in a fair fight. Several violent actions are condoned in the movie: traditionally sanctioned violence demanded by the group (Cooper never questions the lynching; he suffers only because he is forced to abandon his friend); violence brought about by repeated attacks on one's character (Trampas indicates that Cooper is a coward); and violence that redeems the violence Cooper has been forced to commit against his friend. These acts of violence have complete social sanction. Only Cooper's eastern schoolmarm girlfriend fails to condone Cooper's actions; she has not as yet been assimilated into western society.

In the western every man who operates solely with reference to this strict code lives and dies redeemed. He has retained his social and moral honor. The code provides justification; thus it allows for a guiltless existence. On the other hand, we do not know ourselves when, if ever, violence is justifiable. We have great difficulty in forming a personal code and we cannot be sure that this code will conform in any way to the large, impersonal legal code set up to regulate our unwieldy, decaying economic structure. The westerner's code is at once personal and social—if a man lives by it he both conforms to social norms and retains his personal integrity. The source of the satisfaction we get from the western is evident. Momentarily we understand the peace that comes from acting in accord with a coherent moral and social code and forget our fragmented selves. Many critics have seen the western as a glorification of traditional American individualism. On the contrary, the western preaches integration and assimilation and absolute obedience to the laws of the land.

The horror film deals with the conflict between rational or scientific and traditional ways of problem solving. In *Dracula* (Tod Browning, 1930), *Frankenstein* (James Whale, 1931), *The Mummy* (Karl Freund, 1932), and *The Wolf Man* (George Waggner, 1948), the monsters are the embodiment of human evil. They are three-dimensional representations of our uncontrollable will to evil; we must conquer them if society is to survive. Lawrence Talbot ignores the gypsy's warnings, is tainted by a wolf bite, and becomes dominated by evil desires—he kills those he cares for. Dracula, the incarnation of unbridled sensuality, attracts his victims,

8. *Dracula:* The vampire (Bela Lugosi) as the incarnation of unbridled sensuality.

sucks them dry, and condemns them to becoming like him. Before becoming a mummy, an Egyptian prince has unsuccessfully pitted himself against the will of the gods. He, too, represents unbridled sensual appetite, the naked id. Dr. Frankenstein's poor maimed creation is a projection of his own overwhelming will to power and knowledge beyond that granted by God. Because he relies totally on scientific means to ends, he becomes a monster himself—he is redeemed by suffering and by his complete rejection of his heretical drive to uncover the secrets of life and death.

Various groups attempt to overcome the monsters. "Ignorant peasants" (for example, the Egyptian workers or the Carpathian peasants), who believe in the reality of evil but who belong to a traditionally oppressed class, are overcome, or, at best, live out a miserable existence under the monster's sway. The masses are shown to be without sufficient moral strength to overcome the monster themselves. These monsters are at some point opposed by enlightened scientists who, because they believe only in the ability of science to defeat social and physical ills and in rational, demonstrable means to ends, disregard tradition and thus threaten the existing social order. Because these scientists refuse to believe in the power of the irrational will to evil, the monster annihilates them. The monster is finally defeated by members of the upper class who abandon scientific training in favor of belief in the traditional ways in which others before them have overcome evil forces. Dr. Van Helsing, once he realizes that medical science cannot save Dracula's victims, does research, finds what traditionally has been used against Dracula (beheading, garlic, a stake through the heart), and employs these means. The wolfman is killed by a silver-headed cane; the mummy is destroyed by an appeal to the ancient Egyptian gods. Van Helsing makes the required return to tradition with a commitment to articles of faith, as do all those who defeat the evil.

The message is clear: science must not be allowed to replace traditional values and beliefs. Otherwise, chaos will result, as humans cannot control their own evil tendencies or those of the people around them without suprarational help. The social order out of which these monsters spring is posited as good—it must remain unchanged. Only by the benevolent dictatorship of the hereditary aristocracy can these monsters be kept at bay; the existing class structure prevents chaos. Like the German expressionist horror films that preceded them, American horror films (the first and best of which appeared in the early thirties) may be seen as a reaction to a period of economic and social upheaval—the films are, in effect, a plea to go back to older methods of coping. This solution works in the horror film's oversimplified world.

The science fiction film, which developed during the forties and fifties, may be seen as a dramatization of those fears and desires aroused by the cold war. "The other," however strange and alien, has at least some significant relation to those massed hordes of Communists foisted on the American people by such venomous Red-baiters as Joseph McCarthy, Richard Nixon, and Billy Graham. Confronted by "the other," according to these films, there is only one possible response. We must use every scientific means at our disposal to destroy the invader.

As in the horror film, the social order that exists previous to the coming of the aliens is posited as good. The aliens, who are scientifically advanced but who lack emotions (that is, they do not share our values), invade in frightening machines. Often nonviolent communication is established between a few scientists and the aliens. However, these scientists invariably learn that these beings aim to take our bodies, as in *Invasion of the Body Snatchers* (Don Siegel, 1956) or to assume social and political control, as in *Earth vs. the Flying Saucers* (Fred F. Sears, 1956), or to suck our blood, as in *The Thing* (Christian Nyby, 1951). The un-

9. *Invasion of the Body Snatchers* (1956): The "other" invades the home.

easiness Americans feel about scientific advance and intellectuals in general is evident in many of these films—often a wild-haired scientist is willing to hand over the country to the invaders in order to learn more about the secrets of the universe. He is either annihilated by the very invaders he has tried to protect, or he regroups when confronted by the invaders' lack of concern with our traditional values and social structures. Usually, however, the scientists (often they are allied with the military) are the first to recognize the extent of the aliens' ill will and band together to defeat them. Great ingenuity and immediate scientific advance are required to win the fight, but the scientists discover the necessary materials in the nick of time and save the world. Although a few films like *20 Million Miles to Earth* (Nathan Juran, 1957) and *The Day the Earth Stood Still* (Robert Wise, 1951) question the absolute evil of the aliens, these films were not well received. It was those films that gave a single, unequivocal answer to the problem of "the other" which were the most successful. The message of these films was that "the other" will do only evil, no matter what blandishments disguise its true intent. The only recourse is to destroy it utterly. And, so say these films, we can. These films build on fears of the intrusive and the overpowering and thereby promote isolationism. They also imply that science is good only inasmuch as it serves to support the existing class structure.

The best beginning to a discussion of the gangster film is Robert Warshow's description of our reactions to it:

> The gangster is doomed because he is under obligation to succeed, not because the means he employs are unlawful. In the deeper layers of the modern consciousness, *all* means are unlawful, every attempt to succeed is an act of aggression, leaving one alone and guilty and defenseless among enemies: one is *punished* for success. This is our intolerable dilemma: that failure is a kind of death and success is evil and dangerous and—ultimately—impossible. The effect of the gangster film is to embody this dilemma in the person of the gangster and resolve it by his death. The dilemma is resolved because it is his death, not ours. We are safe; for the moment we can acquiesce in our failure, we can choose to fail.[3]

The world of the gangster is made up of a pyramidal hierarchy. Only one man can be the top dog. We follow a single man as he makes his way up the various ranks of the structure. In *The Public Enemy* (William Wellman, 1931), he starts out as a petty thief who sells his loot to a fence a few steps higher up in the system. He quickly graduates to stealing liquor supplies and, finally, to the rank of boss. Unlike Scarface and Little Caesar, who make it all the way, Cagney is undone by his own temper and arrogance before he becomes much more than small-time. However, he is intrepid enough to attempt to revenge another gang's decimation of his own hierarchy, and is killed as a warning to others who might attempt to meddle with the strong. These men are rebels and renegades, but only within the confines of the existing order. They do not wish to establish a different kind of structure, but to fight their way to the top of an existing one. This pyramid is a microcosm of the capitalist structure. We have a very ambivalent response to the competition necessary to survive in our own competitive society. We know that we must defeat other people to succeed ourselves. And because we have reached some worthwhile position through aggression, we are left vulnerable to any competitor who covets our position. We are left with the choice of fighting with all comers—and we know we cannot do that successfully forever—or else failing. As Warshow states, we can exist with our own economic and social failure as we watch the gangster's death. For a moment it becomes acceptable to survive, even at the price of economic anonymity. A gangster film would never suggest that a different sort of social and political structure might allow for more humane possibilities. In fact, the gangster film implicitly upholds capitalism by making the gangster an essentially tragic figure. The insolubility of his problem is not traced to its social cause; rather the problem is presented as growing out of the gangster's character.

His tragic flaw is ambition; his stature is determined by the degree to which he rises in the hierarchy. We are led to believe that he makes choices, not that he is victimized by the world in which he finds himself. The gangster film retains its appeal because our economic structure does not change—we must commit aggressive acts to survive within the confines of our capitalistic structure. And, as Warshow implies, when we see a gangster film—be it *Little Caesar* (Mervyn LeRoy, 1930) or *The Godfather* (Francis Ford Coppola, 1971)—we are moved not to struggle out of our class to question our hierarchical social structure, but to subside and survive.

We may trace the amazing survival and proliferation of the genre films to their function. They assist in the maintenance of the existing political structure. The solutions these films give to the conflicts inherent in capitalism require obeisance to the ruling class and cause viewers to yearn for not less but greater freedom in the face of the insoluble ambiguities surrounding them. Viewers are encouraged to cease examining themselves and their surroundings, and to take refuge in fantasy from their only real alternative—to rise up against the injustices perpetrated by the present system upon its members.

Notes

1. T. W. Adorno, "The Culture Industry," trans. Rafael Cook, *Cinéaste* 5, no. 1, 8–11.

2. Robert Warshow, "Movie Chronicle: The Westerner," in *The Immediate Experience* (New York: Atheneum, 1971), pp. 135–154.

3. Ibid., p. 133.

5. Social Implications in the Hollywood Genres

JEAN-LOUP BOURGET

From the outset, the cinema has been characterized by a certain tension, even a certain conflict, between an apparent content, derived from popular literature, and a number of autonomous stylistic devices (the various uses of actors, sets, camera movements, montage). Strictures traditionally passed on the Hollywood film fail to take into account the basic fact that its conventionality is the very paradoxical reason for its creativity. Conventions inherited from literature have added themselves to social pressures, such as the necessity for self-censorship, and to commercial imperatives, and may well have badly hampered the explicit content and meaning of movies—plot and characterization frequently tending to become stereotyped. But in many instances the newness of the medium made it possible, even mandatory, to resort to a language both visual and aural, whose implicit meaning was far removed from what the mere script might convey. Here are two brief examples. In Griffith's films, we find a tension between the conventional Victorian moralizing of the plot and titles, and the much more subtle meanings of sets, lighting, close-ups of actresses' faces, camera movements, and editing. In Josef von Sternberg's films, there is an open, unresolved conflict between the stereotypes of the plot and dialogue and the "pure poetry" of the visual elements.

Another point that should be borne in mind is that, whenever an art form is highly conventional, the opportunity for subtle irony or distanciation presents itself all the more readily. The director's (that is to say, the camera's) point of view need not coincide with the hero's point of view; or again, and more generally, since a film represents a superposition of texts, it is not surprising that large segments of an audience (notably including literary-minded critics) should decipher only one of these texts and therefore misread the sum total of the various texts. European directors working in Hollywood developed a technique for telling stories with implicit ironical meanings. For example, Ernst Lubitsch's *Trouble in Paradise* (1932) presents a coherent view of contemporary society under the neat gloss of the sophisticated comedy: thieves are capitalists; capitalists are thieves. Similarly, *To Be or Not to Be* (Lubitsch, 1942) is not just a farce: it makes the not altogether frivolous point that the historical Nazis were worse actors than the fictitious bad actors of the Polish underground. The point was completely missed by the contemporary audience, who regarded the film as being in very bad taste. The same remark applies to most of Douglas Sirk's American films. Thus *All That Heaven Allows* (1956) is not a "weepie," but a sharp satire of small-town America; *Written on the Wind* (1957) is not about the glamor of American high society, but about its corruption; *Imitation of Life* (1959) is superficially naïve and optimistic, but profoundly bitter and antiracist.

The conflict between the movie's pre-text (the script, the source of the adaptation) and its text (all the evidence on the screen and sound track) provides us with an analytic tool, because it allows for a reconciliation of two apparently antagonistic approaches: the auteur theory, which claims that a film is the work of one creative individual, and the iconological approach, which assumes that a film is a sequence of images whose real meaning may well be unconscious on the part of its makers. Elsewhere I have tried to show that the original version of *Back Street* (John M. Stahl, 1932), while apparently describing a woman's noble and sad sacrifice, is in fact a melodrama with profound social and feministic implications.[1] I also stated that "melodrama" in its traditional sense was born at the time of the French Revolution and reflected social unrest in a troubled historical period. In the context of the description of society, we may therefore distinguish between melodramas such as *Back Street,* which express a certain state of society, depicting its relative stability and the occasions of potential conflict, and melodramas such as *Orphans of the Storm* (D. W. Griffith, 1922) and *Anthony Adverse* (Mervyn LeRoy, 1936), which comment on actual turmoil. It would probably be possible to give a survey of other popular genres in search of similar examples of these alternative approaches: description of an operative system, description of the breaking up of a given structure.

In the first category—films describing how a given social structure operates—we find many movies belonging to genres that are often dismissed as escapist and alienating. While this may well be true in a majority of cases, it nevertheless remains that escapism can also be used as a device for criticizing reality and the present state of society. A utopian world that calls itself a utopia is not escapist in the derogatory sense of the word; rather, it calls the viewer's attention to the fact that his or her own society is far removed from such an ideal condition. Many films by such Rousseauistic directors as Allan Dwan and Delmer Daves belong to this category; they might best be described as "South Seas adventure dramas"— see Allan Dwan's adaptation of Melville's *Typee* (*Enchanted Island,* 1958) and Delmer Daves's *Bird of Paradise* (1951), *Treasure of the Golden Con-*

dor (1953), and his western *Broken Arrow* (1950). Some of these films suffer from a stylistic incompetence that somewhat forces the implicit meaning back out of the film itself, into the director's generous but unrealized intentions. More to the point are perhaps two films by John Ford, *The Hurricane* (1937) and *Donovan's Reef* (1963). The first film implicitly contrasts Raymond Massey, who embodies the oppressive law, with the Lincoln of other John Ford films, Lincoln being an incarnation of the law which gives life and freedom. In *Donovan's Reef,* a brief scene located in Boston supplies the key to implicit meaning as we are allowed to glimpse a caricatural reality of America opposed to the idealized vision of the Pacific island.

In contradistinction to the legend that in all traditional westerns "the only good Indian is a dead Indian," a closer look at early Hollywood westerns reveals surprising conflicts between explicit and implicit meanings. Thus in DeMille's *The Squawman,* a subject obviously dear to him since he treated it on three different occasions (1913, 1918, 1931), an Englishman who has settled in America is seduced by the "primitive" and therefore "immoral" beauty of an Indian woman drying her naked body by the fire. He lives with her without marrying her, and she bears him a child. Years later, the Englishman's relatives look him up and insist on taking his child to England in order to give him a proper education. Because of her "primitive" mind (as the man puts it), the Indian woman does not understand why her son should be taken away from her, and she commits suicide. Earlier on, she had already been rejected by the child, who had preferred an electric train to the crude wooden horse that she had carved for him. In its treatment of the story, DeMille's point of view is sympathetic to the Indian woman rather than to the Europeans. To him, she is morally superior. This is made clear less by the plot than by the lyricism of the sequences devoted to Lupe Velez "seducing" the Englishman or carving the wooden toy. At the same time, because of its tragic conclusion, the film could hardly be accused of being escapist or naively optimistic. In a much more subtle way, the indictment of white pseudo-civilization is as harsh as in Arthur Penn's *Little Big Man* of 1970. But these cultural tensions remain implicit and unresolved. Obviously, the "deconstruction" of ironical analysis is not synonymous with "destruction." Is this failure to resolve tensions due to weakness in the creative act or rather to the capitalistic mode of film production? In Hollywood, the director's work, however conscious it may be of social alienation, is bound by the same alienation.

Ironical implications of a social breakdown can be embedded in the most highly conventional and least realistic films. Such a movie is *Heidi* (Allan Dwan, 1937), starring Shirley Temple, where kitsch, as is usual, verges on parody. Only in a kitsch film or in a comedy could servants be emblematically described as holding a feather duster. The kitsch movie is often located in Central Europe, and the ideal society it tends to refer to is that of the Hapsburg Empire. There we find a static hierarchical society where everybody is defined by a social function rather than by individual traits. But the providential architecture of this social system is so exaggerated that (whether consciously or unconsciously on the part of the filmmakers) the effect produced is, in the last analysis, satirical. Stylistically, social functions are indicated by emblems (folkloric costumes, pointed helmets, plumes), which look slightly ridiculous. For example, in *Zoo in Budapest* (Rowland V. Lee, 1933), society is neatly divided between the haves and the have-nots, between those with some parcel of authority and those without any. On the one hand, we find certain aristocratic visitors to the zoo and a multitude of characters in quasi-military uniforms: wardens, policemen, bus drivers. On the other hand, we have the peasant visitors in colorful garb, the girls from an orphanage, and the unsociable hero who seeks the company of animals rather than that of men. This amounts to the description of a society so alienated that, in order to be free, one has to live behind bars in a zoo! The last part of the film bursts into nightmare, as all the wild beasts escape from their cages—a suggestion that this neatly organized society is no less prone to explosions and revolutions, notwithstanding the literally incredible ending, which claims to reconcile the feudal system and the individual's happiness.[2]

Similarly, a turn-of-the-century setting seems to be very popular in a variety of genres, from the literary adaptation (*The Picture of Dorian Gray*, Albert Lewin, 1945) to the horror film (*Hangover Square*, John Brahm, 1945), from the romantic drama (*Letter from an Unknown Woman*, Max Ophuls, 1948) to the musical (*Meet Me in St. Louis*, Vincente Minnelli, 1944; *Gigi*, Minnelli, 1958; *My Fair Lady*, George Cukor, 1964). There are probably two reasons for this popularity. For one thing, such a setting has stylistic qualities that readily lend themselves to artistic effects. For another thing, it refers to Western society—usually but not necessarily European—at its most sophisticated, on the eve of the First World War and of the economic collapse of Europe. This presumably accounts for the success of the Viennese film, a genre that has often been wrongly explained in naively biographical and nostalgic terms. The satirical element that is obvious in von Stroheim's films is implicit in the works of other European directors. Josef von Sternberg's *Dishonoured* (1931) contrasts Marlene Dietrich's *amour fou* with the sense of decadence and the collapse of empires, Austrian and Russian. In Anatole Litvak's *Mayerling* (1936), the lovers are doomed, not by fate but by the ominous sign of the Hapsburg Empire, the oppressive Eagle of *raison d'état:* the ball scene in particular opens with the camera seemingly tracking through a glass eagle and ends with the same movement in reverse. In many "Viennese" films, both European and American, Ophuls uses the device of a duel, which points out the way in which a particular class of society goes about solving its private problems when they cannot be kept private any longer.

Such films therefore enable us to put forward a tentative definition of melodrama as opposed to tragedy: in melodrama, fate is not metaphysical but rather social or political. Thus melodrama is bourgeois tragedy, dependent upon an awareness of the existence of society. This echoes Benjamin Constant's own definition of the new tragedy: "Social order, the action of society on the individual, in different phases and at different epochs, this network of institutions and conventions in which we are caught from our birth and which does not break until we die, these are the mainsprings of tragedy. One only has to know how to use them. They are absolutely equivalent to the Fatum of the Ancients." [3]

In several respects, the musical is close to the cinematic melodrama, both having developed from forms of spectacle associated with the conventions of the popular stage. In order to express an implicit meaning, they both have to rely almost exclusively on stylization, at once visual and musical (melodrama is etymologically "drama with music"), for they are both removed from the convention of realism.[4] In the hands of creative individual directors, musicals therefore lend themselves to statements that will pass unnoticed by the majority of the entertainment-seeking audience and by critics who judge the explicit content. Unsurprisingly, some directors have excelled in both genres—above all, Minnelli. *Brigadoon* (1954) is an excellent example of what is meant here: the musical is set against the motif of bustling New York, and the meaning of the supposedly escapist part of the movie can only be induced from the satirized madness of the everyday setting toward the end of the film.

An allegory frequent in the musical is that of Pygmalion, of a member of respectable society raising a girl of the lower classes to his own level of civilized sophistication. It is the particular failure of *My Fair Lady* (George Cukor, 1964) to have used Audrey Hepburn in such a part, because the actress is evidently an extremely sophisticated one. Thus the parable rings false; in order to make it convincing, Cukor should have used an actress of a completely different type, Shirley MacLaine, for example, and have her look like a lady by the end of the film. For the implication should be that there is nothing in high society that a good actor or dancer should not be capable of achieving through imitation. Again, it should suggest a reversal of the apparent roles and functions similar to the one found in Lubitsch's *Trouble in Paradise:* if dancers are ladies, ladies cannot be far different from dancers. The whole oeuvre of such directors as Minnelli and Cukor is based on this underlying assumption, which, hidden behind a playful guise, is both a satire of actual social solidity and an indication of possible social fluidity (see Cukor's films starring Judy Holliday and Minnelli's films starring Judy Garland).

Easter Parade (Charles Walters, 1948) tells a story similar to that of *My Fair Lady,* with Fred Astaire and Judy Garland in roles similar to those of Rex Harrison and Audrey Hepburn. But there the allegory works, and goes farther, because it has serious bearings on woman's status in society. At the end of the film, Judy Garland, tired of waiting to be proposed to, decides that there is no reason why she should not in fact woo Fred Astaire. She adopts the man's traditional role, sends numerous gifts to the object of her thoughts, and compliments him on his beautiful clothes. The musical, like a court jester, is allowed a saturnalian freedom because it is not a "serious" genre. Its self-eulogy ("Be a Clown" in Minnelli's *The Pirate,* 1948; "Make 'Em Laugh" in Donen and Kelly's *Singin' in the Rain,* 1952; and "That's Entertainment" in Minnelli's *The Band Wagon,* 1953) shows its understandable reluctance to part with such a liberty.

Another category of films is not content with describing a system, but portrays its collapse. (Screwball comedies and Busby Berkeley musicals, connected with the Depression, can be mentioned in passing.) [5] The implicit meaning may be more difficult to assert in historical films and epics because they often refer to revolutions or civil wars whose pattern is given as fact and thus not susceptible to an interpretation. Yet a coherent explanation is sometimes to be found hidden behind the historical or adventurous plot. *Anthony Adverse,* referred to earlier, is located in the time of the French Revolution and of the First Empire. It is critical of both the former aristocracy and of the new classes, depicted as a ruthless mob aping the former nobility. The only solution is found in leaving a doomed continent and sailing for the new land and the democratic society of America. A somewhat similar point of view is expressed in *A Tale of Two Cities* (Jack Conway, 1935), where the French Revolution must be shown as almost simultaneously profoundly justified and profoundly unjust. This is achieved in a very interesting way. The first part of the film is, despite a few hints, rather sympathetic to the idea of a revolution, which is shown as inevitable. Even more committed are the sequences of the revolution proper (the storming of the Bastille), which were directed by a different team—Jacques Tourneur and Val Lewton. They are absolutely Eisensteinlike in their depiction of blatant injustice and spontaneous union, Sovietlike, of people and army. From there on, it is impossible to think of any adequate transition; the trick consists in skipping over the transition, in reverting to a title, a pre-text, which claims that the spirit of liberty had been betrayed even before it had triumphed. But such is not the evidence on the screen, and the film embodies a strange, unresolved discrepancy between the sequences directed by Jack Conway (pleasant but traditional in style, faithful to the source of the adaptation) and those by Jacques Tourneur, formally very original, unambiguous in their meaning, and telling a tale of their own.

Conversely, a perfectly coherent film about the French Revolution is *Marie Antoinette* (Woody S. Van Dyke, 1937)—coherent, that is, from a reactionary point of view. Yet, even in this case, we see a tension at work between the explicit argument of the film as signified by the title (a woman's picture, the sad, dignified story of Marie Antoinette) and the implicit political message, according to which the hero/victim is King Louis XVI rather than Marie Antoinette. In the light of the film, she is not much more than a pleasure-loving girl, but he is portrayed as a man of good will who was betrayed by a conspiracy of Freemasons and the Duke of Orleans.

A subgenre of the adventure film that almost inevitably acclaims a pattern of social unrest and revolution (always successful in this case, because it is far removed in time and space, and therefore with no apparent direct bearings on present society) is the swashbuckler, the pirate film. The most "democratic" examples of the genre include two films by Michael Curtiz, *Captain Blood* (1935) and *The Sea Hawk* (1940). In both, an apolitical man is charged with sedition and actually becomes a rebel (cf. a similar parable in John Ford's *Prisoner of Shark Island,* 1936). Both films describe the way a colonial system rests on political oppression, slavery, and torture; they both advocate violent revolution as the only means of destroying such a system. The evidence of the genre therefore conflicts with the evidence of colonial films set in the twentieth century—for example, in British India or in French North Africa—where it is the outlaw who is supposedly guilty of savagery. It might be illuminating to show to what extent a contemporary, politically committed filmmaker like Gillo Pontecorvo has relied on the traditional Hollywood and Cinecittà genre of the pirate film in his 1968 film *Quemada* (*Burn!* in English).

As pointed out before, the danger of certain explicit statements about Robin Hood and pirate figures in distant times or remote places is that the remoteness can be emphasized rather than played down. In historical films about outlaws, the viewer is allowed to walk out with a clear conscience and a dim consciousness. This danger was realized and pointed out by directors more sophisticated than Michael Curtiz. In *Sullivan's Travels* (1942), Preston Sturges satirized the conventions of the social-problem genre that had flourished at Warners under the guidance of Mervyn LeRoy, among others. The bittersweet conclusion of Sturges's film was that directors should not go beyond the camera, that they should not make social statements when they have but the vaguest notions about the condition of society, and should rather devote their time and energy to the making of comedies. But his own film showed that he could somehow do both at the same time: entertain and make valid comments. Similarly, Minnelli's *The Pirate* underlines the conventions of the swashbuckler. It adds another dimension to the meaning of the pirate film. Judy Garland, the governor's daughter, falls in love with Gene Kelly, an actor who parades as Macoco, the fierce pirate. The point is, first, that to make a "revolutionary" and "democratic" pirate film is partly to base the argument on Errol Flynn's—or Gene Kelly's—sex appeal. But this is only the first layer of meaning. The actor, not the pirate, turns out to be the "revolutionary" individual who is going to achieve social change, for he unmasks Walter Slezak (Judy Garland's fiancé), the real Macoco who parades as a respectable citizen. The lesson is therefore that piracy can be identified with respectable bourgeois society, and that the artist (whether an actor or a Hollywood director) emerges as the one person with both a sense of individual freedom and the refusal to oppress others.

Thus the freedom of Hollywood directors is not measured by what they can openly do within the Hollywood system, but rather by what they can imply about American society in general and about the Hollywood system in particular. They can describe in extensive detail how a given social structure operates, but cannot do so openly unless the society in question is remote in time or space; if they describe the breakdown of a social system, they must somehow end on a hopeful note and show that both order and happiness are eventually restored. However, the interplay of implicit meanings, either subtly different from or actually clashing with the conventional self-gratification, allows the Hollywood director to make valid comments about contemporary American society in an indirect way, by "bending" the explicit meaning (Sirk's phrase). Genre conventions can be either used as an alibi (the implicit meaning is to be found elsewhere in the film) or turned upside down (irony underlines the conventionality of the convention). The implicit subtext of genre films makes it possible for the director to ask the inevitable (but unanswerable) question: Must American society be like this? Must the Hollywood system function like this?

Notes

1. Jean-Loup Bourget, "Aspects du mélodrame américain," *Positif*, no. 131 (October 1971): 31–43; for the English version, see "*Back Street* (Reconsidered)," *Take One* 3, no. 2 (November–December 1970): 33–34. The implicit significance of Stahl's *Back Street* is due not to the Fannie Hurst story itself, but to its treatment by Stahl. A confirmation will be found in a comparison with the latest version of the same story (retold by David Miller in 1961), where the meaning is altered, reduced both to its mawkish pretext and to very few fulgurant images listlessly "borrowed" from films by Douglas Sirk.

2. In *Zoo in Budapest*, Gene Raymond and Loretta Young first find happiness in a bear's den overlooking the town, the outside world. Their situation recalls that of Borzage's heroes in *Seventh Heaven* (1927): the "little man" lives in a garret, close to the stars, which allows him symbolic "overlooking" of a world that crushes him in every other way.

3. Benjamin Constant, *Oeuvres* (Paris: Bibl. de la Pléiade, 1957), p. 952, translation mine. Obviously, many cinematic melodramas still pretend to rely on the device of superhuman fate; it is only an analysis of their implicit meanings, of their subtext, which makes it possible to unmask such fate and give it its actual name of social necessity.

4. In fact, what is variously termed "romantic drama," "soap opera," "sudser," "woman's film," etc., spans all the gamut from the operatic formalism of Dietrich's films and Garbo's *Queen Christina* (Rouben Mamoulian, 1933) to the drab realism of the kitchen-sink drama. There are some successful examples of fairly "realistic" melodramas, notably John Cromwell's *Made for Each Other* and *In Name Only* (both 1939). Nevertheless, even such films are highly unrealistic in their catastrophic situations and providential endings. The impression of realism is largely due to the actors (Carole Lombard as opposed to, say, Joan Crawford) rather than to the verisimilitude of plot and setting. As a rule, both the musical and the melodrama are more openly formalized and ritualized than the realistic guise normally allows. This is due to their common theatrical origin and to their disregard of subtle, novelistic psychological analysis.

5. See Jean-Loup Bourget, "Capra et la screwball comedy," *Positif*, no. 133 (December 1971): 47–53.

6. Ideology, Genre, Auteur

ROBIN WOOD

The truth lies not in one dream but in many.
—Arabian Nights (PIER PAOLO PASOLINI, 1974)

Each theory of film so far has insisted on its own particular polarization. Montage theory enthrones editing as the essential creative act at the expense of other aspects of film; Bazin's realist theory, seeking to right the balance, merely substitutes its own imbalance, downgrading montage and artifice; the revolutionary theory centered in Britain in *Screen* (but today very widespread) rejects—or at any rate seeks to "deconstruct"—realist art in favor of the so-called open text. Auteur theory, in its heyday, concentrated attention exclusively on the fingerprints, thematic or stylistic, of the individual artist; recent attempts to discuss the complete "filmic text" have tended to throw out ideas of personal authorship altogether. Each theory has, given its underlying position, its own validity—the validity being dependent upon and restricted by the position. Each can offer insights into different areas of cinema and different aspects of a single film.

I have suggested elsewhere[1] the desirability for critics—whose aim should always be to see the work as wholly as possible, as it is—to be able to draw on the discoveries and particular perceptions of each theory, each position, without committing themselves exclusively to any one. The ideal will not be easy to attain, and even the attempt raises all kinds of problems, the chief of which is the validity of evaluative criteria that are not supported by a particular system. For what, then, *do* they receive support? No critic, obviously, can be free from a structure of values, nor can he or she afford to withdraw from the struggles and tensions of living to some position of "aesthetic" contemplation. Every critic who is worth reading has been, on the contrary, very much caught up in the effort to define values beyond purely aesthetic ones (if indeed such things exist). Yet to "live historically" need not entail commitment to a system or a cause; rather, it can involve being alive to the opposing pulls, the tensions, of one's world.

The past two decades have seen a number of advances in terms of the opening up of critical possibilities, of areas of relevance, especially with regard to Hollywood: the elaboration of auteur theory in its various manifestations; the interest in genre; the interest in ideology. I want here tentatively to explore some of the ways in which these disparate approaches to Hollywood movies might interpenetrate, producing the kind of synthetic criticism I have suggested might now be practicable.

In order to create a context within which to discuss *It's a Wonderful Life* (Frank Capra, 1946) and *Shadow of a Doubt* (Alfred Hitchcock, 1943), I want to attempt (at risk of obviousness) a definition of what we mean by American capitalist ideology—or, more specifically, the values and assumptions so insistently embodied in and reinforced by the classical Hollywood cinema. The following list of components is not intended to be exhaustive or profound, but simply to make conscious, prior to a discussion of the films, concepts with which we are all perfectly familiar:

1. Capitalism, the right of ownership, private enterprise, personal initiative; the settling of the land.

2. The work ethic: the notion that "honest toil" is in itself and for itself morally admirable, this and concept 1 both validating and reinforcing each other. The moral excellence of work is also bound up with the necessary subjugation or sublimation of the libido: "the Devil finds work for idle hands." The relationship is beautifully epitomized in the zoo-cleaner's song in *Cat People* (Jacques Tourneur, 1942):

> Nothing else to do,
> Nothing else to do,
> I strayed, went a-courting
> 'cause I'd nothing else to do.

3. Marriage (legalized heterosexual monogamy) and family—at once the further validation of concepts 1 and 2 (the homestead is built for the woman, whose function is to embody civilized values and guarantee their continuance through her children) and an extension of the ownership principle to personal relationships ("*My* house, *my* wife, *my* children") in a male-dominated society.

4a. Nature as agrarianism; the virgin land as Garden of Eden. A concept into which, in the western, concept 3 tends to become curiously assimilated (ideology's function being to "naturalize" cultural assumptions): e.g., the treatment of the family in *Drums along the Mohawk* (John Ford, 1939).

4b. Nature as the wilderness, the Indians, on whose subjugation civilization is built; hence by extension the libido, of which in many westerns the Indians seem an extension or embodiment, as in *The Searchers* (Ford, 1956).

5. Progress, technology, the city ("New York, New York, it's a wonderful town").

6. Success and wealth—a value of which Hollywood ideology is also deeply ashamed, so that, while hundreds of films play on its allure, very few can allow themselves openly to extol it. Thus its ideological "shadow" is produced.

7. The Rosebud syndrome. Money isn't everything; money corrupts; the poor are happier. A very convenient assumption for capitalist ideology; the more oppressed you are, the happier you are, as exemplified by the singing "darkies" of *A Day at the Races* (Sam Wood, 1937).

8. America as the land where everyone is or can be happy; hence the land where all problems are solvable within the existing system (which may need a bit of reform here and there but no *radical* change). Subversive systems are assimilated wherever possible to serve the dominant ideology. Andrew Britton, in a characteristically brilliant article on Hitchcock's *Spellbound* (1945), argues that there even Freudian psychoanalysis becomes an instrument of ideological repression.[2] Above all, this assumption gives us that most striking and persistent of all classical Hollywood phenomena, the happy ending: often a mere "emergency exit" (Sirk's phrase)[3] for the spectator, a barely plausible pretense that the problems the film has raised are now resolved. *Hilda Crane* (Philip Dunne, 1950) offers a suitably blatant example among the hundreds possible.

Out of this list logically emerge two ideal figures:

9. The ideal male: the virile adventurer, the potent, untrammelled man of action.

10. The ideal female: wife and mother, perfect companion, the endlessly dependable mainstay of hearth and home.

Since these combine into an ideal couple of quite staggering incompatibility, each has his or her shadow:

11. The settled husband/father, dependable but dull.

12. The erotic woman (adventuress, gambling lady, saloon "entertainer"), fascinating but dangerous, liable to betray the hero or turn into a black panther.

The most striking fact about this list is that it presents an ideology that, far from being monolithic, is *inherently* riddled with hopeless contradictions and unresolvable tensions. The work that has been done so far on genre has tended to take the various genres as "given" and discrete, defining them in terms of motifs, iconography, conventions, and themes. What we need to ask, if genre theory is ever to be productive, is less *what* than *why*. We are so used to the genres that the peculiarity of the phenomenon itself has been too little noted. The idea I wish to put forward is that the development of the genres is rooted in the sort of ideological contradictions my list of concepts suggests. One impulse may be the attempt to deny such contradiction by eliminating one of the opposed terms, or at least by a process of simplification.

Robert Warshow's seminal essays on the gangster hero and the westerner (still fruitfully suggestive, despite the obvious objection that he took too little into account) might be adduced here. The opposition of gangster film and western is only one of many possibilities. *All* the genres can be profitably examined in terms of ideological oppositions, forming a complex interlocking pattern: small-town family comedy/sophisticated city comedy; city comedy/film noir; film noir/small-town comedy, and so on. It is probable that a genre is ideologically "pure" (i.e., safe) only in its simplest, most archetypal, most aesthetically deprived and intellectually contemptible form—such as the Hopalong Cassidy films or Andy Hardy comedies.

The Hopalong Cassidy films (in which Indians, always a potentially disruptive force in ideological as well as dramatic terms, are, in general, significantly absent), for example, seem to depend on two strategies for their perfect ideological security: the strict division of characters into good and evil, with no "grays"; and Hoppy's sexlessness (he never becomes emotionally entangled). Hence the possibility of evading all the wandering/settling tensions on which aesthetically interesting westerns are generally structured. (An intriguing alternative: the ideal American family of Roy Rogers/Dale Evans/Trigger.) *Shane* (George Stevens, 1953) is especially interesting in this connection. A deliberate attempt to create an "archetypal" western, it also represents an effort to resolve the major ideological tensions harmoniously.

One of the greatest obstacles to any fruitful theory of genre has been the tendency to treat the genres as discrete. An ideological approach might suggest why they can't be, however hard they may appear to try: at best, they represent different strategies for dealing with the same ideological tensions. For example, the small-town movie with a contemporary setting should never be divorced from its historical correlative, the western. In the classical Hollywood cinema motifs cross repeatedly from genre to genre, as can be made clear by a few examples. The home/wandering opposition that Peter Wollen rightly sees as central to Ford[4] is not central only to Ford or even to the western; it structures a remarkably large number of American films covering all genres, from *Out of the Past* (Tourneur, 1947) to *There's No Business Like Show Business* (Walter Lang, 1954). The explicit comparison of women to cats connects screwball comedy (*Bringing Up Baby*, Howard Hawks, 1938), horror film (*Cat People*), melodrama (*Rampage*, Phil Karlson, 1963), and psychological thriller (*Marnie*, Hitchcock, 1964). Another example brings us to this essay's specific topic: notice the way in which the potent male adventurer, when he enters the family circle, immediately displaces his "shadow," the settled husband/father, in both *The Searchers* and *Shadow of a Doubt*.

Before we attempt to apply these ideas to specific films, however, one more point needs to be especially emphasized: the presence of ideological tensions in a movie, though it may give it an interest beyond Hopalong Cassidy, is not in itself a reliable evaluative criterion. It seems probable that artistic value has always been dependent on the presence—somewhere, at some stage—of an individual artist, whatever the function of art in the particular society and even when (as with the Chartres cathedral) one no longer knows who the individual artists were. It is only through the medium of the individual that ideological tensions come into particular focus, hence become of aesthetic as well as sociological interest. It can perhaps be argued that works are of especial interest when the defined particularities of an auteur interact with specific ideological tensions and when the film is fed from more than one generic source.

The same basic ideological tensions operate in both *It's a Wonderful Life* and *Shadow of a Doubt*. They furnish further reminders that the home/wandering antinomy is by no means the exclusive preserve of the western. Bedford Falls and Santa Rosa can be seen as the frontier town seventy or so years on; they embody the development of the civilization whose establishment was celebrated around the same time by Ford in *My Darling Clementine* (1946). With this relationship to the western in the background (but in Capra's film made succinctly explicit), the central tension in both films can be described in terms of genre: the disturbing influx of film noir into the world of small-town domestic comedy. (It is a tension clearly present in *Clementine* as well: the opposition between the daytime and nighttime Tombstones.)

The strong contrast presented by the two films testifies to the decisive effect of the intervention of a clearly defined artistic personality in an ideological-generic structure. Both films have as a central ideological project the reaffirmation of family and small-town values that the action has called into question. In Capra's film this reaffirmation is magnificently convincing (but with full acknowledgement of the suppressions on which it depends and, consequently, of its precariousness); in Hitchcock's it is completely hollow. The very different emotional effects of the films—the satisfying catharsis and emotional fullness of Capra's, the "bitter taste" (on which so many have commented) of Hitchcock's—are very deeply rooted not only in our response to two opposed directorial personalities but in our own ideological structuring.

One of the main ideological and thematic tensions of *It's a Wonderful Life* is beautifully encapsulated in the scene in which George Bailey (James Stewart) and Mary (Donna Reed) smash windows in a derelict house as a preface to making wishes. George's wish is to get the money to leave Bedford Falls, which he sees as humdrum and constricting, and travel about the world; Mary's wish (not expressed in words, but in its subsequent fulfillment—confirming her belief that wishes don't come true if you speak them) is that she and George will marry, settle down, and raise a family in the same derelict house, a ruined shell that marriage-and-family restores to life.

This tension is developed through the extended sequence in which George is manipulated into marrying Mary. His brother's return home with a wife and a new job traps George into staying in Bedford Falls to take over the family business. With the homecoming celebrations continuing inside the house in the background, George sits disconsolately on the front porch; we hear an off-screen train whistle, to which he reacts. His mother (the indispensable Beulah Bondi) comes out and begins "suggesting" that he visit Mary; he appears to go off in her direction, physically pointed that way by his mother, then reappears and walks away past the mother—in the opposite direction.

This leads him, with perfect ideological/generic logic, to Violet (Gloria Grahame). The Violet/Mary opposition is an archetypally clear rendering of that central Hollywood female opposition that crosses all generic boundaries—as with Susan (Katharine Hepburn) and Alice (Virginia Walker) in *Bringing Up Baby,* Irene (Simone Simon) and Alice (Jane Randolph) in *Cat People,* Chihuahua (Linda Darnell) and Clementine (Cathy Downs) in *My Darling Clementine,* Debby (Gloria Grahame) and Katie (Jocelyn Brando) in *The Big Heat* (Fritz Lang, 1953). But Violet (in front of an amused audience) rejects his poetic invitation to a barefoot ramble over the hills in the moonlight; the good-time gal offers no more solution to the hero's wanderlust than the wife-mother figure.

So back to Mary, whom he brings to the window by beating a stick aggressively against the fence of the neat, enclosed front garden—a beautifully precise expression of his ambivalent state of mind: desire to attract Mary's attention warring with bitter resentment of his growing entrapment in domesticity. Mary is expecting him; his mother has phoned her, knowing that George would end up at her house. Two ideological premises combine here: the notion that the "good" mother always knows, precisely and with absolute certitude, the workings of her son's mind; and the notion that the female principle is central to the continuity of civilization, that the "weaker sex" is compensated with a sacred rightness.

Indoors, Mary shows George a cartoon she has drawn of George, in cowboy denims, lassoing the moon. The moment is rich in contradictory connotations. It explicitly evokes the western and the figure of the adventurer-hero to which George aspires. Earlier, it was for Mary that George wanted to "lasso the moon," the adventurer's exploits motivated by a desire to make happy the woman who will finally entrap him in domesticity. From Mary's point of view, the picture is at once affectionate (acknowledging the hero's aspirations), mocking (reducing them to caricature), and possessive (reducing George to an image she creates and holds within her hands).

The most overtly presented of the film's structural oppositions is that between the two faces of capitalism, benign and malignant. On the one hand, there are the Baileys (father and son) and their building and loan company, its business practice based on a sense of human needs and a belief in human goodness; on the other, there is Potter (Lionel Barrymore), described explicitly as a spider, motivated by greed, egotism, and miserliness, with no faith in human nature. Potter belongs to a very deeply rooted tradition. He derives most obviously from Dickens's Scrooge (the film is set at Christmas)—a Scrooge disturbingly unrepentant and irredeemable—but his more distant antecedents are in the ogres of fairy tales.

The opposition gives us not only two attitudes to money and property but two father images (Bailey, Sr., and Potter), each of whom gives his name to the land (Bailey Park, in small-town Bedford Falls, and Pottersville, the town's dark alternative). Most interestingly, the two figures (representing American choices, American tendencies) find their vivid ideological extensions in Hollywood genres: the happy, sunny world of small-town comedy (Bedford Falls is seen mostly in the daytime) and the world of film noir, the dark underside of Hollywood ideology.

Pottersville—the vision of the town as it would have been if George had never existed, shown him by his guardian angel (Henry Travers)—is just as "real" as (or no more stylized than) Bedford Falls. The iconography of small-town comedy is exchanged, unmistakably, for that of film noir, with police sirens, shooting in the streets, darkness, vicious dives, alcoholism, burlesque shows, strip clubs, and the glitter and shadows of noir lighting. George's mother, embittered and malevolent, runs a seedy boarding-house; the good-time gal/wife-mother opposition, translated into noir terms, becomes an opposition of prostitute and repressed spinster-librarian. The towns emerge as equally valid images of America—validated by their generic familiarity.

Beside *Shadow of a Doubt, It's a Wonderful Life* manages a convincing and moving affirmation of the values (and value) of bourgeois family life. Yet what is revealed, when disaster releases George's suppressed tensions, is the intensity of his resentment of the family and desire to destroy it— and with it, in significant relationship, his work (his culminating action is furiously to overthrow the drawing board with his plans for more small-town houses). The film recognizes explicitly that behind every Bedford Falls lurks a Pottersville, and implicitly that within every George Bailey lurks an Ethan Edwards of *The Searchers*. Potter, tempting George, is

10. *It's a Wonderful Life:* The happy world of small-town comedy.

given the devil's insights into his suppressed desires. His remark, "You once called me a warped, frustrated old man—now you're a warped, frustrated *young* man," is amply supported by the evidence the film supplies. What is finally striking about the film's affirmation is the extreme precariousness of its basis; and Potter survives without remorse, his crime unexposed and unpunished. It may well be Capra's masterpiece, but it is more than that. Like all the greatest American films—fed by a complex generic tradition and, beyond that, by the fears and aspirations of a whole culture—it at once transcends its director and would be inconceivable without him.

Shadow of a Doubt has always been among the most popular of Hitchcock's middle-period films, with critics and public alike, but it has been perceived in very different, almost diametrically opposed ways. On its appearance it was greeted by British critics as the film marking Hitchcock's coming to terms with America; his British films were praised for their humor and "social criticism" as much as for their suspense, and the early American films, notably *Rebecca* (1940) and *Suspicion* (1941), seemed

11. *It's a Wonderful Life:* The disturbing influx of film noir.

like attempts artificially to reconstruct England in Hollywood. In *Shadow of a Doubt* Hitchcock (with the aid of Thornton Wilder and Sally Benson) at last brought to American middle-class society the shrewd, satirical, affectionate gaze previously bestowed on the British. A later generation of French critics (notably Rohmer and Chabrol in their Hitchcock book) praised the film for very different reasons, establishing its strict formalism (Truffaut's "un film fondé sur le chiffre 2") and seeing it as one of the keys to a consistent Catholic interpretation of Hitchcock, a rigorous working out of themes of original sin, the loss of innocence, the fallen world, the exchange (or interchangeability) of guilt.[5] The French noted the family comedy beloved of British critics, if at all, as a mildly annoying distraction.

That both these views correspond to important elements in the film and throw light on certain aspects of it is beyond doubt; both, however, now appear false and partial, dependent upon the abstracting of elements from the whole. If the film is, in a sense, completely dominated by Hitchcock (nothing in it is unmarked by his artistic personality), a complete reading would need to see the small-town-family elements and the Catholic elements as threads weaving through a complex fabric in which, again, ideological and generic determinants are crucial.

The kind of "synthetic" analysis I have suggested (going beyond an interest in the individual auteur) reveals *It's a Wonderful Life* as a far more potentially subversive film than has been generally recognized, but its subversive elements are, in the end, successfully contained. In *Shadow of a Doubt* the Hollywood ideology I have sketched is shattered beyond convincing recuperation. One can, however, trace through the film its attempts to impose itself and render things "safe." What is in jeopardy is above all the family—but, given the family's central ideological significance, once that is in jeopardy, everything is. The small town (still rooted in the agrarian dream, in ideals of the virgin land as a garden of innocence) and the united happy family are regarded as the real sound heart of American civilization; the ideological project is to acknowledge the existence of sickness and evil but preserve the family from their contamination.

A number of strategies can be discerned here: the attempt to insist on a separation of Uncle Charlie from Santa Rosa; his death at the end of the film as the definitive purging of evil; the production of the young detective (the healthy, wholesome, small-town male) as a marriage partner for Young Charlie so that the family may be perpetuated; above all, the attribution of Uncle Charlie's sexual pathology to a childhood accident as a means of exonerating the family of the charge of producing a monster, a possibility the American popular cinema, with the contemporary overturning of traditional values, can now envisage—e.g., *It's Alive* (Larry Cohen, 1974).

The famous opening, with its parallel introductions of Uncle Charlie and Young Charlie, insists on the city and the small town as *opposed,* sickness and evil being of the city. As with Bedford Falls/Pottersville, the film draws lavishly on the iconography of usually discrete genres. Six shots (with all movement and direction—the bridges, the panning, the editing—consistently rightward) leading up to the first interior of Uncle Charlie's room give us urban technology, wreckage both human (the down-and-outs) and material (the dumped cars by the sign "No Dumping Allowed"), children playing in the street, the number 13 on the lodging-house door. Six shots (movement and direction consistently left) leading to the first interior of Young Charlie's room give us sunny streets with no street games (Santa Rosa evidently has parks), an orderly town with a smiling, paternal policeman presiding over traffic and pedestrians.

In Catholic terms, this is the fallen world against a world of apparent prelapsarian innocence; but it is just as valid to interpret the images, as in *It's a Wonderful Life,* in terms of the two faces of American capitalism. Uncle Charlie has money (the fruits of his crimes and his aberrant sexu-

12. Young Charlie (Teresa Wright), Uncle Charlie (Joseph Cotton), and Louise the waitress (Janet Shaw) in *Shadow of a Doubt*.

ality) littered in disorder over table and floor; the Santa Rosa policeman has behind him the Bank of America. The detailed paralleling of uncle and niece can of course be read as comparison as much as contrast, and the opposition that of two sides of the same coin. The point is clearest in that crucial, profoundly disturbing scene where film noir erupts into Santa Rosa itself: the visit to the Til Two bar, where Young Charlie is confronted with her alter ego Louise the waitress, her former classmate. The scene equally invites Catholic and Marxist commentaries; its force arises from the revelation of the fallen world/capitalist-corruption-and-deprivation at the heart of the American small town. The close juxtaposition of genres has implications that reach throughout the whole generic structure of the classical Hollywood cinema.

The subversion of ideology within the film is everywhere traceable to Hitchcock's presence, to the skepticism and nihilism that lurk just behind the jocular facade of his public image. His Catholicism is in reality the lingering on in his work of the darker aspects of Catholic mythology: hell without heaven. The traces are clear enough. Young Charlie wants a "mir-

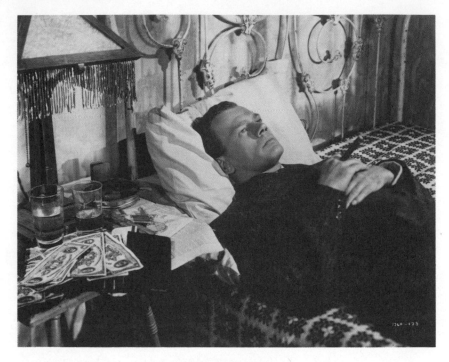

13. Uncle Charlie in repose (*Shadow of a Doubt*).

acle"; she thinks of her uncle as "the one who can save us" (and her mother immediately asks, "What do you mean, *save* us?"); when she finds his telegram, in the very act of sending hers, her reaction is an ecstatic "He heard me, he heard me!" Hitchcock cuts at once to a low-angle shot of Uncle Charlie's train rushing toward Santa Rosa, underlining the effect with an ominous crashing chord on the sound track.

Uncle Charlie is one of the supreme embodiments of the key Hitchcock figure: ambiguously devil and lost soul. When he reaches Santa Rosa, the image is blackened by its smoke. From his first appearance, Charlie is associated consistently with a cigar (its phallic connotations evident from the outset, in the scene with the landlady) and repeatedly shown with a wreath of smoke curling around his head (no one else in the film smokes except Joe, the displaced father, who has a paternal pipe, usually unlit). Several incidents (the escape from the policemen at the beginning, the garage door slammed as by remote control) invest him with a quasi-supernatural power. Rather than restrict the film to a Catholic reading, it seems logical to connect these marks with others: the thread of superstition that runs through the film (the number 13; the hat on the bed; "Sing at table and you'll marry a crazy husband"; the irrational dread of the utterance, however innocent, of the forbidden words "Merry Widow") and the telepathy motif (the telegrams, the tune "jumping from head to head")—the whole Hitchcockian sense of life at the mercy of terrible, unpredictable forces that have to be kept down.

The Hitchcockian dread of repressed forces is characteristically accompanied by a sense of the emptiness of the surface world that represses them, and this crucially affects the presentation of the American small-town family in *Shadow of a Doubt*. The warmth and togetherness, the mutual responsiveness and affection that Capra so beautifully creates in the Bailey families, senior and junior, of *It's a Wonderful Life* are here almost entirely lacking—and this despite the fact, in itself of great ideological interest, that the treatment of the family in *Shadow of a Doubt* has generally been perceived (even, one guesses, by Hitchcock himself) as affectionate.

The most striking characteristic of the Spencers is the separateness of each member; the recurring point of the celebrated overlapping dialogue is that no one ever listens to what anyone else is saying. Each is locked in a separate fantasy world: Emmy in the past, Joe in crime, Anne in books that are read apparently less for pleasure than as a means of amassing knowledge with which she has little emotional contact (though she also believes that everything she reads is "true"). The parents are trapped in a petty materialism (both respond to Young Charlie's dissatisfaction with the assumption that she's talking about money) and reliance on "honest toil" as the means of using up energies. In *Shadow of a Doubt* the ideological image of the small-town happy family becomes the flimsiest facade. That so many are nonetheless deceived by it testifies only to the strength of the ideology—one of whose functions is of course to inhibit the imagining of radical alternatives.

I have argued elsewhere that the key to Hitchcock's films is less suspense than sexuality (or, alternatively, that his "suspense" always carries a sexual charge in ways sometimes obvious, sometimes esoteric); and that sexual relationships in his work are inevitably based on power, the obsession with power and dread of impotence being as central to his method as to his thematic. In *Shadow of a Doubt* it is above all sexuality that cracks apart the family facade. As far as the Hays Code permitted, a double incest theme runs through the film: Uncle Charlie and Emmy, Uncle Charlie and Young Charlie. Necessarily, this is expressed through images and motifs, never becoming verbally explicit; certain of the images depend on a suppressed verbal play for their significance.

For the reunion of brother and sister, Hitchcock gives us an image (Emmy poised left of screen, arrested in mid-movement, Charlie right, under trees and sunshine) that iconographically evokes the reunion of lovers (Charlie wants to see Emmy again as she was when she was "the prettiest girl on the block"). And Emmy's breakdown, in front of her embarrassed friends and neighbors, at the news of Charlie's imminent departure is eloquent. As for uncle and niece, they are introduced symmetrically lying on beds, Uncle Charlie fondling his phallic cigar, Young Charlie, prone, hands behind head. When Uncle Charlie gets off the train he is bent over a stick, pretending to be ill; as soon as he sees Young Charlie, he "comes erect," flourishing the stick. One of his first actions on taking over her bedroom is to pluck a rose for his buttonhole ("deflowering"). More obviously, there is the business with the ring, which, as a symbolic token of engagement, not only links Charlie sexually with her uncle, but also links her, through its previous ownership, to his succession of merry widows. The film shows sexual pathology at the heart of the American family, the necessary product of its repressions and sublimations.

As for the "accident"—that old critical stumbling block—it presents no problem at all, provided one is ready to acknowledge the validity of a psychoanalytical reading of movies. Indeed, it provides a rather beautiful example of the way in which ideology, in seeking to impose itself, succeeds merely in confirming its own subversion. The "accident" (Charlie was "riding a bicycle" for the first time, which resulted in a "collision") can be read as an elementary Freudian metaphor for the trauma of premature sexual awakening (after which Charlie was "never the same again"). The smothering sexual/possessive devotion of a doting older sister may be felt to provide a clue to the sexual motivation behind the merry-widow murders; Charlie isn't interested in money. Indeed, Emmy is connected to the merry widows by an associative chain in which important links are her own practical widowhood (her ineffectual husband is largely ignored), her ladies' club, and its leading light, Mrs. Potter, Uncle Charlie's potential next-in-line.

A fuller analysis would need to dwell on the limitations of Hitchcock's vision, nearer the nihilistic than the tragic; on his inability to conceive of repressed energies as other than evil and the surface world that represses them as other than shallow and unfulfilling. This explains why there can be no heaven corresponding to Hitchcock's hell, for every vision of heaven that is not merely negative is rooted in a concept of the liberation of the instincts, the resurrection of the body, which Hitchcock must always deny. But my final stress is less on the evaluation of a particular film or director than on the implications for a criticism of the Hollywood cinema of the notions of interaction and multiple determinacy I have been employing. Its roots in the Hollywood genres, and in the very ideological structure it so disturbingly subverts, make *Shadow of a Doubt* so much more suggestive and significant a work than Hitchcock the bourgeois entertainer could ever have guessed.

Notes

1. Robin Wood, "Old Wine, New Bottles: Structuralism or Humanism?" *Film Comment* 12, no. 6 (November–December 1976): 22–25.
2. Andrew Britton, "Hitchcock's *Spellbound:* Text and Counter-Text," *Cine-Action!* no. 3/4 (January 1986): 72–83.
3. See *Sirk on Sirk,* edited by Jon Halliday (London: Secker & Warburg/British Film Institute, 1971).
4. Peter Wollen, *Signs and Meaning in the Cinema,* 3d. ed. (Bloomington and London: Indiana University Press, 1972), pp. 94–101.
5. See Eric Rohmer and Claude Chabrol, *Hitchcock: The First Forty-Four Films,* translated by Stanley Hochman (New York: Ungar, 1979), p. 72.

7. "Cinema/Ideology/Criticism" Revisited: The Progressive Genre

BARBARA KLINGER

Since the publication of the Jean-Louis Comolli and Jean Narboni editorial "Cinema/Ideology/Criticism" in *Cahiers du Cinéma* in 1969, there has been strong theoretical and critical attention devoted to the elaboration of the particular relation between cinematic text and ideology as a central aspect of the overall post-1968 concern with the area of cultural production. The terms of this elaboration—advanced fundamentally through a Marxist/feminist perspective that employs, variably, a quartet of textual theories drawn from formalism, structuralism, semiotics, and psychoanalysis—have been as diverse as the textual objects addressed, which range from classic Hollywood cinema to the work of the experimental avant-garde. Vital to and constant within this primarily textual focus of the cinema/ideology inquiry are the twin interrogatives of what constitutes dominant cinematic practices and then what deconstitutes them. These concerns have led to a full-scale critical expedition into the Hollywood cinema as a particularly compelling site for the analysis of dominant aesthetic/cultural production, resulting in the development of a refined set of analytical procedures that designate and differentiate the ideological contours of specific textual practices within this only apparently monolithic mainstream.

Though the pursuit of a "countercinema" has defined encounters with all manner of texts, the subdivision I wish to reconsider here is that which has addressed differing textual "politics" within Hollywood cinema. Part of this work on the signification practices of dominant cinema has involved the critical identification of a series of "rebel" texts within the Hollywood empire. These texts, while firmly entrenched within the system, display certain features that are critically deemed as combative to the conventions governing the "typical" classic text. Ideological criticism, which has so entertained the variability of textual politics within mainstream production, has distinguished a category of films referred to as "progressive" or "subversive."

While this classification has influenced and contributed to developments in both auteur and genre studies, my explanatory emphasis primarily concerns film genre. It is important to note, however, that ideological genre criticism is quite substantially inflected by questions of auteur; within each specific critical argument engaged with defining the progressive coordinates of certain generic periods, auteurist considerations are frequently instrumental. Among film groups that have been of interest to ideological criticism are film noir, the woman's film, the forties and fifties melodrama, the seventies horror film, and the exploitation and B film.[1] This list is by no means exhaustive of the criticism that has addressed the notion of "progressivity," but simply suggestive of the expanse of work that has consistently taken up and elaborated the parameters of the progressive film. What follows is both a reconsideration and reevaluation of the theoretical genealogy and critical terms through which this substantial current in film studies has developed.

NEO-MARXIST AESTHETIC THEORY

The theoretical formulation that underwrites the critical constitution of the "progressive" text originates with the work of Louis Althusser. Though his essays expressly on art—"A Letter on Art in Reply to André Daspre" and "Cremonini, Painter of the Abstract"[2]—are not voluminous meditations on a Marxist theory of the artistic text, they do furnish the basis from which such a theory and its adjacent conceptualization of a critical praxis for film were constructed.

Briefly, the focus of discussion in these essays is on an elaboration of art's specific relation to ideology. For Althusser, the most emphatic aspect of art to be addressed within this inquiry is its essential, definitive epistemology. Art, here, is neither "knowledge in the strictest sense" or unadulterated ideology; rather, it provides a particularly valuable epistemological halfway house between the two. According to Althusser, "What art makes us *see,* and therefore gives us in the forms of '*seeing,*' '*perceiving*' and '*feeling*' . . . is the ideology from which it is born, in which it bathes, from which it detaches itself as art, and to which it alludes."[3] Art is a special perceptual agency that performs a quasi-epistemic function: it literally makes a spectacle of ideology, and in so doing, elucidates, even materially objectifies, the presence and activity of ideology. Further, in this distinction of the epistemological contours of art, certain artists' works are singled out (Balzac, Cremonini) as they exhibit an exceptionally revelatory view of the ideology in which they "bathe." This view, in Althusser's words, "presupposes a *retreat,* an *internal distanciation,* from the very ideology from which their [work] emerged." Similarly, these texts make us "perceive . . . in some sense from the *inside,* by an *internal distance,* that ideology in which they are held."[4] This commentary implies a class of texts with a slightly superior epistemology; that is, it suggests the existence of a textual practice that amplifies the "basic" epistemological dynamics of the aesthetic text, to the point where the text not only objectifies the ideological, but effects a more emphatic distance from it—a "break"—which, in turn, forces the ideological into conspicuous view.

Central to Althusser's discussion of an aesthetic epistemology is the definition of a corresponding, distinctly Marxist critical practice, the function of which is to compose a knowledge of art. This knowledge of art, like all knowledge for Althusser, "presupposes a preliminary *rupture* with the language of *ideological spontaneity,*" and constructs "a body of scientific concepts to replace it."[5] The mission of criticism here is not, as in some traditions, to act in complicity with the aesthetic facade of the text, so as to bolster its consumption, but rather to realize and quantify the internal textual objectification of ideology produced by art's peculiar epistemological character.

Summarily, this theorization of the artistic text and consonant specification of a critical practice of reading promote a strong, explicitly textual focus to questions of the relation of art and ideology. The text is characterized as a site upon which the significant relations of representation and ideology are distilled, almost in bilateral configuration. The language of Althusser's aesthetic epistemology used to describe the text/ideology relation—rupture, break, internal distanciation, deformation—foster this sense of the reflexive, formal geography of the text, which, by critical extension, can be viewed as internally empowered to engineer an "auto-critique" of the ideology in which it is held. The potential of this perspective on the artistic text is elaborated within film studies to produce a critical and aesthetic category of films designated generally as "progressive."

FILM THEORY/CRITICISM: THE PROGRESSIVE FORMULATION

The mobilization of Althusser's precepts into active critical service in film, via the Comolli/Narboni editorial, provides the means through which film texts were purposefully scrutinized anew expressly to ascertain their "textual politics." The overall project of the Comolli/Narboni essay, to differentiate the text's specific relation to the ideology it produces in form and content, results in a seven-category classification of film types, wherein films are appraised according to how they adhere to or depart from predominant expressions of ideology.

The categories most pertinent for discussion here, categories "a" and "e," feature films within the tradition of classical Hollywood cinema—

that tradition recognized as both forming the basis for and exemplifying dominant representational concerns and practices. In this critical scheme, category "a" (the one most populated) typified a "zero degree" state of textual politics; these films act only as conduits for and perpetuators of existing ideological norms, both in content (for instance, as they salute the institutions and premises that define "the American way") and in form (accepting the conventional system of depiction in the cinema). An "e" film, on the other hand, though appearing supportive of the ideology that conditions its existence, hampers the straightforward expression of it through the production of a formally impelled rupture with the veneer of its own premises. The cinematic framework of "e" films "lets us see [the operative ideology] but also shows it up and denounces it," producing "an internal criticism . . . which cracks the film apart . . . [creating] an internal tension . . . simply not there in an ideologically innocuous film." Here Comolli and Narboni identify a textual practice, which while fully integrated within dominant cinema "ends up by partially dismantling the system from within."[6] The "e" category, then, fits the description of the more epistemologically ambitious text outlined by Althusser, which produces ideological critique.

The importance of these particular classifications to the identification of a body of texts as progressive lies in their critical provision for a differential typology of textual politics within dominant cinema, and, crucially, in the essential systemic relationship through which that difference is established. "E" films achieve their preferential "politic" status through their reflexive, deconstructive relation to what is recognized as the standard classic text. This relational distinction, proposed by Comolli and Narboni, informs subsequent and more extensive elaborations of the specific textual parameters of the progressive text and genre. This discrimination is clear in one of the bedrock propositions regulating the critical establishment of progressive textual practice: that the progressive work must exhibit textual characteristics which are strategically reactive to commonplace "classicism." In general, the strong critical investment in designating and elucidating countercinema or progressive cinema is financed through a staunch conception of classic textuality, against which progressive practice relies for its very definition.

PROFILE OF THE PROGRESSIVE GENRE

As Kaplan notes, "The 'classic text' (applicable to genre and nongenre films) describes a *dominant mode of production,* which masks its own operation . . . in terms of covering over ideological tension and contradiction . . . which [then] represents the Truth *vis-à-vis* the film's content and meaning; or in terms of giving the impression that it gives access to the 'real world.'" [7] The classic form subscribes to an ideology of representa-tion—the achievement of the "impression of reality"—and, in so doing, unproblematically broadcasts dominant cultural ideas. A distinguishing mark of the progressive film is its operational refusal of the overall ambi-tion of the classic form toward concealment and transparency, the chief attributes of realism. This formal dynamic embodies a challenge to the conventional means of representing reality in the cinema in such a way as to expose those means as practice, as a product of ideology, and not as a manifest replication of reality. The progressive generic text is, in this sense, antirealist, as it rattles the perfect illusionism transmitted by a major sector of classic cinema. Assessments of progressive texts/genres generally establish the features of departure from convention in this way and subse-quently endow those features with the edifying effects of "rupture."

Pam Cook's essay on exploitation and B films, for example, presents the logic of the progressive genre argument based on the reaction against cer-tain tactics of classic Hollywood cinema. She recommends a critical re-appraisal of these previously considered "low-life" films, because of the way in which they "lay bare" the underlying suppositions and operative principles of Hollywood films with higher production values. Exploitation films almost contradictorily (given their capitalistic fervor) crystallize, ex-aggerate, and expose the "ground rules" from which mainstream films are built. Cook defends exploitation and B films in this way as less objection-able in their representation of women than sophisticated Hollywood or European art films; images of women in the former are obviously stereo-typed, display themselves as such, and so resist the sort of naturalization process Cook believes classic films of "good taste" excel in. In the "better-quality" film, the myth of the star persona (Bette Davis, Katharine Hep-burn, etc.) and/or the density of character traits, which seem to construct fuller, more real characters, do nothing more than camouflage the nor-mative function and actual stereotyped status of the female character in question. Here, then, a film like *Student Nurses* (Stephanie Rothman, 1970) fares better than *An Unmarried Woman* (Paul Mazursky, 1978).

Though the critics engaged in distinguishing progressive genres are not at all homogeneous in methodology (all do not draw explicitly from Althusser; some arguments are more heavily inflected by auteurism than others), the terms in which they identify the requisite characteristics of progressive genres are strikingly similar. The consistent conceptual basis for this constitution involves an exclamation of the genre's reactive differ-ence from what is "classic" in classic Hollywood fare, as well as the estab-lishment of the generic period's insurgent inventional qualities within the diachronic structures that govern its entire system.

Robin Wood, for instance, in his writings on horror films, sets the genre off from Hollywood films in general, because horror films seem to have a special pipeline to the unconscious. They possess the potential, that is, to exhibit as explicit content what most other films soundly repress (the repressiveness of the family vs. the insistent celebration or sentimentalization of family solidarity). This characteristic, according to Wood, gives the horror film a revelatory rather than a complacent relation to ideology. In addition, because horror films have a marginal and disreputable status within Hollywood production, they are "capable of being more radical and subversive in their social criticism, since works of conscious social criticism . . . must always concern themselves with the possibility of reforming aspects of a social system whose basic rightness must not be challenged."[8] Horror films are not obliged in this way; their relentless critique can remain, ultimately, unredemptive. Aside from establishing the "anticlassicism" of the horror film, there is also in Wood's argument an internal set of distinctions produced from a consideration of the genre's conventional/historic trajectory that results in a choice of a specific period therein—the horror of the seventies. *Psycho* (Alfred Hitchcock, 1960) is the film that transforms the genre's formula and instigates the progressive/subversive character of horror films of the seventies like *The Texas Chainsaw Massacre* (Tobe Hooper, 1974), *The Hills Have Eyes* (Wes Craven, 1977), and *Night of the Living Dead* (George Romero, 1968). The formula for the genre, "normality threatened by the monster," which represents the conventional core of narrative/thematic oppositions, is in horror films preceding *Psycho* usually dramatized less problematically: that is, the monster is always foreign, exotic, radically other than the family it threatens, as in the thirties with *Dracula* (Tod Browning, 1931) or *King Kong* (Merian C. Cooper and Ernest B. Schoedsack, 1933) or in the fifties with its proliferation of giant, mutant insects. The strategic importance of *Psycho* within this trajectory is in revealing the locus of horror as specifically familial, as being produced from within the family institution itself; this is a "truth" Wood finds always lurking but repressed in earlier films.

Wood's work on horror is representative of the fundamental operative tenets implicitly required to establish generic "progressivity." Difference from the environment of conventions within which these films exist, then, is a paramount feature of their progressive status, and the rationale by which they are accorded a radical valence. The diverse critical positions that address film noir, the woman's film, the sophisticated family melodrama of the forties and fifties, the horror film of the seventies, and the exploitation and B film are united in particular by an emphasis on the identity of these film groups as alternative or "countercinemas" within the province of dominant cinematic practice. These generic propositions are not forged exclusively on the basis of genre considerations alone, however, but are usually substantially articulated through specific auteurs

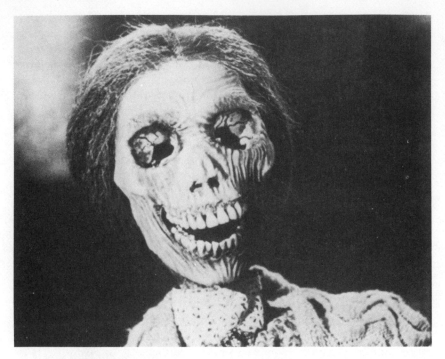

14. *Psycho:* The locus of horror is specifically familial.

and films—evidence the preference of Sirk and Minnelli melodramas over those of Curtiz or Mankiewicz, Wes Craven's horror films over David Cronenberg's, and the emphasis on the woman's films of Dorothy Arzner and Stephanie Rothman. But even given the myriad areas of emphasis within ideological-generic criticism, the ideological "aesthetics" employed in each argument are implicitly dictated through the presence or nonpresence of certain textual attributes necessary to the architecture of the progressive category. What follows is a selective, synthetic exposition of the characteristics that describe the progressive class of films. These traits do not by any means exhaust each individual critical argument but rather display in schematic form the consistent means through which the "progressive" is critically constructed.

A "Pessimistic World View"

Instead of the optimism that characterizes the typical celebratory or complacent view of the American way of life in the classic text, such as *The*

Bells of St. Mary's (Leo McCarey, 1945), the overall atmosphere of these films is bleak, cynical, apocalyptic, and/or highly ironic—as in *Kiss Me Deadly* (Robert Aldrich, 1955), *It's Alive* (Larry Cohen, 1974), *All That Heaven Allows* (Douglas Sirk, 1956)—in such a way as to disturb or disable an unproblematic transmission or affirmative ideology. Thus Sylvia Harvey writes of film noir that it "captures and magnifies the rumbles that shift the hidden foundations of a society and . . . begins the displacement of its characteristic and dominant system of values and beliefs"; Robin Wood writes of seventies horror that it gives "the sense of civilization condemning itself . . . a negativity . . . not recuperable into the dominant ideology, but constituting the recognition of that ideology's disintegration, its untenability"; and Thomas Elsaesser comments on the way in which fifties melodramas portray the "demise of the affirmative culture."[9]

Themes

Associated with this world view, the themes of the progressive film dramatize the demolition of values positively propounded in dominant cinema's characterization of the role and nature of social institutions—such beliefs as the inviolability and/or ultimate benevolence of the law, and the family as an institution of social and sexual "salvation" for the individual members of a couple, especially women. The law and the family are two institutions that come consistently under the remonstrative gun in these films, mainly through an hysterical exaggeration of and attack on their repressive and deforming principles, as in *Shadow of a Doubt* (Hitchcock, 1943), *Mildred Pierce* (Michael Curtiz, 1945), *Home from the Hill* (Vincente Minnelli, 1960), *The Texas Chainsaw Massacre*, and *Jackson County Jail* (Michael Miller, 1976). In film noir, the law is depicted as corrupt and/or ineffectual, and the family, as Harvey indicates, is absent, depicted in either a too-sunny glow of banality or as sterile and monstrous. In the melodrama, the psychic destructiveness of social institutions, often centering on the heterosexual couple, results in a rampant representation of ambition and of romantic love, disquieted through expressions of nymphomania, impotency, suicidal tendencies, obsessions with paternity, and the like (Sirk's 1957 film *Written on the Wind* is an especially rich example of these psychodynamics). There is, in short, no longer any restful identity to be found in the family in these films; the center of hope in most narratives, the romantic couple, is shown as either cloyingly insipid or deranged, two spectral expressions of the same impulse to denaturalize and explode the myth of the happy, unproblematic founding unit of the family.

Narrative Form

It is in the narrative and stylistic elements of progressive films that their dual critique of classic form/classic ideology is substantially generated. There are several structural components that are essential to this critique.

First, the overall narrative structure is refined toward an exposure—rather than a suppression, as in the classic text—of ideological contradictions and tensions. The progressive structure can work, for instance, to conflate oppositions within the dramatic conflict, which usually act to segregate good (that which upholds the existing order) from evil (that which threatens it). So structural correspondences may be drawn between hero and villain and the respective systems they represent. This characteristic is very important to Robin Wood's distinction between Capra's *It's a Wonderful Life* (1946) and Hitchcock's *Shadow of a Doubt*,[10] and to his discussion of seventies horror films like *The Hills Have Eyes*. The concept of structurally impelled contradiction figures prominently in Elsaesser's discussion of cinematic counterpoint in melodrama and in Gledhill's analysis of point-of-view structures in film noir. The parallels wrought by the structural complexity of these films create ambiguity that prevents both easy identification and separation of systems of "good" and "evil."

Most important, the narrative form of the ideologically complex film departs from perceived demands of the classical Hollywood form. The principles of this latter type of construction require a general effect of legibility and transparency, qualities obtained through a well-defined chain of cause and effect ending in satisfying closure. Conventional rules of construction promote the invisibility of the mechanisms at work and the expulsion of any feature that would distract from the hegemony of the narrative line. The progressive film genre conversely departs from the letter of the classical system by either paring it down to its barest essentials (as does the exploitation film) so that cause and effect exist, but merely as the most minimal acknowledgement of that system of construction more than as a systematic illumination of the narrative flow; or by maximizing and exaggerating its principles (as in the structure of reversal in melodrama or the circuitous jungle of cause and effect in film noir), so that the logic of the system is overdetermined in such a way as to stretch its credibility and legibility. Through these distinct mutations of classic narrative rules, represented in such films as *Terminal Island* (Rothman, 1973), *Imitation of Life* (Sirk, 1959), or *The Locket* (John Brahm, 1946), the system is both reflexively exposed and countered.

The issue of closure here is also crucial. The progressive film must escape the compromising forces inherent in the conventional procedure of closure. Whereas closure usually signals the ultimate containment of matters brought out in the narrative—the network of cause and effect is resolved, and the narrative returned to a final state of equilibrium—progressive films end in such a way as to "refuse" closure. The "progressive" critics claim that such an ending cannot contain the excess of meaning produced in the course of the film, cannot solve all the conflicts. Of film noir narratives Harvey writes that "narrative resolutions cannot recuperate their subversive significance."[11] Wood similarly posits that, in contradistinction to "works of conscious social criticism," the finale of the seventies horror film remains ultimately unredemptive. The violence and destructiveness centered upon the social institutions are not adequately resolved merely through the conventional appearance of the device of closure. The circumvention of this process is fostered through the use of certain textual strategies. For example, in the melodrama with the happy ending (especially when that most stalwart of Hollywood conventions is used by Douglas Sirk), there is a veneer of optimism present that is not only unconvincing, but countered by a system of meaning produced stylistically, which imbues the conclusion with unmistakable irony, as in *Written on the Wind* or *Magnificent Obsession* (Sirk, 1954).[12] A combination of "excessive" narrative problems encountered during the film and the manner in which elements of the mise-en-scène undercut the affirmative ending conspire to disturb the harmonizing tendencies of closure. The strong sense of irony or desolation that frequently characterizes these generic endings questions the achievement of "containing" closure and imparts a rather hollow victory to this convention. The terms "excess" and "irony" are central then to the issue of closure, as they wrench the intentions of conventional form to unilaterally resolve contradiction.

Visual Style

These films are basically characterized by stylistic self-consciousness and formal excess, which are seen in varying degrees of specificity as supporting or implementing a vital part of their subversive commentary. This is in contrast to films that do not actively use their visual register to produce meaning—what Elsaesser calls "liberal films of sophistication," such as those of Fred Zinnemann, which "do nothing in terms of visual elaboration to compensate for their verbal explicitness."[13] In the progressive film, there is a foregrounding of visual style, which is manifested so forcefully as to contend with the dominance of the narrative line: in exploitation and B films, the visual register calls attention to itself through its sheer bargain-basement look; in film noir and horror, it is the use of expressionistic chiaroscuro and camera angles; and in melodrama, there

15. *Home from the Hill:* Robert Mitchum's den.

is a similar "baroque" foregrounding of the formal aspects of mise-en-scène and camera—all of which are seen as intensifying the text's internal structure of distanciation.

Character

Rather than the humane, dimensional characters who populate films of "good taste," the excessive sexual stereotyping of genre films is critically preferred, and, again, endowed with a revelatory salience; the stereotype is considered to foreground rather than camouflage the representational basis through which codes of "masculinity" and "femininity" are constructed in the cinema (see Robert Mitchum's den in *Home from the Hill*). Especially evident in the dynamics of gender representation is an intense focus on both the threat and enigma of female sexuality, in all of its psychoanalytic complexity, as in *Psycho, Written on the Wind, Gun Crazy* (Joseph H. Lewis, 1949), and *Caged Heat* (Jonathan Demme, 1974).

16. *Gun Crazy:* The threat and enigma of female sexuality.

THE VALUATION OF "ANTICLASSICAL" DIFFERENCE

The identification of the progressive genre film depends heavily on the critical leverage imparted to the intrinsic inventional characteristics described above, which serve to distinguish these films from the dominant classic cinema and, often, from within their own generic categories as well. So film noir is "recognizably different from other films"; it "stands out as a phase in the development of the gangster/thriller [because of] . . . certain highly foregrounded inflections of plot, character, and visual style which dominated at the expense of narrative coherence and the comprehensible solution of the crime, the usual goal of the thriller."[14] The major axis upon which the progressive argument revolves is this valuation of inventional signifiers, wherein "difference" is conferred with deconstructive capabilities and a subversive effectivity. In addition, the assessment of "textual politics" based on systemic/textual attributes is not consistently considered solely as the product of critical computations derived from a certain reading position, but tends to introject the progressive features as intrinsic, effectual properties of the texts themselves; hence, texts can be labeled "reactionary" or "progressive" according to their internal subscription to or rejection of the classic paradigm and its imputed ideology. The ideological effects of a text come to be identified and ratified through the espoused critical reading.

That the cinema/ideology inquiry has become strongly situated within the province of textual reading is indicated especially in the logic and tenets of the progressive-text argument, wherein specific textual features embody that relation. This emphasis is true even in those genre studies that do attend to the external social/ideological environments that house the production of a given cycle of films. In the descriptions of the historical conditions circumscribing film noir or melodrama, the brunt of the relational analysis tends to spotlight the activity of the textual features as they respond to these conditions. This can assume a one-to-one correlation between social formation and representation, where, for instance, the economic and psychic preoccupations of postwar or corporate capitalist America are seen as both crystallized in and "disturbed" by the mise-en-scène of film noir or melodrama.

While the critical readings of Hollywood films developed from Marxist and feminist film theory have produced invaluable critical perspectives and tools with which to differentiate textual articulations of ideology— an absolutely necessary advance, historically, to ward off competing and reductive theories of Hollywood cinema forwarded by "monolith-mongers" (such as the writers of *Cinéthique* circa 1969), who asserted the basic monolithic ideology of all Hollywood films—there is a strong impulse to overestimate the effectiveness of textual signifiers in determining the text/ideology relation. The central issue here, then, is not a dispute with criticism tuned toward the definition of textual variation as significant in producing a cultural symptomatology, but simply with the prescription of a political value to those differences within a system of representation that is so absolutely based on a univocal, textual-centric consideration of the cinema/ideology relation. In the transit from Althusser's explication of an aesthetic epistemology to the parallel formulation in film studies, there is a marked tendency toward a sort of "textual isolationism," an intrinsic formalization of the cinema/ideology inquiry. In progressive text and genre criticism, this results in an overvaluation and overestimation of inventive, "reactive," textual elements—a phenomenon that bears further and alternative commentary.

GENRE THEORY: "DIFFERENCE" IN CONTEXT

The designation of text and genres as "progressive," which is dependent on a radical valorization of inventional qualities, provokes at least two theoretical problems, which arise directly from other systemic theories as they account for the phenomenon of difference. The valuation of invention in progressive-text criticism enables a disturbance of the system to be felt sheerly through the intervention of invention without sufficient deliberation of how the elements of difference figure within the overall dynamics of the system of representational history or within the system of narrative itself. Indeed, classical narrative is often considered almost nothing more than a backdrop against which the inventions and departures of the progressive text move and have effect. The excesses that mark these genre films are theorized as they distinguish their systemic exceptionalness, not as they may characterize the very mainstays of their mother systems. The overvaluation of invention in these arguments, then, underplays any sense of systemic context for these works that might qualify the progressive assertion. Specifically, when examining the coordinates of the progressive/subversive genre, it seems quite necessary to consider the attributes of the diachronic systems they, as microsystems, inhabit. This emphasis poses both the question of generic/systemic evolution and of genre's relation to classical narrative.

In defining the place of genre within its systemic history, theories emanating from Russian formalist and semiotic accounts of literary evolution are particularly germane. Semiotician Maria Corti, aided and abetted by formalist theories of literary evolution, addresses herself specifically to the question of innovation within the generic system. She writes: "The process of transformation inside a literary genre . . . has regulative power. In every hypersign of strong individuality the program of the literary genre matures and is modified as it becomes a constitutive law of the work itself. . . . From the moment in which such a process takes place, the transformation which was an individual event, becomes another link in the chain that is the path of the literary genre."[15] This view of the literary system parallels the normative evaluation of violation within literary evolution forwarded by such formalists as Jurij Tynjanov and Roman Jakobson. The terms "deviation," "deformation," and "defamiliarization," which are fueled with subversive implications in some ideological criticism, are used in formalism to define the normative dynamics of literary evolution;[16] innovations in the system do not entail sudden and complete renovations, but are mutations that genetically engineer the modifications necessary to the maintenance and perseverance of the system. The chiaroscuro lighting schemes in film noir, for instance, which are critically observed as cuing the disequilibrium and subversive disturbances to the norm, have ancestral ties to German expressionist lighting tactics and, as well, generically extend lighting codes that characteristically signified criminal environments in crime films of the thirties. In short, no film genre is an island. The individual work itself intrinsically reflects and modifies the diachronic characteristics of the system; as Roman Jakobson remarked, "This simultaneous presentation of tradition and breaking away from tradition . . . form the essence of every new work of art."[17]

Here, the notion of difference, even a staunchly innovative one, seems firmly entrenched within the vicissitudes of the system.

The relation of genre to narrative system results in a parallel minimization of the autonomy of difference. The explicit relation of genre to the literary system, theorized by Corti, defines genre as a type of literary process reproducing "like a microcosm those functional variations that generate the very movement of literature." [18] Similarly, rather than privileging overtly inventional genres as "escapees" from the regulations of the classical narrative system, one can argue that they instead be regarded as instances of the system's requisite operation. The "rupture thesis" as it has been developed in the branch of ideological criticism considered here relies on a very restricted formulation of classical narrative, which enables a deviation from the identified principles to be readily gauged as challenging the entire foundation of the system.

In theories of classical Hollywood narrative the work of Stephen Heath, among others, has stressed a less petrified formula for the classic text via a consideration of its principles of structuration and process.[19] Stephen Neale's monograph on genre redefines genre through a Heathian perspective on the operations of the classic narrative. In his view, genre is an instance of the classical Hollywood system par excellence: genres are "modes of this narrative system, regulated orders of its potentiality." [20] This theory of classical narrative relieves the rigidity of definition drawn by the term "classic text" and offers instead the notion of a classical textual system, which is produced from a volatile combination of disequilibrium (excess, difference) and equilibrium (containment, repetition). Neale, like Corti, recognizes disequilibrium/difference not as a partisan component of the subversive text, but as an essential functioning element of the overall system—here, the classic textual system. Genres play an essential role in demonstrating and supporting the principles of this system, which "allow for (regulated) forms of excess, and (regulated) forms of display of its process: part of the very function of genres is precisely to display a variety of possibilities of the semiotic processes of mainstream narrative cinema while containing them simultaneously as genre. Hence the musical with its systematic freedom of space . . . , its shifting balance of narrative and spectacle . . . ; or the film noir, with its display of the possibilities of chiaroscuro lighting, frequently unmotivated, diegetically impossible. . . ." [21] Genre, then, is an exigent permutation of this system which thrives on a play of variation and regulation. Genres provide what Neale calls "regularized variety" and so are directly related to the textual economy of the system in that they "systematize its regime of difference and repetition," providing an "economy of variation, rather than rupture. . . ." [22]

What these contextual perspectives provide is a less inflammatory reading of the impact of moments of textual difference, by projecting the dynamics of difference/innovation as system-descriptive rather than system-subversive. The question of the nature and processes of both systemic-historic evolution and classical narrativity does not efface the cogent results of textually oriented ideological analyses, but qualifies contentions about the ideological effectivity of texts that are presumed "rupturous." In the case of progressive-text criticism, "textual isolationism" invites an assessment of textual politics based on a rather rigid sense of both what "makes" and "breaks" the system. This streamlining critical position seems especially difficult to maintain, logically, in the face of the overall phenomenon of generic textuality—which is so explicitly heterogeneous due to the "pluralizing" forces of both diachronic and synchronic factors that impinge upon the internal contours and reception/consumption of the genre film. The critical assumptions that measure the subversiveness of a genre, based on its anticlassical formal attributes, selectively overstate the radical valency of inventional signifiers and underestimate the means through which supervising systems negotiate a normative function for even the most excessive, foregrounded, deformative textual tendencies.

Notes

1. Among such pieces involving mainstream productions are Christine Gledhill, "*Klute:* A Contemporary Film Noir and Feminist Criticism," and Sylvia Harvey, "Woman's Place: The Absent Family of Film Noir," in *Women in Film Noir,* edited by E. Ann Kaplan (London: British Film Institute, 1978), pp. 6–21 and 22–33, respectively; Claire Johnston, "Women's Cinema as Counter Cinema," in *Sexual Stratagems,* edited by Patricia Erens (New York: Horizon Press, 1979), pp. 133–143; Claire Johnston, ed., *The Work of Dorothy Arzner: Towards a Feminist Cinema* (London: British Film Institute, 1975); Thomas Elsaesser, "Tales of Sound and Fury: Observations on the Family Melodrama," *Monogram,* no. 4 (1973): 2–15 (reprinted in this volume); Robin Wood, "Ideology, Genre, Auteur," *Film Comment* 13, no. 1 (January–February 1977): 46–51 (reprinted in this volume); *The American Nightmare,* edited by Robin Wood and Richard Lippe (Toronto: Festival of Festivals, 1979); and Pam Cook, "Exploitation Films and Feminism," *Screen* 17, no. 2 (1976): 122–127.

2. Louis Althusser, *Lenin and Philosophy and Other Essays,* translated by Ben Brewster (New York: Monthly Review Press, 1971), pp. 221–227, 228–242.

3. Ibid., p. 222.

4. Ibid., p. 241.

5. Ibid.

6. Jean-Louis Comolli and Jean Narboni, "Cinema/Ideology/Criticism," *Screen* 12, no. 1 (Spring 1971): 27–36.

7. Kaplan, "Introduction," in *Women in Film Noir,* p. 2.

8. Robin Wood, "Introduction," in *The American Nightmare,* p. 13.

9. Harvey, "Woman's Place," in *Women in Film Noir,* p. 22; Wood, *The American Nightmare,* p. 22; Elsaesser, "Tales of Sound and Fury," p. 15.

10. See Wood, "Ideology, Genre, Auteur."

11. Harvey, "Woman's Place," p. 33.

12. Elsaesser, "Tales of Sound and Fury," p. 6.

13. Ibid., p. 8.

14. *Women in Film Noir,* pp. 2, 13–14.

15. Maria Corti, *An Introduction to Literary Semiotics,* translated by Margherita Bogat and Allen Mandelbaum (Bloomington: Indiana University Press, 1978), p. 16.

16. A more extensive discussion of this point can be found in Tony Bennett, *Formalism and Marxism* (London: Methuen, 1979).

17. Roman Jacobson, "The Dominant," in *Readings in Russian Poetics,* edited by L. Matejka and K. Pomorska (Cambridge: MIT Press, 1971), pp. 76–77.

18. Corti, *Literary Semiotics,* p. 134.

19. Stephen Heath, "Film and System," *Screen* 16, no. 1 (Spring 1975): 7–77, and no. 2 (Summer 1975): 91–113.

20. Stephen Neale, *Genre* (London: British Film Institute, 1980), p. 20.

21. Ibid., p. 31.

22. Ibid.

8. The Structural Influence: New Directions in Film Genre Study

THOMAS SCHATZ

There has been in recent years a rather dramatic upsurge of scholarly interest in the Hollywood film—particularly the genre film—as a "product" of a conventionalized production system. One might suggest a number of reasons for this interest: the overwhelming auteurism of the 1960s, the influence of such critical methodologies as structuralism and semiotics, and also our natural inclination to perform an autopsy on the studio system now that its death has been verified by the New Hollywood. Aside from the issue of its motivation, however, this broadened perspective would seem to indicate an increased consideration in film study for the Hollywood movie as an industrial and cultural document as well as an autonomous aesthetic artifact.

Perhaps the most evident manifestation of this concern for the conventionalized nature of American movies and their production is in the burgeoning field of popular culture, which itself is founded on something of a structuralist concept in its basic assumption that members of a mass-mediated society develop and participate in complex systems of unexamined beliefs. This culturally responsive perspective already has been evident in structuralist film theory—whether semiological or psychoanalytic—which seeks to delineate the various signification systems that inform virtually all Hollywood films. More recently, this perspective has influenced film history and criticism as well, and further promises to delimit or at least clarify the generally artificial boundaries that traditionally have distinguished the study of film history, theory, and criticism. Such historical studies as Robert Sklar's *Movie-Made America* (1976) and Michael Wood's *America in the Movies* (1976) as well as genre studies like Stuart Kaminsky's *American Film Genres* (1974), Will Wright's *Sixguns and Society* (1975), and Stanley Solomon's *Beyond Formula* (1976) all rely for their conceptual thrust upon some degree of sensitivity to the Hollywood film's industrial and cultural context.

Both Sklar's and Wood's studies represent efforts to treat the complex relationship between the Hollywood cinema and American culture (or what a decade ago might have been termed American ideology) by examining the virtual "world" that the studios projected onto neighborhood movie screens throughout this century. Sklar, whose book is subtitled *A Cultural History of the Movies*, assumes a rather traditional historical approach, treating chronologically the patterns of American thought as reflected in its national cinema, whereas Wood is much more eclectic in his effort to trace the "fragments of myth" incorporated in the Hollywood films of the 1940s and 1950s.

Sklar's study marks a considerable advance over Arthur Knight's and Gerald Mast's historical surveys, although Sklar ultimately offers only tentative suggestions as to precisely how America has been "moviemade." It is Wood's study, despite its conversational tone and general disdain for scholarly discipline, that is of special interest here. His conception of American movie production as a mythmaking process in which both the Hollywood studios and the mass audience reciprocally participate is an idea that promises to redefine the study of Hollywood film genres. In his effort to examine the "classic" Hollywood era (which Wood defines, somewhat arbitrarily, as spanning the late thirties to the early sixties), he in fact does develop an extended generic analysis, identifying various cinematic forms and conventions in terms of the myths—or "clusters of worries"—that characterize them. So even though Wood views the Hollywood cinema from a personalized and often somewhat self-indulgent perspective, it would seem that there are certain methodological and conceptual aspects of his work that are directly applicable to recent developments in film genre study.

Regarding genre study, the most significant implication of Wood's cultural history is that we can begin finally to confront film genres as something other than individual, isolated narrative formulae. In each of the genre studies cited above, for example, there is an effort—even if only a marginal one—to treat the notion of genre per se, to address the "genreness" of repetitive cinematic forms and the reasons why only certain forms have been refined into genres. But while both Kaminsky and Solomon examine several genres, ranging from screwball comedy to science fiction, only in their suggestive but ultimately underdeveloped introductions do they consider what these varied forms might have in common beyond their being termed film genres. After prefatory comments regarding cultural and narrative patterns, both analysts proceed to deal with each genre as a distinct and unique conventionalized system, as a bundle of formalized elements that individual filmmakers animate in the course of production. Consequently, these studies recall both Jim Kitses's introduction to *Horizons West* and Colin McArthur's opening chapters to *Underworld USA*, which presented litanies of generic conventions manipulated by cinematic auteurs whose films somehow "transcended" the genres in which they worked. Despite their initial allusions to the role of genre films in contemporary culture, each of these analysts displays an overt traditionalist bias in emphasizing the distinctive aesthetic value as opposed to the shared ritualistic value of Hollywood genre films.

It is somewhat ironic that Will Wright's *Sixguns and Society,* a perceptive but limited structural study of the western, finally comes closest to tapping that form's broad appeal as cultural ritual and hence its relationship to other generic forms. His synthesis of the seminal ideas of Claude Lévi-Strauss, Vladimir Propp, and Kenneth Burke in their respective studies of mythic, narrative, and symbolic form proves to be both enlightening and unwieldy when applied to the western genre. But more important, it does indicate the sort of conceptual perspective from which we might consider the fundamental popular appeal and cultural value of seemingly disparate cinematic forms. As such, Wright's work is something of a watershed in the general study of Hollywood film genres, even though he deals only with the western genre. One comes away from Wright's rather tedious analysis of scores of westerns wishing he had broadened his inquiry to consider other generic forms as well, a project that seems most appropriate to his methodological approach.

As Wright's work indicates, recent developments not only in cultural studies but also in such varied fields as structural anthropology, mythology, and linguistics suggest the vital importance of both cultural and formal conventions in every commercial cinematic product. The importance of these conventions is most pronounced, of course, in genre films, in those westerns and musicals and gangster films in which a tacit "contract" has been established through the reciprocal studio-audience relationship. From the audience's viewpoint, this contract represents a distinct cluster of narrative, thematic, and iconographic patterns that have been refined through exposure and familiarity into systems of reasonably well-defined expectations. I would suggest that it is this high degree of audience familiarity with the Hollywood generic product, and thus the audience's active but indirect participation in that product's creation, that provides the basis for whatever claims might be made for the genre film as a form of cultural ritual and for its status as contemporary myth.

I accept the fact, somewhat grudgingly, that the elitist biases implicit in most traditional film study have done a great deal to promote both popular and scholarly interest in the Hollywood cinema, but not until we examine the genre film in its ritualistic capacity will we fully appreciate its cultural and aesthetic value. We might recall in this context an observation by André Bazin, whose cultural sensibilities generally have been underrated, that "the cinema's existence precedes its essence."[1] Neither Bazin nor I would wish to minimize the commercial cinema's status as a contemporary art form. There clearly is a need, however, for those very attributes of the commercial cinema which have been considered its shortcomings—its popularity with a mass audience, its obvious marketability, its system of production—to be reconsidered in a broader cultural perspective. This perspective should encourage new approaches to the study of American film, redirecting at least a portion of our critical and theoretical energies away from the traditionalist aesthetics that have inhibited certain areas of film study.

As I indicated earlier, a number of genre analysts have noted its ritualistic and socially functional character, although few have pursued it beyond the level of casual observation. In his brief but illuminating essay on film genre, Thomas Sobchack describes this process in classical terms, stating that "the cathartic potentials of the genre film can be seen in the way in which the tensions of cultural and social paradoxes inherent in human experience can be resolved."[2] John G. Cawelti assumes a more direct approach in his analysis of the western entitled *The Six-Gun Mystique*. Cawelti observes that an important dimension of the western "is social and cultural ritual,"[3] and he later defines ritual as "a means of affirming certain basic cultural values, resolving tension and establishing a sense of continuity between present and past."[4]

This view of the genre film as a contemporary folktale leads us even further into an area of investigation that genre analysts have consistently recognized as important and yet have never profitably developed—the relationship of the genre film to myth. In his introduction to *American Film Genres,* Kaminsky offers an insight that he regrettably does not pursue, stating that "on one level one can argue that the genre films, television, and literature have to a great extent replaced more formal versions of mythic response to existence such as religion and folk tale."[5] John Fell follows this line of reasoning when he suggests that "the conjunction of the terms 'popular culture' and 'myth' poses a central issue of genre study."[6] Fell pursues this central issue for only a single paragraph, concluding that the genre film incorporates a "corrupted form" of myth, a notion clearly borrowed from Northrop Frye.

More detailed and influential genre studies, especially those of Cawelti and Kitses, have also demonstrated a recognition of the importance of ritual and myth in the popular arts generally, and particularly in the Hollywood genre film. But due once again to an admitted allegiance to the position of literary genre analyst Northrop Frye, they both assume an aesthetically oriented definition of myth. Consequently, Kitses concludes that the idea of myth, "ever in the air when the [western] form is discussed, clouds the issue completely."[7] Cawelti's position is similar, as he opts for the term "formula" rather than "genre" specifically to avoid the issue of myth. "For Frye myths are universal patterns of action," observes

Cawelti, and he argues that as such they cannot exist within a medium that is essentially culturally specific in terms of both imagery and ideology.[8]

These arguments are derived from a definition of myth which, for these analysts as well as for Frye, is dependent upon a classical conception of myth as a formal vehicle for sacred or pantheistic narrative content. Kitses's stance, for example, is indicative of that assumed by the majority of genre theorists when confronted with the issue of myth and ritual. According to Kitses, "In strict classical terms of definition myth has to do with the activity of the gods and as such the western has no myth."[9] It is interesting that Kitses's analysis of the structure of the western brings him quite close to some recently developed ideas about mythic structure, but his allegiance to Frye's classical position prevents him from making that connection. On the one hand, he cites the presence of a functional or dualistic—in his words a "dialectical"—structure of the western, but when confronted with the concept of myth in the generic sense, he defines it in terms of narrative content rather than structure or function.

As numerous mythologists and also cultural and structural anthropologists have recently observed, however, a ritualized form, whether religious or secular, does not *have* a myth; it *is* a myth—or rather it serves a mythic function. Myth is not defined by the repetition of some classical content or universal narrative; it is defined according to its function as a unique conceptual system that embodies elements specific to the culture which realizes it. Bronislav Malinowski, one of the fathers of modern anthropology, observes that myth fulfills "an indispensable function; it expresses, enhances, and codifies belief; it safeguards and enforces morality; it vouches for the efficiency and contains practical rules for the guidance of man."[10]

In describing Ernst Cassirer's reflections on myth, anthropologist David Bidney states that "according to Cassirer, mythical thinking is a unitary form of consciousness with its specific and characteristic features. There is no unity of *object* in myth but only a unity of function expressed in a unique mode of experience."[11] In *The Myth of the State,* Cassirer contends that the function of myth is not that of explanation but is, instead, practical and social, to promote a feeling of unity and harmony between the members of a society and also with the whole of nature or life.[12]

This view of myth recalls both Sobchack's earlier premises that genre films resolve the "tensions of cultural and social paradoxes" and also Cawelti's view of the western film as "cultural and social ritual." As a ritualization of collective ideals, the genre film necessarily treats the relationship between the individual and the community, thereby considering the value of that community within the natural world of which the individual is sensually and emotionally a part. Sobchack finds these conflicts—" between the individual and the group, between self-realization and communal conformity"—to be the seminal characteristics of the genre film. He also contends that because of the specific nature of the ritualized form, "the resolution of the tension between the two poles will always be in favor of the community." [13]

This conception of the genre film as a unique functional structure is closely akin to the work of Claude Lévi-Strauss in his structural analyses of myth. Lévi-Strauss defines mythical thought as "a whole system of references which operates by means of a pair of cultural contrasts: between the general and the particular on the one hand and nature and culture on the other." [14] Lévi-Strauss, along with linguist Roman Jakobson, argues that myth as a functional structure is analogous to language in that we do not define it by the content of its sentences but rather by its syntax, by the rules governing the sentences' construction. As Lévi-Strauss states: "If there is meaning to be found in mythology, this cannot reside in the isolated elements which enter into the composition of a myth, but only in the way the elements are combined." [15] This observation is itself indebted to Ferdinand de Saussure's insight distinguishing *langue* from *parole* in verbal language. Saussure held that the speakers' and listeners' shared knowledge of the rules of grammar comprising the language system (*langue*) enables them to develop and understand a virtually unlimited and even grammatically incorrect range of individual utterances (*parole*). [16]

Like language and myth, the film genre as a textual system represents a set of rules of construction that are utilized to accomplish a specific communicative function. In his metaphor describing the variation of individual folktales that constitute a mythic structure, Lévi-Strauss might just as easily be describing the individual films within a genre:

> Thus, a myth exhibits a "slated" structure which seeps to the surface, if one may say so, through the repetition process. However, the slates are not absolutely identical to each other. And since the purpose of myth is to provide a logical model capable of overcoming a contradiction, . . . a theoretically infinite number of slates will be generated, each one slightly different from the others. [17]

The concept of genre as a filmic system must be characterized, like that of myth, by its function; its value is determined not according to what it is, but rather according to what it does. In its ritualistic capacity, a film genre transforms certain fundamental cultural contradictions and conflicts into a unique conceptual structure that is familiar and accessible to the mass audience. The issue of cultural specificity, a cinematic characteristic that encouraged Cawelti to avoid altogether the concepts of genre and myth in dealing with the western, is actually vital to any mythic structure. Edmund Leach, in his study of the works of Lévi-Strauss, holds that myth is "the expression of unobservable realities in terms of observable phenomena." [18] Lévi-Strauss himself points out that different cultures "express their different originalities by manipulating the resources of a dialectical system of contrasts and correlations within the framework of a common conceptual world." [19]

Thus, a mythic structure must indeed be incorporated within a culturally specific context, or else it would be unrecognizable or meaningless to the members of the culture who experience it. When Cawelti argues that cinematic formulas "relate to culture rather than to the generic nature of man," he is in fact addressing two sides of the same mythic coin. [20] The mythic ritual of the folktale is, to paraphrase Lévi-Strauss, a society collectively speaking to itself, confronting basic human issues in a familiar context. The "generic nature of man" that Cawelti refers to is precisely that mythmaking faculty by which individuals deal with the culturally specific in order to make palatable certain truths about the human condition that people have always found it difficult to contemplate. [21]

When we assume this view of the genre film functioning as a form of contemporary mythic ritual, we establish a basis for examining genres not only as individual, isolated forms, but also as related systems that exhibit fundamentally similar characteristics. In this context, we can begin to treat two vitally important questions regarding the study of film genre that thus far have gone unanswered: first, why only certain narrative-thematic structures have been refined into genres in the American cinema; second, what cultural appeal and conceptual basis endows these forms with their generic identity, with their "genre-ness," as it were.

Considering the genre film as a popular folktale assigns to it a mythic function that generates its unique structure, whose function is the ritualization of collective ideals, the celebration of temporarily resolved social and cultural conflicts, and the concealment of disturbing cultural conflicts behind the guise of entertainment, behind what Michael Wood terms "the semitransparent mask of a contradiction." [22] By assuming this mythic perspective when analyzing the genre film, we must necessarily consider the collective audience's participation in the studio system of production, which further substantiates the role of that production system in the contemporary mythmaking process. This role has been suggested by various analysts, but it generally has been done without initially delineating the interaction of the studio system with the audience and thereby recognizing the audience's collective participation in the generation and development of film genres. [23] This reciprocal studio-audience relationship provides the cultural context in which the genre film has been produced, endowing that film with its distinctive ritualistic character and providing the foundation for any theoretical approach that treats the genre film in terms of its mythic function.

In treating the Hollywood genre film as a form of mythic expression within a popular art form, we should not fail to consider certain basic qualifications imposed by the nature of the commercial cinematic medium that necessarily affect the narrative and thematic composition of that expression. That is, there are a number of general cinematic codes indigenous to the Hollywood production system that influence (and ultimately characterize) all of its products, including genre films. Beyond the obvious consideration of the cinema's incorporating an audiovisual as opposed to an oral or written mode of mythic expression, we might also consider Hollywood's penchant for narrative as opposed to documentary or abstract films, its "closed" economic system that made independent feature film production virtually impossible in America until the 1960s, its nurturing of the star system, and other related aspects of production. Whereas these considerations by no means undercut the notion of genre films representing an idealized cultural self-image in a ritualized form—indeed, the deification of such stars as John Wayne and Fred Astaire seem to underscore it—they do testify to the fact that the Hollywood cinema's mode of production provides a unique context for mythic expression.

Perhaps the characteristic of the commercial cinema that marks its most significant departure from traditional forms of ritual is the tendency, even within the conservative Hollywood system, toward rapid evolution of certain aspects of its popular narrative forms. Films within a genre represent variations on a theme, so to speak; the theme itself, as a manifestation of fundamental cultural preoccupations, may remain essentially consistent, but without variation the form necessarily will stagnate. The widespread exposure of genre films to the audience and the demand that filmmakers sustain audience interest in popular forms encourage continued manipulation of generic conventions if the genre is to maintain its vitality and cultural significance. As Robert Warshow has observed in his study of the western: "We do not want to see the same movie over and over again, only the same form." [24]

The western genre, for example, has enjoyed a life span roughly equivalent to that of the commercial American cinema itself, and throughout that span it has dealt with the basic oppositions of social order and anarchy as manifested in various dualities (East versus West, town versus wilderness, garden versus desert, group versus individual, and so on). While consistently focusing upon these oppositions, the genre has undergone considerable evolutionary development, both in terms of its historical depiction of the western environment and its casting of the western hero, who has tended in more recent films to be aligned with the forces of anarchy rather than those of social order.

In his structural study of the western, sociologist Will Wright views this evolutionary development in terms of extracinematic social and economic change. Wright suggests that "the narrative structure varies in accordance with the changing social actions and institutions. The oppositions, on the other hand, create images of social types that are fundamental in the consciousness of the society." [25] From his sociological perspective, Wright tends to minimize the creative input of the Hollywood production system. I would complement Wright's position with the suggestion that once the generic conventions have been established (which may take several decades, as with the western, or only a few years, as with the gangster film), filmmakers are stimulated, either by economic or aesthetic impulse, to take considerable liberties with the basic forms that are readily comprehensible in the context of audience familiarity and expectations. Thus, the "psychological" westerns of the early 1950s or the more recent celebration of the western outlaw should seem to the mass audience a reasonable extension of the genre's conventional ritualization of the forces of social order, progress, and individual freedom.

Our consideration of the genre film, then, is qualified by something of a dual perspective. It is, on the one hand, a product of a commercial, highly conventionalized popular art form and subject to certain demands imposed by both the audience and the cinematic system itself. On the other hand, the genre film represents a distinct manifestation of contemporary society's basic mythic impulse, its desire to confront elemental conflicts inherent in modern culture while at the same time participating in the projection of an idealized collective self-image. Having suggested the value of this perspective, I would like to close with a brief comment on what seem to be certain dangers inherent in this approach. As Wood's cultural study of the Hollywood film indicates, we might extend the previously elaborated methodological inquiry to yet a "higher" level, considering the Hollywood product generally as a contemporary manifestation of the human being's mythic impulse. But while there is certainly a degree to which virtually every mass-mediated cultural artifact can be examined from such a perspective, there appears to be a point at which we tend to lose sight of the initial object of inquiry.

Symptomatic of this brand of scholarly myopia—and again Wood's study is perhaps the most appropriate example—is the propensity either to expound generalizations about popular culture of such breadth and scope as to be essentially meaningless, or else to lapse into highly personal, impressionistic recollections of preadolescent Saturday afternoons spent with the Duke or Garbo or Godzilla. If we avoid overextending its reach, it would seem that the ultimate value of the form of analysis outlined here is that it enables students of the Hollywood genre film to broaden their analytical perspective without violating the integrity of the individual films or the genres in which they participate. Consequently, we can consider the genre film and the film genre in the same analytical context, examining westerns and musicals, screwball comedies and war films, from a culturally responsive perspective that acknowledges their shared as well as their distinctive individual qualities.

Notes

1. André Bazin, "In Defense of Mixed Cinema," in *What Is Cinema?* edited and translated by Hugh Gray (Berkeley: University of California Press, 1971), 1:71.

2. Thomas Sobchack, "Genre Film: A Classical Experience," *Literature/Film Quarterly* 3, no. 3 (Summer 1975): 201. Reprinted in this volume.

3. John G. Cawelti, *The Six-Gun Mystique* (Bowling Green, Ohio: Bowling Green University Popular Press, [1970]), p. 32.

4. Ibid., p. 73.

5. Stuart M. Kaminsky, *American Film Genres: Approaches to a Critical Theory of Popular Film* (Chicago: Pflaum, 1974), p. 3.

6. John C. Fell, *Film: An Introduction* (New York: Praeger, 1975), p. 116.

7. Jim Kitses, *Horizons West* (Bloomington: Indiana University Press, 1969), p. 13.

8. Cawelti, *Six-Gun Mystique*, p. 30. This issue of "cultural specificity" provides the basis for much recent discussion concerning the viability of myth in various cultures. As I intend to elaborate throughout this paper, the denial by Cawelti, Kitses, and Frye that a culturally specific narrative form *itself* can be mythic is in direct opposition to recent studies in mythology and structural anthropology.

9. Kitses, *Horizons West*, p. 13.

10. Bronislav Malinowski, *Myth in Primitive Psychology* (New York: W. W. Norton, 1926), p. 13.

11. David Bidney, "Myth, Symbolism, and Truth," *Journal of American Folklore* 68, no. 270 (October–December 1955): 381.

12. Ibid., p. 384.

13. Sobchack, "Genre Film," p. 201.

14. Claude Lévi-Strauss, *The Savage Mind* (Chicago: University of Chicago Press, 1966), p. 135.

15. Claude Lévi-Strauss, "A Structural Study of Myth," in *The Structuralists*, edited by Richard T. DeGeorge and Fernande M. DeGeorge (Garden City: Doubleday, 1972), p. 105.

16. Ferdinand de Saussure, *A Course in General Linguistics* (Paris: Bally and Sechehaye, 1972), p. 16.

17. Lévi-Strauss, "Structural Study of Myth," p. 109.

18. Edmund Leach, *Claude Lévi-Strauss* (New York: Viking, 1970), p. 58.

19. Claude Lévi-Strauss, *The Raw and the Cooked: Introduction to a Science of Mythology* (Evanston, Ill.: Harper and Row, 1969), p. 8.

20. Cawelti, *Six-Gun Mystique*, p. 31.

21. Robert Scholes, *Structuralism in Literature: An Introduction* (New Haven: Yale University Press, 1974), p. 68.

22. Michael Wood, *America in the Movies* (New York: Basic Books, 1975), p. 80.

23. See, for example, Will Wright's *Sixguns and Society: A Structural Study of the Western* (Berkeley: University of California Press, 1975), an entire volume devoted to the western film genre that does not once mention the studio system or the influence of the audience in the generation and development of the form.

24. Robert Warshow, "The Westerner," in *The Immediate Experience* (Garden City: Doubleday, 1962), p. 147.

25. Wright, *Sixguns and Society*, p. 27.

9. Genre Film: A Classical Experience

THOMAS SOBCHACK

In *An Illustrated Glossary of Film Terms,* Harry M. Geduld and Ronald Gottesman define *genre* as a "category, kind, or form of film distinguished by subject matter, theme, or techniques." [1] They list more than seventy-five genres of film, both fiction and nonfiction. There are categories within categories and categories which overlap and are not mutually exclusive. In light of the difficulty of accurately defining the individual genres, I would rather sidestep the problem by considering the fictional genre film as a single category that includes all that is commonly held to be genre film—i.e., the western, the horror film, the musical, the science fiction film, the swashbuckler—in order to show that all of these films have a common origin and basic form. Bound by a strict set of conventions, tacitly agreed upon by filmmaker and audience, the genre film provides the experience of an ordered world and is an essentially classical structure predicated upon the principles of the classical world view in general and indebted to the *Poetics* of Aristotle in particular; in the genre film the plot is fixed, the characters defined, the ending satisfyingly predictable.

Because the genre film is not realistic, because it is so blatantly dramatic, it has been condescendingly treated by many critics for its failure to be relevant to contemporary issues, philosophies, and aesthetics. Yet the truth of the matter is that the genre film lives up to the guiding principle of its classical origins: "there is nothing new under the sun," and truth with a capital T is to be found in imitating the past. The contemporary and the particular are inimical to the prevailing idea in classical thought that knowledge is found in the general conclusions that have stood the test of time. Thus originality, unique subject matter, and a resemblance to actual life are denigrated as values, while conformity, adherence to previous models, and a preoccupation with stylistic and formal matters are held to be the criteria for artistic excellence.

The subject matter of a genre film is a story. It is not about something that matters outside the film, even if it inadvertently tells us something about the time and place of its creation. Its sole justification for existence is to make concrete and perceivable the configurations inherent in its ideal form. That the various genres have changed or gone through cycles of popularity does not alter the fact that the basic underlying coordinates of a genre are maintained time after time. From *The Great Train Robbery* (Edwin S. Porter, 1902) to *The Cowboys* (Mark Rydell, 1972) or *True Grit* (Henry Hathaway, 1968), the western has maintained a consistency of basic content; the motifs, plots, settings, and characters remain the same. What is true of the western is also true of the adventure film, the fantasy film, the crime film, and the musical, or any fictional genre one can identify. Any particular film of any definable group is only recognizable as part of that group if it is, in fact, an imitation of that which came before. It is only because we have seen other films that strongly resemble the particular film at hand that we can say it is a horror film or a thriller or a swashbuckler. Consciously or unconsciously, both the genre filmmaker and the genre audiences are aware of the prior films and the way in which each of these concrete examples is an attempt to embody once again the essence of a well-known story.

This use of well-known stories is clearly a classical practice. Homer, the Greek dramatists, Racine, Pope, Samuel Johnson, and all the other great figures of the classical and neoclassical periods used prior sources for their stories. The formative principle behind the creation of classical art has always been the known and the familiar. The Greeks knew the stories of the gods and the Trojan War in the same way we know about hoodlums and gangsters and G-men and the taming of the frontier and the never-ceasing struggle of the light of reason and the cross with the powers of darkness, not through first-hand experience but through the media. For them it was tales told around the hearth and the yearly ritual of plays; for us it is the newspapers, television, and the movies themselves.

The body of stories is, to use Balazs's terms, the "material" out of which the "content" of a genre film can be made. And it is a strictly de-limited area: other films may have the whole of life experience to choose from, but the genre film must be made from certain well-known and immediately recognizable plots—plots usually dealing with melodramatic incidents in which obvious villains and heroes portray the basic conflict of good versus evil. No matter how complicated the plot of a genre film may be, we always know who the good guys and the bad guys are; we always know whom to identify with and for just how long. Sam Spade may be considered by real-life standards to be a man of dubious moral character, but in the world of *The Maltese Falcon* (John Huston, 1941) he is clearly the hero akin to Odysseus threading his way through the obstacles of a hostile universe, using lies and deceit if necessary to complete his task.

Aristotle used the word *mimesis* to describe what a play is about. Supposedly it means imitation. Aristotle goes on to say that a plot is an imitation of a human action, and there are those who see in this definition the prescription for a kind of literal realism, holding the mirror up to life. But Greek drama, from which Aristotle drew his conclusions, was never that at all. Very few people in fifth-century Athens killed their fathers and slept with their mothers. The story of Oedipus, no matter how rife with Freudian implications for us today, was after all simply a story, albeit a kind of horror tale of its time, as were most of the stories upon which Greek writing was based. In practical terms Greek writings are imitations of prior stories, redone, reshaped, given dramatic form or epic form as the case may be, but nevertheless imitations of fictions.

Genre films operate on the same principle. They are made in imitation not of life but of other films. True, there must be the first instance in a series or cycle, yet most cases of the first examples of various film genres can be traced to literary sources, primarily pulp literature. Even the gangster films of the thirties derive not from life itself but from newspaper stories; the musical film, from the musical stage. And once the initial film is made, it has entered the pool of common knowledge known by filmmaker and film audience alike. Imitations and descendants—the long line of "sons of," "brides of," and "the return of"—begin.

One of the paradoxes of a classical approach to form is aptly demonstrated in the genre film's unrelenting pursuit of imitation. Classical theory insists upon the primacy of the original. It is that which must be imitated, and the basic and fundamental elements must not be changed. Therefore, to avoid an exact duplicate, subsequent imitations can merely embroider and decorate, which in most cases destroys the elegance and simplicity of the original design. The Doric column came first, simple, balanced, proportioned, direct. As the years passed, the Doric gave way to the Ionic, and the Ionic to the Corinthian, the last column so cluttered and intricate that it diluted the original idea. Classical painting and architecture give way to the rococo and the baroque. The decorations increase; the power and the purity of the original are somehow dissipated.

We can see the same process at work in the genre film, and it explains why so often the original version or the "classic" version seems so much better than any of its followers. The original Draculas, silent and sound, *Little Caesar* (Mervyn LeRoy, 1930) and *The Public Enemy* (William Wellman, 1931), *The Iron Horse* (John Ford, 1924) and *The Covered Wagon* (James Cruze, 1923), Busby Berkeley musicals, *The Maltese Falcon*—not only were they progenitors of their kind and therefore to be venerated as examples from the Golden Age, but seen today they have a sparseness and an economy of means that put most of the recent remakes to shame. Christopher Lee cannot compare to Bela Lugosi, and full-color blood cannot make up for the spectral mysteriousness of F. W. Murnau's *Nosferatu* (1922).

A genre film, no matter how baroque it may become, however, still differs fundamentally from other films by virtue of its reliance on preordained forms, known plots, recognizable characters, and obvious iconographies; it is still capable of creating the classical experience because of this insistence on the familiar. It is what we expect in a genre film and what we get. Other fiction films are not genre films precisely because they do the opposite; they go out of their way to be original, unique, and novel. They appear more realistic, more true to life. Their characters are more highly individualized, their actions physically and psychologically more believable, and the events of the plot, employing random events and inconsequential details, well within the realm of possibility.

There are grey areas, of course—films that seem to be closer to genre than others depending on the total effect of the film, the way in which the realistic elements are emphasized or deemphasized, the way in which generic elements are used or abused. Yet for most films the issue is more clear-cut. The ideas and attitudes informing genre films are diametrically opposed to the other kind of fiction film. Although there is a detective (the reporter) and a mystery (what's Rosebud?), it would be difficult to make a case for *Citizen Kane* (Orson Welles, 1941) as a detective or mystery genre film. Though it has certain generic elements, they are not prominent, nor are they the sole justification for the creation of the film. On the other hand, Sherlock Holmes films, the Thin Man series, Charlie Chan movies, and others exist primarily to flesh out the idea of the detective story on film. They exist as variations on the motif of sleuthing. "Who dun it?" is the primary question raised and answered by these movies. No matter how rich a gold mine of interpretation one may find in *The Maltese Falcon*, for example, the basic question dealt with is still "Who dun it?" and not "Who am I?" or "What is the discrepancy between what a man appears to be and what he really is?" This is not to say that something of the latter question is not raised by Sam Spade's character, but certainly the film does not invite the general audience to take the question seriously, even if critics do.

One of the most important characteristics of the classical complex is a concern with form. Genre films, as suggested, are invariably more involved with formal matters both in content and in style, since they begin in imitation of other formal objects and not in imitation of life. In keeping with this notion, the form of a genre film will display a profound respect for Aristotelian dramatic values. There is always a definite sense of beginning, middle, and end, of closure, and of a frame. The film begins with

"Once upon a time . . ." and ends only after all the strings have been neatly tied, all major conflicts resolved. It is a closed world. There is little room in the genre film for ambiguity anywhere—in characters, plots, or iconography. But even when seeming ambiguities arise in the course of a film, they must be either deemphasized or taken care of by the end of the film.

The most important single aspect of the genre film that gives it this compact sense of shape is the plot. It's what happens that is most important, not why. Incident crowding on incident, reversal after reversal, all strung out like beads on a string (or a rosary), to be counted one after another until the final shoot-out, the burning of the castle, the destruction of the fiend, the payment of the mortgage on the Big Top, or the return of the spacecraft to earth. Inherent and implicit in the beginning of any genre plot is the end; the elements presented in the exposition at the beginning are all clearly involved with the inevitable conclusion. Nothing extraneous to the plot can be introduced at random, somewhere in the middle. The best genre films always seem shorter than they really are. The classical virtue of economy of means may have been forced upon the genre film because of its usually low production budget, but it has maximized this possible defect. Only those scenes that advance the plot are permitted. Only that dialogue which will keep things moving is allowed. The adage attributed apocryphally to Hitchcock, that you should never use dialogue when you can show it in pictures, is often reversed in the genre film— even in Hitchcock's films. Whenever it takes too long to show it, say it instead. Do anything and everything to keep the plot moving, to create the sense of gathering momentum, of inevitable causality.

To further speed comprehension of the plot, genre films employ visual codes, called iconographies, in order to eliminate the need for excessive verbal or pictorial exposition. Strictly speaking, beyond the use of masks, there is nothing in Greek drama comparable to the iconography of the genre film, for as Aristotle pointed out, "spectacle"—what we see—is the least important element of a play, while it is obviously a primary aspect of film. A more appropriate analogy can be found in the Greek narrative art—the epic poems. Homer is an exceptionally visual poet, particularly when he is describing the armor and weapons of his heroes in *The Iliad; The Odyssey,* too, pictorializes costumes, metamorphoses, monsters, and settings in a way that brings to mind the vividness of the modern equivalent—the genre film.

Iconography consists of certain photographed objects, costumes, and places composing the visible surface of a genre film that creates economically the context and milieu, the field of action on which the plot will unravel itself. Over a period of use in many films, these visual elements have become encrusted with shared meanings, so that dialogue and camera can concentrate on revealing the twists and turns of the plot. Iconography, like familiar plot situations and stereotypical characters, provides a shorthand of mutually recognizable communications that neither filmmaker nor audience need ponder: the jungle is treacherous, the castle that towers darkly over the village is sinister, the flat horizon of the desert is unyielding. Capes and evening clothes create threatening figures unless they are in a musical; laboratories with bubbling liquids are occupied by men tampering with things no human being should.

Like the epithet—a descriptive, characterizing tag line in the epic poems (the "wine-dark sea," the "bronze-shot arrows," the "cunning Odysseus")—the icons of genre films serve to remind the viewer of the internal consistency and familiarity of the characters and places in the film. These places and characters do not change in the course of a film, and very little from film to film. The visual appearance of a western town in one film is just about the same as in other films. The landscape in a sci-fi picture can be depended upon. The world of the musical is always a glittering unreality poised somewhere between our doughty old world and heaven, whether it is set backstage at the Broadway Theater or high in the Swiss Alps.

As indicated above, characterization in a genre film often uses the shorthand of iconography. We know a person by what he wears as opposed to what he says and does. And once known, the character cannot change except in the most limited ways. Curiously enough, the Greek word for *character* as applied to human beings was the same as that applied to a letter of the alphabet. That is, the root word means the "stamp" that imprints the letter on the paper, or the stamp that imprints the character onto the person. Right up until the end of the classical era—and the neoclassical—in the eighteenth century, the prevailing opinion was that human character was imprinted at birth and that it did not develop or change. Though the subsequent revolutions of thought in the nineteenth and twentieth centuries have all but wiped out this idea, the genre film continues to employ this extremely classical concept.

Frequently generalized and known by their vocation, genre characters are conveyed through iconographical means—costumes, tools, settings, and so on. The man who wears a star, whether he is a figure in the crowd or a major character, has a limited range of responses to situations. The same is the case with men who wear lab coats, carry sawed-off shotguns, or drink their whiskey straight. These men are their functions in the plot. Revealed to us through costume, dialogue, or physiognomy, they remind us of other sheriffs, private eyes, and mad scientists from other movies we've seen. Typecasting in the genre film is a bonus, not a debit. It is just one more way of establishing character quickly and efficiently. John Wayne is the character type John Wayne, his face no more expressive than the painted masks used in ancient times by the Greeks. Other performers like Bela Lugosi, Peter Lorre, and Vincent Price are instantly "knowable" as genre figures.

In addition to establishing character with speed and directness, the use of less individualized characters sets up the basis for the existence of Aristotelian catharsis by allowing for an increase in empathy by the audience. Being so much their exteriors, genre characters allow us to easily assume their roles. The fact that we know that they are not realistic, not part of our real world, lets us slip into their trench coats or boots with ease. We can identify so strongly and safely with their roles that we leave the theater walking a little bow-legged or pulling up the collar of a nonexistent trench coat to ward off the wind. Genre characters, because they are so unrealistic and without depth, because they are so consistent and unwavering in their purpose, because they are never forced to come to terms with themselves—they have no "self" in one sense—invite identification with the role or type; that identification releases us from the ordinary and mundane realism of our own lives. We can say, "I wish I were like him"— so tough, so hard-boiled, so ruthless, so lucky, so pure, so wonderfully one-dimensional, so bent on destruction or revenge, or on saving the world that eating and sleeping and other everyday occurrences and responsibilities can never interfere. While we may all live quiet lives of desperation, genre characters do not. We are all Walter Mittys, and for a few short hours we can be lifted out of our inconsequential existences into a world of heroic action.

This difference in level between our world and the world of the genre film I would regard as fulfilling Aristotle's dictum that the characters of drama be elevated. Genre characters are certainly far superior to us in what they can do; they may be limited as ordinary human beings, but they are unlimited as far as action. They can do what we would like to be able to do. They can pinpoint the evil in their lives as resident in a monster or a villain, and they can go out and triumph over it. We, on the other hand, are in a muddle. We know things aren't quite right, but we are not sure if it is a conspiracy among corporations, the world situation, politicians, our neighbors down the street, our boss, our spouse; but whatever it is, we can't call it out of the saloon for a shoot-out or round up the villagers and hunt it down. Genre characters inhabit a world that is better than ours, a world in which problems can be solved directly, emotionally, in action. It is in a sense an ideal plane, a utopia, as far removed from our world as was the world of kings and nobles and Olympian gods from the lives of the Athenians who attended the plays and heard the epics.

That we desire to witness such worlds and to experience classical catharsis is demonstrated by the current phenomenal attendance at martial arts films, the newest of film genres; it would be impossible to count the number of people who partake of such experiences through the older genres as offered on their television screens, both in reruns of theatrical films and the made-for-TV variety. The emotional involvement and subsequent release that Aristotle called catharsis is an obviously desired tonic in our postromantic modern world. Critics, sociologists, psychologists, and politicians may argue over the social impact of literature and films that depict violent action—are they only a reflection of the times or are they a cause of the violence in our culture?—but Aristotle's position is quite clear: there is a social benefit, a point at which art and the good of the community come together. If spectators identify strongly with the figures of the drama, feeling pity and fear as drawn out by the activities going on before their eyes and ears, then, when properly concluded, given the appropriate ending, these emotions are dissipated, leaving viewers in a state of calm, a state of stasis in which they can think rationally and clearly. Properly conceived and executed, the genre film can produce this effect.

The cathartic potentials of the genre film can also be seen as a way in which the tension of cultural and social paradoxes inherent in a human experience can be resolved. Freud in *Civilization and Its Discontents* and Nietzsche in *The Birth of Tragedy* and *The Death of Tragedy* discuss the issue at length. Nietzsche identifies the two poles of human behavior as the Apollonian and the Dionysian. The Apollonian is the urge to individuate the self from others and the Dionysian is the urge to submerge the self into a group, mob, clan, family, or chorus.

Since the conflict between the individual and the group, between self-realization and communal conformity, between the anxiety and loneliness engendered by the freeing of the self and the security of passive identification with the crowd, is so all-pervasive an element of human life, it is not surprising to find this tension between individual needs and community needs metaphorically represented in genre films, not only in gangster films, as Warshow has suggested, or in western films, as Cawelti has stated, but in all genre films. This tension, being so universal, may appear in other films as well, but because of the classical nature of the genre film, the resolution of the tension between these two poles will always be in favor of the community. The human being is after all a social animal. Thus, in classical thought, anything that can relieve or diffuse conflicting emotions and purge them from the individual can only be seen as a social good. Group values must be continually reinforced in the individual; in the old days religion did the job, but in post-Reformation times the burden has moved elsewhere. Patriotic nationalism and world communism have sought to pick up the standard in real life, but the only twentieth-century art that has consistently reenacted the ritual of reaffirmation of group values has been the genre film. Simply enough, it is the form of the genre film, its repetitive quality, its familiarity, and violent plotting that has made this work. During the course of a genre film we can vicariously play out our desire for individuation by identifying with the protagonist free from the anxiety of group censure. Personal fears of actually acting out our fantasies of sex and power are eliminated because we know it is only a movie. There are no penalties to pay, as there are in real life, for being either hero or villain. A short survey of several plot structures found in various genres will serve to show how genre plots are the key to the dispersal of the tension between individual and group.

In the war film, for example, the most popular plot involves a group of men, individuals thrown together from disparate backgrounds, who must be welded together to become a well-oiled fighting machine. During the course of the film, the rough edges of the ornery and the cantankerous, the nonjoiners, the loners, like John Garfield in Hawks's *Air Force* (1943), must be smoothed down to make them fit. They must all hang together or all hang separately. The emphasis is on the team. And, of course, for the war film the end goal of the fighting is always the even larger group, the nation. Or peace in the world, to protect us all from some peculiarly successful individuals—Hitler or Hirohito or the kaiser. The hero's primary function is to mold the group and personally oppose the idea of individualism whenever it rears its head in its own cause and not that of the group effort. What better metaphor than the coward—the man interested only in saving his own skin, who somehow or other must be forced into changing his attitude or else destroyed before he infects the rest of the group. The hero, not just in the war film but in all genre films, is always in the service of the group, of law and order, of stability, of survival, not of himself but of the organization or the institution, no matter how individual his activities, while a villain could be defined as a man who ruthlessly looks after his own needs first and who works for and will sacrifice himself for no one or nothing but himself.

In the swashbuckler, the Errol Flynn character must restore the true social order, and though he may appear to be an outlaw now (which allows him to do all sorts of antisocial actions like killing and robbing), by the end of the film his crimes against the crown have been pardoned since they were all done in a good cause. He kneels to his liege lord and marries the girl (marriage traditionally having connotations of responsibility to the social order).

The police or detective film follows the same general pattern. The cops can do violent antisocial acts (acts which all of us would like to do) with impunity, for they are fulfilling their primary function to catch the guilty party and restore order. At first glance the private-eye film doesn't seem to fit this pattern, but it does. Sam Spade and the police are really on the same side, protecting the mindless masses (who seldom play a central role in the films) from evil. True, the police may be corrupt or stupid or slow to figure things out, yet the end goal is the same. The ideal of commitment to square dealing and presumably to a community of square dealers is demonstrated in the moral integrity of the private eye who can't be bought. Hence we may understand that in the particular social order shown, the police may be stupid or even corrupt, but that there is somewhere a moral order of community and group benefit as opposed to personal and material benefit, an ideal vindicated by the private eye's sending to prison the girl he's fallen in love with.

Horror films and monster films need no elaboration on this point, nor do science fiction films. Though the latter may leave us slightly wondering if the community shown in the film will survive in the future, there is the implicit assertion that there is no survival without the group. Science, that corporate analytical endeavor, will save us if anything can—not any individual. Westerns are also clearly involved with the eventual triumph of the forces of civilization, law and order, even as they are tinged with melancholy for the loss of individual freedom.

The musical will often end with a wedding or the promise of one as the boy and girl come together after overcoming all obstacles—a perfect example of a socially regenerative action, as Northrop Frye has pointed out in his discussion of New Comedy in *The Anatomy of Criticism*. In those musicals in which a star is born, in which it seems as though an individual is rising to the heights of individual achievement, it usually turns out that the star must go on despite personal tragedy, again emphasizing the group—the Broadway show, the production, standing as a metaphor for society.

Any brief rundown of basic plots should serve to demonstrate that the catharsis engendered in genre films is a basic element of their structure. The internal tension between the opposing impulses of personal individuation and submission to the group, which normally is held in check by the real pressures of everyday living, is released in the course of a genre film as the audience vicariously lives out its individual dreams of glory or terror, as it identifies with the stereotyped characters of fantasy life. But in the end those impulses to antisocial behavior (acts of individuation no matter how innocuous or permissible are still tinged with an element of the antisocial) are siphoned off as we accept the inevitable justice of the social order: the group is always right, and we know in our hearts that it is wrong to think otherwise.

In recent years it has become the fashion for some directors to use the elements of the genre film—the plots, characters, and iconographies—to create an antigenre film. That is, they will use everything according to the normal pattern, but simply change the ending so as not to satisfy the audience's expectations of a conventional group-oriented conclusion. If the detective finally gives in and takes the money and the girl, if the crook gets away with it, if an individual solves his problems so as to enhance his position vis-à-vis the world, that is, to increase the distance between his values and the values of the group—then the film has turned its back on the idea of genre. It violates the basic principle of the genre film: the restoration of the social order. Instead of justifying the status quo, these films intend the opposite. They suggest that individuals can succeed in individual schemes, that separation from the group can be had without consequences. In this sense they are not classical but romantic in their tenor.

The genre film is a structure that embodies the idea of form and the strict adherence to form that is opposed to experimentation, novelty, or tampering with the given order of things. The genre film, like all classical art, is basically conservative, both aesthetically and politically. To embody a radical tenor or romantic temper in a classical form is to violate that form at its heart. One can parody the conventions, one can work against the conventions, one can use the conventions with great subtlety and irony. To hold up individual ideals as superior to group ideals, however, changes the whole frame of reference. When a seeming genre film merely changes the ending in a final reversal, catharsis is restricted. The audience is unprepared by what has come before. There is no release of tensions, since the inevitable conclusion for which the audience has come and which would send them back into the real world smiling has not taken place. Rather than stasis, such endings produce agitation, discomfort, a vague anxiety. The guilt of having identified with the scoundrel or hero is never dissipated and viewers must bear the responsibility for their individual desires all alone.

In *Charlie Varrick* (Don Siegel, 1973), an otherwise conventional caper movie, the title character gets away with a million dollars scot-free at the end, which denies the audience the opportunity of saying, "That's the way it is. Nobody gets away with fighting against the mob or syndicate." His escape from just punishment for daring to wrest something of value from the Olympians of today, the banks, the corporations, the Mafia, makes him a Prometheus figure who doesn't get caught. It induces in the audience a kind of irrational radicalism as opposed to a reasonable conformism: "If he can do it, then maybe I, too, can fight the system, the institutions, and win." This is not what ordinary people—fated to a life in society in which they are relatively powerless to change the course of things—like to comfort themselves with and not what a true genre film provides.

For the time that genre characters play out their lives upon the screen we can safely identify with them, confident that the group will assert its overwhelming force in the end—like the chorus in a Greek play, always having the last word, reminding us that "That's the way it is. If you reach beyond your grasp, you will fall." We need not feel guilty; our surrogates will take the blame. We will switch allegiance by the end and become a member of the chorus. Our split personality is no longer split. Crime doesn't pay. True love wins out. The monster is destroyed. The forces of evil and darkness are vanquished by faith and reason. All is for the best in this best of all possible worlds. We have achieved the stasis that Aristotle mentions as the product of catharsis—a quiet calm. This is not to say that this feeling lasts long after we leave the theater, but at least we have been internally refreshed by our brief sojourn in a realm of cosmos, not chaos. If nothing else, the genre film is a paradigm of ritual and order.

The genre film is a classical mode in which imitation not of life but of conventions is of paramount importance. Just as in the classical dramas of Greece, the stories are well known. Though there may be some charm in the particular arrangement of formula variables in the most current example of a genre, the audience seeks the solid and familiar referrents of that genre, expecting and usually receiving a large measure of the known as opposed to the novel. Elevated and removed from everyday life, freed from the straitjacket of mere representationalism, genre films are pure emotional articulation, fictional constructs of the imagination, growing essentially out of group interests and values. Character takes a second place to plot, in agreement with Aristotle's descriptions of drama. And it is this emphasis on the plot that makes genre films the most cinematic of all films, for it is what happens in them, what actions take place before our eyes that are most important. They move; they are the movies.

Note

1. Harry M. Geduld and Ronald Gottesman, *An Illustrated Glossary of Film Terms* (New York: Holt, Rinehart and Winston, 1973), p. 73.

10. Experience and Meaning in Genre Films

BARRY KEITH GRANT

It is an essential quality of the cinematic medium (with the exception, perhaps, of certain "structuralist" films) that the spectator is engaged during the viewing experience. In fact, it would seem that this engagement is consistently more intense, more complete, with film than with any other art. The technological requirement that the projector gears grab the sprocket holes of the celluloid to move it through the gate thus provides an apt metaphor for the way we commonly relate to movies. While viewing a film one is able simultaneously to say something to the effect of "It's only a movie," yet also have distinct physiological responses—sweating palms, for instance, or an unsettled stomach in a sequence like the car chase through the sloping streets of San Francisco in *Bullitt* (Peter Yates, 1968)—a phenomenon observed at least fifty years ago by the aesthetician and psychologist Rudolf Arnheim.[1]

Of course the very perception of a *motion* picture begins with the synthesis by the spectator's eye of the individual still frames. But movies also engage us in more complex ways. The viewer's willing suspension of disbelief and propensity for character identification, for example, are especially encouraged in the cinema, where one experiences images and sounds larger and louder than life. (It is just this ability of cinema to "magnify" reality that explains the medium's apparent affinity for the melodramatic, the fantastic, and the spectacular—modes that tend to magnify reality in different ways.) In fact, the cinema's greatest artists in one manner or another have all been concerned with the nature of film experience. The films of directors who exploit the viewer's emotions, such as Alfred Hitchcock, Claude Chabrol, or Francois Truffaut, for example, take as their recurrent theme the psychological/sociological dimension of the viewing experience, and often are structured in such a way as to depend upon audience identification and involvement for their meaning. Similarly, more intellectual and politically committed filmmakers such as Sergei Eisenstein, Jean-Luc Godard, and Rainer Werner Fassbinder construct their films in ways that comment upon the ideological implications of the viewing experience. Even the so-called "closed" cinema of Fritz Lang derives both its effect and meaning from audience involvement no less than the "open," participatory cinema of Jean Renoir: the former encourages judgments in the viewer that are subsequently exposed as morally corrupt, the latter invites suspension of judgment.[2] Other directors—Luis Buñuel, Federico Fellini, and Jean Cocteau, for instance—exploit the cinema's special contiguity with fantasy and the dream; their film practice illustrates well Suzanne Langer's contention that "cinema is 'like' dream in the mode of its presentation: it creates a virtual present, an order of direct apparition."[3] In short, whether directors consider emotional or intellectual involvement of paramount importance, they all mobilize elements of the viewing experience as an essential structural element of their film work.

Although generally acknowledged in film criticism, however, the qualities of the cinematic experience have implications that for the most part have remained unexplored; rather, analysis has tended to focus on film texts as discrete objects—as expressions of a director's personality and vision or as a network of signifying practices. I would like to suggest that while the exploration of the viewing experience is always relevant to film, it is of central importance to a consideration of those movies that can be subsumed under generic categories. The idea of genre is comprised of two essential elements: the function of generic works as secular myth and the assumed "contract" between filmmaker and film viewer that allows for their existence—their system of production, distribution, and consumption—in the first place. Genre criticism has concentrated primarily on the former aspect, enumerating the conventions, iconography, plots, themes, and characters that distinguish the various genres and carry their mythic meanings. However, it would seem impossible to appreciate in any meaningful way individual genre films without considering the special manner in which we experience them. Because a genre, as Andrew Tudor reminds us, is "what we collectively believe it to be"[4] and because what we believe a genre to be sets up expectations that condition our responses to a genre film from the very first shot—indeed, often even before the lights in the cinema are dimmed—an analysis of the generic contract in operation, its actual dynamics, becomes crucial.

Commonly invoking the work of such anthropologists as Bronislav Malinowski and Claude Lévi-Strauss, genre criticism has viewed both film genres and genre films—that is, both a tradition of common works and individual instances of that tradition—as contemporary versions of social myth.[5] Indeed, genre films are directly related to lived experience, their traditions clearly connected to communal values. While most filmgoers do not go to the literal extreme of attempting to live generic conventions directly, as do both the Jean-Paul Belmondo character in *A bout de souffle* (Jean-Luc Godard, 1959) and the Dennis Christopher character in the more recent *Fade to Black* (Vernon Zimmerman, 1980), audiences do model their values and behavior to a significant degree according to those conventions.

For example, the resurgence in the early seventies of the outlaw-couple cycle of gangster films—*Bonnie and Clyde* (Arthur Penn, 1967), *Badlands* (Terrence Malick, 1973), *Thieves Like Us* (Robert Altman, 1974), *Aloha Bobby and Rose* (Floyd Mutrux, 1975), and *The Sugarland Express* (Steven Spielberg, 1974), to mention the most notable—can be seen as an expression of that period's youthful disaffection with the Establishment. These films, with their young romantic couple on the fringes of society pursued by an unyielding authority, invite a reading relevant to the contemporary zeitgeist. This attitude influenced not only popular film but also popular music (for example, Georgie Fame's hit song "The Ballad of Bonnie and Clyde" and Bob Dylan's numerous ballads about outlaws and outsiders), politics (Tom Hayden and Jane Fonda), and fashion (the nostalgic return to the styles of the thirties—particularly, for some reason, in the decor of aspiring upscale restaurants). Then, as a sense of political disaffection deepened during the trauma of the Nixon administration and spread to other social groups, the outlaw-couple films were replaced by a resurgence of both political conspiracy films (*The Parallax View*, Alan J. Pakula, 1974; *Executive Action*, David Miller, 1973; *All the President's Men*, Pakula, 1976) and disaster films, with their equally obvious metaphors. *The Towering Inferno* (John Guillerman, 1974), for example, depicted the dangers of corruption in the capitalist edifice, while *Earthquake* (Mark Robson, 1974) rocked the very foundations of American society. The shared convention of these films, wherein a cross section of social types is faced with the same crisis and the good seem to perish indiscriminately along with the evil, blunts the clear moral polarization of the outlaw-couple film but pointedly expresses the increasingly prevalent social dis-ease of the time. *The Poseidon Adventure* (Ronald Neame, 1972) literally inverts society by turning the microcosmic ship upside down, forcing isolated groups of individuals to struggle to escape by ascending to the bottom of the ship in a Dantesque vision of contemporary society as hell.

Surely one of our basic ways of understanding film genres, and of explaining their evolution and changing fortunes of popularity and production, is as collective expressions of contemporary life that strike a particularly resonant chord with audiences. It is virtually a given in genre criticism that, for example, the thirties musicals are on one level "explained" as an escapist Depression fantasy; that film noir in the forties expressed first the social and sexual dislocations brought about by World War II and then the disillusionment when it ended; and that the innumerable science fiction films of the fifties embodied cold-war tensions and nuclear anxiety new to that decade. In short, it can be said that because they are so integral to our cultural consciousness, genre films provide us with what John Dewey in *Art as Experience* considers to be true aesthetic experience—for such movies are indeed "a product, one might almost say a by-product, of continuous and cumulative interaction of the organic self with the world" in which "the conventions themselves live in the life of the community."[6] Of course, such a description may apply as well to many nongenre films, from popular movies like *Casablanca* to the more art-house allegories of Ingmar Bergman; but it is their reliance on communally shared conventions that brings genre films so close so often to our continual negotiations between the world and the self.

The conventional nature of genre films has been cited most frequently to support the argument that genres have become the contemporary equivalent of tribal ritual and myth for mass-mediated society. But it equally well supports the claim for genre films as art (if, indeed, such an argument any longer needs to be made) primarily because of their potential richness as experience (by contrast, a relatively novel argument), if we understand works of art, again, in the sense that Dewey uses it. For him, the phrase "work of art" implies an action, an interaction with the text, an aesthetic experience rather than object. As Dewey says, "Art is the quality of doing and of what is done. Only outwardly, then, can it be designated by a noun substantive. . . . The product of art—temple, painting, statue, poem—is not the *work* of art. The work takes place when a human being cooperates with the product so that the outcome is an experience that is enjoyed because of its liberating and ordered properties."[7] This is something substantially different from the claim for genre films as art either because of their characteristic economy of expression (a concentrated use of conventions) or because of their individual variation (unusual inflections of conventions).

To take an obvious but vivid example, consider how the meaning of *Psycho* (Alfred Hitchcock, 1960) would be severely reduced if we did not take into account our relation to it, our interaction with it—particularly the manner in which we first identify with the character of Marion Crane (Janet Leigh) and then, when that is frustrated by her sudden death, how we shift our identification to Norman Bates (Anthony Perkins). Robin Wood convincingly points out the many stylistic and narrative devices Hitchcock uses in the first part of the film to encourage the viewer's identification with Marion, and how this affects our response to what follows.[8] The viewer's intense identification with Marion is even further strengthened when, after meeting Norman, she decides to return the money she has stolen.

This apparent moral redemption, visually underscored by the cleansing shower, promises us the expected, typical generic pleasure of having it both ways—here, specifically, the invitation to identify with a character engaging in antisocial actions and at the same time to remain free of the burden of guilt. The film until this point has concentrated on Marion's crime, the robbery of $40,000, and is therefore likely to invoke further expectations raised by the gangster film, which operates according to a very similar dynamic. In that genre, however, gangsters conventionally pay for their flamboyant denial of social restraint, which the audience has experienced vicariously, by being obligatorily gunned down in the closing minutes. Thus the death of Marion in *Psycho* is all the more shocking and our strategic shift of point of view to Norman that much more necessary because the criminal/protagonist here dies at an unexpected (unconventional) moment in the narrative.

It is true that *Psycho* encourages viewer identification with Marion only to transfer it later to Norman; but it is also true that the profoundly disturbing and frightening quality of this experience (and hence of the film's essential meaning) depends largely upon generic expectations: the horror icon of the Victorian (in California?) house on the hill as opposed to the clean, modern motel room; the unexpected death of the protagonist; and so on. Such a response is deepened by both our past experience of thrillers and horror films and by Hollywood cinema itself as an institution, with certain seemingly inviolable rules entrenched across genres. One of these primary rules is that the protagonist/hero does not die, especially after being redeemed by a correct moral choice. The notable exception to this is, of course, the war film, but in this case we are already prepared for such a possibility by generic category. The essential concern of the war film (until recently, at least) is to show the importance of a group working together to achieve a common goal; individuals must be welded together into a unit, a platoon, in which each works for the good of all and a clear, mutually accepted hierarchy is established.

The narrative turn of Marion's death in *Psycho* was virtually unprecedented in previous thrillers or horror films; but this in no way reduces this sequence to a mere shock effect, for it becomes thematically functional in the manner in which it implicates the viewer in the immoral desires of the characters (the $40,000 going to waste, the momentary halt of the car as Norman sinks it in the swamp, the emphasis on voyeurism). Robin Wood of course understands this, emphasizing that the film is a particularly salient example of what he calls Hitchcock's therapeutic theme: "*Psycho* is Hitchcock's ultimate achievement to date in the techniques of audience-participation. . . . The characters of *Psycho* are *one* character, and that character, thanks to the identification the film evokes, is us."[9] But while Wood's analysis convincingly emphasizes the importance of viewer response more than most film criticism, he does not go far enough in identifying the nature of this response, the extent to which it is generically influenced.

In his book *The Basis of Criticism in the Arts,* which takes as its project the organization of all possible critical approaches and methods within four basic categories, the aesthetician Stephen C. Pepper coined the term *contextualism* to describe that type of critical practice that acknowledges and places value upon experience in formulating aesthetic judgments. Although Pepper nowhere in the book specifically addresses the film medium, his notion of aesthetic experience seems particularly germane to the cinema. According to Pepper, contextualism views as positive aesthetic value the work of art's instrumentality in achieving what he describes as "the intensification and clarification of experience." [10] For contextualism, the pleasure of an aesthetic experience, while not disregarded, is secondary to its force: "*The more vivid the aesthetic experience and the more extensive and rich its quality,*" Pepper declares, "*the greater its aesthetic value.*" [11] He adds that the specific nature or "quality" of this experience—"the character, the mood, and you might almost say, the personality" of it—becomes the central focus of the contextualist approach. [12] Thus contextualism, as Pepper notes, is the only aesthetic theory that can account adequately for the pleasures involved in the experience of classical tragedy—and, by extension, melodrama and horror. As D. L. White has written, a horror film is more than simply a bundle of conventions and icons; it is "not just a sequence of certain events . . . but the unity of a certain kind of action." [13] More precisely, as the exemplary case of *Psycho* reveals, it is a certain kind of *inter*action that characterizes the horror film; and this dynamic, the degree to which our experience of horror is examined or exploited may also serve, as Bruce Kawin has shown, to distinguish the aesthetically better horror films from the rest. [14] In Dewey's terms, it is precisely this interaction which marks the crucial difference between a product of art and a work of art, between a thesis and a demonstration.

Now, it may at first seem odd to attempt to fit contextualist theory to film genre, primarily since most genre films are, quite simply, conventional. They are by definition predictable: classically, they resolve conflicts in favor of the status quo, and therefore apparently they cannot engage the viewer in any significant way. It is for this reason that Morris Dickstein has claimed that the horror film "washes over us without really reaching us," that such works are a vicarious experience, no more challenging than a ride on a roller coaster or a parachute jump. [15] In this sense horror films may be seen as paradigmatic examples of the limitations many critics view as integral to all of popular culture. As Abraham Kaplan puts it, popular art is "never a discovery, only a reaffirmation," and, so to speak, it merely "tosses baby in the air a very little way and quickly catches him again." [16] Pepper himself is quite careful to point out that "habit," which he defines as "convention, tradition, and the like," reduces aesthetic value because it "simply dulls experience and reduces it to routine." [17] In terms of contemporary film theory, this view of popular culture and its genres is one that sees the spectating subject as "positioned" by generic conventions, themselves determined by the dominant ideology, so as to contain desire and structure perception to reinforce itself.

But if this view of genre films were in fact correct, then contextualist aesthetics would necessarily devalue them. Pepper's notion of habit, I think, applies primarily to those movies that are, in Robin Wood's phrase, "pure" genre films [18]—that is, ones that are full of their generic elements but lack an interpretive perspective upon them or that present them in ways that they have commonly been presented before. For Wood, then, a genre film is truly interesting only insofar as it is filtered through the consciousness of an auteur, whose concerns provide a "tension" with the basic generic material. If the richer genre films do indeed result from such a tension, then contextualist aesthetics actually proves itself particularly relevant here. Pepper would substitute the term "conflict" for "tension": while there is of course aesthetic virtue to be found in the formal unity of a work (or rather, a *product*) of art, he asserts that "it is something new in aesthetic theory to discover the aesthetic value of conflict. This side of his theory is what a contextualist should exploit. The integration he should stress is an integration of conflicts." [19] Pepper's main example of the positive value of conflict consists of a detailed analysis of a Shakespearean sonnet, in which the conflict between the poem's theme (sadness) and its form (the accentuation of "brightness" implied by the tone of the final rhymed couplet) is said to increase its aesthetic value, as the reader is enlivened by this tension. [20] In the general context of film genre, conflict may be seen to exist inherently in the shifting ideological relationships between mainstream American cinema as an institution; its forms of expression (genres); those social and economic forces that encourage generic modification; the auteurs who, working within or against this system, animate these forms; and the audience viewing the generic work.

The "pure" genre movie falls into that group of films that Jean-Louis Comolli and Jean Narboni, in their discussion of the possible ways films relate to ideology, label category "a": "those films which are imbued through and through with the dominant ideology in pure and unadulterated form, and give no indication that their makers were even aware of the fact." [21] Such films constitute the largest and most common category of both genre and nongenre films. However, many films embody ideological tensions, either intentionally or inadvertently, stylistically or thematically, or by a combination of both (categories "b," "c," and "e"). It is these films that are said to reveal "cracks" or "fissures" in their narrative and in their articulation of what is normally presented as the seamless, calm surface of bourgeois illusionism. The genre films that work in this manner gain considerably from their very nature as generic instances, from their position within a clear tradition, for it is precisely their conventionally conservative generic qualities that "anchor" the potentially subversive elements.[22]

For example, the context of genre is perhaps the most significant factor in determining a star's persona or iconographical meaning. As Maurice Yacowar has said, "The film actor is all image, hence all fluid associative potential, so his performance is continuous over a number of roles."[23] This is especially true of genre films, in which actors are typecast (see Eisenstein's notion of *typage*)[24] from film to film within the same genre. The character actors and supporting players who populate genre films provide the firmament for the stars to shine. Fred Astaire, John Wayne, and Edward G. Robinson have been in films that were not musicals, westerns, or gangster films, respectively; but their significance as "fluid associative potential" would be virtually nil if not for their work in those genres. For example, the moral authority and rugged independence of Wayne, as depicted in his films with John Ford, deepen our experience of his roles in the westerns of Howard Hawks, particularly *Red River* (1948), when the western code of behavior as embodied in Wayne's Ringo Kid from *Stagecoach* (1939) is revealed as a monomania in his portrayal of Dunston.

In the case of Robinson, his roles in crime films such as *Little Caesar* (Mervyn LeRoy, 1930) inform not only his performance as a meek clerk with a gangster double in Ford's *The Whole Town's Talking* (1935), but also his henpecked husband with apron and kitchen knife in *Scarlet Street* (Fritz Lang, 1945). In this film the viewer is signaled from the beginning by the appearance of a number of icons of the gangster genre, including the presence of the actor Robinson, to expect the character he plays, Christopher Cross, to stab his wife one evening as he is subjected to one of her shrill harangues while slicing bread. Lang teasingly raises the viewer's expectation here, then thwarts it, as nothing happens, only to fulfill it later when Cross wildly hacks to death the woman he has loved with an ice pick. In this way the film has suggested not only that the most abject and repressed of men may reveal themselves as little Caesars and that it may happen suddenly and unexpectedly, but also that this is true for us, too—for we have been implicated in imagining (even hoping) that Cross will murder his wife. The casting of Henry Fonda as the brutal villain in Sergio Leone's *Once upon a Time in the West* (1969) or the appearance of John Wayne in *The Fighting Seabees* (Edward Ludwig, 1944) are two more of many possible examples in which meaning is generated

17. Edward G. Robinson as Caesar Enrico Bandello in *Little Caesar*.

by generic association of actors—the former another instance of generic subversion through casting.

Just as a genre film possesses the capability to play upon an actor's image, so it may play with the conventional diegetic structures of genre. George Romero's *Night of the Living Dead* (1968), which predates but inspired the rise of the dreadful "slice and dice" films, may serve as a particularly vivid example. With *Psycho* and *Scarlet Street* it shares the theme of the monster within us, although it is significant for the boldness and originality with which it locates the monster, in a movie overpopulated by monsters, within society. Romero's films have not yet received their critical due, and so in order to explain fully the contextualistic complexity of *Night of the Living Dead*, the discussion below temporarily shifts into the first person.

When I viewed the film for the first time, two years after its original release, I immediately noticed that the film was shot in black and white, and so assumed it was made on a low budget. Thus I quickly formed the expectation that the film would be something like the classic black and white horror films, the Universal films of the thirties or Val Lewton's RKO cycle in the forties—movies that elicited horror by suggestion rather than through graphic presentation. I reasoned to myself that this movie, with-

18. Robinson as Christopher Cross in the opening dinner scene in *Scarlet Street*.

out color, would not be as graphic as the more recent British Hammer Studio horror films (aside from Roger Corman's Poe cycle, the only group of horror films photographed in color). Yet within minutes I found myself struggling to adapt to each of its generic alterations and violations: the black hero (something never commented on by the other characters, even the despicable Harry Cooper, but nonetheless charged with meaning at the time of the film's release in 1968); the disorganized and unheroic military; the graphic depiction of entrails; the death of the teenage romantic couple. The film also consistently eliminates the conventional means of such narratives for dealing with monsters, since both religion and reason ultimately prove ineffective in halting the threat of the living dead.

Most disturbing of all was that, unlike most horror films up to that point, *Night of the Living Dead* withholds any explanations for its bizarre events until it is almost half over. And then, when we are given an explanation, it is difficult to hear because the television newsman who offers the long-awaited explanation is periodically drowned out by the protagonist's noisy construction of defensive barriers and by the govern-

19. Christopher Cross, the henpecked husband in *Scarlet Street*.

ment's evasive responses to the reporter's pressing questions (and by extension, ours). And so a tension is created as Ben's immediate concern for survival conflicts with and thwarts our generically reinforced desire either to find the *cause* of the living dead or, on an intellectual level, to know what they *mean*—and so make them manageable and safe. However, I renewed my "contractual" faith in the text by remembering that it is only a horror film, after all; I looked forward to the traditional resolution that I was now hoping, but no longer securely assuming, would come. And, sure enough, it didn't. When the long night seemed over and survival finally achieved, the film shook my complacency irretrievably: for with the arrival of the sheriff and his vigilante posse, the resourceful and morally admirable Ben is shot from a distance, insensitively mistaken for one of the living dead he has been fighting so hard against.

The ending, while certainly constituting a considerable shock at the time, is in fact consistent with the theme of the film. For even then I thought of the events of the Democratic National Convention in Chicago in 1968, the same year as the film's release, and I began to understand,

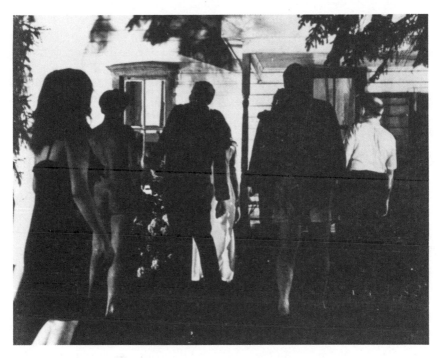

20. *Night of the Living Dead:* The zombies look like average folk.

first, that the night of the living dead is not the evening of the film's narrative but the darkness in the human spirit brought about by the absence of compassion and understanding; and, second, who the living dead really are—not the lurching zombies but average folk like Harry Cooper, the sheriff and his men, and, ultimately, myself. The film didn't preach this to me, but was instrumental in providing me with an experience with which I had to admit this truth; for I remembered that, given a choice in the resolution of the tension concerning my wish to have the zombies explained and Ben's frenzy to secure his position in the farmhouse, I would have, in effect, "sacrificed" Ben, even as I identified with him, to satisfy that wish. Like the repulsive Harry Cooper, I was instinctively looking out for Number One, an attitude that the film suggests is analogous to the desensitized state of the zombies.

D. H. Lawrence once referred to those people who did not fully embrace what he perceived as the life principle as the "living dead," saying that they were both angels and devils, at once vibrant and corrupt.[25] *Night of the Living Dead* similarly forces us to acknowledge that we have the capacity to be both Ben and Harry, however repugnant this notion might be. From other approaches, *Night of the Living Dead* may seem like cheap exploitation filmmaking; but when one is open to it as potential experience, it is a rich film indeed.

One of the key characteristics of aesthetic experience, according to Pepper, is the possibility of repeated interactions with the art object. Pepper calls this "funding," the building and enriching of aesthetic experience through subsequent encounters with the physical work of art, each instance of which is likely to be different in quality. In its simplest form, funding occurs when, say, we reread a poem and in this subsequent reading discover new linguistic potential previously unnoticed. Of course this is a common enough experience. But it assumes special relevance in the context of genre, where there exists not only the possibility of funding one's experience of a particular work by seeing it again, but also, because of our generic expectations of the text, the inevitability of instantly funding our experience by the composite sum of all the other films of that genre we have seen. A similar idea informs T. S. Eliot's description of an artistic tradition as an "existing order which is complete before the new work arrives"; but with the appearance of this new work "the relations, proportions, values of each work of art toward the whole are readjusted"—a point that Eliot insists is "a principle of aesthetic, not merely historical criticism." [26] And since our relationship to genre films is synchronic rather than diachronic, these "new works" need not necessarily be experienced in chronological sequence. Just as *Red River* funds our experience of earlier westerns, so too does *The Godfather* fund our experience of earlier gangster films and *Pennies from Heaven* (Herbert Ross, 1981) our experience of preceding musicals. In this sense the experience of funding is similar to the way we understand the films of auteurs, since the later films often shed light on the earlier ones. So our experience of, say, Ford's *Stagecoach* or *Wagonmaster* (1950) is made richer by already knowing the later *Cheyenne Autumn* (1964) or *The Man Who Shot Liberty Valance* (1962). And any of these westerns by Ford gains not only from a knowledge of earlier westerns by, for example, Griffith, but also from later westerns by Hawks or Peckinpah.

Subsequent viewings of genre films help not only to sort through the medium's inherent encouragement of emotional response, but also to clarify that considerable part of aesthetic experience that is ideologically determined. Obviously, the more one studies something, the better one understands how it works. But with those genre films that incorporate generic expectations into their meaning, the result can be an experience that illuminates the nature of genre itself and thus its function within ideology. If, for example, we acknowledge the monstrous within ourselves in certain horror films, enjoy a Sirk melodrama, or laugh at the indignities inflicted on solid citizens by wacky protagonists in screwball comedies, we are in some way forced to deal with the cultural construction of social values. The collapse of the brontosaurus skeleton at the end of *Bringing Up Baby* (Howard Hawks, 1938), for instance, is a vivid image for the social implications of laughing at the many frustrations experienced by the rational Cary Grant in his research and, by extension, of the genre of screwball comedy itself.

Nowhere in his discussion of experience and contextualism does Pepper acknowledge the shaping power of ideology. For him the spectator would seem to exist apart from ideology, an "ideal" subject. Yet this omission, crucial as it is, does not diminish the value of the approach. On the contrary, given film criticism's recently renewed interest in the spectating subject, it is now particularly appropriate. Even the scientific semioticians have acknowledged the importance of experience. In the lovely words of Christian Metz, "I am at the cinema, attending a film show. ATTENDING. Like a midwife who attends at a birth, and thereby also helps the woman, I am present to the film in two (inseparable) ways: witness and helper; I watch, and I aid. In watching the film I help it to be born, I help it to live, since it is in me that it will live and it was made for that. . . ."[27]

Genre criticism of course should continue to map out, to describe, generic structures, their differences, and—more recently—their similarities. But it must address more directly the nature of the audience contract and generic experience as well as the connections between them. Pepper says of subjective response that it is most often "explained away . . . called merely subjective," but that it in fact cannot be, because it is an undeniable aspect of aesthetics, and "one cannot explain an ultimate fact."[28] Genre criticism may indeed be past the point where it is necessary for it to remain detached, "objective," simply descriptive, in the manner of Northrop Frye. Yet if most genre films fail the contextualist criterion of value, they are all of considerable interest as ideological constructs. And the aspects of myth and ritual so central to genre films require us to understand not only the logic behind their construction but our individual and collective responses to them as well.

Notes

1. Rudolf Arnheim, "Selections Adapted from *Film*," in *Film as Art* (Berkeley: University of California Press, 1971), pp. 8–160.

2. This distinction is persuasively examined by Leo Braudy in *The World in a Frame* (Garden City: Anchor, 1977).

3. Suzanne K. Langer, "A Note on the Film," in *Feeling and Form: A Theory of Art* (New York: Macmillan, 1953), p. 412.

4. Andrew Tudor, *Theories of Film* (New York: Viking Press, 1973), p. 139.

5. See, for example, Will Wright, *Sixguns and Society* (Berkeley and Los Angeles: University of California Press, 1975), and Thomas Schatz, *Hollywood Genres* (New York: Random House, 1981). See also Thomas Schatz, "The Structural Influence: New Directions in Film Genre Study," *Quarterly Review of Film Studies* 2, no. 3 (August 1977): 302–311; reprinted in this volume.

6. John Dewey, *Art as Experience* (New York: Capricorn, 1958), pp. 220, 152.

7. Ibid., p. 214.

8. Robin Wood, *Hitchcock's Films* (London and New York: Zwemmer/ Barnes, 1965), pp. 114–124.

9. Ibid., p. 119.

10. Stephen C. Pepper, *The Basis of Criticism in the Arts* (Cambridge: Harvard University Press, 1965), p. 57.

11. Ibid. Italics in the original.

12. Ibid., p. 59.

13. Dennis L. White, "The Poetics of Horror," in *Film Genre: Theory and Criticism,* edited by Barry K. Grant (Metuchen, N.J.: Scarecrow Press, 1977), p. 130.

14. See Kawin's "Children of the Light" in Part Two of this volume.

15. Morris Dickstein, "The Aesthetics of Fright," *American Film* 5, no. 10 (September 1980): 35; reprinted in *Planks of Reason: Essays on the Horror Film,* edited by Barry K. Grant (Metuchen, N.J.: Scarecrow Press, 1984), pp. 65–78.

16. Abraham Kaplan, "The Aesthetics of the Popular Arts," *Journal of Aesthetics and Art Criticism* 24, no. 3 (Spring 1966): 354–355.

17. Pepper, *Basis of Criticism,* p. 65.

18. Robin Wood, "Ideology, Genre, Auteur," *Film Comment* 13, no. 1 (January–February 1977): 47–48; reprinted in this volume.

19. Pepper, *Basis of Criticism,* p. 66.

20. Ibid., pp. 120–123.

21. Jean-Louis Comolli and Jean Narboni, "Cinema/Ideology/Criticism (1)," in *Screen Reader 1: Cinema/Ideology/Politics* (London: SEFT, 1977), p. 5.

22. This is demonstrated in a somewhat different context in Jean-Loup Bourget, "Social Implications in the Hollywood Genres," reprinted in this volume.

23. Maurice Yacowar, "An Aesthetic Defense of the Star System in Films," *Quarterly Review of Film Studies* 4, no. 1 (Winter 1979): 41.

24. See Sergei M. Eisenstein, "Form and Content: Practice," in *The Film Sense,* translated and edited by Jay Leyda (New York: Harcourt, Brace & World, 1947), p. 172.

25. D. H. Lawrence, "The Reality of Peace," in *Phoenix: The Posthumous Papers of D. H. Lawrence,* edited by Edward D. McDonald (New York: Viking Press, 1968), p. 677.

26. T. S. Eliot, "Tradition and the Individual Talent," in *Selected Essays of T. S. Eliot* (New York: Harcourt, Brace and World, 1960), pp. 4–5.

27. Christian Metz, "History/Discourse: A Note on Two Voyeurisms," in *Theories of Authorship,* edited by John Caughie (London and Boston: Routledge and Kegan Paul//British Film Institute, 1981), p. 227.

28. Pepper, *Basis of Criticism,* p. 63.

11. Genre and Performance: An Overview

RICHARD DE CORDOVA

Although performance has been central to the definition of a couple of genres, it has had a fairly marginal place in most genre studies. One explanation for this is that genres have been defined largely in terms of their most pertinent features. Thus, work on the musical has quite naturally assigned a central position to performance, while discussions of other genres have focused on other features—visual style, narrative structure, and thematic oppositions. What this explanation fails to explain, however, is why performance is so readily excluded from the field of pertinence in these discussions. Performance is an important part of our experience of such genres as the western, film noir, and the melodrama, and each, it can be argued, renders performance according to genre-specific rules.

The reason for this exclusion undoubtedly lies in the difficulty of the notion of performance itself. Other aspects of film seem to lend themselves to conceptualization in a way that performance does not. Once we have accepted a particular model of narrative structure, for instance, we have little trouble applying it to a wide range of genres. It is not clear that a model of performance exists that affords this kind of generality, however.[1] In fact, performance manifests itself so differently in different genres that it seems to call into question the coherence of the concept itself. Can we talk about acting in melodrama in the same terms that we talk about an Astaire dance number or a Keaton gag? Perhaps, but the diversity of these forms and traditions of performance poses an obstacle to such efforts.

Our notion of performance lacks a certain coherence largely because of the differential existence of these performances in a system of genre. The examination of the ways that different genres circumscribe the form and position of performance in film is an important and underdeveloped area of genre studies. The work to be done in this area must be accompanied by a more general reflection on film performance, however, if performance is to be extricated from its status as a catchall category and emerge as an object of theory.

The following overview of the way in which performance has entered into the definitions of the musical, historical fiction, film noir, and melodrama is offered with this in mind. I am interested in examining both the conceptualization that performance has received in the work on these different genres as well as the claims that have been made in this work concerning the generic specificity of certain forms of performance. Finally, I want to consider the question of whether a more coherent, general account of film performance can be gleaned from the somewhat prismatic treatment it has received in these various genre studies. The musical has prompted the most serious and sustained discussions of film performance.[2] There are at least four different levels at which performance has been figured in these discussions. The first, which appears most explicitly in the work of Jim Collins and Jane Feuer, views performance insofar as it incorporates a specific mode of address, one that distinguishes it both from performances in nonmusicals and nonperformances within the musical itself. This mode of address proceeds through a number of the features of the musical number—the lyrics of the song, the performer's glance into the camera, the proscenium space, and so on. The general argument is that the musical performance involves a more direct mode of address than other cinematic forms. This notion of address is informed by the work of the French linguist Emile Benveniste.[3] In many ways, his distinction between *histoire* and *discours* and the subsequent descriptions of the cinema as *histoire* provided the impetus for the examination of the discursive characteristics of the musical.[4] The musical places an obvious and extraordinary emphasis on the relations it establishes with the spectator, and it does this through performance. The performer seems to address the spectator quite directly.

Performance in the musical has also been approached in terms of its syntagmatic specificity.[5] It not only involves an appeal to the spectator; it also has an identifiable beginning and end and therefore a kind of integrity as a segment. Of course this integrity is particularly overdetermined in the musical—by the length of the song and dance; by the general opposition between singing and dancing, on the one hand, and walking and talking, on the other; and by the specific form of address sustained throughout the performance and discontinued at its end. Thus, the syntagmatic parameters of performance are more clearly marked in the musical than in other genres.

A third level of inquiry concerns the way in which performance fits into the structure and the strategy of the film as a whole. This involves, in part, an examination of the relation between the performance and the narrative sequences surrounding it. The question here typically concerns the form and degree of the performance's motivation within the narrative. This varies within the genre and even within individual films. The song

21. *The Band Wagon:* Performers in musicals seem to address the spectator directly.

may be part of a show, or it may comment indirectly on the fictional situation. Or it may fulfill a narrative function, almost in the Proppian sense, assuming a crucial role in furthering the narrative. The seduction, for instance, is quite frequently articulated through performance in the musical. Above, a number of aspects were noted that separate and distinguish the performance segments of the musical from the narrative. Here we can see a more global strategy that works to integrate these segments back into the narrative's linear movement.

The examination of the way in which performance fits into the strategy of the film as a whole cannot be restricted to these purely linear relations, however. Broader structural and thematic oppositions are articulated through performance in the musical. In films that pose popular entertainment against high art, for instance, the song or dance accrues a symbolic weight through its opposition with other performances within the film. Performance enters quite explicitly into the thematics of the musical as it is taken up in a system of differences that gives it a stable meaning.

The significance of the musical number extends beyond the strategy of the individual film, of course. It has an institutional or ideological function as well, and this constitutes a fourth level at which performance has been considered. Jane Feuer's work[6] has given the most comprehensive view of this function. For her, the musical number is the site at which a whole series of oppositions is negotiated. These oppositions may or may not be figured directly in the fiction. Their importance lies in the way they set efforts to depict film as a folk art against the evidence that film is in fact a carefully engineered, mechanically reproduced product of capitalism. Thus, a kind of disavowal proceeds through the musical performance, which has as its object this capitalistic aspect of the cinema as institution. The song or dance, typically put forward as the spontaneous creation of amateurs, becomes a misleading but extremely malleable metaphor for the cinema as a whole.

This is, of course, a very schematic summary of the considerable work that has been done on performance in the musical. What should be noted here are the different aspects of performance that have been dealt with in this work and how, taken together, they form a fairly comprehensive view of the functioning of performance in the musical. One can note, by contrast, how little work of this sort has been done on other genres.

In fact, my attention to the historical fiction is not due to the existence of any kind of general account of performance in the genre but rather to a few restricted comments that Jean-Louis Comolli makes in his article "Historical Fiction: A Body Too Much."[7] As the title indicates, Comolli is interested in the inscription of the body within the genre. He argues that two bodies potentially coexist in any fiction film—the body acting and the body acted (actor and character). In most films, he claims, there is a fairly unproblematical fit between the two, largely because the character, being fictional, has no existence *outside* of the actor's body. The situation is somewhat more complicated in the historical film, however; the character has a real historical referent, and thus a clear disjunction between the two bodies is evident from the start.

Comolli's emphasis is on the effect this has on structuring the spectator's belief. In any fiction film the spectator knows very well that the actor and character are not the same, yet at the same time must believe that they are for the film to work.[8] This denegation proceeds with a special difficulty in the historical fiction since the historical character can never be fully embodied by the actor. However, what results is not a failure of belief but rather a more direct play upon it.

The importance of Comolli's article lies both in its identification of the split between actor and character and in its conceptualization of the mechanisms of belief that this split sets in motion. Comolli's claim that historical fiction involves particular difficulties in the negotiation of the split between character and actor is well founded. However, his assumption that the split is resolved more simply in other films is somewhat misguided. The problem is that Comolli generally stresses the presence of the body to the exclusion of its activity. Here, a distinction must be made between casting (something which remains constant in a film) and performance (something which vacillates in a film and is emphasized only at certain points). The two are obviously related. But Comolli's emphasis is on the effect that Pierre Renoir has in *La Marseillaise* (Jean Renoir, 1938) solely by virtue of his *appearance* as Louis XVI. Further attention to the presence of the body, in the context of genre studies, might lead to an investigation of the way in which certain actors appear as icons of specific genres. John Wayne's association with the western is among the clearest examples of this. However, although this emphasis on casting is certainly a legitimate one, it stops short of the question of performance, which is a matter not so much of the presence of the body as its activity. In fact, it is along these lines that we can see the split between character and actor assert itself in films other than historical fictions. In those moments in films in which acting comes to the fore and is noticed, there is a split between actor and character as agents of two different actions. At the end of *Dark Victory* (Edmund Goulding, 1936), for instance, the spectator's recognition and appreciation of the performance depends on the simultaneous existence of the actions of two figures. The actor (Bette Davis) acts while the character (Judith Traherne) responds to the fictional situation, telling her friend Ann to leave her to her death. The body that appears on the screen is not at odds with another historical body in this case (Judith is fictional, without historical referent); rather, these two agents are disjoined within the same body. This splitting of agency at particular moments in a film involves more complex mechanisms of belief than Comolli allows for.

The problem of performance in film noir has not been dealt with by anyone in any detail. However, many of the aspects that have been prominent in the description of the genre have a direct bearing on it. The voice-over, for instance, though it has been approached largely in terms of its narrational function, plays a crucial role in structuring performance.[9] Categories that have entered into the discussion of performance in other genres, such as address, are applicable to the voice-over in film noir. The voice-over, like the musical number, involves a direct address to the spectator. Whether it is motivated within the fiction, such as the confession to a coworker, for example, in *Double Indemnity* (Billy Wilder, 1944) or not, the voice-over always exceeds the bounds of *histoire* as described by Benveniste and Metz. It may comment on a chronology of actions, but it is never reducible to one. The voice-over is defined, in fact, by its discursive characteristics; it is put forward as a performance for someone—implicitly, at least, the spectator.

A second area of inquiry follows from Comolli's work and concerns the

22. *Sunset Boulevard:* The voice-over is by the dead Joe Gillis (William Holden).

way the body is inscribed in film noir. The voice-over in film noir works to problematize the body by introducing a variety of disjunctions between the bodily image and the voice.[10] One result of this is an added emphasis on the performative aspects of the voice as it is freed from its supposedly realistic link with the image and assigned a more active role in relation to it. A particularly self-conscious example of the possibilities of disjoining voice and body occurs in *Sunset Boulevard* (Wilder, 1950): the voice-over is ascribed to a man we see floating dead in a swimming pool at the beginning of the film.

This brings up another major issue that has not yet been touched upon: the relation between performance and specific features of the cinematic apparatus. In film noir it is clear that performance functions, in part, through the split between sound and image. However, one can also note in this and other genres instances in which such devices as lighting, framing, camera movement, and the close-up ally themselves with the body of the actor and work to produce effects of performance. These forms of alliance need to be described more carefully and their generic features delineated.

The voice-over is only one site at which performance manifests itself in film noir. Performance has a more general function in the fictional strategy of these films, one that relates to the problem of verisimilitude and the negotiation of the spectator's belief. In his work on the detective novel, Todorov argues that the production of any discourse involves relations of verisimilitude, but that the detective novel specifically treats verisimilitude as its object and theme.[11] This theme is articulated particularly strongly through performance in the detective film (and more generally in film noir). We have noted that a certain problem of belief is inherent in the split between actor and character in the fiction film; at the level of enunciation it is taken up by the fiction as well in film noir.

The dynamics of this can be seen in the example of *The Maltese Falcon* (John Huston, 1941). When O'Shaughnessy first appears in Spade's office, she gives a performance that, if we recognize it as such (by calling into play the aesthetic category of acting), we must attribute to the actor, Mary Astor. Later, however, we find out that it was not Astor's performance but rather that of the character O'Shaughnessy, as she tried to deceive both Archer and Spade. We can see a fairly active play on the division between actor and character here, but the performance is finally grounded in the character. The problems of verisimilitude and belief at the level of the enunciation become couched in the fiction in a series of questions that bear upon the movement of truth in the film. Is the character lying or not lying, performing or not performing? Performance, as it is given a place in the diegesis of film noir, essentially follows a model of dissimulation.

This dissimulation would have little force in film noir if it was not read against another model of performance: that of performance as expression. If this model of performance is not properly melodramatic, then it at least receives its fullest rendering within the melodrama. The genre places an overriding emphasis on the inner emotional states of the characters, and it works to represent them through elements of the mise-en-scène. The scenic excesses that often arise in this effort have been the object of a great deal of interest. For example, Geoffrey Nowell-Smith has attempted to explain these excesses through an analogy with Freud's notion of conversion hysteria.[12] He claims that the emotional material that cannot be expressed in the actions of the character finds its expression in the body of the film. What has not been sufficiently explored in this regard is the relation between the body of the film in this sense and the body within the film. This latter body, as has been noted elsewhere, belongs ambiguously to both character and actor. As character, this body is what the mise-en-

23. *The Maltese Falcon:* Is Brigitte O'Shaughnessy (Mary Astor) lying or telling the truth, performing or being?

scène acts upon, the focus of the represented emotion; as actor, however, it is an active part of the mise-en-scène which works in alliance with such features as decor and music to produce the other, fictional body. The split between these two bodies and their relation to other features of the cinematic language is not fixed at the beginning of the film but rather put in process throughout it. It is primarily at those moments of the melodrama when the performative dimension comes to the fore that the body of the actor becomes an issue in the film, and, at those moments, the spectator is involved in a particularly complex play of identification and belief.

This results in a specific textual effect, but it also relates to the broader institutional functioning of performance in the melodrama. Performance is perhaps the principal critical standard by which audiences have judged films, and there is little doubt that the melodrama, in its emphasis on acting as expression, has provided the ideal object for the application of such a standard. The melodrama has, in fact, been central to the cinema's claim for aesthetic legitimacy because it has supported, more than any other genre, the claim that film incorporates the art of acting.[13]

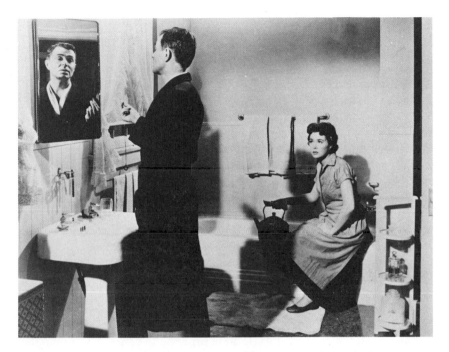

24. *Bigger Than Life:* Madness in the melodrama is strongly marked as performance.

Another question that seems important to note here concerns the fictional conditions under which performance manifests itself in the melodrama. It is clear that certain melodramatic scenes are written as showcases for performance. What is striking is how often these scenes engage the same types of fictional material. Suffering, hysteria, and madness not only become topics of melodrama; they also mark out a highly conventionalized space within which the scene of performance can unfold. *Bigger than Life* (Nicholas Ray, 1956), *Splendor in the Grass* (Elia Kazan, 1961), and *Possessed* (Curtis Bernhardt, 1947) are good examples of this. In each, a character's mental disturbance in the fiction is accompanied, at the level of the enunciation, by the placement of the actor in a number of strongly marked scenes of performance.

The subject of enunciation in the cinema is not a coherent, unitary position. The sites at which one might locate an organizing productivity within a given film are multiple, and the negotiation of these different sites becomes crucial both for the strategy of the individual film and the institution of the cinema at large. The question of performance specifically concerns the way in which the actor enters into the enunciative apparatus of the cinema as subject—under what conditions and within what kind of process.

Genre studies, insofar as they have dealt with this problem, have extended discussions of performance beyond the question of the talent of the individual performer and have attempted to outline broader generic conventions that determine the place of the performer as subject within a film. Unfortunately, as we have seen, these attempts have been too fleeting and unfocused to provide a general account of performance and its role within an economy of genres. If such an account is to be arrived at, at least two lines of inquiry must be pursued. First, there must be a close analysis of the way in which performance is structured within particular films and particular genres. The kind of detail that textual analysis has brought to discussions of the narrative structure of films needs to be brought to discussions of performance as well. Second, a more comparative approach to the problem of genre and performance needs to be taken. As it stands, the work in this area exists as a number of isolated and unnecessarily circumscribed claims. The concept of performance needs to be rescued from this dispersed existence and given to a common field of questions. For instance, does performance generally involve a shift in address, and, if so, how does address function in genres other than the musical? How does the musical negotiate the shift between actor and character that Comolli describes in his work on historical fiction? The answers to these and other questions suggested by this overview should give us a much more precise sense not only of performance but of genre as well.

Notes

1. A body of analytical work on performance has begun to appear recently, however. The special issue of *Cinema Journal* 20, no. 1 (Fall 1980), is of particular note. See also Charles Affron, *Star Acting: Gish, Garbo and Davis* (New York: E. P. Dutton, 1977), and Virginia Wright Wexman, "Kinesics and Film Acting: Humphrey Bogart in *The Maltese Falcon* and *The Big Sleep*," *Journal of Popular Film and Television* 7, no. 1 (1978): 42–55.

2. See, for instance, Jim Collins, "Toward Defining a Matrix of the Musical Comedy: The Place of the Spectator within the Textual Mechanisms," in *Genre: The Musical*, edited by Rick Altman (London: Routledge and Kegan Paul, 1981), pp. 134–146; Jane Feuer, *The Hollywood Musical* (Bloomington: Indiana University Press, 1982); Patricia Mellencamp, "Spectacle and Spectator: Looking through the American Musical Comedy," *Ciné-Tracts* 1 (Summer 1977): 28–35; and Dana B. Polan, "It Could Be Oedipus Rex: Denial and Difference in *The Band Wagon*, or the American Musical as American Gothic," *Ciné-Tracts*, no. 14 (Summer 1981): 15–26.

3. Emile Benveniste, *Problems in General Linguistics* (Miami: University of Miami Press, 1971).

4. Benveniste argues that *discours* (discourse) contains a number of formal markings that stake out the position of its producer (the "I") and its receiver (the "you"). *Discours* is therefore characterized by a clearly marked system of address. *Histoire* (story, history), on the other hand, effaces all of the marks that would point to the conditions of its own production. As Benveniste says, "There is . . . no longer even a narrator. The events are set forth chronologically, as they occurred. No one speaks here; the events seem to narrate themselves" (p. 208). Christian Metz has argued that the classical cinema functions as *histoire*. See "Story/Discourse (A Note on Two Kinds of Voyeurism)," in *The Imaginary Signifier* (Bloomington: Indiana University Press, 1982), pp. 89–98.

5. See, for instance, Mellencamp, "Spectacle and Spectator."

6. See Feuer, *The Hollywood Musical.*

7. Jean-Louis Comolli, "Historical Fiction: A Body Too Much," *Screen* 19, no. 2 (Summer 1978): 41–53.

8. Comolli's work on the negotiation of the spectator's belief (and the work of Metz before him) draws heavily on O. Mannoni, *Clefs pour l'imaginaire ou l'autre scène* (Paris: Editions de Seuil, 1969).

9. For an excellent account of the general functioning of the voice-over, see Mary Ann Doane, "The Voice in the Cinema: The Articulation of Body and Space," *Yale French Studies* 60 (1980): 33–50.

10. Alan Williams has noted the importance of a different kind of disjunction between voice and image in "The Musical Film and Recorded Popular Music," in *Genre: The Musical,* pp. 147–158.

11. Tzvetan Todorov, "Du vraisemblable que l'on ne saurait éviter," *Communications* 11 (1968): 145–147.

12. Geoffrey Nowell-Smith, "Minnelli and Melodrama," *Screen* 18, no. 2 (Summer 1977): 113–118.

13. For an account of the role of acting in establishing the cinema's aesthetic legitimacy after 1907, see Richard de Cordova, "The Emergence of the Star System in America," *Wide Angle* 6, no. 4 (Winter 1984): 4–13.

Part Two: SELECTED GENRE CRITICISM

12. The Western (Genre and Movies)

DOUGLAS PYE

The generic and individual identities of narrative works are created by a large number of elements in combination, many (all?) of which are necessary to those identities without any one or small group being sufficient to define them. In the American cinema, characteristics of the narrative tradition that run across generic boundaries contribute to our sense of what "the western" is as greatly as those features most obviously characteristic of the genre.

In an essay called "The Use of Art for the Study of Symbols," E. H. Gombrich describes a parlor game he remembers from his childhood to illuminate the process of symbol formation in the visual arts. It is also evocative in relation to genre.

> We would agree, for instance, that the person to be guessed would be a film star. . . . The task would be to guess his identity through a series of appropriate emblems or comparisons. The guesser would ask the group in the know such questions as: If he were a flower what would he be? Or what would be his emblem among animals, his style among painters? . . . You might compare each of the answers to the indices of letters and numbers on the sides of an irregular map which combine to plot a position. The psychological category of bearlike creatures sweeps along a wide zone of the metaphorical field, and so does the category of thistly characters, but the two categories are sufficiently distant to determine an area that can be further restricted by further plottings.

Later, Gombrich remarks of the categories that might be employed: "None of these, of course, can be said to have an intrinsic meaning, but they can interest through their very multiplicity and generate meaning within suitably narrow contexts." [1]

The recognition of works as belonging to a specific genre may be seen as the result of a similar process—the intersection of a range of categories, the interplay of which generates meaning within a context narrow

Note: This chapter is excerpted from a longer essay published previously.

enough for recognition of the genre to take place but wide enough to allow enormous individual variation. If the categories are thought of as involving conventions of various kinds, it is easy to see why exhaustive classification of generic elements is impossible. Given the number and possible combinations of elements within a field, the range of meanings and associations that can be generated through the constant movement of narrative and mise-en-scène will be infinite.

Within the American cinema in general, narrative traditions can be characterized in a number of ways: in terms of linearity, psychological involvement, dramatic and temporal-spatial unity, illusionism, and so on.[2] In approaching the western I want to concentrate on a limited number of conventions, some of which relate to broad tendencies of narrative (inside and outside the cinema) and others of which seem more obviously determined by the historical moment, national tradition, and local circumstances.

Certain broad tendencies of narrative can be approached through a theory of fictional modes of the kind Northrop Frye constructs in *The Anatomy of Criticism*.[3] He distinguishes five modes, defined in terms of the range and power of action of the protagonist:

1. Myth, in which the protagonist is superior in kind to other men and his environment. The hero is in fact a god.

2. Romance, in which the hero is superior in degree to other men and his environment. Here the hero is mortal, but his actions are marvelous and the laws of nature tend to be to some extent suspended.

3. The high mimetic mode, in which the protagonist is superior in degree to other men but not to his environment. The hero in this mode is a leader whose authority, passions, and power of expression are greater than ours but who is subject to social control and to the order of nature. This is the mode of tragedy and most epic.

4. The low mimetic mode, in which the protagonist is superior neither to other men nor to the natural world. He is one of us; we respond to his common humanity and demand the same canons of probability we find in our own lives. This is the mode of most realistic fiction.

5. The ironic mode, in which the protagonist is inferior in power or intelligence to ourselves, so that we have a sense of looking down on a scene of frustration or absurdity.

Frye's framework is a useful one if we bear in mind that the modes are not mutually exclusive but form points on a sliding scale, so that they can occur in various combinations in individual works. Frye also adds a further distinction that is relevant here, between tragedy and comedy. Again, these are tendencies, not exclusive categories, and can be found together with any one or more of the five modes. In tragedy the hero is isolated from his society in his fall and death, and in comedy the theme is the reverse: the integration of the hero with his society. From the five modes and the tragedy/comedy axis, several sources of conflict within the narrative emerge as characteristic—the nature of those conflicts and their outcome contributing to the structure, theme, and mood of the work. The major sources of conflict will be between one human being and another, human beings and nature, and the human being and society—personal/heroic, elemental, and social.

Whatever validity Frye's poetics have, such distinctions are helpful in pointing to issues that must be significant in any discussion of narrative genres.[4] Although Frye's modes are unsatisfactory as final categories, for the purposes of this article, the notion of modes remains useful. Tendencies of this kind may well have a lot to do with genre recognition. At this level, literary and filmic narrative can be seen as continuous, and we may find common tendencies across a number of genres we commonly think of as distinct. Generic differences emerge from the combination of these basic tendencies and the more local conventions.

A further general, and perhaps rather obvious, point. In classical aesthetics, "levels of style" were prescribed for each major kind of literary work: a particular manner accompanied the subject matter. So, in tragedy, the fall and death of a hero would be handled in a serious and elevated style. These levels of style never completely dominated Western literature,[5] but they remained important for each succeeding classicizing movement. Since the early nineteenth century, however, and the achievement of the realist novel, levels of style have effectively broken down, with important consequences. There is no longer any necessary correlation between subject matter and the manner in which it is treated. In the terms I have already used, a fictional mode does not determine a level of style. For instance, a work may contain strong elements of Romance and yet be realized (in its setting, characterization, treatment of action) in a manner that might be called low mimetic, or realistic. This fluid relationship between mode and manner of realization, and especially between a low mimetic manner and high mimetic or romantic mode, is important for the western, the genre I intend to concentrate on.

Apart from the conventions that relate to broad tendencies of narrative are others more obviously determined by local conditions of various kinds. They might include the following:

1. *Plot.* It might be possible to identify within a genre recurring plots that carry with them associations and expectations.

2. *Other structural features.* These might relate both to mode and to plot: recurring "block" constructions, day and night, journey and rest, action and repose.

3. *Character.* Individual incarnations of both central and peripheral figures. In the western, both the distribution of identification figures and the expected hero, heroine, villain configuration. A large list of conventional types can easily be drawn up for the western, together with their most common roles in the action.

4. *Time and space.* Not just the expected temporal-spatial continuity, but recurring historical and geographical settings.

5. *Iconography.* In the western, this would include landscape, architecture, modes of transport, weapons and clothes, and even soundtrack, including recurrent sounds, voices, and kinds of speech.

6. *Themes.* Particular concerns associated with or arising from a complex of elements.

Each of these contains a wide range of possibilities—in combination, the possibilities are enormously multiplied and, with the conventions of mode and so on, the permutations are endless. The variable combination of elements within the western will therefore make each individual work unique in some respects even if it appears highly stereotyped, but it will be unique within a field plotted by the intersection of these various matrices. In terms of Gombrich's game, the field would therefore be narrow enough to register as familiar to an audience and to invoke a wide spectrum of expectations that are aroused, defined, confirmed, or surprised by the moment-to-moment conjunction of elements within each film. The number of more or less familiar elements within the total work is very large, and the movement, both on the screen and in the narrative, creates a dynamic that produces new combinations at each moment of the film.

Seen in this way, a genre will be capable of taking an enormously wide range of emphasis, depending on the interests and intentions of the individual artist. Any one or more than one element can be brought to the foreground while others may all but disappear. Plot, character, theme— each can become central. The relationship of character to the natural world may be a major issue in some westerns while in others landscape may be simply a background to the action; characters can be fully individualized, given complex or conflicting motivation, or presented schematically as morality play figures, embodiments of abstract good or evil. Part of the western's richness must be due to this potential range of emphasis and situation, but underlying this is the peculiar impurity of its inheritance, the convergence of various currents that achieve a special resonance in America.

One current that seems of particular importance is romantic narrative, in Frye's sense. In this mode, the hero is superior in degree to other men and to his environment, but he is mortal—a hero but not a god. His actions in the story tend to be marvelous—he performs wonders—and he often lives in close harmony with the natural world. When such a hero dies, it creates the sense of a spirit passing out of nature, coupled with a melancholy sense of the passing of time, the old order changing and giving way to the new. The mood that is evoked when the hero dies Frye calls "elegiac." At the other end of the scale of romance for Frye is romantic comedy, and he describes the mood corresponding to the elegiac in romantic comedy as "idyllic." In this form, the simple life of the country or frontier is idealized, and the close association with the natural world recurs in the sheep and pleasant meadows of pastoral. Interestingly, Frye identifies the western as the pastoral of modern popular literature, with cattle and ranches instead of sheep and pleasant pastures. But it is clear that the western as we know it is more complex than such a definition will allow. It seems more rewarding to think of its debt from romance as dual, with elements of the elegiac and idyllic modes.

This duality is present in Fenimore Cooper's Leatherstocking tales, the first significant fiction of the West and a formative influence on the tradition of western fiction through the nineteenth century. The five novels present an ambivalent vision of the process of westward expansion—the encroachment of civilization on the wilderness—centering on the scout and hunter, Natty Bumppo. The setting of the tales moves gradually west from New York State to the Great Plains of *The Prairie,* in which Natty, now a very old man, dies facing the setting sun. Natty is in some ways very much the hero of romance (although his social status gave Cooper difficulties): he has talents that set him apart from all other characters, and, more important, he is endowed with an infallible moral sense—he has the ability to know good from evil. Natty lives outside the settlements, which he regards with deep suspicion as corrupt and ungodly, wasteful of the goods God has provided for human use. And yet, although his values are presented as ideal, the westward expansion of society encroaches more and more on the wilderness, pushing Natty farther and farther west. His death, and in fact the tone of more than one of the tales, can be described as elegiac in Frye's sense. At the same time, Natty lives in harmony with the natural world, reading the wilderness as the book of God, so that images of perfected natural life recur in the tales, images in which the natural and moral worlds are united, as they are in Frye's idyllic mode. Characteristically, the tales end with the genteel heroes and heroines, the army officers and their ladies, the kidnapped aristocratic girls, being reintegrated into society—the movement Frye describes as characteristic of comedy—while Natty remains estranged from it, a movement into isolation that evokes the elegiac mood, the inevitable passing of an ideal order.

In Cooper, this current of romantic narrative, capable of inflection in more than one direction, meets other currents of thought associated particularly with the idea of the West and its significance for America, and this conjunction of romantic mode and complex thematic gave a basic shape to the western. It isn't necessary to do more than refer to the complex of ideas about the West that dominated so much of nineteenth-century American thought, since many of the ideas have become commonplaces in the discussion of American literature and film. But it is important to stress the variable associations of the terms "West" and "frontier." From the earliest times, these concepts could mean several things, some of them apparently contradictory. If the West was seen as a potential Eden, the garden of the world, it was also seen as the wilderness, the great American desert. The life of the frontier was both ennobling, because it was close to nature, and primitive, at the farthest remove from civilization. The Indian could be both a child of nature, primitive but innocent, and the naked savage. In Cooper, this dual vision of the Indian is a feature of most of the tales—the virtuous tribe of the Mohicans set against the unredeemable evil of the Mingoes. These very familiar oppositions of garden/desert, civilization/savagery, which are at the heart of ideas about the West, were bound up with the western from the earliest times. They were not always overt, or as important to meaning as they are in Cooper, but they are always at least latent within the material of the genre, providing the western with a unique potential for reflecting on American themes. It is also worth emphasizing the continuity of the developing images of the West in America with much older ideas and myths. So, the images of the garden connect with much earlier images—the Garden of the Hesperides and other earthly paradises to be found in the direction of the sunset—and the opposition of garden and desert can easily take up the biblical images of the Promised Land and the wilderness. Similarly, views of the Indian are at least partially formed from earlier images of the noble savage.

The western is founded, then, on a tremendously rich confluence of romantic narrative and archetypal imagery modified and localized by recent American experience—the potential source of a number of conflicting but interrelated streams of thought and imagery.

After Cooper, the thematic concern with ideas of the West is not maintained at the same level of fiction.[6] Stories of pioneers feed into existing molds of ideas and into existing romantic structures to create the story of western adventure, less concerned with American identity than with action and excitement. In dime novels, the western tale became increasingly extravagant and fantastic, although it was fed by actual events—the Indian wars, the adventures of outlaws and lawmen, the cattle drives. Actual people became the basis of heroes of dime-novel sagas in a constant process of romanticizing actuality in the service of sentimental fiction and the adventure story. The western was also taken up on the stage, becoming one form of melodrama, sometimes with famous western characters playing themselves, and in the Wild West show.

In addition to these developments, the representations of the West in American painting may well have influenced attitudes and helped to create a specifically visual repertoire of western imagery. It is difficult to locate with any precision the film western's debt to these sources, but there are several potentially interesting areas. It is plausible to suggest that landscape painters, themselves probably influenced by contemporary attitudes, should in turn have contributed to ways in which the American landscape was thought of, both in terms of its sublimity and wildness and in terms of the American mission of domesticating the wilderness.[7] Through most of the nineteenth century, there were also painters whose major interest was in recording the appearance and customs of the Indians and frontiersmen, a documentary impulse that retains an important grip on the tradition. Thus the fantastic invention of the dime novelists and their cover designers coexisted with the much more sober accuracy of painters (and photographers) interested in recording what they saw; in between these extremes were various shades of invention, distortion, and interpretation.

Frederic Remington, whose work was disseminated by *Harper's* and *Collier's* weeklies in the years between 1886 and 1909, contains in himself various impulses that indicate the range of visual responses to the West during the period.[8] Many of his drawings of Indians, hunters, and cowboy life are straightforwardly factual, but even here Remington presents a range of incidents that define life on the range for his audience. A second category is more overtly dramatic—narrative pictures with strong romantic or melodramatic feeling ("Fight over a Water Hole," "A Misdeal"). There are others that are moralistic or thematic, the equivalent of much Victorian anecdotal painting: "Solitude" (a solitary buffalo in an open, hilly landscape and near it, a single buffalo skull); "The Twilight of the Indian" (an Indian behind a plough with a fence behind him and in the background both wooden shack and tepee). It is very difficult to separate different impulses in Remington—the categories I have indicated are by no means clearly defined—and this is a crucial point about the western tradition in general: by the end of the nineteenth century, there is no possibility of disentangling the confused and conflicting impulses within the tradition.

I mentioned earlier the importance for the western of the breakdown of levels of style, the split between the mode of fiction and its manner. With the development of the film western, manner—the nature of the presented world—becomes particularly important. From early on, the western film gravitated toward exteriors and a comparative solidity and fullness in the presentation of the fictive world (something we see already in Remington and other painters). However fabulous the story, there tends to be a kind of verisimilitude of surface. We can see this if we compare the minimal setting and costumes that will convey the idea of "western town" in a musical or in a number in a TV spectacular—flats seen in silhouette only, a pair of saloon doors, and a cast wearing jeans and wide-brimmed hats—with almost any town scene in a film or TV western. Clearly, the film setting is stylized, but it has a solidity of appearance that creates a sense of reality—an inhabitable world. The "realism" reveals itself in the large level of repetition and redundancy in such a scene. Many details duplicate or double each other, providing much more than the bare minimum that would signify a western town, enough detail to convince us of the solidity of the presented world.

Obviously enough, this kind of realism is not peculiar to the western—it is a feature of most narrative genres in the American cinema. But a tension between a realism of presentation and a much greater degree of abstraction at other levels does seem characteristic of many westerns—the low mimetic realization "anchors" and gives credence to other, more abstract elements: romantic narrative structures, plots inherited from melodrama, the simple moral framework of sentimental fiction. In the last section of this essay I want to illustrate this kind of tension as one way in which the conflicting elements of the tradition contribute to the richness of the western.

In some films, this tension produces a resonance we tend to associate with symbol. The simultaneous presence of the solid surface and a high degree of abstraction elsewhere causes an oscillation of response from one level to another, an awareness that the narrative flow is not the sole source of meaning, but that it is accompanied by another dimension, intimately tied to it but supplying another kind of meaning. Neither the realism of the surface nor the underlying abstraction dominates in such a context, but a balance is achieved between the two, a relationship analogous to that between denotation and connotation in Roland Barthes.[9]

The famous dance sequence in John Ford's *My Darling Clementine* (1946) seems to me to work like this. The whole passage is something of an interlude in the main development of the narrative, contributing nothing to the revenge plot and little to the Doc Holliday interest. In fact, the episode tends to unbalance the film structurally by being so markedly different from what has gone before. Yet it is partly the reduction of narrative interest that gives the passage its particular force. The interruption of the main channel of communication has the effect of throwing others into relief, while the specific detail is maintained at a level high enough to retain the solidity of the presented world—in the acting, for instance, there is a splendid fullness and individuality.

The abstraction is present in the particularly bold conjunction of elements Ford brings together to form the central complex of the sequence: the landscape of Monument Valley, which is barren and inhospitable but beautiful, with the desert coming right to the edge of the town; the partly built church; the stars and stripes; the dance itself. All these things have associations of their own, but together they form an enormously rich associative cluster. At the simplest level we see the dedication of Tombstone's first church, one milestone in the town's growth. But the church is also a tangible sign of community identity and solidarity and of the faith of the settlers (less in religion perhaps than in their own abilities and their social future); and the flag is the emblem of their sense of national identity. These ideas are fused with the more personal human values of family and community in the dance, while the bold juxtaposition of desert and town suggests broader ideas of the conquering of the wilderness, the growth of American civilization. The abstractions invoked are given particular force and the whole scene great emotional weight by the presentation of the dance itself: the inexpert musicians, the naive enthusiasm and lack of pretension, and the homeliness of dances and dancers—the density, at this level, of circumstantial detail "grounds" the symbolized aspiration, giving it concrete form.

The sequence achieves formal completeness with the integration of Wyatt Earp (Henry Fonda) and Clementine (Cathy Downs) into the dance, and they too have both individual and representative significance, as characters within the narrative and also as representatives of East and West—Clementine the embodiment of Eastern refinement, Earp of the "natural," untutored virtues of the frontier. Their walk away from the town toward the dance is given, through their bearing and the visual presentation, a formality and dignity that inevitably suggests a couple walking down the aisle, but a couple that unites the traditional East/West opposition. The interruption of the dance as Earp and Clementine reach the floor has none of the tension or disruptive force interrupted dances take on in other Ford westerns; it is a prelude to a greater harmony, the community joining the dance around the marshal and "his lady fair"— an image that points toward the possibility of a perfected society in the West that will reconcile opposing forces in an ideal harmony.

The ideas invoked in the sequence are commonplaces of the tradition, and Ford asserts them with extraordinary economy in a kind of visual shorthand, so that both the basic image structure of the sequence and its conceptual foundation are highly abstract. But it is impossible to respond only at this denuded level of meaning. If the conceptual, symbolized meaning in a sense robs the scene of its individual life to confer a wider, representative significance on it, the concrete realization constantly reasserts its specific and detailed life in which the objects, people, movement, and music are of this moment only and refuse to be contained by any

25. *My Darling Clementine:* Wyatt Earp (Henry Fonda) and Clementine Carter (Cathy Downs) walk toward the dance.

schematic framework. Response oscillates between the levels of meaning, unable to choose definitely one or the other, rather in the way Barthes describes as characteristic of myth.

Different forms of this tension, in which other elements are in the foreground, can be found in many westerns. The famous "silent" opening of *Rio Bravo* (Howard Hawks, 1959), for instance, is in its way equally abstract, without invoking themes to do with westward expansion at all. The abstraction here is in the characters and action. The main characters are readily identifiable genre types characterized in largely conventional ways: the drunk, the smiling killer, the unbending sheriff. Their presentation is so unambiguous and familiar, and the intense and violent action so compressed in time, that the sequence is almost melodramatic in effect and quite bewildering in the opening moments of the film. Because it is the opening, we rely not on a context for action established by the director during the film, but almost exclusively on genre recognition and expectation, and Hawks plays directly on our experience in his use of Dean Martin, John Wayne, and Claude Akins. His use of conventions of character and action is more than economical, although it is certainly that—it involves a kind of balancing act in which the emblematic presentation of

26. The dance on the church platform (*My Darling Clementine*).

character and the extreme compression of intense action border on the unacceptably schematic. But abstraction is in fact necessary to the sequence's functions in establishing the basic situation of the film and stating its central theme. It is precisely the abstraction that signals the scene so clearly as thematic statement. The rest of the film can be seen as developing and exploring in various forms the issue of self-respect, between the moral poles presented so boldly in the opening action. In fact, the abstraction remains within dramatically acceptable limits partly because Hawks makes his statements not in dialogue but through action that has a specific life of its own in addition to its thematic role, and partly (a related point) because the whole scene is sufficiently grounded in the detail we conventionally expect of a saloon: decor, other characters, actions, costume, and so on. But even so, there is a remarkably low level of redundancy in the sequence, as in fact throughout the film: Hawks excludes a great many familiar western elements and narrows his focus to a small group of characters in, for a western, a very restricted setting. More than any other conventions, he invokes those of character and action, excluding virtually all thematic material related to history and never activating the symbolic potential of the form as Ford does so frequently. This is interesting in relation to Hawks's earlier westerns, *Red River* (1948) and *The Big Sky* (1952), which involve wider "epic" and historical dimen-

27. Earp and Clementine are integrated into the dance (*My Darling Clementine*).

sions in which Hawks seems only marginally interested. In both films, the central concern is a very small group of characters and their relationships, but the presence of the epic material has the effect of dissipating to some extent the effectiveness of that focus. The compression of *Rio Bravo* is the result of a self-discipline based on understanding the possibilities inherent in the generic material.

Concentration on positively valued films like *My Darling Clementine* and *Rio Bravo* inevitably tends to suggest that one can ignore the vast mass of western movies and TV series that constitute the bulk of the genre. In practice, this huge number of more or less undistinguished films *is* ignored by criticism, and it is difficult to conceive of a situation in which they will ever receive detailed study. But it is important to bear in mind that these films have made possible the achievements of the recognized directors, keeping alive the conventions. The elements of the tradition are found in all westerns, of whatever quality.

For example, *The Lone Ranger* (William Witney and John English, 1938), which had a long run in the cinema and on TV as a children's series, exists at the pulp end of the western spectrum, while *The Searchers*

(John Ford, 1956) is by one of the acknowledged masters of the American cinema and is arguably one of the greatest westerns ever made. It is not a juxtaposition that can be held very long, but long enough to point to common elements. *The Lone Ranger* represents the inheritance of romantic narrative in one of its simplest forms; it centers on the anonymous masked hero who possesses extraordinary powers that set him apart from ordinary men. He is virtually invulnerable—the nearest thing to a god without being immortal. He rides a horse of incredible beauty, which, like its master, has extraordinary gifts. And he is accompanied by a faithful Indian companion—a fact which draws attention to the direct line of descent from Fenimore Cooper. In fact, *The Lone Ranger* can be seen as a debased and simplified version of Cooper's tales, with the hero riding off from the settlements after each adventure, away from all human company except that of his Indian friend, retaining his emotional isolation and his celibacy. There is none of Cooper's complexity, of course, but instead a simple moral scale of polarized good and evil, with the basic terms and the hero's status never questioned.

The Searchers incorporates elements of romance that are very similar, and again the line of descent from Cooper can be fairly easily traced. One thread within the film is the idea of the solitary, invulnerable, wandering hero, Ethan Edwards (John Wayne), for whom life within the settlements is impossible. He appears from the wilderness as the story opens, and when his job is finished he returns to the desert again. In common with the hero of Frye's romantic mode, Ethan's power of action is greater than that of other men. At the same time the film is structured around a version of the romantic quest, which brings to mind the grail quest (Ethan's grail being Debbie), and is largely set in desert terrain that evokes the imagery of the Waste Land familiar from versions of the grail legend but also, through the repeated biblical allusions, the journey of the Israelites to the Promised Land and their years wandering in the wilderness. The settlers are in a sense both attempting to find a Promised Land and are still wandering in the wilderness, living in the barren landscape of Monument Valley. They are also led by an Old Testament soldier-priest in the figure of the Reverend Samuel Johnson Clayton, captain of the Texas Rangers. These elements are very powerful in *The Searchers,* but they are combined with others in such a way that they are never dominant. In particular, Ford gives great complexity to the romance structure by combining it with features more characteristic of lower modes. So, unlike the Lone Ranger, Ethan is humanized, his mortality and human needs emphasized. The aspiration to achieve autonomy and emotional isolation is held in tension with the love for his sister-in-law that binds him to the settlements, and this tension contributes to the psychic split that brings him close to madness. Again, Ethan does not possess the perfect moral sense of Cooper's Leatherstocking; in this respect, he is more like the characteristic heroes of realist fiction, only too fallible morally.

I think it is reasonable to claim that *The Searchers* consistently achieves the resonance of symbolic drama that *My Darling Clementine* achieves only in one passage, and that it does so partly as a result of the fusion of modes and impulses that are held in productive tension: romantic narrative and a version of the hero of romance with a low mimetic insistence on human needs and moral fallibility; a high level of abstraction (or unreality) in the setting—the farm set in the middle of barren desert—with a fullness of naturalistic detail in the presentation of the settlers' lives. Part of any claim for the greatness of *The Searchers* needs to be based on these tensions, which make what could have been simply a story of Indian savagery and revenge into a work that can be seen as a film about America— a symbolic representation of the American psyche—as one might discuss the Leatherstocking tales or *Moby Dick*. Ford's achievement is based on a profound understanding of his tradition. Even the comic domestic scenes, the grotesquery of sexual relationships in the film, which are often ignored or apologized for, belong to a tradition stretching back to "Rip Van Winkle," in which marriage and settlement are presented as crippling or at least inhibiting, a tradition that Leslie Fiedler has discussed at some length.[10]

Less complex than *The Searchers*, but interesting in this context, is Delmer Daves's *3:10 to Yuma* (1957). What is most frequently commented on in the film is its "realism," its evocation of an unusually barren and unromanticized West in which environment dominates people, as well as its refusal of "romantic" (in both senses) characterization. From the outset, the barren landscape suggests the bleakness of life in this West. The holdup that follows the extended shot of the stage approaching across the desert is undramatic, unclear, shrouded in dust. The iconographical profile of the hero, Evans (Van Heflin), when he appears, conflicts with expectation—he is with his two sons, dressed in functional, worn working clothes, without a gun, and he is almost immediately deprived of his horse and forced to chase his cattle on foot. The insistence on the harshness of the environment is reinforced by discussion of the drought that dominates the lives of the ranchers in the area. The hero is also unusually motivated exclusively by money—his need to raise cash to buy water for his parched ranch. This need is played on throughout, the captured outlaw Wade (Glenn Ford) tempting him with offers of more and more money if he will release him. Both towns in the film are unprepossessing, dominated by harsh sunlight and hard shadows; the inhabitants are reluctant to risk anything over the outlaw, as if the heat and drought have sapped physical and moral resolve. These elements of the film are firmly low mimetic, in terms of the relationship between the human and natural worlds and the stature of the hero (he is one of us). Daves goes even further in this direction by handcuffing Glenn Ford when he is first captured, and so effectively preventing the possibility of conventional confrontations between hero and villain.

But it is partly, perhaps, the consistency with which the low mimetic manner is maintained that begins to suggest, paradoxically, through its absence for most of the film, the existence of another dimension. Daves consistently refuses possible developments through action in favor of a concentration on the tension between Evans's desperate need for money (his motive for taking in Wade), with its accompanying sapping of moral energy, and the moral obligation to complete his undertaking in the face of Wade's bribes. The film moves toward Evans's final decision to take Wade from the hotel to the train, not as a moral obligation or a way of making the necessary money (it is going to be paid anyway) but as a completely free act. It is at this point that the suppressed dimension of the film emerges clearly with the thunder which accompanies the buildup to Evans's decision but which his wife somehow fails to hear. He takes the thunder as promising the long-needed rain but also, it seems clear, as confirmation of the rightness of his resolve. The simultaneity of moral climax and thunder signals dramatically an other than contingent relationship between the human and the natural worlds, the drought as expression of and punishment for the spiritual state of the people. Their atrophy of will and resigned selfishness stand in a necessary relationship to the blight on the land in a way that clearly evokes the wasteland of Grail legends. Evans's action ends the drought as the quester's can in legend. It is free of the considerations of money and family that have dominated him earlier—"The awful daring of a moment's surrender/Which an age of prudence can never retract." What is interesting in *3:10 to Yuma* is not the presence of this romantic dimension but its sudden revelation. Not only does the selective hearing of the characters (we hear the thunder, why can't the wife?) break with the established naturalism of the film's manner, but the climactic thunder, which is acceptable in other conventions, has such obvious dramatic and symbolic significance in this resolutely low mimetic context that the context cannot contain it. The thunder and the rain at the end assert with melodramatic force the existence of, on the whole, unprepared dimensions (the solemn sympathy of human beings and nature characteristic of romance) in a way that seems to threaten the film's unity. In other words, there seems in *3:10 to Yuma* a collision of mode and manner rather than a productive tension between them, a capitulation of sense to meaning, which makes the end of the film unfortunately glib.

These attempts to approach particular films in terms of genre are necessarily tentative. The description of tendencies within generic traditions needs finally to be based on more detailed study of the available materials. In this respect, the western is likely to remain central to genre criticism. It is unique in the accessibility of its prehistory and the continuity of its traditions, which make an accurate description of the evolution of conventions adopted by the cinema both possible and necessary. Comparative work is needed on the antecedents of other genres, the tendencies that seem to contribute to their recognition, and most especially on the ways in which modes intersect other, often more obvious conventions. Inevitably this kind of emphasis will contribute to the modification of notions of authorship in the American cinema. It may also provide materials for other approaches—accounts, for instance, of the sociological and psychological contexts of genre—which should tell us more about the social significance of popular forms and the ways in which conventions are sustained.

Notes

1. E. H. Gombrich, "The Use of Art for the Study of Symbols," in *Psychology and the Visual Arts,* edited by James Hogg (Baltimore: Penguin, 1969), pp. 149–170.

2. See, for instance, Thomas Elsaesser, "The American Cinema II: Why Hollywood," *Monogram,* no. 1 (April 1971): 4–10.

3. Northrop Frye, *Anatomy of Criticism* (Princeton: Princeton University Press, 1957). See especially the theory of fictional modes.

4. For a critique of Frye's theory of modes, see Tzvetan Todorov, *The Fantastic: A Structural Approach to a Literary Genre,* translated by Richard Howard (Cleveland and London: Case Western Reserve University Press, 1973).

5. Eric Auerbach, *Mimesis* (New York: Doubleday, 1957).

6. Henry Nash Smith traces the development of western fiction after Cooper in chapters 7 through 10 of *Virgin Land* (Cambridge, Mass.: Harvard University Press, 1950).

7. *American Frontier: Images and Myths,* catalogue of the 1974 London Exhibition of paintings of the West, July 26–Sept. 16, 1973 (New York: Whitney Museum of American Art, 1973), contains a useful introduction on this topic. Roderick Nash, *Wilderness and the American Mind,* 3d ed., revised (New Haven: Yale University Press, 1982), deals in greater detail with developing American attitudes to wilderness.

8. *Frederic Remington: 173 Drawings and Illustrations* (New York: Dover Books, 1972).

9. Roland Barthes, "Myth Today," in *Mythologies,* translated by Annette Lavers (London: Jonathan Cape, 1972).

10. Leslie Fiedler, *Return of the Vanishing American* (London: Jonathan Cape, 1968).

13. Apes and Essences: Some Sources of Significance in the American Gangster Film

EDWARD MITCHELL

Most of the study of film genres is taken up with an examination of formulas, icons, motifs—in short, the elements of repetitive patterning common to all the films that we call detective films, or westerns, or gangster films. This is as it should be. Indeed, no serious discussion of genre is possible without recourse to those elements that a particular genre film shares with others of its kind. But what concerns me at the moment is not so much those elements that give a particular film meaning within a context of other similar films. Rather, I am concerned with the patterns emerging from a culturally shared and habitual structuring of thought, the usually unexamined convictions that bestow value—in other words, the patterns that give an entire genre significance whatever the meaning of any particular film.

For the American gangster film there are three such patterns: a secularized Puritanism; the ideas and attitudes that came to be known as Social Darwinism; and the Horatio Alger myth. For the present generation, Puritanism has been reduced in meaning until it is virtually synonymous with a narrow sexual morality. But at one time it was, and in some unlabeled ways continues to be, a statement about the nature of God, the meaning of good and evil, and the nature of a person's precarious relationship to each. Briefly, Puritanism à la Calvin held that people were conceived and born in sin, helplessly depraved and without hope of redemption except for those few whom an omnipotent and omniscient God elected to save. The reasons for such salvation were totally unfathomable by the common person, but the signs of election were clear, generally manifested in increased material prosperity. Whatever their material fortunes, however, Puritans were admonished to look on them with equanimity because they were saved to, not by, virtue, and a person's primary responsibility was to attempt to avoid evil in what could be a winning game only by the "grace of God."

For our purposes, there are three chief respects in which Puritanism framed the all-important relationship between human beings and their

world. The first is condemnation: we are guilty, and nothing alters that—
"in Adam's fall we sinned all." Second, we are helpless: election, if it
comes, is an action initiated by God over which we have no influence.
Finally, we are inescapably moral agents: we are born in sin, there is no
neutrality. We cannot escape the onus of choice even if that choice is on-
tologically meaningless.

From Puritanism to Social Darwinism, at least in the subconscious
convictions of a culture, is less of a leap than it might appear. Thanks to
Spencer's interpretation of Darwin, an intractable nature came to be substituted for an all-powerful God. Human beings are a product of evolution, and by a process of natural selection (which the Social Darwinists
found it convenient to translate to "survival of the fittest"), the adaptive
ends of evolution are served. In short, Social Darwinism was a determinism, a kind of naturalistic Calvinism in which human beings were subju-
gated to their environment rather than to the will of God.[1] But the thought
that either could be influenced or altered was, as William Graham Sumner
succinctly put it, "absurd," since to attempt to influence the process of
evolution was in effect to attempt to subvert a natural law. Like Calvinism, Social Darwinism placed the individual in a passive role—at least
in theory. But in the notion of survival of the fittest lay an emphasis on
adaptability, which could be, and was, interpreted to mean that nature
favored the more dynamic, the most aggressive and intelligent (which
came to mean most cunning) of the species. Thus in practice Social Darwinism served as a rationalization for economic and geographic rapaci-
ousness while numbing moral judgment with the comforting assurance of
a slow but inevitable progress up the evolutionary ladder.

The boy hero of Horatio Alger, Jr., at first glance may appear misplaced
in company with the concepts and convictions making up Puritanism and
Social Darwinism. But like Natty Bumppo or George Babbitt, Alger's
hero lives on in the American imagination quite independently of his novelistic origins. Moreover, while the Alger novels were the most immediate
historical antecedents of the gangster film, popular myths have a way of
mixing and combining with little or no regard for history. The basic pattern of the Alger books is simple and can be found with minor variations
in each of the novels. The hero is a young lad, who, either through mis-
fortune or the machinations of relatives, has been separated from his family and deprived of his rightful inheritance. The chief task of the hero
is either to win back the family homestead for himself and his aging
mother, or, if no apparent family exists, to rise from his status as urban
waif to a position of monetary security and respectability. His chief weapons in this struggle are the manly fortitude and traditional virtues that
Alger signified by "pluck," and the continuous stream of fortuitous cir-

cumstances, "luck," which provided occasion for the employment of that fortitude and those virtues.

For our purposes the important point is that all of Alger's plots play upon the theme of disinheritance. In Alger's fictional world, security means above anything else being confident of one's identity and of one's position in the world. Thus the retention of "home" or the securing of a comfortable middle-class job becomes a metaphor for the orderly and respectable life. Moreover, except for the conveniences of plot and the maintenance of an artificial suspense, the outcome is never in doubt. The Alger hero *is* the rightful heir, and his recognition as the long-lost son merely completes the pattern of temporary dispossession and eventual restoration. Thus the Alger hero's task is not so much to earn his success as it is to maintain his traditional values until the inevitable justification and restoration occur.

Now even this cursory review of Puritanism, Social Darwinism, and the Horatio Alger myth reveals the basis for a welter of potential conflicts and contradictions. Perhaps the weakest chink in the Puritan armor was the very remoteness of the wrathful God who ostensibly governed the Puritan's destiny. In any case, the burgeoning New England villages and towns were concrete and immediate, and the material well-being they generated became inextricably linked in the Puritan mind with moral worth. In the everyday world, therefore, hard work, perseverance, and ingenuity yielded a material wealth with palpable consequences, while the question of damnation or salvation, or at least the consequence of that question, was postponed to an eschatological future. In its turn, Social Darwinism was in many ways the rationalization generated to account for a complex, largely urbanized society riding the crest of the Industrial Revolution. Consequently, the individual guilt that could haunt the Puritan mind became detoxified in a process of evolution that tended to render value judgments irrelevant by insisting that evolution was self-justifying. However, by its mutual insistence on both the dominance of the environment and the idea of survival of the fittest, Social Darwinism reopened the door of ambivalence and ambiguity in human conduct. On the one hand a man or woman was a "product of the environment," while on the other he or she was enjoined to observe those "fittest" who not only survived but exploited that environment.

The conflict between the inevitability of passive acceptance and the demand for adaptive strategies produced anxiety, and it is precisely that anxiety which the Horatio Alger stories, at the mythic level, were designed to relieve. By adapting the encounters of a picaresque tale, Alger kept the surface of his plot busy with action, making it appear that his hero is actively struggling with the forces arrayed against him. However, by the time we reach the happy ending it is evident that Alger's hero has always been simply himself, steadfastly waiting out adversity and practicing homely virtues until he is restored to a position of identity, security, and comfort that really has always been his except for this temporary interruption. In other words, by the dexterity always practiced in the products of popular culture, Alger has managed, temporarily, to achieve an apparent synthesis among contradictory elements. While paying homage to adaptive "pluck," Alger ensures that the plot will turn on a stroke of "luck" for which the hero is prepared but not responsible. Moreover, that synthesis is further aided by a general pejoration of all consequences. Salvation, which is really due the hero anyway, is reduced to the monetarily secure, middle-class life. Evil, insofar as it is dealt with at all, is equated to greedy relatives seeking self-preferment, while punishment consistently takes the form of a pay cut.

So, what has all this to do with the issue of significance in American gangster films? First of all, more than any other film genre, gangster films are the home of the conflict between good and evil.[2] This may take the form of the well-dressed, antiseptic, technology-oriented T-men versus the malevolent, psychotic Cody Jarrett (James Cagney) in *White Heat* (Raoul Walsh, 1949). Or the good and evil elements may be mixed in a single character, such as Roy Earle (Humphrey Bogart) in *High Sierra* (Raoul Walsh, 1941). Or perhaps a director will undertake to examine and question the very basis upon which conventional notions of good and evil rest, as does Fritz Lang in *The Big Heat* (1953). But whatever its form, taint and corruption pervade the gangster film and have consequences that the characters cannot escape.

There has always been something "fated" about the main character in American gangster films. We know that no matter what happens, somehow the gangster will "get his." Although he is often dispatched by minions of the law, death comes to the gangster not as a result of a social or legal process, but because he has sinned. Occasionally we are permitted to see the effects of that sin, as in the hysterical pleading of Tony Camonte (Paul Muni) before he is machine-gunned by police in *Scarface* (Howard Hawks, 1932), or in the penultimate scene of hospital repentance before the body of Tommy Powers (James Cagney) is brutally dumped in his mother's living room by a rival gang in *The Public Enemy* (William Wellman, 1931). The law may be the instrument of the gangster's demise, but is never really the cause. Thus even in a semidocumentary like Richard Wilson's *Al Capone* (1959), Capone (Rod Steiger) is ritualistically but unauthentically stoned into bloody unconsciousness by his fellow prisoners in Alcatraz while the narrator reminds us that Capone died insane, totally debilitated by a "social disease." While it is never overtly related to a

28. *The Big Heat:* Conventional notions of good and evil are questioned.

wrathful God, justice, or at least punishment, usually in the form of an early and violent death, inevitably awaits the gangster.

Yet, while he somehow cannot succeed, the film gangster hero insidiously demands our admiration. His is a violent and hostile environment, a labyrinth of dark alleys and concrete canyons, a warren of mean streets from which danger constantly threatens. The gangster survives as long as he does against heavy odds because of his energy, cunning, and bravura. His adaptive strategies are simple and classically summed up by Tony Camonte when he regales his partner Little Boy (George Raft). Forefinger extended, thumb up, he says, "Do it first, do it yourself, and keep on doing it." Roy Earle commands our respect precisely because he will not adapt to a changing environment composed of self-serving renegade cops, unprofessional punks, and shallow, pleasure-seeking "nice" girls. Ivan Martin (Jimmy Cliff) sings "The Harder They Come, the Harder They Fall," lyrics that become ironic in *The Harder They Come* (Perry Henzell, 1973). Ivan is a "badass," temporarily but flamboyantly defying rural ignorance, the cops, exploitative capitalism—in short, every oppressive element in his environment.

Still, although the environment may mold and motivate the gangster, it never wholly determines him. Tommy Powers is more attractive than the Putty Noses or Paddy Ryans he comes in contact with. He retains possibilities that were never theirs. Nor can one seek in the environment an explanation for Michael, Tommy's law-abiding, hard-working, middle-class brother. The pervasive corruption that defines the environment in *The Big Heat* becomes finally almost irrelevant. It is the innate depravity, the universal capacity for rage, revenge, and murder which is the motivating force in this film. And Francis Ford Coppola's *Godfather II* (1975) is most revealing in regard to the issue of environment. On the surface Michael Corleone (Al Pacino) appears to be *the* most successful adaptor. He has risen to and held power in the face of rival "families," treacherous relatives, Senate investigating committees, and changing economic and political conditions. Yet, at the film's somber close, he sits staring emptily at his vacant Reno mansion. He is utterly alone in a world depopulated by his own orders.

Following the lead of Robert Warshow, many critics have pointed to the perverted Horatio Alger pattern especially evident in early gangster films.[3] The evidence is everywhere: in the steady rise to position and power of Rico (Edward G. Robinson) in *Little Caesar* (Mervyn LeRoy, 1930); the neon sign flashing "The World Is Yours" to Tony Camonte in *Scarface;* Cody Jarrett demonically screaming "Top of the world, Ma" as a fireball of exploding gas tanks carries him into oblivion in *White Heat.* Interestingly enough, however, the traditional Alger message has always been savagely undercut in the gangster film. Uneasy in its ersatz synthesis of conflicting elements, the Horatio Alger myth seems particularly vulnerable to the chilling facts of a Depression or the sobering realities of Third World exploitation. The opening scenes of *The Harder They Come* are accompanied by Jimmy Cliff singing "You Can Get It If You Really Try." The pathetic falsity of that claim becomes ever more painfully clear as the film progresses. Ivan's will, sagacity, courage, and style, his fundamental demand for his "propers," is futile. He is a man without a home in country or city. He is ultimately borne down by the system—too much money, influence, and finally firepower—everything connoted by "the man." But mostly Ivan is defeated by his own illusions. The harder they come, the harder they *do* fall. He is not an idol of the silver screen scattering baddies before him (although he clearly identifies himself with that image), nor will the military police send out "one baaad man" to shoot it out on the empty beach.

Despite the fact that social mobility and bank-book morality are held out to and eagerly adopted by the American film gangster, he finally proves heir to nothing but calamity. What the Horatio Alger myth chiefly affirms is precisely what the American gangster film denies. The gangster *is* disinherited—permanently. Socially and financially he is a usurper. While the gangster may feel that he is restoring to himself some rightful

29. *White Heat:* Cody Jarrett (James Cagney) shouts "Top of the world, Ma."

position, status, or power, the films repeatedly reveal that nothing could be farther from the truth. While retaining most of the surface trappings of the Horatio Alger myth, the gangster film denies its meaning at the source and returns to other, and conflicting, cultural convictions—chiefly, a pervasive sense of alienation and impending doom, a punishment that cannot be escaped for a fault that cannot be irradicated.

Perhaps more recent gangster films suggest a moving away from the patterns I have been discussing. But this is true more in appearance than in reality. Martin Scorsese's *Mean Streets* (1973) seems to jettison the Horatio Alger myth. Charlie is not motivated by a desire to "get ahead" or supplant his Uncle Giovanni. His guilt and his need to aid the damaged people like Teresa and Johnny Boy overpower his desire to take over the restaurant and thus rise in the Mafiosi-dominated family business. Nor does Scorsese fall back on a simplistic environmental determinism. While he immerses us in an environment that is almost claustrophobic, Scorsese never permits the audience to use it as the basis for normative judgments. It is simply there, sufficient for and ignored by those who live in it. Yet calamity does come. And, ironically, it is brought about by Michael

30. *Little Caesar:* The gangster's rise . . .

(Richard Romanus), who *does* take himself seriously, who sees himself rising to the top in this world of punks, and who affects the expensive clothes, big cars, and strong-arm methods that compose the traditional icons of the gangster film. But, more important, it is the basic depravity, the capacity for evil, which ultimately surfaces in this film. Thus it is no accident that it is a parallel scene from *The Big Heat* which Uncle Giovanni is watching on television as a wounded Charlie drags himself from a demolished automobile across town.

In summation, what I am suggesting is that the elements of Puritanism, Social Darwinism, and the Horatio Alger myth are hopelessly contradictory. And it is precisely these contradictions which the American gangster film embodies and which, because they remain unresolved in America's collective consciousness, provide the imbalances, ambiguities, and am-

31. . . . and fall: Cagney in *The Roaring Twenties*.

bivalences with which the gangster film abounds. However, this does not at all imply that individual gangster films are without meaning or that the genre lacks significance. It is exactly the contradictory attitudes toward freedom and fate; the irreconcilable conflicts regarding the sources and signs of good and evil; the simultaneous and mutually exclusive admonition to accept/wait and adapt/initiate which form at least part of the dynamics of the American mind. These same dynamics provide the bases for the significance of American gangster films.

Notes

1. For a more detailed account of the origin and influence of the ideas we call Social Darwinism, see Richard Hofstadter, *Social Darwinism in American Thought* (Philadelphia: University of Pennsylvania Press, 1944).

2. For example, consider the issue of good and evil in most westerns. While the western is considered the province of the "good guys" and the "bad guys," that conflict is seldom central to the western. More often the western hero is pursuing

some private vendetta or finds himself in the "man in the middle" position, fighting to usher in a civilization which, once established, will have no place for him. For more on this issue see John Cawelti, *The Six-Gun Mystique* (Bowling Green: Bowling Green University Popular Press, [1970]).

3. Robert Warshow, "The Gangster as Tragic Hero," in *The Immediate Experience* (New York: Atheneum, 1977), pp. 127–133.

14. Notes on Film Noir

PAUL SCHRADER

In 1946 French critics, seeing the American films they had missed during the war, noticed the new mood of cynicism, pessimism, and darkness that had crept into the American cinema. The darkening stain was most evident in routine crime thrillers, but was also apparent in prestigious melodramas. The French cineastes soon realized they had seen only the tip of the iceberg: as the years went by, Hollywood lighting grew darker, characters more corrupt, themes more fatalistic, and the tone more hopeless. By 1949 American movies were in the throes of their deepest and most creative funk. Never before had films dared to take such a harsh uncomplimentary look at American life, and they would not dare to do so again for twenty years.

Hollywood's film noir has recently become the subject of renewed interest among moviegoers and critics. The fascination that film noir holds for today's young filmgoers and film students reflects recent trends in American cinema: American movies are again taking a look at the underside of the American character, but compared to such relentlessly cynical examples of film noir as *Kiss Me Deadly* (Robert Aldrich, 1955) or *Kiss Tomorrow Goodbye* (Gordon Douglas, 1959), the newer self-hate cinema of *Easy Rider* (Dennis Hopper, 1969) and *Medium Cool* (Haskell Wexler, 1969) seems naive and romantic. As the current political mood hardens, filmgoers and filmmakers will find the film noir of the late forties increasingly attractive. The forties may be to the seventies what the thirties were to the sixties.

Film noir is equally interesting to critics. It offers writers a cache of excellent, little-known films (film noir is oddly both one of Hollywood's best periods and least known) and gives auteur-weary critics an opportunity to apply themselves to the new questions of classification and transdirectorial style. After all, what is a film noir?

Film noir is not a genre, as Raymond Durgnat has helpfully pointed out

Note: This chapter is excerpted from a longer essay published previously.

over the objections of Higham and Greenberg's *Hollywood in the For-ties*.[1] It is not defined, as are the western and gangster genres, by conven-tions of setting and conflict but rather by the more subtle qualities of tone and mood. It is a film "noir," as opposed to the possible variants of film "gray" or film "off-white." Film noir is also a specific period of film his-tory, like German expressionism or the French New Wave. In general, film noir refers to those Hollywood films of the forties and early fifties that portrayed the world of dark, slick city streets, crime and corruption.

Film noir is an extremely unwieldy period. It harks back to many previ-ous periods: Warner's thirties gangster films, the French "poetic realism" of Carné and Duvivier, Sternbergian melodrama, and ultimately German Expressionist crime films (Lang's Mabuse cycle). Film noir can stretch at its outer limits from *The Maltese Falcon* (John Huston, 1941) to *Touch of Evil* (Orson Welles, 1958), and most every dramatic Hollywood film from 1941 to 1953 contains some noir elements. There are also foreign off-shoots of film noir, such as *The Third Man* (Carol Reed, 1949), *Breathless* (Jean-Luc Godard, 1959), and *Le Doulos* (Jean-Pierre Melville, 1963).

Almost every critic has his or her own definition of film noir, along with a personal list of film titles and dates to back it up. Personal and descriptive definitions, however, can get a bit sticky. A film of urban nightlife is not necessarily a film noir, and a film noir need not necessarily concern crime and corruption. Since film noir is defined by tone rather than genre, it is almost impossible to argue one critic's descriptive defini-tion against another's. How many noir elements does it take to make a film noir? Rather than haggle about definitions, I would rather attempt to reduce film noir to its primary colors (all shades of black), those cultural and stylistic elements to which any definition must return.

INFLUENCES

At the risk of sounding like Arthur Knight, I would suggest that there were four influences in Hollywood in the forties that brought about the film noir. (The danger of Knight's *Liveliest Art* method is that it makes film history less a matter of structural analysis and more a case of artistic and social forces magically interacting and coalescing.) Each of the fol-lowing four catalytic elements, however, can define the film noir; the dis-tinctly noir tonality draws from each of these elements.

War and Postwar Disillusionment

The acute downer that hit the United States after the Second World War was, in fact, a delayed reaction to the thirties. All through the Depres-sion, movies were needed to keep people's spirits up, and, for the most

32. *You Only Live Once:* Crime films became darker in the late thirties.

part, they did. The crime films of this period were Horatio Algerish and socially conscious. Toward the end of the thirties a darker crime film began to appear (*You Only Live Once,* Fritz Lang, 1937; *The Roaring Twenties,* Raoul Walsh, 1939), and, were it not for the war, film noir would have been at full steam by the early forties.

The need to produce Allied propaganda abroad and promote patriotism at home blunted the fledgling moves toward a dark cinema, and the film noir thrashed about in the studio system, not quite able to come into full prominence. During the war the first uniquely film noir appeared in *The Maltese Falcon, The Glass Key* (Stuart Heisler, 1942), *This Gun for Hire* (Frank Tuttle, 1942), and *Laura* (Otto Preminger, 1944), but these films lacked the distinctly noir bite the end of the war would bring.

As soon as the war was over, however, American films became markedly more sardonic—and there was a boom in the crime film. For fifteen years the pressures against America's ameliorISTIc cinema had been building up, and, given the freedom, audiences and artists were now eager to take a less optimistic view of things. The disillusionment that many soldiers, small businessmen, and housewife/factory employees felt in returning to a peacetime economy was directly mirrored in the sordidness of the urban crime film.

This immediate postwar disillusionment was directly demonstrated in films like *Cornered* (Edward Dmytryk, 1945), *The Blue Dahlia* (George Marshall, 1946), *Dead Reckoning* (John Cromwell, 1947), and *Ride the Pink Horse* (Robert Montgomery, 1947), in which a serviceman returns from the war to find his sweetheart unfaithful or dead, or his business partner cheating him, or the whole society something less than worth fighting for. The war continues, but now the antagonism turns with a new viciousness toward American society itself.

Postwar Realism

Shortly after the war, every film-producing country had a resurgence of realism. In America it first took the form of films by such producers as Louis de Rochemont (*House on 92nd Street*, Henry Hathaway, 1945; *Call Northside 777*, Hathaway, 1948) and Mark Hellinger (*The Killers*, Robert Siodmak, 1946; *Brute Force*, Jules Dassin, 1947) and directors like Hathaway and Dassin. "Every scene was filmed on the actual location depicted," the publicity for the 1947 de Rochemont-Hathaway *Kiss of Death* proudly proclaimed. Even after de Rochemont's particular "March of Time" authenticity fell from vogue, realistic exteriors remained a permanent fixture of film noir.

The realistic movement also suited America's postwar mood; the public's desire for a more honest and harsh view of America would not be satisfied by the same studio streets they had been watching for a dozen years. The postwar realistic trend succeeded in breaking film noir away from the domain of the high-class melodrama, placing it where it more properly belonged, in the streets with everyday people. In retrospect, the pre–de Rochemont film noir looks definitely tamer than the postwar realistic films. The studio look of films like *The Big Sleep* (Howard Hawks, 1946) and *The Mask of Dimitrios* (Jean Negulesco, 1944) blunts their sting, making them seem polite and conventional in contrast to their later, more realistic counterparts.

The German Expatriates

Hollywood played host to an influx of German expatriates in the twenties and thirties, and these filmmakers and technicians had, for the most part, integrated themselves into the American film establishment. Hollywood never experienced the "Germanization" some civic-minded natives

33. *The Big Combo* adapted the old expressionist techniques to the new desire for realism.

feared, and there is a danger of overemphasizing the German influence in Hollywood.

But when, in the late forties, Hollywood decided to paint it black, there were no greater masters of chiaroscuro than the Germans. The influence of expressionist lighting has always been just beneath the surface of Hollywood films, and it is not surprising, in film noir, to find it bursting out into full bloom. Neither is it surprising to find a larger number of Germans and East Europeans working in film noir: Fritz Lang, Robert Siodmak, Billy Wilder, Franz Waxman, Otto Preminger, John Brahm, Anatole Litvak, Karl Freund, Max Ophuls, John Alton, Douglas Sirk, Fred Zinnemann, William Dieterle, Max Steiner, Edgar G. Ulmer, Curtis Bernhardt, Rudolph Maté.

On the surface the German expressionist influence, with its reliance on artificial studio lighting, seems incompatible with postwar realism, with its harsh unadorned exteriors; but it is the unique quality of film noir that it was able to weld seemingly contradictory elements into a uniform style. The best noir technicians simply made all the world a sound stage, directing unnatural and expressionistic lighting onto realistic settings. In films like *Union Station* (Maté, 1950), *They Live by Night* (Nicholas Ray, 1948), and *The Killers,* there is an uneasy, exhilarating combination of realism and expressionism.

Perhaps the greatest master of noir was Hungarian-born John Alton, an expressionist cinematographer who could relight Times Square at noon if necessary. No cinematographer better adapted the old expressionist techniques to the new desire for realism, and his black-and-white photography in such gritty examples of film noir as *T-Men* (Anthony Mann, 1948), *Raw Deal* (Mann, 1948), *I, the Jury* (Harry Essex, 1953), and *The Big Combo* (Joseph H. Lewis, 1955) equals that of such German expressionist masters as Fritz Wagner and Karl Freund.

The Hard-Boiled Tradition

Another stylistic influence waiting in the wings was the "hard-boiled" school of writers. In the thirties, authors such as Ernest Hemingway, Dashiell Hammett, Raymond Chandler, James M. Cain, Horace McCoy, and John O'Hara created the "tough," a cynical way of acting and thinking that separated one from the world of everyday emotions—romanticism with a protective shell. The hard-boiled writers had their roots in pulp fiction or journalism, and their protagonists lived out a narcissistic, defeatist code. The hard-boiled hero was, in reality, a soft egg compared to his existential counterpart (Camus is said to have based *The Stranger* on McCoy), but he was a good deal tougher than anything American fiction had seen.

When the movies of the forties turned to the American "tough" moral understrata, the hard-boiled school was waiting with preset conventions of heroes, minor characters, plots, dialogue, and themes. Like the German expatriates, the hard-boiled writers had a style made to order for film noir; and, in turn, they influenced noir screenwriting as much as the Germans influenced noir cinematography.

The most hard-boiled of Hollywood's writers was Raymond Chandler himself, whose script of *Double Indemnity* (from a James M. Cain story) was the best written and most characteristically noir of the period. *Double Indemnity* (Billy Wilder, 1944) was the first film that played film noir for what it essentially was: small-time, unredeemed, unheroic; it made a break from the romantic noir cinema of *Mildred Pierce* (Michael Curtiz, 1945) and *The Big Sleep.* In its final stages, however, film noir adapted and then bypassed the hard-boiled school. Manic, neurotic post-1948 films such as *Kiss Tomorrow Goodbye, D.O.A.* (Maté, 1950), *Where the Sidewalk Ends* (Preminger, 1950), *White Heat* (Raoul Walsh, 1949), and

The Big Heat (Fritz Lang, 1953) are all post–hard-boiled: the air in these regions was even too thin for old-time cynics like Chandler.

STYLISTICS

There is not yet a study of the stylistics of film noir, and the task is certainly too large to be attempted here. Like all film movements, film noir drew upon a reservoir of film techniques, and given the time one could correlate its techniques, themes, and casual elements into a stylistic schema. For the present, however, I'd like to point out some of film noir's recurring techniques.

1. The majority of scenes are lit for night. Gangsters sit in offices at midday with the shades pulled and the lights off. Ceiling lights are hung low and floor lamps are seldom more than five feet high. One always has the suspicion that if the lights were all suddenly flipped on, the characters would shriek and shrink from the scene like Count Dracula at sunrise.

2. As in German expressionism, oblique and vertical lines are preferred to horizontal. Obliquity adheres to the choreography of the city, and is in direct opposition to the horizontal American tradition of Griffith and Ford. Oblique lines tend to splinter a screen, making it restless and unstable. Light enters the dingy rooms of film noir in such odd shapes— jagged trapezoids, obtuse triangles, vertical slits—that one suspects the windows were cut out with a penknife. No character can speak authoritatively from a space that is being continually cut into ribbons of light. Anthony Mann and John Alton's *T-Men* is the most dramatic example, but far from the only one, of oblique noir choreography.

3. The actors and setting are often given equal lighting emphasis. An actor is often hidden in the realistic tableau of the city at night, and, more obviously, his face is often blacked out by shadow as he speaks. These shadow effects are unlike the famous Warner Brothers lighting of the thirties in which the central character was accentuated by a heavy shadow; in film noir, the central character is likely to be standing *in* the shadow. When the environment is given an equal or greater weight than the actor, it, of course, creates a fatalistic, hopeless mood. There is nothing the protagonists can do; the city will outlast and negate even their best efforts.

4. Compositional tension is preferred to physical action. A typical film noir would rather move the scene cinematographically around the actor than have the actor control the scene by physical action. The beating of Robert Ryan in *The Set-Up* (Robert Wise, 1949), the gunning down of Farley Granger in *They Live by Night*, the execution of the taxi driver in *The Enforcer* (Bretaigne Windust, 1951) and of Brian Donlevy in *The Big*

34. *T-Men:* Oblique and vertical lines splinter the screen.

Combo are all marked by measured pacing, restrained anger, and oppressive compositions, and seem much closer to the film noir spirit than the rat-tat-tat and screeching tires of *Scarface* (Howard Hawks, 1932) twenty years before or the violent, expressive actions of *Underworld U.S.A.* (Samuel Fuller, 1960) ten years later.

5. There seems to be an almost Freudian attachment to water. The empty noir streets are almost always glistening with fresh evening rain (even in Los Angeles), and the rainfall tends to increase in direct proportion to the drama. Docks and piers are second only to alleyways as the most popular rendezvous points.

6. There is a love of romantic narration. In such films as *The Postman Always Rings Twice* (Tay Garnett, 1946), *Laura, Double Indemnity, The Lady from Shanghai* (Orson Welles, 1949), *Out of the Past* (Jacques Tourneur, 1947), and *Sunset Boulevard* (Billy Wilder, 1950), the narration creates a mood of *temps perdu:* an irretrievable past, a predetermined fate, and an all-enveloping hopelessness. In *Out of the Past* Robert Mitchum relates his history with such pathetic relish that it is obvious there is no hope for any future: one can only take pleasure in reliving a doomed past.

7. A complex chronological order is frequently used to reinforce the feelings of hopelessness and lost time. Such films as *The Enforcer, The Killers, Mildred Pierce, The Dark Past* (Maté, 1948), *Chicago Deadline* (Lewis Allen, 1949), *Out of the Past,* and *The Killing* (Stanley Kubrick, 1956) use a convoluted time sequence to immerse the viewer in a time-disoriented but highly stylized world. The manipulation of time, whether slight or complex, is often used to reinforce a noir principle: the *how* is always more important than the *what.*

THEMES

Raymond Durgnat has delineated the themes of film noir in an excellent article in the British *Cinema* magazine,[2] and it would be foolish for me to attempt to redo his thorough work in this short space. Durgnat divides film noir into eleven thematic categories, and although one might criticize some of his specific groupings, he covers the whole gamut of noir production, thematically categorizing over 300 films. In each of Durgnat's noir themes (whether Black Widow, killers-on-the-run, *doppelgangers*), one finds that the upwardly mobile forces of the thirties have halted; frontierism has turned to paranoia and claustrophobia. The small-time gangster has now made it big and sits in the mayor's chair, the private eye has quit the police force in disgust, and the young heroine, sick of going along for the ride, is taking others for a ride.

Durgnat, however, does not touch upon what is perhaps the overriding noir theme: a passion for the past and present, but also a fear of the future. Noir heroes dread to look ahead, but instead try to survive by the day, and if unsuccessful at that, they retreat to the past. Thus film noir's techniques emphasize loss, nostalgia, lack of clear priorities, and insecurity, then submerge these self-doubts in mannerism and style. In such a world style becomes paramount; it is all that separates one from meaninglessness. Chandler described this fundamental noir theme when he described his own fictional world: "It is not a very fragrant world, but it is the world you live in, and certain writers with tough minds and a cool spirit of detachment can make very interesting patterns out of it."[3]

PHASES

Film noir can be subdivided into three broad phases. The first, the wartime period (1941–1946 approximately), was the phase of the private eye and the lone wolf, of Chandler, Hammett, and Greene, of Bogart and Bacall, Ladd and Lake, classy directors like Curtiz and Garnett, studio sets, and, in general, more talk than action. The studio look of this period was reflected in such pictures as *The Maltese Falcon, Casablanca* (Michael Curtiz, 1942), *Gaslight* (George Cukor, 1944), *This Gun for Hire, The Lodger* (Brahm, 1944), *The Woman in the Window* (Lang, 1945), *Mildred Pierce, Spellbound* (Alfred Hitchcock, 1945), *The Big Sleep, Laura, The Lost Weekend* (Wilder, 1945), *The Strange Love of Martha Ivers* (Lewis Milestone, 1946), *To Have and Have Not* (Howard Hawks, 1944), *Fallen Angel* (Preminger, 1946), *Gilda* (Charles Vidor, 1946), *Murder My Sweet* (Dmytryk, 1944), *The Postman Always Rings Twice, Dark Waters* (Andre de Toth, 1944), *Scarlet Street* (Fritz Lang, 1945), *So Dark the Night* (Joseph H. Lewis, 1946), *The Glass Key, The Mask of Dimitrios,* and *The Dark Mirror* (Siodmak, 1946).

The Wilder/Chandler *Double Indemnity* provided a bridge to the postwar phase of film noir. The unflinching noir vision of *Double Indemnity* came as a shock in 1944, and the film was almost blocked by the combined efforts of Paramount, the Hays Office, and star Fred MacMurray. Three years later, however, *Double Indemnity*s were dropping off the studio assembly lines.

The second phase was the postwar realistic period from 1945 to 1949 (the dates overlap and so do the films; these are all approximate phases for which there are exceptions). These films tended more toward the problems of crime in the streets, political corruption, and police routine. Less romantic heroes like Richard Conte, Burt Lancaster, and Charles McGraw were more suited to this period, as were proletarian directors like Hathaway, Dassin, and Kazan. The realistic urban look of this phase is seen in such films as *The House on 92nd Street, The Killers, Raw Deal, Act of Violence* (Zinnemann, 1949), *Union Station, Kiss of Death, Johnny O'Clock* (Robert Rossen, 1947), *Force of Evil* (Abraham Polonsky, 1948), *Dead Reckoning, Ride the Pink Horse, Dark Passage* (Delmer Daves, 1947), *Cry of the City* (Siodmak, 1948), *The Set-Up, T-Men, Call Northside 777, Brute Force, The Big Clock* (John Farrow, 1948), *Thieves' Highway* (Dassin, 1949), *Ruthless* (Ulmer, 1948), *The Pitfall* (de Toth, 1948), *Boomerang!* (Elia Kazan, 1947), and *The Naked City* (Dassin, 1948).

The third and final phase of film noir, from 1949 to 1953, was the period of psychotic action and suicidal impulse. The noir hero, seemingly under the weight of ten years of despair, started to go bananas. The psychotic killer, who had in the first period been a subject worthy of study (Olivia de Havilland in *The Dark Mirror*), and in the second a fringe threat (Richard Widmark in *Kiss of Death*), now became the active protagonist (James Cagney in *Kiss Tomorrow Goodbye*). There were no excuses given for the psychopathy in *Gun Crazy* (Joseph H. Lewis, 1949)—it was just "crazy." James Cagney made a neurotic comeback, and his instability was matched by that of younger actors like Robert Ryan and Lee Marvin. This was the phase of the B noir film and of psycho-analytically inclined directors like Ray and Walsh. The forces of personal disintegration are reflected in such films as *White Heat, Gun Crazy, D.O.A., Caught* (Max Ophuls, 1949), *They Live by Night, Where the Sidewalk Ends, Kiss Tomorrow Goodbye, Detective Story* (William Wyler, 1951), *In a Lonely Place* (Ray, 1950), *I, the Jury, Ace in the Hole* (Wilder, 1951), *Panic in the Streets* (Kazan, 1950), *The Big Heat, On Dangerous Ground* (Ray, 1952), and *Sunset Boulevard.*

This third phase is the cream of the film noir period. Some critics may prefer the early "gray" melodramas, others the postwar "street" films, but film noir's final phase was the most aesthetically and sociologically piercing. After ten years of steadily shedding romantic conventions, the later noir films finally got down to the root causes of the period: the loss of public honor, heroic conventions, personal integrity, and, finally, psychic stability. The third-phase films were painfully self-aware; they seemed to know they stood at the end of a long tradition based on despair and disintegration and did not shy away from that fact. The best and most characteristically noir films—*Gun Crazy, White Heat, Out of the Past, Kiss Tomorrow Goodbye, D.O.A., They Live by Night,* and *The Big Heat*—stand at the end of the period and are the results of self-awareness. The third phase is rife with end-of-the-line noir heroes: *The Big Heat* and *Where the Sidewalk Ends* are the last stops for the urban cop, *Ace in the Hole* for the newspaper man, the Victor Saville–produced Spillane series *I, the Jury, The Long Wait* (Victor Saville, 1954), and *Kiss Me Deadly* for the private eye, *Sunset Boulevard* for the Black Widow, *White Heat* and *Kiss Tomorrow Goodbye* for the gangster, *D.O.A.* for the John Doe American.

Appropriately, the masterpiece of film noir was a straggler, *Kiss Me Deadly,* produced in 1955. Its time delay gives it a sense of detachment and thoroughgoing seediness—it stands at the end of a long sleazy tradition. The private-eye hero, Mike Hammer, undergoes the final stages of degradation. He is a small-time "bedroom dick," and has no qualms about it because the world around him isn't much better. Ralph Meeker, in his best performance, plays Hammer, a midget among dwarfs. Robert Aldrich's teasing direction carries noir to its sleaziest and most perversely erotic. Hammer overturns the underworld in search of the "great whatsit," and when he finally finds it, it turns out to be—joke of jokes—an exploding atomic bomb. The inhumanity and meaninglessness of the hero are small matters in a world in which the Bomb has the final say.

By the middle fifties film noir had ground to a halt. There were a few notable stragglers—*Kiss Me Deadly,* the Lewis/Alton *The Big Combo,* and film noir's epitaph, *Touch of Evil*—but for the most part a new style of crime film had become popular.

As the rise of McCarthy and Eisenhower demonstrated, Americans were eager to see a more bourgeois view of themselves. Crime had to move to the suburbs. The criminal put on a grey flannel suit, and the footsore cop was replaced by the "mobile unit" careening down the expressway. Any attempt at social criticism had to be cloaked in ludicrous affirmations of the American way of life. Technically, television, with its demand for full lighting and close-ups, gradually undercut the German influence, and color cinematography was, of course, the final blow to the noir look.

New directors like Seigel, Fleischer, Karlson, and Fuller, and TV shows like *Dragnet, M-Squad, Lineup,* and *Highway Patrol* stepped in to create the new crime drama. This transition can be seen in Samuel Fuller's 1953 *Pickup on South Street,* a film that blends the black look with the red scare. The waterfront scenes with Richard Widmark and Jean Peters are in the best noir tradition, but a later, dynamic fight in the subway marks Fuller as a director who would be better suited to the crime school of the middle and late fifties.

Film noir was an immensely creative period—probably the most creative in Hollywood's history—at least, if this creativity is measured not by its peaks but by its median level of artistry. Picked at random, a film noir is likely to be a better made film than a randomly selected silent comedy, musical, western, and so on. (A Joseph H. Lewis B film noir is better than a Lewis B western, for example.) Taken as a whole period, film noir achieved an unusually high level of artistry. Film noir seemed to bring out the best in everyone: directors, cameramen, screenwriters, actors. Again and again, a film noir will make the high point on an artist's career graph. Some directors, for example, did their best work in film noir (Stuart Heisler, Robert Siodmak, Gordon Douglas, Edward Dmytryk, John Brahm, John Cromwell, Raoul Walsh, Henry Hathaway); other directors began in film noir and, it seems to me, never regained their original heights (Otto Preminger, Rudolph Maté, Nicholas Ray, Robert Wise, Jules Dassin, Richard Fleischer, John Huston, André de Toth, and Robert Aldrich); and other directors who made great films in other molds also made great film noir (Orson Welles, Max Ophuls, Fritz Lang, Elia Kazan, Howard Hawks, Robert Rossen, Anthony Mann, Joseph Losey, Alfred Hitchcock, and Stanley Kubrick). Whether or not one agrees with this particular schema, its message is irrefutable: film noir was good for practically every director's career. (Two interesting exceptions to prove the case are King Vidor and Jean Renoir.) Film noir seems to have been a creative release for everyone involved. It gave artists a chance to work with previously forbidden themes, yet had conventions strong enough to protect the mediocre. Cinematographers were allowed to become highly mannered, and actors were sheltered by the cinematographers. It was not until years later that critics were able to distinguish between great directors and great noir directors.

Film noir's remarkable creativity makes its long-time neglect the more baffling. The French, of course, have been students of the period for some time (Borde and Chaumeton's *Panorama du film noir* was published in 1955), but American critics until recently have preferred the western, the musical, or the gangster film to the film noir.

Some of the reasons for this neglect are superficial; others strike to the heart of the noir style. For a long time film noir, with its emphasis on corruption and despair, was considered an aberration of the American character. The western, with its moral primitivism, and the gangster film, with its Horatio Alger values, were considered more American than the film noir.

This prejudice was reinforced by the fact that film noir was ideally suited to the low-budget B film, and many of the best noir films were B films. This odd sort of economic snobbery still lingers on in some critical circles: high-budget trash is considered more worthy of attention than low-budget trash, and to praise a B film is somehow to slight (often intentionally) an A film.

The fundamental reason for film noir's neglect, however, is the fact that it depends more on choreography than sociology, and American critics have always been slow on the uptake when it comes to visual style. Like its protagonists, film noir is more interested in style than theme, whereas American critics have been traditionally more interested in theme than style. American film critics have always been sociologists first and scientists second: film is important as it relates to large masses, and if a film goes awry, it is often because the theme has been somehow "violated" by the style. Film noir operates on opposite principles: the theme is hidden in the style, and bogus themes are often flaunted ("middle-class values are best") that contradict the style. Although, I believe, style determines the theme in every film, it was easier for sociological critics to discuss the themes of the western and gangster film apart from stylistic analysis than it was to do for film noir.

Not surprisingly, it was the gangster film, not the film noir, which was canonized in *The Partisan Review* in 1948 by Robert Warshow's famous essay, "The Gangster as Tragic Hero." Although Warshow could be an aesthetic as well as a sociological critic, in this case he was interested in the western and gangster film as "popular" art rather than as style. This sociological orientation blinded Warshow, as it has many subsequent critics, to an aesthetically more important development in the gangster film—film noir.

The irony of this neglect is that in retrospect the gangster films Warshow wrote about are inferior to film noir. The thirties gangster was primarily a reflection of what was happening in the country, and Warshow analyzed this. The film noir, although it was also a sociological reflection, went further than the gangster film. Toward the end film noir was engaged in a life-and-death struggle with the materials it reflected; it tried to make America accept a moral vision of life based on style. That very contradiction—promoting style in a culture that valued themes—forced film noir into artistically invigorating twists and turns. Film noir attacked and interpreted its sociological conditions and, by the close of the noir period, created a new artistic world that went beyond a simple sociological reflection, a nightmarish world of American mannerism that was by far more a creation than a reflection.

Because film noir was first of all a style, because it worked out its conflicts visually rather than thematically, because it was aware of its own identity, it was able to create artistic solutions to sociological problems. And for these reasons films like *Kiss Me Deadly, Kiss Tomorrow Goodbye,* and *Gun Crazy* can be works of art in a way that gangster films like *Scarface, The Public Enemy,* and *Little Caesar* can never be.

Notes

1. Raymond Durgnat, "Paint It Black: The Family Tree of Film Noir," *Cinema* (U.K.), nos. 6–7 (August 1970): 49–56.
2. Ibid.
3. Raymond Chandler, "The Simple Art of Murder," in *Detective Fiction: Crime and Compromise,* edited by Dick Allen and David Chacko (New York: Harcourt Brace Jovanovich, 1974), p. 398.

15. *Chinatown* and Generic Transformation in Recent American Films

JOHN G. CAWELTI

One of the fascinating things about Roman Polanski's *Chinatown* (1974) is that it invokes in so many ways the American popular genre of the hard-boiled detective story. Most of us, I suppose, associate this tradition particularly with two films, both of which starred Humphrey Bogart: John Huston's *The Maltese Falcon* (1941) and Howard Hawks's *The Big Sleep* (1946). But these are only the two most remembered and perhaps the most memorable versions of a narrative formula that has been replicated in hundreds of novels, films, and television programs. Next to the western, the hard-boiled detective story is America's most distinctive contribution to the world's stock of action-adventure stories, our contemporaneous embodiment of the drama of heroic quest that has appeared in so many different cultures in so many different guises. Unlike the western—the heroic quest on the frontier—which can perhaps be traced back as far as the Indian captivity narratives of the late seventeenth century and certainly to Cooper's Leatherstocking saga of the early nineteenth century, the hard-boiled detective story is of quite recent origin. It developed in the twenties through the medium of short action stories in pulp magazines like the famous *Black Mask*. By 1929, Dashiell Hammett had produced in *Red Harvest* the first hard-boiled detective novel. Before retiring into literary silence in the mid-thirties, Hammett had created a basic core of hard-boiled adventure in his Continental Op stories and his novels—*The Dain Curse* (1929), *The Maltese Falcon* (1930), *The Glass Key* (1931), and *The Thin Man* (1934). In very short order, the hard-boiled detective made the transition from novel to film. *The Maltese Falcon* appeared in two film versions in the early thirties, before John Huston made the definitive version in 1941. *The Glass Key* was produced in the early thirties and in the forties; *The Thin Man* became one of the great movie successes of the later thirties, so popular that it led to a number of invented sequels. And while the hard-boiled detective flourished in film, Hammett's example was followed in novels by writers whose literary approach ranged from the subtlety and depth of Raymond Chandler and

Ross Macdonald to the sensational—and bestselling—crudity of Mickey Spillane. Radio and television, too, made many series based on the figure of the hard-boiled detective and his quest for justice through the ambiguous landscape of the modern American city. If a myth can be defined as a pattern of narrative known throughout the culture and presented in many different versions by many different tellers, then the hard-boiled detective story is in that sense an important American myth.

Chinatown invokes this myth in many different ways. Its setting in Los Angeles in the 1930s is very much the archetypal "hard-boiled" setting, the place and time of Hammett's and Chandler's novels. While it is true that many hard-boiled novels and films are set in different places and times— Mickey Spillane's Mike Hammer stories in New York City, John D. Macdonald's Travis McGee saga in Florida—the California city setting of Hammett and Chandler and the approximate time of their stories, memorialized in the period furnishings, visual icons, and style of the great hard-boiled films of the 1940s, have become for us the look and the temporal-spatial aura of the hard-boiled myth. It is this aura that Polanski generates, though there is something not quite right, something disturbingly off about it. In this case, it is the color. The world of the hard-boiled myth is preeminently a world of black and white. Its ambience is that compound of angular light and shadow enmeshed in webs of fog that grew out of the visual legacy of German expressionism in drama and film, transformed into what is now usually called film noir by its adjustment to American locales and stories. Polanski carefully controls his spectrum of hue and tone in order to give it the feel of film noir, but it is nonetheless color with occasional moments of rich golden light—as in the scene in the dry riverbed. These moments of warm color often relate to scenes that are outside the usual setting or thematic content—for example, scenes in the natural landscape outside the city—which are themselves generally outside the world of the hard-boiled detective story. The invocation of many other traditional elements of the hard-boiled myth, the film noir tone and the 1930s setting cue us to expect the traditional mythical world of the private-eye hero. But the presence of color, along with increasing deviations from established patterns of plot, motive, and character give us an eerie feeling of one myth colliding with and beginning to give way to others.

Let us begin by examining *Chinatown*'s relation to the traditional myth of the hard-boiled detective. The established narrative formula of the hard-boiled story has as its protagonist a private investigator who occupies a marginal position with respect to the official social institutions of criminal justice. The private eye is licensed by the state, but though he may be a former member of a police force or district attorney's staff, he is not now connected with such an organization. In the course of the story, he is very likely to come into conflict with representatives of the official machinery, though he may also have friends who are police officers. His position on the edge of the law is very important, because one of the central themes of the hard-boiled myth is the ambiguity between institutionalized law enforcement and true justice. The story shows us that the police and the courts are incapable of effectively protecting the innocent and bringing the guilty to appropriate justice. Only the individual of integrity who exists on the margins of society can solve the crime and bring about true justice.

The marginal character of the private-eye hero is thus crucial to his role in the myth. It is also central to his characterization. We see him not only as a figure outside the institutionalized process of law enforcement, but as the paradoxical combination of a man of character who is also a failure. The private eye is a relatively poor man who operates out of a seedy office and never seems to make very much money by his exploits; he is the most marginal sort of lower-middle-class quasi professional. Yet unlike the usual stereotype of this social class, he is a man of honor and integrity who cannot be made to give up his quest for true justice. He is a compelling American hero type, clearly related to the traditional western hero who manifests many of the same characteristics and conditions of marginality.

The story begins when the hard-boiled hero is given a mission by a client. It is typical that this initial mission is a deceptive one. Either the client is lying, as Brigid O'Shaughnessy lies to Sam Spade in *The Maltese Falcon*, or the client has been deceived and does not understand what is really at stake in giving the detective the case, as with General Sternwood in *The Big Sleep*. Often the detective is being used as a pawn in some larger plot of the client's. Whatever his initial impetus to action, the detective soon finds himself enmeshed in a very complex conspiracy involving a number of people from different spheres of society. The ratiocinative English detectives of authors like Dorothy Sayers, Agatha Christie, or Ngaio Marsh investigate crimes by examining clues, questioning witnesses, and then using their intellectual powers of insight and deduction to arrive at the solution. The hard-boiled detective investigates through movement and encounter; he collides with the web of conspiracy until he has exposed its outlines. The crime solved by the ratiocinative detective is usually that of a single individual. With this individual's means and motives for the criminal act rationally established, he or she can be turned over to the law for prosecution. But the hard-boiled detective encounters a linked series of criminal acts and responsibilities; he discovers not a single guilty individual, but a corrupt society in which wealthy and respectable people are linked with gangsters and crooked politicians. Because it is society that is corrupt, and not just a single individual, the official machinery of law enforcement is unable to bring the guilty to justice.

The hard-boiled detective must decide for himself what kind of justice can be accomplished in the ambiguous urban world of modern America, and he himself must, in many instances, undertake to see this justice through. There have always been two different tendencies within the hard-boiled myth. Some writers, like Mickey Spillane and his many current followers, place their emphasis on the hero playing the role of executioner as well as detective and judge. More complex and artistic writers, like Hammett, Chandler, and Ross Macdonald, develop instead the theme of the hero's own relationship to the mythical role of lawman-outside-the-law. Their versions of the story rarely end with the detective's execution of the criminal; they prefer instead either to arrange for the criminal's self-destruction, as in Chandler's *Farewell, My Lovely,* or simply to bring about the criminal's exposure and confession, as in *The Maltese Falcon.* But this latter trend, though it has produced greater literature, is perhaps best understood as a humane avoidance of the true thrust of the myth, which is, I think, essentially toward the marginal hero becoming righteous judge and executioner, culture hero for a society that has profoundly ambiguous conflicts in choosing between its commitment to legality and its belief that only individual actions are ultimately moral and just.

One further element of the hard-boiled myth needs to be particularly noted: the role of the feminine antagonist. In almost every case, the hard-boiled hero encounters a beautiful and dangerous woman in the course of his investigations and finds himself very much drawn toward her, even to the point of falling in love. Sometimes the woman is his client, sometimes a figure in the conspiracy. In a surprising number of cases (*The Maltese Falcon, The Big Sleep, Farewell, My Lovely, I, the Jury,* and many others) the woman turns out to be the murderess and, in Spillane at least, is killed by her detective-lover. This murky treatment of the "romance" between detective and dangerous female is occasionally resolved happily, as in the Bogart-Bacall relationship at the end of the film version of *The Big Sleep* (in the novel this romantic culmination does not take place). However, such an outcome is rare. Even if the beautiful woman does not turn out to be a murderess, the detective usually separates from her at the end to return to his marginal situation, basically unchanged by what has happened to him and ready to perform more acts of justice when the occasion arises.

We can see from this brief resumé of the hard-boiled formula how close a resemblance *Chinatown* bears to it. But the film deviates increasingly from the myth until, by the end of the story, the film arrives at an ending almost contrary to that of the myth. Instead of bringing justice to a corrupt society, the detective's actions leave the basic source of corruption untouched. Instead of protecting the innocent, his investigation leads to the death of one victim and the deeper moral destruction of another. Instead of surmounting the web of conspiracy with honor and integrity intact, the detective is overwhelmed by what has happened to him.

True, the action of *Chinatown* increasingly departs from the traditional hard-boiled formula as the story progresses; however, there are, from the very beginning, a number of significant departures from the standard pattern. The choice of Jack Nicholson and Faye Dunaway as leading actors is a good instance of this. Nicholson and Dunaway have certain physical and stylistic resemblances to Bogart and Bacall, and these are obviously played up through costume, makeup, and gesture. Indeed, there is one early scene in a restaurant that is almost eerily reminiscent of the famous horse-racing interchange between Bogart and Bacall in *The Big Sleep*. But much as they echo the archetypal hard-boiled duo in a superficial way, Nicholson and Dunaway play characters who are very different. Dunaway has a neurotic fragility, an underlying quality of desperation that becomes even more apparent as her true situation is revealed. She never generates the sense of independence and courage that Bacall brought to her hard-boiled roles; her qualities of wit and sophistication—those characteristics that made Bacall such an appropriate romantic partner for the hard-boiled detective—are quickly seen to be a veneer covering depths of anguish and ambiguity. Nicholson also portrays, at least early on, a character who is not quite what he seems. His attempt to be the tough, cynical, and humorous private eye is undercut on all sides; he is terribly inept as a wit, as his attempt to tell his assistants the Chinese joke makes clear. Nor is he the tough, marginal man of professional honor he pretends to be at the beginning; actually, he is a successful small businessman who has made a good thing out of exploiting the more sordid needs of his fellowmen. One of the most deeply symbolic clichés of the traditional hard-boiled formula is the hero's refusal to do divorce business, in fact one of the primary functions of the private detective. By this choice the traditional private eye of the myth established both his personal sense of honor and his transcendent vocation, distinguishing himself from the typical private investigator. However, from the beginning of *Chinatown*, it is clear that the accumulation of evidence of marital infidelity is Jake Gittes's primary business. He is, indeed, drawn into the affairs of Noah Cross, his daughter, and her husband by a commission to document a supposedly clandestine affair between the latter and a much younger woman. The name, J. J. Gittes, which Polanski and Robert Towne, the screenwriter, chose for their protagonist, is a good indication of this aspect of his character. Think of the names of the traditional hard-boiled detectives: Sam Spade, with its implication of hardness and digging beneath the surface; Philip Marlowe, with its aura of knightliness and chivalry; Lew Archer, with its mythical overtones. Gittes, or "Gits," as Noah

Cross ironically keeps pronouncing it, connotes selfishness and grasping and has, in addition, a kind of ethnic echo very different from the pure Anglo of Spade, Marlowe, and Archer.

Yet, qualified and even "antiheroic" as he is, Gittes is swept up into the traditional hard-boiled action. His initial and deceptive charge involves him in the investigation of a murder, which in turn leads him to evidence of a large-scale conspiracy involving big business, politics, crime, and the whole underlying social and environmental structure of Los Angeles. Like the traditional hard-boiled detective, Gittes begins as a marginal individual, but gradually finds himself becoming a moral agent with a mission. At the same time he becomes romantically involved with a character deeply implicated in the web of conspiracy, the mysterious widow of the man who has been murdered. By the middle of the film Gittes is determined to expose the political conspiracy that he senses beneath the surface, and also to resolve the question of the guilt or innocence of the woman to whom he has been so strongly attracted. Thus far, the situation closely resembles that of *The Maltese Falcon* and *The Big Sleep*. It is at this point, however, that the action again takes a vast departure from that of the traditional hard-boiled story. Instead of demonstrating his ability to expose and punish the guilty, Gittes steadily finds himself confronting a depth of evil and chaos so great that he is unable to control it. In relation to the social and personal depravity represented by Noah Cross and the world in which he can so successfully operate, the toughness, moral concern, and professional skill of Gittes not only seem ineffectual, but lead to ends that are the very opposite of those intended. At the end of the film, Noah Cross is free to continue his rapacious depredations on the land, the city, and the body of his own daughter-granddaughter; and the one person who might have effectively brought Cross to some form of justice—his daughter-mistress—has been destroyed. Gittes's confrontation with a depth of depravity beyond the capacity of the hard-boiled ethos of individualistic justice is, I think, the essential significance of the Chinatown motif in the film. Chinatown becomes a symbol of life's deeper moral enigmas, those unintended consequences of action that are past understanding and control. Gittes has been there before. In another case his attempts at individual moral action had led to the death of a woman he cared for. It is apparently this tragedy that motivated him to leave the police force and set up as a private investigator. Now he has been drawn back into moral action, and it is again, in Chinatown, that his attempt to live out the myth of individualistic justice collides with the power of evil and chance in the world. The result is not heroic confrontation and the triumph of justice, but tragic catastrophe and the destruction of the innocent.

35. *Chinatown:* The antiheroic detective J. J. Gittes (Jack Nicholson) gets his nostril sliced for nosing around.

Chinatown places the hard-boiled detective story within a view of the world that is deeper and more catastrophic, more enigmatic in its evil, more sudden and inexplicable in its outbreaks of violent chance. In the end, the image of heroic, moral action embedded in the traditional private-eye myth turns out to be totally inadequate to overcome the destructive realities revealed in the course of this story. This revelation of depths beneath depths is made increasingly evident in the film's relentless movement toward Chinatown, the symbolic locus of darkness, strangeness, and catastrophe; but it also appears in the film's manipulation of action and image. The themes of water and drought, which weave through the action, not only reveal the scope of Noah Cross's conspiracy to dominate a city by manipulating its water supply, but create a texture of allusion that resonates with the mythical meanings traditionally associated with water and drought. Polanski's version of Los Angeles in the 1930s reveals the transcendent mythical world of the sterile kingdom, the dying king, and the drowned man beneath it—the world, for example, of Eliot's *The*

Waste Land and before that of the cyclical myths of traditional cultures. Another of the film's motifs, its revelation of the rape-incest by which Noah Cross has fathered a daughter on his own daughter and is apparently intending to continue this method of establishing a progeny through the agency of his daughter-granddaughter, is another of the ways in which the hard-boiled myth is thrust into depths beyond itself. Though traditionally an erotically potent figure, the private eye's sexuality seems gentility itself when confronted with the potent perversity embodied in the figure of Noah Cross. Cross is reminiscent of the primal father imagined by Freud in *Totem and Taboo,* but against his overpowering sexual, political, and economic power, our hero-Oedipus in the form of J. J. Gittes proves to be tragically impotent, an impotence symbolized earlier in the film by the slashing of his nose and the large comic bandage he wears throughout much of the action.

In its manipulation of a traditional American popular myth and the revelation of the tragic inadequacy of this myth when it collides with a universe that is deeper and more enigmatic in its evil and destructive force, *Chinatown* is one of the richest and most artistically powerful instances of a type of film of which we have seen many striking instances in the last decade. It is difficult to know just what to call this type of film. On one level, it relates to the traditional literary mode of burlesque or parody in which a well-established set of conventions or a style is subjected to some form of ironic or humorous exploitation. Indeed, many of the most striking and successful films of the period have been out-and-out burlesques of traditional popular genres, such as Mel Brooks's *Blazing Saddles* (1974, westerns), his *Young Frankenstein* (1974, the Frankenstein horror cycle), and his *High Anxiety* (1977, Hitchcock's psychological suspense films). However, burlesque and parody embody a basically humorous thrust, and many of the most powerful generic variations of the last decade or so—films like *Bonnie and Clyde* (Arthur Penn, 1967), *The Wild Bunch* (Sam Peckinpah, 1968), *The Godfather* (Francis Ford Coppola, 1972), and *Nashville* (Robert Altman, 1975)—tend more toward tragedy than comedy in their overall structures. It seems odd to speak of a tragic parody or a doomed burlesque. Therefore, one is at first tempted to conclude that the connection between *Blazing Saddles* and *The Wild Bunch,* or *The Black Bird* (David Giler, 1975) and *The Long Goodbye* (Altman, 1973) is only superficial. Yet it is clear that in many of these films the line between comedy and tragedy is not so simply drawn. What, for example, of the extraordinary combination of Keystone Cops chase scenes and tragic carnage in *Bonnie and Clyde,* or the interweaving of sophomoric high jinks and terrible violence in Altman's *M*A*S*H* (1970)? This puzzling combination of humorous burlesque and high seriousness seems to be a mode of expression characteristic of our period, not only in film, but

36. *Young Frankenstein:* A burlesque of the Frankenstein horror cycle.

in other literary forms. It is at the root of much that is commonly described as the literature of the absurd or of so-called black humor, and is,
as well, characteristic of the style of major contemporary novelists like
Thomas Pynchon. By adopting this mode, American movies have, in a
sense, become a more integral part of the mainstream of postmodernist
literature, just as, through their frequent allusion to the narrative conventions of American film, contemporary novelists and dramatists have created a new kind of relationship between themselves and the traditions of
popular culture.

The linkage between these many different kinds of contemporary literary, dramatic, and cinematic expression is their use of the conventions of
traditional popular genres. Basically, they do in different ways what Polanski does in *Chinatown:* set the elements of a conventional popular
genre in an altered context, thereby making us perceive these traditional
forms and images in a new way. It appears to me that we can classify the
various relationships between traditional generic elements and altered
contexts into four major modes.

First, there is the burlesque proper. In this mode, elements of a conventional formula or style are situated in contexts so incongruous or exaggerated that the result is laughter. There are many different ways in which this can be done. The formulaic elements can be acted out in so extreme a fashion that they come into conflict with our sense of reality, forcing us to see these aspects of plot and character as fantastic contrivances. A good example of this is the burlesque image of the gunfighter in *Cat Ballou* (Elliott Silverstein, 1965). In this film we are shown how, by putting on his gunfighter costume, a process that involves strapping himself into a corset within which he can barely move, an old drunk can become the terror of the bad guys. Or, in a closely related type of altered context, a situation that we are ordinarily accustomed to seeing in rather romanticized terms can be suddenly invested with a sense of reality. This is how the famous campfire scene in *Blazing Saddles* operates. The cowboys sit around a blazing campfire at night, a scene in which we are accustomed to hearing mournful and lyrical cowboy ballads performed by such groups as the Sons of the Pioneers. Instead we are treated to an escalating barrage of flatulence. Anyone who knows the usual effect of canned wilderness fare is likely to be delighted at this sudden exposure of the sham involved in the traditional western campfire scene. Sam Peckinpah's *Ride the High Country* (1962) offers another instance of the humorous effect of the sudden penetration of reality into a fantasy when one of his aging heroes attempts to spring gracefully into the saddle and is suddenly halted by a twinge of rheumatism.

In addition to these sudden confrontations with "reality," conventional patterns can be turned into laughter by inverting them. A good example of this is the device of turning a character who shows all the marks of a hero into a coward, or vice versa. A favorite manifestation of this in recent films and novels is what might be called the hard-boiled schlemiel, the private detective who turns out to be totally unable to solve a crime or resist villains except by accident. This type of burlesque is even more effective when the inverted presentation actually seems to bring out some latent meanings that were lurking all the time in the original convention. Mel Brooks is a particular master of this kind of burlesque. In his *Young Frankenstein,* the monster attacks Frankenstein's fiancée Elizabeth—a moment of tragic violence in the original novel—and the result is complete sexual satisfaction on both sides, something most of us had suspected all along.

These two primary techniques of burlesque, the breaking of convention by the intrusion of reality and the inversion of expected implications, have frequently appeared in the history of literature as a response to highly conventionalized genres. Just as the Greek tragedies gave rise to their burlesque counterparts in the plays of Aristophanes, the western, one of our most formally distinctive genres, has been the inspiration of parody and burlesque throughout its history from Twain and Harte's assaults on James Fenimore Cooper to Brooks's send-up of *Shane* and *High Noon*. Thus, there is nothing particularly new in the penchant toward humorous burlesque so evident in recent films. What is more striking in the films of the last decade is their use of these techniques of generic parody for ultimately serious purposes.

The second major mode of generic transformation is the cultivation of nostalgia. In this mode, traditional generic features of plot, character, setting, and style are deployed to recreate the aura of a past time. The power of nostalgia lies especially in its capacity to evoke a sense of warm reassurance by bringing before our mind's eye images from a time when things seemed more secure and full of promise and possibility. Though one can, of course, evoke nostalgia simply by viewing films of the past, a contemporary nostalgia film cannot simply duplicate the past experience, but must make us aware in some fashion of the relationship between past and present. Attempts to evoke nostalgia merely by imitating past forms, as was the case with the television series *City of Angels,* do not generally work because they seem simply obsolescent. A truly successful nostalgia film—like Henry Hathaway's *True Grit* (1969), one of the last highly popular westerns—succeeds because it set its highly traditional generic content in a slightly different context, thereby giving us both a sense of contemporaneity and of pastness. In *True Grit,* this was done in a number of ways. First of all, the central character played by Kim Darby represented an extremely contemporary image of adolescent girlhood. She was independent, aggressive, and full of initiative, a shrewd horse trader and a self-confident, insistent moralist, unlike the shy desert rose of the traditional western. John Wayne, aging and paunchy, did not attempt to cover up the ravages of the years and reaffirm without change the vigorous manhood of his earlier films. Instead, with eyepatch, unshaven face, and sagging flesh, he fully enacted his aging. Similarly, the film's images of the western landscape were in many ways deromanticized. But out of this context of contemporaneity there sprang the same old story of adventure and heroism culminating in an exuberant shoot-out that seemed to embody everybody's best dreams of Saturday matinees. The same quality of nostalgic reinvocation of the past played an even more powerful role in Peckinpah's *Ride the High Country,* in which two tired, aging, and obsolescent heroes ride again, and in Dick Richards's recent version of Raymond Chandler's *Farewell, My Lovely* (1975), where a sagging Robert Mitchum moves out of the malaise of modernity and reenacts once more the ambiguous heroic quest of the hard-boiled detective of the 1930s and 1940s.

The difference between nostalgic reincarnation of an earlier genre like

37. John Wayne as the Ringo Kid in *Stagecoach* . . .

Farewell, My Lovely and the more complex ironies of *Chinatown* and Robert Altman's *The Long Goodbye* is considerable. It is a difference similar to the one between *True Grit* and neowesterns like Altman's *McCabe and Mrs. Miller* (1971) or Arthur Penn's *Little Big Man* (1970). In the former case, nostalgia is the end result of the film. In the latter nostalgia is often powerfully evoked, but as a means of undercutting or ironically commenting upon the generic experience itself. This brings us to the third and, in many respects, the most powerful mode of generic transformation in recent films: the use of traditional generic structures as a means of demythologization. A film like *Chinatown* deliberately invokes the basic characteristics of a traditional genre in order to bring its audience to see that genre as the embodiment of an inadequate and destructive myth. We have seen how this process of demythologization operates in *Chinatown* by setting the traditional model of the hard-boiled detective's quest for justice and integrity over and against Polanski's sense of a universe so steeped in ambiguity, corruption, and evil that such individualistic moral enterprises are doomed by their innocent naiveté to end in tragedy and self-destruction.

38. . . . and as Rooster Cogburn in *True Grit.*

The work of Arthur Penn has also explored the ironic and tragic aspects of the myths implicit in traditional genres. His *Night Moves* (1975), a transformation of the detective story, was, like *Chinatown,* the ambiguous enactment of a reluctant quest for the truth about a series of crimes. As the detective approaches a solution to the crimes, he becomes morally and emotionally involved in the quest, making it more and more difficult for him to integrate truth, feeling, and morality. In the end, like Polanski's Jake Gittes, he is more dazed than fulfilled by the catastrophe his investigation has brought about.

In other films, such as *The Left-Handed Gun* (1958), *Bonnie and Clyde,* and *Little Big Man,* Penn created a version of the western or the gangster film in which traditional meanings were inverted, but the effect was tragic rather than humorous. In *Little Big Man,* for example, the conventional western opposition between Indians and pioneers serves as the basis of the plot, which embodies two of the most powerful of our western myths, the Indian captivity and the massacre. However, the con-

39. *Little Big Man:* Jack Crabbe (Dustin Hoffman) in his gunfighter phase.

ventional renderings of these myths pit the humanely civilizing thrust of
the pioneers against the savage ferocity and eroticism of the Indians and
thereby justify the conquest of the West. Penn reverses these implications.
In his film it is the Indians who are humane and civilized, while the pioneers are violent, corrupt, sexually repressed, and madly ambitious. By
the end, when Custer's cavalry rides forward to attack the Indian villages,
our sympathies are all with the Indians. From this perspective, the conquest of the West is demythologized from the triumph of civilization into
a historical tragedy of the destruction of a rich and vital human culture.

   Despite its many virtues, the film version of *Little Big Man* was less
artistically successful than Thomas Berger's novel, on which it was based,
primarily because as the film proceeds, Penn loses the ironic detachment
that Berger successfully maintains throughout the novel. Penn's portrayal
of Custer as a lunatic symbol of aggressive American imperialism is over-

stated, and toward the end the cinematic *Little Big Man* tends to fall back from the serious exploration of mythical meanings into melodramatic burlesque. This is an artistic problem common to films in the mode of demythologization of traditional genres. Penn was far more successful in *Bonnie and Clyde,* which will remain one of the major masterpieces of recent American film. Taking off from the traditional gangster film with its opposition between the outlaw and society, *Bonnie and Clyde* establishes a dialectic between conventional and inverted meanings that is far richer and more powerfully sustained throughout the film. In the traditional gangster film, a powerful individual, frustrated by the limitations of his lower-class origin, is driven to a life of crime. Initially the audience is inclined to sympathize and identify with this character, but as he becomes involved in criminal actions, he overreaches himself and becomes a vicious killer who must be tracked down and destroyed by the representatives of society. The underlying myth of this genre affirms the limits of individual aggression in a society that tolerates and even encourages a high degree of personal enterprise and violence. The gangster becomes a tragic figure not because he is inherently evil, but because he fails to recognize these limits. The myth assures us that society is not repressive or violent; instead it shows how criminal violence evokes its own inevitable doom.

It is this comforting myth of proper and improper violence that Penn demythologizes in *Bonnie and Clyde.* As in *Little Big Man,* meanings become inverted. Instead of representing a limit to aggression and violence, society is portrayed as its fountainhead, while the outlaw protagonists are seen as victims of society's bloodlust. Throughout the film, we are shown a society of depression and chaos that yearns for action, and projects this yearning into a vicarious excitement about the robberies and murders of the Barrow gang. Penn effectively develops this theme through his representation of the newspapers which so avidly report the gang's adventures and by the reactions of witnesses to the gang's attacks on banks. Finally, its lust for the hunt aroused, society itself takes up the pursuit in packs and posses, and, in a final ambush that set a new level in explicit screen violence, the doomed Bonnie and Clyde are shot to pieces. But the inversion of generic meanings is still more complex, for Penn refuses to make the opposition between gangster and society a simple reversal of traditional generic meanings as he does in *Little Big Man.* The protagonists of *Bonnie and Clyde* are not simply victims of society. They are themselves very much a part of the society they are attacking. They share its basic aspirations and confusions, and they yearn above all to be reintegrated with it. In many respects, their actions reflect a desperate and misconceived attempt to achieve some measure of the status, security, and sense of belonging that ought to be among the basic gifts of a society to its members. Instead of simply reversing the meanings conventionally ascribed to the opposing forces of criminal and society in the gangster genre, *Bonnie and Clyde* expressed a more complex and dark awareness that this basic opposition was itself a mythical simplification, and showed us the deeper and more difficult irony of the twisted and inseparable fates of individuals and their society. This was in its way a recognition of that skein of ambiguous inevitability which Polanski summed up in the symbol of Chinatown and which Francis Ford Coppola developed through the fateful intertwining of individuals, "families," and society in *The Godfather.*

Though the demythologization of traditional genres has been primarily evident in the work of younger directors, it has also had some influence on the later work of some of the classic filmmakers, most noticeably perhaps in the later westerns of John Ford, particularly *The Searchers* (1956), *Cheyenne Autumn* (1964), and *The Man Who Shot Liberty Valance* (1962). Indeed, in the last-named film, Ford symbolized the conquest of the West through a story in which the territory's last major outlaw was killed in a shootout by a man destined to lead the territory into the blessings of civilization. In fact, the legend of Senator Stoddard's heroic deed was a myth, the actual shooting of Liberty Valance having been done by another man. Toward the end of the film, the newspaper editor to whom Senator Stoddard confesses the truth about his past makes the famous and ambiguous comment, "When the legend becomes a fact, print the legend." But is this an ironic comment on the falsity of legends and newspapers alike, or is it some kind of affirmation of the significance of myth in spite of its unreality? Ford was apparently inclined to the latter interpretation, for he once told Peter Bogdanovich, "We've had a lot of people who were supposed to be great heroes and you know damn well they weren't. But it's good for the country to have heroes to look up to." [1]

This brings us to a fourth and final mode of generic transformation that might be described as the affirmation of myth for its own sake. In films in this mode, a traditional genre and its myth are probed and shown to be unreal, but then the myth itself is at least partially affirmed as a reflection of authentic human aspirations and needs. This is the element that becomes dominant in Ford's later westerns, in which he seems to see the heroic ethos of the West in critical terms and becomes more and more sympathetic with the Indian victims of the westward movement. Yet, at the same time that he became more cynical about the reality of the West, he seemed to feel even more strongly the need to affirm its heroic ideals. Thus, in his powerful late film *The Searchers,* Ford turns to the old western theme of Indian captivity, portraying the mad obsessive hatred with which a white man pursues a band of Indians who have captured and adopted his niece. Yet Ford also accepted a change in the ending of the original novel, where this mad Indian-hater was finally destroyed by his obsession, in order to reaffirm at the end the heroism and self-sacrifice of this obsessive quest. *The Searchers* is a powerful and beautiful film, yet one feels uncomfortable at the end, as if the gap between Ford's sense of historical reality and his feelings about genre and myth have come into collision.

Sam Peckinpah's *The Wild Bunch,* for all its ugliness and violence, is a more coherent example of the destruction and reaffirmation of myth. Throughout the film, Peckinpah points up the gap between the conventional western's heroic struggle between pioneers and outlaws. His pioneer lawmen are despicable bounty hunters in the employ of the railroad, and they kill the guilty and the innocent indiscriminately. His outlaws are not much better; they are brutal, coarse, and quite capable of leaving a wounded comrade behind. Moreover, their type of criminal operation has become absurdly obsolescent in the early twentieth-century West of the film. In the end, Peckinpah's outlaw protagonists are drawn into a ridiculously destructive shoot-out with an entire Mexican village full of troops and are completely wiped out in the process. Yet the film also leaves us with a sense that through their hopeless action these coarse and vicious outlaws have somehow transcended themselves and become embodiments of a myth of heroism that people need in spite of the realities of their world.

While I have separated the four modes of generic transformation—humorous burlesque, evocation of nostalgia, demythologization of generic myth, and the reaffirmation of myth as myth—into separate categories in order to define them more clearly, most films that employ one of these modes are likely to use another at some point. Probably the best films based on generic transformation employ some combination of several of these modes in the service of one overriding artistic purpose; *Chinatown* uses both humorous burlesque and nostalgic evocation as a basis for its devastating exploration of the genre of the hard-boiled detective and his myth. Some directors seem to have a primary predilection for one of these modes; Brooks is primarily oriented toward burlesque, Bogdanovich toward nostalgia, Penn toward demythologization, and Peckinpah toward reaffirmation. Some directors—Robert Altman springs particularly to mind—have, in their best films, worked out a rich and fascinating dialectic between different modes of generic transformation. In films like *McCabe and Mrs. Miller, The Long Goodbye, Thieves Like Us* (1974), and *Nashville* it is quite difficult to decide at the end whether Altman is attacking or reaffirming the genre on which he has based each particular work. In fact, until the last two or three years, Altman's filmography has looked almost as if he had planned a systematic voyage through the major traditional film genres. That generic transformation has been so important a source of artistic energy to the most vital younger directors suggests that it is a central key to the current state of the American film.

There are probably many reasons for the importance of these modes of filmmaking in the last decade, but in conclusion I will comment briefly on what seem to me the most important factors involved in the proliferation of this kind of film. I think it is not primarily the competition of television. Though television has been somewhat more conservative in its use of generic transformation than film, the same modes seem to be turning up with increasing frequency in television series. Instead I would point to the tendency of genres to exhaust themselves, to our growing historical awareness of modern popular culture, and finally, to the decline of the underlying mythology on which traditional genres have been based since the late nineteenth century. Generic exhaustion is a common phenomenon in the history of culture. One can almost make out a life cycle characteristic of genres as they move from an initial period of articulation and discovery, through a phase of conscious self-awareness on the part of both creators and audiences, to a time when the generic patterns have become so well-known that people become tired of their predictability. It is at this point that parodic and satiric treatments proliferate and new genres gradually arise. Our major traditional genres—the western, the detective story, the musical, the domestic comedy—have, after all, been around for a considerable period of time, and it may be that they have simply reached a point of creative exhaustion.

In our time, the awareness of the persistence of genres has been intensified by an increasing historical awareness of film. A younger generation of directors has a sense of film history quite different from many of their predecessors who, like Ford and Hawks, were involved with the art of film almost from its beginnings. Similarly, audiences have a kind of sophistication about the history of genres different from earlier film publics because of the tremendous number of past films now regularly shown on television and by college film societies.

But I am inclined to think that there is more to it than that. The present significance of generic transformation as a creative mode reflects the feeling that not only the traditional genres but the cultural myths they once embodied are no longer fully adequate to the imaginative needs of our time. It will require another essay to explain and justify this assertion, but if I may hazard a final prediction, I think we will begin to see emerging out of this period of generic transformation a new set of generic constructs more directly related to the imaginative landscape of the second half of the twentieth century. Thus, the present period of American filmmaking will seem in retrospect an important time of artistic and cultural transition. Like many transition periods, it may also turn out to be a time of the highest artistic accomplishment.

Note

1. Quoted in Jon Tuska, *The Filming of the West* (Garden City: Doubleday, 1976), p. 519.

16. Shoot-Out at the Genre Corral: Problems in the "Evolution" of the Western

TAG GALLAGHER

"The Western," writes Thomas Schatz in *Hollywood Genres*, "is with-out question the richest and most enduring genre of Hollywood's reper-toire."[1] Without question it has been the richest and most enduring genre for genre critics as well. Certain writings on the western, however—notably works by Robert Warshow, John G. Cawelti, Philip French, Jack Nachbar, Will Wright, Frank D. McConnell, Leo Braudy, and Thomas Schatz[2]—have, it seems to me, been marred by flaws in theory and prac-tice so similar that, despite the scholarly illumination these writers have otherwise cast upon the western, their similar flaws reflect upon genre criticism itself.

Genre criticism has tended to ignore the evidence.

"There is," writes French, "general agreement that . . . the Western has changed significantly since World War II, becoming more varied, com-plex, and self conscious."[3] But French, concerned mostly with post-1950 westerns, offers no supporting evidence for changes, and the other seven critics, although they concur, fail as well to defend this position. "Of course," asserts McConnell, "artistic forms evolve under their own impe-tus, and it was inevitable that sooner or later the Western film should have achieved the self-consciousness [of 1959]."[4] The western's "ritualistic af-firmations of progress and success become more and more ambiguous and strained," claims Cawelti.[5] "In most contemporary Westerns . . . he-roes are no longer necessarily heroic, the civilized no longer necessarily civilized," states Nachbar, in comparison to the past.[6] "Even the horses," sighs Warshow, "grow tired and stumble more often than they did."[7]

   Probably no one makes stronger claims for the western's "evolution" than Schatz. After citing Christian Metz to the effect that westerns, from 1939 to 1959 or so, progressed, as audiences and filmmakers grew in-creasingly "self-conscious," from "classic" treatments, to "parody," to "contestation" (straining the conventions), to "deconstruction" (self-critiquing the conventions), Schatz draws an analogy with Henri Focillon's observation that styles in art pass through various clear stages: the *experimental,* when stylistic conventions become established; the *classical,* when they have been accepted by the public; *refinement,* when style becomes more elaborate; and *mannerist,* when style becomes self-reflective.[8] Schatz feels that genres evolve similarly to styles. Although he does not detail the evolution of the western through four phases, his perceptions of differences between later (c. post-1950) and earlier westerns resemble those of the seven other genre critics and are basically three in number: (1) the later western projects a less optimistic and more unflattering vision of the West's potential synthesis of nature and culture; (2) the western hero, once an agent of law and order, has become a renegade, a professional killer, an antihero, neurotic, psychotic, less integratable into a synthesis; (3) the later western is less simple, tidy, and naive, more ambiguous, complex, and ironic, more self-critical and into the "art of telling."

It is a curious testament to the continued vitality of the western that Warshow back in 1954 found differences between early-1950s and prewar westerns almost identical to those which critics like Schatz and company detect a quarter-century later between westerns of the 1970s and early 1950s. Perhaps older westerns, like olden times, will always strike the modern mind as less complex, less amoral, and above all less vivid— particularly when the modern mind feels it unnecessary to examine the past in any detail. Collectively, our octet of genre critics evinces only the scantiest acquaintance with 1939–1940 prewar westerns, and infinitely less acquaintance with earlier and silent westerns. "In earlier Westerns," writes Braudy, apparently referring back to 1939, "while basics of the form were being worked out"—in 1939?!—"the issues were more patterned and the individual played a more stereotyped role."[9] In any other academic discipline one would suppose that Braudy's authority for such a statement rested upon a judicious survey of the more than five thousand westerns made before World War II; in actual fact, however, there is no such authority and Braudy's phrase smacks of pure conjecture. Wright's is the most rigorous evolutionary essay, purporting to examine westerns from 1931 through 1972, but, having already excluded the first thirty-five years of western cinema, Wright then disqualifies from his study any western that has not grossed at least $4,000,000. Not surprisingly, given inflation in ticket prices from 10¢ to $4.00, of Wright's sixty-four sample films only three were made before 1939, while fifty-eight were made since the war. Wright's survey is obviously inadequate. Western buffs might further object that blockbuster westerns tend to be unrepresentative of the genre in any case—is this true?—and that Wright would have done better to have considered only westerns that grossed *under,* say, $500,000.

Every argument that evolution exists at all comes down not to evidence mustered through representative sampling but either to bald assertions or to invidious comparisons between a couple of titles—a "classic" western versus a "self-conscious" western—selected specifically to illustrate the assertion. A film is considered "classic" when it matches a critic's paradigm of the ideal western. But the paradigm is entirely arbitrary, with the result that there is some disagreement about which pictures are "classic" and which have evolved astray. Warshow, for example, is intent on showing how the 1943 *Ox-Bow Incident* (William Wellman), the 1950 *Gunfighter* (Henry King), and the 1952 *High Noon* (Fred Zinnemann) transformed the primeval western into a vehicle for social criticism, in comparison with Victor Fleming's naively archetypal 1929 *Virginian*. Thus he found an "unhealthy preoccupation with style," an "aestheticizing tendency," in *Stagecoach* (John Ford, 1939), *My Darling Clementine* (Ford, 1946), and *Shane* (George Stevens, 1954) that he felt "violat[ed] the Western form." [10] Later genre critics regard the last three pictures as "classic" and regard as "self-conscious" movies such as *The Man Who Shot Liberty Valance* (Ford, 1962), *Hour of the Gun* (John Sturges, 1967), *Chisum* (Andrew V. McLaglen, 1970), and *The Wild Bunch* (Sam Peckinpah, 1969).

In sum, while it is undoubtedly true that each age's westerns reflect each age, and that westerns of recent years, *like almost every film made,* evince sorts of violence, pornography, and cynicism that probably were not present to the same degree in the same ways during the 1940s, little evidence has been brought forward to support the theory that there has been growing "self-consciousness"—or any other sort of linear evolution—in and specific to the western. Indeed, the evidence has not even been considered. So perhaps the opposite is true.

Schatz asserts that "the earliest Westerns (many of which actually depicted then-current events) obviously were based on social and historical reality. But as the genre developed, it gradually took on its own reality." [11] This may be obvious, but is it true? Granted, *The Great Train Robbery* (Edwin S. Porter, 1902) has reference to a current event (although note that even in this case an antihero is being glorified and the use of the antihero's close-up firing, outside of the movie's diegesis, at the audience constitutes a species of self-reflexivity); but no such basis was required in 1904 and 1905, when the only historical reality in many westerns was their conventionality. The bulk of westerns in this period were—like the very first western novels—produced for European markets, mostly by European film companies, and romantic myth rather than reality, current or otherwise, was the standard. In fact, so popular were westerns during narrative cinema's formative years (1903–1911) that it may well be that, rather than the cinema having invented the western, it was the western, already long existent in popular culture, that invented the cinema. Picturesque scenery, archetypal characters, dialectical story construction, long

40. *The Great Train Robbery:* The bandit fires at the audience.

shots, close-ups, parallel editing, confrontational cross-cutting, montaged chases—all were explicit in the western before the Lumières cranked their first camera. By 1909, and during the next six years, there were probably more westerns released *each* month than during the entire decade of the 1930s. Hyperconsciousness of the genre resulted. Almost all the observations of our octet of genre critics were commonplace in pre–World War I writings on the western. More subtly, westerns were then divided into quite distinct subgenres, each of which was known to possess its own specific conventions—among them, frontier dramas, Indian dramas, Civil War dramas, western comedies. Not only did the mode of exhibition (the average theater changing its bill frequently, the average moviegoer attending several times per week) and the mode of criticism (a host of thick weekly trade and popular magazines reviewing every new release, along with lengthy plot summaries) encourage both generic consciousness and self-consciousness, but so did the mode of production: each "studio" was subdivided into semiautonomous troupes, so that a core group of director, writer, cameraman, and actors worked together regularly and were expected to turn out one, sometimes two, new pictures (fifteen to sixty minutes long) each week. Instruction booklets, moreover, were available by mail order for nascent scenarists, in which all the basic plots and their many variations within each genre were carefully outlined.

Anything novel was instantly seized upon and copied voraciously. Will Wright in 1975 proposes as fresh insight "my argument . . . that within each period the structure of the [western] myth corresponds to the conceptual needs of social and self understanding required by the dominant social institutions of that period," but no one thought otherwise back in 1913. Any news event or fashion trend—labor actions, bloomers, Apaches, prohibition, female suffrage, Balkan crises, and a myriad of forgotten issues of the day—were zealously incorporated not only into westerns but into whatever other genres were currently popular, the western hero and the nature of his struggles altering accordingly.

The actual number of genres was considerably greater in these years than at any time since, and there was far more awareness of generic specificities: each new picture was labeled as belonging to a given genre by its producers and in the trade journals. Exhibitors, critics, and filmmakers grumbled constantly about the hackneyed versus the original, the stale versus the new, in character, story, and theme. No one complained in 1956 when a baddy's presence in *Rio Bravo* (Howard Hawks) is revealed when his blood drips down from the floor above; but when the same gag was used back in 1918 in Ford's *The Scarlet Drop* it was contemptuously dismissed as "old hat" by *Exhibitors' Trade Review*.

Schatz, along with his colleagues, assumes that the earliest westerns were somehow more realistic, primitive, and unself-conscious. But, quite the contrary, "realism" was a big issue in 1907 because people thought that the western was too much a parody and concerned only with its own conventions. Some years later, William S. Hart was campaigning against, and Harry Carey was spoofing, the dandy cowboy hero represented by Bronco Billy, Tom Mix, and others. Carey, in 1919, talked longingly about wanting to "Jack Londonize the Western cowboy—that is, present him as he really is in life . . . totally unlike the one we see in [movies]. He has his distinctive characteristics and they are amusing enough without exaggeration." [12] Without exaggeration, clichés are already an issue. Self-reflexivity in the early teens was often evident as well in the form of films within films: characters frequently fall asleep and dream, friends deceive friends with elaborate masquerades (put-on kidnappings and the like), Remington paintings (as in Ford's 1918 *Hell Bent*) come alive in an onlooker's fantasy—all methods of critiquing generic conventions. In fact, so familiar had western conventions become by 1913 that Universal announced its despair of ever again doing anything new, and—two years before Griffith's *The Birth of a Nation*—said it was giving up frontier, Indian, and Civil War pictures.[13]

Heroes before World War I evince many of the complex, "self-conscious" qualities Schatz and Braudy assign to the evolved western. The "double" character Braudy traces from *Jesse James* (Henry King) in 1940[14] was of course the basis of innumerable "good badmen" heroes in early Ford (most of Harry Carey's roles in 25 Ford pictures, as well as those of other directors), Anderson (Bronco Billy), Ince (William S. Hart), and others. In the remarkable series of 101-Bison westerns initiated by Thomas Ince and Francis Ford in 1912, heroes were almost routinely ambivalent, endings unresolved, and visions tragic. In fact, tragic endings were quite modish before the war, but by 1919 the weather vane had clearly shifted away from the morally daring and innovative hero. *Exhibitors' Trade Review* (November 21, 1918) sternly lectured Harry Carey for "consistently portray[ing] a rough character throughout [Ford's *Three Mounted Men*]. The only wonder of it is that anyone should attempt to heroize such a type. There may be such men in the west, but it is best on the screen to show them up as horrible examples of what a man may be." The change in audience and producer attitudes after World War I is typified, I suspect,[15] by the case of Ford's *Straight Shooting,* in which, as originally issued in 1917, the hero, a hired killer who finds his conscience in the film's course, declines to settle down with the woman who loves him and goes off into the sunset instead. When the picture was rereleased in 1925, however, its title was changed to *Straight Shootin'* (parody?), and the hero, by dint of some clumsy reediting, is made to accept marriage.[16]

It is surprising that none of our genre critics, well-armed as each of them is with battalions of analytic theory gleaned from literary studies, psychology, anthropology, communications, sociology, and political science, seems aware of the rich roles played by genre films in the years before World War I. Immense research into actual movies, or at least into surviving accounts of them, ought, one would think, to precede attempts to theorize their development. Yet the teens and preteens are not the only periods of cinema history of which our knowledge is vague and our cant deceptive. My own glance at the pre–World War I western—cursory, superficial, and undetailed as it is—nonetheless suggests strongly that, while a genre does reflect its era, no such evolutionary process as described by Metz or our octet of critics has ever occurred in which, because audiences and filmmakers demand variations, reexaminations, more complications, and stylistic embellishments, a form is first established and then elaborated upon.[17]

Quite the contrary, pictures such as *Stagecoach, Shane,* or *The Searchers* (John Ford, 1956), even *Once Upon a Time in the West* (Sergio Leone,

1968) show that audiences respond forcibly to stark apotheoses of the genre's most primeval elements—even, in the case of *Star Wars* (George Lucas, 1977), after eighty years of repetition. "Self-consciousness" is too readily assumed to have come to movies only in reaction against Holly-wood's so-called "classic codes" (whose existence, never demonstrated, is at least to be questioned), while such consciousness has traditionally been considered a necessary ingredient of any mature work of art and would certainly seem to be abundant in pictures of the 1930s, where style, far from being "invisible," is so overwhelming. It is perhaps natural that people today, attuned to contemporary film styles and only vaguely ac-quainted with the past, should feel they are onto something new when in an ostentatiously revisionist film by Robert Altman (*McCabe and Mrs. Miller,* 1971, or *Buffalo Bill and the Indians,* 1976) they perceive references to motifs and conventions from other westerns made twenty or thirty years earlier and thus cast forcibly into a "straight man's" role for the revisionist's lampooning. But they forget that even such putatively na-ive classics as *Stagecoach* were similarly perceived by audiences in 1939; indeed, *Stagecoach* in particular is a virtual anthology of gags, motifs, conventions, scenes, situations, tricks, and characters drawn from past westerns, but each one pushed toward fresh intensities of mythic ex-tremism, thus consciously revisiting not only the old West but old west-erns as well, and reinterpreting at the same time these elements for mod-ern minds.

A superficial glance at film history suggests cyclicism rather than evolu-tion. Despair and an appetite for realism were modish before World War I, escapism and genuinely happy endings became mandatory after the war. Films were moody and depressed during the early years of the De-pression, when both surrealism and realism were in fashion; then with the censorship codes of 1934 films turned escapist and during the next ten years were awesomely repressed. A demonic period after World War II precedes a mingling of optimism and anguish in the 1950s, followed by extremism and schizophrenia in the 1960s, escapism mingling with se-rious concern in the late 1970s and 1980s. It would be easy to cite apt examples for each period; but it would be just as easy to cite exceptions. But nothing suggests the western changed separately from film produc-tion as a whole.

Genre critics tend to be unsympathetic to the subtleties of "old" movies.

Like neo-Wagnerites who loved Mozart and Haydn only for their sweet-ness, "modernist"-inclined genre critics tend to love "old" movies only for their supposed naiveté. In misinterpreting these pictures—by failing to grasp the subtleties of so-called "classic" styles and the conventions of earlier decades—while yet using these pictures as the "fall guys" for invidious comparisons, these genre critics necessarily misperceive the history of the cinema.

Stagecoach (1939) and *My Darling Clementine* (1946) are among the pictures used most frequently as antipodes to the recent western, and Schatz uses these pictures within Ford's career to exemplify an alleged evolution. But how do Schatz and his colleagues regard these movies?

Nachbar, for example, begins his essay by stating that Wyatt Earp's motives are "very clear" in *My Darling Clementine:* he has "both the right and the duty to kill the Clantons [who killed Earp's two brothers and stole his cattle]. It is no surprise, then, that after the famous battle, Earp is recognized as the hero of the community and will soon be rewarded by wedding the lovely maiden from the East, Clementine Carter." In contrast, in *Hour of the Gun* (John Sturges, 1967), Wyatt "contemptuously hides under the law to satisfy his near-psychotic lust for violent revenge. Obviously between 1946 and 1967 there were some important changes in the legend of Wyatt Earp." [18]

The problem is that Nachbar misreads Earp's character as badly as he misreads *My Darling Clementine*'s plot.[19] The films of the sixties had to work harder, had to be more strident and dissonant, in order to try to express the same notions as earlier films. Eroticism, for example, has not necessarily increased along with nudity, although it may seem to have, for those incapable of getting emotionally involved with the types of people in 1930s films. Similarly, violence and ugliness do not necessarily increase as they are denuded. In the case of Ford's Wyatt Earp, charm hides a self-righteous prig, and a marshal's badge and noble sentiments hide a "near-psychotic lust for violent revenge" even from Earp himself; but this upstanding Wyatt is all the more ambivalently complex a character for the sublimation of his hypocrisy and violence. Schatz, who like Nachbar sees Wyatt as a naive archetype, describes him as a stoic, laconic militarist who uses force only when necessary and disdains Holliday's penchant for gunplay.[20] But Wyatt clearly relishes lording it over people without using his gun, and Ford is far too much of a moralist to accept Earp simply as a "redeemer" (Schatz) who has an unequivocal "right and duty to kill" (Nachbar). Wyatt, in any case, morally abdicates his "right to kill" when, just before the battle, he declines the assistance of the town mayor and parson, calling his feud with the Clantons "strictly a family affair"; he is thus left only with "duty" to kill—that is, vengeance duty. Duty, however, as a myopic, negative quality, is an obsessive theme throughout Ford's oeuvre, while the major theme of *My Darling Clementine* is wrapped around musing over whether one can ever have the right or duty to kill, whether one should "be or not be" (i.e., the staging of Shakespeare's *Hamlet* soliloquy), and the fearsome cost wreaked by vengeance: Wyatt loses a second brother in trying to avenge the first; Chihuahua and Doc Holliday also perish amid Wyatt's efforts. Contrary to Nachbar, there is no recognition in the film of Wyatt as "hero of the community": Ford cuts directly from the battle's last death to Wyatt's solitary farewell to Clementine virtually outside of town. Nor is there any "reward" of a wedding: Wyatt has known Clementine only two days, the great love of her life has just been killed, and the forlorn feelings in the air—Wyatt must go to California and tell his father that two sons are dead—suggest he may never "pass through here again someday" (an intimation strengthened by the gone-forever "Clementine" song).[21]

The question, then, of whether heroes change in the 1960s is not as simple as some critics would have us believe. Perhaps heroes sometimes merely disappear, allowing, as they did at times during earlier decades, the fellows who play supporting roles to step to center stage. Perhaps heroes merely stop shaving. Ford's heroes, in any case, fail to act in accordance with the model Schatz proposes—that is, electing civilization in early westerns, choosing wilderness in later westerns, remaining distinct from either civilization or wilderness in still later westerns. Ford's heroes in *Three Bad Men* elect wilderness in 1926, as do the Ringo Kid in 1939, Wyatt Earp in 1946, and Cheyenne Harry in 1917. But John Wayne in *Three Godfathers* in 1948 and Ben Johnson in *Wagon Master* in 1950 choose civilization, while Ethan Edwards in *The Searchers* (1956) represents not wilderness but the purity of civilized values: he values home and family, loathes Indians, and execrates miscegenation. *The Man Who Shot Liberty Valance* shows the hero's surrender to civilization, the antihero's corruption by it.

Schatz bases much of his argument on an extended comparison between *Stagecoach* (1939) and *Liberty Valance* (1962). But to assume, as he does and as many people seem routinely to do, that *Stagecoach* proffers a more optimistic vision of synthesis between nature and civilization than does *Liberty Valance*—merely because Ringo and Dallas ride off into the sunrise to start their lives together in 1939, whereas Ranse and Hallie sadly recognize their failure at the end of their lives in 1962—is to ignore rather than perceive the conventions of the films' times.

First of all, it is never sufficiently acknowledged to what degree the much-maligned Hollywood "happy ending" during the whole Depression era, but markedly during the 1939–1941 years, is tacked onto narrative structures whose abysmally despairing logic the happy endings arbitrarily contradict. Deus ex machina conclusions patently escape the dismal messages that Mr. Smith is doomed in Washington, that the western dream has vanished completely from *Stagecoach*'s ramshackle frontier towns, that the Joad family has hopelessly disintegrated at the end of *The Grapes of Wrath* (Ford, 1940), that family and village are completely

41. *Stagecoach:* The intolerant ladies of the law and order league force the prostitute (Claire Trevor) to leave town.

destroyed at the end of *How Green Was My Valley* (Ford, 1941); even Dorothy's search for the Wizard of Oz fizzles out. What is my point? That these films, and many more, deliver the sorts of messages Schatz finds typical of evolved genres (messages questioning official ideology or generic expectations and values), but that by giving audiences tacked-on happy endings, producers provided *formal* satisfaction *plus* a telling interaction between form and message; whereas in the late 1960s and 1970s—when until *Breaking Away* (Peter Yates, 1979) it was difficult to find *any* happy ending or unneurotic film—aesthetic form was the mere maidservant of message: exactly the opposite of what Schatz contends. In short, *Stagecoach*'s vision is not optimistic merely because it has a sort of happy end tacked on.

Second, Ransom Stoddard in *Liberty Valance* spends a lifetime figuring out what everyone knows already in *Stagecoach*—that civilization is corrupting. In malodorous, dirty, sleazy Lordsburg and Tonto, full of the mean, intolerant, aggressive people inhabiting *Stagecoach,* one finds nothing of the idealism, progressivism, and enlightenment shared by virtually everyone in *Liberty Valance*'s Shinbone. As a hero, moreover,

Stagecoach's Ringo implies no solutions, no syntheses. He ignores society rather than confronting it; he is less an outlaw than oblivious, an unconscious god. Who else would nonchalantly save three bullets to kill three men? Naturally Ringo can pluck up Dallas and spirit her away to never-never land. But who of *us* resembles Ringo? How is *his* solution reason for optimism for us? We are neither outlaws, never-never land's gods, nor detachable from civilization. (In any case, far from representing a synthesis between nature and civilization, as Schatz contends, Ringo and Dallas are explicitly "saved from the blessings of civilization," as Doc tells the sheriff.) If we fantasize with Ringo, it is only because hope is more primal than reason.

My point in this section is not that I disagree with certain interpretations of certain films by certain genre critics, nor even that such interpretations *can* be questioned. My point is that in each case rich lodes of ambivalence are overlooked in order to bolster a specious argument that "classic" westerns are simple and naive. That genre critics tend to be oblivious, as I see it, to the complexities of "classic" westerns is perhaps due to a more deeply endemic flaw in their methodology.

Genre critics deal not with the phenomenon of cinema art but with a derived abstraction—narrative.

Taking the case of Ford, as Schatz does, it seems at first obvious that change has occurred over fifty years. But the more closely one looks, the less such change seems definable as an increase in self-consciousness, self-criticism, or pessimism, and the more it becomes difficult to specify *what* has changed, or even how. Granted, Ford's career closed with two blackly suicidal tragedies, *Cheyenne Autumn* (1964) and *7 Women* (1965), but are we entitled to conclude an *evolution* in his sensitivity on that account? Shakespeare, after all, ended with two happy idyllic romances, but we do not thereby conclude that he was repudiating *Hamlet* and *King Lear,* or even that his vision of life had changed. Actually, in Ford's case, his last picture would have been a comedy, *The Miracle of Merriford,* but his funding disappeared a week before shooting was to begin. And, in any case, Ford's oeuvre is arguably the most melancholic in the American cinema. Lost illusion, cynicism, tragedy, and moral trauma permeate his pictures—particularly during the decade before the war—as in *Air Mail* (1932), *Pilgrimage* (1933), *The Whole Town's Talking* (1935), *The Informer* (1935), *The Prisoner of Shark Island* (1936), *The Hurricane* (1937), *The Grapes of Wrath, Young Mr. Lincoln* (1939), and *How Green Was My Valley.* The sunny pictures of the early 1950s—*She Wore a Yellow Ribbon* (1949), *Wagon Master,* and *The Quiet Man* (1952)—are outstanding exceptions. And John Ford, finally, is the worst possible paradigm with which to attempt to illustrate the evolution of the western, for the cyclical alterations in Ford's vision and style occur regardless of the genre in which he is working. Since the "feel" and narrative structures of a given western will at any given date resemble closely those of the non-westerns, Schatz's and Braudy's arguments of some internally generated evolution specific to the western genre cannot be verified. And since the changes they note in all, not just Ford's, westerns over the decades resemble changes they do not note in all contemporaneous genres and non-genre films, their arguments tend to collapse.

Surely a great artist's powers become more acute during the artist's lifetime, at least in certain moments; but can the perturbations of soul that aestheticize great cinema be accounted for by plot twists? The human being is more than that, and so are movies. Whatever the ontology of cinematic art, it is certainly not, as Warshow describes the western, "an art form for connoisseurs, where the spectator derives his pleasure from the appreciation of minor variations within the working out of a pre-established order." [22] Really? Is my pleasure in loving a woman in my appreciation of her minor variations from other women? Do I enjoy a good dish of pasta through appreciating its variations from chop suey? Schatz apparently does: "Our ultimate goal is to discern a genre film's quality, its social and aesthetic value. To do this, we will attempt to see its relation to the various systems that inform it." [23] What of the *thing itself*? Granted, comparisons, classifications, contrasts may aid us, but is not their illumination ultimately peripheral to the work itself?

Alas. Every one of our octet of genre critics virtually equates *experience* of a movie with analytic apperception of its narrative! Everything that can be is abstracted into literature. An "icon" is catalogued, and immediately is stripped of its iconicity and transformed into a verbal symbol. "A white hat in a Western," writes Schatz, "is significant because it has come to serve a specific symbolic function within the narrative system." [24] It has, then, no significance more important than that? Apparently not. And, similarly, land and nature become "land" and "nature," abstractions from the real world photographed in the movie, abstractions reduced into the essentially verbal background symbols they become in bad O'Neill plays.

Genre criticism seems almost endemically antiphenomenological. [25] It cannot conceive the true nature of cinema. It cannot recognize that extraction of a "narrative" is distant indeed from experience of cinema, that narrative analysis of cinema, when divorced from a phenomenological approach, is virtually as irrelevant to cinematic criticism as narrative summaries of operas are to music criticism. Literary critics exalt the "idea," but they regard its actualization as a mere illustration. They concern themselves with narrative because they comprehend cinema chiefly in terms of what happens, as *becoming,* as "action." Cinema critics, on the other hand, tend to comprehend cinema more as *being,* as a world and soul experienced in an immediate now. A rose is a rose in cinema, or at least nearly so: its value lies primarily in its being a real image of a real rose; symbolic accretions are imposed subsidiarily. But a "rose" is not a rose in literature: it is primarily a sign, rich in accretions but universally abstracted from any actual rose. For these reasons, narrative is more important than character in literature, because character can be suggested only through event, whereas in cinema character is more important than narrative, because cinema gives us direct and immediate experience of another person, and an event is more the personality of the doer than the deed that is done. What is nearly impossible in literature—virtually direct experience of the world—is the essence of cinema. And thus it is that many of cinema's greatest works—among them, certain pictures of Sternberg, Ophuls, Dreyer, Ford, and Rossellini—offer little more for the grist of narrative criticism than platitudinous plots, stereotyped characters, and hackneyed dialogue. But genre criticism tends—not always, but frequently enough—to delete the sensuous from the dialectic between sensuousness and logic that creates art; in so doing, such criticism emasculates cinema of its aesthetic dimension and transforms it into an effete, conceptual vehicle. Art becomes an academic exercise, pornography or propaganda, raped of its capability, its *aesthetic* capability, to give us knowledge of ourselves and our world.

Notes

1. Thomas Schatz, *Hollywood Genres: Formulas, Filmmaking, and the Studio System* (New York: Random House, 1981), p. 45.

2. Robert Warshow, "Movie Chronicle: The Westerner," in *The Immediate Experience* (New York: Atheneum, 1979), pp. 135–154; John G. Cawelti, *The Six-Gun Mystique* (Bowling Green, Ohio: Bowling Green University Popular Press, [1970])—a more cautious essay than the author's subsequent "Reflections on the New Western Films," in *Focus on the Western,* edited by Jack Nachbar (Englewood Cliffs, N.J.: Prentice Hall, 1974), pp. 113–117; Philip French, *Westerns: Aspects of a Movie Genre* (New York: Viking Press, 1973); Jack Nachbar, "Riding Shotgun: The Scattered Formula in Contemporary Western Movies," in *Focus on the Western,* pp. 101–112; Will Wright, *Sixguns and Society: A Structural Study of the Western* (Berkeley: University of California Press, 1975); Frank D. McConnell, *The Spoken Seen* (Baltimore: Johns Hopkins University Press, 1976); and Leo Braudy, *The World in a Frame* (Garden City: Anchor Press/Doubleday, 1976). Many others have written on the western as a genre, of course, without exhibiting the flaws cited in my essay.

3. French, *Westerns,* pp. 12–13.

4. McConnell, *The Spoken Seen,* p. 158.

5. Cawelti, *Six-Gun Mystique,* p. 74.

6. Nachbar, "Riding Shotgun," pp. 102–103.

7. Warshow, "Movie Chronicle," p. 144.

8. Schatz, *Hollywood Genres*, p. 37. See Christian Metz, *Language and Cinema* (New York: Praeger, 1975), pp. 148–161, and Henri Focillon, *Life of Forms in Art* (New York: George Wittenborn, 1942), p. 10.

9. Braudy, *The World in a Frame*, p. 135.

10. Warshow, "Movie Chronicle," pp. 149–150.

11. Schatz, *Hollywood Genres*, p. 36.

12. *Moving Picture World*, March 29, 1919, p. 1768.

13. Ibid., May 10, 1913, p. 582.

14. Schatz, *Hollywood Genres*, pp. 135–139.

15. Many pictures of the teens were reissued in the twenties; one would have to compare published plot summaries. But reediting was a common occurrence, making a picture shorter or longer, depending upon the new use planned for it, and it seems reasonable to assume that story material would have been updated when possible. But the matter should be checked. Pictures made between 1929 and 1934 were frequently reedited when reissued during the next twenty years in order to conform to the more stringent censorship codes.

16. (*Universal*) *Motion Picture Weekly* of August 17, 1917, and the concurrent number of *Moving Picture World* describe the original ending. The later ending is described in (*Universal*) *Motion Picture Weekly* of January 1925. The clumsy editing may be seen in extant copies of the movie itself, all of which descend from a print from the Czech Film Archives into which new title cards have been interpolated, so that they incorrectly bear the original rather than the reissue title.

17. Schatz, *Hollywood Genres*, p. 38. See also Braudy, *The World in a Frame*, p. 179: "Change in genre occurs when the audience says, 'That's too infantile a form of what we believe. Show us something more complicated.'" Braudy offers no data to support his conjectures about what audiences say or when, nor about audiences influencing change.

18. Nachbar, "Riding Shotgun," pp. 101–102. In fact, history, not legend, had changed. The heroic portrait of Earp in Stuart N. Lake's *Wyatt Earp, Frontier Marshall* (Boston: Houghton Mifflin, 1931) had been discredited by the revisionist history in Frank Waters, *The Earp Brothers of Tombstone* (Lincoln: University of Nebraska Press, 1960), in which Earp and Holliday are revealed to have been partners in a hold-up racket who massacred the Clantons in an ambush (not a battle) and hung their bodies up in the butcher-shop window. Ford, who had based his *My Darling Clementine* on Lake's book, acknowledged the new truth three years before 1967 with a salacious version of Earp in *Cheyenne Autumn* (and with a salacious marshal in *Two Rode Together* in 1961). But since Ford had known Earp personally in the teens, he tempered his 1946 Earp with undercutting criticism.

19. Similarly, McConnell in *The Spoken Seen* misreads the nature of society and hero in *Stagecoach*: "The society of *Stagecoach* is the explicitly nomadic one of the travelers in the coach to Lordsburg . . . The Ringo Kid (John Wayne) saves the group and holds it together against danger from within and without . . ." (p. 155). Half of *Stagecoach* occurs in the two towns; most of what we see of the

voyage occurs at the two way-stations. Is this "nomadic"? The Ringo Kid does not specifically save the group or hold it together, either from within or from without; he is captured, held against his will, fails to escape only because Indians appear, and places his personal vengeance above saving the group by holding back the three bullets.

20. Schatz, *Hollywood Genres*, pp. 67–69.

21. For elaboration of these and subsequent arguments about Ford, see Tag Gallagher, *John Ford* (Berkeley: University of California Press, 1985).

22. Warshow, "Movie Chronicle," p. 146.

23. Schatz, *Hollywood Genres*, p. 21.

24. Ibid., p. 22.

25. An exposition of a phenomenological approach to cinema theory may be found in J. Dudley Andrew, *The Major Film Theories* (New York: Oxford University Press, 1976), pp. 242–254.

17. The Bug in the Rug: Notes on the Disaster Genre

MAURICE YACOWAR

Disaster films constitute a sufficiently numerous, old, and conventionalized group to be considered a genre rather than a popular cycle that comes and goes. The disaster film is quite distinct from the science fiction genre Susan Sontag discusses in "The Imagination of Disaster,"[1] though like sci-fi, the disaster film exploits the spectacular potential of the screen and nourishes the audience's fascination with the vision of massive doom.

The disaster genre is older than Griffith's *Intolerance* (1916). One might argue that the first disaster film was Méliès's happy accident whereby a jammed camera transformed an ordinary autobus into a hearse. There we have the essence of the genre: a situation of normalcy erupts into a persuasive image of death. More obvious examples could be found in Méliès's *Collision and Shipwreck at Sea* (1898), perhaps in *The Misfortunes of an Explorer* (1900) and *The Interrupted Honeymoon* (1899), but certainly in *The Eruption of Mount Pelée* (1902) and *The Catastrophe of the Balloon "Le Pax"* (1902).

THE BASIC TYPES

At least eight types of disaster film can be distinguished. Of course, there will be overlap between them and even with other genres.

Natural Attack

The most common disaster type pits a human community against a destructive form of nature. The attack may be by an animal force, such as rats—*Willard* (Daniel Mann, 1970), *Ben* (Phil Karlson, 1972). It may be ants—either normal (*The Naked Jungle*, Byron Haskin, 1954) or abnormal (*Them!*, Gordon Douglas, 1954; *Phase IV*, Saul Bass, 1975). It may be fish (*Jaws*, Steven Spielberg, 1975) or fowl (*The Birds*, Alfred Hitchcock, 1961) or amphibian (*Frogs*, George McCowan, 1972). It may be a rampage of natural monsters (*Elephant Walk*, William Dieterle, 1954) or of giant forms of natural monsters, like *King Kong* (Merian C. Cooper and Ernest B. Schoedsack, 1933), *The Giant Gila Monster* (Ray Kellogg, 1959), or *Tarantula* (Jack Arnold, 1955). Or they can be fantasy monsters, like Honda's *Godzilla* (1955), Mothra, Reptilicus, Gappa, Rodan, and the rest of the boys in that band. In *The Lost World* (Harry Hoyt, 1924) an aquatic dinosaur rips up London Bridge, as *Gorgo* was to do again for Eugene Lourie in 1961.

Or it may be an attack by the elements, as in John Ford's *The Hurricane* (1937), or in the ever-popular flood movie, such as *The Rains Came* (Clarence Brown, 1939) and *The Rains of Ranchipur* (Jean Negulesco, 1955). Volcanoes figure in *The Last Days of Pompeii* (Maggi, 1908), *Volcano* (Dieterle, 1953), and of course *Krakatoa, East of Java* (Bernard Kowalski, 1969), about the volcano Krakatoa, which is west of Java. The flood and volcano films, wherever they are set, bear the moral weight of the urban renewal sagas of Pompeii, Sodom, and Gomorrah. Mark Robson's *Earthquake* (1974) is a variation on this type.

A third type of natural attack is by an atomic mutation, as the giant ants of *Them!*, the giant grasshoppers of Bert Gordon's *The Beginning of the End* (1953), *The Cyclops* (Gordon, 1957), *The Terror Strikes* (Gordon, 1958; also called *War of the Colossal Beast*), *Kronos* (Kurt Neumann, 1957), *The Creature from the Black Lagoon* (Arnold, 1954), *The Beast from 20,000 Fathoms* (Lourie, 1953), and *It Came from beneath the Sea* (Robert Gordon, 1955). Or it may be the disaster of mutation or radioactive effect, as in *The Incredible Shrinking Man* (Arnold, 1957), *The Amazing Colossal Man* (Bert Gordon, 1957), and *The Atomic Kid* (Leslie Martinson, 1954).

In all three types, the natural disaster film dramatizes people's helplessness against the forces of nature. In the 1950s, obsession with atomic disasters showed human beings diminished by their own technology, as in the credits of *The Incredible Shrinking Man*, where the human outline dwindles as the mushroom cloud swells. The animal films typically dramatize the power of familiar, small creatures, like ants and frogs, often developing the threat out of domesticated animals, like cats and birds. In *The Birds* a complacent society is attacked by birds for no logical reason. *Willard* is an impure disaster film, for the rats' power and malice are at first released under a human's control. Generally, the animal-attack films provide a frightening reversal of the chain of being, attributing will, mind, and collective power to creatures usually considered to be safely without these qualities. At the end of *Willard*, however, the ungentle Ben sniffs smugly in close-up, ominously free of human control, dominant.

The Ship of Fools

The dangers of an isolated journey provide the most obviously allegorical disaster films, given the tradition of "the road of life." Such westerns as *Stagecoach* (John Ford, 1939) and *Hombre* (Martin Ritt, 1967) are cousins in another form, where the savagery of Indians or outlaws is the threatening disaster.

The most common travel disaster involves flying. So we have Walter Booth's *Battle in the Clouds* (1909), *No Highway in the Sky* (Henry Koster, 1951), *The High and the Mighty* (William Wellman, 1954), *Zeppelin* (Etienne Perier, 1971), *The Hindenburg* (Robert Wise, 1976), and the spawn of *Airport* (George Seaton, 1969), *Airport 1975* (Jack Smight, 1975), and indeed any air films that involve massive threat of destruction without the elements of human warfare. Hawks's *Only Angels Have Wings* (1939) has elements of the disaster film, but not *Tora! Tora! Tora!* (Richard Fleischer, Toshio Masuda, and Kinji Fukasaku, 1970), which belongs in the neighboring genre of war films. The flying disasters are based on the audience's familiar sense of insecurity in flight and upon the tradition of punishment for the hubris of presuming to fly. It's even hubristic to float, as in *Titanic* (Negulesco, 1953) and *A Night to Remember* (Roy Baker, 1958). The same anxiety is addressed by the horrors of underground disaster in Gary Sherman's powerful *Death Line* (1972; in America, *Raw Meat*) and, with the modification by human malevolence, in *The Incident* (Larry Peerce, 1967) and *The Taking of Pelham One Two Three* (Joseph Sargent, 1974). Godard works round to a disaster vision in his traffic jam at the end of *Weekend* (1967), but the fullest extension of the auto mythology into disaster is Peter Weir's *The Cars That Ate Paris* (1974).

The City Fails

Here people are most dramatically punished for placing their faith in their own works and losing sight of their maker. So their edifices must crumble about them. This type dates back to Ernest Schoedsack's *The Last Days of Pompeii* (1935), E. A. Martin's *War o' Dreams* (1915), Mary Pickford's *Waking Up the Town* (1925), Luitz Morat's *La Cité foudroyée* (1924), Lang's *Metropolis* (1926), G. W. Pabst's *Atlantis* (1932), *Earthquake,* John Guillermin's *The Towering Inferno* (1974) and so on. In *The Neptune Factor* (Daniel Petrie, 1973) an underwater lab and living experiment is threatened by giant fish and eels bred by undersea volcanoes, so both the monster and failed-city forms converge.

In this type the advances of civilization are found to be fragile and dangerous. In *The Incredible Shrinking Man* the world of commonplace objects overwhelms the hero, until he resolves in mystic humility to enjoy

42. *The Incredible Shrinking Man:* The world of commonplace objects overwhelms the hero (Grant Williams).

his disappearance, his fade into the rich nothingness of God. As we learned from the coffee tin he passed, "Use less for best results." In *Invasion USA* (Alfred E. Green, 1952) and *Red Planet Mars* (Harry Horner, 1952) we enjoy visions of the cataclysmic destruction of America and Russia respectively.

The Monster

Natural and aberrant monsters were listed under the natural-attack category above. But the beast may come from the vast beyond, as in *X from Outer Space* (Kazui Nihonmatsu, 1967). Space monsters are terrifying even when they are not malevolent, as in *20 Million Miles to Earth* (1957) and *The Day the Earth Stood Still* (Robert Wise, 1951). The monster can be a vegetable (*The Day of the Triffids,* Steve Sekely, 1963; *The Thing,* Howard Hawks, 1951). It can be constructed by human beings (*Der Golem,* Wegener, 1920; *Frankenstein,* James Whale, 1931). Or it can be bacterial, as in *Shivers* (David Cronenberg, 1975). It can even be a computer, as in *Westworld* (Michael Crichton, 1974), *2001* (Stanley Kubrick, 1968), *Colossus: The Forbin Project* (Sargent, 1969). The beast can be a shapeless evil, like that in *The Quatermass Experiment* (Val Guest, 1955), *The H-Man* (Honda, 1958), *X the Unknown* (Leslie Norman, 1956), *The Blob* (Irving A. Yeaworth, 1958), and *The Green Slime* (Kinji Fukasaku, 1969). Even the destruction scenes in *The Exorcist* (William Friedkin, 1974) satisfied the appetite for disaster.

Often the monster threatens dehumanization, not death: *Shivers, Night of the Blood Beast* (Bernard Kowalski, 1958), *Attack of the Crab Monsters* (Roger Corman, 1957), *Not of This Earth* (Corman, 1957), *It Conquered the World* (Corman, 1956), *Invasion of the Body Snatchers* (Don Siegel, 1956). Often the monster is a zombie: *Night of the Living Dead* (George Romero, 1968), *Plan 9 from Outer Space* (Edward D. Wood, Jr., 1956), *The Undead* (Corman, 1956), *The Plague of the Zombies* (John Gilling, 1966), and Ray Dennis Stecker's *The Incredibly Strange Creatures Who Stopped Living and Became Zombies* (1962). Humans are occupied by alien, dehumanizing forces in *Invasion of the Body Snatchers* and *The Earth Dies Screaming* (Terence Fisher, 1964). Then we have the host of vampire films. These all work as black parodies of the mystique of Christian inspiration/possession. The form shades off into the gothic horror tale in the one direction—*Nosferatu* (F. M. Murnau, 1922) and *Dracula* (Tod Browning, 1931)—and into the science fiction genre in the other—*Zombies of the Stratosphere* (Fred Brannon, 1953)—according to its iconography (settings, costumes, etc.). Large-scale destruction characterizes the films of the disaster type.

The monster is often a projection of or a metaphor for the character's psychological state. In *Forbidden Planet* (1956), Herbert Wilcox's clever variation on *The Tempest*, the beast is explicitly an externalization of the human id. (The planet Altair was once the empire of the Krel, whose "mindless beast" impulses destroyed their highly technical civilization.) In *Willard* the rats express Martin's corruption but Willard's mousiness.

Survival

A respectable variety of disaster films detail the problems of survival after a disastrous journey—*Lifeboat* (Hitchcock, 1943), *Marooned* (John Sturges, 1970), *The Naked Prey* (Cornell Wilde, 1966), *Flight of the Phoenix* (Robert Aldrich, 1966), *Sands of the Kalahari* (Cy Endfield, 1965), *The Savage Is Loose* (George C. Scott, 1974)—or after the brawl is over—*Soylent Green* (Richard Fleischer, 1973), *The War Game* (Peter Watkins, 1967), *Planet of the Apes* (Franklin Schaffner, 1968), *The World, the Flesh and the Devil* (Ranald MacDougall, 1959), *On the Beach* (Stanley Kramer, 1959), *Panic in the Year Zero* (Ray Milland, 1962), *The*

Omega Man (Boris Segal, 1971), *Zero Population Growth* (Michael Campus, 1971), *Teenage Caveman* (Corman, 1958).

War

The war film becomes a disaster film when the imagery of carnage and destruction predominates over the elements of human conflict. Thus *The War Game, Fires Were Started* (Humphrey Jennings, 1943), and the destruction scenes of *Gone with the Wind* (Victor Fleming, 1939) and *Slaughterhouse Five* (George Roy Hill, 1972) could qualify. In the fifties the atomic threat provided a host of visions of the day of judgment: *The Day the Earth Stood Still, The Day the Earth Caught Fire* (Val Guest, 1962), *The Day the Sky Exploded* (Paolo Heusch, 1958), and *The Day the World Ended* (Corman, 1956).

The Historical

A separate classification should be made of disasters set in remote times, either past (*San Francisco*, Van Dyke, 1936; *The Last Days of Pompeii*; *Cabiria*, Pastrone, 1914) or future (*Planet of the Apes*; *When Worlds Collide*, Rudolph Mate, 1951; *War of the Worlds*, Haskin, 1953; *Things to Come*, Menzies, 1936). The disaster film characteristically depends upon the audience's sense of contemporaneity, but these films belong by the power and centrality of their doom imagery.

The Comic

There are three types of comic disaster film. In the first type, the disaster can provide a happy ending, as in DeMille's spectaculars *Samson and Delilah* (1949) and *The Ten Commandments* (1923, 1956), assuming that one's critical perspective is not that of the Philistines or the Egyptians. Here there is a discrepancy between the destruction in the image and its constructive spirit. More recent affirmations through disaster include the balletic explosion of the house and contents at the end of Antonioni's *Zabriskie Point* (1970) and at the ending of John Boorman's *Leo the Last* (1970).

In the second type, the destruction can be extended into exuberant absurdity, as in the snowballing destruction in certain films by Laurel and Hardy, in the Mack Sennett smashups, and Stanley Kramer's *It's a Mad, Mad, Mad, Mad World* (1963). In Olsen-Johnson and in the Crosby-Hope road films, delight is taken in the violation of the logic and integrity of the image itself. This is a comic kind of violence. Then, too, there is the comedy among the ruins that one finds in two brilliant films, Richard

43. *The Big Bus:* Full-scale parody of the trip disaster film.

Lester's *The Bed-Sitting Room* (1968) and L. Q. Jones's *A Boy and His Dog* (1976). In the comic disaster film, the audience's delight in seeing familiar treasures smashed—an element in all disaster films—is freest.

The third type of disaster comedy is parody. Among the various film parodies in Woody Allen's *Everything You Always Wanted to Know about Sex* (1972), for example, is the invasion of an isolated countryside by a giant breast. "I can handle boobs," the hero confidently avers, but as usual, the monster is an externalization of the hero's own phobia/obsession/boobishness.

A genre comes of age when its conventions are well enough known to be played for laughs in a parody. *The Big Bus* (James Frawley, 1976) is a full-scale parody of the trip disaster film. A twelve-million-dollar nuclear-powered bus is attempting to make the first nonstop journey from New York to Denver. No one, of course, asks "Why bother?" Much of the comedy involves mock heroic twists. So the hero's brawl has him wielding a broken milk carton, supported by a man with a broken candle. This sends up every bar fight ever fought on screen. In Joseph Bologna's os-tracized driver the film parodies the ostracism of Richard Barthelmess in *Only Angels Have Wings*. But generally the parody is of such contemporary films as *The Hindenburg* and *Airport '75*. As Dana Andrews crashes a small plane into the jet in *Airport '75*, here a farmer rams his half-ton into the bus. The bus itself is a ludicrous demonstration of technology extended into absurdity: its self-washing mechanism and exploding tire-changer, its system of jettisoning the soda pop, its luxurious fittings in washroom, bowling alley, dining room, and pool, and the alternately fastidious and sloppy handling of radioactive matter. The details of the parody in *The Big Bus* brings us to the conventions of the genre as it is played seriously.

THE CONVENTIONS

There are numerous conventions that operate in the disaster film.

1. Except in the historical/fantasy type, there is no distancing in time, place, or costume, so the threatened society is ourselves. The disaster film aims for the impact of immediacy. So in the American film of *The War of the Worlds* the setting was changed from H. G. Wells' London to contemporary Los Angeles. When the American *No Blade of Grass* (Wilde, 1970) was set in England, it was to emphasize the tradition of culture and sophistication ("Keep up your Latin, David; it will stand you in good stead"!!) that is destroyed by the famine and anarchy.

The device of Sensurround purported to provide the physical sensation of *Earthquake*. Significantly, the first tremor felt is when a character is shown at a movie—that is, when there is a precise continuity between the threatened character's situation and the viewer's. Similarly, one of the liveliest frights in *Night of the Living Dead* is when the zombies attack the girl cowering in her automobile. The movie was made for drive-in showings, where the subjective shots here would have had heightened impact. In the horror genre, Peter Bogdanovich's *Targets* (1968) works a similar effect.

2. Given this immediacy, it is difficult to define an iconography for the disaster film as one can do for the western, the gangster film, even the musical and gothic horror. The basic imagery of the disaster film would be disaster, a general, spectacular destruction, but usually this imagery occurs only at the end, though often with brief and promising samples along the way. More than by its imagery, then, the genre is characterized by its mood of threat and dread. Thus films as different as the B space monster films and Bunuel's *The Exterminating Angel* (1962) and Bergman's *The Seventh Seal* (1957) can properly be considered disaster films.

3. The entire cross section of society is usually represented in the cast. The effect is the sense of the entire society under threat, even the world, instead of a situation of individual danger and fate. The ads for *The Big*

Bus typically presented a line of head-and-shoulder pictures of its many main characters, each labeled.

Often the stars depend upon their familiarity from previous films, rather than developing a new characterization. Plot more than character is emphasized, suspense more than character development. In *The Towering Inferno* an inherited sentiment plays around Jennifer Jones and Fred Astaire, Robert Vaughn repeats his corrupt politician from *Bullitt* (Peter Yates, 1968), and Richard Chamberlain reprises his corrupt all-American from *Petulia* (Lester, 1968), itself an ironic inversion of his Kildare. In *The Big Bus* Ruth Gordon provides both a parody of the Helen Hayes figure in *Airport* and an extension of her own salty-old-lady act from *Where's Poppa?* (Carl Reiner, 1970) and *Harold and Maude* (Hal Ashby, 1972).

Similarly, in *Earthquake* the romantic legend of Ava Gardner keys us to expect that husband Charlton Heston will gravitate toward her in the crunch, particularly when his mistress is lightly accented as an alien (French Canadian Genevieve Bujold). When Marjoe Gortner's amiable grocer turns out to be a sadistic fascist, we're prepared by our knowledge of the actor's career as a duplicitous evangelist. In *Airport 1975* Gloria Swanson is Gloria Swanson and Linda Blair is a poor little sick girl about to have her kidney exorcised.

4. The disaster film often dramatizes class conflict. Thus we have the racial concerns in Arch Oboler's *Five* (1951), *The World, the Flesh and the Devil,* and the tensions between John Hodiak and Tallulah in *Lifeboat.* In *The Big Bus* posh designer Lynn Redgrave allows her secret new styles to be worn as some vague part of the company's rescue scheme. A hustling businessman is common in the form, like Henry Hull's Rittenhouse in *Lifeboat* or Theodore Bikel in *Sands of the Kalahari.* Gig Young acts suspicious in *The Hindenburg* but only out of his concern for a cunning business deal. The material concerns—and our differences—of daily life are supposed to pale in the shadow of death cast off in disaster films. In *Earthquake,* the villains are the officials of the Seismology Institute who ignore the graduate student's warnings because they fear loss both of face and of a possible foundation grant.

5. Particularly in American films, gambling is a recurrent device. There is a card game in *Lifeboat,* two sharks on *The Hindenburg,* and overall much drawing of straws, flipping of coins, and poetic justice, suggesting the inscrutability of fate and the pettiness of people's attempts to alter their doom. Superstition is a fossil of piety. Life is a gamble.

6. The exception to the cross-section drama is where a family is beset by the disaster. In *The Birds, The Savage Is Loose, Frogs,* and *Food of the Gods* (Bert I. Gordon, 1976), one of the central issues is the family's reluc-

44. *The Birds:* The family is reluctant to admit an outsider to the intimacy of the family unit.

tance to admit an outsider to the intimacy of the basic unit. In *Zero Population Growth* the parents at first refuse to share their parenthood with the couple who have found them out. The horrific climax in *Night of the Living Dead* is when the daughter eats the father, who had frantically kept outsiders out of the family basement. In *Lifeboat* the "family" of Americans must deal with the attempt of Germans to join them, including the German American Schmidt/Smith. Many disaster films will develop the image of an inner circle or haven being defended against invasion, with a near-sexual tinge to the entrance (in *The Birds,* the pecking through the wood and the invasion of the attic).

7. The disaster film is predicated upon the idea of isolation. No help can be expected from the outside. Further, the threatened characters are jammed together, without escape, without relief from each other. The disaster is often directed at an island community (*The Birds, Frogs*) or one isolated by its remoteness (*The Thing*) or cut off from others by the disaster (*The Towering Inferno*). Then there are all the survival films

set in remote areas. Sometimes even a connection with someone will heighten the isolation: the separated family talking ship-to-shore in *Juggernaut* (Lester, 1974) or in *The Hindenburg,* when the ostensible villain, Boeth, learns that the Gestapo has killed his girlfriend.

The isolation is an important convention of the genre. Westerns and musicals both assume strong human community. But the disaster film draws its anxiety from its conception of human beings as isolated and helpless against the dangers of their world.

8. The characters' isolation is exacerbated by the various conflicts between them. The basic point of the genre is that people must unite against calamity, that personal or social differences pale beside the assaulting forces in nature.

In *Jaws* there is a hostility between the noble savage, Quint, and the wealthy college man, Hooper, that is only briefly glossed over by their drunken camaraderie—and by their sharing of wounds! The town knows Amity in its name only. Both in *Jaws* and in *Grizzly* (William Girdler, 1976), the hero and his political superior quarrel over the danger of the animal threat. In *The Poseidon Adventure* (Ronald Neame, 1972), the rivalry between the Reverend Scott (Gene Hackman) and the policeman Rogo (Ernest Borgnine) seems like the Renaissance debate between the orders of grace and nature.

Here lies the essential relationship between the disaster film and the war film. In both, a society at odds within itself unites against a common threat. In the war film the threat is human; in the disaster film, natural or supernatural. But both genres provide the mimetic harmonizing of a shattered community. War films and disaster films seem to arrive in an alternating cycle, both performing the same general function but with significant shifts of emphasis. War films are at a peak during periods of war and express nationalist confidence. Disaster films express the triviality of human differences in the face of cosmic danger.

The politics of Vietnam did not find expression in war films, because the climate of opinion about the war was so widely and deeply divided in America; but it did emerge in the cycles of amoral cop and spy thrillers, with their ambiguous myths of militant police action on the local or international scale. The disaster cycle of the 1970s followed the slow ending of the American presence in Vietnam. The subsequent cycle of war films was possibly spurred by the fervor of the Bicentennial, but it continued the successful elements of the disaster film: suspense, spectacle, formulaic characterization, and the drama of a divided society seeking vital reconciliation.

In *The Big Bus* there is a variety of comic reconciliations. At home base Scotty gets his lover/attendant back at the end. The passionate and quarrelling couple, Sybil and Claude, fight, divorce, then are remarried. The driver is reconciled to the woman he abandoned at the altar and to the woman whose father he ate (granted, "Just one foot!").

9. The war and disaster genres share the further sense that savagery continues to underlie a pretense to civilization. Thus disasters usually breed a lawless anarchy, as Gortner personifies in *Earthquake,* or the selfishness of Ralph Meeker in *Food of the Gods,* the savagery of *No Blade of Grass;* or states of rigorous repression, as in *Zardoz* (Boorman, 1973), *1984* (Michael Anderson, 1955), and the underworld of *A Boy and His Dog.* In *Sands of the Kalahari* Theodore Bikel asks the typical question: "Look at us. Victims of civilization. Are we lost now or were we lost all those years before?" Technology leads people to disaster, by plane or ship, by their dominating creations. They build towers higher than their fire hoses can reach (*The Towering Inferno*). Often their works survive them, like the Rolls Royce abandoned on a hilltop in *No Blade of Grass,* while the sound track repeats a car commercial. People's works are dangerous, like their robots, their monsters, their transports of delight, even the earphone transistors which in *The Towering Inferno* deafen the boy to the danger around him. In *The Savage Is Loose* the father systematically rejects the paraphernalia of society: the pocket watch, the alphabet, and the guilt-edged family Bible.

And yet, there is an optimism in the genre. The center holds even when chaos has broken loose. The maniacs and fascists are in a minority in the film vision of anarchy. Gortner's fascist is quickly subdued. Order is reasserted. Even in *The Savage Is Loose,* having tried to kill his father, the lad still comes to his mother gently, like a lover, not a rapist. War is hell, but the disaster world is only an earth of brief disturbance. Pessimistic visions without relief, without hope, are rare: Watkins's *The War Game,* for example, and *No Blade of Grass.* Few films raise a disaster that cannot be survived or that does not bring out the best in the characters and our society.

10. Among the recurring character types is the specialist—the various Edmund Gwenn or Cecil Kellaway scientists or professors, or the amateur ornithologist in *The Birds,* whose knowledge provides the basic factual framework for the drama. Significantly, these specialists are almost never able to control the forces loose against them. Specialists are there to measure the force of the mystery by their impotence. For the form serves the principle of the unknowable, the superhuman, the mystery that dwarfs science.

Usually there is also someone of ominous complacency. Sometimes he is the scientist, as Carrington in *The Thing.* Or he may be a businessman/politician, like the mayor in the sharkskin grey suit in *Jaws.* "We *are* the ugly rich," Ray Milland smugly admits in *Frogs.* This confidence represents the extreme form of the security which the audience brings into the theatre for playful threatening—and perhaps the deeper need to be punished for possessing it.

11. There is rarely a religious figure in the disaster film, because faith would temper the dread, a sense of God's abiding support would nullify the suspense. In *The Big Bus* René Auberjonois plays a doubting priest who wants to date, who gloats over God's giving him the window seat, and who finally, his faith recovered, leads them all in a singsong, but a secular one. But he is not proof of a common type. He seems a specific parody of Hackman's priest in *The Poseidon Adventure,* whose religion is based on secular confidence and self-help. He learns a nonreligious kind of humility and sacrifice through the events of the film. The singing nun in *Airport 1975* is safely Helen Reddy. Her song—something about your being your own best friend because no one looks after you better than you do—is strikingly oblivious of Jesus. Moreover, the film turns on the salvation from a lover from earth. God is no copilot in the current disaster film and probably never was. For only in wars, not in the upheavals of peacetime, can one claim that God is on one's side.

Instead of church figures, the form presents evangelical crackpots, like the drunken seer in *The Birds.* This coheres with the literary tradition of disaster visions, deriving out of the irregular, outcast prophets of the Old Testament, proclaiming doom and destruction for the godless pride and corruption of the human race.

12. All systems fail in the disaster. Politicians are corrupt, save the Sam Ervin type of mayor of *The Towering Inferno.* The church is usually absent, as irrelevant. The police are either absent or skeptical about anything beyond the familiar. James Whitmore in *Them!* is virtually unique as a policeman hero of a disaster film. George Kennedy is a heroic cop in *Earthquake,* but he is disillusioned with and suspended from the force.

In *War of the Worlds* the Martians attack the three basic authorities of 1950s America: church, army, and science. The courageous pastor is immediately converted into steaming ash. The army and science fail in turn to assert their powers stronger than faith. The Martians are finally vanquished by earthly bacteria ("For best results use less"!). Nature alone holds sway in the disaster world.

13. The hero is usually a layman with practical sense but without specialized knowledge. In *The Birds* Mitch the lawyer can board up a house. A black handyman is the hero of *Night of the Living Dead.* The modest sheriff saves the day in *Jaws,* when both the savvy of the savage and the knowledge of the scholar have failed. The specialist in *Grizzly,* Richard Jaeckel, dies twice, because he presumed to live in the hide of his prey. In *The Towering Inferno* Paul Newman is a specialist, an architect, but his knowledge is leavened by his rusticity. Heston plays an industrialized ex-

athlete in *Earthquake,* and his achievement in *Airport 1975* is acrobatic as much as aviational. Cornell Wilde's persona in his socially conscious period reverses his old image of easy, swashbuckling triumph.

14. Almost invariably there is a romantic subplot. Romance is a vital aspect of the tension between social instinct and selfishness. So the romance is not just a matter of box-office concession (few things that traditionally work could be!). The romantic byplay dramatizes the virtue of emotionally responsive humanity.

The romance is risible in *Food of the Gods,* where the scientist is sexually aroused by Marjoe Gortner from the strain of fighting giant rats. The theme is worked out most explicitly in *The Thing,* where the hero's emotional capacity opposes him to the foolish Carrington, to whom the monster is the perfect creature: no heart, no emotions, no pleasure or pain. For the hero, the icy landscape is a garden spot, for his romantic response to the lady expresses his feeling and joy of life. The icy landscape is a projection of Carrington's soul. To Carrington, "Knowledge is greater than life," but to the hero the pleasures and vulnerabilities of the heart are more important than science. Thus the hero preserves the animal quality of the human being against the vegetable values of The Thing and Dr. Carrington. Similarly, in *The Neptune Factor* Yvette Mimieux's love for the lost Ed McGibbon causes her to cut the Neptune loose, risking everyone and everything, to recover her lost lover—and the lost laboratory. Her love opposes the unsentimental logistics of Captain Ben Gazzara.

The romance is a variation upon the primary antithesis between a selfish, fragmented society and a community impelled by other-concern. Libertinism is to be punished by disaster (Pompeii, Sodom, the opening murder in *Jaws*). In *Earthquake* Heston must die for his infidelity—and as a reward for his courage and final faithfulness, his death saves him from the long pain of a loveless marriage. The ability to love is the primary virtue of the disaster hero, promiscuity and coldness the main though opposite faults. In *The Poseidon Adventure,* Rogo's wife, Stella Stevens, is an ex-prostitute. Her early demise is ordained by the same tradition that has the saloon gal intercept the bullet intended for the white-hatted hero and that claims Heston's life in *Earthquake.*

In *The Andromeda Strain* (Robert Wise, 1970) James Olson wears a prophylactic rubber sheath to approach the infected survivors, but to save everyone he must break through his sterile invulnerability. In *The Omega Man* Heston valiantly fights off plague-riddled inferiors until he falls in love with the negress. His new susceptibility costs him his life, but he dies with a fertile and romantic gesture, passing on the serum from his blood to another.

The romantic strain is so familiar that variations can be played by implication. In *The Hindenburg* the Scott and Atherton characters, a questioning Nazi and a German resistance youth, are kindred spirits for having girlfriends. The nobility of ex-lovers Scott and Bancroft harkens back to the warmth of an earlier Germany. In *The Forbin Project* we have a romantic attachment between two computers who plot to be reunited when their political masters, the United States and Russia, break their connection. The romantic element is introduced when Colossus watches voyeuristically over Forbin's affair and pours his martinis. In *The Savage Is Loose* the romantic dilemma moves to the center of the film; the incestuous solution is but an extension of the romantic values of the genre. In *No Blade of Grass* the middle-class daughter must reject the gentleman ordinarily esteemed in her class, in favor of the coarser, rougher man, who can afford her better protection. That slight inflection of the romantic convention speaks volumes in the film.

15. Often the disasters have a contemporary significance. In *The Big Bus* there is topical comedy in Stockard Channing's blowsy parody of Liz Taylor and in the doctor's fear of a malpractice suit. Something of post-Nixon America is expressed in *Airport '75,* in the image of an airplane heading toward the mountains with a hole where its pilots used to be. Whether Gerald Ford is played by Karen Black or Charlton Heston is a matter of party politics, but Larry Storch as the press must be an Agnew invention. *The Towering Inferno* is a modern Babel, people building to the heavens without talking to those who might help them. *Earthquake* is an image of a society with its footing shaken out from under it, both personal and professional responsibilities rent asunder. Its climax of the bursting Hollywood Dam is an image of what happens when personal codes are abandoned.

In *Demons of the Swamp* (Bernard L. Kowalski, 1959; also called *The Giant Leeches*) the monster is a reasonable squid. The leeching is done by various interloping humans, a congenital poacher, and parasitic exploiters of the merchant's wife and shame. The hero is a game warden committed to preserving animal rights and property.

In *Frogs* the Crockett family is attacked by reptiles and amphibians, as if to punish them for having tampered with the balance of nature. Young Crockett starts the film by upsetting the canoe of the ecologist hero. The Crocketts may recall pioneers to us, but the animals avenge themselves against them as smug intruders. The frogs can be taken as the process of nature; thus one Crockett lady reports her aging in terms of froglike bags under her eyes. The indictment becomes a national one when father Crockett celebrates his birthday on the Fourth of July. The film abounds in striking images: a snake in the crystal chandelier; a frog on the Old Glory birthday cake; Clint's wife devoured by a turtle ("Slow and steady . . ."); a lizard casually upsetting a canister of insecticide to asphyxiate the grandson; Crockett at the end among his now-menacing hunting trophies, covered by frogs. In one sly irony, the daughter who earlier complained that her profits were reduced by the cost of antipollution devices is lured by a butterfly into the swamp, then bled by leeches. The large close-ups of the frogs suggest they sit in judgment of human beings for their arrogant abuse of nature, with a force hitherto restrained. The film articulates the concern of the 1970s with the abuse of the environment. So does *Food of the Gods,* where nature itself provides a dangerous food that will turn small creatures into monsters, once catalyzed by human greed.

Walon Green's *The Hellstrom Chronicle* (1971) avoids the fictional form in favor of a documentary pretense, but it has the effect of a disaster film, dramatizing the smallness and vulnerability of human beings in the context of the smaller creatures of nature. Its science and pseudoscience give the film the air of newspaper factuality, as the atomic dramas seemed to have amid the red and bomb scares of the 1950s. The anxiety fostered by "Dr. Hellstrom" recalls the dislocation Gulliver suffers in going from Lilliput to Brobdignag. The film achieves that kind of reorientation of the viewer's senses.

Both *The Hellstrom Chronicle* and *Fantastic Voyage* (Richard Fleischer, 1966) were produced in the early years of the LSD phenomenon, when society was excited with prospects of revolutionary perception. So Hellstrom makes a gigantic, compelling world out of the insect close-ups. And *Fantastic Voyage* sets an adventure story in "inner space," the body providing the kind of eerie spectacle previously found in interplanetary travel. The final danger in that adventure is the explosion of the heroes into full size while still within the host body. Premature explosion is a danger that is not remote in any dream that exploits the presence of Raquel Welch.

16. Poetic justice in disaster films derives from the assumption that there is some relationship between a person's due and his or her doom. Hitchcock's *The Birds* is distinctive in not providing a cause for the birds' attack, but typical in presenting the characters as selfish, complacent figures who generally deserve to be shaken up. So do we all, or we wouldn't go to disaster films.

Specific flaws need not cause the disaster, but some inference of guilt by association may be drawn. In *San Francisco* the earthquake is not just due to the San Andreas Fault, but seems at least partly a response to the moral atmosphere in which Clark Gable could knock down priest Spencer Tracy for banning a scantily clad performance by Jeanette Macdonald.

In one respect poetic justice breaks down in disaster films. Often the good die with the evil. In *The Poseidon Adventure* prostitute, priest, and generous swimmer die alike. No logic dictates who will live and who will die in the crash of the *Hindenburg.* The mortality rate among stars and

45. *Shivers* works against the romantic conventions of the genre and the liberated sensuality of its day.

heroes is higher in the disaster film than in any of the other didactic popular genres.

THE APPLICATION

The main purpose in defining a genre is to establish a context for the approach to an individual work. David Cronenberg's *Shivers* might serve as an example of a film illuminated by the sense of the disaster genre.

Shivers opens with a media-sell voice-over, oozing with the complacency that in disaster films is doomed for downfall. It is an assured voice of brittle normalcy, selling the joys of the Starliner apartment building on an island in Montreal. The company prides itself on the apartment's self-containment. The setting is thus developed into an image of the enislement of the sensually obsessed. The facilities cater to nothing but the appetites and the image of the beautiful life. Yet the inhabitants are lonely, insular people, condemned to sad privacy until the disaster frees them for unbridled lust, a horrible parody of community and love.

The disaster is an attack of red, phallic little critters that have been bred by the mad Dr. Emil Hobbes, combining the effects of VD and aphrodisiac. To save people from having tragically lost contact with their physical nature, Hobbes would convert the world into a gigantic orgy.

The Starliner presents life as a trip, a new, exciting ultramodern exploration. The film is about the "sex trip," about the use of free sex as an escape from the ostensible stasis of the responsible and restrained life. The film works against the romantic conventions of the genre and against the liberated sensuality of its day, by making the sexual connection between people the horror, not the cure. The parasite is spread by figures representative of the current sexual liberation: a precocious nymphet, an adulterer, the old swinger with his megavitamin virility, the Swedish couple, the bachelor swingers, hetero and gay.

Cronenberg's Emil Hobbes has a connection to the real world, the philosopher Thomas Hobbes who in *Leviathan* argued the primacy of the physical nature of man and his universe. As Hobbes provided the rationale for Restoration libertinism, Cronenberg reverts to his name for his reversal, a horrific vision of our exalted libertinism. Our sensual togetherness Cronenberg makes more horrifying than the initial loneliness of his characters. The parasites appear as a cross between your standard red phallus and miniature whales, to confirm the Hobbes connection.

As so often in the genre, the monsters are only partly threats from the external world and partly projections of the characters' mental or emotional states. In this case the parasites are images of the characters' sexual compulsions. So when they attack Barbara Steele they come up from within the drainage system, through the plugged drain pipe of her tub, sexually to enter her. She had been moping around in a premasturbatory lethargy, lying open in her tub, loosening up with a large brandy, as if in unconscious hope for sexual engagement.

The hero is a young doctor (Paul Hampton) who restrains his sexual responses. He chats coolly on the phone while his nurse strips for him. The audience, both out of vicarious appetite and by its acquaintance with the conventional romance of the genre, expects and wants him to curtail his call and make love to the nurse. But Cronenberg's hero puts science and duty ahead of casual lust. That is the central moral thrust of the film.

Cronenberg makes the lusting creatures his zombies, against the tradition of the genre. His orgiasts' hyperactivity belies their void in will, soul, and sense. Cronenberg dramatizes the depersonalization of "liberated" sexuality. It is unsettling to find that the zombies are the characters fulfilling our fondest fantasies—sex unlimited by law or capacity.

The film closes with a completion of the media-sell frame. A disc jockey assures his audience that nothing dangerous has happened. While the beautiful people drive out in their performance cars to infest the world with debilitating appetite, all in the name of love and freedom, the disaster itself is hushed up by the loud confidence of the announcer.

Shivers is a powerful, unnerving film. Even its supporters are repelled by it. Much of its anxiety derives from the effective way that Cronenberg has inflected—and in some cases radically reversed—the conventions of the disaster film, the cultivated but unwritten expectations of his audience. That is one of the things that a genre is supposed to do.

Note

1. Susan Sontag, "The Imagination of Disaster," in *Against Interpretation* (New York: Delta, 1966), pp. 209–225.

18. Children of the Light

BRUCE F. KAWIN

There are a lot of ways to play host. Many flowers provide food, comfort, and even shelter to the insects that, in exchange for the pollen they consume, carry pollen on their bodies to other flowers and thus keep the host species alive. Some plants, like some spiders, say "Come and sit in this little room which is really my belly." Dracula is the host who consumes his guest, and the parallel between him and the natural parasites is an important theme in F. W. Murnau's *Nosferatu* (1922). The question is this: What kind of host is the horror film? What does it give to the guest and what does it take? Or, to be clearer about this, what do we as audience expect it to take? Our lives, our peace, our anxiety, our afternoon, our date's self-control, our anger, our idealism? Are its threatening but beautiful figures, like Dracula's wolves, "children of the night" or of the light?

Imagine that what is coming at you is a shuffling, gruesome, unstoppable crowd of zombies; imagine that they want to eat you and that they haven't brushed their teeth since before they died. Did you make up the details of the scene you're now imagining, or borrow them from memories of George Romero's *Night of the Living Dead* (1968)? Is it safer—does it make it "all theater"—to imagine that this is a film, or does that bring the threat somehow closer and make it more frightening? In other words, does it put the horror more in the terms of your own imagination, and has your imagination begun to model itself on film? Have you accepted the horror film as an acceptable source of imagery, stuffed your attic with its particular taste in furniture? Has the part of your mind that imagines horrors adopted the perspectives and structures of the narrative horror film, and if so, is that a way of controlling the anxiety by phrasing it in terms you recognize as artificial, or is that a way of making it more frightening? And why would that make it more frightening?

Now imagine that the zombies are from Romero's film and that the film is being shown in a darkened theater. The audience is "undead," and they are enjoying the film; it makes them feel at home. They become aware of your presence. They come after you. The only light is that provided by the projector, so that the room is, in this particular case, lit by the figures of Romero's zombies. The figures closing in on you are the children of the night; the ones on the screen are the children of the light. This scene is taken, more or less, from Peter Straub's novel *Ghost Story,* a book that examines with intelligence and care the ways that horror stories—whether portrayed on film or in literature or told in serious tones around a firelit circle—can lead us into temptation and deliver us to evil. Straub presents the ghost story as a mirror in which we can find ourselves, but only if we are willing to seek what we have found there, only if we confront our desire to be lost in horror and darkness.

In a good horror story, nobody gets off easy. In a bad horror story like *The Giant Gila Monster* (Ray Kellogg, 1959) or *Friday the 13th* (Sean S. Cunningham, 1980) a lot of people get killed, but no one really cares about them; the audience's attention skips from victim to victim until it finds the survivor, the one with whom it is thrilling but safe to identify. If there turns out to be no survivor, or if the survivor is threatened again at the end of the picture, it doesn't make much difference in the basic formula. Those shock/reversal endings, modeled on the good one in *Carrie* (Brian De Palma, 1976), work only because they play off the norm, which is that there will be at least one survivor. One way to respond to this new cliché is to regard it as a cheap but fashionable negativism. Another response, which few contemporary horror films have deserved, is to entertain the possibility that this particular horror is being extended or repeated because it is deathless, that it will recur—as in the forties paradigm of the Mummy sequels or the ending of *Halloween* (John Carpenter, 1978)—and that this recurrence has some kind of point. But here we are treading on the territory of the good horror film. In any case, it is important not to be misled by the clutch of victims into thinking that a film like *Friday the 13th* deals with real pain or loss; it deals with spectacle, and is no more threatening or profound than the fifties spectacle of a downtown crowd running and screaming with a dinosaur at their heels. As Joanna Russ observed, what passes for ethics and judgment in these films can often be reduced to "Giant ants are bad/People are good."[1] Often, but not always.

A good horror film takes you down into the depths and shows you something about the landscape; it might be compared to Charon, and the horror experience to a visit to the land of the dead, with the difference that this Charon will eventually take you home, or at least drop you off at the borders of the underworld. The seeker, who is often the survivor, confronts his or her own fallibility, vulnerability, and culpability as an aspect of confronting the horror object, and either matures or dies. ("Matures" in this sense refers to the adult act of making peace with the discrepancy between self and self-image.) Both *The Turn of the Screw* and *Heart of Darkness* are straightforward literary examples of this generic imperative.

Karl Freund's *Mad Love* (1935) offers a cinematic example at its climax, where Stephen and Yvonne Orlac manage to survive only by agreeing to function in the terms in which the villain, Dr. Gogol, has cast them. Yvonne's problem is that Dr. Gogol has confused her with her image; he gets sexually excited watching her sadomasochistic performances on stage, takes a wax statue of her into his home (and plays the organ for it, imagining that his love might make it come to life, on the model of Pygmalion—though the audience is encouraged to remember the more tragic model of *The Phantom of the Opera*), and eventually attempts to control and possess her as he has controlled and possessed her image (i.e., both the statue and the image Yvonne projects, as actress, into his fantasy life). Stephen's problem is that Dr. Gogol has grafted onto his wrists the hands of a murderous knife-thrower, Rollo, and that these hands not only cannot play the piano (Stephen's forte before a railroad accident smashed his hands) but also control him, virtually forcing him to throw knives when he is angry. At the climax, Yvonne faces her statue, accidentally breaks it, and must pretend to be her statue (i.e., her image) in order to buy time and delude Dr. Gogol, whose delusion was to confuse her and her image. When Dr. Gogol decides to perfect his control of what he believes is a statue come to life and begins to strangle her while quoting poetry (Wilde's "Ballad of Reading Gaol" and Browning's "Porphyria's Lover"), Stephen and the police arrive. Stephen saves his wife by accurately throwing a knife into Dr. Gogol's back. Earlier the doctor had tried to drive Stephen mad by convincing him that he had killed his own father with a knife. That knife, which had made its way onto the police chief's desk, is the one Stephen throws into Dr. Gogol with Rollo's hands. Although it is obvious that Dr. Gogol has created the means and exact terms of his own destruction, it is less obvious but just as true that Dr. Gogol has, by those same actions, created the terms by which Yvonne and Stephen survive. They survive by accepting those aspects of themselves that reflect Dr. Gogol's influence on their lives, the ways in which the horror has changed them. It is only by becoming a knife-wielding killer that Stephen overcomes his castration crisis and is able to save his wife and himself—though he will never again become "a great pianist" (Yvonne's phrase, which she says so rapidly that it almost sounds like "penis"). It is only by becoming her image that Yvonne survives long enough to be tortured and saved for the last time. Neither of them gets off easy.

Although it might raise the specter of knee-jerk Freudian criticism to speak of a castration crisis in *Mad Love*, to notice such a crisis does not commit one to analyze it in narrowly Freudian terms. The Gestalt psychologists, under the guidance of Fritz Perls, have developed methods of exploring dream fields that appear at least as valid, in their own terms, as Freud's and that have a more natural connection with the analysis of visual structures. Social psychology, in which it is possible to speak of the lower classes as somehow "repressed," also has its relevance, and the Jungian archetypes present another framework that can be useful in sorting out recurrent figures and images in the horror film, many of which come from classical mythology for a good reason. But there is a great deal of phallic imagery in *Mad Love,* and it is fairly obvious: the pianist who cannot play, the man who has lost his hands, the man who throws only knives and pens, the man who throws his first knife at his taunting father (but does not hurt him; it is Dr. Gogol who does the killing later on). In fact, Stephen and Yvonne are setting out for a delayed honeymoon when disaster intrudes, and the implication is that they must go through a horror phase, something identified with Dr. Gogol and his "mad love," before they can settle into their marriage, which in this case is an emblem of (interrupted) sexual and social stability.

This turns out to be a relatively consistent pattern in the horror films of the twenties, thirties, and forties: a perverse or somehow unsatisfactory love triangle among the boy, the girl, and the monster; a happy coupling of the surviving couple that depends on their dealing with the monster or coming to some kind of understanding with the forces it represents (the same question is at issue in *Nosferatu,* even though the wife dies at the end); and a romantic resolution that bodes well for the society at large. ("Well" is, of course, usually defined in terms of the prevailing ideology of the culture that produces the film, but it often appears that the genre itself has a built-in ideology or at least a regularly preferred state of affairs.) Whatever relationship there is between the monster and the girl must be resolved, and this can be a matter—in the dumbest prototype—of monster steals girl, boy kills monster, girl kisses boy. In the more complex films, like *Mad Love,* John Badham's recent *Dracula* (1979), or—to pick another Freund film—*The Mummy* (1932), there is some real emotional and ethical intercourse between monster and survivor, in the course of which both are changed. Consider, for instance, the serious girl-and-werewolf relationships in George Waggner's *The Wolf Man* (1941) and John Landis's *An American Werewolf in London* (1981) or the really complex situation of the newscaster in *The Howling* (Joe Dante, 1981), who is both girl and monster and has to save/sacrifice herself.[2] In any case, this triangle is an important psychological structure, and the device of the delayed honeymoon—which carries over from *Frankenstein* (James Whale, 1931) to *The Bride of Frankenstein* (Whale, 1935), as poor Henry (Victor in the novel) only gradually gets the idea that he would do better to create life with the aid of a human female—reminds the viewer that there is something that needs to be settled before the characters can be considered healthy. Another aspect of the triangle, as in the example of Cocteau's *Beauty and the Beast* (1946), is that the boy and the monster often represent two sides of the girl's own sexual desire (i.e., of her own sexual self-image), and the implication is that she cannot choose Mr. Right without first confronting her desire for—or to be—Mr. Wrong. Essentially this is the same issue as that of Stephen Orlac's phallic crisis, because it demonstrates how the horror film functions as a mirror or series of mirrors in which aspects of the self demand to be confronted.

This confrontation is usually in the interests of the health of the protagonists, and almost any great horror film can send ripples down our understanding of the therapies of Freud, Jung, and Perls, as suggested before. In Freudian terms, it is possible to think of the horror object as an idlike force that compels attention through compulsive repetition, that often expresses itself in dream formats, complete with displacement and secondary revision (i.e., if films are like dreams, or work in similar ways with the "language" of the unconscious in a situation where the audience is as apparently passive as the dreamer, then horror films can be fruitfully compared with nightmares), and that must be unmasked if healing is to take place. In Jungian terms, the monster often plugs into our shared sense of the archetypes, and in the horror film we often indulge our nostalgia for the world of myth and magic. In a Perls framework, the monster is often a projection split off from the wholeness of the protagonist (or audience), so that health is achieved not by releasing some widely shared trauma—knee-jerk Freudianism—but by taking the projection back into oneself, in other words by deeply acknowledging the connection between the monster and the official self. A Gestalt reading of *The Wizard of Oz* (Victor Fleming, 1939), for instance, would consider how Dorothy, the dreamer, projects aspects of her personality into the figures that populate Oz, leaving the image of "Dorothy Gale from Kansas" less than whole. Part of her is the Wicked Witch and can use the ruby slippers correctly (and might even want to get rid of Toto!); part of her is the Wizard, who knows what everybody needs and knows that what they need, they already have. The Scarecrow is already smart, the Tin Woodman already sentimental, the Cowardly Lion already a parody of the military hero; thus the resolution scene, in which they come into the wholeness they unknowingly already enjoy, is an emblem of the psychological value system that underlies the film as well as of the way Dorothy dreams (and, in this dream, explains to herself the nature of her own power, a little sermon on re-owning projections that is credibly motivated by her experience of powerlessness in the prologue). In many ways this reading is just as useful as a Freudian reading of the Wicked Witch as bad mother and the Wizard as helpless or castrated father, or a Jungian reading of the Witch and Wizard as archetypes. In many ways, the deployment of elements within the field of the artwork is the one aspect of artistic psychology most congenial to Gestalt analysis and one that might prove especially valuable in sorting out how genres are constituted. It is, in any case, extremely useful in understanding the horror love triangle, the genesis and role of the monster, and the problem of effecting a resolution between self and self-image.

Now this is only one aspect of one horror formula, and I will be advancing toward larger generalizations later, but for the moment it makes the basic point: good horror films try to be good hosts. They lead us through a structure that shows us something useful or worth understanding. Because so many of them are psychologically oriented or psychoanalyzable, what they often map out is the terrain of the unconscious, and in that connection they often deal with fantasies of brutality, sexuality, victimization, repression, and so on. (How much violence they include is irrelevant; what matters is the tone and point of that violence. In the work of Tobe Hooper, for example, I would argue that *The Texas Chain Saw Massacre* [1974], *The Funhouse* [1981], and *Poltergeist* [1983] are equally valuable films.) Because they deal with the unconscious in a larger-than-Freudian sense, they often involve some disguised journey into the Jungian territory of the land of the dead,[3] which can be thought of in terms of the lawyer's glimpses of "the other side" or "the dream time" in Peter Weir's *The Last Wave* (1977) or of the intrusion of the guardians of the dead into the bland America of the post-Freund Mummy sequels. Robin Wood, among others, has argued that repressed political and social discontent, the urge to smash the system and subvert its values, is another more or less unconscious element that the horror film temporarily liberates.[4] What science fiction films do, in contrast, is to address not the unconscious but the conscious—if not exactly the scientist in us, then certainly the part of the brain that enjoys speculating on technology, gimmicks, and the perfectible future. What bad horror films do, in contrast to both of these, is to present a spectacle for the simple purpose of causing pain in the viewer's imagination—not just scaring the hell out of us, or us into hell, but attacking and brutalizing us on a deep level. Perhaps I am making a further distinction here between a bad film and a pernicious or evil film, because a badly made horror film like *Ghost Story* (John Irvin, 1981) doesn't do much more than sadden the audience at the waste of time and talent, while a pernicious film like *Friday the 13th* or *My Bloody Valentine* (George Mihalka, 1981) fuses a bizarre and destructive connection between sexuality and bloody awful death that can be hard to shake off and teaches nothing of value, coming very close to the structures, devices, and audience appeal of the sickest and most violent pornography. Since the latter is the impression of horror films most people seem to have these days, it seems important to point out how many of the real classics of film history—*Nosferatu* and *Vampyr* (Carl Dreyer, 1932), for example—have been horror films and to sketch out what the good ones did and are still doing. I would now like to posit a distinction between horror and science fiction, in the interest of working toward a definition of horror as a genre, and go on from there to outline a pattern that is as common as that of the boy-girl-monster triangle, the remarkably consistent use of reflexive devices in the good horror film.

Stephen King has said that it is hard to imagine a more boring, profitless, and terminally academic pastime than that of discriminating between horror and science fiction.[5] It seems to me that we will never fully understand the horror film until we agree on a definition of the genre, and that the genre with which horror is most regularly confused is that of science fiction. Some people have called *The Thing (from Another World)* (directed by Christian Nyby with a good deal of input from Howard Hawks, 1951), for example, a horror film, while others list it among the greatest science fiction films ever made.[6] The difficulty—which may date back to the birth of Frankenstein's monster in a scientific laboratory—is that *The Thing* deploys elements associated with both genres; the problem is that the film will reveal different meanings and emphases according to the generic context against which it is set.

Horror is, in the first place, the older literary form, with roots in folklore, mythology, classical tragedy (e.g., *Medea* and, though this may be stretching matters, *The Bacchae*), the gothic novel, and the work of Romantics from Coleridge and Mary Shelley to Poe. Indeed, in literary terms it is fairly easy to conceptualize the difference between horror and science fiction in terms of the obvious differences between Henry James and H. G. Wells, between H. P. Lovecraft and John Campbell, Jr., or between Shirley Jackson and Arthur C. Clarke. In film, however, the lines have proved much harder to draw, and this may have something to do with the role of the BEM, or bug-eyed monster, in the pulp science fiction magazines of the thirties and forties. In most cases science fiction is cross-fertilized by imagination and scientific premise: What would happen if . . . ? What would happen if there were space travel, if cloning were practical, if time travel were voluntary and multidirectional, if there were parallel worlds, if robots could think, if a police detective could read minds, if parthenogenesis were practical? Largely because of the influence of Campbell, as editor of *Astounding,* writers were expected to back up their ifs with a reasonable amount of hard science and logical speculation. (Discussing films, Campbell said that *Destination Moon* [Irving Pichel, 1950] and *Fail-Safe* [Sidney Lumet, 1964] were good examples of science fiction, while most were "totally unrealistic fantasies"; as ex-

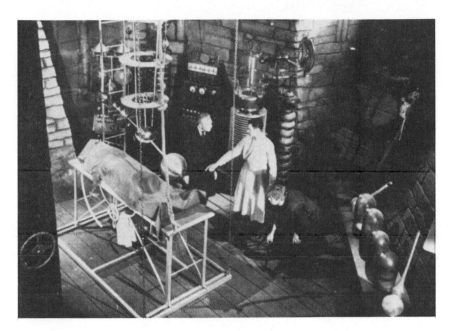

46. *Frankenstein:* The doctor (Colin Clive) at work in his lab.

amples of the latter he offered *Gojira* [*Godzilla, King of the Monsters,* 1954] and *The Beast from 20,000 Fathoms* [Eugene Lourie, 1953].)[7] But one of the writers Campbell nurtured was A. E. Van Vogt, who perfected the tale of the space travelers who encounter the absolutely malevolent monster, and it became commonplace to refer to such pieces as science fiction, along with the horde of less original pieces in which a space voyage was hardly worth describing if it did not include some variety of extraterrestrial BEM. Science fiction provided a wide range of settings and nurturing environments for many frightening creatures, and it is out of that association of story elements that the present confusion seems to have come, particularly since the "Golden Age" pulps and the low-budget films of the fifties drew on many of the same writers and appealed to much the same audience (as the horror film of the forties shared its audience and many of its characteristic devices with the radio mystery melodrama). As a member of the fifties matinee generation and a devotee of both E. C. horror comics and the "idea literature" of the science fiction magazines, I remember going to a horror movie with the expectation of being scared—of seeing something horrible—and to a science fiction movie with the expectation of having my imagination stretched to include

47. *Alien:* More horror than science fiction film.

new possibilities, of seeing something interesting that I had probably never thought of. Space ships meant travel to the stars; monsters meant trouble. After a while, when the market became dominated by BEM movies and hard-core science fiction purists had to wait out the hiatus between *Destination Moon* and *2001: A Space Odyssey* (Stanley Kubrick, 1968), I recall that we came to call any speculative fantasy "science fiction," while "horror films" were what the local stations played after 11:30 on Friday evenings and after the cartoons on Saturday mornings. It is probably true to say that the fifties were a decade of transition in which both genres borrowed each other's terms—*Forbidden Planet* (Fred McLeod Wilcox, 1956) is a good example of a meld—but since the genres diverged later and since it is still clear that *Friday the 13th* is not science fiction and *Close Encounters of the Third Kind* (Steven Spielberg, 1977) not horror, it seems evident that the genres remained ultimately intact and capable of definition.

Genres are determined not just by plot elements but also by *attitudes* toward plot elements. (In a recent article,[8] Rick Altman posited a very useful integration of "semantic" and "syntactic" genre strategies, taking account both of a genre's recurring terms or semantic units—e.g., horses

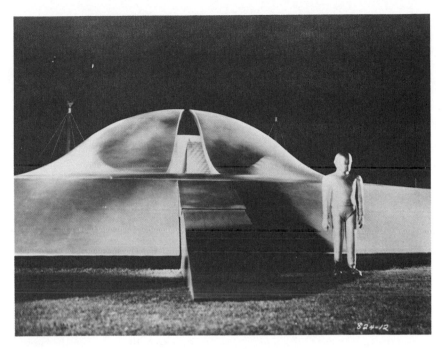

48. *The Day the Earth Stood Still:* An extraterrestrial of science fiction, not horror.

in westerns—and the recurring ways in which those elements are deployed and interrelated—e.g., that in many westerns there is a conflict between the semantic elements of "garden" and "desert." My use of the term "attitude" is more value-laden than his "syntactic" construct and perhaps less useful, but it is in the syntactic area that the value structures I address are generated, and we agree that the presence of certain semantic elements is inadequate to define a genre.) It not only impoverishes one's sense of these films, but also is simply inaccurate to say that "it's a horror film if it has a monster in it, a science fiction film if it has a scientist," or "it's a horror film if the monster is humanoid or an aspect of human psychology, and science fiction if the monster is a machine or the product of a machine." *Frankenstein,* for example, fits *all* of these descriptions, and so does *Alien* (Ridley Scott, 1979)—and as far as I can tell, they both are horror films even if they use elements that regularly crop up in science fiction, even if science fiction writers venerate the novel *Frankenstein,* and even if *Alien* closely follows the Van Vogt formula.

To unscramble some of this, I wrote an article for *Dreamworks* in which I suggested that *The Day the Earth Stood Still* (Robert Wise,

1951) was clearly a science fiction film while *The Thing* was clearly a horror film, although both had essentially the same plot elements—encounters between the intelligent pilots of flying saucers and a complex of military, scientific, and civilian personnel—and both were produced under similar conditions, in 1951 in American studios during the cold war. Taken together, *The Day the Earth Stood Still* and *The Thing* seemed an ideal test case:

> *The Day the Earth Stood Still* . . . is the story of a spaceman, Klaatu (Michael Rennie), who sets down his flying saucer in Washington, D.C., with the intention of putting Earth on notice: anything resembling nuclear violence will be punished by the obliteration of the planet, courtesy of a race of interstellar robot police. The spaceman has three forces to contend with: the army, which wants to destroy him; the scientists, who are willing to listen to him; and a woman (Patricia Neal) who understands and helps him. The central scientist (Sam Jaffe) is a kooky but open-minded and serious figure. Although it is suggested that earthlings understand violence better than most kinds of communication, they do respond to a nonviolent demonstration of Klaatu's power, and he does manage to deliver his message—perhaps at the expense of his life. The film's bias is in favor of open-minded communication, personal integrity, nonviolence, science, and friendship. The major villain (Hugh Marlowe) is a man who values personal fame and power more than integrity and love; he is willing to turn Klaatu over to the army, which shoots first and asks questions later—even if it means losing Neal, his fiancée.
>
> *The Thing (from Another World)* . . . is the story of a team of military men sent to an arctic station at the request of its scientists, to investigate what turns out to be the crash of a flying saucer. The saucer's pilot (James Arness) is a bloodsucking vegetable that is described as intelligent but spends most of its time yelling and killing and leaving evidence of plans for conquest. The minor villain is a scientist (Robert Corthwaite) who wants to communicate with the Thing rather than destroy it and who admires the alien race for its lack of sexual emotion. The Thing, however, has no interest in the scientist, and the human community (from which the scientist wishes to exclude himself), led by an efficient, hard-headed, and sexually active Captain (Kenneth Tobey), manages to electrocute the "super carrot." The film's bias is in favor of that friendly, witty, sexy, and professionally effective—Hawksian—human community, and opposed to the dark forces that lurk outside (the Thing as *Beowulf's* Grendel). The film also relates the lack of a balanced professionalism (the scientist who becomes indifferent to the human community and whose professionalism approaches the fanatical, as opposed to the effective Captain and the klutzy but less seriously flawed reporter) to what was meant in that paranoid time by the term communism (we are all one big vegetable or zombie with each cell equally conscious).

This is how the oppositions between these two movies stack up:

1. *Army vs. scientists.* In both films the army and the scientists are in conflict with each other. The army sees the alien as a threatening invader to be defended against and, if necessary or possible, destroyed. The scientists see

the alien as a visitor with superior knowledge, to be learned from and, if possible, joined. In *The Thing* the army is right, and the scientist is an obsessive visionary who gets in the way of what obviously needs to be done. In *The Day* the scientists are right, and the army is an impulsive force that is almost responsible for the end of the world (hardly a far-fetched perspective).

2. *Violence vs. intelligence.* The Thing is nonverbal and destructive; Klaatu is articulate and would prefer to be nonviolent. The army, which meets violence with violence, is correct in *The Thing* and wrong in *The Day* because of the nature of the alien; but what I am suggesting here is that the alien has its nature because of each genre's implicit attitude toward the unknown. The curious scientist is a positive force in *The Day* and a negative force in *The Thing*, for the same reasons.

3. *Closing vs. opening.* Both horror and science fiction open our sense of the possible (mummies can live, men can turn into wolves, Martians can visit), especially in terms of community (the Creature walks among us). Most horror films are oriented toward the restoration of the status quo rather than toward any permanent opening. *The Day* is about man's opportunity to join an interstellar political system; it opens the community's boundaries and leaves them open. *The Thing* is about the expulsion of an intruder and ends with a warning to "watch the skies" in case more monsters show up; in other words, the community is opened against its will and attempts to reclose. What the horrified community has generally learned from the opening is to be on guard and that chaos can be repressed.

4. *Inhuman vs. human.* Science fiction is open to the potential value of the inhuman: one can learn from it, take a trip with it (*Close Encounters*), include it in a larger sense of what is. Horror is fascinated by transmutations between human and inhuman (wolfmen, etc.), but the inhuman characteristics decisively mandate destruction. This can be rephrased as Uncivilized vs. Civilized or as Id vs. Superego, suggesting the way a horror film allows forbidden desire to find masked expression before it is destroyed by more decisive repression. . . .

5. *Communication vs. silence.* This links most of the above. The Thing doesn't talk; Klaatu does. (Or: Romero's Living Dead are completely nonverbal, while the climax of *Close Encounters* is an exchange of languages.) What one can talk with, one can generally deal with. Communication between species is vital in *The Day*, absurd in *The Thing*. The opened community can be curious about and learn from the outsiders, while the closed community talks only among itself. Horror emphasizes the dread of knowing, the danger of curiosity, while science fiction emphasizes the danger and irresponsibility of the closed mind. Science fiction appeals to consciousness, horror to the unconscious.[9]

Horror and science fiction, then, are different because of their attitudes toward curiosity and the openness of systems, and comparable in that both tend to organize themselves around some confrontation between an unknown and a would-be knower. Where a given film includes scientists, space travel, *and* monsters—as in *This Island Earth* (Joseph M. Newman, 1955), for instance—the important thing is to discover the dynamics of the situation, the attitude toward the question of discovery; in the case of *This Island Earth,* such an investigation would, I think, lead to its being identified as science fiction. In *The Fly* (Kurt Neumann, 1958), as in *Frankenstein,* the vital elements are that the scientist and his creation are intimately interrelated and that the white-headed fly is destroyed rather than saved. When a scientist agrees that "there are things man is not meant to know," it is a safe bet that one is in the realm of horror rather than that of science. In *Forbidden Planet,* which might at first appear a nearly perfect example of genre crossover, the Krel science, the brain booster, Robbie the Robot, and the notion of humans traveling in a flying saucer all seem to outweigh, as genre-definitive elements, the "monster from the id" that the father/scientist unleashes in the absence of conscious control and that would, on its own, fit perfectly into the repertoire of the horror film. The moral of the story of the Krel monster and the subsequent decision to destroy its planet fit explicitly into a horror world view, but it seems important that the robot (as one aspect of Krel science, yet built by a human) is integrated into the human crew and that the human race is presented as being on a positive evolutionary course. It is also significant that the scientist, by becoming conscious of his accountability for the actions of his unconscious, denies the Krel monster and releases himself and his daughter from their Oedipal nightmare. (He cannot deny the monster without first accepting that it is *his* monster.) Ultimately *Forbidden Planet* is a "myth of human adaptability," [10] a phrase Joanna Russ has used to characterize science fiction in contrast to fantasy and one that is substantially in agreement with my notion of the perfectible, open community.

   Alien, on the other hand, is emphatically a horror film, if for no other reason than because the scientist (who may well have been modeled on the scientist played by Robert Corthwaite in *The Thing*) is a soulless robot rather than an authentic visionary and because the humans are presented as trapped between an efficient monster and a monstrously efficient military-industrial complex. The computer in *Alien,* who is called "Mother," is addressed as "You bitch!" when she supports the company, protects the robot, and takes her self-destruct program a bit too far; the monster is the "son" of the "bitch." The threat behind all of these is an organization that values military efficiency and heartless strength more than human life and love, and in comparison with the power of that theme, the space travel setting does not have much weight. In Robert Wise's *Star Trek* (1979), on the other hand—which is set, like *Alien,* primarily on a threatened spaceship—the relations between human love and curiosity on the one hand and advanced computer technology on the other are integrated in a positive way. What begins as a story of a threat from outer space turns into a love story in which a sexual and romantic apotheosis creates a new order of being. Although most people seem to dislike Wise's film, particularly in comparison with its excellent sequels, all three *Star Treks* (like the TV series) are similar in their emphasis on humanistic values, the importance of friendship, the excitement of discovery, the mysteries opened by science, and of course the nastiness of the bad guys, whether they be Klingons or Earth-bound bureaucrats. Like *The Day the Earth Stood Still*, *La Jetée* (Chris Marker, 1963), and *2001*, the *Star Trek* films are useful examples of pure as well as great science fiction.

It may seem at this point as if I were arguing that science fiction is the more positive and healthful genre, but what I am really getting at is that science fiction and horror each promote growth in different ways. By appealing to the conscious, to the spirit of adventure, to the imaginative province of the medieval romance, and to the creative use of intelligent curiosity, science fiction allows us to explore our evolution and to begin the creation of the future, something it accomplishes both in cautionary tales of the dangers of technology and in adventurous celebrations of human capacity and resourcefulness. It opens the field of inquiry, the range of possible subjects, and leaves us open.

Where much science fiction is limited is in its sometimes boyish sense of adventure, its tendency to extend into some hypothetical time and place the unexamined assumptions of the present culture (e.g., the patriarchy), and its relative lack of interest in the unconscious. Where science fiction stands or falls is often in the *idea* that supports the fiction and in how far the tale is willing to follow that idea. What *The Day the Earth Stood Still* shares with Harry Bates's "Farewell to the Master" (the story on which it is based) is the idea that once human beings have passed a certain evolutionary level, it is technology that masters them; both story and movie, each in its own way, pursue this idea to logical conclusions. In the standard science fiction world of the story, which is organized around one gee-whiz daring boyish reporter, the emphasis is on the robot's invention of a device that recreates beings from sound recordings and the startling discovery that Klaatu is the beloved pet of the robot, who is "the monster." In the cold-war world of the movie, which has a much more interesting human story, the relevance of this conceit is made explicit in terms of the way people are forced to learn that they must submit to the authority of the robots because they have—without knowing it—already become the servants of nuclear technology. By this ingenious twist, the Wise film offers human beings the option of mastering the atomic bomb while it extends the essence of the story's original, chilling idea. And the same often applies to horror, because what distinguishes fictions like *Franken-stein*, Matheson's *I Am Legend*, and King's *Salem's Lot* or films like

Don't Look Now (Nicolas Roeg, 1973), *Dawn of the Dead* (George Romero, 1979), or *The Last Wave* is their pushing good ideas as far as possible.

What *The Thing* does not share with the story on which it is based (Campbell's "Who Goes There?") is an interesting idea. Even if both story and movie, in this case, explore the problem of the human community undermined by the presence of a monster, the monster in *The Thing* is fundamentally not interesting, merely a loud hulk, whereas the monster in "Who Goes There?" is a shape-shifter capable of ingesting and imitating every man and animal in the environment, a monster that threatens the notions of trust and community so seriously that Hawks and Nyby apparently felt unable to handle it (though they could well have been stopped by the problem of finding adequate special effects), with the result that they produced a movie more Hawksian than it is anything else, and as much a comedy as it is a thriller, about witty people with a less complex but still dirty job to do. It would, I think, have been a more interesting and frightening movie if the idea of Campbell's monster had been followed to its logical conclusion, as John Carpenter's remake (1982) would have been better if it had projected a more viable and engaging vision of the isolated human community.

The really scary films turn out to be those organized around a good idea, and while that may not be a scientific premise, it is often a well-struck nerve, a resonant psychological intersection, as is the case in fictions like *Heart of Darkness, The Turn of the Screw,* and *Frankenstein* and films like *The Wolf Man* (George Waggner, 1941), *Mad Love,* and *Peeping Tom* (Michael Powell, 1960). In a case like *Night of the Living Dead,* for example, the *premise* that the dead could rise and would want to eat the living is what I find scary; Romero's ghoulish imagery dramatizes that premise and would not have, on its own, the same force—a lesson that the slasher films will eventually learn.

The direction in which the horror film leads its audience—into the unconscious and through the implications of evil and of dream—can prove beneficial to the audience, and here we return to the problem of the good host. What the best horror films offer is another image of human perfectibility, and not always through the exclusion of the unconscious impulse or the lower classes (since, after all, to go to a horror film is to let the inner monster, whether psychological or social, find expression, no matter what happens at the end of the film). Sometimes what these movies offer is integration with the horror, as in the example of *Mad Love,* or reconciliation with what is valuable in the horror, as in *The Bride of Frankenstein,* or personal growth in a tragic context, as in *The Howling.* The effect of the good horror film is to show us what we are not comfortable seeing but may need to look at anyway. As a strategic aspect of its programmatic project—its intention to show us what we are comfortable ignoring—the horror film often turns reflexive, reminding us that we are watching a movie, that we have chosen to have this nightmare experience, and that we must take responsibility for submitting to a category of illusion. This is, in a nutshell, the difference between *Psycho* (Alfred Hitchcock, 1960), which implicates the audience in the voyeurism of the mad killer, and almost every mad slasher movie that pretends to pay homage to *Psycho* but has no interest in raising the consciousness of the audience and concentrates on techniques that reinforce illusion and defeat self-examination.

The first thing that happens in *Mad Love,* for instance, is that a fist smashes the glass on which the credits have been painted. This is followed by a brilliant series of image/reality fake-outs of which the most subtle is the use of Frances Drake (who plays the real Yvonne) in close shots of Yvonne's statue, which forces the audience to compare the image of Drake as Yvonne, which is supposed to be "real," and the image of Drake as the statue of Yvonne, which is supposed to be an "image"—the sort of joke that Keaton exploited so well at the end of *Sherlock Jr.* (Buster Keaton, 1924). Under the pressure of conflicting desires, Gogol's identity fragments into a series of mirrored self-images. For a while Gogol is the victim of illusions as well as a cheerfully ruthless creator of delusions in the mind of his patient, but at the climax he is entirely unable to distinguish image from reality, which is the central feature of his madness and the twist that makes his obsessiveness interesting. But of course the point of the opening fake-outs and a number of closely related tropes throughout the film is that the audience of *Mad Love* regularly confuses image and reality and is, to the extent that it responds to the story and believes its illusions, nearly mad—and all of that is tied securely, via a series of verbal and visual allusions, to *The Cabinet of Dr. Caligari* (Robert Wiene, 1919) and its theme of the unreliability of surface impressions and the danger of a controlling illusion, whose political implications were certainly not lost on Karl Freund. (The allusion to *Dr. Caligari* is one of many; *Mad Love* anchors itself firmly in the history of the genre, making particularly good use of *The Phantom of the Opera* and—outside the genre—*The Last Laugh* [F. W. Murnau, 1924], which Freund of course photographed.)

To take a more familiar example of flagrant reflexivity in the horror film, the first line in *King Kong* (1933) is "Is this the moving picture ship?" And the finest irony in the film is that Denham starts out to make a movie, decides instead to bring the monster home (i.e., creates not film but theater), and is reproached by the audience—while the curtains are still closed—because they have expected to see a movie, to really "see something." For *King Kong*'s audience to smile knowingly at this re-

49. *King Kong:* The giant gorilla is the live attraction instead of a movie.

mark—Lady, are you going to see something, and it's not a movie, it's real!—is to be brought suddenly up against the fact that *King Kong*'s audience is seeing a movie and that all this is not real. This elegant twist is supported by a labyrinth of authorially self-conscious in-jokes whereby the principal screenwriter, Ruth Rose, and her husband, Ernest B. Schoedsack, together with Merian C. Cooper, set up Ann Darrow, Jack Driscoll, and Carl Denham, respectively, as their surrogates, who are attempting to make a movie that will satisfy those who feel that adventure films ought to have a love interest—which is precisely what the filmmakers, irritated at the reception of *Chang* (1927) and *Rango* (1930), were doing in *King Kong*—all of that complicated by the fact that Rose and Schoedsack had met and fallen in love while on an expeditionary ship whose name is very like that used in *King Kong*. The audience of 1933 would not have gotten most of these jokes, though they might have remembered *Chang* and so might have been able to see themselves in the New York audience or in the images of the producers alluded to at the start, but they would certainly have been aware of the movie/theater dichotomy that informs Denham's turnaround.

These are only two examples from the thirties, and it is possible to come up with examples from virtually any decade or industry. Even a wretched knife-and-sex picture like *He Knows You're Alone* (original title, *Blood Wedding*, Armand Mastroianni, 1980) opens with a young woman being stabbed through the back of her theater seat while unwillingly watching a movie in which a young woman is threatened by a psychopathic killer. Even *Friday the 13th* plays a lot of games with dreams and the fulfillment of dreams (games that are extended and complicated in the superior Parts 2 and 3), as does *Halloween II* (Rick Rosenthal, 1981), a film that is almost entirely organized around the implications of the song that runs under the closing credits, "Mister Sandman, bring me a dream; / Make him the cutest that I've ever seen." (And then: "Please turn on your magic beam"!) My favorite example from the forties is *The Mummy's Ghost* (Reginald LeBorg, 1944), in which not even the priest can believe that "Kharis—still *lives*?"; in which a student suggests to his obsessed professor that "maybe that was a man made up as a mummy, to fool the people"; and in which a museum guard ignores an accurate preview of his own death that presents itself as a silly radio mystery. There was less of this sort of thing in the fifties, which was a bad period for self-consciousness in the first place and one in which Hollywood was particularly interested in selling illusions, but there were some reflexive elements in *House of Wax* (Andre deToth, 1953), *The 5,000 Fingers of Dr. T.* (Roy Rowland, 1953), *The House on Haunted Hill* (William Castle, 1958), *The Tingler* (Castle, 1959), and *Invasion of the Body Snatchers* (Don Siegel, 1956), and it is arguable that the shift into more overt and problematic reflexivity that was announced in the great British film *Peeping Tom* and its American contemporary *Psycho* was the core of the shift into the sixties themselves. *Psycho*, of course, did not come out of nowhere, and in terms of the argument I am advancing here, it is not difficult to read *Vertigo* (Hitchcock, 1958) and to a lesser extent *Rear Window* (Hitchcock, 1954) as working with horror-film material in the genre format of the mystery; all three of these films are centrally concerned with the problem of the image and its relation to the real world, each of which is presented as a category of obsession, and in *Vertigo* and *Psycho* the figure who insists on living his dream is perceived as a destructive but fascinating force. It is these films, with Powell's *Peeping Tom*, that most prefigure the labyrinthine reflexivity of such sixties horror films as *Targets* (Peter Bogdanovich, 1968) and *Kwaidan* (Masaki Kobayashi, 1965). The seventies and early eighties have already been discussed at some length, so I would like to close with two particularly arresting reflexive images, one from Dreyer's *Vampyr* and one from De Palma's *Blow Out* (1981).

It is not necessary for a horror film to have a transcendental or even a dream element. There are horror stories that are not ghost stories and

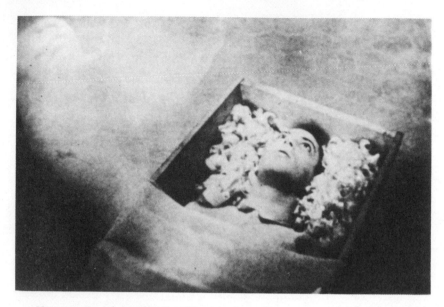

50. *Vampyr:* David Gray (Julian West) in the coffin.

horror stories that are not psychologically oriented. There are, very broadly, three subcategories of the genre: monster stories, supernatural stories, and psychosis stories.[11] Often they overlap. The present knife-and-sex cycle is an unfortunate but apt example of the psychosis story; more fortunate examples include *Dr. Caligari, Mad Love, Peeping Tom,* and *Repulsion* (Roman Polanski, 1965). *King Kong* is a straightforward monster story, as is *Them!* (Gordon Douglas, 1954), while *Vampyr,* like *Dracula* (Tod Browning, 1931), *The Wolf Man,* and *The Mummy,* is a monster story with strong supernatural elements. *The Last Wave* is supernatural but has no monsters. The means by and ends to which consciousness is raised in the horror film depend to a certain extent on which of these subcategories is involved, and in *Vampyr* the notion of the film as dream is inseparable from its view of the night world haunted by supernatural agencies. *Vampyr* is about light and shadows, about categories of illusion and revelation, and its climax comes when the central protagonist, David Gray, gives up some of his blood and has two dreams, the first of which is an accurate warning of a forced suicide attempt and the second of which presents him to himself as trapped—dead yet sentient—in a coffin whose window first is compared to and then actually becomes the rectangle of the movie screen; this suggests to the audience that it is entombed in a dark room whose window is the image, and that the whole film is a dream or image field whose limits and dangers are only now becoming clear. In a paradoxical way, this makes the horrors real as it makes the film accountable for presenting an illusion. At the very least it makes the audience conscious of submitting to a dream field, a willing suspension of belief that results, as I have argued elsewhere,[12] in an all the more compelling trap of belief, because there is no innocent way to dismiss the artwork as an illusion once it has presented itself as being aware of being an illusion.

Blow Out, which starts as a psychosis story and turns quickly into a paranoia film[13] about the evils of Watergate, is not interested in metaphysics and has little to say about dreams or shadows, but it is much more clearly focused on the ethics of self-consciousness than either of the films on which it is modeled (*Blow Up* [Michelangelo Antonioni, 1966] and *The Conversation* [Francis Ford Coppola, 1974]) and is in its own way as serious about the problem of knowledge and illusion as *Vertigo* or *Vampyr*. It opens with a terrible sequence from a bad horror film about a slasher in a girl's dormitory; it turns out that the protagonist of *Blow Out* is a sound engineer who needs a good scream to complete this sequence, which, we discover, he is helping to edit. Eventually he becomes involved in a complicated murder-and-politics story, falls in love with a prostitute who is entangled in that intrigue, wires her for sound so that he can save her life and capture the bad guy, and loses his entire library of sound effects when the bad guy invades his territory with a bulk eraser. What happens is that he is too late to save the woman; all he has left of her is the tape of her dying screams. In the final seconds of the film, we see the protagonist again editing the bad horror film; we realize that he has not told the authorities what he knows, because he knows that would change nothing. Then comes the moment when the girl in the bad film screams, and we recognize the scream as that of the dying prostitute. In that moment *Blow Out* becomes a real horror film, setting itself in relation to and judging the category of illusion represented by the dumb slasher movie, absolutely scaring the hell out of the audience while shifting reality gears and tackling the whole problem of action and guilt in contemporary America. This is an America disillusioned from its idealism, and therefore not realistic but helpless, and so prey to the illusion of escapism—whereas the rest of the point is of course that there is no escape from politics any more than there is a way to forget who is screaming and under what circumstances. It becomes a horror film that by critiquing its own level of illusion addresses the reality of horror—as in all great horror films, its terrible message and unpleasant imagery are meant not to destroy us but to show us something that we need to see.

Not just in film but throughout our experience of the world, vision is both an opportunity and a problem. To the extent that the world or the imagination is a darkened theater, the shadow images created by the integrated forces of projected light and masking/filtering silver—a silver that, for once, allows vampires to cast a reflection—are the children of the light. The horror film creates an opportunity for vision even as it dramatizes its dialectical partner—utter darkness, the refusal to see clearly. For even as its threatening figures advance toward the audience out of the night, the "music they make" is still the music of light, and while the image of human perfectibility that they generate may seem to have chosen odd, often monstrous terms for its expression, it is still the exploration of the human condition and the burden of knowledge to which they are dedicated. We are still on the outskirts of Eden, expelled from an easy paradise because we wanted to know the "things man is not meant to know," a knowledge that could make us like gods. Although both horror and science fiction, as genres, are dubious about the value of the apple, they are dubious in different ways. Science fiction has its challenging apple full of challenging possibilities, and horror has its dangerous apple full of destructive potential; the difference between these attitudes is the difference between the last line of *The Thing*—"Keep watching the skies!"—and the last line of *Brainstorm* (Douglas Trumbull, 1983)—"Look at the stars!" In both cases the apple will be bitten, and whether it introduces us to the world of the undead (as it did Snow White) or gives us an idea for an entirely new kind of pie, that bite will still prove nourishing.

Notes

1. Joanna Russ, "What Can a Heroine Do? or Why Women Can't Write," in *Images of Women in Fiction: Feminist Perspectives,* edited by Susan Koppelman Cornillon (Bowling Green, Ohio: Popular Press, 1972), p. 18. A similar observation was made by Susan Sontag in her widely reprinted essay, "The Imagination of Disaster," which first appeared in Sontag, *Against Interpretation* (New York: Delta, 1966), pp. 209–225, but Russ's is the better article.

2. For an extensive discussion of reflexive devices and their carefully manipulated moral implications, see Bruce Kawin, *"The Funhouse* and *The Howling,"* *Film Quarterly* 35, no. 1 (Fall 1981): 30–32.

3. Bruce Kawin, "The Mummy's Pool," *Dreamworks* 1, no. 4 (Summer 1981): 291–301; reprinted in *Planks of Reason: Essays on the Horror Film,* edited by Barry K. Grant (Metuchen, N.J.: Scarecrow Press, 1984), pp. 3–20, and *Film Theory and Criticism,* 3d ed., edited by Gerald Mast and Marshall Cohen (New York: Oxford, 1985), pp. 466–481.

4. "An Introduction to the American Horror Film," in *The American Nightmare,* edited by Robin Wood and Richard Lippe (Toronto: Festival of Festivals, 1979), pp. 7–28; reprinted in *Planks of Reason,* ed. Grant, pp. 164–200.

5. Stephen King, *Danse Macabre* (New York: Everest House, 1981), pp. 15–17, 29–30. I think, however, that even King would be irritated if someone called *Pet Sematary* "science fiction."

6. See *Focus on the Horror Film*, edited by Roy Huss and T. J. Ross (Englewood Cliffs, N.J.: Prentice-Hall, 1972), p. 129, and *Focus on the Science Fiction Film*, edited by William Johnson (Englewood Cliffs, N.J.: Prentice-Hall, 1972), pp. 69, 154–156.

7. *Focus on the Science Fiction Film*, pp. 153–154.

8. Rick Altman, "A Semantic/Syntactic Approach to Film Genre," *Cinema Journal* 23, no. 3 (Spring 1984): 6–18; reprinted in this volume.

9. Kawin, "The Mummy's Pool," pp. 293–294. A point I have not had time to make here is that "Who Goes There?"—with its careful emphasis on scientifically explaining the horror—is science fiction.

10. Russ, "What Can a Heroine Do?" p. 18. See also Russ, "The Image of Women in Science Fiction," pp. 79–94. These are two of the finest essays on the subject, and I am clearly indebted to them both.

11. Huss and Ross arrived at a similar breakdown of subcategories: gothic horror, monster terror, and psychological thriller. See *Focus on the Horror Film*, pp. 1–10.

12. Bruce Kawin, *The Mind of the Novel: Reflexive Fiction and the Ineffable* (Princeton: Princeton University Press, 1982).

13. For the term "paranoia film," see Bruce Kawin, "Me Tarzan, You Junk: Violence, Sexism, and Moral Education in the Paranoia Film," *Take One* 6, no. 4 (March 1978): 29–33.

19. Monsters from the Id

MARGARET TARRATT

Few things reveal so sharply as science fiction the wishes, hopes, fears, inner stresses and tensions of an era, or define its limitations with such exactness.[1]

Most writers in English on science fiction films view them as reflections of society's anxiety about its increasing technological prowess and its responsibility to control the gigantic forces of destruction it possesses. Francis Arnold, for instance, was typical in relating the upsurge of science fiction films in the 1950s and 1960s to the existence of the Bomb and the first Sputnik.[2] It has long been a critical commonplace to deplore the introduction of the "love interest" into science fiction films. Richard Hodgens, while praising *War of the Worlds* (Byron Haskin, 1953), complained that "one unnecessary modern addition . . . was an irrelevant boy and girl theme, because [George] Pal apologized 'Audiences want it.'"[3] Penelope Houston refers cynically to "the inevitable girl" in such films.[4] The plot synopsis of *20 Million Miles to Earth* (Nathan Juran, 1957) in the *Monthly Film Bulletin*[5] omits the hero's romance, and this is no isolated example. Yet the "love interest" in science fiction films, far from being extraneous to the central concern of the works, usually forms an integral part of their structure, as certain French critics have recognized.

F. Hoda dwells with interest on the "camouflaged sensuality" of the genre,[6] pointing out that many of the situations in films of this kind could be reduced to representations of aggressive sexuality, disguised to a greater or lesser degree. Jean Loth suggested that film monsters should be regarded as embodiments of women's virginal sexual fantasies—a cross between fear and desire.[7] Raymond Lefèvre noticed the masking of sadism and eroticism by fantastic decor and poetic effects,[8] while Fereydoun Hoveyda suggested that the importance of the science fiction film lay in its tentative breakdown of certain limitations concerning the representation on the screen of love and hate and of human relationships.[9] None of these writers, however, gives any detailed illustration in support of their theses. The fullest analysis along these lines so far is in Tom Milne's study of Mamoulian's *Dr. Jekyll and Mr. Hyde* (1931),[10] but this film is not examined in a science fiction context.

Although the majority of science fiction films appear to express some kind of concern with the moral state of contemporary society, many are more directly involved with an examination of our inner nature. Curt Siodmak maintained:

> In its day, *Frankenstein*, the forerunner of a generation of admitted mumbo jumbo and lots of entertainment, was a true trail blazer, and in effect opened up Hollywood-produced motion pictures to both psychiatry and neuro-surgery. What now seems primitive in *Metropolis* or the Jekyll-Hydean cycle of werewolf pictures are simply variations on the theme which Siegfried Kracauer in *From Caligari to Hitler* characterised as a "deep and fearful concern with the foundations of the self." [11]

This article will argue that these films are deeply involved with the concepts of Freudian psychoanalysis and seem in many cases to derive their structure from it. They may deal with society as a whole, but they arrive at social comment through a dramatization of the individual's anxiety about his or her own repressed sexual desires, which are incompatible with the morals of civilized life. Freud described this process in "Anxiety and Instinctual Life" thus: "The commonest cause of anxiety neurosis is unconsummated excitation. Libidinal excitation is aroused but not satisfied, not employed; apprehensiveness then appears instead of this libido that has been directed from its employment. . . . What is responsible for anxiety in hysteria and other neurosis is the process of repression." [12]

The battles with sinister monsters or extraterrestrial forces are an externalization of the civilized person's conflict with his or her primitive subconscious or id. Freud writes of the id in the following manner:

> We approach the Id with analogies; we call it a chaos, a cauldron full of seething excitations. . . . It is filled with energy reaching it from the instincts, but it has no organisation, produces no collective will, but only a striving to bring about the satisfaction of the instinctual needs subject to the observance of the pleasure principle. . . . Contrary impulses exist side by side, without cancelling each other out or diminishing each other. . . . No alteration in its mental processes is produced by the passage of time. Wishful impulses which have never passed beyond the id, but impressions, too, which have been sunk into the id by repression are virtually immortal; after the passage of decades they behave as if they had just occurred. They can only be recognized as belonging to the past, can only lose their importance and be deprived of their cathexis of energy when they have been made conscious by the work of analysis. . . . The id, of course, knows no judgments of value; no good and evil; no morality. . . . Instinctive cathexes seeking discharge—that, in our view, is all there is in the id. [13]

Forbidden Planet (Fred McLeod Wilcox, 1956) provides an explicit, if somewhat crude, example of the id in action. The events take place several centuries in the future, when human beings have penetrated what is significantly termed "inner" as opposed to "outer" space. A party is sent

51. *Forbidden Planet:* The innocent siren Altaira (Anne Francis) and Robby the Robot.

to discover what has happened to a group who had attempted to colonize the planet Altair 420 years before. As they try to land, they are warned off by Captain Morbius (Walter Pidgeon), leader of the original expedition, who claims he is the only survivor, needs no help, and cannot be held responsible for the consequences of their landing. They are entertained by Morbius, who lives in the height of automated luxury. Unexpectedly, his daughter Altaira (Ann Francis), appears in the room, an innocent, briefly clad siren whom Morbius had been trying to keep away from the men. She shows considerable admiration for the clean-limbed heroic spacemen, who become rivals for her affection until Commander Adams (Leslie Nielsen) wins. When he kisses her, her pet tiger, which had hitherto been harmless when in her presence, no longer recognizes her and advances, snarling, until the captain is forced to shoot it. Meanwhile, in the spaceship at night a curiously sexual, heavy panting noise is heard, the ship is smashed up, and one of the men is later found torn to bits. Eventually they see and fight the monster, a leaping tigerish shape outlined in electrical sparks. Morbius, talking to the captain, explains that

52. The monster from the id appears in electrical sparks (*Forbidden Planet*).

the planet was originally the domain of the Krel, a humane and hyperintelligent species whose scientific discoveries he is able to make use of with the help of a patent brain booster. They became extinct at a time when they were on the threshold of dispensing with their physical bodies. The captain, finding the monster is immune to all weapons, decides to have a brain boost himself in order to work out a strategy against it. Returning to Morbius's house with his scientist colleague (whose IQ is considerably higher than his own), he persuades the doctor's daughter to marry him and leave with him for Earth. Dr. Morbius opposes this plan violently, declaring that he and his daughter are "joined, body and soul." Meanwhile the captain's companion, who had sneaked off to get a brain boost himself, returns to die, gasping with his last breath: "The monster is from the id."

"The id—what's that?" asks the captain. "An obsolete term once used to describe the elementary structure of the subconscious," replies Morbius. The captain, with commendable celerity, now grasps the root of the problem. The Krel, in the passion for scientific advancement, had ignored the "mindless beast" of their own subconscious, which had ultimately destroyed them. "That thing out there is you!" he accuses the doctor, indicating the monster which is once more advancing; "We are all part monsters in our subconscious—that's why we have laws and religion. You sent your secret id out, a primitive, more enraged and inflamed with each frustration. You still have the mind of a primitive." The doctor was destroying the spacemen who threaten his relationship with his daughter. In despair, Morbius recognizes the truth, turns off the electric current which animates the monster of his id and significantly addresses the captain as "Son." The word *incest* is never mentioned, but his suppressed incestuous desires are clearly implied to be at the root of all the trouble.

Forbidden Planet has aspects in common with many science fiction films. Space travel is commonly accompanied by publicly recognized sexual frustration among the all-male crew. The scientist with his total dedication to advanced knowledge is an unbalanced figure, ruthless in defense of his own research. The hero is an ordinary man with a healthy physique, leadership qualities, a controlled sexual drive, and only average intellect—a good all-rounder.

As Kingsley Amis pointed out,[14] this film has strong structural and thematic connections with Shakespeare's *Tempest*—especially in its distrust of advanced science and its influence on human beings. In *Forbidden Planet* science has advanced to a point at which it becomes the equivalent of Prospero's occult study. Morbius has entered the realm of "forbidden knowledge," both sexually and intellectually, a realm both enticing and fearful to characters such as Baron Frankenstein or Colonel Merritt in *Conquest of Space* (Byron Haskin, 1955), who dies attempting to sabotage his sacrilegious mission.

Traditionally, the idea of forbidden knowledge has had a sexual as well as an intellectual connotation stemming from the myth of Adam and Eve. Science fiction films take up this dual interpretation. With them, we return to the problems and anxieties of the Middle Ages, when people feared to inquire too closely into the elements, thought to be inhabited by evil demons. Bacon's famous challenge to the fear of natural science, in his *Advancement of Learning,* is a challenge that seems to confront the heroes of science fiction. Freud drew a parallel between the anxieties of modern man and the "demonological neurosis" of the seventeenth century: "The states of possession correspond to our neurosis, for the explanation of which we resort to psychical powers. In our eyes the demons are bad and reprehensible wishes, derivatives of instinctual impulses that have been repudiated and repressed. We merely eliminate the projection of these mental entities into the external world, which the middle ages carried out; instead we regard them as having arisen in the patient's internal life where they have their abode."[15]

One of the classics of the science fiction genre, *The Thing (from Another*

53. Male bonding in *The Thing* (1951) . . .

World) (Christian Nyby, 1951), provides an outstanding example of the "demonological neurosis." A group of American airmen in Alaska are called in by scientists working on secret research at the North Pole. Much emphasis is laid on the freezing conditions as well as the lack of women. A radioactive craft has landed, embedding itself in the ice.

Captain Pat Hendry, in charge of rescuing the spacecraft, is subjected to a good deal of ragging about an alleged romance with the chief scientist's secretary, Nikki (Margaret Sheridan). We learn that they have spent a disastrous evening on leave together in which Hendry got drunk and made a heavy pass at her, only to wake up and find her gone back to base. This incident has become common knowledge in the camp. Hendry, to some extent ignorant of his own drunken behavior, complains about Nikki's action and is enlightened by the indignant girl: "You had moments like an octopus—I never saw so many hands in all my life." Hendry suggests that their relationship started off on the wrong footing and asks if they can begin again. Following this is the film's best sequence, in which the men attempt to extricate the spacecraft by means of explosives, but destroy it while salvaging its occupant, who is frozen into a slab of ice. On the return journey, the Thing is not shown, but a couple of dogs in the plane whine. One of the men recalls an incident in the war when he was stranded with a bomber group: "An army nurse came ashore and caused as much disturbance as this man from Mars."

54. . . . and bondage between Nikki Nicholson (Margaret Sheridan) and Captain Patrick Hendry (Kenneth Tobey).

On their arrival back at base, Hendry resists the pressure of Dr. Carrington, who wishes to be allowed to examine the creature immediately, believing it necessary to keep it alive at all costs. The captain insists on awaiting instructions and organizes a twenty-four-hour watch to be kept. In another interlude with Nikki, she declares: "You're much nicer when you're not mad" and offers to buy him a drink. "That sounds promising," he replies, "You can tie my hands if you want." In a subsequent scene we see him "bound" to a chair, discussing men and women's relationships. "If a man tries to kiss you the first time, he is a wolf. But after 1,000 drinks and 1,000 dinners he isn't?" asks Hendry. She agrees. "Can't I be untied now?" he asks. Later she kisses him and remarks that she would not have been able to be so nice to him were he untied. Finally, when her back is turned, he loosens his bonds. Nikki: "How long have you been loose?" Hendry: "Long enough!"

Later that night, the captain is told how the man on watch is terrified by the monster's hands and eyes, and there is speculation as to whether or not it is alive. The guard covers the ice with his electric blanket so he will not see it, and the creature thaws out. Observing it free, the watchman attacks it in blind panic, and in a subsequent struggle with the airmen, it escapes into the Arctic night, leaving part of its arm and hand behind. It later grows a new one. Examining the severed arm, Dr. Carrington observes that it is entirely composed of vegetable matter and concludes that on Mars, vegetables have evolved in the same way that animals evolved on earth. He also discovers a pocket of seed pollen in the palm of the hand and marvels at the Thing's method of reproduction—"No pain, pleasure, emotions or heart. How superior!" The Thing is later found to feed off blood, but in spite of this, Carrington longs to communicate with the superior intelligence, at whatever cost to human life. Again the captain resists his pressures, stressing the need for the creature to be locked up. Later, it becomes necessary to destroy it. As it seems invulnerable to firearms they attempt to burn it with kerosene, but it escapes, leaving Hendry slightly wounded in the hand, to be ministered to by Nikki. Plans are made to electrocute the Thing. Dr. Carrington steps out to save it, urging it to communicate with them on a rational basis, but is sent flying by a violent blow from the creature's arm. Once the creature has been destroyed, the men joke: "Our worries are over, whilst our captain. . . ." Taking the hint, Hendry proposes to Nikki and she accepts. Meanwhile, the newspaper reporter radios the story he has been burning to deliver: "One of the world's greatest battles has just been fought by the human race. . . ."

The plot of this film could not meaningfully be described in less detail. A parallel is drawn between Captain Hendry and the monster, most clearly through the motif of the hand. We do not need Freud to suggest the phallic significance of this limb in dream symbolism since, in this film, the hand is explicitly established as a sexual organ. In the conflicts between the captain and Nikki, his hands are his sexual weapon, and in his use of them he becomes octopuslike or monstrous. When he is bound to his chair the purpose is to put his hands out of action. While the Thing is seen lying in its ice prison, the guards are particularly frightened by his eyes and hands and by whether or not he is alive. The scientists establish not only that his hand is his sexual organ, but that it grows again when severed—a human fantasy symbolically warding off castration. In the struggle against this monster of his id, Hendry is slightly wounded in the hand, which is tended by Nikki. He undergoes a kind of emasculation that makes him acceptable to her. The struggle against the Thing draws them closer together; by conquering the Thing he wins Nikki in marriage. His facing up to the Thing and the desires of unbridled virility that it represents is a dramatization of Freud's description of the instincts of the id being overcome when brought up into the level of consciousness through analysis. As with the demonological neurosis of the seventeenth century, the instinctual impulses are externalized and dramatized. The Thing clearly represents Hendry's repressed sexual desires, the impulses of the id. We are reminded of the parallel drawn by an airman between the arrival of a single woman in the midst of an all-male military group and the arrival of the Thing among the airmen. Like the Thing, Hendry is initially "frozen." The Arctic landscape provides an objective correlative for his emotional and sexual life, repressed in the all-male disciplined environment of an isolated base. Hendry, too, has his own accidental thaw, through drink, when on leave. His subsequent instinctual predatory behavior is as unacceptable to Nikki as that of the Thing to the airmen. His renewed courtship of Nikki is subject to a joking but rigid control of the instincts symbolized by the binding of his hands. Only in this "civilized" manner can he awaken desire in her—the repeated ritual of drinks, dinner, and restrained behavior cited by Kinsey [16] as the acceptable norm. In his courtship he must fight his surging primitive instincts, a conflict we see settled in the destruction of the Thing. The manner in which he handles the military situation created by the Thing's presence is an image of the way in which he handles himself in relation to Nikki. Unlike the scientist whose greed for knowledge leads him into questionable moral paths, Hendry fears the dangers of examining the Thing. Once it is free, he hopes to control it, to keep it alive but contained. He takes up his general's cry of "Close the door," voicing the necessity to protect human beings from the extremes of nature, whether human or climatic. The Thing is found to be incompatible with human life and must consequently be destroyed, however fascinating it may be. As in Freud's description of the id, the Thing cannot respond to human reason. Hendry's wounded hand suggests the forcible taming of his aggressive sexuality that civilized society demands. The structure of this film can only be understood in a Freudian context. A number of films, some less artistically accomplished than *The Thing,* are structured in a similar manner.

One such example can be found in Nathan Juran's *20 Million Miles to Earth* (1957), in which a U.S. rocketship returning from a flight to Venus crashes into the sea off Sicily. Its one survivor, Colonel Calder (William Hopper), is tended by a zoologist's niece, Marisa (Joan Taylor). A child finds a sealed cylindrical container and sells it to the zoologist, Dr. Leonardo, who finds a glutinous jelly inside. Out of this appears to hatch a small prehistoric type of monster with a long tail. It is extremely aggressive and found to grow at an alarming rate, and eventually escapes. Recaptured and paralyzed by electric shock, it is kept in a Rome zoo for the scientists to examine, but breaks loose again during a power failure. After a spectacular fight with an elephant it is finally killed in the Colosseum. A small circle of men stand around the corpse, regarding it with expressions of regret.

This film has a number of aspects in common with *The Thing*. At the outset, Colonel Calder and Marisa have an antagonistic relationship. Her concern is for his health, while he is obsessed with the need to safeguard his cargo. The first appearance of the creature, as it struggles to free itself from its prison of jelly, follows the goodnight wish of Dr. Leonardo to his niece: "Pleasant dreams." The monster is a clear phallic symbol with its thrashing tail, its absence of internal organs, its dramatic growth, and its reawakening to activity after it has been overpowered. Significantly, the planet it comes from is Venus, also the name of the goddess of love. We are told that the atmosphere on Venus is such that humans cannot breathe and survive in it for long. Eight of the colonel's crew died from exposure to it. The colonel wishes the creature to be kept alive so that scientists may examine it to see under what conditions life could survive on Venus. We do not have to stretch the interpretation too far to recognize this as concern as to how far the aggressive male sexual urge can be liberated in a love relationship without causing injury to the civilized way of life. The threat to civilization from man's destructive urge has been voiced at the beginning of the film with the image of an exploding atomic bomb, and this idea is kept in mind at several points in the film, especially in the Roman background with its ancient crumbling ruins and the Colosseum setting for the battle with the elephant, which remind us of the fall of the Roman Empire, popularly reputed to have sprung from an era of sexual decadence.

As in *The Thing*, battles with the monster are interspersed with increasingly romantic interludes. The more committed the colonel becomes to controlling the creature, the less antagonistic is his relationship to Marisa. She is profoundly disturbed by its appearance and is at one point attacked by it when it stretches out an arm from within its cage. Like Captain Hendry in *The Thing*, Colonel Calder is wounded in the arm—again a symbolic semiemasculation—when he tries to master it, declaring airily: "It's just a matter of controlling the beast." Once he has been wounded, his relationship with Marisa becomes milder and more romantic. He apologizes for his aggression and looks forward to a time when they can pursue their relationship in a darkened cafe at a table with a candle burning and a bottle of wine. This is a symbolic representation of intercourse, the flame of the candle symbolizing desire rather than destruction. This is made clear in a later scene, when Marisa tells the colonel of her nightmare, in which the candle in the dark cafe is burning lower and lower. Soon it will be out. "If we hurry," suggests the colonel, "perhaps we'll be in time." The situation in which they can enjoy this dreamed-of intercourse can only arise when the monster from Venus is put down, as the colonel ultimately recognizes. If it is not quickly destroyed, their romance will have burned itself out. The colonel is unusual in this kind of film in combining the role of scientist and hero. Like Dr. Carrington in *The Thing,* he wishes the monster to be scientifically examined, but, like *The Thing,* the monster has potentially destructive power that renders this too dangerous a course of action. In *The Thing,* the refrain is "Close the door." In *20 Million Miles to Earth* it is "Shut the gate." In order to maintain the mores of civilization, some instincts must be quelled the moment they become apparent. Both films suggest the fear of the violent primitive drives of the male id. The women are almost asexual figures of Arthurian romance offering themselves to the knight once he has slain the beast.

In *The Day the Earth Stood Still* (Robert Wise, 1951), the imperfect human male, a mixture of outward politeness and inner violence, is contrasted with the refined Martian Klaatu (Michael Rennie), who comes to Earth to warn men against the violence of their lives. Significantly, the heroine's husband has been killed in a war. A gentle asexual figure, Klaatu is tended by a powerful robot named Gort, who seems to represent man's violence and even his sexuality (in the scene where he advances threateningly on the cringing heroine and carries her off to the spaceship, as F. Hoda observed). [17] Out of control, Gort's powers are dangerous. Under Klaatu's orders he is an invaluable weapon. After the girl, Helen Benson (Patricia Neal), has been in contact with Klaatu, she is unable to go through with the marriage that her jealous and selfish fiancé urges on her. As Klaatu enters his spaceship to return to Mars, she looks at him wistfully. He is a man whose "baser instincts" or id, in the figure of Gort, are held firmly under control. The film suggests a concept of an ideal man separated from his most primitive instincts, using them only as a source of energy to aid his "higher" civilized aims.

It Came from Outer Space (Jack Arnold, 1953) is another film in which a similar pattern develops with slight variations. The hero, John Putnam (Richard Carlson), a dreamer-scientist who wishes to hasten his marriage to his slightly reluctant fiancée Ellen (Barbara Rush), is the only man in his town to realize that Earth has been invaded by alien beings. The creatures begin to take over the bodies of people in the town so that they seem simultaneously to be themselves, yet not themselves; something is different. The scientist, who quickly comes to terms with the fact that they have been invaded, tries to convince the sheriff (who, as a friend of Ellen's family, opposed his marriage), but is repeatedly ridiculed and ignored. Eventually Ellen is held as a hostage. When she is seen again, her light-colored girlish summer dress has been exchanged for a black one, and she has adopted something of the air of the femme fatale. All the invaders wish to do is to mend their spaceship and take off again. A pact, sensibly made between humans and invaders by Putnam, is finally broken by the sheriff, whose overriding instinct is to attack once he has been forced to accept their existence. The creatures manage to escape, but not before they have been compelled to "show" themselves as they really are—indistinct phallic shapes with an enormous eye (a symbol of the genitals) in the middle of their heads.[18]

In this film, society, as epitomized by the sheriff, is unwilling to probe beneath the surface and refuses to believe anything that does not accord with its own "civilized" desires. Hence, the thoughtful scientist, who recognizes the strength of his own sexual desire and who sees in marriage something more than a mere social alliance, is automatically a suspect figure. The invaders assume human form because they recognize the human weakness of being unable to confront the existence of sexuality. But the existence of the genitals cannot be ignored. Even the "nice" girl Ellen is forced to reveal her innate sexuality. Putnam's dealings with the invaders suggest that some form of harmony can be established between the civilized and sexual aspects of human beings (a more sophisticated and humane view than that in the films previously discussed), but society in the form of the sheriff, made to confront its own sexual nature, can only attempt to overcome what is, in fact, a superior force.

This film, like many science fiction films, provides a good illustration of the tensions, examined by Kinsey,[19] between publicly accepted social and sexual mores and the actual sexual needs of the individual. *Forbidden Planet, The Thing, 20 Million Miles to Earth, The Day the Earth Stood Still*, and *It Came from Outer Space* are all films concerned with the clash between the public and private individual, unwilling to defy convention but disturbed by secret impulses and desires that are incompatible with the social superego to which they aspire. The legal proscription, still widespread in the United States, of all sexual relationships outside marriage, reflected in the bourgeois consciousness of right and wrong, becomes a nagging source of disquiet, particularly in *The Thing, It Came from Outer Space*, or Mamoulian's *Dr. Jekyll and Mr. Hyde*.

The conquest of the "monster of the id" is the structural raison d'être of many science fiction films. There are also some science fiction films which, while based on psychoanalytical concepts, concern themselves with a variation on this theme. A number of them deal with impotence and frigidity. This group includes such films as *Spider Woman* (Roy William Neill, 1944), *Wasp Woman* (Roger Corman, 1960), and *The Fly* (Kurt Neumann, 1958), which explore insect phobia—fear of castration and dread of the phallic mother. One of the earliest science fiction films to look at the sexual nature of woman is James Whale's *The Bride of Frankenstein* (1935). *Frankenstein* (Whale, 1931) itself provides a fairly straightforward example of the kind of film discussed earlier, which examines the tension between subconscious sexual desires and the mores of civilization. *The Bride* assumes a knowledge of the earlier film in its continued exploration of such secret desires. The film opens with a conversation between Shelley, Byron, and Mary Shelley, author of the novel *Frankenstein.* Byron professes some amazement that such a dark story could have been created by Mary, who appears a graceful feminine figure. She is undisturbed by his suggestion of the monstrous fantasies that lurk in her inner nature. Considering Byron's claim to be the "world's greatest sinner" and Shelley's to be the "world's greatest poet," Mary suggests that a simple love story would never have done for such an audience: "So why shouldn't I write of monsters?" She then offers to continue the tale, and her narration is carried over the opening shots of the fire in which the monster is thought to have met his death.

As with Hendry and the Thing, there is a close parallel relationship between Frankenstein and his monster in the Frankenstein films. Just as, at the beginning of *The Bride of Frankenstein,* the monster, thought to be dead, shows himself very much alive, so Frankenstein (Colin Clive), brought home as a corpse on his wedding night, is revived in the presence of his wife, who, incidentally, had once been warned to beware her wedding night. As with the creature in 20 *Million Miles to Earth,* this reawakening process symbolizes what Freud describes as "the revival of libidinal desires after they have been quenched through being sated." [20]

The wedding night proceeds with a scene in which Frankenstein, still weakened through illness, lies alone in bed and with reawakening enthusiasm discusses the temptations of aspiring to be a creator with his wife (Valerie Hobson). She responds with shocked arguments that what he desires is "blasphemous." "We are not meant to know such things. It is the work of the Devil." They are clearly discussing the act of procreation or some form of sexual intercourse. The analogy between love and science is taken up a little later by the eminent scientist Dr. Pretorius (Ernest Thesiger)—a man booted out of the university for knowing too much: "The creation of life is enthralling," he declares, "Science, like love, has her little surprises." In his efforts to convince Frankenstein to continue his experiments in creation, he points to the Bible, quoting the exhortation to "increase and multiply." As if to underline his point he reveals some homunculi he has created, imprisoned in glass jars—a king, queen, archbishop, devil, and ballerina. The king, watched primly by the archbishop and gleefully by the devil (who is said to resemble Pretorius), makes frenzied attempts to climb out of his jar and make love to the queen. The queen remains still, chattering anxiously. The ballerina, unaware of anything, dances to one tune. As in the relationship between Frankenstein and his wife, the male is the active transgressor, attempting from sexual motives to overcome the limits set by his creator. The female adheres to the conventions, an innocent insipid performer, seeking admiration like the ballerina, issuing anxious warnings against the predatory actions of the male, like the queen.

The wedding night is disturbed by Pretorius, whose temptations to create life once more Frankenstein is unable to resist. He is symbolically separated from his wife, and in a subsequent scene she hears a noise and cries out, "Is that you, Henry?" She then turns to find that she is being menaced by the monster (Boris Karloff), who kidnaps her. Thus the connection between Frankenstein and his monster is emphasized. Pretorius and the monster insist that Frankenstein's wife will not be returned to him until he creates a mate for the monster.

Clearly, Frankenstein's primitive sexual drives are an estranging factor between himself and his wife. She speaks to her husband and is answered by a monster. His only chance of survival is to discover the secrets of her sexual nature in order to meet the needs of his own erotic impulses. The female monster he creates is played by Elsa Lanchester, significantly the same actress who plays Mary Shelley in the film's prologue. The slow, tense attempts to stimulate this corpselike figure to life eventually succeed. She seems to look to Frankenstein for reassurance, but when confronted with the monster lets out a blood-curdling scream of terror and revulsion. The dual role played by Elsa Lanchester indicates the identification that should be made between the ultracivilized Mary Shelley and the primitive world of her subconscious from which she draws her monster fantasies. Valerie Hobson, as the gracious, civilized Elizabeth, is another substitute for Mary Shelley in the film. The suggestion is that even when woman's sexuality is most strongly aroused, she can only meet the sexual male with complete frigidity. There appears to be no distinction between woman's conscious and unconscious desires. This is why Mary Shelley is undisturbed by Byron's innuendos. It is, after all, man who is the "great sinner." The point is made; the baffled monster threatens violence, and at that moment Elizabeth, escaped from the monster's prison, knocks on the door, calling to Frankenstein. The monster, about to pull the lever that will destroy the whole building and its occupants, agrees to Frankenstein's escape: "Yes, you go; [to Pretorius] you stay. We belong dead." The innate female frigidity suggested by the reaction of the female monster to the monster shows Frankenstein the impossibility of satisfying his sexual nature. It can only destroy, and he escapes thankfully with his wife, tacitly agreeing that this part of himself should be obliterated.

Much of the dialogue has a familiar ring to those acquainted with later science fiction films—the assertion of an area of knowledge forbidden to man, Biblical quotation to support argument, as in *Conquest of Space* or *Them!*, the optimistic but ill-judged comment on the monster: "it just wants someone to handle it" (cf. *The Thing* or *20 Million Miles to Earth*). Another film that looks at the nature of woman from a man's point of view in rather different terms is *The Incredible Shrinking Man* (Jack Arnold, 1957).

In this, as in most science fiction films, the apparently casual details of the opening scene are crucially important to the film's thematic development. A couple are seen sunbathing on a boat. The man, Scott (Grant Williams), says he is thirsty and wants the woman, Louise (Randy Stuart), to fetch him some beer. She refuses until he makes a bargain with her that he will make the dinner if she does so. They then act out a scene in mock sixteenth-century dialogue, in which he calls her "wench" and orders her down to the galley in imitation of a time when man was master and woman served him—a complete contrast to their own relationship. They reveal that they have been living together for six years and decide to get married. While the woman fetches the drinks a cloud of mist appears on the horizon and rolls toward the boat, finally enveloping the man and leaving him freezing cold.

In the next scene they are shown to be married. He comments on a loss of weight, suggesting jokingly, "Maybe it's the cooking round here." A little later, when they kiss, he observes with dawning fear, "You used to have to stretch when you kissed me." As he grows rapidly smaller from day to day, he finds out that his sickness has been caused by the radioactive mist to which he had been exposed and to which the doctors and scientists can find no antidote. "I want you to start thinking about us," he says to his wife, "—about our marriage. There's a limit to your obligation." A model of patience and understanding, she stands by him, tolerating his increasing bad temper. "Every day I become smaller. Every day I become more tyrannical in my domination of Louise. I don't know how she stood it. Burning inside was my desperate need for her." He starts up a friendship with a female midget his own size but abandons it when he finds he cannot stop shrinking. We see him dwarfed by a low coffee table, with Louise, enormous in the foreground. Eventually, he is to be found living for safety in a dollhouse in the living room, complaining at the noise of his wife's feet as she appears to crash down the stairs. She answers him patiently and goes out shopping, inadvertently letting the cat in as she does so. A terrifying scene follows in which the gigantic predatory animal peers through the dollhouse window and makes a grab for him with its paw. In the ensuing struggle, he escapes and falls through the stairs to the cellar, from which he is unable to escape. In his new universe, away from Louise's cooking, his main object must be to find food. He sees a piece of cheese, but it is contained in a lethal mousetrap that could well destroy him; a piece of bread lies as bait in a spider's web, and his adversary, a monstrous spider, prowls round the cellar. "I had an enemy, the most terrifying beheld by human eyes," he comments. There is an immediate cut to Louise, upstairs, preparing to leave the house. He finds a weapon for himself in a nail which in proportion to him is the size of a sword, and he decides to pit his wits against the spider. At one point, unarmed and threatened by the creature, he retrieves his weapon: "With these, I was a man again . . . I no longer felt hatred for the spider. My enemy was not a spider but every unknown terror in the world. . . . One of us had to die." He finally kills the spider in a nauseating scene in which he impales her on his nail while black drops ooze onto his shoulder. After the spider's death, "there was no thought of hunger or shrinking." Completely reconciled to his state, he turns to philosophizing about his role: "What was I, still a human being, or a man of the future?"

Fear of castration by the female is the overriding theme of this film, and we are aware of the popular myth of the dominant American woman, served by an emasculated spouse. The opening scene observes the aggressive sexual equality of modern times and looks back to the male-dominated situation it replaces. Our first image of the couple's married life is outside the house. Louise feeds the cat and prepares breakfast. His laughing fear of what her cooking may be doing to him is taken up more strongly in the cellar scenes, where food is left as bait to lure mice and flies to their destruction—an analogy of the married woman's social and sexual relationship to her husband. In the dollhouse he is reduced to the status of a toy. The giant clawing cat is a replacement for Louise. She lets it in unconsciously. Freud wrote of animal phobias: "The anxiety felt in animal phobias is . . . an affective reaction on the part of the ego in danger: and the danger which is being signalled in this way is the danger of castration. This anxiety differs in no respect from the realistic anxiety which the ego normally feels in situations of danger, except that its content remains unconscious and only becomes conscious in the form of a distortion." [21]

This film is a first-person narrative from the man's point of view. Superficially, he and his wife at first have a good relationship. Later Louise behaves "perfectly" while he feels guilt at his resentment of her. The film is clearly concerned with his fear of her influence on him within the marriage relationship, which turns him into a toy and gradually engulfs him.

In the cellar sequences, which symbolize his subconscious, his adversary comes out into the open, a female trying to trap him with food, implicitly associated with his wife in the cut mentioned above. He specifies that his real enemy is "every unknown terror in the world." By this, he means what Freud describes as fear, not merely of the mother but of the "*phallic* mother, of whom we are afraid; so that the fear of spiders expresses dread of mother-incest and horror of the female genitals." [22] Feeling "a man again" with his weapons, he impales her with his sword/penis. By confronting her sexually he proves his ability to resist her attacks and to conquer. After the fight neither the bait of food nor the fear of "shrinking," or castration, holds any power over him. He has freed himself from the constricting area of female domination and senses a new freedom for himself in the world, comforting himself that perhaps he will not be the only one to undergo this liberating experience in the future.

Don Siegel's *Invasion of the Body Snatchers* (1956) is not concerned with fears of woman but looks at a society characterized by lack of passion in every aspect. In some ways it has something in common with *It Came from Outer Space*. This film shows a silent conspiracy by which people are taken over by some curious plant life and as a result no longer feel pain, fear, or joy, merely a vegetable contentment. Miles (Kevin McCarthy) and Becky (Dana Wynter) both have broken marriages behind them. Years ago at college they had been boyfriend and girlfriend but did not have sufficient courage or passion to leave to get married, as one of their friends in similar circumstances had done. Miles's conversations reveal the extent to which his interior and sex life has been dried up and destroyed by the humdrum processes of everyday life. He claims that the reason his marriage broke up was that as a doctor, "I never was there when the food was on the table"—a comment both on the empty ritualization of the institution of marriage but also, at another level, implying that his job never left him enough time to sustain the sexual relationship. Both he and Becky pay more than lip service to society's clichés about human relationships. He chaffs his pretty nurse, telling her if she were not married, hers would have been a lost cause long ago. To Becky, he suggests that a doctor's wife needs infinite patience and the understanding of an Einstein. "What about love?" she asks. "That's for the specialists," he replies. Despite their growing feeling for each other, Becky resists a sexual relationship with conventional excuses that it is madness and the whole thing is so sudden—a point that is factually untrue, as he observes. Around them, the number of zombielike creatures grows. A child rejects his mother, saying she is not his mother. She is the same as she was before but all feeling has vanished. The sickness is contagious, as more and more people conspire to place the giant pods in contact with other victims. The psychiatrists, themselves afflicted with the common illness, suggest that worry about what is going on in the world causes the alienation problems: "The trouble is inside you." In an impassioned speech, the doctor describes how he has watched humanity draining away from his patients—"People I've known all my life. Only when we have to fight to stay human do we realize how precious it is." When he argues that love cannot so easily be discounted, with those who try to infect him, they reply cynically: "You've been in love before. It doesn't last." Becky cries out that she wants his children, but she finally succumbs from exhaustion, becoming "an inhuman enemy bent on my destruction." Standing on the motorway, he yells at people in cars to stop and help him escape to tell the truth. They assume he is drunk or insane and pass by regardless. "You fools!

55. *Them!* The labyrinthine lair of the mutated ants.

You're next!" he yells. The film ends on a false note of optimism, and he is finally believed, but this is not the ending that Siegel wanted and certainly not the logical ending to the film.

All the films discussed so far have been firmly structured around coherent themes relating the tensions of sexual drives and the obligations on behavior imposed by civilized society. They are saturated with an awareness of Freudian concepts. The symbols are established from within the narrative context. There is also a large group of films in which such tensions are latent but not fully explored. The films do not appear to create their own symbolism. *Them!* (Gordon Douglas, 1954) is a good example of this. It incorporates a skeleton romance between two people working to destroy a plague of monstrous aggressive ants—mutants from radioactive fallout. Those who see the creatures view them with horror and revulsion, and there is a long scene in which the ants are pursued through the nest they have made for themselves in the city's sewers and an attempt is made to locate and destroy the central egg chamber. This labyrinthine motif might be seen as a fantasy of anal birth,[23] but the interpretation does not clarify the preoccupations of the film in any significant way. The hero of *The Projected Man* (Ian Curteis, 1966), who has himself been hurled through space to prove a scientific point to the corrupt authorities, is clearly motivated to an equal extent by jealousy of the romance between his assistants, one of them his former girlfriend (Mary Peach). Returning from the experiment with his face hideously burned and scarred, his aggression knows no bounds, and he indulges in what might appear to be a gratuitous form of sexual menace as he carries off the office secretary, who is conveniently stripped to her underwear. His horrible appearance is the visible sign of the transformation he has undergone through jealousy, yet once more, nothing is closely worked out.

The Day the Earth Caught Fire (Val Guest, 1961) interweaves the imagery of the climatic changes with the story of a developing sexual attraction—at times it is not clear whether the hero and heroine are talking about themselves or about the weather. In the face of the potential destruction of the earth by fire, their intolerant antagonism is shown to be petty and irrelevant. The reporter is brought to shake hands with his ex-wife's husband and to wish him well.

There are other science fiction films that are firmly entrenched in exploring different areas. *2001* (Stanley Kubrick, 1968), for example, is concerned with moral and metaphysical speculation combined with a delight in technical virtuosity for its own sake. A quasi documentary such as *Destination Moon* (Irving Pichel, 1950) was an attempt to give a realistic picture of what the first moon landing might involve. *Marooned* (John Sturges, 1969) takes up the question most people were asking at the time of the first moon landing. What happens to the spacemen if their apparatus fails them and they cannot get back to earth? Such films, with their masculine emphasis and concentration on the mechanics of space flight, suggest an image of man marveling at his own genitals. They do not have the social orientation of the heterosexual films.

This article has attempted to describe and analyze only one large and probably central area within the amorphous science fiction genre and to point out some of the major preoccupations in these films with the problem of reconciling the desires of the individual as both sexual animal and social being. Although the current emphasis in science fiction films seems to be toward some form of pseudoscientific "documentary," this is just a more subtle disguise for the overriding concern of the genre with "inner space" and "monsters from the id."

Notes

1. H. L. Gold, editor of *Galaxy Science Fiction*, quoted by Kingsley Amis in *New Maps of Hell* (London: Gollancz, 1961), p. 64.

2. Francis Arnold, "Out of This World," *Films and Filming* 9, no. 9 (June 1963): 14–18.

3. Richard Hodgens, "A Brief Tragical History of the Science Fiction Film," *Film Quarterly* 13 (Winter 1959(: 32.

4. Penelope Houston, "Glimpses of the Moon," *Sight and Sound* 22 (April–June 1953): 187.

5. *Monthly Film Bulletin* 24, no. 290 (November 1957): 141.

6. F. Hoda, "Epouvante et science fiction," *Positif* (November–December 1954): 1–16.

7. Jean Loth, "Le Fantastique erotique ou l'orgasme qui fait peur," *Cinema* '57, July–August 1957, pp. 9–14.

8. Raymond Lefèvre, "Le Décor de la peur," *Image et Son*, no. 192 (May 1966): 31–36.

9. Fereydoun Hoveyda, "La Science-fiction à l'ère des Spoutniks," *Cahiers du Cinéma* 11, no. 80 (February 1958): 9–16.

10. Tom Milne, *Mamoulian* (London: Thames and Hudson, 1969), pp. 39–50.

11. Curt Siodmak, "Sci-Fi or Sci-Fact?" *Films and Filming* 14, no. 12 (November 1968): 64.

12. Sigmund Freud, "Anxiety and Instinctual Life," *New Introductory Lectures on Psycho-Analysis: The Standard Edition of the Complete Psychological Works of Sigmund Freud,* 24 vols., translated by James Strachey in collaboration with Anna Freud (London: Hogarth Press and the Institute of Psycho-Analysis, 1953–1974), 22:82–83. Subsequent references to Freud are from this edition.

13. Freud, "The Dissection of the Psychical Personality," 22:73–74.

14. Amis, *New Maps of Hell,* p. 30.

15. Freud, "Introduction: A Seventeenth-Century Demonological Neurosis," 19:72.

16. Alfred C. Kinsey, Wardell B. Pomeroy, and Clyde E. Martin, *Sexual Behaviour in the Human Male* (Philadelphia and London: Saunders, 1949), p. 268.

17. Hoda, "Epouvante et science fiction," pp. 1–16.

18. Freud, "The Uncanny," 17:231.

19. Kinsey, Pomeroy, and Martin, *Sexual Behaviour in the Human Male,* pp. 263–296.

20. Freud, "The Acquisition and Control of Fire," 22:191.

21. Freud, "Inhibitions, Symptoms and Anxiety," 20:126.

22. Freud, "Revision of Dream Theory," 22:24.

23. Ibid., p. 25.

20. Tales of Sound and Fury: Observations on the Family Melodrama

THOMAS ELSAESSER

Asked about the color in *Written on the Wind* (1957), Douglas Sirk replied: "Almost throughout the picture I used deep-focus lenses which have the effect of giving a harshness to the objects and a kind of enamelled, hard surface to the colours. I wanted this to bring out the inner violence, the energy of the characters which is all inside them and can't break through." It would be difficult to think of a better way of describing what this particular movie and indeed most of the best melodramas of the fifties and early sixties are about. Or, for that matter, how closely in this film style and technique are related to theme.

I want to pursue an elusive subject in two directions: first, to indicate the development of what one might call the melodramatic imagination across different artistic forms and in different epochs; second, prompted by Sirk's remark, to look for some structural and stylistic constants in one medium during one particular period (the Hollywood family melodrama between roughly 1940 and 1963) and to speculate on the cultural and psychological context that this form of melodrama so manifestly reflected and helped to articulate. Nonetheless, this isn't an historical study in any strict sense, nor a *catalogue raisonné* of names and titles, for reasons that have something to do with my general method as well as with the obvious limitations imposed on film research by the unavailability of most of the movies. Thus I lean rather heavily on half a dozen films, notably *Written on the Wind*, to develop my points. This said, it is difficult to see how references to twenty more movies would make the argument any truer. For better or worse, what I have to say should at this stage be taken to be provocative rather than proven.

HOW TO MAKE STONES WEEP

Bearing in mind that everybody has some idea of what is meant by "melodramatic" (whatever one's scruples about an exact definition), any discussion of the melodrama as a specific cinematic mode of expression has to start from its antecedents—the novel and certain types of "entertainment" drama—from which scriptwriters and directors have borrowed their models.

The first thing one notices is that the media and literary forms that have habitually embodied melodramatic situations have changed considerably in the course of history and, further, that they differ from country to country. In England it has mainly been the novel and the literary gothic where melodramatic motifs persistently crop up (though the Victorian stage, especially in the 1880s and 1890s, knew an unprecedented vogue for the melodramas of R. Buchanan and G. R. Sims, plays in which "a footbridge over a torrent breaks under the steps of the villain; a piece of wall comes down to shatter him; a boiler bursts, and blows him to smithereens").[1] In France, it is the costume drama and historical novel; in Germany, "high" drama and the ballad, as well as more popular forms like *Moritat* (street songs); finally, in Italy the opera rather than the novel reached the highest degree of sophistication in the handling of melodramatic situations.

Two currents make up the genealogy. One leads from the late medieval morality play, the popular *gestes,* and other forms of oral narrative and drama, like fairy tales and folk songs, to their romantic revival and the cult of the picturesque in Scott, Byron, Heine, and Hugo, which has its lowbrow echo in barrel-organ songs, music-hall drama, and what in Germany is known as *Bänkellied,* the latter coming to late literary honors through Brecht in his songs and musical plays, *The Threepenny Opera* or *Mahagonny.* The characteristic features for our present purposes in this tradition are not so much the emotional shock tactics and the blatant playing on the audience's known sympathies and antipathies, but rather the nonpsychological conception of the dramatis personae, who figure less as autonomous individuals than to transmit the action and link the various locales within a total constellation. In this respect, melodramas have a myth-making function, insofar as their significance lies in the structure and articulation of the action, not in any psychologically motivated correspondence with individualized experience.

Yet what particularly marks the ballad or the *Bänkellied* (i.e., narratives accompanied by music) is that the moral/moralistic pattern which furnishes the primary content (crimes of passion bloodily revenged, murderers driven mad by guilt and drowning themselves, villains snatching children from their careless mothers, servants killing their unjust masters) is overlaid not only with a proliferation of "realistic" homely detail, but also "parodied" or relativized by the heavily repetitive verse form or the mechanical up-and-down rhythms of the barrel organ, to which the voice of the singer adapts itself (consciously or not), thereby producing a vocal parallelism that has a distancing or ironic effect, to the extent of often crisscrossing the moral of the story by a "false" or unexpected emphasis. Sirk's most successful German melodrama, *Zu neuen Ufern* (To New Shores, 1937), makes excellent use of the street ballad to bring out the tragic irony in the courtroom scene, and the tune which Walter Brennan keeps playing on the harmonica in King Vidor's *Ruby Gentry* (1952) works in a very similar way. A variation on this is the use of fairgrounds and carousels in films like *Some Came Running* (Vincente Minnelli, 1958) and *The Tarnished Angels* (Sirk, 1957), or more self-consciously by Hitchcock in *Strangers on a Train* and *Stage Fright* (both 1951) and Welles in *Lady from Shanghai* and *The Stranger* (both 1946) to underscore the main action and at the same time "ease" the melodramatic impact by providing an ironic parallelism. Sirk uses the motif repeatedly, as, for instance, in *A Scandal in Paris* (1946) and *Take Me to Town* (1952). What such devices point to is that in the melodrama the *rhythm* of experience often establishes itself against its value (moral, intellectual).

Perhaps the current that leads more directly to the sophisticated family melodrama of the 1940s and 1950s, though, is derived from the romantic drama which had its heyday after the French Revolution and subsequently furnished many of the plots for operas, but which is itself unthinkable without the eighteenth-century sentimental novel and the emphasis put on private feelings and interiorized (puritan, pietist) codes of morality and conscience. Historically, one of the interesting facts about this tradition is that its height of popularity seems to coincide (and this remains true throughout the nineteenth century) with periods of intense social and ideological crisis. The prerevolutionary sentimental novel— Richardson's *Clarissa* or Rousseau's *Nouvelle Héloise*, for example—go out of their way to make a case for extreme forms of behavior and feeling by depicting very explicitly certain external constraints and pressures bearing upon the characters, and by showing up the quasi-totalitarian violence perpetrated by (agents of) the "system." (Lovelace tries everything, from bribing her family to hiring pimps, prostitutes, and kidnappers in order to get Clarissa to become his wife, only to have to rape her after all.) The same pattern is to be found in the bourgeois tragedies of Lessing (*Emilia Galotti*, 1768) and the early Schiller (*Kabale und Liebe*, 1776), both deriving their dramatic force from the conflict between an extreme and highly individualized form of moral idealism in the heroes (again, nonpsychological on the level of motivation) and a thoroughly corrupt yet seemingly omnipotent social class (made up of feudal princes and petty state functionaries). The melodramatic elements are clearly visible in the plots, which revolve around family relationships, star-crossed lovers, and forced marriages. The villains (often of noble birth) demonstrate their superior political and economic power invariably by sexual aggression and attempted rape, leaving the heroine no other way than to commit suicide or take poison in the company of her lover. The ideological "message" of these tragedies, as in the case of *Clarissa,* is transparent: they record the struggle of a morally and emotionally emancipated bourgeois consciousness against the remnants of feudalism. They pose the problem in political terms and concentrate on the complex interplay of ethical principles, religious-metaphysical polarities, and the idealist aspirations typical of the bourgeoisie in its militant phase, as the protagonists come to grief in a maze of economic necessities, realpolitik, family loyalties, and through the abuse of aristocratic privilege from a still divinely ordained and therefore doubly depraved absolutist authority.

Although these plays and novels, because they use the melodramatic-emotional plot only as their most rudimentary structure of meaning, belong to the more intellectually demanding forms of melodrama, the element of interiorization and personalization of what are primarily ideological conflicts, together with the metaphorical interpretation of class conflict as sexual exploitation and rape, is important in all subsequent forms of melodrama, including that of the cinema. (The latter in America, of course, is a stock theme of novels and movies with a "Southern" setting.)

Paradoxically, the French Revolution failed to produce a new form of social drama or tragedy. The restoration stage (when theaters in Paris were specially licensed to play melodramas) trivialized the form by using melodramatic plots in exotic settings and by providing escapist entertainment with little social relevance. The plays warmed up the standard motif of eighteenth-century French fiction and drama, that of innocence persecuted and virtue rewarded, and the conventions of melodrama functioned in their most barren form as the mechanics of pure suspense.

What before the revolution had served to focus on suffering and victimization—the claims of the individual in an absolutist society—was reduced to ground glass in the porridge, poisoned handkerchiefs, and last-minute rescues from the dungeon. The sudden reversals of fortune, the intrusion of chance and coincidence, had originally pointed to the arbitrary way feudal institutions could ruin the individual unprotected by civil rights and liberties. The system stood accused of greed, willfulness, and irrationality through the Christlike suffering of the pure virgin and the selfless heroism of the right-minded in the midst of court intrigues and callous indifference. Now, with the bourgeoisie triumphant, this form of drama lost its subversive charge and functioned more as a means of consolidating an as yet weak and incoherent ideological position. Whereas the prerevolutionary melodramas had often ended tragically, those of the Restoration had happy endings; they reconciled the suffering individual to his or her social position by affirming an "open" society where everything was possible. Over and over again, the victory of the "good" citizen over "evil" aristocrats, lecherous clergymen, and the even more conventional villains drawn from the lumpenproletariat was reenacted in sentimental spectacles full of tears and high moral tones. Complex social processes were simplified either by blaming the evil disposition of individuals or by manipulating the plots and engineering coincidences and other dei ex machina, such as the instant conversion of the villain, moved by the plight of his victim, or suddenly struck by divine grace on the steps of Notre Dame.

Since the overtly "conformist" strategy of such drama is quite evident, what is interesting is certainly not the plot structure, but whether the conventions allowed authors to dramatize in their episodes actual contradictions in society and genuine clashes of interests in the characters. Already during the Revolution plays such as Monvel's *Les Victimes cloîtrées* or Laya's *L'Ami des lois,* though working with very stereotyped plots, conveyed quite definite political sympathies (the second, for instance, backed the Girondist moderates in the trial of Louis XVI against the Jacobites) and were understood as such by their public.[2]

Even if the form might act to reinforce attitudes of submission, the actual working out of the scenes could nonetheless present fundamental social evils. Many of the pieces also flattered popular sympathies by giving the villains the funniest lines, just as Victorian drama playing east of Drury Lane was often enlivened by low-comedy burlesque put on as curtain-raisers and by the servants' farces during the intermission.

All this is to say that there seems a radical ambiguity attached to the melodrama, which holds even more for the film melodrama. Depending on whether the emphasis fell on the odyssey of suffering or the happy ending, on the place and context of rupture (moral conversion of the villain, unexpected appearance of a benevolent Capucine monk throwing off his pimp's disguise), that is to say, depending on what dramatic mileage was got out of the heroine's perils before the ending (and one only has to think of Sade's Justine to see what could be done with the theme of innocence unprotected), melodrama would appear to function either subversively or as escapism—categories that are always relative to the given historical and social context.[3]

In the cinema, Griffith is a good example. Using identical dramatic devices and cinematic techniques, he could create, with *Intolerance* (1916), *Way Down East* (1920), or *Broken Blossoms* (1919), if not exactly subversive, at any rate socially committed melodramas, whereas *Birth of a Nation* (1915) or *Orphans of the Storm* (1921) are classic examples of how melodramatic effects can successfully shift explicit political themes onto a personalized plane. In both cases, Griffith tailored ideological conflicts into emotionally charged family situations.

The persistence of the melodrama might indicate the ways in which

56. *Orphans of the Storm:* The shifting of explicit political themes onto a personalized level.

popular culture has not only taken note of social crises and the fact that the losers are not always those who deserve it most, but has also resolutely refused to understand social change in other than private contexts and emotional terms. In this, there is obviously a healthy distrust of intellectualization and abstract social theory—insisting that other structures of experience (those of suffering, for instance) are more in keeping with reality. But it has also meant ignorance of the properly social and political dimensions of these changes and their causality, and consequently it has encouraged increasingly escapist forms of mass entertainment.

However, this ambivalence about the "structures" of experience, endemic in the melodramatic mode, has served artists throughout the nineteenth century for the depiction of a variety of themes and social phenomena while remaining within the popular idiom. Industrialization, urbanization, and nascent entrepreneurial capitalism have found their most telling literary embodiment in a type of novel clearly indebted to the melodrama, and the national liberals in Italy during the Risorgimento, for example, saw their political aspirations reflected in Verdi's operas (as in the opening of Luchino Visconti's *Senso* [1954]). In England, Dickens, Collins, and Reade relied heavily on melodramatic plots to sharpen social conflicts and portray an urban environment where chance encounters, coincidences, and the side-by-side existence of extreme social and moral contrasts were the natural products of the very conditions of existence—crowded tenement houses, narrow streets backing up to the better residential property, and other facts of urban demography of the time. Dickens in particular uses the element of chance, the dream/waking, horror/bliss switches in *Oliver Twist* or *Tale of Two Cities*, partly to feel his way toward a portrayal of existential insecurity and moral anguish that fiction had previously not encompassed, but also to explore deep psychological phenomena for which the melodrama—as Freud was later to confirm—has supplied the dynamic motifs and the emotional-pictorial decor. What seems to me important in this form of melodrama (and one comes across a similar conception in the sophisticated Hollywood melodramas) is the emphasis Dickens places on discontinuity, on the evidence of fissures and ruptures in the fabric of experience, and the appeal to a reality of the psyche—to which the notions of sudden change, reversal, and excess lend a symbolic plausibility.

In France it is the works of Sue, Hugo, and Balzac that reflect most closely the relation of melodrama to social upheaval. Sue, for example, uses the timeworn trapdoor devices of cloak-and-dagger stage melodrama for an explicitly sensationalist, yet committed journalism. In a popular form and rendered politically palatable by the fictionalized treatment, his *Mystères de Paris* were intended to crusade on such issues as public health, prostitution, overcrowding and slum housing, sanitation, black-market racketeering, corruption in government circles, opium smoking, and gambling. Sue exploited a "reactionary" form for reformist ends, and his success, both literary and practical, proved him right. Twenty years later Victor Hugo, who had learnt as much from Sue as Sue had picked up from *Nôtre-Dame de Paris*, produced with *Les Misérables* a supermelodrama spectacular that must stand as the crowning achievement of the genre in the novel. The career of Jean Valjean, from convict and galley slave to factory owner and capitalist, his fall and literal emergence from the sewers of Paris to become a somewhat unwilling activist in the 1848 revolution, is staged with the help of mistaken identities, orphans suddenly discovering their noble birth, inconvenient reappearance of people long thought dead, hair-breadth escapes and rescues, multiple disguises, long-suffering females dying of consumption or wandering for days through the streets in search of their child—and yet, through all this Hugo expresses a hallucinating vision of the anxiety, the moral confusion, the emotional demands, in short, the metaphysics of social change and urban life between the time of Waterloo and 1848. Hugo evidently wanted to bring together in a popular form subjective experiences of crises while keeping track of the grand lines of France's history, and he succeeds singularly well in reproducing the ways in which individuals with different social backgrounds, levels of awareness, and imaginations respond to objective changes in the social fabric of their lives. For this, the melodrama, with its shifts in mood, its different *tempi,* and the mixing of stylistic levels, is ideally suited: *Les Misérables,* even more so than the novels of Dickens, lets through a symbolic dimension of psychic truth, with the hero in turn representing very nearly the id, the superego, and finally the sacrificed ego of a repressed and paranoid society.

Balzac, on the other hand, uses melodramatic plots to a rather different end. Many of his novels deal with the dynamics of early capitalist economics. The good/evil dichotomy has almost disappeared, and the Manichaean conflicts have shifted away from questions of morality to the paradoxes of psychology and economics. What we see is a Schopenhauerian struggle of the will: the ruthlessness of industrial entrepreneurs and bankers; the spectacle of an uprooted, "decadent" aristocracy still holding tremendous political power; the sudden twists of fortune with no-good parasites becoming millionaires overnight (or vice versa) through speculation and the stock exchange; the antics of hangers-on, parvenus, and cynical artist-intellectuals; the demonic, spellbinding potency of money and capital; the contrasts between abysmal poverty and unheard-of affluence and waste, which characterized the "anarchic" phase of industrialization and high finance. All were experienced by Balzac as both vital and melodramatic. His work reflects this more in plot and style than through direct comment.

To sum up, these writers understood the melodrama as a form that carried its own values and already embodied its own significant content: it served as the literary equivalent of a particular historically and socially conditioned mode of experience. Even if the situations and sentiments defied all categories of verisimilitude and were totally unlike anything in real life, the structure had a truth and a life of its own, which artists could make part of their material. This meant that those who consciously adopted melodramatic techniques of presentation did not necessarily do so out of incompetence or always from a cynical distance, but, by turning a body of techniques into a stylistic principle that carried the distinct overtones of spiritual crisis, they could put the finger on the texture of their social and human material while still being free to shape this material dramatically. For there is little doubt that the whole conception of life in nineteenth-century Europe and England and especially the spiritual problems of the age were often viewed in categories we would today call melodramatic—one can see this in painting, architecture, the ornamentation of gadgets and furniture, the domestic and public mise-en-scène of events and occasions, the oratory in parliament, and the tractarian rhetoric from the pulpit as well as the more private manifestations of religious sentiment. Similarly, the timeless themes that Dostoyevsky brings up again and again in his novels—guilt, redemption, justice, innocence, freedom—are made specific and historically real not least because he was a great writer of melodramatic scenes and confrontations, and they more than anything else define that powerful irrational logic in the motivation and moral outlook of, say, Raskolnikov, Ivan Karamasov, or Kirilov. Finally, how different Kafka's novels would be if they did not contain those melodramatic family situations, pushed to the point where they reveal a dimension at once comic and tragically absurd—perhaps the existential undertow of all genuine melodrama.

PUTTING MELOS INTO DRAMA

In its dictionary sense, melodrama is a dramatic narrative in which musical accompaniment marks the emotional effects. This is still perhaps the most useful definition, because it allows melodramatic elements to be seen as constituents of a system of punctuation, giving expressive color and chromatic contrast to the story line, by orchestrating the emotional ups and downs of the intrigue. The advantage of this approach is that it formulates the problems of melodrama as problems of style and articulation.

Music in melodrama, for example, as a device among others to dramatize a given narrative, is subjective and programmatic. But because it is also a form of punctuation in the above sense, it is both functional (i.e., of structural significance) and thematic (i.e., belonging to the expressive content) in formulating certain moods—sorrow, violence, dread, suspense, happiness. The syntactic function of music has, as is well known, survived into the sound film, and the experiments conducted by Hanns Eisler and T. W. Adorno are highly instructive in this respect.[4] A more practical demonstration of the problem can be gleaned from the almost farcical account that Lillian Ross gives of Gottfried Reinhard and Dore Shary reediting John Huston's *Red Badge of Courage* (1951) to give the narrative a smoother dramatic shape by a musical build-up to the dramatic climaxes, which is exactly what Huston had wanted to avoid when he shot it.[5]

Because it had to rely on piano accompaniment for punctuation, all silent film drama—from *True Heart Susie* (Griffith, 1919) to *Foolish Wives* (Erich von Stroheim, 1922) or *The Lodger* (Alfred Hitchcock, 1926)—is "melodramatic." It meant that directors had to develop an extremely subtle and yet precise formal language (of lighting, staging, decor, acting, closeup, montage, and camera movement), because they were deliberately looking for ways to compensate for the expressiveness, range of inflection and tonality, rhythmic emphasis, and tension normally present in the spoken word. Having had to replace that part of language which is sound, directors like Murnau, Renoir, Hitchcock, Mizoguchi, Hawks, Lang, and Sternberg achieved in their films a high degree (well recognized at the time) of plasticity in the modulation of optical planes and spatial masses, which Panofsky rightly identified as a "dynamization of space."[6]

Among less gifted directors this sensitivity in the deployment of expressive means was partly lost with the advent of direct sound, since it seemed no longer necessary in a strictly technical sense—pictures "worked" on audiences through their dialogue, and the semantic force of language drowned out and overshadowed the more sophisticated pictorial effects and architectural values. This perhaps helps to explain why some major technical innovations, such as color, wide-angle and deep-focus lenses, crane and dolly, have in fact encouraged a new form of sophisticated melodrama. Directors (quite a sizeable proportion of whom came during the 1930s from Germany, and others were clearly indebted to German expressionism and Max Reinhardt's methods of theatrical mise-en-scène) began showing a similar degree of visual culture as the masters of silent film-drama: Ophüls, Lubitsch, Sirk, Preminger, Welles, Losey, Ray, Minnelli, Cukor.

Considered as an expressive code, melodrama might therefore be described as a particular form of dramatic mise-en-scène, characterized by a dynamic use of spatial and musical categories, as opposed to intellectual or literary ones. Dramatic situations are given an orchestration that will allow for complex aesthetic patterns: indeed, orchestration is fundamental to the American cinema as a whole (being essentially a dramatic cinema, spectacular, and based on a broad appeal) because it has drawn the aesthetic consequences of having the spoken word more as an additional "melodic" dimension than as an autonomous semantic discourse. Sound, whether musical or verbal, acts first of all to give the illusion of depth to the moving image, and by helping to create the third dimension of the spectacle, dialogue becomes a scenic element, along with more directly visual means of the mise-en-scène. Anyone who has ever had the bad luck of watching a Hollywood movie dubbed into French or German will know how important diction is to the emotional resonance and dramatic continuity. Dubbing makes the best picture seem visually flat and dramatically out of sync: it destroys the flow on which the coherence of the illusionist spectacle is built.

That the plasticity of the human voice is quite consciously employed by directors for what are often thematic ends is known: Hawks trained Lauren Bacall's voice so that she could be given "male" lines in *To Have and*

Have Not (1944), an effect that Sternberg anticipated when he took great care to cultivate Marlene Dietrich's diction, and it is hard to miss the psychological significance of Robert Stack's voice in *Written on the Wind,* sounding as if every word had to be painfully pumped up from the bottom of one of his oil wells.

If it is true that speech and dialogue in the American cinema lose some of their semantic importance in favor of their aspects as sound, then conversely lighting, composition, and decor increase their semantic and syntactic contribution to the aesthetic effect. They become functional and integral elements in the construction of meaning. This is the justification for giving critical importance to the mise-en-scène over intellectual content or story value. It is also the reason why the domestic melodrama in color and wide screen, as it appeared in the 1940s and 1950s, is perhaps the most highly elaborated, complex mode of cinematic signification that the American cinema has ever produced, because of the restricted scope for external action determined by the subject, and because everything, as Sirk said, happens "inside." To the "sublimation" of the action picture and the Busby Berkeley/Lloyd Bacon musical into domestic and family melodrama corresponded a sublimation of dramatic conflict into decor, color, gesture, and composition of frame, which in the best melodramas is perfectly thematized in terms of the characters' emotional and psychological predicaments.

For example, when in ordinary language we call something melodramatic, what we often mean is an exaggerated rise-and-fall pattern in human actions and emotional responses, a from-the-sublime-to-the-ridiculous movement, a foreshortening of lived time in favor of intensity— all of which produces a graph of much greater fluctuation, a quicker swing from one extreme to the other than is considered natural, realistic, or in conformity with literary standards of verisimilitude: in the novel we like to sip our pleasures rather than gulp them. But if we look at, say, Minnelli, who had adapted some of his best melodramas—*The Cobweb* (1955), *Some Came Running, Home from the Hill* (1960), *Two Weeks in Another Town* (1962), *The Four Horsemen of the Apocalypse* (1962)— from extremely long, circumstantially detailed popular novels by James Jones, Irving Shaw, and others, it is easy to see how in the process of having to reduce seven to nine hours of reading matter to ninety-odd minutes or so, such a more violent "melodramatic" graph almost inevitably produces itself, short of the narrative becoming incoherent. Whereas in novels, especially when they are staple pulp fare, size connotes solid emotional involvement for the reader, the specific values of the cinema lie in its concentrated visual metaphors and dramatic acceleration rather than in the fictional techniques of dilation. The commercial necessity of compression (being also a formal one) is taken by Minnelli into the films themselves and developed as a theme—that of a pervasive psychological pressure on the characters. An acute sense of claustrophobia in decor and locale translates itself into a restless and yet suppressed energy surfacing sporadically in the actions and the behavior of the protagonists—a dialectic that is part of the subject of a film like *Two Weeks in Another Town,* with hysteria bubbling all the time just below the surface. The feeling that there is always more to tell than can be said leads to very consciously elliptical narratives, proceeding often by visually condensing the characters' motivation into nonessential sequences of images, seemingly lyrical interludes not advancing the plot. The shot of the Trevi fountain at the end of a complex scene where Kirk Douglas is making up his mind in *Two Weeks* is such a metaphoric condensation, and so is the silent sequence, consisting entirely of what might appear to be merely impressionistic dissolves, in the *Four Horsemen,* when Glenn Ford and Ingrid Thulin go for a ride to Versailles, but which in fact tells and foretells the whole trajectory of their relationship.

Sirk, too, often constructs his films in this way: the restlessness of *Written on the Wind* is not unconnected with the fact that he almost always cuts on movement. His visual metaphors ought to have a chapter to themselves: a yellow sportscar drawing up the gravelled driveway to stop in front of a pair of shining white doric columns outside the Hadley mansion is not only a powerful piece of American iconography, especially when taken in a plunging high-angle shot, but the contrary associations of imperial splendor and vulgar materials (polished chrome plate and stucco plaster) create a tension of correspondences and dissimilarities in the same image, which perfectly crystallizes the decadent affluence and melancholy energy that give the film its uncanny fascination. Sirk has a peculiarly vivid eye for the contrasting emotional qualities of textures and materials, and he combines them or makes them clash to very striking effect, especially when they occur in a nondramatic sequence: again in *Written on the Wind,* after the funeral of Hadley, Sr., a black servant is seen taking an oleander wreath off the front gate. A black silk ribbon gets unstuck and is blown by the wind along the concrete path. The camera follows the movement, dissolves, and dollies in on a window, where Lauren Bacall, in an oleander-green dress, is just about to disappear behind the curtains. The scene has no plot significance whatsoever. But the color parallels black/black, green/green, white concrete/white lace curtains provide an extremely strong emotional resonance in which the contrast of soft silk blown along the hard concrete is registered the more forcefully as a disquieting visual association. The desolation of the scene transfers itself onto the Bacall character, and the traditional fatalistic association of the wind reminds us of the futility implied in the movie's title.

These effects, of course, require a highly self-conscious stylist, but they are by no means rare. The fact that commercial necessities, political censorship, and the various morality codes have restricted directors in what they could tackle as a subject has entailed a different awareness of what constituted a worthwhile subject, a change in orientation from which sophisticated melodrama benefited perhaps most. Not only did they provide a defined thematic parameter, but they encouraged a conscious use of style-as-meaning, the mark of a modernist sensibility working in popular culture. To take another example from Minnelli: his theme of a character trying to construct the world in the image of an inner self, only to discover that this world has become uninhabitable because it is both frighteningly suffocating and intolerably lonely (as in *The Long, Long Trailer* [1954] and *The Cobweb*) is transformed and given social significance in the recurrent melodrama plot of the woman who, having failed to make it in the big city, comes back to the small-town home in the hope of finding her true place at last, but who is made miserable by meanmindedness and bigotry and then suffocated by the sheer weight of her none-too-glorious, still-raw-in-the-memory past (*Hilda Crane* [Philip Dunne, 1956], *Beyond the Forest* [King Vidor, 1949], *All I Desire* [Sirk, 1953]).[7] But in Minnelli, it becomes an opportunity to explore in concrete circumstances the more philosophical questions of freedom and determinism, especially as they touch the aesthetic problem of how to depict characters who are not constantly externalizing themselves into action, without thereby trapping them in an environment of ready-made symbolism.

Similarly, when Robert Stack shows Lauren Bacall her hotel suite in *Written on the Wind,* where everything from flowers and pictures on the wall to underwear, nail polish, and handbag is provided, Sirk is not only characterizing a rich man wanting to take over the woman he fancies body and soul or showing the oppressive nature of an unwanted gift. He is also making a direct comment on the Hollywood stylistic technique that "creates" a character out of the elements of the decor and that prefers actors who can provide as blank a facial surface and as little of a personality as possible.

Everyone who has at all thought about the Hollywood aesthetic wants to formulate one of its peculiar qualities: that of direct emotional involvement—whether one calls it "giving resonance to dramatic situations" or "fleshing out the cliché" or whether, more abstractly, one talks in terms of identification patterns, empathy, and catharsis. Since the American cinema, determined as it is by an ideology of the spectacle and the spectacular, is essentially dramatic (as opposed to lyrical—i.e., concerned with mood or the inner self) and not conceptual (dealing with ideas and the structures of cognition and perception), the creation or reenactment of situations that the spectator can identify with and recognize (whether this recognition is on the conscious or unconscious level is another matter) depends to a large extent on the aptness of the iconography (the "visualization") and on the quality (complexity, subtlety, ambiguity) of the orchestration for what are transindividual, popular mythological (and therefore generally considered culturally "lowbrow") experiences and plot structures. In other words, this type of cinema depends on the ways "melos" is given to "drama" by means of lighting, montage, visual rhythm, decor, style of acting, music—that is, on the ways the mise-en-scène translates character into action (not unlike the pre-Jamesian novel) and action into gesture and dynamic space (comparable to nineteenth-century opera and ballet).

This granted, there seems to be a further problem that has some bearing on the question of melodrama: although the techniques of audience orientation and the possibility of psychic projection on the part of the spectator are as much in evidence in a melodrama like *Home from the Hill* or *Splendor in the Grass* (Elia Kazan, 1961) as they are in a western or adventure picture, the difference of setting and milieu affects the dynamics of the action. In the western, especially, the assumption of "open" spaces is virtually axiomatic; it is indeed one of the constants that makes the form perennially attractive to a largely urban audience. Yet this openness becomes problematic in films that deal with potential melodrama themes and family situations. The complex father-son relationships in *The Left-Handed Gun* (Arthur Penn, 1958), the Cain-Abel themes of Mann's *Winchester 73* (1950) and *Bend of the River* (1952), the conflict of virility and mother-fixation in Jacques Tourneur's *Great Day in the Morning* (1956) and *Wichita* (1955), or the search for the mother (-country) in Fuller's *Run of the Arrow* (1957) seem to find resolution because the hero can act positively on the changing situations where and when they present themselves. In Raoul Walsh's adventure pictures, as Peter Lloyd has shown,[8] identity comes in an often paradoxical process of self-confirmation and overreaching, but always through direct action, while the momentum generated by the conflicts pushes the protagonists forward in an unrelentingly linear course.

The family melodrama, by contrast, though dealing largely with the same Oedipal themes of emotional and moral identity, more often records the failure of the protagonist to act in a way that could shape the events and influence the emotional environment, let alone change the stifling social milieu. The world is closed, and the characters are acted upon. Melodrama confers on them a negative identity through suffering, and the progressive self-immolation and disillusionment generally end in resignation: they emerge as lesser human beings for having become wise and acquiescent to the ways of the world.

The difference can be put in another way. In one case, the drama moves

57. *Double Indemnity:* Walter Neff (Fred MacMurray) is lured by the femme fatale (Barbara Stanwyck).

toward its resolution by having the central conflicts successively externalized and projected into direct action. A jail break, a bank robbery, a western chase or cavalry charge, and even a criminal investigation all lend themselves to psychologized, thematized representations of the heroes' inner dilemmas and frequently appear that way, as in Walsh's *White Heat* (1949) or *They Died with Their Boots On* (1941), Losey's *The Criminal* (1960), Preminger's *Where the Sidewalk Ends* (1950). The same is true of the melodrama in the *série noire* tradition, where the hero is edged on or blackmailed by the femme fatale—the smell of honeysuckle and death in *Double Indemnity* (Billy Wilder, 1944), *Out of the Past* (Jacques Tourneur, 1947), or *Detour* (Edgar G. Ulmer, 1946)—into a course of action that pushes him farther and farther in one direction, opening a narrowing wedge of equally ineluctable consequences that usually lead the hero to wishing his own death as the ultimate act of liberation, but where the mechanism of fate at least allows him to express his existential revolt in strong and strongly antisocial behavior.

Not so in the domestic melodrama. The social pressures are such, the frame of respectability so sharply defined, that the range of "strong" ac-

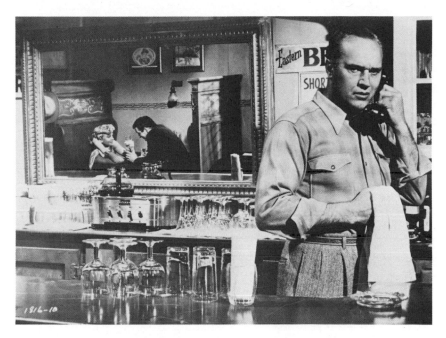

58. *Written on the Wind:* Real and metaphorical mirrors in Sirk.

tions is limited. The tellingly impotent gesture, the social gaffe, the hysterical outburst replaces any more directly liberating or self-annihilating action, and the cathartic violence of a shoot-out or a chase becomes an inner violence, often one that the characters turn against themselves. The dramatic configuration, the pattern of the plot, makes them, regardless of attempts to break free, constantly look inward, at each other and themselves. The characters are, so to speak, each others' sole referent; there is no world outside to be acted on, no reality that could be defined or assumed unambiguously. In Sirk, of course, they are locked into a universe of real and metaphoric mirrors, but quite generally what is typical of this form of melodrama is that the characters' behavior is often pathetically at variance with the real objectives they want to achieve. A sequence of substitute actions creates a kind of vicious circle in which the close nexus of cause and effect is somehow broken and—in an often overtly Freudian sense—displaced. James Dean in *East of Eden* (Elia Kazan, 1955) thinks up a method of cold storage for lettuce, grows beans to sell to the army, falls in love with Julie Harris, not to make a pile of money and live happily with a beautiful wife, but in order to win the love of his father and oust his brother—neither of which he achieves. Although very much on the surface of Kazan's film, this is a conjunction of puritan capitalist ethic and psychoanalysis that is sufficiently pertinent to the American melodrama to remain exemplary.

The melodramas of Ray, Sirk, or Minnelli do not deal with this displacement-by-substitution directly, but by what one might call an intensified symbolization of everyday actions, the heightening of the ordinary gesture and a use of setting and decor so as to reflect the characters' fetishist fixations. Violent feelings are given vent on "over-determined" objects (James Dean kicking his father's portrait as he storms out of the house in *Rebel without a Cause* [Ray, 1955]), and aggressiveness is worked out by proxy. In such films, the plots have a quite noticeable propensity to form a circular pattern, which in Ray involves an almost geometrical variation of triangle into circle and vice versa,[9] whereas Sirk (*nomen est omen*) often suggests in his circles the possibility of a tangent detaching itself—the full-circle construction of *Written on the Wind* with its linear coda of the Hudson-Bacall relationship at the end, or even more visually apparent, the circular race around the pylons in *The Tarnished Angels* broken when Dorothy Malone's plane in the last image soars past the fatal pylon into an unlimited sky.

It is perhaps not too fanciful to suggest that the structural changes from linear externalization of action to a sublimation of dramatic values into more complex forms of symbolization, and which I take to be a central characteristic of the melodramatic tradition in the American cinema, can be followed through on a more general level where it reflects a change in the history of dramatic forms and the articulation of energy in the American cinema as a whole.

As I have tried to show in an earlier article,[10] one of the typical features of the classical Hollywood movie has been that the hero was defined dynamically, as the center of a continuous movement, often both from sequence to sequence as well as within the individual shot. Perceptually, in order to get its bearing, the eye adjusts almost automatically to whatever moves, and movement, together with sound, completes the realistic illusion. It was on the basis of sheer physical movement, for example, that the musicals of the 1930s (Lloyd Bacon's *Forty-Second Street* [1933] being perhaps the most spectacular example), the gangster movie, and the B thriller of the 1940s and early 1950s could subsist with the flimsiest of plots, an almost total absence of individual characterization, and rarely any big stars. These deficiencies were made up by focusing to the point of exaggeration on the drive, the obsession, the *idée fixe*—that is to say, by a concentration on the purely kinetic-mechanical elements of human motivation. The pattern is most evident in the gangster genre, where the single-minded pursuit of money and power is followed by the equally single-minded and peremptory pursuit of physical survival, ending in the hero's apotheosis through violent death. This curve of rise and fall—a wholly stylized and external pattern that takes on a moral significance—can be seen in movies like *Underworld* (Josef von Sternberg, 1927), *Little Caesar* (Mervyn LeRoy, 1930), *The Roaring Twenties* (Raoul Walsh, 1939), and *The Rise and Fall of Legs Diamond* (Budd Boetticher, 1960) and depends essentially on narrative pace, though it permits interesting variations and complexities, as in Fuller's *Underworld USA* (1961). A sophisticated director, such as Hawks, has used speed of delivery and the pulsating urgency of action to comic effect (*Scarface* [1932], *Twentieth Century* [1934]) and has even applied it to films whose dramatic structure did not naturally demand such a treatment (notably *His Girl Friday* [1940]). In parenthesis, Hawks's reputed stoicism is itself a dramaturgical device, whereby sentimentality and cynicism are played so close together and played so fast that the result is an emotional hot-cold shower that is apt to numb the spectator's sensibility into feeling a sustained moral charge, where there is more often simply a very skilled switchboard manipulation of the same basic voltage. I am thinking especially of films like *Only Angels Have Wings* (1939).

This unrelenting internal combustion engine of physical and psychic energy, generically exemplified by the hard-boiled, crackling aggressiveness of the screwball comedy, but which Walsh diagnosed in his Cagney heroes as psychotic (*White Heat*) and a vehicle for extreme redneck republicanism (*A Lion Is in the Streets* [1953]), shows signs of a definite slowing down in the 1950s and early 1960s, where raucous vitality and instinctual "lust for life" is deepened psychologically to intimate neuroses and adolescent or not so adolescent maladjustments of a wider social significance. Individual initiative is perceived as problematic in explicitly political terms, as in *All the King's Men* (Robert Rossen, 1949), after having previously been merely stoically and heroically antisocial, as in the film noir. The external world is more and more riddled with obstacles that oppose themselves to personal ambition and are not simply overcome by the hero's assertion of a brawny or brainy libido. In Mann's westerns the madness at the heart of the James Stewart character only occasionally breaks through an otherwise calm and controlled surface, like a strong subterranean current suddenly appearing above ground as an inhuman and yet somehow poetically apt thirst for vengeance and primitive biblical justice, where the will to survive is linked to certain old-fashioned cultural and moral values of dignity, honor, and respect. In the films of Sirk, an uncompromising, fundamentally innocent energy is gradually turned away from simple, direct fulfillment by the emergence of a conscience, a sense of guilt and responsibility, or the awareness of moral complexity, as in *Magnificent Obsession* (1953), *Sign of the Pagan* (1954), *All That Heaven*

Allows (1955), and even *Interlude* (1957)—a theme that in Sirk is always interpreted in terms of cultural decadence.

WHERE FREUD LEFT HIS MARX IN THE AMERICAN HOME

There can be little doubt that the postwar popularity of the family melodrama in Hollywood is partly connected with the fact that in those years America discovered Freud. This is not the place to analyze why the United States should have become the country in which his theories found their most enthusiastic reception anywhere or why they became such a decisive influence on American culture, but the connections of Freud with melodrama are as complex as they are undeniable. An interesting fact, for example, is that Hollywood tackled Freudian themes in a particularly "romantic" or gothic guise, through a cycle of movies inaugurated possibly by Hitchcock's first big American success, *Rebecca* (1940). Relating his Victorianism to the Crawford-Stanwyck-Davis type of "women's picture," which for obvious reasons became a major studio concern during the war years and found its apotheosis in such movies as John Cromwell's *Since You Went Away* (1944) (to the Front, that is), Hitchcock infused his film, and several others, with an oblique intimation of female frigidity producing strange fantasies of persecution, rape, and death—masochistic reveries and nightmares that cast the husband into the role of the sadistic murderer. This projection of sexual anxiety and its mechanisms of displacement and transfer is translated into a whole string of movies often involving hypnosis and playing on the ambiguity and suspense of whether the wife is merely imagining it or whether her husband really does have murderous designs on her. Hitchcock's *Notorious* (1946) and *Suspicion* (1941), Minnelli's *Undercurrent* (1946), Cukor's *Gaslight* (1944), Sirk's *Sleep, My Love* (1947), Tourneur's *Experiment Perilous* (1944), and Lang's *Secret beyond the Door* (1948) all belong in this category, as does Preminger's *Whirlpool* (1949) and in a wider sense Renoir's *Woman on the Beach* (1946). What strikes one about this list is not only the high number of European émigrés entrusted with such projects, but that virtually all of the major directors of family melodramas (except Ray) in the fifties had a (usually not entirely successful) crack at the Freudian feminist melodrama in the forties.

More challenging, and difficult to prove, is the speculation that certain stylistic and structural features of the sophisticated melodrama may involve principles of symbolization and coding that Freud conceptualized in his analysis of dreams and later also applied in his *Psychopathology of Everyday Life*. I am thinking less of the prevalence of what Freud called "Symptomhandlungen" or "Fehlhandlungen," that is, when slips of the tongue project inner states into interpretable overt behavior. This is a way of symbolizing and signaling attitudes common to the American cinema in virtually every genre and perhaps more directly attributable to the metonymic use of detail in the realist novel rather than to any Freudian influence. However, there is a certain refinement of this in the melodrama—it becomes part of the composition of the frame, more subliminally and unobtrusively transmitted to the spectator. When Minnelli's characters find themselves in an emotionally precarious or contradictory situation, it often affects the balance of the visual composition; wine glasses, a piece of china, or a tray full of drinks emphasizes the fragility of their situation—e.g., Judy Garland over breakfast in *The Clock* (1945), Richard Widmark in *The Cobweb*, explaining himself to Gloria Grahame, or Gregory Peck trying to make his girlfriend see why he married someone else in *Designing Woman* (1957). When Robert Stack in *Written on the Wind*, standing by the window he has just opened to get some fresh air into an extremely heavy family atmosphere, hears of Lauren Bacall expecting a baby, his misery becomes eloquent by the way he squeezes himself into the frame of the half-open window, every word his wife says to him bringing torment to his lacerated soul and racked body.

Along similar lines, I have in mind the kind of condensation of motivation into metaphoric images or sequences of images mentioned earlier, the relation that exists in Freudian dream work between manifest dream material and latent dream content. Just as in dreams certain gestures and incidents mean something by their structure and sequence rather than by what they literally represent, the melodrama often works, as I have tried to show, by a displaced emphasis, by substitute acts, by parallel situations and metaphoric connections. In dreams one tends to "use" as dream material incidents and circumstances from one's waking experience during the previous day, in order to "code" them, while nevertheless keeping a kind of emotional logic going, and even condensing their images into what, during the dream at least, seems an inevitable sequence. Melodramas often use middle-class American society, its iconography, and the family experience in just this way as their manifest material, but "displace" it into quite different patterns, juxtaposing stereotyped situations in strange configurations and provoking clashes and ruptures that not only open up new associations but also redistribute the emotional energies that suspense and tensions have accumulated in disturbingly different directions. American movies, for example, often manipulate very shrewdly situations of extreme embarrassment (a blocking of emotional energy) and acts or gestures of violence (direct or indirect release) in order to create patterns of aesthetic significance that only a musical vocabulary might be able to describe accurately and for which psychoanalysis or anthropology might offer some explanation.

One of the principles involved is that of continuity and discontinuity.

What Sirk has called the "rhythm of the plot" is what makes a movie hang together. This, it seems to me, is a particularly complex aspect of the sophisticated melodrama. A typical situation in 1950s American melodramas occurs where the plot builds up to an evidently catastrophic collision of counterrunning sentiments, but a string of delays gets the greatest possible effect from the clash when it does come. In Minnelli's *The Bad and the Beautiful* (1952) Lana Turner plays an alcoholic actress who has been "rescued" by producer Kirk Douglas, giving her a new start in the movies. After their premiere, flushed with success, self-confident for the first time in years, and in happy anticipation of celebrating with Douglas, with whom she has fallen in love, she drives to his home armed with a bottle of champagne. However, we already know that Douglas isn't emotionally interested in her ("I need an actress, not a wife," he later tells her) and is spending the evening with a broad in his bedroom. Turner, suspecting nothing, is met by Douglas at the foot of the stairs. At first too engrossed in herself to notice how cool he is, she is stunned when the other woman suddenly appears at the top of the stairs in Douglas's dressing gown. Her nervous breakdown is signaled by the car headlights flashing against her windshield like a barrage of footlights and arc lamps as she drives home.

Letting the emotions rise and then bringing them suddenly down with a thump is an extreme example of dramatic discontinuity, and a similar, vertiginous drop in the emotional temperature punctuates a good many melodramas—almost invariably played out against the vertical axis of a staircase.[11] In one of the most paroxysmic montage sequences that the American cinema has known, Sirk has Dorothy Malone in *Written on the Wind* dance like some doomed goddess from a Dionysian mystery while her father is collapsing on the stairs and dying from a heart attack. Again, in *Imitation of Life* (1959), John Gavin gets the brush-off from Lana Turner as they are going downstairs, and in *All I Desire* Barbara Stanwyck has to disappoint her daughter about not taking her to New York to become an actress, after the girl has rushed downstairs to tell her father the good news. Ray's use of the staircase for similar emotional effects is well known and most spectacular in *Bigger Than Life* (1956). In Henry King's *Margie* (1946), a film following rather closely Minnelli's *Meet Me in St. Louis* (1944), the heroine, Jeanne Crain, about to be taken to the graduation ball by a blind date (whom we know to be her father) since her poetry-loving bespectacled steady has caught a cold, comes tearing down from her bedroom when she hears that the French master, on whom she has a crush, has dropped in. She virtually rips the bouquet of flowers out of his hands and is overwhelmed by joy. With some embarrassment, the poor man has to explain that he is taking someone else to the ball, that he has only come to return her papers. Margie, mortified, humiliated, and cringing with shame, has just enough time to get back upstairs before she dissolves in tears.

All this may not sound terribly profound on paper, but the orchestration of such a scene can produce strong emotional effects, and the strategy of building up to a climax so as to throttle it the more abruptly is a form of dramatic reversal by which Hollywood directors have consistently criticized the streak of incurably naive moral and emotional idealism in the American psyche, first by showing it to be often indistinguishable from the grossest kind of illusion and self-delusion and then by forcing a confrontation when it is most wounding and contradictory. The emotional extremes are played off in such a way that they reveal an inherent dialectic, and the undeniable psychic energy contained in this seemingly vulnerable sentimentality is utilized to furnish its own antidote, to bring home the discontinuities in the structures of emotional experience that give a kind of realism and toughness rare if not unthinkable in the European cinema.

What makes these discontinuities in the melodrama so effective is that they occur, as it were, under pressure. Although the kinetics of the American cinema are generally directed toward creating pressure and manipulating it (as suspense, for example), the melodrama presents in some ways a special case. In the western or the thriller, suspense is generated by the linear organization of the plot and the action, together with the kind of "pressure" that spectators bring to the film by way of anticipation and a priori expectations of what they hope to see; melodrama, however, has to accommodate the latter type of pressure, as already indicated, in what amounts to a relatively closed world.

This is emphasized by the function of the decor and the symbolization of objects: the setting of the family melodrama is almost by definition the middle-class home, filled with objects, which in a film like Philip Dunne's *Hilda Crane*, typical of the genre in this respect, surround the heroine in a hierarchy of apparent order that becomes increasingly suffocating. From Father's armchair in the living room and Mother's knitting, to the upstairs bedroom, where after five years' absence dolls and teddies are still neatly arranged on the bedspread, home not only overwhelms Hilda with images of parental oppression and a repressed past (which indirectly provoke her explosive outbursts that sustain the action), it also brings out the characteristic attempt of the bourgeois household to make time stand still, immobilize life, and fix forever domestic property relations as the model of social life and a bulwark against the more disturbing sides in human nature. The theme has a particular poignancy in the many films about the victimization and enforced passivity of women—women waiting at home, standing by the window, caught in a world of objects into which they are expected to invest their feelings. Cromwell's *Since You*

Went Away has a telling sequence in which Claudette Colbert, having just taken her husband to the troop train at the station, returns home to clear up after the morning's rush. Everything she looks at or touches—dressing gown, pipe, wedding picture, breakfast cup, slippers, shaving brush, the dog—reminds her of her husband, until she cannot bear the strain and falls on her bed sobbing. The banality of the objects, combined with the repressed anxieties and emotions, forces a contrast that makes the scene almost epitomize the relation of decor to characters in the melodrama: the more the setting is filled with objects to which the plot gives symbolic significance, the more the characters are enclosed in seemingly ineluctable situations. Pressure is generated by things crowding in on them, life becomes increasingly complicated because it is cluttered with obstacles and objects that invade the characters' personalities, take them over, stand for them, become more real than the human relations or emotions they were intended to symbolize.

It is again an instance of Hollywood stylistic devices supporting the themes or commenting on each other. Melodrama is iconographically fixed by the claustrophobic atmosphere of the bourgeois home and/or the small-town setting; its emotional pattern is that of panic and latent hysteria, reinforced stylistically by a complex handling of space in interiors (Sirk, Ray, and Losey particularly excel in this) to the point where the world seems totally predetermined and pervaded by "meaning" and interpretable signs.

This marks another recurrent feature, already touched on: that of desire focusing on the unobtainable object. The mechanisms of displacement and transfer, in an enclosed field of pressure, open a highly dynamic, yet discontinuous cycle of nonfulfillment, where discontinuity creates a universe of powerfully emotional but obliquely related fixations. In melodrama, violence, the strong action, the dynamic movement, the full articulation, and the fleshed-out emotions so characteristic of the American cinema become the very signs of the characters' alienation and thus serve to formulate a devastating critique of the ideology that supports it.

Minnelli and Sirk are exceptional directors in this respect, not least because they handle stories with four, five, or sometimes six characters all tied up in a single configuration, and yet give each of them an even thematic emphasis and an independent point of view. Such skill involves a particularly "musical" gift and a very sensitive awareness of the harmonizing potential contained in contrasting material and the structural implications of different characters' motives. Films like *Home from the Hill, The Cobweb, The Tarnished Angels,* or *Written on the Wind* strike one as "objective" films, since they do not have a central hero (though there may be a gravitational pull toward one of the protagonists). Nonetheless they cohere, mainly because each of the characters' predicaments is made plausible in terms that relate to the problems of the others. The films are built architecturally, by a combination of structural tensions and articulated parts, and the overall design appears only retrospectively, as it were, when with the final coda of appeasement the edifice is complete and the spectator can stand back and look at the pattern. But there is, especially in the Minnelli movies, also a wholly "subjective" dimension. Because the parts are so closely organized around a central theme or dilemma, the films can be interpreted as emanating from a single consciousness, which is testing or experiencing in dramatic form the various options and possibilities flowing from an initially outlined moral or existential contradiction. In *The Cobweb* John Kerr wants both total self-expression and a defined human framework in which such freedom is meaningful, and George Hamilton in *Home from the Hill* wants to assume adult responsibilities while at the same time he rejects the standards of adulthood implied in his father's aggressive masculinity. In the latter the drama ends with a "Freudian" resolution of the father being eliminated at the very point when he has resigned himself to his loss of supremacy, but this is underpinned by a "biblical" one which fuses the mythology of Cain and Abel with that of Abraham blessing his firstborn. The interweaving of motifs is achieved by a series of parallels and contrasts. Set in the South, the story concerns the relations of a mother's boy with his tough father, played by Robert Mitchum, whose wife so resents his having a bastard son (George Peppard) that she won't sleep with him. The plot progresses through all the possible permutations of the basic situation: lawful son/ natural son, sensitive George Hamilton/hypochondriac mother, tough George Peppard/tough Robert Mitchum, both boys fancy the same girl, Hamilton gets her pregnant. Peppard marries her, the girl's father turns nasty against the lawful son because of the notorious sex life of his father, etc. However, because the plot is structured as a series of mirror reflections on the theme of fathers and sons, blood ties and natural affinities, Minnelli's film is a psychoanalytical portrait of the sensitive adolescent— but placed in a definite ideological and social context. The boy's consciousness, we realize, is made up of what are external forces and circumstances, his dilemma the result of his social position as heir to his father's estate, unwanted because felt to be undeserved, and an upbringing deliberately exploited by his mother in order to get even with his father, whose own position as a Texas landowner and local big-shot forces him to compensate for his wife's frigidity by proving his virility with other women. Melodrama here becomes the vehicle for diagnosing a single individual in ideological terms and objective categories, while the blow-by-blow emotional drama creates the second level, where the subjective aspect (the immediate and necessarily unreflected experience of the characters) is left intact. The hero's identity, on the other hand, emerges as a kind of picture puzzle from the various pieces of dramatic action.

Home from the Hill is also a perfect example of the principle of substitute acts, mentioned earlier, which is Hollywood's way of portraying the dynamics of alienation. The story is sustained by pressure that is applied indirectly and by desires that always chase unattainable goals: Mitchum forces George Hamilton to "become a man" though he is temperamentally his mother's son, while Mitchum's "real" son in terms of attitudes and character is George Peppard, whom he cannot acknowledge for social reasons. Likewise, Eleanor Parker puts pressure on her son in order to get at Mitchum, and Everett Sloane (the girl's father) takes out on George Hamilton the sexual hatred he feels against Mitchum. Finally, after his daughter has become pregnant he goes to see Mitchum to put pressure on him to get his son to marry the girl, only to break down when Mitchum turns the tables and accuses him of blackmail. It is a pattern that in an even purer form appears in *Written on the Wind*: Dorothy Malone wants Rock Hudson, who wants Lauren Bacall, who wants Robert Stack, who just wants to die. *Le Ronde à l'américaine*. The point is that the melodramatic dynamism of these situations is used by both Sirk and Minnelli to make the emotional impact carry over into the very subdued, apparently neutral, sequences of images that so often round off a scene and that thereby have a strong lyrical quality.

One of the characteristic features of melodramas in general is that they concentrate on the point of view of the victim: what makes the films mentioned above exceptional is the way they manage to present *all* the characters convincingly as victims. The critique—the questions of "evil," of responsibility—is firmly placed on a social and existential level, away from the arbitrary and finally obtuse logic of private motives and individualized psychology. This is why the melodrama, at its most accomplished, seems capable of reproducing more directly than other genres the patterns of domination and exploitation existing in a given society, especially the relation between psychology, morality, and class consciousness, by emphasizing so clearly an emotional dynamic whose social correlative is a network of external forces directed oppressingly inward and with which the characters themselves unwittingly collude to become their agents. In Minnelli, Sirk, Ray, Cukor, and others, alienation is recognized as a basic condition, fate is secularized into the prison of social conformity and psychological neurosis, and the linear trajectory of self-fulfilment so potent in American ideology is twisted into the downward spiral of a self-destructive urge seemingly possessing a whole social class.

This typical masochism of melodrama, with its incessant acts of inner violation, its mechanisms of frustration and overcompensation, is per-

59. *Written on the Wind:* Building on the metaphoric possibilities of alcohol.

haps brought most into the open in characters who have a drinking problem (*Written on the Wind, Hilda Crane, Days of Wine and Roses* [Blake
Edwards, 1963]). Although alcoholism is too common an emblem in
films and too typical of middle-class America to deserve a close thematic
analysis, drink does become interesting in movies where its dynamic significance is developed and its qualities as a visual metaphor recognized:
wherever characters are seen swallowing and gulping their drinks as if
they were swallowing their humiliations along with their pride, vitality
and the life force have become palpably destructive, and a phony libido
has turned into real anxiety. *Written on the Wind* is perhaps the movie
that most consistently builds on the metaphoric possibilities of alcohol
(liquidity, potency, the phallic shape of bottles). Not only is its theme an
emotional drought that no amount of alcohol, oil pumped by the der-
ricks, or petrol in fast cars and planes can mitigate, it also has Robert
Stack compensate for his sexual impotence and childhood guilt feelings
by hugging a bottle of raw corn every time he feels suicidal, which he proceeds to smash in disgust against the paternal mansion. In one scene,
Stack makes unmistakable gestures with an empty martini bottle in the

direction of his wife, and an unconsummated relationship is visually underscored when two brimful glasses remain untouched on the table, as Dorothy Malone does her best to seduce an unresponsive Rock Hudson at the family party, having previously poured her whiskey into the flower vase of her rival, Lauren Bacall.

Melodrama is often used to describe tragedy that doesn't quite come off: either because the characters think of themselves too self-consciously as tragic or because the predicament is too evidently fabricated on the level of plot and dramaturgy to carry the kind of conviction normally termed "inner necessity." In some American family melodramas inadequacy of the characters' responses to their predicament becomes itself part of the subject. In Cukor's *The Chapman Report* (1962) and Minnelli's *The Cobweb*—two movies explicitly concerned with the impact of Freudian notions on American society—the protagonists' self-understanding as well as the doctors' attempts at analysis and therapy are shown to be either tragically or comically inadequate to the situations that the characters are supposed to cope with in everyday life. Pocket-size tragic heroes and heroines, they are blindly grappling with a fate real enough to cause intense human anguish, which as the spectator can see, however, is compounded by social prejudice, ignorance, and insensitivity on top of bogus claims to scientific objectivity by the doctors. Claire Bloom's nymphomania and Jane Fonda's frigidity in the Cukor movie are seen to be two different but equally hysterical reactions to the heavy ideological pressures that American society exerts on the relations between the sexes. *The Chapman Report,* despite having apparently been cut by Darryl F. Zanuck, Jr., remains an extremely important film partly because it treats its theme both in the tragic and the comic mode without breaking apart, underlining thereby the ambiguous springs of the discrepancy between displaying intense feelings and the circumstances to which they are inadequate—usually a comic motif but tragic in its emotional implications.

Both Cukor and Minnelli, however, focus on how ideological contradictions are reflected in the characters' seemingly spontaneous behavior—the way self-pity and self-hatred alternate with a violent urge toward some form of liberating action, which inevitably fails to resolve the conflict. The characters experience as a shamefully personal stigma what the spectator (because of the parallelisms between the different episodes in *The Chapman Report* as well as the analogies in the fates of the seven principal figures of *The Cobweb*) is forced to recognize as belonging to a wider social dilemma. The poverty of the intellectual resources in some of the characters is starkly contrasted with a corresponding abundance of emotional resources, and as one sees them helplessly struggling inside their emotional prisons with no hope of realizing to what degree they are the victims of their society, one gets a clear picture of how a certain individualism reinforces social and emotional alienation, and of how the economics of the psyche are as vulnerable to manipulation and exploitation as is a person's labor.

The point is that this inadequacy has a name, relevant to the melodrama as a form: irony or pathos, which both in tragedy and melodrama is the response to the recognition of different levels of awareness. Irony privileges the spectator vis-à-vis the protagonists, for he or she registers the difference from a superior position of knowledge. Pathos results from noncommunication or silence made eloquent—people talking at cross-purposes (Lauren Bacall telling Robert Stack she's pregnant in *Written on the Wind*), a mother watching her daughter's wedding from afar (Barbara Stanwyck in *Stella Dallas* [King Vidor, 1937]), or a woman returning unnoticed to her family, watching them through the window (Barbara Stanwyck in *All I Desire*). These highly emotional situations are underplayed to present an ironic discontinuity of feeling or a qualitative difference in intensity, usually visualized in terms of spatial distance and separation.

Such archetypal melodramatic situations activate very strongly an audience's participation, for there is a desire to make up for the emotional deficiency, to impart the different awareness, which in other genres is systematically frustrated to produce suspense: the primitive desire to warn the heroine of the perils looming visibly over her in the shape of the villain's shadow. But in the more sophisticated melodramas this pathos is most acutely produced through a "liberal" mise-en-scène which balances different points of view, so that the spectator is in a position of seeing and evaluating contrasting attitudes within a given thematic framework—a framework which is the result of the total configuration and therefore inaccessible to the protagonists themselves. The spectator, say in Otto Preminger's *Daisy Kenyon* (1947) or a Nicholas Ray movie, is made aware of the slightest qualitative imbalance in a relationship and also sensitized to the tragic implications that a radical misunderstanding or a misconception of motives might have, even when this is not played out in terms of a tragic ending.

If pathos is the result of a skillfully displaced emotional emphasis, it is frequently used in melodramas to explore psychological and sexual repression, usually in conjunction with the theme of inferiority; inadequacy of response in the American cinema often has an explicitly sexual code. Male impotence and female frigidity is a subject that allows for thematization in various directions, not only to indicate the kinds of psychological anxiety and social pressures that generally make people sexually unresponsive, but as metaphors of a lack of freedom (Hitchcock's frigid heroines) or as a quasi-metaphysical "overreaching" (as in Ray's *Bigger Than Life*). In Sirk, where the theme has an exemplary status, it is treated as a problem of decadence—where intention, awareness, and yearning outstrip sexual, social, and moral performance. From the Willi Birgel character in *Zu neuen Ufern* onward, Sirk's most impressive characters are never up to the demands that their lives make on them, though some are sufficiently sensitive, alive, and intelligent to feel and know about this inadequacy of gesture and response. It gives their pathos a tragic ring, because they take on suffering and moral anguish knowingly, as the just price for having glimpsed a better world and having failed to live it. A tragic self-awareness is called upon to compensate for lost spontaneity and energy, and in films like *All I Desire* or *There's Always Tomorrow* (Sirk, 1956), where as so often, the fundamental irony is in the titles themselves, this theme which has haunted the European imagination at least since Nietzsche, is absorbed into an American small-town atmosphere, often revolving around the questions of dignity and responsibility, of how to step down, how to yield when confronted with true talent and true vitality—in short, those qualities that dignity is called upon to make up for.

In Hollywood melodrama characters made for operettas play out the human tragedies (which is how they experience the contradictions of American civilization). Small wonder they are constantly baffled and amazed, as Lana Turner is in *Imitation of Life*, about what is going on around them and within them. The tensions of seeming and being, of intention and result, register as a perplexing frustration, and an ever-increasing gap opens between the emotions and the reality they seek to reach. What strikes one as the true pathos is the very mediocrity of the human beings involved, putting such high demands upon themselves, trying to live up to an exalted vision of the human being, but instead living out the impossible contradictions that have turned the American dream into its proverbial nightmare. It makes the best American melodramas of the fifties not only critical social documents but genuine tragedies, despite or rather because of the happy ending: they record some of the agonies that have accompanied the demise of the "affirmative culture." Spawned by liberal idealism, they advocated with open, conscious irony that the remedy is to apply more of the same idealism. But even without the national disasters that were to overtake America in the late sixties, this irony, too, almost seems now to belong to a different age.

Notes

1. Pierre Marie Augustin Filon, *The English Stage*, translated by Frederic Whyte (1897; reprint Port Washington, N.Y.: Kennikat Press, 1970), p. 195. Filon also offers an interesting definition of melodrama: "When dealing with Irving, I asked the question, so often discussed, whether we go to the theatre to see a

representation of life, or to forget life and seek relief from it. Melodrama solves this question and shows that both theories are right, by giving satisfaction to both desires, in that it offers the extreme of realism in scenery and language together with the most uncommon sentiments and events" (p. 196).

2. See Jean Duvignaud, *Sociologie du théâtre* (Paris: Presses Universitaires du France, 1965), 4, no. 3, "Théâtre sans révolution, révolution sans théâtre."

3. About the ideological function of nineteenth-century Victorian melodrama, see Maurice Willson Disher, *Blood and Thunder: Mid-Victorian Melodrama and Its Origins* (London: F. Muller, 1949): "Even in gaffs and saloons, melodrama so strongly insisted on the sure reward to be bestowed in this life upon the law-abiding that sociologists now see in this a Machiavellian plot to keep democracy servile to Church and State. . . . There is no parting the two strains, moral and political, in the imagination of the nineteenth-century masses. They are hopelessly entangled. Democracy shaped its own entertainments at a time when the vogue of Virtue Triumphant was at its height and they took their pattern from it. . . . Here are Virtue Triumphant's attendant errors: confusion between sacred and profane, between worldly and spiritual advancement, between self-interest and self-sacrifice" (pp. 13–14). However, it ought to be remembered that there are melodramatic traditions outside the puritan-democratic world view: Catholic countries, such as Spain and Mexico (cf. Buñuel's Mexican films) have a very strong line in melodramas, based on the themes of atonement and redemption. Japanese melodramas have been "high-brow" since the Monogatari stories of the sixteenth century, and in Mizoguchi's films (*O Haru, Shinheike Monogatari*) they reach a transcendence and stylistic sublimation rivalled only by the very best Hollywood melodramas.

4. Hanns Eisler, *Composing for Film* (London: Dobson, 1981).

5. Lilian Ross, *Picture* (London: Penguin, 1958).

6. Erwin Panofsky, "Style and Medium in the Motion Pictures," in *Film: An Anthology*, ed. Daniel Talbot (Berkeley: University of California Press, 1969), p. 18.

7. The impact of *Madame Bovary* via Willa Cather on the American cinema and the popular imagination would deserve a closer look.

8. Peter Lloyd, "Raoul Walsh," *Brighton Film Review*, no. 14 (November 1969): 9; "Raoul Walsh: The Hero," ibid., no. 15 (December 1969): 8–12; "Raoul Walsh," ibid., no. 21 (June 1970): 20–21.

9. I have not seen *A Woman's Secret* (1949) or *Born to Be Bad* (1950), either of which might include Ray in this category, and the Ida Lupino character in *On Dangerous Ground* (1952)—blind, living with a homicidal brother—is distinctly reminiscent of this masochistic strain in Hollywood feminism.

10. Thomas Elsaesser, "Nicholas Ray (Part 1)," *Brighton Film Review*, no. 19 (April 1970): 13–16; "Nicholas Ray (Part 2)," ibid., no. 20 (May 1970): 15–16.

11. As a principle of mise-en-scène the dramatic use of staircases recalls the famous *Jessner-treppe* of German theater. The thematic conjunction of family and height/depth symbolism is nicely described by Max Tessier: "Le heros ou l'héroine sont ballotés dans un véritable scenic-railway social, ou les classes sont rigoureusement compartimentées. Leur ambition est de quitter à jamais un milieu

moralement dépravé, physiquement éprouvant, pour accéder au Nirvana de la grande bourgeoisie. . . . Pas de famille, pas de mélo! Pour qu'il y ait mélo il faut avant tout qu'il y ait faute, péché, transgression sociale. Or, quel est le milieu idéal pour que se développe (cette gangrène, sinon cette cellule familiale, liée à une conception hiérarchique de la société)?" (*Cinéma* 71, no. 161, p. 46).

21. Romantic Comedy Today: Semi-Tough or Impossible?

BRIAN HENDERSON

1

It is a scandal of culture that there has never been a widely accepted theory of comedy to organize the general sense of the subject and to orient particular studies within it. Since Aristotle's *Poetics* there has been a theory of tragedy, more or less the same one. (Hegel's and Bradley's theories have different emphases but are compatible with it and relate to their object in a similar way.) Lacking such a founding text and oddly unable to form a later tradition, theorists of comedy have operated in a vacuum, each writer setting out boldly to do the whole job.[1]

As bad as the state of affairs itself is that we do not know *why* it is so. Determining its causes may be equal to solving the theoretical problem itself and as difficult. A speculation: each theory of comedy faces a double task—to account for comic forms (i.e., the laws of comic discourse, literary, dramatic, and filmic) and to account for the phenomenon of laughter, and of course to relate the two. Perhaps in different ways each theory of comedy has shattered or distended itself on the double task. The more successful theories, notably Freud's, tend to concentrate on one of the tasks and to ignore the other, though this entails incompleteness.

No theory can deal with both questions successfully; yet each must try to do so because the questions are linked. Producing laughter is a fundamental effect of comic discourse,[2] hence it is a part of the art of comedy writing, directing, and acting that no treatise can leave out. The two phenomena are linked but they seem to lie along different axes.

Henri Bergson's theory of comedy as the mechanical encrusted on the organic is exposed as simplistic by the case that it seems to fit best: Buster Keaton. The latter's creative misadaptation of objects to various survival needs is a positive evolutionary force. So is his turning his body into machines of various sorts to surmount various perils, such as becoming a pendulum to rescue his fiancée from a waterfall in *Our Hospitality* (Keaton, 1923).

Freud's *Jokes and Their Relation to the Unconscious*[3] may well be the best book on the subject, but it limits itself to the simplest of comic discourses, the minimal unit of humor—the joke, epigram, or humorous remark. Hence it is of more limited value to our inquiry than might appear. A comic film such as *Bringing Up Baby* (Howard Hawks, 1938) contains many jokes and instances of humor in Freud's sense but is not reducible to them. Its construction, effects, and humor operate on several levels at once. No single element may be understood by itself either discursively or in regard to spectator relation, only in relation to the multitiered whole. Although the book is one of his most brilliant, Freud was no more satisfied than the reader seeking a full treatment of comedy. James Strachey reports that Freud's other books of the period (*Interpretation of Dreams, Psychopathology of Everyday Life, Three Essays*) were expanded and modified almost out of recognition in their later editions. Half a dozen small additions were made to *Jokes* in 1912, but no further changes were ever made in it. References to it are rare in the other works, but in the *Introductory Lectures* he speaks of it having temporarily led him aside from his path; in the *Autobiographical Study* there is an apparent depreciatory reference to it. Twenty years later, in 1927, he returned to the problem with a short paper entitled "Humor," which recasts the subject by the metapsychological scheme id-ego-superego.

Although there is no satisfactory theory of the subject, there are of course traditions of comedy. These are far more diverse than traditions of tragedy and far more subject to change with changing conditions. Ben Jonson, an avowed classicist even in his comedies, nevertheless assigns the following speech to Cordatus in *Every Man out of His Humor:*

> No, I assure you, signor. If those laws you speak of had been delivered us *ab initio*, and in their present virtue and perfection, there had been some reason of obeying their powers; but 'tis extant that that which we call *Comoedia* was at first nothing but a simple and continued song sung by only one person, til Susario invented a second; after him, Epicharmus a third; Phormus and Chionides devised to have four actors, with a prologue and chorus; to which Cratinus, long after, added a fifth and sixth; Euppolis more; Aristophanes, more than they; every man in the dignity of his spirit and judgment supplied something. And though that in him this kind of poem appeared absolute and fully perfected, yet how is the face of it changed since! in Menander, Philemon, Cecilius, Plautus, and the rest, who have utterly excluded the chorus, altered the property of the persons, their names, and natures, and augmented it with all liberty, according to the elegancy and disposition of those times wherein they wrote. I see not then, but we should enjoy the same license or free power to illustrate and heighten our invention as they did; and not be tied to those strict and regular forms which the niceness of a few, who are nothing but form, would thrust upon us.[4]

2. FIFTEEN KINDS OF SNOW

In "Literature as Equipment for Living," Kenneth Burke observes: "The Eskimos have special names for many different kinds of snow (fifteen, if I remember rightly) because variations in the quality of snow greatly affect their living. . . . A different name for snow implies a different kind of hunt. Some names for snow imply that one should not hunt at all."[5]

Romantic comedy: a genre, a family of genres (marriage, manners, screwball), a category of production and marketing, a category of analysis, a realm of specialties (Ernst Lubitsch, Gregory La Cava), a notion. Definition, even delimitation, is difficult or impossible because all Hollywood films (except some war films) have romance and all have comedy. We might specify "comic *about* the romance," but nearly always at least some of the comedy concerns some of the romance. A workable subset "romantic comedy" might refer to those films in which romance and comedy are the primary components or to those without other such components as crime, detection of crime, western adventure, war, and so forth. But what is "primary" in a given case is difficult to determine where romance and comedy are pervasive. Moreover, even if crime films, westerns, and war films are eliminated, the remainder is vast and its modes of conjoining romance and comedy myriad.

3. SPECIAL NAMES

It may be that subdividing romantic comedy into its component types or genres will further analysis of it. The definition that is elusive might be easier to accomplish at a level of greater particularity. Let us take "screwball comedy," a term one finds in critical contexts of all sorts. Beneath the common term, however, there is no agreement, neither from critic to critic nor within the work of a single critic. The weekly critics use the term again and again without definition, implicit or explicit, or even an approximate sense. In the hands of its users, "screwball" seems to refer to a general impression of zaniness received by the critic.

A working definition is provided by Howard Hawks in speaking of *Bringing Up Baby:* "I think the picture had a great fault and I learned an awful lot from it. There were no normal people in it. Everyone you met was a screwball. Since that time I have learned my lesson and I don't intend ever again to make everybody crazy. If the gardener had been normal, if the sheriff had been just a perplexed man from the country—but as it was they were all way off center."[6] Hawks defines screwball comedy as a film in which everyone is a screwball. He seems to limit the category to one instance and claims to regret that as a mistake, but Hawks's definition does have to do with structural factors, not with impressions of

60. *Bringing Up Baby:* Everyone you meet is a screwball.

craziness. Its import is clarified by these observations on ancient comedy: "The representation of manners always supposes some philosophy of conduct, some standard by which we judge, and some method of discovering it. . . . Aristotle had only put it into form when he laid down his doctrine of the Mean. This doctrine is at the root of Theophrastus's *Characters*, and is everywhere implied by such comedies as Menander's. . . . Virtue once admitted to be the mean, it became necessary to define all the extremes, the too little and too much of the social appearances of man."[7] Against this backdrop screwball comedy is that which omits (or departs from) the philosophy of conduct traditional to comedy. In a comedy of characters who are all crazy, there can be no mean or standard. Even to say that all are in excess implies an external standard since there is no inner one.

But in what is called screwball comedy there often *is* comparative judgment of behavior and therefore at least an inchoate "philosophy of conduct." It is certainly not abstract like Aristotle's *Ethics*; it may be closer to Lévi-Straussian "savage thought," a thinking with empirical entities. In

The Awful Truth (Leo McCarey, 1937) and *His Girl Friday* (Hawks, 1940) the Ralph Bellamy character is exemplar and an exaggeration of conventional morality—both a character norm against which to contrast the eccentricities of the leads and a social norm against which the film directs its satire. (These functions are not always embodied in a single character.) The main characters are screwballs in relation to him, but this is not mere madness, for it exemplifies the value of spontaneity, which reigns supreme in thirties romantic comedy, where it stands in for and includes wit, intelligence, genuine feeling vs. conventional response, adaptable moral response, vitality, and life. In films without a Bellamy type, less prominent background figures such as policemen, judges, store-keepers, and relatives perform one or both functions. In both these films, the heroines plan to marry Bellamy at one point, which indicates that they waver between the two moralities.

Holiday (George Cukor, 1938) would not be called a screwball com-edy by most. The action is carefully plotted, emerging logically from con-sistent, well-motivated characters. It is a well-made film of a well-made play. Yet the main characters Linda and Casey (and the Potters) are cele-brated as some kind of screwballs in contrast to the convention-bound, predictable other characters. Its philosophy of conduct is clear-cut, but it champions a pair of semiscrewballs. Is it a screwball comedy?

A different instance is Preston Sturges, in whose films all characters speak a heady, epigrammatic prose, improbably in all but a few cases. Probability is violated in this respect and in some outrageous plot twists (usually at the end), but there are few if any screwball characters if screw-ball means to *act* spontaneously and crazily. The dialogue is the main crazy element, usually the only one. The actions, events, and plots some-times are rather conventional and predictable. The characters played by Joel McCrea, Henry Fonda, Eddie Bracken, even William Demarest are not "spontaneous." They perform no "flips" like Johnny Case in *Holiday* and hardly if ever run, as the characters in *Bringing Up Baby* do con-stantly. They rarely laugh, sigh, sing, or do slapstick like McCarey's char-acters. Mainly they exchange words—it is the words which flip, sigh, run, get out of breath. But at this level, the lines themselves are screwball. They may come out of any figure in the frame and very often express sur-prising sentiments. Character consistency is often sacrificed for a good speech—another screwball element (or is it?).

We have chased the notion of screwball around the clock of filmic ele-ments. We went in one door and came out another without encountering an iota of certainty or consistency, not even a vector between two points that pointed in a definite direction.

4

If we cannot define romantic comedy, can we talk about it at all? Aristotelian logic says no. Wittgensteinian logic says yes:

> Instead of producing something common to all that we call language, I am saying that these phenomena have no one thing in common which makes us use the same word for all, but that they are *related* to one another in many different ways. . . . Consider for example the proceedings that we call "games." I mean board-games, card-games, ball-games. Olympic-games, and so on. What is common to them all? Don't say "There *must* be something, or they would not be called 'games'" but *look and see* whether there is anything common to all. For if you look at them you will not see something that is common to *all,* but similarities, relationships, and a whole series of them at that . . . we see a complicated network of similarities overlapping and crisscrossing: sometimes overall similarities, sometimes similarities of detail. . . . I can think of no better expression to characterize these similarities than "family resemblances . . ."[8]

5

Romantic comedy is a family of resemblances. Filmic romantic comedy is one branch of that family but also, as we have seen, a family in itself with diverse subbranches. Since the branches of romantic comedy include entire art forms and their traditions—ballet, drama, painting, novel, opera, poem, symphony—it is necessarily true that the differences among them, which are material, are greater than the similarities, which are semantic, abstract, thematic (as is the heading "romantic comedy" itself). This is why transformations of subjects or themes from one medium to another are never automatic and never equal and why they offer an excellent perspective on the signifying processes of both, especially on the second or receiving system, on which the burden of transformation falls.

Consider the oft-told story of Ben Hecht's adaptation of Noel Coward's *Design for Living* (Lubitsch, 1933)—what is its point? Hecht is said to have boasted that he had kept only one line of the original (or was it a line from *Hay Fever*?), but critics agree that the film is far inferior to the play, even those virtually uncritical of Lubitsch's work. This story, like all Hollywood stories, emphasizes personalities, but far more important is the work process. Under the prevailing censorship, a woman could not live sexually with a man if they were not married, let alone two. The suggestion that Leo and Otto had been or were lovers was also inadmissible. The play (or its title, though even that no longer made sense) had to be turned toward an acceptable category, in this case competition between two men for a girl, with the twists that it remains cheerful to the end and

61. The romantic triangle in *Semi-Tough* (left to right, Kris Kristofferson, Jill Clayburgh, Burt Reynolds).

that there is no final choice. For Hecht or any Hollywood writer the project was the same—to turn *Design for Living* into a romantic comedy.

6

Semi-Tough is a nonromantic comedy, a football/sex/Texas-boy novel by Dan Jenkins. (Of course, the book has its own comedy and its own romance, but these were transformed entirely in making it into a romantic comedy.) The novel was transformed by Walter Bernstein into a romantic comedy of the same name (Michael Ritchie, 1977) at a time when the concept of romantic comedy itself seems vaguely problematic, extinct, or transformed. Thus in considering this problem, we are defining and pursuing an equation with two unknowns. What is romantic comedy now? How is this particular nonromantic comedy transformed into one? There are also two (more or less) knowns that we may use—what romantic comedy used to be and what this nonromantic comedy was before transformation.

The book's plot concerns three childhood friends from Texas who now live in New York—football pros and roommates Billy Clyde and Shake Tiller and a woman, Barbara Jane Bookman. Barbara Jane comes from the highest class in the region; Shake's father owned a paint store; Billy Clyde was an orphan and an outcast. (The three characters' parallel to Becky Thatcher, Tom Sawyer, and Huck Finn is evident.) The book builds to a double climax of pregame orgy and Super Bowl. A third climax concerns the dawning of love between Billy Clyde and Barbara Jane. Shake and Barbara Jane have been romantically involved since childhood. Billy Clyde, who is the book's narrator, tells of Shake's not appearing after the big game, of Barbara Jane's suggestions that the two of them get together, and of his own persistent refusals to do so, even after Shake has written from afar telling them to get together. At the end of his account—after an interval in which he has presumably worked through his inhibitions—Billy Clyde describes their finally hitting the right mood and beginning to make love, then stops.

7

The film drops nearly all of the book's football and casual sex and all of its material about the characters' shared childhood. It also makes the three friends roommates. It eliminates the love relationship between Shake and Barbara Jane—none of the three has apparently had sex with another when the film opens. This has been called the film's *Design for Living* premise, but it is not that. In the play the three try each of three possible pairings before they go off to live as three at the final curtain. The initial arrangement of *Semi-Tough* is merely a set-up for romantic comedy of a more usual sort—a competition of two men for a woman who will favor first one then the other.

Barbara Jane returns from a long absence, during which time Shake has gotten involved with a movement called BEAT—"It changed my life." Barbara Jane admires his new self-mastery, they become closer, and by the next road game they are sleeping together. Billy Clyde's distress is expressed in various ways (to the audience only), though the exact cause is unclear. He counterattacks by proposing to write a book, but he blows this bid for Barbara Jane's esteem by making a joke of it. Shake saves a life through BEAT; Barbara Jane's anxiety at the event becomes hysterical admiration for Shake and they decide to marry. At this point Billy Clyde drops his book project and carries the battle to the enemy's territory by faking his way through a BEAT weekend and pretending to have IT, just as Barbara Jane suffers through to please Shake and does not get IT. During the wedding preparations Billy Clyde plays off Shake's anxieties that a "mixed marriage" will not work. Shake says "I don't" at the altar, the ceremony becomes a brawl, and Billy Clyde and Barbara Jane escape. He says they should go to Hawaii; they walk together down the beach.

On this romantic comedy framework, the script and film develop a rather extensive satiric inventory of various kinds of psychotherapies, body therapies, and human potential movements. Much of the time, indeed, the writer and director seem more interested in lampooning the therapy craze than in the love story itself. This loss of faith in the interest of romance as a subject suggests the decline and perhaps the impossibility of romantic comedy today.

8

George Cukor once remarked, "He [Philip Barry] was a subtle writer, but nothing muddy about him. A clarity at the back of it all. I don't like muddiness, I like clarity. It has nothing to do with being literal, and it doesn't cut out mystery—of course, there are times when you don't want to say everything—but I like to know that I can look into the pool of water when I want to and find it clear at the bottom."[9]

Would sophisticated characters walk into this drama machine so naively or be so surprised by pitfall no. 1, sexual jealousy? The book's characters might discuss the proposal amusingly, but each would vote no at the end. The film begins with three friendships and moves to one love match, then to another. What is the nature and strength of the friendships, of the loves, how and why do they arise or fall apart when they do? On these points the film is unclear.

When do Billy Clyde's feelings for Barbara Jane change? When the Shake–Barbara Jane romance starts, Billy Clyde is evidently unhappy but why—exclusion by friends, jealousy of Barbara Jane, sex rivalry with Shake, or slow-ripening love for Barbara Jane quickened by the pressure of events? These are confused or insufficiently differentiated—Billy Clyde's quest remains ambiguous.

Friendship is partway established between Shake and Barbara Jane and between Billy Clyde and Barbara Jane but not between the two men. Though they are said to be old and close friends, what we see is Billy Clyde competing with Shake ruthlessly for Barbara Jane. "Nobody ever said it wasn't going to be semi-tough." The book's line and title refer to the Super Bowl. In the film Billy Clyde speaks the line to himself about breaking up the wedding and winning Barbara Jane. Thus the film's displacement of competition from sport to love and its elimination of friendship and teamwork.

9

Basic to romantic comedy is the dyad old love/new love. Nearly all romantic comedies may be divided according to it. *Bringing Up Baby* and *Holiday* treat new love; *The Awful Truth, His Girl Friday,* and *Twentieth Century* (Hawks, 1934) treat old love. *The Philadelphia Story* (Cukor, 1940) treats both, though the new is only a flash, as do most films by Lubitsch.

Semi-Tough is a story of new love and of new rivalries for it, wherein ruthlessness, stunts, and dissembling are traditional. But when a story of new love is laid over a story of old friendship, the results are unsavory and unattractive. Were Cary Grant the close friend and work partner of Ralph Bellamy, his taunts and ruses would not be so funny. A work that faced squarely this disturbing mixture and its consequences might well be interesting. But if it insists on the new love quest and sweeps the residues under the rug, as this film does, then the viewer will be confused and disturbed at the end, perhaps without knowing why. This happens here when the hero is shown triumphant in love, but his friend lies slain by him just off-screen.

10

Friendship must be established and built, not just posited, even if (especially if) the friends later fall out over a love object. This is proven by the films of Hawks and Ford, as it is by Coward's *Design for Living.*

In *Semi-Tough* both friendship and love are posited abstractly. We must infer Billy Clyde's love for Barbara Jane from his writing and disrupting the wedding, not from the way the two relate to each other on-screen. Their confrontations, in brief, tangential scenes, are awkward. Another "obligatory" scene that is missing is one between Shake and Billy Clyde confronting the issue of Barbara Jane. As BEAT follower, Shake might propose the talk, though follow through glibly. Billy Clyde might become tense or refuse to take it seriously or actually speak his feelings. How it was done would not matter; their usual banter would suffice, so long as it were banter under pressure.

Another posit: Billy Clyde is said to like only fucking and football, but neither liking is shown. He has two meager sexual encounters—why only this for an alleged stud? Because even a semi-intense scene between Billy Clyde and a woman might throw off his alleged passion for Barbara Jane and the campaign he is mounting to fulfill it. (In very skillful hands such a scene could be used to clarify his feelings for Barbara Jane.) In all these respects the film lives a life of denial to protect its house-of-cards premise. It might have been better to accept the weakness of the premise and go after some old-fashioned character interaction. In this way the premise might have been abandoned or rediscovered or changed or developed.

It is true that some classic films present love indirectly—to be consistent with hard-bitten heroes and/or the conflict of strong egos too proud to submit to love. This is the case in scripts by Jules Furthman, especially those directed by Josef von Sternberg and Hawks (*Morocco* [von Sternberg, 1930], *Shanghai Express* [von Sternberg, 1932], *Only Angels Have Wings* [Hawks, 1939], *To Have and Have Not* [Hawks, 1944], *Rio Bravo* [Hawks, 1959]). Each of these films presents the love attraction early and with great vividness, often in great set pieces, so that later when we see the characters choking on the attraction as it slowly turns to love, we know what they are choking on. Furthman's law is that the hero cannot say "I love you"—hence the messages on mirrors, carvings on tables, two-headed coins, threatened handbills, tickets for the morning stage, bus, plane, and boat. But the attraction has to be felt viscerally first if the later doubts, hesitations, betrayals, the goings back and forth, and the complex movement toward resolution are to have dramatic impact and emotional force. Otherwise one creates a set of logical complications that have no referent; the plot gets more and more abstract as it doubles over, achieving new levels of tangles in relation to its basic love premise— it refers to nothing in the viewer's emotional memory of the film. Of course this is a fine strategy for modernist films that proceed systematically, like Marguerite Duras's *Woman of the Ganges* (1972) and Yvonne Rainer's films, but we are not speaking of that here.

11. HEROINE

At the start of the film, the Barbara Janes of film and book seem close— the changes do not seem to matter, but if we compare them at the end of the film, the difference is enormous. At the end, Barbara Jane has just come close to a third marriage, been spurned by Shake, and hustled away by Billy Clyde. It dawns on her slowly that she has been a fool about Shake (going against her nature to learn BEAT), and that Billy Clyde has contrived to break up the wedding, therefore he must love her. She asks him, "Do you want to marry me?" When he says no and suggests a trip to Hawaii, she asks like a child, "What will we do there?" The last-minute rescue from a bad wedding is a fixture of romantic comedy, but the pathetic dependence of the heroine on the rescuer is not. In thirties comedies the heroine might turn on her benefactor at rescue point and strip him of his pretensions. In *Morgan!* (Karel Reisz, 1966), Vanessa Redgrave laughs at the disorder caused by her psychotic rescuer and is thereby complicit in it. Even *The Graduate* (Mike Nichols, 1967) does a better wedding breakup by playing it as drama rather than comedy and by having the heroine come to the hero. (When will we see a film in which the woman does the rescuing?) In *Semi-Tough* the heroine does nothing after the rescue except to be catatonic. We do not notice this on first viewing because the wedding brawl creates a slight sense of breathlessness that almost lasts through the final scene. The latter is very short anyway but is made to seem longer through a trick. The new couple takes a long slow walk down the beach as the camera watches them, a shot that continues as the credits come up. This fills out a sense of time while providing no new information or emotion. The hollowness of the film's romantic-comedy premise surfaces here.

Billy Clyde's breakup and refusal may be meant to cure Barbara Jane of her marriage compulsion. He may sense that she marries knowing it will not work, therefore he will live with her to make their relationship last. This is a kindly guess, as the script supplies few clues. Nor are there enough to evaluate such a supposition on Billy Clyde's part. In any case it implies a psychiatrist-patient or parent-child relation, not a romantic-comedy one.

The final scene marks the collapse of the filmic Barbara Jane—it reveals that there never was a character at all. With her collapse, the film collapses. There can be no romantic comedy without strong heroines.

12

He'd [Jules Furthman] been writing a thing for Bacall for an introduction— really good scene, where she'd had her purse stolen. He said, "What do you think of it?" and I said, "Well, Jules, if anything makes me sexually excited it's a girl who's lost her purse." And he looked bemused and began to stare at me. "You son of a bitch," he said, and he walked out. And he came in and he wrote a story about how the girl stole a purse. Made a lot better picture.

—HOWARD HAWKS [10]

We need not review Hegel on the master-slave dialectic or Simone de Beauvoir on the man-woman dialectic to observe that a fictive mode that debases the heroine thereby debases the hero also and thereby subverts itself. We note also that the novel's Barbara Jane is strong, independent, and virtually equal to her two friends. It is she who pursues Billy Clyde at the end, as the mate she believes best for her. The long last chapter concerns the overcoming of Billy Clyde's reservations. This makes the film's transformations especially alarming. As an answer to the question "What is romantic comedy now?" it is even more alarming.

Romantic comedy posited men and women willing to meet on a common ground and to engage all their faculties and capacities in sexual dialectic. Later work such as the Kanin-Gordon-Cukor films brought work, political dispute, and psychological complications to this engaged ground and extended the age range of its participants. What we begin to see now in films is a withdrawal of men and women from this ground (or of it from them). Or we see—in effect the same thing—false presences in the sexual dialectic or divided ones (one realizes at the end that one did not want to play the game at all) or commitments for trivial stakes only. It seems that when the new self pulls itself together, it is away from the ground of full sexual dialectic. To argue this is to argue the death of romantic comedy.

13. KING SUN

One need not subscribe to any theory of art as mimesis to recognize that social and political changes have transformed the making and reception of romantic comedy since the classical period. These changes are vast, complex, interwoven, and not yet sufficiently understood in themselves to permit application to subtopics like our own. This is true even if we limit ourselves to changes in the family and in sexual life: the doubling of the divorce rate in the last decade, the rise of the single parent, the political and social impact of feminist movements and gay rights movements, and so on. One factor, the rise of working women, has been called "a revolution in the roles of women that . . . is a worldwide phenomenon, an integral part of a changing society. Its secondary and tertiary consequences are really unchartable." [11] The striking fact is how little these changes have made their way into films of any kind, whether comedies, dramas, or documentaries.

Another factor, perhaps a simpler one, is the sharply increased movement of the American population from Eastern cities to the Sunbelt in the last ten years. Since 1970 the nation's eight largest metropolitan areas have declined in population growth. This development stands in contrast with practically all preceding periods since 1790. The more rapid growth of large urban concentrations as compared to nonmetropolitan territory has been one of the most persistent of American demographic trends. Five of the eight areas had a net loss of population during this period. During the next fifteen years there will be a pronounced shift of income away from the Northeast and North Central regions of the country to the Southern and Western regions. "The question is not so much one of decline but one of: Can the Northeast age gracefully?" [12]

The romantic comedy has always been urban and urban-oriented, aggressively, smugly assuming the superiority of city over country. This pattern of thought and response is old and deep in both U.S. and European culture. It characterizes the great age of industrialism and capitalist expansion, which is now beginning to be over.

In sophisticated films and plays, the sticks were always ridiculed, especially the visitor from the sticks, and the immigrant to the city from the country. The full fury of urban scorn was vented on those who retained any narcissistic pride in the provinces. The immigrant had to adapt to capitalism and its life ways in a hurry. Thus, in *The Awful Truth*: "What's wrong with Oklahoma City?" "Nothing, Bruce, nothing." Jokes based on urban superiority had an unquestioned sense for audiences for 180 years and more that they are beginning not to have. What sense does Walter Burns's put-down of Albany make (in *His Girl Friday*) now that New York City is dependent on Albany for survival?

What a cinema of the Sunbelt will be we do not know. Perhaps *Badlands* (Terrence Malick, 1974) and *Three Women* (Robert Altman, 1977) are versions of this. To quote Pascal, "The silence of those infinite spaces terrifies me."

14. ENUNCIATION

Enunciation signifies the act of uttering a message. It is opposed to *enoncé*, which signifies what is uttered. The system of enunciation that governs particular acts of enunciation is in turn governed by the semiotic system involved—which creates a limited number of enunciation possibilities—and by historical, social, and other contextual factors. French linguist Emile Benveniste distinguishes two distinct and complementary systems of enunciation, that of story (*l'histoire*) and that of discourse (*discours*). In language these systems divide up all verb tenses between them—what does not belong to discourse (only the aorist) belongs to history:

> The historical utterance . . . characterizes the narration of past events. These three terms "narration," "event," and "past," are of equal importance. Events that took place at a certain moment of time are presented without any intervention of the speaker in the narration. In order for them to be recorded as having occurred, these events must belong to the past.[13]

> Discourse must be understood in its widest sense: every utterance assuming a speaker and a hearer, and in the speaker, the intention of influencing the other in some way. It is primarily every variety of oral discourse of every nature and every level . . . But it is also the mass of writing that reproduces oral discourse or that borrows its manner of expression and its purposes: correspondence, memoirs, plays, didactic works, in short, all the genres in which someone addresses himself to someone, proclaims himself as the speaker, and organizes what he says in the category of person.[14]

Histoire suppresses or hides all traces of its telling; it refers neither to speaker or listener but only to the events it relates. The effects of different modes of enunciation on the receiver is a complex, largely uncharted area, but it is clear that *histoire* in general is used to make the events related seem more real, vivid, present, whereas *discours* modes continually break such illusions, or at least may do so.

Applying these concepts in film analysis creates several problems, the first of which is that films are apparently perceived as told in the present. That in any case is its most transparent mode, and in this it resembles *histoire*. Romantic comedies of all decades belong to this mode. They are dramatic—they present what is happening now, without mediation. Pace and timing are important, and there is a sense that the characters are under pressure and must react quickly. Lines of dialogue are delivered fast, often unexpectedly, and must be countered fast. Of course this is a carefully engineered illusion, but it is the impression that romantic comedy must create if it is to achieve the effects which define it.

Related to this enunciative mode is a thematic constant of romantic comedy (at least in the thirties)—an ethos of spontaneity. Not only are lines of dialogue rendered spontaneously, so are physical actions. We see Johnny Case's excited face and rising inflections in *Holiday* and suddenly he does a "flip," lands on his feet, utters a few more lines, and goes out the door. Any evidence of enunciation in this passage would ruin the effect of the scene. Imagine a film noir like *Raw Deal* (Anthony Mann, 1944) with ghostly voice-over, eerie music, expressionist lighting, and webbed, tangled mise-en-scène: "I did a flip on my way out the door. As I stood there looking at my friends it seemed to me that everything was upside down. The room was going round and round . . . I knew that I had to get to Helen, who was waiting in the car, but I could not move." The example is ridiculous, I beg your indulgence, but it should make clear the difference between enunciation that is heavily marked and enunciation that is transparent and—very roughly—the kinds of subjects traditionally appropriate to each. (Film noir is especially interesting because its plethora of signifier chains, its multichanneled redundancy, works as often to pull the viewer in—i.e., the film naturalizes itself as "complex world"—as to distance the viewer.)

Works of *histoire* suppress signs of enunciation, but no work can do this completely. The analyst must look more carefully in such cases, but all works betray signs of their telling. The first close-up in *Bringing Up Baby,* about a third of the way through, shows us Susan's distress at hearing that David is to be married. This shot betrays a previously transparent discourse—someone is showing us this detail, is marking it as important (so that we will understand Susan's behavior later). In *The Awful Truth* there is a gap after Bellamy departs—an affair for Jerry is needed in a hurry so that Lucy may play disrupter and the film continue. The film presents a rather typical montage of society column excerpts, with shots of the couple at racetrack, watching polo, and motorboating before the music dies down and the next funny scene starts. Here it is the banality of the presentation, the simplicity and obviousness of the message, the tediousness of its "process" that calls attention to the enunciation, as well as its marked difference from the rest of the film and its odd placement in its late middle, perhaps also the switching from dramatic/improvisational to narrational mode and from a constant use of scenes to a bracket syntagm. Thus a passage's difference from a film's principal mode of enunciation can mark one mode of transparent enunciation from its fellows.

Romantic comedy's banishment of enunciation marks is reflected in *Semi-Tough,* too. The book has an interesting enunciation structure: not only a first-person but a second-person, too. Billy Clyde narrates the book to Jim Tom, a reporter friend who will edit it. Every so often he asks Jim Tom if he's listening and tells him what to disregard if he wishes. At times he speculates alone or in imaginary colloquy with Jim Tom what the publisher's editor is likely to think. Billy Clyde sometimes describes himself taping, the presence of others while he's taping; he also has to account for all his comings and goings that relate to the taping—such as why he can tape now. And of course he cannot both play football and narrate what is happening on the field. This requires continual maneuver. The film eliminates these complexities in one stroke, opting for the dramatic mode of entirely present action and dialogue rather than narration.[15] In doing so it maximizes the values of spontaneity and vividness and diminishes those of perspective, layering, and temporal and presentational complexity. In short, it adopts the enunciative mode that has always been obligatory for romantic comedy. This dictates in part the transformation pattern that romantic comedy imposes on its diverse materials—which is to say that it is part of the definition of romantic comedy.

15

At one point in *Semi-Tough* the heroine says to the hero, "How come we never fucked?" It is arguable that romantic comedy depends upon the suppression of this question and that with its surfacing romantic comedy becomes impossible.

The sexual question always circulates in romantic comedy; it is its utterance that is forbidden. On this prohibition romantic comedy stands. Indeed one can see the entire spectrum of romantic comedy as so many variations on this unuttered question. In comedies of old love, the unspoken question is "Why did we stop fucking?" In comedies of new love, it is "Why don't we fuck now?" There is a virtual Freudian declension system operating here, the terms of which define the principal modes of romantic comedy.[16]

It seems, then, that the various modes of romantic comedy posit a condition of nonfucking. In comedies of new love this is the initial situation;

62. *It Happened One Night:* The "Walls of Jericho" between Ellen (Claudette Colbert) and Peter (Clark Gable).

the plot extends it by prolonging aversion or indifference, by mistaken identity, and/or by a repetition of frustrating encounters. Old love come- dies posit a cessation of fucking, due to suspected infidelity (*The Awful Truth*), to "leaving the newspaper business to settle down" (*His Girl Fri- day*), or whatever. In comedies of both kinds it is the entire film, but no line in it, that poses and explores the question "Why are we not fucking?" and "How can we get (back) to fucking?" Romantic comedy lives on the problem of nonfucking and is over when, and only when, it is resolved, when fucking starts or resumes. This is explicit in *The Awful Truth,* when the boy and girl figures on the clock finally go through the same door, just before "The End"; and in *It Happened One Night* (Frank Capra, 1934) when the "Walls of Jericho" come down at the same mo- ment. These films end just as the characters begin to fuck. In *Holiday* and other films, the film ends as the characters "go off" together, marking the same occasion less literally. *Semi-Tough* concludes this way, but the over- all film is muddied because the characters are childhood friends—it is the story both of new love complications and of exploring an old bar, "Why haven't we ever fucked?" In fact the second question is not explored—beyond a throwaway from Billy Clyde about how they had meant too much to each other for "fun" sex along the way.

An exception is Lubitsch's *One Hour with You,* a 1933 remake of *The Marriage Circle* and a romantic comedy about a happy couple. Of course the plot turns on a slow-building threat to the marriage, but it breaks them up for only a short time (one night) before they get back together.

Note that in romantic comedy resolution of the problem of nonfucking involves both a theoretic question and a pragmatic one (as in psychoanalysis). Determining why we are not fucking and overcoming the barrier by actually fucking are quite different things, though romantic comedies and their characters consistently confuse them. The theoretic answer to the question does not necessarily lead to the desired result, and achievement of the desired result does not necessarily imply that the theoretic question has been answered. Perhaps it is anxiety over the problem and the desire for its pragmatic overcoming, both overdetermined, that are the mainspring of the genre. Seeking theoretic knowledge is one solution among others that are tried, with no very strict housekeeping as to which one actually works. For one thing, there is not the time, patience, or mental calm necessary to try one solution at a time—the notion itself is comic (though not romantic)—all are tried at once. This is a realm in which "savage thought" and *bricolage* dominate, despite a surface appearance of rationality.

Although romantic comedy is about fucking and its absence, this can never be said nor referred to directly. This is perhaps the fascination of romantic comedy. It implies a process of perpetual displacement, of euphemism and indirection at all levels, a latticework of dissembling and hiding laid over what is constantly present but denied, unspoken, unshown. We perceive the sublimation system and the thing itself at every point, a system of repression suffused with a libidinal glow. In "Humor" Freud defined humor (as opposed to jokes) as proceeding from the super-ego, in reward for a survival-enhancing act or attitude.

Language in romantic comedy has a special status. What stands between sexual desire and its fulfillment is language. In romantic comedy language is the medium in which all things occur, arise, and are discharged or not. Visual metaphors like figures on a clock and walls trumpeted down as well as actions such as "going off" are resorted to for the absolutely unsayable. In romantic comedy, it is the past sex lives of the characters and present sexual problems that constitute a referent that cannot be named directly. *Angel* (Lubitsch, 1937) and *The Awful Truth,* both concerned with the possible infidelity of a marriage partner, cleverly make the enunciative conditions of romantic comedy the predicament of the inquiring characters—they have only indirect, oblique signs to interpret. Also in both the question is never resolved, for the character or for us. The enunciation system is inscribed by displacement in the plot. Lubitsch's dollies into and static shots of closing bedroom doors do the same thing at a different level.

The effective prohibitions of romantic comedy are prohibitions within language. It is this that makes speaking the question "Why haven't we ever fucked?" destructive of romantic comedy. It wrecks the language game on which it rests. In that game you can refer to anything but cannot speak of it. (See again the works of Lubitsch.)

The first reason that *Semi-Tough* says "How come we never fucked?" is that it can say it. In the thirties such language and such linguistic reference were prohibited—nor could you say "Why haven't we ever made love?" That you can say something does not mean that you must do so. But has any realm of art invented for itself a system of censorship not imposed upon it? On this ground alone, it may be that romantic comedy is not an art that can flourish in this period.

Notes

1. Some scholars have argued that Aristotle wrote a second part of his *Poetics,* now lost, dealing with comedy. See G. M. A. Grube, *The Greek and Roman Critics* (London: Methuen, 1965); W. D. Ross, *Aristotle,* 5th ed. (London: Methuen, 1964); and Lane Cooper, *An Aristotelian Theory of Comedy* (New York: Harcourt, 1922). Wimsatt and Brooks ingeniously sketch an Aristotelian theory of comedy by connecting and rationalizing fragments on the subject from several of his books. See William K. Wimsatt, Jr., and Cleanth Brooks, *Literary Criticism: A Short History* (New York: Random House, 1967). Neither the possibility of a lost work nor later attempts at reconstruction overcome that gap of nearly twenty-five hundred years of which I speak here.

2. Dare one call laughter a rhetorical effect? No, because the figure may be written and no one laugh. In comedy, we identify the figure with the effect—as though metaphor were dependent on audience effect to be that.

3. Sigmund Freud, *Jokes and Their Relation to the Unconscious,* translated by James Strachey (New York: Norton, 1960).

4. Reprinted in *Literary Criticism: Plato to Dryden,* edited by Allan H. Gilbert (Detroit: Wayne State University Press, 1962), pp. 537–538.

5. Kenneth Burke, *The Philosophy of Literary Form* (New York: Random House, 1957), pp. 253–254.

6. Interview with Howard Hawks by Peter Bogdanovich, *Movie,* no. 5 (n.d.): 11.

7. G. S. Gordon, "Theophrastus and His Imitators," in *English Literature and the Classics,* edited by G. S. Gordon (New York: Russell & Russell, 1969), pp. 52–53.

8. Ludwig Wittgenstein, *Philosophical Investigations,* translated by G. E. M. Anscombe (Oxford: London, 1953), pp. 31e–32e.

9. Gavin Lambert, *On Cukor* (New York: Putnam, 1972), p. 123.

10. Interview with Howard Hawks by Peter Lehman et al., *Wide Angle* 1, no. 2 (Summer 1976): 57.

11. "Vast Changes in Society Traced to the Rise of Working Women," *New York Times*, November 29, 1977, pp. 1, 28.

12. "Influx of Population Down in Urban Areas," *New York Times*, June 16, 1975, pp. 1, 7.

13. Emile Benveniste, *Problems in General Linguistics*, translated by Mary Elizabeth Meek (Coral Gables: University of Miami Press, 1971), p. 206.

14. Ibid., pp. 208–209.

15. Although the film eliminates Billy Clyde's narration, his book project is retained as a narrative episode—a few scenes show him writing and taping. This has only to do with the enounced (the told), whereas the taping is the enunciation principle of the entire book as well as sometimes part of the enounced, as when Billy Clyde describes himself speaking to the recorder. The film plays Gene Autry songs almost constantly, sometimes diegetically when the characters listen to them and react, sometimes nondiegetically over a football game, etc. Perhaps the ubiquitous voice of Autry, with its recurring "I" and "I'm," stands in for the absent narrational voice of Billy Clyde as a displaced principle of enunciation.

16. From his analysis of Schreber's memoirs, Freud concluded that the principal forms of paranoia can all be represented as contradictions of the single proposition "I (a man) love him (a man)," and that they exhaust all the possible ways in which such contradictions can be formulated.

22. The Self-Reflexive Musical and the Myth of Entertainment

JANE FEUER

Within the musical film the most persistent subgenre has involved kids (or adults) "getting together and putting on a show." *The Jazz Singer* (Alan Crosland, 1927) featured a show-business story, and during the talkie boom that followed (1929–1930), a large percentage of the early musicals took for their subjects the world of entertainment: Broadway, vaudeville, the Ziegfeld Follies, burlesque, night clubs, the circus, Tin Pan Alley, and, to a lesser extent, mass entertainment media in the form of radio or Hollywood itself. Warner Brothers' *Forty-Second Street* (Lloyd Bacon, 1933) precipitated a second cycle of musicals. The *Forty-Second Street* spinoffs tended to feature a narrative strategy typical of the backstage musical: musical interludes, usually in the form of rehearsal sequences detailing the maturation of the show, would be interspersed with parallel dramatic scenes detailing maturation of the off-stage love affairs. Even a radio story such as *Twenty Million Sweethearts* (Ray Enright, 1934) took its narrative structure from this paradigm. Perhaps these "art" musicals fulfilled a need for verisimilitude; perhaps the audience felt more comfortable viewing musical numbers within the context of a show than seeing fairy-tale queens and princes suddenly feel a song coming on in the royal boudoir. Whatever the explanation of its origins, the backstage pattern was always central to the genre. Incorporated into the structure of the art musical was the very type of popular entertainment represented by the musical film itself. The art musical is thus a self-referential form.

All art musicals are self-referential in this loose sense. But given such an opportunity, some musicals have exhibited a greater degree of self-consciousness than others. *Dames* (Enright, 1934) climaxes its show-within-the-film with an apology for its own mode of entertainment, appropriately entitled "Dames." Moreover, the "Dames" number resolves a narrative in which the forces of Puritanism do battle with the forces of entertainment. It is the victory of what might be termed the "prurient ethic" over the Puritan ethic that the final show celebrates within the film

63. *Forty-Second Street:* The backstage musical.

and that the "Dames" number celebrates within that show. In similar fashion, the Fred Astaire–Ginger Rogers cycle at RKO (1933–1939) began to reflect upon the legends created in its dancing stars.[1]

Shall We Dance (Mark Sandrich, 1937) culminates in a show merging popular dancing with ballet. Yet that merger consists not in an equal union but rather in the lending of youth, rhythm, and vitality to the stiff, formal, classical art of ballet. Once again, a musical film has affirmed its own value for the popular audience.

Dames and *Shall We Dance* are early examples of musicals that are *self-reflective* beyond their given self-referentiality. Historically, the art musical has evolved toward increasingly greater degrees of self-reflectivity. By the late forties and into the early fifties, a series of musicals produced by the Freed unit at MGM used the backstage format to present sustained reflections upon, and affirmations of, the musical genre itself. Three of these apologies for the musical (all scripted by Betty Comden and Adolph Green), *The Barkleys of Broadway* (Charles Walters, 1949), *Singin' in the Rain* (Stanley Donen and Gene Kelly, 1952), and *The Band Wagon* (Vincente Minnelli, 1953) involve contrasts between performances that fail to please audiences and performances that are immediately audience-pleasing.[2] Performances in these films are not restricted to onstage numbers. Multiple levels of performance and consequent multiple levels of audience combine to create a myth about musical entertainment permeating ordinary life. Through the work of these filmic texts all successful performances, both in art and in life, are condensed into the MGM musical.

To say that entertainment is "mythified" is to institute a triple play upon conventional meanings of the word "myth." Most simply, it means that entertainment is shown as having greater value than it actually does. In this sense musicals are ideological products; they are full of deceptions. As students of mythology have demonstrated, however, these deceptions are willingly suffered by the audience. In *American Vaudeville as Ritual,* Albert F. McLean attempts to explain this contradiction in his definition of myth as "a constellation of images and symbols, whether objectively real or imaginary, which brings focus and a degree of order to the psychic (largely unconscious) processes of a group or society and in so doing endows a magical potency upon the circumstances of persons involved."[3] McLean's notion of myth as "aura" occupies a pole opposite that of myth as "untruth" in constituting the myth of entertainment.

According to Claude Lévi-Strauss, the seemingly random surface structure of a myth masks contradictions that are real and therefore unresolvable.[4] Art musicals are structurally similar to myths, seeking to mediate contradictions in the nature of popular entertainment. The myth of entertainment is constituted by an oscillation between demystification and remythicization.[5] Musicals, like myths, exhibit a stratified structure. The ostensible or surface function of these musicals is to give pleasure to the audience by revealing what goes on behind the scenes in the theater or Hollywood—that is, to demystify the production of entertainment. But the films remythicize at another level that which they set out to expose. Only unsuccessful performances are demystified. The musical desires an ultimate valorization of entertainment; to destroy the aura, reduce the illusion, would be to destroy the myth of entertainment as well.[6] For the purpose of analysis, the myth of entertainment can be subdivided into three categories: the myth of spontaneity, the myth of integration, and the myth of the audience. In the films, however, the myth makes its impact through combination and repetition. Thus, a single musical number can be highly overdetermined and may be discussed under all three categories.

THE MYTH OF SPONTANEITY

Perhaps the primary positive quality associated with musical performance is its spontaneous emergence out of a joyous and responsive attitude toward life. The musical buffs' parlor game that attempts to distinguish Fred Astaire's screen persona from Gene Kelly's ignores the overriding similarities in both dancers' spontaneous stances.[7] *The Barkleys of*

Broadway, Singin' in the Rain, and *The Band Wagon* contrast the spontaneity of Astaire or Kelly with the prepackaged or calculated behavior of other performers.

In *Singin' in the Rain,* spontaneous talent distinguishes Don, Cosmo, and Kathy from Lina Lamont. Lina's laborious attempts to master basic English are followed by Don Lockwood's elocution lesson. Don and Cosmo seize upon the tongue-twister to turn the lesson into a spontaneous, anarchic dance routine, "Moses Supposes." Spontaneous self-expression through song and dance characterizes the three positive performers: Cosmo in "Make 'Em Laugh," Don in "Singin' in the Rain," and all three in "Good Mornin'," which evolves out of their collective solution to the problems of "The Dueling Cavalier."

In addition, the impression of spontaneity in these numbers stems from a type of *bricolage*; the performers make use of props at hand—curtains, movie paraphernalia, umbrellas, furniture—to create the imaginary world of the musical performance. This *bricolage,* a hallmark of the post–Gene Kelly MGM musical, creates yet another contradiction: an effect of spontaneous realism is achieved through simulation.

The Barkleys of Broadway opposes strained, artificial "serious" performances to spontaneous and natural musical comedy performances. Dinah Barkley's sparkling costume and demeanor in the title sequence with Astaire ("Swing Trot") contrasts with her subdued garb and sullen demeanor as a dramatic actress. Early in the film we see Dinah truncating her understudy's carefully calculated audition, doing a brief warm-up, and going into a perfectly executed rehearsal of a tap routine with her husband. The rehearsals of "Young Sarah" (a play about Sarah Bernhardt's *struggle* to become an actress) are quite the opposite. Josh (Astaire), the musical comedy director-performer, is always spontaneous and natural. In the parallel sequence to Dinah's labors over "Young Sarah," we see Josh doing a completed number from his new show. "Shoes with Wings On" presents musical comedy dancing as an involuntary response, like breathing. Dancing is so spontaneous for Josh that animated shoes pull him into performance. The Astaire character never changes; he is presented as an utterly seamless monument of naturalness and spontaneity. Others must adapt to his style. Dinah can succeed as a performer only in a musical setting with Josh. Even their offstage performances stem from a spontaneous responsiveness to ordinary life, as when their dance to "You'd Be Hard to Replace" evolves out of the natural movements of putting on robes.

Similar oppositions between spontaneous and canned performers structure *Singin' in the Rain* and *The Band Wagon.* Astaire's trademark, "reflex" dancing, has its counterpart in the "Gotta Dance" motif that informs Kelly's "Broadway Ballet," part of the ultimately successful film-

64. *The Band Wagon:* Dancing and the myth of spontaneity.

within-the-film. *The Band Wagon* cuts from Tony Hunter's (Astaire's) spontaneous eruption into song and dance at the penny arcade to Jeffrey Cordova in *Oedipus Rex*. The moaning sounds in the background of this production are later associated with the reactions of an audience to Cordova's laborious musical version of *Faust*. We are shown Cordova from the point of view of Tony and the Martons in the wings (almost always a demystifying camera position), as he segues from his curtain calls as Oedipus into his offstage pomposity. Although Cordova's *Oedipus* is said to be successful with audiences in the film, the extent to which it is demystified for us undercuts its status as a successful show. Cordova is characterized throughout the first half of the film by the mechanical nature of his actions and utterances. He continually gives rehearsed speeches such as the one about Bill Shakespeare's immortal lines and Bill Robinson's immortal feet. On the first day of rehearsals, Cordova tells the cast exactly what will happen to them before the show opens. Not until he dances with Astaire (and in Astaire's style) in the top hat, white tie, and tails softshoe number in the second "Band Wagon" does Cordova achieve true spontaneity as a performer.

Almost every spontaneous performance in *The Band Wagon* has a matched segment that parodies the lack of spontaneity of the high art world. Tony drops Gaby while attempting a lift during the rehearsal of a ballet number for the first show; later in "The Girl Hunt," a jazz ballet, he lifts her effortlessly. Tony and Gaby's relaxed offstage rehearsal of a dance to "You and the Night and the Music" literally explodes onstage at the dress rehearsal. A prepackaged orchestra rendition of "Something to Remember You By" at the official New Haven cast party dissolves into a vocal version of the same song spontaneously performed by the "kids" at the chorus party. Spontaneity thus emerges as the hallmark of a successful performance.

The myth of spontaneity operates through what we are shown of the work of production of the respective shows as well as how we are shown it. In *Singin' in the Rain,* we see the technical difficulties involved with filming and projecting "The Dueling Cavalier," including Lina's battle with the microphone and the failure of the film when its technological base is revealed to the preview audience. "The Dancing Cavalier," in contrast, springs to life effortlessly. The film shows an awareness of this opposition between the foregrounding of technology in "The Dueling Cavalier" and the invisibility of technology in "The Dancing Cavalier." "The Broadway Ballet" is presented in the context of an idea for a production number, and one of the biggest jokes in the film concerns the producer's inability to visualize what we have just been shown, elaborate and complete. Yet at many other points in *Singin' in the Rain* this awareness is masked, often in quite complex ways.[8] In "You Were Meant for Me" the exposure of the wind machine figures prominently in the demystification of romantic musical numbers. Yet in a dialogue scene outside the soundstage just prior to this number, Kathy's scarf had blown to the breeze of an invisible wind machine. Even after we are shown the tools of illusion at the beginning of the number, the camera arcs around and comes in for a tighter shot of the performing couple, thereby remasking the exposed technology and making the duet just another example of the type of number whose illusions it exposes. Demystification is countered by the reassertion of the spontaneous evolution of musical films. Perhaps the ultimate in spontaneous evolution of a musical number occurs in *The Barkleys of Broadway.* At the end of the film, the couple decides to do another musical. Josh describes a dance routine which, unlike "Young Sarah," will have *tempo,* and the couple goes into a dance, framed to the right of a curtain in their living room. As they spin, there is a dissolve to the same step as part of an elaborate production number in the new show.

In *The Band Wagon* the labor of producing the first show eclipses the performances. Never do we see a completed number from the first show. Technical or personal problems prevent the completion of every number shown in rehearsal, as when Tony walks out or when Cordova is levitated by the revolving stage. It is not because high art (ballet) and popular art (musical comedy) are inherently mutually exclusive that Cordova's show fails. After all, it is Tony's impressionist paintings that pay for the successful show. Rather, the film suggests that Cordova fails because he has been unable to render invisible the technology of production in order to achieve the effect of effortlessness by which all entertainment succeeds in winning its audience.

Of course spontaneous performances that mask their technology have been calculated, too—not for audiences within the films but for audiences *of* the film. The musical, technically the most complex type of film produced in Hollywood, paradoxically has always been the genre that attempts to give the greatest illusion of spontaneity and effortlessness. It is as if engineering were to afirm *bricolage* as the ultimate approach to scientific thought. The self-reflective musical is aware of this in attempting to promulgate the myth of spontaneity. The heavily value-laden oppositions set up in the self-reflective films promote the mode of expression of the film musical itself as spontaneous and natural rather than calculated and technological. Musical entertainment thus takes on a natural relatedness to life processes and to the lives of its audiences. Musical entertainment claims for its own all natural and joyous performances in art and in life. The myth of spontaneity operates (to borrow Lévi-Strauss's terminology) to make musical performance, which is actually part of culture, appear to be part of nature.

THE MYTH OF INTEGRATION

Earlier musicals sometimes demonstrated ambiguous attitudes toward the world of musical theater, perceiving conflicts between success on the stage and success in the performers' personal lives. In *Ziegfeld Girl* (Robert C. Leonard, 1941), Lana Turner is destroyed when she forsakes the simple life in Brooklyn for the glamour of the Follies. In *Cain and Mabel* (Lloyd Bacon, 1936), Marion Davies has to be physically dragged onto the stage after deciding to retire to a garage in Jersey with prize-fighter beau Clark Gable. But the self-reflective musical asserts the integrative effect of musical performance. Successful performances are intimately bound up with success in love, with the integration of the individual into a community or a group, and even with the merger of high art with popular art.

In *Singin' in the Rain*, the success of the musical film brings about the final union of Don and Kathy. This consummation takes place on the stage at the premiere in front of a live audience and in the form of a duet. The music is carried over to a shot of the lovers embracing in front of a billboard of Don and Kathy's images. But the successful show on the billboard is no longer "The Dancing Cavalier"; it is *Singin' in the Rain,* that is, the film itself. This hall-of-mirrors effect emphasizes the unity-giving function of the musical both for the couples and audiences *in* the film and for the audience *of* the film. In *The Barkleys of Broadway,* Josh and Dinah are reunited when she realizes she wants "nothing but fun set to music," that is, the type of performance associated with the MGM musical. Gaby, in *The Band Wagon,* learns the value of popular entertainment as she learns to love Tony. "Dancing in the Dark" imitates the form of a sexual act as it merges two kinds of dancing previously set in conflict. The number combines the ballet movements associated with Gaby and her choreographer beau Paul Byrd with the ballroom dancing associated with Astaire. At the end of the film the long run of their successful show is used by Gaby as a metaphor for her relationship with Tony.

The right kind of musical performance also integrates the individual into a unified group just as the wrong kind alienates. *The Band Wagon* traces Tony's repeated movements from isolation to the joy of being part of a group. At the beginning of the film, Tony sings "By Myself" isolated by the tracking camera; as he enters the crowded terminal, the camera stops moving to frame him against the crowd, a mass that becomes an audience for Tony's antics with the Martons. The arcade sequence repeats this opening movement. Once again Tony overcomes his sense of isolation by reestablishing contact with an audience through spontaneous musical performance. The "?" machine at the arcade symbolizes the problem/solution format of the narrative. When Tony answers the question of how to make a comeback by dancing with a shoeshine man, the machine bursts open and his audience rushes to congratulate him. Another such movement occurs when, after the failure of the first show, Tony finds himself the only guest at the official cast party. "I Love Louisa" marks his renewal of contact with yet another audience—this time the common folk of the theater itself. At the end of the film, Tony moves from a reprise of "By Myself" into the final integration—a symbolic marriage to Gaby and to the rank and file of the theater. The myth of integration makes itself felt through the repetitive structure of the film.

Paralleling Tony's movement from isolation to integration and also paralleling the integration of the couple is Gaby's integration into the populist world of musical theater from the elitist world of high art. We first see Gaby in a ballet performance in which she functions as prima ballerina backed by the corps. At Cordova's, the two worlds are spatially isolated as the representatives of high art (Gabrielle and Paul) and those of popular art (Tony and the Martons) occupy separate rooms. The possibility of movement between the two worlds is stressed by the precisely parallel actions taking place in each room as well as by Cordova's role as mediator between the two rooms (worlds). Cordova prevents a terminal clash between Tony and Gaby by rushing into the neutral space of the front hall and drawing the representatives of both worlds back into his own central space.

Gabrielle begins her integration into the world of popular art through a renewal of contact with the common folk in Central Park, a process which culminates in "I Love Louisa" with Gaby serving as part of the chorus. Paul Byrd draws Gaby away from the group into an isolated space symbolic of the old world of ballet; the camera frames the couple apart from the mass. The colors of their isolated space—subdued shades of brown and white—contrast with the vibrant colors of the chorus's costumes, which have just filled the frame. In leaving this isolated space to return to the group, Gaby has taken the side of the collective effort that will produce the successful musical. "New Sun in the Sky," the first number in the new show, again finds Gaby backed up by a chorus, but this time the mood is celebratory—the bright golds and reds as well as the lyrics of the song emphasize Gaby's rebirth. Even the musical arrangement of the song, upbeat and jazzy, contrasts with the more sedate balletic arrangement we heard in that rehearsal for the Faustian *Band Wagon* in which Tony dropped Gaby. At the end of the film, Gaby expresses her feelings for Tony by speaking for the group, the chorus framed in back of her as she speaks.

Everyone knows that the musical film was a mass art produced by a tiny elite for a vast and amorphous consuming public; the self-reflective musical attempts to overcome this division through the myth of integration. It offers a vision of musical performance originating in the folk, generating love and a cooperative spirit that includes everyone in its grasp and that can conquer all obstacles. By promoting audience identification with the collectively produced shows, the myth of integration seeks to give the audience a sense of participation in the creation of the film itself. The musical film becomes a mass art that aspires to the condition of a folk art—produced and consumed by the same integrated community.

THE MYTH OF THE AUDIENCE

It follows that successful performances will be those in which the performer is sensitive to the needs of the audience and which give the audience a sense of participation in the performance. Josh Barkley berates Dinah for her participation in the performance in the subway scene because "the audience wants to cry there and you won't let them." Cordova is more concerned with the revolving stage than with delivering audience-pleasing performances; his canned speeches of solidarity with the cast are undercut by his delivering them with his back to the group, oblivious to their response. Tony Hunter, on the other hand, is willing to leave the self-enclosed world of the theater to regain contact with the folk who make up his audience. "Dancing in the Dark" is precipitated by observing ordinary people dancing in Central Park.

The insensitive performer also attempts to manipulate the audience. Cordova wants to control the timing of the curtain, the actress's exit pace, and the placing of an amber spot in *Oedipus*. Lina Lamont masks the fact that she is unable to speak for herself either onstage or onscreen.

Yet while setting up an association between success and lack of audience manipulation, the musicals themselves exert continuous control over the responses of their audiences. The film musical profits rhetorically by displacing to the theater the myth of a privileged relationship between musical entertainment and its audience. Popular theater can achieve a fluidity and immediacy in this respect that the film medium lacks. The out-of-town tryout, the interpolation of new material after each performance, the instantaneous modulation of performer-to-audience response—none of these common theatrical practices is possible for film. Hollywood had only the limited adaptations made possible by the preview system and the genre system itself, which accommodated audience response by making (or not making) other films of the same type. The backstage musical, however, manages to incorporate the immediate performer-audience relationship into films, thus gaining all the advantages of both media. Musical numbers can be shot from the point of view of a front-row theatrical spectator and then move into filmic space—combining the immediate contact of the theater with the mobility of perspective of the camera. Numbers that begin within theatrical space merge, often quite imperceptibly, into filmic space. Extended musical sequences such as "Shoes with Wings On" and "The Girl-Hunt Ballet" start within a proscenium frame and then become fully edited filmic sequences, in a tradition stemming from the early Berkeley musicals.

The Band Wagon uses this double perspective to manipulate the film audience's point of view. In "That's Entertainment," Cordova and the Martons try to convince Tony that all successful art is entertainment. The number takes place on the stage of an empty theater with the first refrain of the song shot from camera positions that approximate the point of view of a spectator *on* the stage (angles available only to the cinema). Midway through the number, at the point where Tony is convinced, the action shifts to the performing area of the stage and the point of view shifts to that of a spectator in the theater. The film audience sees, from the point of view of a theater audience, the number performed in the empty theater becoming a direct address to the film's audience. The effort to convince Tony has become an effort to convince *us*. In the reprise of "That's Entertainment" at the film's finale, the point of view shifts from over-the-shoulder shots to frame the performers directly in front of the

65. *Dames:* Musical numbers can be shot from filmic space.

camera as they ask us to celebrate once again the merging of all art into entertainment, this time in the form of the film *The Band Wagon* itself (an effect quite like that of the billboard at the end of *Singin' in the Rain*). "Make 'Em Laugh" is much more subtle in shifting point of view. Starting from a subjective shot over Don's shoulder, the number begins as an affirmation of the value of entertainment as Cosmo attempts to cheer up his friend; however, the point of view quickly shifts so that the message is addressed to the film's audience. We quickly lose track of Don's point of view, and the number never returns to it.

The use of theatrical audiences *in* the films provides a point of identification for audiences *of* the film. Even *Singin' in the Rain* emphasizes the responses of live audiences at previews and premieres. Although inserted shots of applauding audiences can be used as a trick similar to television's use of canned laughter, self-reflective musicals tend to use audiences within the film more subtly. In *The Barkleys of Broadway,* Astaire and

Rogers dance "Swing Trot," a routine designed to arouse nostalgia for the famous team, under the film's titles. At the end of the number there is a cut to a side angle, and we see the couple taking a bow before a live audience. The audience in the film is there to express the adulation the number itself sought to arouse from the film's audience.

MGM musicals make use of natural, spontaneous audiences that form around offstage performances.[9] "Shine on Your Shoes" in *The Band Wagon* demonstrates Astaire's ability to adapt his dancing to any occasion and any audience as well. In "I Love Louisa" the chorus serves first as an audience for Tony and the Martons' clowning, and then participates in the dance, providing a vicarious sense of participation for the film audience. Audiences in the films suggest a contagious spirit inherent in musical performance, related to the suggestion that the MGM musical is folk art; the audience must be shown as participating in the production of entertainment.

Intertextuality and star iconography can be a means of manipulating audience response. Many of the later MGM musicals play upon the audience's memories of earlier musicals. *The Barkleys of Broadway* plays on the Astaire-Rogers legend from its first shot of the couple's feet, which echoes the title sequence of *Top Hat* (Sandrich, 1935). The couple's reunion performance to "You Can't Take That Away from Me" harks back to *Shall We Dance,* with the dance itself reminiscent of one of their old routines. Such attempts to evoke nostalgia play on the star system's desire to erase the boundaries between star persona and character, between onscreen and offscreen personalities. *The Barkleys of Broadway* thus celebrates the return of Ginger Rogers to musical comedy after a series of straight dramatic films, suggesting that the only way she can succeed with an audience is by dancing with Astaire in musicals.[10]

Other self-reflective musicals make use of audience response to songs from previous stage musicals or films. Most of the songs in *Singin' in the Rain* were written for the earliest MGM film musicals. *The Band Wagon* takes its music from stage reviews of the same period, the late twenties to early thirties. In the interim many of these songs had become standards, and the films were able to play upon the audience's familiarity with the lyric. "Dancing in the Dark," for example, is used only in instrumental arrangement, thus inviting the audience to participate by supplying the lyric. Two related practices of the Freed unit—biopics fashioned around a composer's hit songs and the purchase of a song catalog around which to construct an original musical—depended upon audience familiarity (through both filmic and nonfilmic intertexts) for their effectiveness.

CONCLUSION

Self-reflective musicals mediate a contradiction between live performance in the theater and the frozen form of cinema by implying that the MGM musical *is* theater, possessing the same immediate and active relationship to its audience. Both the myth of integration and the myth of the audience suggest that the MGM musical is really a folk art, that the audience participates in the creation of musical entertainment. The myth of integration suggests that the achievement of personal fulfillment goes hand in hand with the enjoyment of entertainment. And the myth of spontaneity suggests that the MGM musical is not artificial but rather completely natural. Performance is no longer defined as something professionals do on stage; instead, it permeates the lives of professional and nonprofessional singers and dancers. Entertainment, the myth implies, can break down the barriers between art and life.

The myth of entertainment, in its entirety, cannot be celebrated in a single text or even across three texts. Different aspects of the myth achieve prominence in different films, but the myth is carried by the genre as a whole. The notion of breaking down barriers between art and life, for example, is more prominent in Vincente Minnelli's *The Pirate* than in any of the films discussed here. It might be said that the elements of the myth of entertainment constitute a paradigm that generates the syntax of individual texts.

Ultimately, one might wonder why these films go to such lengths to justify the notion that all life should aspire to the conditions of a musical performance. That is, why expend so much effort to celebrate mythic elements the audience is likely to accept anyway? Answering this question involves an awareness both of the function of ritual and of the ritual function of the musical. All ritual involves the celebration of shared values and beliefs; the ritual function of the musical is to reaffirm and articulate the place that entertainment occupies in its audience's psychic lives. Self-reflective musicals are then able to celebrate myths created by the genre as a whole.

Yet the extremes of affirmation in *The Band Wagon* need further justification in terms of its function for MGM as well as for the popular audience. At a time when the studio could no longer be certain of the allegiance of its traditional mass audience, *The Band Wagon*, in ritual fashion, served to reaffirm the traditional relationship. For the musical was always the quintessential Hollywood product: all Hollywood films manipulated audience response, but the musical could incorporate that response into the film itself; all Hollywood films sought to be entertaining, but the musical could incorporate a myth of entertainment into its aesthetic discourse. As Thomas Elsaesser says, "The world of the musical becomes a kind of ideal image of the [film] medium itself." [11]

Nowhere is Lévi-Strauss's notion of myth more applicable to the musical than in the relationship of the genre to the studio system that produced it. Faced with declining attendance due to competition from television, the studio could suggest, through *Singin' in the Rain*, that making musicals can provide a solution to any crisis of technological change. Faced with charges of infantilism from the citadels of high art, the studio could suggest, through *The Barkleys of Broadway*, that all successful performances are musical performances. Faced with the threat of changing patterns of audience consumption, the studio could suggest, through *The Band Wagon*, that the MGM musical can adapt to any audience. *The Band Wagon* ends where *That's Entertainment* (Jack Haley, Jr., 1974) and *That's Entertainment, Part 2* (Gene Kelly, 1976) commence, in an attempt to recapture the aura of the "Golden Age" of the Freed/MGM musicals. It is not surprising that the "That's Entertainment" number from *The Band Wagon* should have been inserted into the contemporary sequences of the nostalgia compilations. For the ending of *The Band Wagon* already marked the genre's celebration of its own (and Hollywood's) economic death and ritual rebirth.

Self-reflectivity as a critical category has been associated with films, such as those of Godard, which call attention to the codes constituting their own signifying practices. The term has been applied to aesthetically or politically radical films that react against so-called classical narrative cinema by interrogating their own narrativity. Thus we tend to associate reflexivity with the notion of deconstruction within filmmaking practice. The MGM musical, however, uses reflexivity to perpetuate rather than to deconstruct the codes of the genre. Self-reflective musicals are conservative texts in every sense. MGM musicals have continued to function both in the popular consciousness and within international film culture as representatives of the Hollywood product at its best. I hope to have shown that this was the very task these texts sought to accomplish.

Notes

1. See Leo Braudy, *The World in a Frame* (New York: Anchor Press/Doubleday, 1976), pp. 143–147, for a discussion of self-consciousness in *Shall We Dance*.

2. *The Barkleys of Broadway* presents Josh and Dinah Barkley (Fred Astaire and Ginger Rogers) as the Lunts of musical comedy. Dinah leaves musical comedy to do a serious play ("Young Sarah"), and finally learns the lesson that there's no difference between serious acting and musical comedy acting. She returns to do a musical at the end of the film. *Singin' in the Rain* depicts the coming of sound to Hollywood. An early talkie that fails ("The Dueling Cavalier") is remade as a mu-

sical that succeeds ("The Dancing Cavalier"). *The Band Wagon* also involves a second production of a show that flops (a musical version of the Faust story called "The Band Wagon") into a musical revue that succeeds (again called "The Band Wagon").

3. Albert F. McLean, *American Vaudeville as Ritual* (Lexington: University of Kentucky Press, 1965), p. 223.

4. Claude Lévi-Strauss, "The Structural Study of Myth," in *Structural Anthropology* (New York: Basic Books, 1963), p. 220. I am also indebted to Lévi-Strauss for other ideas contained in the same essay: first, that a myth works itself out through repetition in a number of texts; second, that myth works through the mediation of binary oppositions.

5. These terms are taken from Paul Ricoeur, *Freud and Philosophy* (New Haven: Yale University Press, 1970), p. 54. Ricoeur uses them to refer to two schools of hermeneutics that nevertheless constitute "a profound unity." I find them equally applicable to texts that seek to interpret themselves.

6. The inseparability of demystification from its opposite (remythicization) is best illustrated by *A Star Is Born* (George Cukor, 1954), at once the last bearer of the studio's myth of entertainment and the first of the antimusicals. Even the supposedly Brechtian antimusical *Cabaret* (Bob Fosse, 1972) merely inverts the backstage paradigm while maintaining its narrative strategy.

7. See Braudy, *The World in a Frame*, pp. 147–155, for a discussion of the function of spontaneity in the Astaire and Kelly personas.

8. See David Lusted, "Film as Industrial Product—Teaching a Reflexive Movie," *Screen Education* 16 (Autumn 1975): 26–30, for detailed examples of the mystification-demystification dynamic in *Singin' in the Rain*.

9. Other good examples of "natural audiences" in the MGM musical include "By Strauss," "I Got Rhythm," and "'S Wonderful" in *An American in Paris* (Minnelli, 1951); "Nina" in *The Pirate* (Minnelli, 1948); and "I Like Myself," Gene Kelly's dance on roller skates in *It's Always Fair Weather* (Kelly, 1955). The history of this device in the musical film may be traced from Jolson to Chevalier to Astaire to Kelly and back to Astaire, spontaneity of performance providing the link among the major male musical stars.

10. The extreme example of this phenomenon is *A Star is Born*, the signification of which depends upon the audience's knowledge of Judy Garland's offscreen life as the negation of her MGM onscreen image.

11. Thomas Elsaesser, "The American Musical," *Brighton Film Review* 15 (December 1969): 13.

23. Footnote to Fact: The Docudrama

SETH FELDMAN

"It's either news or drama, but obviously this shows that mixing the two doesn't work."[1] The quote comes from a Canadian lawyer on the occasion of his successfully suing for damages inflicted on his client by a CBC docudrama entitled *The Tar Sands*. In retrospect, that 1982 decision appears to have been part of an international decline in the currency and credibility of "mixing the two," i.e., of docudrama itself. Publicists have finally tired of affixing the term to anything remotely resembling realist drama. Conventional documentarians no longer see the genre as a threat to their tiny share of the public imagination. And the many legal battles begun by the outraged prototypes for docudrama protagonists seem to be winding down.

What remains of docudrama are the lessons it has to teach about the metageneric concerns of "mixing the two." In a larger historical context, the docudrama seems to have been a response to an explosion of public interest in nonfiction dating at least from Truman Capote's "nonfiction novel" *In Cold Blood* (filmed by Richard Brooks, 1966). The New Journalism, the immense rise in popularity of news magazines (published and televised) and soft news formats (e.g., tabloids, *Real People*) are all indicators of that trend sustaining itself into the early 1980s. At the same time, the fine arts have witnessed a rebirth of a representational aesthetic in postmodernism. Whether the result of public pressure, a more desperate world situation, or simple aesthetic fatigue, creators in the Western world have spent the better part of the last two decades turning away from abstraction toward new modes of presenting an objectively recognizable world.

As any comparison of the 1920s to the 1930s would indicate, the swing in interest from abstract to representational creativity is not without precedent. Within the context of cinema—a medium that straddles the extremes of mimesis and the fantastic—these reorientations have become all but routine. In this regard, docudrama is simply the most recent set of conventions used by audiences to tread their way between these extremes.

66. *Nanook of the North:* Mediation between purportedly straightforward observation and narrative manipulation.

The process is nearly as old as the medium itself. Turn-of-the-century
"newsreels" depicting the sinking of a toy *Maine* and Boer War atrocities
in the English countryside now appear so outrageously contrived as to
make us wonder at the audacity of their promoters and gullibility of early
cinema audiences. And certainly those audiences may have been discon-
certed by a medium too new to establish its parameters of veracity. But
they may also have been working out an understanding of that medium—
a negotiated space between being amazed (by the films of Méliès and his
imitators) and being informed (by the straightforward and, by then,
somewhat repetitious Lumière and Edison clips). Two decades later,
Robert Flaherty's *Nanook of the North* (1922) offered a similar mediation between purportedly straightforward observation and narrative manipulation. John Grierson's systematic formulation of the classical documentary in his writings and as a producer in Britain and Canada built
upon Flaherty's mediation. The Griersonian documentary, with its bom-

bastic music, Soviet editing, and voice-of-God narration, is looked at to-day more for its art (or artifice) than as an objective representation of its subject. Cinéma vérité—ostensibly a far less manipulative aesthetic—is nevertheless analyzed in much the same manner.[2]

What docudrama appears to add to this long tradition of documentary manipulation is the recognition that script, actors, and sets may be used as conventions in the presentation of documentary reality. Yet, upon closer scrutiny, there is certainly no lack of performance within documentary and news. Both come to us with scenes that are (acknowledged or not) reconstructions of the original incidents. Even within the cinema verité footage of films such as the Maysles Brothers' *Salesman* (1969) and *Grey Gardens* (1975), one may point to narrative structures that have the effect of making real people going about their business into performers engaged in dramatic plots. Nor does there seem to be a substantial difference between the precise scripting and well-rehearsed performance of onstage characters and that of documentary narrators and their descendants on the six o'clock news.[3]

If documentary performance may be seen as an antecedent of the docudrama, then the equally ubiquitous tradition of the realist narrative cinema provides it with direct stylistic precedents. Indeed, the formula for docudrama is to be found as early as *Birth of a Nation* (D. W. Griffith, 1915). Griffith creates an interplay between the scrupulous accuracy of his historical tableaux and the eye-level experience of history as depicted by his performers. Much of Griffith's defense of the film was based on the accuracy of these reconstructed panoramas, as if that accuracy negated the possibility of interpretation in script, performance, direction, or, for that matter, the Thomas Dixon novel from which the film was adapted. What followed in Hollywood's long history of histories, biographies, and topical dramas was the assumption that an essentially correct set of tableaux (sets, costuming, resemblance to historical figures) distracted from and, in a sense, forgave melodrama, anachronisms (including moral and ideological anachronisms), and the otherwise implausible convolutions of motivation and interpersonal response. History—here in the traditional bourgeois understanding—became a fixed backdrop distinct in its veracity from the far more artificial struggles of recreated or invented individuals.

Docudrama, as practiced in the last fifteen years, is, to an extent, a recognition of this distinction and, at its best, a step toward its redress. In their article "Docudrama on American Television," Tom W. Hoffer and Richard Alan Nelson categorized nine variations of docudrama "ranging from the 'pure' form based on investigatory and trial records recreating events in the lives of actual persons . . . to programs utilizing historical personages or themes which include some fictionalization."[4] It is in its "pure" manifestation that docudrama attempts to transcend or at least to speak to the artificiality of Hollywood's schism between the individual and society. Limiting dialogue to a transcript (as in, for instance, Emile de Antonio's *In the King of Prussia* [1982]) homogenizes background realities with foregrounded action at least to the degree that the editing of the transcript, the direction, the actors' interpretations, and the very act of recreation allow. The Berrigan brothers and their colleagues, for all the dramatic value of their performance, remain intricately detailed recreations: action and its historic milieu are one.

It was just this dramatic unity based on accuracy that stood as the ideal for docudrama. In discussing the Canadian *For the Record* series, producer Sam Levene, wishing to disassociate himself from the widespread hyping of the term, demanded it be limited to these "pure" forms: "I can't get anybody who writes about television in this country to refer to this series without calling us the CBC's docu-drama. The docu-drama is a dramatic recreation of a true story as it happened using for the most part, real characters and real names. What we do is simply contemporary, topical drama which is issue oriented."[5] As an historian of the documentary, Brian Winston went a step further: "I think there are very limited circumstances where you can claim a validity above and beyond the norms of our drama and our dramatic tradition. I think if you've had a bug in the wall, and you actually have a *verbatim* account of some event—if you've got a court transcript, and so on, that sort of thing—then you can say 'this is docudrama.' Anything else is absolutely spurious."[6]

Despite these admonitions, the topical dramas and even more "spurious" productions (e.g., *Roots* [David Greene, 1977]) that populate the categories far removed from Hoffer and Nelson's idea of "pure" docudrama are, in fact, the programs that seem to have achieved a greater deal of public attention. The same may also be said of the cinema, where a star-studded recreation like *Silkwood* (Mike Nichols, 1984), a topical drama like *The China Syndrome* (James Bridges, 1977), or even a conventional Hollywood biography like *Gandhi* (Richard Attenborough, 1982) have received far more popular attention than "pure" work like *In the King of Prussia, The Battle of Algiers* (Gillo Pontecorvo, 1965), or *Raging Bull* (Martin Scorsese, 1980). Docudrama in the extreme—either as illustrated transcripts or scrupulously illustrated research—seems to have been geared to minority tastes (the same people, one would guess, who have always watched documentary). The British, who set the standard for scrupulous recreation from *Culloden* (Peter Watkins, 1964) to *Oppenheimer* (Barry Davies, 1981), have enjoyed no more success in elevating these works to levels of acceptance enjoyed by their topical dramas (e.g., *Cathy Come Home* [Ken Loach, 1966], *Boys from the Blackstuff* [Peter Saville, 1982]).

The public perception of the docudrama's parameters may, in the long run, be more relevant than the qualms of its practitioners or professional critics. Productions using "real" names or court transcripts as their scripts are (paradoxically) so unusual as to call attention to themselves as media events—i.e., highly mediated interventions. *In the King of Prussia* results not in a greater acceptance of de Antonio's version of the trial but rather an automatic scepticism regarding the impact of the film's few fictional interventions (e.g., Martin Sheen's performance). The "privileging" a given text (to use Brian Winston's term) is not necessarily a product of its purist conventions. Rather, it seems more logical to see this "privileging" as taking place through the perceptions of the spectator or, to be more precise, the alignment achieved between an accepted version of a personality or event and the presentation's depiction of it. Simply put, a film or television drama becomes a docudrama if it is accepted as such, if it becomes a useful embodiment of fact. As Andrew Tudor writes in his *Theories of Film,* "Genre is what we collectively believe it to be."[7]

This populist understanding of docudrama is, at the very least, an aid in tracing the interest in the form during the 1970s. Hoffer and Nelson offer the opinion that the "revival of the docudrama on American commercial television was directly conditioned by public interest in newsmakers and the Watergate scandals, network experimentation to build mid-1970 audience ratings on primetime TV, and the appeals inherent in the American Bicentennial."[8] These, along with the more generalized interest in nonfiction cited above, yielded what Peter Davis, a producer of more conventional documentaries, had labeled a "hunger" for factually oriented fiction:

> . . . they're kind of strip-mining the headlines, these people that make docudramas. And really, they're trading in on the same voyeuristic passions that the *National Enquirer* does. It's the same thing: I'll show you the *real* story of Princess Di—and so you make up a character that you invest with both your own fantasies and those qualities that you think Princess Diana might have, if she had grown up next door to you, only with a lot more money. I think that there's a terrific hunger for real true stories, and what docudramas do is feed that hunger without really nourishing it, and without really filling the void.[9]

Seen from a slightly different perspective, docudramas in the 1970s came to operate as ritual. Events, persons, or even prominent works of fiction were *recognized* (in both senses of the word) by repeating them in another medium. The idea was not only to achieve further insight by scrutinizing the subject a second time ("filling the void," as Davis puts it) as it was to affirm the subject's worth with additional attention. Remaking Princess Di's ascendancy as TV docudrama is the modern equivalent of a regal imprint on coins of the realm.

The act of seeing the recreation after being taught the history, reading the news, or living through the period is essentially narcissistic; we are looking at something that is already part of ourselves. Further satisfaction is derived from the communal sharing of an event and the mass catharsis inherent in jointly exposing social anxieties, experiencing the retelling of a familiar horror. Thus, the three most popular manifestations of the genre—*Roots, Holocaust* (Marvin Chomsky, 1978), and *The Day After* (Nicholas Meyer, 1984)—were firmly grounded in events that had already achieved a central place in the public imagination. What all three programs then spoke to were the personal, psychological reasons for that centrality: essentially, fears of disruption in conventional familial and sexual relations. The varying sociopolitical realities of slavery, racism, Nazism, and nuclear war were presented solely through a single set of consequences: impotent fathers, violated wives, and children destroyed. Despite the devastation they present, all three series end with a reaffirmation of the worth of familial order: the escape at the end of *Roots*, Part I; finding "the old African" at the end of Part II; the son's taking children to Palestine at the end of *Holocaust*; the father's return to the rubble of his home in *The Day After*. The ultimate satisfaction they offer to their audiences is not a deeper understanding of historical forces; rather, it is the durability of that familial order.

The melodramatic nature of *Roots, Holocaust,* and *The Day After* points to a traditional role of melodrama in providing explanations of an incomprehensible world to the disenfranchised (a role, it should be noted, that Grierson hoped to usurp with the conventional documentary). Similarly, docudrama may be taken in the context of Barthes's understanding of myth, the making of culture into nature—i.e., what history and politics produce are human events as "natural" as family interaction. But perhaps the most apt analogy is that of the fable, particularly in Bruno Bettelheim's understanding of the fable as a tool with which the individual may find a comfortable alien context where sensitive personal issues may be aired. This approach would see the docudrama as consistent with Hollywood's traditional demarcation between an essentially anachronistic personalized foreground and an accurate but secondary historical milieu. *The Day After* is not about the Third World War so much as it is a dissection of otherwise taboo family mores made possible through the imposition of an historical abstraction. Fact (or, in this case, factually based speculation) becomes the key to never-never land.

If docudrama may be equated with the fable, it is not surprising to find that the programs lend themselves to some form of Proppian analysis. Characterization in either "pure" docudrama or topical dramas provides us with a familiar array of folktale characters. Protagonists overcome obstacles and gather information in order to work their way toward an awareness that will fundamentally change them. They are likely to be guided by informants, onscreen embodiments of the old voice-of-God narrator. Jason Robards in *The Day After* is our sacrificial victim, guided by various informants through the realities of nuclear war. The informants tell the protagonist (and us) the meaning of what has happened and provide inevitably correct predictions of what is to come. Errant views and incorrect information are provided by the central characters' primary antagonists. These are people without a cause whose function it is to represent the evils of the status quo (the more mindless Nazis in *Holocaust*, the reddest necks in *Roots*). Secondary antagonists are those who have their reasons. Their function is to provide an element of realism by softening the melodramatic implications of black and white distinctions between good and evil. Unenlightened as to the implications of ignorance and compromises, they are as much as the protagonist victims of the process or event under scrutiny. The secondary antagonists are, in a sense, the viewer before watching the presentation, perched atop a slippery slope that leads to passive acceptance of the general malaise. And finally, there are those characters who serve as a kind of human scenery contributing to the authenticity of the docudrama's background—lithographs, newspaper photos in action.[10]

Of course, docudrama is not the only form of mass media presentation that attempts to mediate history and current events in this manner. Dramatized history and journalism find their way into situation comedies and adventure shows that serve as a kind of electronic Kabuki. The slowly changing interpretations of a few basic plots and characters are used to tell television audiences the real news, the manner in which events are to be digested at a personal level. *All in the Family* was a forum for the resolution of issues that divided Americans in the 1960s and 1970s; *Hill Street Blues* similarly tells audiences today that their social and personal worlds are equally under siege and, if they are to be rescued at all, that it will come through the traditional acceptance of a functioning multiculturalism under the direction of level-headed middle management.

Our post-McLuhan understanding of television seems to point to this role as central to the nature of the medium itself. John Fiske and John Hartley, for instance, in their monograph *Reading Television* write of the essential bardic nature of the medium: "The bardic mediator tends to articulate the negotiated central concerns of its culture, with only limited and often overmediated references to the ideologies, beliefs, habits of thought and definitions of the situation which obtain in groups which are for one reason or another peripheral."[11] In their analyses of the various facets of television, Fiske and Hartley repeatedly define the medium as a vehicle that blurs the distinction between producer and audience in favor of a ritual validation of what is being depicted as a universal ideology.

Although the two authors do not undertake an analysis of docudrama, their central contention is echoed by John Caughie when he complains that "the documentary drama produces within itself a self-confirming integration and produces a spectator who is already confirmed in an already determined position." [12] On his part, Albert Hunt in *The Language of Television* suggests that the heritage of the medium has established an essential duality that lends itself to the mixture of entertainment and social document to be found in docudrama:

> Television teaches us that we have a right to be entertained in our own home. It also teaches us that this right can only be exercised by the grace of authority which ordains that entertainment can only be provided as part of a public service which is legally obliged to provide us with information and education as well.
>
> Television teaches that the information services are "serious" and "responsible." The information offered is "true" and "impartial" and concerned with real life. Television produces an official picture of reality.
>
> Television also teaches that entertainment has nothing to do with real life and is simply escapist. But happily some of the entertainment programmes have a hidden curriculum of their own. They teach us to look with less reverence at the official version of reality that "serious" television has to offer. [13]

Television, then, comes to us with a promise of responsibility, a subversion of that promise (through the mindless entertainment that it in fact supplies) and then a subversion of that subversion through the possibilities of decoding that entertainment. To an extent, the production of docudramas represents an institutionalization of that process. We are shown entertainments whose social messages have been prepackaged by the officialdom that started the ball rolling in the first place. We are asked either indirectly (through the scheduling and publicity of a particular program) or directly (through forewarnings and disclaimers; e.g., the discussion kits and panel discussions arranged for the airing of *The Day After*) to frame what we are going to see in the context of "entertainment to be taken seriously."

These self-proclaimed media contexts might be seen as secondary were it not for the qualitative implications of television's massive global infrastructure. To paraphrase the Soviet constructivists' definition of communism ("collectivization plus electrification"), we might be tempted to see docudrama as collective experience plus electronic dissemination. Lest this seem too natural a conclusion, the student of docudrama should bear in mind the practical realities of a television and film industry that has come to be dominated entirely by the United States. The values that underlie *Roots, Holocaust,* and *The Day After* are fundamentally American values; non-American audiences are left to read these fables in entirely different contexts. American audiences may have found *Holocaust* to be a revelation of forgotten events; but despite American expectations, German audiences saw the series as a rather soapy foreign intrusion into their own unremitting media considerations of the Nazi era. While for their part, Polish viewers found that the survivors depicted in *The Day After* didn't have it so bad compared to their actual wartime experiences.

If American docudramas have some trouble abroad, the phenomenon of docudrama per se has proven useful in pointing out cultural differences in the role of television, film, and the documentary tradition in mediating reality. In speculating upon the genesis of American docudrama, Hoffer and Nelson also cite links to the "Golden Age" of American television in the 1950s and to prestige programming on both the commercial networks and PBS.[14] Inherent in their assertion is the assumption that Americans produce and perhaps view television in the traditional puritannical context of temptation and redemption. The pursuit of "worthy" programming by either producer or consumer is the pursuit of humility before a cultural edifice and the decorum of a well-ordered household. It is also the rescue of television as a whole from the natural (materialistic) forces that led to Newton Minow's condemnation of it as a "vast wasteland." [15] To view the docudrama is to reenter the garden where we are innocent of the knowledge that quality (if not sanctity) and pleasure are incompatible.

For the British, the evolution of docudrama was not so much a return to an earlier ethic as it was a continuing interaction between feature filmmakers and the social realist commitment inherent in Grierson's original concept of the documentary. The working-class wartime fiction films (e.g., *Fires Were Started* [Humphrey Jennings, 1943]) and postwar documentaries of the Free Cinema movement (*Every Day except Christmas* [Lindsay Anderson, 1957], *We Are the Lambeth Boys* [Karel Reisz, 1958]) saw their fruition in the Angry Young Man features made by the Free Cinema's directors in the late 1950s and early 1960s (*This Sporting Life* [Anderson, 1963], *Saturday Night and Sunday Morning* [Reisz, 1966], *The Loneliness of the Long Distance Runner* [Tony Richardson, 1962]). At the BBC, Tony Garnet and Ken Loach brought this tradition of realist filmmaking to audiences with films like *The Lump* (Jack Gold, 1967), *Five Women* (Roy Battersby, 1968), and *The Big Flame* (Loach, 1969). Beyond these were the "pure" docudramas originated by Peter Watkins in *Culloden* and *The War Game* (1966). Kenith Trodd, a producer of documentary dramas for the BBC, saw the interaction of documentary and drama as essential for the expression of points of view in the face of the network's "fairness" doctrine:

> The Trojan Horse that we managed to slip into the building by using documentary drama was above all extrinsically that we could say, "Look, this is not a piece of propaganda. This is not a documentary. This is a *play*"—which

is the word they like rather than film—"this is one man's view of a piece of the world." And next week, there can be another man's view of the piece of the world, directed by somebody else, produced by somebody else. And if the organization is witty and astute enough to get it, the view can be a total counter-view and the two people should co-exist and compete on the grounds of their talent as writers—not of the relevance of what they have to say as propagandists, because we don't acknowledge that he's here as a *propagandist*, he's here as a *creator*. And because . . . these works managed to get acclaim as films and pieces of creation, it meant that they didn't have to defend themselves every time, because they were passionately and politically concerned with their subject.[16]

The function of docudrama on British television, then, seems to be much in the tradition of the ploys used by Grierson in the 1930s to obtain public and private support for a countercinema. If Grierson's "Trojan Horse" was the promise of better public relations, the promise made by Trodd and his colleagues is that of high-quality, inscrutable (and thus socially harmless) artistic intentions. Yet for both Grierson and the contemporary "creators" of docudrama in Britain, the promises are a facade for a commitment to widespread social change. Trodd's own 1980 production, *United Kingdom* (directed by Roland Joffe), presents detailed speculation upon the formation of local rebellions against the Draconian economic policies of the Thatcher government. What Trodd has said of the early BBC docudramas is no less true of current work or, for that matter, the documentaries produced by Grierson and the Angry Young Man films: "These were all pioneering works which established and developed the tradition, and what they had in common was that they had a writer's name on it, that they all used actors, that they were not based on particular historical, verifiable incidents, and that they were radically motivated. Radical in that sense is a bit of a euphemism—they had a left wing orientation, and that made them both notorious and, with certain people, unpopular."[17] For the British, then, docudrama is not so much an evocation of the higher purposes of television as it is in Hoffer and Nelson's evaluation of American docudrama. Rather, it is a continuation of the long tradition of reconciling the bourgeois ideal of the idiosyncratic artist with the need for addressing social change.

Canada has used docudrama in a manner quite different from the American and British models. Part of this stems from the intrinsically realist nature of Canadian arts and letters, including the work of the Canadian feature film industry.[18] This is reflected in the enormous influence of the documentary-oriented National Film Board. Equally significant, though, is the nature of broadcasting in Canada. As is the case with most nations in the Western world, the main function of Canadian television often appears to be the retransmission of American and, to a lesser extent, British products. Indigenous programming—though mandated by law—is almost entirely modeled on the far more popular American programs. True local content is restricted to news, sports (both of which use American style formats), and some variations of game and variety shows. Added to these factors are budgetary restrictions that seldom permit more than half a season's production of even the most popular series.

The role of docudrama in Canada is, in the face of these characteristics, developmental. The CBC's *For the Record* has kept alive the talents of the country's best writers, actors, and directors during the frequent doldrums in the feature film industry. More importantly, docudrama has taken advantage of the nation's heritage of realist literature and the documentary film exemplified by the National Film Board and used a topical imperative as a means to search for the details that will eventually compose a uniquely English Canadian milieu. For audiences used to American genre conventions, an accurately depicted Canadian courtroom, detective, or city becomes a building block for self-recognition. At the same time, the recognition of a Canadian issue as being worthy of reenactment or illustration through enactment[19] creates the groundwork for collective awareness and a claim for control in setting the national agenda.

It is this last ideal of using docudrama as a mediator in the transformation of reality into mythology that makes a consideration of it most germaine to the understanding of genre itself. In his concluding remarks on the nature of film genres, Stephen Neale has noted:

> Any one genre is, simultaneously, a coherent and systematic body of film texts, and a coherent and systematic set of expectations. As well as providing a means of regulating desire across a series of textual instances, and of offering a variety of the discursive possibilities of cinema itself, genres also provide a means of regulating memory and expectation, a means of containing the possibilities of reading. Overall, they offer the industry a means of controlling demand, and the institution a means of containing coherently the effects that its products produce.[20]

On one hand, we may question whether docudrama in any of the ways we have attempted to define it here can qualify as a genre according to Neale's criteria. Rather than being "a coherent and systematic body of film texts," we have found a wide spectrum of work, much of which successfully operates as docudrama without fitting any single strict or "pure" definition. In addressing the "expectations" aroused by docudrama, we may find that the central nature of the pursuit is to mix established codes, to play upon and frustrate the "coherence" of expectation as its modus vivandi. As John Caughie has observed: ". . . the rhetoric of the drama inscribes the document within narrative and experience; the rhetoric of the documentary establishes the experience as an experience of the real and places it within a system of guarantees and confirmations." [21] The implication of Caughie's observation is that it is the activist spectator working as an arbiter between these two filmic codes who creates the perception of docudrama. Perhaps, then, docudrama does not so much "regulate" as it stimulates, forcing a recognition of genre and generic limitations; docudrama disturbs rather than "contains" the "possibilities of reading." As suggested above, the spectator may read docudrama as fable. But he or she may also use it to read the process of documentary signification per se, finding within the works an invitation to reassess the conventions of fact and fiction.

If these measures of docudrama point to a metageneric understanding of it, a note of caution may be drawn from the final sentence of Neale's conclusion. In practical terms, docudrama offers the "industry" and the "institution" far greater leverage in "containing coherently the effects that its products produce." Docudrama may serve as the institutionalization of news, a step beyond even the strict control of newscasts and soft news offshoots. The facts to be examined and conclusions to be drawn from history and current affairs are determined at the writing stage. Once in production, docudramas are far more expensive than documentaries on the same subjects. This, too, works in favor of larger media institutions. If credibility becomes dependent upon high production values and highly paid stars, it is that much more difficult for decentralized independent producers to compete. Upping the ante in information programming squeezes out the diversity of voices which, to a studio or network executive, may interfere with the orderly "containment" of history or news as "product."

Seen in this perspective, the mixed codification of docudrama may be less important than the manner in which this codification succeeds in presenting an acceptable fictionalization of reality embodying the values of those responsible for the production. If anything, docudrama's greater claim (than, say, the western or gangster film) to nonmediation makes it that much more suspect. Nor does the gradual disappearance of the term itself make the practice or those claims any less prevalent. The mixing of news or history and drama will continue to be a useful way to embody fact. The final understanding of these works lies with this question: useful to whom? Docudrama as genre has been perpetuated by an audience in search of a sounding board on which to work out generalized social anxieties and, more particularly, anxieties concerning the representation of actuality. The manipulation of that genre is more than simply the manipulation of convention. It is, rather, a pointedly effective predigestion of history itself.

Notes

1. "CBC to Pay Lougheed $82,500 to Settle Suit over Oil Sands Drama," *Toronto Globe & Mail,* May 11, 1982, p. 2. The statement was made by Roderick McLennan, lawyer for the premier of Alberta, Peter Lougheed. Lougheed had sued CBC over a docudrama entitled *The Tar Sands,* in which he had been portrayed by an actor. Because of a technicality in Alberta's libel laws, CBC settled shortly before the beginning of the trial. Since the settlement of the case, it has not broadcast this form of "pure" docudrama.

2. See, for instance, Bill Nichols's discussion of the work of Frederick Wiseman in his *Ideology and the Image* (Bloomington: Indiana University Press, 1981), pp. 208–236.

3. I have attempted to describe this in some detail in "Documentary Performance," *Canadian Drama* 5, no. 1 (Spring 1979): 11–24.

4. Tom W. Hoffer and Alan Nelson, "Docudrama on American Television," *Journal of the University Film Association* 30, no. 2 (Spring 1978): 21.

5. Quoted by John Kent Harrison, "Inside CBC Drama," *Cinema Canada,* no. 75 (July 1981): 17.

6. Quoted by Seth Feldman, *Styles of Truth: Decoding the Documentary* (Toronto: CBC Transcripts, 1982), p. 27.

7. Andrew Tudor, *Theories of Film* (New York: Viking Press, 1973), p. 139.

8. Hoffer and Nelson, "Docudrama on American Television," p. 27.

9. Quoted by Feldman, *Styles of Truth,* p. 20.

10. Examples of the presentation of these archetypes are developed in my "The Electronic Fable: Aspects of the Docudrama in Canada," *Canadian Drama* 9, no. 1 (1983): 39–48.

11. John Fiske and John Hartley, *Reading Television* (London: Methuen, 1978), p. 89.

12. John Caughie, "Progressive Television and Documentary Drama," *Screen* 21, no. 3 (1980): 32.

13. Quoted in ibid., p. 30.

14. Hoffer and Nelson, "Docudrama on American Television," p. 27.

15. Minow's widely quoted remarks were originally made at the 1961 meeting of the National Association of Broadcasters. See Erik Barnouw, *Tube of Plenty* (London: Oxford University Press, 1975), p. 299.

16. Quoted by Feldman, *Styles of Truth,* p. 23.

17. Ibid., p. 22.

18. I am referring here entirely to the English Canadian experience. The cultural heritage and subsequent media production of French-speaking Canada have developed in relative isolation and thus differ markedly. The two most useful collections of critiques of English Canadian and Quebecois cinema are my and Joyce Nelson's *Canadian Film Reader* (Toronto: Peter Martin Associates, 1977) and my *Take Two: A Tribute to Film in Canada* (Toronto: Irwin Publishing, 1984).

19. This reenactment has taken the form of topical drama rather than "pure" docudrama. The one exception has been Peter Pearson's *The Tar Sands.*

20. Stephen Neale, *Genre* (London: British Film Institute, 1980), pp. 54–55.

21. Caughie, "Progressive Television and Documentary Drama," p. 32.

24. The Body Snatchers: Genre and Canadian Cinema

JIM LEACH

> But they'd killed the heron anyway. It doesn't matter what country they're from, my head said, they're still Americans, they're what's in store for us, what we are turning into. They spread themselves like a virus, they get into the brain and take over the cells and the cells change from inside and the ones that have the disease can't tell the difference. Like the Late Show sci-fi movies, creatures from outer space, body snatchers injecting themselves into you, dispossessing your brain. . . . If you look like them and talk like them and think like them then you are them . . . you speak their language, a language is everything you do.[1]

Margaret Atwood's ironic allusion to the feat of being "taken over" that dominates much of American popular culture (*us* versus *them*) offers a basic insight into the relationship between Canadian fears of assimilation and the subtle colonizing effects of the American mass media. The influence of Hollywood has affected many film industries throughout the world, but the problem is made particularly acute in Canada by geographical proximity. Canada is largely controlled by U.S. corporations. As Atwood makes clear, however, the problem is also psychological: the "Americans" in *Surfacing* whose mindless cruelty is exhibited in the killing of the heron are in fact Canadians. "Americans" are modern "human beings," the products of the affluent society and the concrete city, totally alienated from their land, their gods, and (in Canada's case) their languages. In terms of film, this alienation can be expressed as a struggle between an attempt to evolve a film language capable of responding to the Canadian experience and the temptation to take over (or be taken over by) the ready-made language of the American genres.

The issue is not confined to cinema or to Canada. As Ronald Sutherland has pointed out, there is a continuity between the Quebecois' fear of being taken over by "the Anglo-Saxon mentality or way of life," the English Canadian fear of "Americanization," and the American experience of "the furious dehumanization of the age."[2] As far as the Canadian cinema is concerned, the problem has always been aggravated by the economic and aesthetic pressure exerted by the mass-production techniques of the American cinema. The development of the American genres has been traced back to the emergence during the First World War of "mass production" methods that brought with them "the concomitant of all economies of scale: standardisation." The use of formulas thus had an economic base, but the social function of the genres was also highly conservative: "The very existence of a set of conventionalized genre parameters constrains movies towards a norm. A genre is a relatively fixed culture pattern. It defines a moral and social world, as well as a physical and historical environment. By its nature, its very familiarity, it inclines towards reassurance."[3] The reliance on established genres provides a general security blanket: the producer knows what he or she is investing in, the distributor has an "angle" to exploit, the director knows that the film will find an audience, and the audience knows what to expect and how to respond. This sense of security is precisely what is lacking, almost by definition, in the more traditional (or progressive?) Canadian cinema that explores (often painfully) the uncertainties of the Canadian experience.

One alternative for Canadian cinema has been found in the documentary tradition established by John Grierson, who developed the National Film Board to set the social concern of the documentary movement against the glamorous escapism of Hollywood. More recently, Pierre Perrault, whose documentaries explore the basis for identity in Quebec, has set that exploration against the simplifications of the genre film: "There is an essential difference between a good western in which the good and bad are easily identifiable . . . and reality. Moreover the films that we make do not seek to divide the world between the good and the bad but to look reality in the face and if possible to reflect it. . . . If sometimes there is spectacle it is in the auditorium. . . . This cinema puts the film-makers themselves in question."[4] Although it has become increasingly difficult to tell the good from the bad (or the ugly) in recent westerns, Perrault does point to a basic opposition between a cinema of provocation and a cinema of consumption. Perrault sees the advance of a consumer society as the greatest threat to the survival of Quebec: "The dream that comes in a box, in a can, on a disc, on film, threatens to assimilate us, to send us to sleep forever."[5] His strategy involves not only the rejection of genre and spectacle but also of fiction. Such an extreme solution is obviously limited as a means of combating the influence exercised by the formulas of the American fiction film through cinema and television, but the experience of the documentary cannot be overlooked in an attempt to distinguish a Canadian perspective.

The documentary experience was certainly a major factor in 1963 when the Canadian fiction film finally established itself, simultaneously in English and French, with the appearance of Don Owen's *Nobody Waved Goodbye* and Gilles Groulx's *Le Chat dans le sac*.[6] Both films originated as documentary projects within the NFB, and they were followed by a number of small-budget fiction films influenced by the techniques of direct cinema and rooted in the specifics of experience in Canada's different regions.[7] These regional films were often better received by U.S. than by Canadian critics, but they generally failed to reach large audiences, not only because of the audience's familiarity with the American formulas that define "popular" cinema but also because of the lack of commitment to these films of the largely U.S.-controlled distribution system in Canada. The search for popular audiences has confirmed the truth of Atwood's vision, as the indigenous regional films have given way to genre films, sometimes filmed in the United States, more often in unidentified Canadian locations or in Canadian settings labeled with U.S. names.[8] Thus Peter Medak's *The Changeling* (1979) was shot in Ontario and Vancouver, but its settings were identified as northern New York State and Seattle, and David Cronenberg's *The Dead Zone* (1983) made Ontario stand in for New Hampshire. Before the body snatchers finally took over, however, there was a transition period (the early seventies) during which a number of Canadian filmmakers tried to adapt the American genres to deal with the specifically Canadian experiences that had provided the basis for the regional films. With the benefit of hindsight, it could be said that these films paved the way for the body snatchers, but the strategies that they developed help to illuminate some of the problems of Canadian popular culture as it tries to define itself within or against the popular formulas established in another country.

These films appeared at a time when the American genres were themselves under pressure. The American dream had turned into something of a nightmare, and the sense of communal values that animated the genres had largely disappeared. In the films of Peckinpah, Altman, and others, the familiarity of the genre material no longer offers reassurance, and the established norms are disturbingly questioned. An increased self-consciousness in the use of genres and the absence of widely accepted norms suggest a possible drawing together of the American and Canadian experiences on this common ground of uncertainty. Two of the most popular American genres of this period were the heist film and the disaster film: in the valueless world of the former, the criminals are caught (if at all) not through the efficiency of the forces of law and order but by pure chance; in the latter a society, normal to the point of banality, is shaken by forces over which it has no control. The tension between a world without norms and a world of aggressive normality becomes the basis for the Canadian genre film.

The absence of normality is thoroughly developed in Harvey Hart's crime thriller *The Pyx* (1973). In the convent where she is undergoing a drug cure, a friend tells Elizabeth (Karen Black) that she doesn't know what the word "normal" means and later, when Elizabeth's homosexual friend doubts whether his reactions are "normal," the detective (Christo-

67. *The Pyx:* The detective (Christopher Plummer) seeks to restore social order.

pher Plummer) replies that after twenty-four years on the police force he doesn't know what that word means. The double structure, in which the investigation of Elizabeth's death is intercut with the events leading up to it, reveals strong parallels between the lives of the prostitute and the detective. Montreal is presented as a city of extremes, with its illuminated cross presiding over prostitution and homosexuality, gangsters and drug addiction, convents and devil worship. The process by which the detective discovers the truth represents not a restoration of social order but a loss of control in the face of an all-pervasive corruption and exploitation. Like Elizabeth, he is a "bad" Catholic, but, whereas her death can be seen as a redemption in that it is caused by her refusal to commit sacrilege against the host, his discovery of the world in which she lived leads him to commit an act of violence that violates the law that he is supposed to uphold.

This grotesque underworld can be seen as the perversion of the instinctual life that has been repressed to make the "normal" life of bourgeois society possible. The "normal" world is glimpsed only briefly in

The Pyx in the unsatisfying, and almost irrelevant, relationship of the detective and his girlfriend, but a number of Canadian films have been concerned with building up a strong sense of normality and security that is then undermined. David Cronenberg's *Shivers* (1974) opens with a smooth soft-sell voice extolling the self-contained luxury of the apartment building that is to be victimized; in William Fruet's *Death Weekend* (1976) the invasion of the dentist's elegant country mansion by violent thugs exposes the fragility of bourgeois illusions of affluence and security; while Don Shebib's *Second Wind* (1976) draws on the sports genre to set Roger's obsession with running against the deadening banality of suburban life. Whereas in the American context the sterility of a life based on consumption and possession signifies the collapse of the American dream, these Canadian films relate the concern with material security to the "Americanization" of Canadian life. What is missing from the plastic and packaged world of each of these films is what gave the American dream its vitality: a sense of challenge. In *Second Wind,* for example, Roger turns to competitive running because, surprisingly, his job at the stock exchange offers no challenges.

The aggressiveness of the normal and the urge toward standardization only serve to emphasize the absence of a felt Canadian identity. The measuring of Canadian culture and society against American standards becomes (implicitly or explicitly) a major concern of Canadian genre films. Dillon in Peter Pearson's *Paperback Hero* (1972) tries to invest his life with a glamor drawn from American westerns that is hopelessly at variance with the drab reality of his small-town existence in Saskatchewan; Don Shebib's *Between Friends* (1973) begins with a smoothly efficient heist in California and ends with a disastrous attempted holdup at a mine in the wastelands of Ontario's nickel belt; Jacques Godbout's *La Gammick* (1974) shows the Montreal underworld to be controlled by American bosses; and Don Owen's *Partners* (1976) deals with the reactions of characters whose backgrounds are American or English to an attempt by an American corporation to take over a Canadian company. Since all these films make explicit their concern with the squeezing of Canadian life into an American mold, their use of the genres is highly ironic: they stress the gulf between Canadian reality and the dreams that once sustained the American genres.

This feeling of disillusionment could also be found in American genre films of the time, but in Canada it was coupled with a tendency to define reality as what happens south of the border. Genre films, of course, are not the only ones to express this tendency: the visits to the Chicago riots in Robin Spry's *Prologue* (1969) and to the poor people's camp in Washington in Claude Jutra's *Wow* (1969) confront Canadian youths searching for identity and commitment with "real" political events. The point is

68. *Between Friends:* The disastrous attempted holdup.

not that Canadian problems are unreal but that they are intangible, that the political battle in the United States seems (or seemed in the late sixties) to be clear-cut while the Canadian identity crisis grows out of the absence of norms against which to rebel. Peter Harcourt has aptly described the reminiscence of John Ford's westerns when Will sings "We Shall Gather at the River" during Coker's funeral in *Between Friends* as "an allusion to an absence," and the whole film is suffused with images of impotence, failure, and absence.[9] This mood also dominates *Paperback Hero,* which is concerned not only with Dillon's failure to become a western hero but also with the way in which his ideal destroys any other possibility for his life. Robert Fulford has referred to "a sense of uselessness to come that places him firmly within the tradition of recent American westerns," but Pearson presents us less with the decline of a heroic past than with the sterility of a present shaped by imported dreams.[10]

The bleakness of outlook presented by most Canadian genre films offers little comfort to audiences, and critics constantly bemoan the absence of the traditional virtues. "If one is looking for a tight, suspenseful, and a fast-paced tingler," writes Nat Shuster, "*The Pyx* is a nix."[11] The demand for a smooth-flowing narrative and an aggressive pace is an attempt to confine Canadian genre films within the Hollywood norms, to

69. *Paperback Hero:* Dillon (Keir Dullea) fails in his attempt to become a western hero.

make them more comfortable and less disturbing. This attempt to impose a preconceived form can be related to the use of a preexisting iconography that is basic to the genre film; and the adoption of the conventions of a genre can result in a failure to take into account the viewing habits developed by that genre. Quebec critics, for example, have complained that the political point of Jean-Claude Lord's *Bingo* (1973) is undermined by its concern to generate the suspense expected of a political thriller; since the spectators are treated as consumers not implicated in the action, the film's structure becomes a reflection of the oppressive political structures that it tries to denounce.[12] An even more extreme case is Denis Héroux's *Born for Hell* (1975), which opens with a powerful vision of a society in which violence has become all-pervasive but which then proceeds to treat its spectators as voyeurs by its graphic depiction of a series of sex murders.

Of course, the best of American genre films do not demand a simple and passive response from their spectators, but the inherent conservatism of the genre system does create a strong pull in that direction. The subversive intentions of filmmakers can easily be negated by the expectations aroused by the genre in which they are working. George McCowan's *Face-Off* (1971), for example, seems to relate the plight of the hockey player (tied to one team, owned by the establishment, and forced to be

competitive and aggressive) to a more general social malaise, but the climactic freeze-frame of Duke stepping onto the ice to save the Leafs conforms to genre expectations and seems to endorse the way things are.
Coupled with this pull toward reassurance, however, is the problem faced
by all genre films of balancing vision and narrative, of ensuring that the
film's themes are not submerged by the details required to embody them
in "realistic" narrative form. In *Shivers* Cronenberg builds up a vision of
a "normal" world that conceals the perversion and frustration of its inhabitants, but the detailed depiction of the parasites' destruction of this
world and the refusal to leave anything to the imagination finally communicate little more than a strong sexual disgust. The graphic depiction of
violent death in *Death Weekend* (throat-cutting, burning alive, being
sucked into a swamp, being run down by a car) arouses our interest in
the mechanics of the illusion but undermines the disturbing vision of a
consumer society with which the film opens (or is death the ultimate
consumer?).

As if to counter this smothering of tensions by the violent detail associated with the genre, *Death Weekend* ends on a note of ambiguity: Diane
has survived the assault of the thugs by answering violence with violence
but is haunted by her memory of her encounter with the leader of the
gang with whom she seems to have some "mystic" connection. Similar "open" endings occur in *Shivers,* in which the infected apartment-
dwellers drive out into the city, and in *Second Wind,* in which it is left
unclear whether Roger has thrown away his running shoes for good.
Whereas genre films normally move from tension to resolution, each of
these films begins in a world in which all ambiguity has been denied and
ends with an image that can be taken as resolution or question. But such
ambiguity seems imposed on films that have previously depended on conventions and stereotypes, an evasion of the issues that the film might have
raised rather than a challenge to the spectator. What these films do demonstrate, however, is the need for stronger and more consistent measures
to counteract the demands of the genre and the difficulty of finding new
perspectives from which to view the old assumptions.

The problem of creating a critical detachment from these assumptions
is stressed by Quebec filmmaker Denys Arcand. He argues that even
when directors set out to separate themselves from "the social positions
of the dominant bourgeoisie . . . , the use of a cinematic form of expression whose rules normally carry the established philosophy leads in the
end to the denial, on the screen, of the original intentions so praiseworthy
in themselves." Arcand's solution is a radical "deconstruction" of the
genre, the denial of genre expectations so as to "produce an uneasiness in
the spectator which will be difficult to identify to begin with because it is
caused by a modification of the cinematic language itself." [13] As in Ar-

cand's own films, this strategy demands a rejection of the heavy editing and brisk rhythms of the American genre film, as well as a lessening of emphasis on "action" and on violence as a solution to all problems. This approach has been adopted, to widely varying effect, in Arcand's own *La Maudite Galette* (1972), Shebib's *Between Friends*, Godbout's *La Gammick*, and Jean-Pierre Lefebvre's *Pigs Are Seldom Clean* (1973).[14]

Arcand has described *La Maudite Galette* as "a false crime thriller" and as "a deconstructed thriller." Like all of these films, it stresses waiting and frustration rather than the action expected of its genre. Its use of single-shot sequences, within which small variations of tone and gesture build up a sense of disturbance and unease, relates it closely to nongenre films like Jacques Leduc's *On est loin du soleil* (1971), which expresses the Quebec experience in terms of "the natural duration of beings to whom nothing happens."[15] The violence of the robbery breaks through the sense of inertia so far built up and creates a sense of direction, but the movement thus initiated leads ultimately to the abandonment of Quebec (by the old couple who end up with the money and drive their new American car to Florida). Arcand's "strategy of slowness" prevents any identification with the characters or emotional gratification from the violence: "Instead of asking yourself what is happening to the heroes, you ask yourself why it is happening. You are led to interrogate yourself on the society which produces this kind of individual."[16] In documentaries like *On est au coton* (1970) and *Quebec: Duplessis and After* (1972), Arcand had already explored the social, economic, and political factors that gave birth to terrorism in Quebec; in his genre films, his interest shifts from terrorism to gangsterism (and its alliance with capitalism), but his vision remains consistent in its concern with the social roots of violence.[17]

Arcand's method in his genre films—*La Maudite Galette, Réjeanne Padovani* (1973), and *Gina* (1975)—is to create frustration in the spectator by developing a tension between "a cinema of the look and a cinema of action."[18] Whereas in the American genre film violent action usually resolves tensions, in these films action only manages to intensify the contradictions that it tries to resolve. Moreover, in a world in which traditional values have crumbled, the opposition between the criminal and "straight" society no longer has any real meaning. After their son has been gunned down in their kitchen in *La Maudite Galette*, his old parents calmly hide the stolen money before the police arrive; similarly, in Lefebvre's *Pigs Are Seldom Clean*, Bob Tremblay both pushes drugs and informs on the users to an RCMP officer who smokes pot himself, and Chico in Godbout's *La Gammick* tries to expose American crime bosses on an open-line radio show but is betrayed by the host and gunned down by police. In *La Maudite Galette* and *Réjeanne Padovani*, as in *Between*

Friends, the family no longer functions as a social force but is instead the source of the violence. In *Pigs Are Seldom Clean* Bob Tremblay acts as a double agent to fulfill his dream of a suburban family life. There is no clear dividing line between domesticity and criminality, and if crime rarely pays, it is because the characters in these films are mostly small-time operators who are as alienated from the world of big crime as they are from the closely related world of big business. Vincent Padovani survives unscathed, while his wife Réjeanne ends up buried in the concrete highway that his company has built as a result of his political connections.

The conventional boundaries that were so important to the genre film no longer exist, and one of the themes of all these films is the search for meaningful boundaries. *Pigs Are Seldom Clean* is set in the divided city of Ottawa-Hull: Bob Tremblay (whose Anglo French name expresses division) works for the police in Ottawa and pushes drugs among the young people of Hull.[19] Despite the boundary between the two cities (and provinces), much of the film takes place in a no-man's land, the two societies having in common their nondescript buildings and, of course, the Canadian winter. More commonly the boundary is that between Canada and the United States: for the American corporate underworld of *La Gammick* the border exists only as a minor nuisance; in *Between Friends* the border is not shown but the California surf remains in Toby's mind as a memory of a past to which he cannot return and as a dream of a future that he does not have. America is both dream and reality; Canada is uncomfortably posed between the two.

Given this absence of well-defined boundaries, the sharply defined conflicts of the genre film cease to be appropriate. Lefebvre leaves us to contemplate a moral vacuum, eliminating all suspense by the opening teletype message that succinctly describes the final killings; Godbout fills the second half of his film almost entirely with Chico's monologue on a hotline radio show, a monologue that becomes an expression of his impotence and a challenge to the viewer to examine its implications; while Shebib begins with the successful Californian heist and ends with the botched Canadian job, these action sequences come to seem almost irrelevant to a film concerned with empty spaces (between friends) and unfulfilled dreams.

In these films, the whole generic context becomes an allusion to an absence. They are now part of Canadian film history and can be seen as transitional works between Canadian regional cinema and the anonymous films of Hollywood North. But they should not be condemned automatically because of what followed them; rather, it would be better to determine how successfully each film has coped with the aesthetic and ideological issues raised by the chosen genre. These Canadian genre films may offer insights into the social and cinematic forces that still threaten to

70. *Pigs Are Seldom Clean* is set in a divided city in the Canadian winter.

"take over" the Canadian cinema. For geographical and linguistic reasons, Canada is especially vulnerable to these forces. In Quebec, the French language does provide some protection, but the essential issue is one of film language. As Atwood suggests in *Surfacing,* "a language is everything you do," and the tensions explored in this article can also be found in many national cinemas that must define themselves in relation to the dominant codes of the American genres.

Notes

1. Margaret Atwood, *Surfacing* (New York: Simon and Schuster, 1972), p. 148.

2. Ronald Sutherland, *Second Image: Comparative Studies in Québec/Canadian Literature* (Don Mills, Ontario: New Press, 1971), p. 22.

3. Andrew Tudor, *Image and Influence* (London: Allen and Unwin, 1974), pp. 180–181.

4. Michel Brûlé, Fernand Dumont, and Pierre Perrault, "De la notion de pays à la représentation de la nation," *Cinéma Québec* 1, no. 1 (May 1971): 26–27.

5. Michel Delahaye and Louis Marcorelles, "L'Action parlée: Entretien avec Pierre Perrault," *Cahiers du Cinéma,* no. 165 (April 1965): 36.

6. I have tried to translate French titles where possible, but Quebec film-

makers often contribute to the politics of language in Canada by using colloquial titles that resist translation into English. The title of *Le Chat dans le sac*—literally, "The Cat in the Bag"—refers to the hero's feelings of suffocation, of being in a cul-de-sac. For earlier attempts to create a Canadian fiction cinema, see Pierre Véronneau and Piers Handling, eds., *Self Portrait: Essays on the Canadian and Quebec Cinemas* (Ottawa: Canadian Film Institute, 1980). For the relationship between Hollywood and the Canadian film industry, see Pierre Berton, *Hollywood's Canada: The Americanization of Our National Image* (Toronto: McClelland and Stewart, 1975).

7. Quebec is, of course, more than simply a "region" of Canada; but Quebec nationalism did inspire a concern to develop cinematic images that would reflect the immediate environment, and these images are often close to those found in English Canadian regional films. See my "Second Images: Reflections on the Canadian Cinema(s) in the Seventies," *Dalhousie Review* 62, no. 2 (Summer 1982): 181–195; reprinted in *Take Two: A Tribute to Film in Canada*, edited by Seth Feldman (Toronto: Irwin Publishing, 1984), pp. 100–110.

8. Another controversial aspect of these films is the frequent use of American stars to ensure international distribution. There have also been several "coproductions" with Britain and France.

9. Peter Harcourt, "Men of Vision: Don Shebib," *Cinema Canada*, no. 32 (November 1976): 40; reprinted in *Canadian Film Reader*, edited by Seth Feldman and Joyce Nelson (Toronto: Peter Martin Associates, 1977), p. 216.

10. Robert Fulford, *Marshall Delaney at the Movies* (Toronto: Peter Martin Associates, 1974), p. 72.

11. Nat Shuster, "Canadian Film View," *Motion* (November–December 1973): 30.

12. See Pierre Vallieres, "*Bingo* sur une foire de confusion," *Cinéma Québec* 3, nos. 6/7 (April–May 1974): 33.

13. Denys Arcand, "*La Maudite Galette*," *Cinéma Québec* 2, no. 1 (September 1972): 11.

14. *La Maudite Galette* means "Damned Money," using a colloquial term for money; *La Gammick* (from the English *gimmick*) refers to the activities of the gangsters that Chico unmasks; *Pigs Are Seldom Clean* is the title of the English-dubbed print of Lefebvre's *On n'engraisse pas les cochons à l'eau claire*, roughly "Pigs don't grow fat on clear water."

15. André Leroux, "L'Evidence mise à nue," *Cinéma Québec* 1, no. 5 (November 1971): 7. *On est loin du soleil* could be translated as "We are far from the sun."

16. "*La Maudite Galette*, interview with Denys Arcand," *Cinéma Québec* 1, no. 9 (May–June 1972): 29.

17. *On est au coton*, Arcand's controversial documentary on the cotton industry in Quebec, was banned by the NFB, but the issues it raises were incorporated into the fiction film *Gina* (1974). The title includes an untranslatable pun, since "coton" means "cotton" but is also part of a colloquial expression meaning "we're fed up."

18. Richard Gay, "Notre condition de violés," *Cinéma Québec* 4, no. 2 (April 1975): 14.

19. Lefebvre does not show the tourist sites in Canada's federal capital, but he does contrast the affluence of the predominantly English-speaking city on the Ontario side of the border with the less prosperous French-speaking city of Hull across the river in Quebec.

Bibliography

Theory

Alloway, Lawrence. "The Iconography of the Movies." *Movie*, no. 7 (February–March 1963). Reprinted in *Movie Reader*, edited by Ian Cameron. New York and Washington: Praeger, 1972.

Altman, Charles F. "Towards a Theory of Genre Film." In *Film: Historical-Theoretical Speculations; The 1977 Film Studies Annual*, ed. Ben Lawton and Janet Staiger, Part II, pp. 31–43. Pleasantville, N.Y.: Redgrave, 1977.

Altman, Rick. "A Semantic/Syntactic Approach to Film Genre." *Cinema Journal* 23, no. 3 (Spring 1984): 6–18.

Amelio, Ralph J. *The Filmic Moment: An Approach to Teaching American Genre Film through Extracts*. Dayton, Ohio: Pflaum, 1974.

Andrew, Dudley. "Valuation [of Genres and Auteurs]." Chap. 7 in *Concepts in Film Theory*. New York: Oxford, 1984.

Braudy, Leo. "Film Genre: A Dialogue—The Thirties, the Forties." *Post Script* 1, no. 3 (1982): 27–29.

———. *The World in a Frame*. Garden City: Anchor Doubleday, 1977.

Cavell, Stanley. "Types; Cycles or Genres." Chap. 5 in *The World Viewed: Reflections on the Ontology of Film*. New York: Viking, 1971.

Cawelti, John G. *Adventure, Mystery and Romance: Formula Stories as Art and Popular Culture*. Chicago: University of Chicago Press, 1976.

———. "The Concept of Formula in the Study of Popular Culture." *Journal of Popular Culture* 3, no. 3 (Winter 1969): 381–390.

———. "The Question of Popular Genres." *Journal of Popular Film and Television* 13, no. 2 (Summer 1985): 55–61.

———. *The Six-Gun Mystique*, Part 4. Bowling Green, Ohio: Bowling Green University Popular Press, 1971.

Collins, Richard. "Genre: A Reply to Ed Buscombe." *Screen* 11, nos. 4–5 (August–September 1970): 66–75.

Deinstfrey, Harris. "Hitch Your Genre to a Star." *Film Culture* 34 (Fall 1964): 35–37.

Dooley, Roger. *From Scarface to Scarlett: American Films in the 1930's*. New York: Harcourt Brace Jovanovich, 1981.

Easthope, Antony. "Notes on Genre." *Screen Education*, nos. 32–33 (Autumn–Winter 1979–1980): 39–44.

Eberwein, Robert T. "Genre and the Writerly Text." *Journal of Popular Film and Television* 13, no. 2 (Summer 1985): 62–68.

Eidsvik, Charles. "Story Conventions." Chap. 6 in *Cineliteracy: Film among the Arts*. New York: Random House, 1978.

Film Reader 3, edited by Valentin Almendarez et al. Evanston, Ill.: Northwestern University, 1978.

Frye, Northrop. *Anatomy of Criticism: Four Essays*. New York: Atheneum, 1970.

———. *The Secular Scripture: A Study of the Structure of Romance*. Cambridge, Mass.: Harvard University Press, 1976.

Grant, Barry K., ed. *Film Genre: Theory and Criticism*. Metuchen, N.J.: Scarecrow Press, 1977.

———. "Impressionism and Ideology: The State of Recent Film Genre Criticism." *Canadian Review of American Studies* 14, no. 1 (Spring 1983): 107–118.

———. "Tradition and the Individual Talent: Poetry in the Genre Film." In *Narrative Strategies: Original Essays in Film and Prose Fiction*, edited by Syndy M. Conger and Janice R. Welsch, pp. 93–103. Macomb: Western Illinois University Press, 1981.

Kaminsky, Stuart M. *American Film Genres: Approaches to a Critical Theory of Popular Film*. Dayton, Ohio: Pflaum, 1974.

Kolker, Robert P. "Film Genre: A Dialogue—The Eighties." *Post Script* 1, no. 3 (1982): 30–32.

Landrum, Larry N. "Recent Work in Genre." *Journal of Popular Film and Television* 13, no. 3 (Fall 1985): 151–158.

Lehman, Peter, et al. "American Film Genre: An Interview with John Cawelti." *Wide Angle* 2, no. 2 (1978): 50–57.

Lévi-Strauss, Claude. *The Raw and the Cooked: Introduction to a Science of Mythology*, translated by John and Doreen Weightman. New York: Harper and Row, 1969.

———. "Structural Study of Myth." In *The Structuralists from Marx to Lévi-Strauss*, edited by Richard and Fernande deGeorge, pp. 169–194. Garden City: Doubleday, 1972.

Lukow, Gregory, and Steven Ricci. "The 'Audience' Goes 'Public': Intertextuality, Genre, and the Responsibilities of Film Literacy." *On Film*, no. 12 (Spring 1984): 28–36.

Mast, Gerald, and Marshall Cohen. "Film Genres." *Film Genre and Criticism*, 3d ed., edited by Gerald Mast and Marshall Cohen. New York: Oxford, 1985.

Mayer, Geoff. "Formula and Genre, Myths and Patterns." *Australian Journal of Screen Theory* 4 (1978): 59–65.

McConnell, Frank D. "Legends and History: The Problem of Film Genre." Chap. 5 in *The Spoken Seen: Film and the Romantic Imagination*. Baltimore and London: Johns Hopkins University Press, 1975.

Manchell, Frank. "A Representative Genre of the Film." In *Film Study: A Resource Guide*. Rutherford, N.J.: Fairleigh Dickenson University Press, 1973.

Neale, Stephen. *Genre*. London: British Film Institute, 1980.

Petlewski, Paul. "Complication of Narrative in the Genre Film." *Film Criticism* 4, no. 1 (Fall 1979): 18–24.

Poague, Leland A. "The Problem of Film Genre: A Mentalistic Approach." *Literature/Film Quarterly* 6, no. 2 (Spring 1978): 152–161.

Propp, V. *Morphology of the Folk Tale*. Austin and London: University of Texas Press, 1968.

Ryall, Tom. "The Notion of Genre." *Screen* 11, no. 2 (March–April 1970): 22–32.

Sacks, Sheldon. "The Psychological Implications of Genre Distinctions." *Genre* 7 (April 1968): 106–115.

Schatz, Thomas. *Hollywood Genres: Formulas, Filmmaking, and the Studio System*. New York: Random House, 1981.

———. "New Directions in Film Genre Study (A Reply to Charles F. Altman)." In *Film: Historical-Theoretical Speculations: The 1977 Film Studies Annual*, Part II, pp. 44–52. Pleasantville, N.Y.: Redgrave, 1977.

———. *Old Hollywood/New Hollywood*. Ann Arbor: UMI Research Press, 1982.

Schiff, Stephen. "The Respectable Experience." *Film Comment* 18, no. 2 (1982): 34–36.

Small, Edward S. "Literary and Film Genres: Toward a Taxonomy of Film." *Literature/Film Quarterly* 7, no. 4 (1979): 209–219.

Sobchack, Thomas, and Vivian C. Sobchack. "Genre Films." Chap. 4 in *An Introduction to Film*. Boston: Little, Brown, 1980.

Sobchack, Vivian. "Genre Film: Myth, Ritual, and Sociodrama." In *Film/Culture: Explorations of Cinema in Its Social Context*, edited by Sari Thomas, pp. 147–165. Metuchen, N.J.: Scarecrow Press, 1982.

Solomon, Stanley J. *Beyond Formula: American Film Genres*. New York: Harcourt Brace Jovanovich, 1976.

Todorov, Tzvetan. *The Fantastic: A Structural Approach to a Literary Genre*, translated by Richard Howard. Cleveland and London: Case Western Reserve University Press, 1973.

Tudor, Andrew. "Critical Method: Auteur and Genre." Chap. 5 in *Theories of Film*. New York: Viking, 1974.

———. "Genre: Theory and Malpractice in Film Criticism." *Screen* 11, no. 6 (1970): 33–43.

Williams, Alan. "Is a Radical Genre Criticism Possible?" *Quarterly Review of Film Studies* 9, no. 2 (Spring 1984): 121–125.

Yacowar, Maurice. "Recent Popular Genre Movies: Awash and Aware." *Journal of Popular Film* 4, no. 4 (1975): 297–305.

Comedy Films

Agee, James. "Comedy's Greatest Era." In *Agee on Film*, Vol. 1, pp. 1–20. New York: Grosset and Dunlap, 1967.

Bergman, Andrew. *We're in the Money*. New York: Harper and Row, 1972.

Bergson, Henri. "Laughter." In *Comedy,* edited by Wylie Sypher, pp. 61–190. New York: Doubleday, 1956.

Callenbach, Ernest. "The Comic Ecstasy." *Films in Review* 5, no. 1 (January 1954): 24–26.

Cavell, Stanley. "Leopards in Connecticut." *Georgia Review* 30, no. 2 (Summer 1976): 233–262.

———. "Pursuits of Happiness: A Reading of *The Lady Eve.*" *New Literary History* 10 (1979): 581–601.

———. *Pursuits of Happiness.* Cambridge: Harvard University Press, 1981.

Clipper, Lawrence J. "Archetypal Figures in Early Film Comedy." *Western Humanities Review* 28, no. 4 (Autumn 1974): 355–366.

Durgnat, Raymond. *The Crazy Mirror: Hollywood Comedy and the American Image.* New York: Delta, 1972.

Dyer, Peter John. "They Liked to Break the Rules." *Films and Filming* 6, no. 1 (October 1959): 12–14, 38–39.

Earley, Steven C. *An Introduction to American Movies.* New York: Mentor, 1978.

Eberwein, Robert. "Comedy and the Film within a Film." *Wide Angle* 3, no. 2 (1979): 12–17.

Everson, William K. "Screwball Comedy: A Reappraisal." *Films in Review* 34, no. 10 (1983): 578–584.

Eyles, Allen. *American Comedy since Sound.* New York: A. S. Barnes, 1973.

Geduld, Carolyn, and Harry Geduld. "From Kops to Robbers: Transformation of Archetypal Figures in the American Cinema of the 20's and 30's." *Journal of Popular Culture* 1, no. 2 (1967–1968): 389–394.

Gerhing, Wes D. "McCarey vs. Capra: A Guide to American Film Comedy of the 30's." *Journal of Popular Film and Television* 7, no. 1 (1978): 67–84.

Grant, Barry K. "Film Comedy of the Thirties and the American Comic Tradition." *West Virginia University Philological Papers* 26 (August 1980): 21–29.

Higham, Charles, and Joel Greenberg. *Hollywood in the Forties.* London: Zwemmer; New York: Barnes, 1968.

Kaminsky, Stuart M. "History and Social Change: Comedy and Individual Expression." Chap. 9 in *American Film Genres: Approaches to a Critical Theory of Popular Film.* Dayton, Ohio: Pflaum, 1974.

Keane, Marian. "The Authority of Connection in Stanley Cavell's *Pursuits of Happiness.*" *Journal of Popular Film and Television* 13, no. 3 (Fall 1985): 139–150.

Kehr, David. "Funny Peculiar." *Film Comment* 18, no. 4 (1982): 9–11, 13–16.

Kerr, Walter. *The Silent Clowns.* New York: Knopf, 1975.

Kracauer, Siegfried. "Silent Film Comedy." *Sight and Sound* 21 (August–September 1951): 31–32.

Krutnik, Frank. "The Clown-Prints of Comedy." *Screen* 25, nos. 4–5 (July–October 1984): 50–59.

Lahue, Kalton C. *World of Laughter: The Motion Picture Comedy Short, 1910–1930.* Norman: University of Oklahoma Press, 1972.

Leach, Jim. "The Screwball Comedy." In *Film Genre: Theory and Criticism,* edited by Barry K. Grant, pp. 75–89. Metuchen, N.J.: Scarecrow Press, 1977.

Lehman, Peter, ed. "Film Comedy." *Wide Angle* 3, no. 2 (1979). Special issue.

McCaffrey, Donald W. "The Evolution of the Chase in the Silent Screen Comedy." *Cinema Journal* 4 (1964): 1–8.

———. *The Golden Age of Sound Comedy: Comic Films and Comedians of the Thirties.* South Brunswick, N.J.: A. S. Barnes, 1973.

Maltin, Leonard. *The Great Movie Comedians.* New York: Crown/Harmony Books, 1982.

———. *Movie Comedy Teams.* New York: New American Library, 1970.

Mast, Gerald. *The Comic Mind: Comedy and the Movies,* 2d ed. Chicago: University of Chicago Press, 1979.

Monaco, James. *American Film Now.* New York: New American Library, 1979.

Montgomery, John. *Comedy Films, 1894–1954.* London: George Allen and Unwin, Ltd., 1968.

Olson, Elder. *The Theory of Comedy.* Bloomington and London: Indiana University Press, 1968.

Robinson, David. *The Great Funnies: A History of Film Comedy.* New York: Dutton, 1969.

Schatz, Thomas. *Hollywood Genres: Formulas, Filmmaking and the Studio System.* New York: Random House, 1981.

Seidman, Steve. *Comedian Comedy: A Tradition in the Hollywood Film.* Ann Arbor: UMI Research Press, 1981.

Sennett, Ted. *Lunatics and Lovers: The Golden Age of Hollywood Comedy.* New York: Limelight Editions, 1985.

Sklar, Robert. "Chaos, Magic, Physical Genius and the Art of Silent Comedy." Chap. 7 in *Movie-Made America.* New York: Random House, 1975.

Surfin, Mark. "The Silent World of Slapstick (1912–1916)." *Film Culture* 2, no. 4 (1956): 21–22.

Wood, Robin. "The American Family Comedy: From *Meet Me in St. Louis* to *The Texas Chain Saw Massacre.*" *Wide Angle* 3, no. 2 (1979): 5–11.

Crime Films*

Alloway, Lawrence. *Violent America: The Movies, 1946–1964.* New York: Museum of Modern Art, 1971.

Baxter, John. "Something More than Night." *Film Journal* 2, no. 4 (1975): 4–9.

Cameron, Ian. *A Pictorial History of Crime Films.* London: Hamlyn, 1975.

Cauliez, Armand Jean. *Le Film criminel et le film policier.* Paris: Editions du Cerf, 1956.

Cawelti, John G. *Adventure, Mystery and Romance: Formula Stories as Art and Popular Culture.* Chicago: University of Chicago Press, 1976.

*In the genre of crime films I have included detective films, police films, mystery films, and spy films—in short, all films dealing with the perpetration or prevention of crime (with the exception of the gangster film, since the body of critical work on this distinct group of films is substantial enough to warrant a separate listing). This classification avoids the intentional fallacy inherent in the dubiously labeled genre "thriller," a term which is more appropriately used to describe tone and which, unlike the horror film, is much too vague as a generic category.—Ed.

Chabrol, Claude. "Evolution du film policier." *Cahiers du Cinéma* 54 (1955): 27–33.

Clarens, Carlos. *Crime Movies: An Illustrated History.* New York: Norton, 1980.

———. "Hooverville West: The Hollywood G-Man, 1934–1945." *Film Comment* 13, no. 3 (May–June 1977): 10–16.

Connor, Edward. "The Mystery Film." *Films in Review* 5, no. 3 (March 1954): 120–123.

Cutts, John. "Oriental Eye." *Films and Filming* 3, no. 11 (August 1957): 16.

Davis, Brian. *The Thriller.* London: Studio Vista; New York: Dutton, 1973.

Deming, Barbara. *Running Away from Myself.* New York: Grossman, 1969.

Douglass, Wayne J. "The Criminal Psychopath as Hollywood Hero." *Journal of Popular Film and Television* 8, no. 4 (Winter 1981): 30–39.

Durgnat, Raymond. "Spies and Ideologies." *Cinema* (U.K.), no. 2 (March 1969): 5–13.

Everson, William K. *The Detective in Film.* Secaucus, N.J.: Citadel Press, 1972.

French, Philip. "Cops." *Sight and Sound* 43, no. 2 (Spring 1974): 113–115.

Godfrey, Lionel. "Martinis without Olives." *Films and Filming* 14, no. 7 (April 1968): 10–14.

Gow, Gordon. *Suspense in the Cinema.* Cranbury, N.J.: A. S. Barnes, 1968.

Grace, Harry A. "A Taxonomy of American Crime Film Themes." *Journal of Social Psychology* 42 (August 1955): 129–136.

Gregory, Charles. "Knight without Meaning? Marlowe on the Screen." *Sight and Sound* 42, no. 3 (Summer 1973): 155–159.

Hammond, Laurence. *Thriller Movies.* Secaucus, N.J.: Derbibooks, 1975.

Haralovich, Mary Beth. "Sherlock Holmes: Genre and Industrial Practice." *Journal of the University Film Association* 31, no. 2 (Spring 1979): 53–57.

Haydock, Ron. *Deerstalker: Holmes and Watson on Screen.* Metuchen, N.J.: Scarecrow Press, 1978.

Henry, Clayton R., Jr. "Crime Films and Social Criticism." *Films in Review* 2, no. 5 (1951): 31–34.

Higgins, George V. "The Private Eye as Illegal Hero." *Esquire* 77, no. 6 (December 1972): 348, 350–351.

Houston, Penelope. "The Private Eye." *Sight and Sound* 26, no. 1 (1956): 22–23, 55.

McConnell, Frank D. "Leopards and History: The Problem of Film Genre." Chap. 5 in *The Spoken Seen: Film and the Romantic Imagination.* Baltimore and London: Johns Hopkins University Press, 1975.

Miller, Don. "Private Eyes: From Sam Spade to J. J. Gittes." *Focus on Film*, no. 22 (Autumn 1975): 15–35.

Oliver, Bill. "*The Long Goodbye* and *Chinatown*: Debunking the Private Eye Tradition." *Literature/Film Quarterly* 3, no. 3 (Summer 1975): 240–248.

Parish, James Robert, and Michael R. Pitts. *The Great Spy Pictures.* Metuchen, N.J.: Scarecrow Press, 1974.

Park, William. "The Police State." *Journal of Popular Film and Television* 6, no. 3 (Fall 1978): 229–237.

Pitts, Michael R. *Famous Movie Detectives*. Metuchen, N.J.: Scarecrow Press, 1979.

Reck, Tom S. "Come Out of the Shower and Come Out Clean." *Commonweal* 26 (September 1969): 588–591.

Rubenstein, Lenny. *The Great Spy Films*. Secaucus, N.J.: Citadel Press, 1979.

———. "The Politics of Spy Films." *Cinéaste* 9, no. 3 (Spring 1979): 16–21.

Sarris, Andrew. "Films in Focus." *Village Voice* 22 (July 1971): 55.

Schatz, Thomas. *Hollywood Genres: Formulas, Filmmaking and the Studio System*. New York: Random House, 1981.

Shadoian, Jack. *Dreams and Dead Ends: The American Gangster/Crime Film*. Cambridge, Mass.: MIT Press, 1977.

Skene Melvin, David, and Ann Skene Melvin, comps. *Crime, Detective, Espionage, Mystery and Thriller Fiction and Film: A Comprehensive Bibliography of Critical Writing through 1979*. Westport, Conn.: Greenwood Press, 1980.

Sobchack, Thomas. "New York Street Gangs or the Warriors of My Mind." *Journal of Popular Film and Television* 10, no. 2 (Summer 1982): 77–85.

Solomon, Stanley J. *Beyond Formula: American Film Genres*. New York: Harcourt Brace Jovanovich, 1976.

Telotte, J. P. "The Detective as Dreamer: The Case of *The Lady in the Lake*." *Journal of Popular Film and Television* 12, no. 1 (Spring 1984): 4–15.

Thomson, David. "Man and the Mean Street." Chap. 6 in *America in the Dark: Hollywood and the Gift of Unreality*. New York: William Morrow, 1977.

Thomson, H. Douglas. "Detective Films." *Sight and Sound* 4, no. 13 (Spring 1935): 10–11.

Tuska, Jon. *The Detective in Hollywood*. New York: Doubleday, 1978.

Tyler, Parker. "The Good Villain and the Bad Hero." Chap. 5 in *The Hollywood Hallucination*. New York: Simon and Schuster, 1970.

Van Wert, William. "Philip Marlowe: Hardboiled to Softboiled to Poached." *Jump Cut*, no. 3 (1974): 10–13.

Waller, Gregory A. "Mike Hammer and the Detective Film of the 1980s." *Journal of Popular Film and Television* 13, no. 3 (Fall 1985): 109–125.

Westlake, Mike. "The Classic Television Detective Genre." *Framework* 13 (1980): 37–38.

Wolfe, Tom. "Pause, Now, and Consider Some Tentative Conclusions about the Meaning of the Mass Perversion Called Porno-Violence . . ." *Esquire* 68, no. 1 (July 1967): 59, 110–111.

Disaster Films

Annan, David. *Catastrophe: The End of the Cinema?* New York: Bounty Books, 1975.

Kaplan, Fred. "Riches from Ruins." *Jump Cut*, no. 6 (March–April 1975): 3–4.

Rosen, David N. "Drugged Popcorn." *Jump Cut*, no. 8 (August–September 1975): 19–20.

Epic Films

Baxter, John. *Hollywood in the Sixties*. London: Tantivy; New York: Barnes, 1972.

Campbell, Richard H., and Michael R. Pitts. *The Bible on Film: A Checklist, 1897–1980*. Metuchen, N.J.: Scarecrow Press, 1981.

Durgnat, Raymond. "Epic, Epic, Epic, Epic, Epic." *Films and Filming* 10, no. 3 (December 1963): 9–12. Reprinted in *Film Genre: Theory and Criticism*, edited by Barry K. Grant, pp. 108–117. Metuchen, N.J.: Scarecrow Press, 1977.

Dyer, John Peter. "Some Mighty Spectacles." *Films and Filming* 4, no. 5 (February 1958): 13–15, 34.

Earley, Steven C. *An Introduction to American Movies*. New York: Mentor, 1978.

Everson, William K. "Film Spectacles." *Films in Review* 5 (November 1954): 459–471.

Richards, Jeffrey. *Swordsmen on the Screen*. London: Routledge and Kegan Paul, 1980.

Robinson, David. "Spectacle." *Sight and Sound* 25, no. 1 (Summer 1955): 22–27, 55–56.

Solomon, John. *The Ancient World in the Cinema*. Cranbury, N.J., and London: Barnes/Tantivy, 1978.

Whitehall, Richard. "Days of Strife and Nights of Orgy." *Films and Filming* 9, no. 6 (March 1963): 8–14.

Wood, Michael. "Shake the Superflux." Chap. 8 in *America in the Movies*. New York: Delta, 1975.

Erotic Films*

Atkins, Thomas, ed. *Movies and Sexuality*. Hollins College, Va.: *Film Journal*, 1973.

Bazin, André. "Marginal Notes on Eroticism in the Cinema." In *What Is Cinema?* Vol. 2, pp. 169–175. Berkeley: University of California Press, 1971.

Blake, Roger. *The Porno Movies*. Cleveland: Original Century Books, 1970.

Botto, Louis. "They Shoot Dirty Movies, Don't They?" *Look*, November 3, 1970, pp. 56–57, 59–60.

Buckley, Peter. "A Dirty Movie Is a Dirty Movie Is a Dirty Movie." *Films and Filming* 18, no. 11 (August 1972): 24–29.

Chappell, Fred. "Twenty-Six Propositions about Skin-Flicks." In *Man and the Movies*, edited by W. R. Robinson, pp. 53–59. Baltimore: Penguin, 1967.

Corliss, Richard. "Cinema Sex: From *The Kiss* to *Deep Throat*." *Film Comment* 9, no. 1 (January–February 1973): 4–5.

de Beauvoir, Simone. *Brigitte Bardot and the Lolita Syndrome*. London: New English Library, 1960.

*I've chosen this term over other possibilities for the pragmatic reason that it seems the most workable for approaching these films generically.—Ed.

Dowdy, Andrew. *The Films of the Fifties: The American State of Mind*. New York: Morrow, 1975.

Durgnat, Raymond. *Eros in the Cinema*. London: Calder and Boyars, 1966.

———. "Eroticism in Cinema, Part 1: The Dark Gods." *Films and Filming* 8, no. 1 (October 1961): 14–16, 40–41.

———. "Eroticism in Cinema, Part 2: The Deviationists." *Films and Filming* 8, no. 2 (November 1961): 33–34, 46.

———. "Eroticism in Cinema, Part 3: Cupids vs. the Legions of Decency." *Films and Filming* 8, no. 3 (December 1961): 16–18, 46.

———. "Eroticism in Cinema, Part 4: The Subconscious: From Pleasure Castle to Libido Motel." *Films and Filming* 8, no. 4 (January 1962): 13–15, 46.

———. "Eroticism in Cinema, Part 5: The Sacred and the Profane: Flames of Passion." *Films and Filming* 8, no. 5 (February 1962): 16–18.

———. "Eroticism in Cinema, Part 6: "Some Mad Love and the Sweet Life." *Films and Filming* 8, no. 6 (March 1962): 16–18, 41.

———. "Eroticism in Cinema, Part 7: Symbolism." *Films and Filming* 8, no. 7 (April 1962): 13–15, 38–41.

———. "Eroticism in Cinema, Part 8: Midnight Sun." *Films and Filming* 8, no. 8 (May 1962): 21–23, 46–49.

Ellis, John. "Photography/Pornography/Art/Pornography." *Screen* 21, no. 1 (Spring 1980): 81–108.

Georgakas, Dan. "Porno Power." *Cinéaste* 6, no. 4 (1974): 13–15.

Hanson, Gillian. *Original Skin: Nudity and Sex in Cinema and Theatre*. London: Tom Stacy, Ltd., 1970.

Heard, Colin. "Sexploitation." *Films and Filming* 15, no. 11 (August 1969): 24–29.

Hoffman, Frank A. "Prolegomena to a Study of Traditional Elements in the Erotic Film." *Journal of American Folklore* 78 (April–June 1965): 143–148.

Knight, Arthur, and Hollis Alpert. "The History of Sex in Cinema." 20 pts. *Playboy* 12, no. 4 (April 1965)–16, no. 1 (January 1969).

Kurti, Laszlo. "Dirty Movies—Dirty Minds: The Social Construction of X-Rated Films." *Journal of Popular Culture* 17, no. 2 (Fall 1983): 187–192.

Kyrou, Ado. *Amour—érotisme & cinéma*. Paris: Le Terrain Vague, 1966.

Lehman, Peter, ed. "Sexual Difference." *Wide Angle* 5, no. 1 (1982). Special issue.

Lo Duca, Guiseppe. *L'Erotisme au cinéma*. 3 vols. Paris: Jean-Jacques Pauvert, 1957.

Meyers, Richard. *For One Week Only: The World of Exploitation Films*. Piscataway, N.J.: New Century, 1983.

Northland, John. "Porno Films: An In-Depth Report." *Take One* 4, no. 4 (March–April 1973): 11–17.

Paul, William. "Emerging Paradoxes of the New Porn." *Village Voice* 3 (June 1971): 63, 73.

Rhode, Eric. "Sensuality in the Cinema." *Sight and Sound* 30, no. 2 (Spring 1961): 93–95.

Robinson, David. "When Is a Dirty Film . . . ?" *Sight and Sound* 41, no. 1 (Winter 1971–1972): 28–30.

Rollin, Roger B. "Triple X: Erotic Movies and Their Audience." *Journal of Popular Film and Television* 10, no. 1 (1982): 2–21.

Rostler, William. *Contemporary Erotic Cinema*. New York: Penthouse/Ballantine, 1973.

Sarris, Andrew. "Reflections on the New Porn." *Village Voice*, September 1, 1975, pp. 71–72.

Slade, Joseph W. "The Porn Market and Porn Formulas: The Feature Film of the Seventies." *Journal of Popular Film* 6, no. 2 (1977): 168–186.

Sontag, Susan. "The Pornographic Imagination." In *Styles of Radical Will*. New York: Delta, 1969.

Turan, Kenneth, and Stephen F. Zito. *Sinema: American Pornographic Films and the People Who Make Them*. New York: New American Library, 1975.

Tyler, Parker. *Screening the Sexes: Homosexuality in the Movies*. New York: Doubleday, 1973.

Vogel, Amos. *Film as a Subversive Art*. New York: Random House, 1974.

Waller, Gregory A. "Auto-Erotica: Some Notes on Comic Softcore Films for the Drive-In Circuit." *Journal of Popular Culture* 17, no. 2 (Fall 1983): 135–141.

Walker, Alexander. *Sex in the Movies*. Baltimore: Penguin, 1968.

Williams, Linda. "Film Body: An Implantation of Perversions." *Ciné-Tracts* 3, no. 4 (Winter 1981): 19–35.

Wortley, Richard. *Erotic Movies*. London: Roxby, 1975.

Youngblood, Gene. "Flamingo Hours." *Take One* 5, no. 10 (July–August 1977): 50–51.

Film Noir

Appel, Alfred. "The End of the Road: Dark Cinema and Lolita." *Film Comment* 10, no. 5 (September–October 1974): 25–31.

Borde, Raymond, and Etienne Chaumeton. *Panorama du film noir américain: 1941–1954*. Paris: Editions d'Aujourd'hui, 1975.

———. "À propos du film noir américain," *Positif* 19 (1956): 52–57.

———. "Vingt ans après: Le Film noir des années 70." *Ecran* 32 (January 1975): 5–8.

Butler, Jeremy G. "Miami Vice: The Legacy of Film Noir." *Journal of Popular Film and Television* 13, no. 3 (Fall 1985): 127–138.

Cohen, Mitchell S. "Villains and Victims." *Film Comment* 10, no. 6 (November–December 1974): 27–29.

Damico, James. "Film Noir: A Modest Proposal." *Film Reader*, no. 3 (1978): 48–57.

Durgnat, Raymond. "The Family Tree of Film Noir." *Film Comment* 10, no. 6 (November–December 1974): 6–7.

———. "Paint It Black: The Family Tree of Film Noir." *Cinema* (U.K.), nos. 6/7 (1970): 49–56.

Dyer, Richard. "Homosexuality and Film Noir." *Jump Cut*, no. 16 (1977): 18–21.

Earley, Steven C. *An Introduction to American Movies*. New York: Mentor, 1978.

Farber, Stephen. "Violence and the Bitch Goddess." *Film Comment* 10, no. 6 (November–December 1974): 8–11.

Film Reader 3, edited by Valentin Almendarez et al. Evanston, Ill.: Northwestern University, 1978.

Flinn, Tom. "*The Big Heat* and *The Big Combo*: Rogue Cops and Mink-Coated Girls." *Velvet Light Trap* 11 (1974): 23–28.

Gross, Larry. "Film après Noir." *Film Comment* 12, no. 4 (July–August 1976): 44–49.

Higham, Charles, and Joel Greenberg. *Hollywood in the Forties*. Cranbury, N.J.: A. S. Barnes, 1968.

Hirsch, Foster. *The Dark Side of the Screen: Film Noir*. San Diego: A. S. Barnes, 1981.

Jameson, Richard T. "Son of Noir." *Film Comment* 10, no. 6 (November–December 1974): 30–33.

Kaplan, E. Ann, ed. *Women in Film Noir*. London: British Film Institute, 1978.

Karimi, A. M. *Toward a Definition of the American Film Noir (1941–1949)*. New York: Arno Press, 1976.

Kerr, Paul. "Out of What Past? Notes on the B Film Noir." *Screen Education*, nos. 32–33 (Autumn–Winter 1979–1980): 45–65.

Krutnik, Frank. "Desire, Transgression and James M. Cain: Fiction into Film Noir." *Screen* 23, no. 1 (1982): 31–44.

Ottoson, Robert. *A Reference Guide to the American Film Noir: 1940–1958*. Metuchen, N.J.: Scarecrow Press, 1981.

Place, J. A., and L. S. Peterson. "Some Visual Motifs of Film Noir." *Film Comment* 10, no. 1 (January–February 1974): 30–32. Reprinted in *Movies and Methods*, edited by Bill Nichols, pp. 325–338. Berkeley: University of California Press, 1976.

Porfirio, Robert G. "No Way Out: Existential Motifs in the Film Noir." *Sight and Sound* 45, no. 4 (Autumn 1976): 212–217.

Ray, Robert B. *A Certain Tendency of the Hollywood Cinema, 1930–1980*. Princeton: Princeton University Press, 1985.

Selby, Spencer. *Dark City: The Film Noir*. Jefferson City, N.C.: McFarland, 1984.

Shadoian, Jack. "Dark Transformations: The Descent into *Noir*." Chap. 2 in *Dreams and Dead Ends: The American Gangster/Crime Film*. Cambridge, Mass.: MIT Press, 1977.

Silver, Alain, and Elizabeth Ward, eds. *Film Noir: An Encyclopedic Reference to the American Style*. Woodstock, N.Y.: Overlook Press, 1979.

Telotte, J. P. "Film Noir and the Dangers of Discourse." *Quarterly Review of Film Studies* 9, no. 2 (Spring 1984): 101–112.

———. "Talk and Trouble: *Kiss Me Deadly*'s Apocalyptic Discourse." *Journal of Popular Film and Television* 13, no. 2 (Summer 1985): 69–79.

Tuska, Jon. *Dark Cinema: American Film Noir in Cultural Perspective*. Westport, Conn.: Greenwood Press, 1984.

Vernet, Marc. "La Transaction filmique." In *Le Cinéma américain: Analyses de films*, vol. 2, edited by Raymond Bellour and Patrick Brion, pp. 122–143. Paris: Flammarion, 1980. Translated as "The Filmic Transaction: On the Openings of Film Noirs," *Velvet Light Trap*, no. 20 (Summer 1983): 2–9.

Whitney, John S. "A Filmography of Film Noir." *Journal of Popular Film* 5, nos. 3–4 (1976): 321–371.

Wood, Michael. "The Intrepidation of Dreams." Chap. 5 in *America in the Movies*. New York: Delta, 1975.

Wood, Nancy. "Women in Film Noir." *Ciné-Tracts* 2, no. 2 (Spring 1979): 74–79.

Gangster Films

Alloway, Lawrence. *Violent America: The Movies, 1946–1964.* New York: Museum of Modern Art, 1971.

Barthes, Roland. "Power and 'Cool.'" In *The Eiffel Tower and Other Mythologies,* translated by Richard Howard, pp. 43–45. New York: Hill and Wang, 1979.

Baxter, John. *The Gangster Film.* New York: A. S. Barnes; London: A. Zwemmer, 1970.

Bergman, Andrew. *We're in the Money.* New York: Harper and Row, 1972.

Douglass, Wayne J. "The Criminal Psychopath as Hollywood Hero." *Journal of Popular Film and Television* 8, no. 4 (Winter 1981): 30–39.

Earley, Steven C. *An Introduction to American Movies.* New York: Mentor, 1978.

Farber, Manny. "The Outlaws." *Sight and Sound* 37, no. 4 (Autumn 1968): 170–176.

Gabree, John. *Gangsters: From Little Caesar to the Godfather.* New York: Galahad Books, 1973.

Geduld, Carolyn, and Harry Geduld. "From Kops to Robbers: Transformation of Archetypal Figures in the American Cinema of the 20's and 30's." *Journal of Popular Culture* 2, no. 2 (1967–1968): 389–394.

Kaminsky, Stuart M. "The Individual Film: *Little Caesar* and the Gangster Film" and "Variations on a Major Genre: The Big Caper Film." Chaps. 2 and 6 in *American Film Genres: Approaches to a Critical Theory of Popular Film.* Dayton, Ohio: Pflaum, 1974.

Karpf, Stephen. *The Gangster Film: Emergence, Variation and Decay of a Genre, 1930–1940.* New York: Arno Press, 1973.

Kinder, Marsha. "The Return of the Outlaw Couple." *Film Quarterly* 27, no. 4 (Summer 1974): 2–10.

Lukow, Gregory, and Steven Ricci. "The 'Audience' Goes 'Public': Intertextuality, Genre, and the Responsibilities of Film Literacy." *On Film,* no. 12 (Spring 1984): 28–36.

McArthur, Colin. *Underworld U.S.A.* New York: Viking, 1972.

Parish, James Robert, and Michael R. Pitts. *The Great Gangster Pictures.* Metuchen, N.J.: Scarecrow Press, 1976.

Peary, Gerald. "Notes on Early Gangster Comedy." *Velvet Light Trap,* no. 3 (Winter 1971–1972): 16–18.

Rosow, Eugene. *Born to Lose: The Gangster Film in America.* New York: Oxford University Press, 1978.

Sacks, Arthur. "An Analysis of the Gangster Movies of the Early Thirties." *Velvet Light Trap,* no. 1 (June 1971): 5–11, 32.

Sarris, Andrew. "Big Funerals: The Hollywood Gangster, 1927–1933." *Film Comment* 13, no. 3 (May–June 1977): 6–9.

Schatz, Thomas. *Hollywood Genres: Formulas, Filmmaking and the Studio System.* New York: Random House, 1981.

Shadoian, Jack. *Dreams and Dead Ends: The American Gangster/Crime Film.* Cambridge, Mass.: MIT Press, 1977.

Silver, Alain, and Elizabeth Ward, eds. *Film Noir: An Encyclopedic Reference to the American Style.* Woodstock, N.Y.: Overlook Press, 1979.

Solomon, Stanley J. *Beyond Formula: American Film Genres.* New York: Harcourt Brace Jovanovich, 1976.

Thompson, David. "Man and the Mean Street." Chap. 6 in *America in the Dark: Hollywood and the Gift of Unreality.* New York: William Morrow, 1977.

Tudor, Andrew. *Image and Influence: Studies in the Sociology of Film.* London: George Allen and Unwin, Ltd., 1974.

Warshow, Robert. "The Gangster as Tragic Hero." In *The Immediate Experience,* pp. 127–133. New York: Atheneum, 1970.

Whitehall, Richard. "Crime, Inc.: A Three-Part Dossier on the American Gangster Film, Part 1: Rackets and Mobs in American Gangster Films." *Films and Filming* 10, no. 4 (January 1964): 7–12.

———. "Crime, Inc.: A Three-Part Dossier on the American Gangster Film, Part 2: G-Men and Gangsters." *Films and Filming* 10, no. 5 (February 1964): 17–22.

———. "Crime, Inc.: A Three-Part Dossier on the American Gangster Film, Part 3: Public Enemies." *Films and Filming* 10, no. 6 (March 1964): 39–44.

———. "Some Thoughts on Fifties Gangster Films." *Velvet Light Trap,* no. 11 (Winter 1974): 17–19.

Horror Films

Brock, Bower. "The Vulgarization of American Demonology." *Esquire* 61 (June 1964): 94–99.

Brustein, Robert. "Reflections on Horror Movies." *Partisan Review* 25, no. 2 (Spring 1958): 288–296.

Butler, Ivan. *Horror in the Cinema.* New York: A. S. Barnes, 1970.

Carroll, Noel. "Nightmare and the Horror Film: The Symbolic Biology of Fantastic Beings." *Film Quarterly* 34, no. 3 (Spring 1981): 16–25.

Cawelti, John G. *Adventure, Mystery and Romance: Formula Stories as Popular Culture.* Chicago: University of Chicago Press, 1976.

Clarens, Carlos. *An Illustrated History of the Horror Film.* New York: Capricorn Books, 1968.

Dadoun, Roger. "Fetishism in the Horror Film." *Enclitic* 1, no. 2 (1979): 39–63.

Daniels, Les. *Living in Fear: A History of Horror in the Mass Media.* New York: Charles Scribner's Sons, 1975.

de Coulteray, George. *Sadism in the Movies,* translated by Steve Hult. New York: Medical Press, 1965.

Derry, Charles. "The Horror of Personality." *Cinéfantastique* 3, no. 3 (Fall 1974): 15–19.

Dickstein, Morris. "The Aesthetics of Fright." *American Film* 5, no. 10 (September 1980): 32–37, 56–59. Reprinted in *Planks of Reason: Essays on the Horror Film,* edited by Barry K. Grant, pp. 65–78. Metuchen, N.J.: Scarecrow Press, 1984.

Dillard, R. H. W. "Even a Man Who Is Pure at Heart: Poetry and Danger in the Horror Film." In *Man and the Movies,* edited by W. R. Robinson, pp. 60–69. Baltimore: Penguin, 1967.

———. *Horror Films.* New York: Monarch Press, 1976.

Douglas, Drake. *Horror.* New York: Macmillan, 1966.

Dyer, Peter John. "All Manner of Fantasies." *Films and Filming* 4, no. 9 (June 1958): 13–15, 34–35.

———. "The Roots of Horror." In *International Film Annual,* no. 3, edited by William Whitebair, pp. 60–69. New York: Taplinger, 1959.

———. "Some Nights of Horror." *Films and Filming* 4, no. 10 (July 1958): 13–15, 34–35.

Earley, Steven C. *An Introduction to American Movies.* New York: Mentor, 1978.

Ebert, Roger. "Why Audiences Aren't Safe Anymore." *American Film* 6, no. 5 (March 1981): 54–56.

Eisner, Lotte. *The Haunted Screen.* Berkeley: University of California Press, 1973.

Ellison, Harlan. "Three Faces of Fear." *Cinema* 3, no. 2 (March 1966): 4–8, 13–14.

Evans, Walter. "Monster Movies and Rites of Initiation." *Journal of Popular Film* 4, no. 2 (1975): 124–142.

———. "Monster Movies: A Sexual Theory." *Journal of Popular Film* 11, no. 4 (Fall 1973): 353–365. Reprinted in *Planks of Reason: Essays on the Horror Film,* edited by Barry K. Grant, pp. 53–64. Metuchen, N.J.: Scarecrow Press, 1984.

Everson, William K. *Classics of the Horror Film.* Secaucus, N.J.: Citadel Press, 1974.

———. "A Family Tree of Monsters." *Film Culture* 1, no. 1 (January 1955): 24–30.

———. "Horror Films." *Films in Review* 5, no. 1 (January 1954): 12–23.

Eyles, Allen, et al. *The House of Horror: The Story of Horror Films.* London: Lorrimer, 1973.

Fell, John L. "Melogenre." *North Dakota Quarterly* 51, no. 3 (Summer 1983): 100–110.

Figenshy, Tom. "Screams of a Summer Night." *Film Comment* 15, no. 5 (September–October 1979): 49–53.

Fisher, David. "The Angel, the Devil and the Space Traveller." *Sight and Sound* 23, no. 3 (January–March 1954): 155–157.

Fox, Julian. "The Golden Age of Terror." 5 pts. *Films and Filming* 22, no. 9 (June 1976): 16–23; no. 10 (July 1976): 18–24; no. 11 (August 1976): 20–24; no. 12 (September 1976): 20–25; 23, no. 1 (October 1976): 18–25.

Frank, Alan. *The Horror Film Handbook.* Totowa, N.J.: Barnes and Noble, 1982.

Frank, Alan G. *Horror Movies: Tales of Terror in the Cinema.* London: Octopus, 1974.

Gifford, Denis. *Movie Monsters.* New York: Dutton, 1967.

————. A *Pictorial History of Horror Movies*. New York: Hamlyn, 1973.

Glut, Donald F. *Classic Movie Monsters*. Metuchen, N.J.: Scarecrow Press, 1978.

————. *The Frankenstein Catalog*. Jefferson City, N.C.: McFarland, 1984.

Grant, Barry K., ed. *Planks of Reason: Essays on the Horror Film*. Metuchen, N.J.: Scarecrow Press, 1984.

Greenburg, Harvey R. *The Movies on Your Mind*. New York: Saturday Review Press/Dutton, 1975.

Halliwell, Leslie. "The Baron, the Count and Their Ghoul Friends." 2 pts. *Films and Filming* 15, no. 9 (June 1969): 13–16; no. 10 (July 1969): 12–16.

Higham, Charles, and Joel Greenberg. *Hollywood in the Forties*. London: Zwemmer; New York: A. S. Barnes, 1968.

Hill, Derek. "Horror." *Sight and Sound* 28, no. 1 (Winter 1958–1959): 6–11.

Huss, Roy, and T. J. Ross, eds. *Focus on the Horror Film*. Englewood Cliffs, N.J.: Prentice-Hall, 1972.

Hutchinson, Tom. *Horror and Fantasy in the Cinema*. London: Studio Vista, 1974.

Kaminsky, Stuart M. "Psychological Considerations: Horror and Science Fiction." Chap. 7 in *American Film Genres: Approaches to a Critical Theory of Popular Film*. Dayton, Ohio: Pflaum, 1974.

Kane, Joe. "Beauties, Beasts and Male Chauvinist Monsters." *Take One* 4, no. 4 (March–April 1973): 8–10.

Kapsis, Robert E. "Dressed to Kill." *American Film* 7, no. 5 (1982): 52–56.

Kennedy, Harlan. "Things That Go Howl in the Id." *Film Comment* 18, no. 2 (1982): 37–39.

King, Stephen. *Danse Macabre*. New York: Everett House, 1981.

Laclos, Michel. *Le Fantastique au cinéma*. Paris: Jean-Jacques Pauvert, 1958.

Lavery, David. "The Horror Film and the Horror of Film." *Film Criticism* 7, no. 1 (Fall 1982): 47–55.

Lazar, Moshe, ed. *The Anxious Subject: Nightmares and Daydreams in Literature and Film*. Malibu: Undena Publications, 1983.

Lee, Walt, ed. *Reference Guide to Fantastic Films: Science Fiction, Fantasy and Horror*. 3 vols. Los Angeles: Chelsea-Lee Books, 1972.

Lenne, Gerard. *Le Cinéma "fantastique" et ses mythologies*. Paris: Editions du Cerf, 1970.

————. "Monster and Victim: Women in the Horror Film." In *Sexual Strategems*, edited by Patricia Erens, pp. 31–40. New York: Horizon Press, 1979.

Lentz, Harris M., III. *Science Fiction, Horror and Fantasy Film and Television Credits*. 2 vols. Jefferson City, N.C.: McFarland, 1983.

Losano, Wayne A. "The Vampire Rises Again in Films of the Seventies." *Film Journal* 2, no. 2 (1973): 60–62.

Lowry, Edward. "Genre and Enunciation: The Case of Horror." *Journal of Film and Video* 36, no. 2 (1984): 13–20, 72.

McCarty, John. *Splatter Movies*. New York: St. Martin's Press, 1984.

McConnell, Frank. "Rough Beasts Slouching: A Note on Horror Movies." *Kenyon Review* 128 (1970): 109–120.

Manchel, Frank. *Terrors of the Screen*. Englewood Cliffs, N.J.: Prentice-Hall, 1970.

Mank, Gregory W. *It's Alive! The Classic Cinema Saga of Frankenstein.* San Diego: A. S. Barnes, 1981.

Modleski, Tania. "The Terror of Pleasure: The Contemporary Horror Film and Postmodern Theory." University of Wisconsin at Milwaukee, Center for 20th Century Studies, Working Paper, no. 8 (Fall 1984).

Monaco, James. "Aaaiieeaaraggh!: Horror Movies." *Sight and Sound* 49, no. 2 (Spring 1980): 80–81.

Naha, Ed. *Horrors from Screen to Scream.* New York: Avon, 1975.

Pendo, Stephen. "Universal's Golden Age of Horror." *Films in Review* 26, no. 3 (March 1975): 155–161.

Peters, Nancy Joyce. "Backyard Bombs and Invisible Rays: Horror Movies on Television." *Cultural Correspondence,* nos. 10–11 (Fall 1979): 39–42.

Pirie, David. *A Heritage of Horror: The English Gothic Cinema, 1946–1972.* London: Gordon Fraser, 1973.

———. *The Vampire Cinema.* New York: Crescent, 1977.

Pitts, Michael R. *Horror Film Stars.* Jefferson, N.C.: McFarland, 1981.

Prawer, S. S. *Caligari's Children: The Film as a Tale of Terror.* New York: Oxford University Press, 1980.

Riccardo, Martin V. *Vampires Unearthed: The Vampire and Dracula Bibliography of Books, Articles, Movies, Records, and Other Material.* New York: Garland, 1983.

Rockett, W. H. "The Door Ajar: Structure and Convention in Horror Films That Would Terrify." *Journal of Popular Film and Television* 10, no. 3 (Fall 1982): 130–136.

———. "Landscape and Manscape: Reflection and Distortion in Horror Films." *Post Script* 3, no. 1 (Fall 1983): 19–34.

Russell, Sharon. "The Witch in Film: Myth and Reality." In *Film Reader 3,* edited by Valentin Almendarez et al., pp. 80–89. Evanston, Ill.: Northwestern University, 1978. Reprinted in *Planks of Reason: Essays on the Horror Film,* edited by Barry K. Grant, pp. 113–125. Metuchen, N.J.: Scarecrow Press, 1984.

Solomon, Stanley J. *Beyond Formula: American Film Genres.* New York: Harcourt Brace Jovanovich, 1976.

Steiger, Brad. *Monsters, Maidens and Mayhem: A Pictorial History of Horror Film Monsters.* New York: Merit, 1965.

Tarratt, Margaret. "Monsters from the Id." 2 pts. *Films and Filming* 17, no. 3 (December 1970): 38–42; no. 4 (January 1971): 40–42. Reprinted in *Film Genre: Theory and Criticism,* edited by Barry K. Grant, pp. 161–181. Metuchen, N.J.: Scarecrow Press, 1977.

Telotte, J. P. "The Doubles of Fantasy and the Space of Desire." *Film Criticism* 7, no. 1 (Fall 1982): 56–68.

———. "Faith and Idolatry in the Horror Film." *Literature/Film Quarterly* 8, no. 3 (1980): 143–155. Reprinted in *Planks of Reason: Essays on the Horror Film,* edited by Barry K. Grant, pp. 21–37. Metuchen, N.J.: Scarecrow Press, 1984.

Tropp, Martin. *Mary Shelley's Monster.* Boston: Houghton Mifflin, 1976.

Tudor, Andrew. *Image and Influence: Studies in the Sociology of Film.* London: George Allen and Unwin, Ltd., 1974.

Twitchell, James B. "*Frankenstein* and the Anatomy of Horror." *Georgia Review* 37, no. 1 (1983): 44−78.

———. "A Psychoanalysis of the Vampire Myth." *American Imago* 37 (1980): 83−92.

Tyler, Parker. "Supernaturalism in the Movies." *Theater Arts* 29, no. 6 (June 1945): 362−369.

Ursini, James, and Alain Silver. *The Vampire Film*. New York: A. S. Barnes; London: Tantivy, 1975.

Welsh, Jim, and John Tibetts. "Visions of Dracula." *American Classic Screen* 5, no. 1 (November−December 1980): 12−16.

White, Dennis L. "The Poetics of Horror: More than Meets the Eye." *Cinema Journal* 10, no. 2 (Spring 1971): 1−18. Reprinted in *Film Genre: Theory and Criticism*, edited by Barry K. Grant, pp. 124−144. Metuchen, N.J.: Scarecrow Press, 1977.

Williams, Linda. "When the Woman Looks." In *Re-Vision: Essays in Feminist Film Criticism*, edited by Mary Ann Doane and Linda Williams, pp. 83−99. Frederick, Md.: University Publications, 1983.

Williams, Tony. "American Cinema in the 70's: Family Horror." *Movie*, nos. 27−28 (1981): 117−126.

Willis, Don. *Horror and Science Fiction Films: A Checklist*. Metuchen, N.J.: Scarecrow Press, 1972.

———. *Horror and Science Fiction Films 2*. Metuchen, N.J.: Scarecrow Press, 1982.

Wood, Robin. "The American Family Comedy: From *Meet Me in St. Louis* to *The Texas Chain Saw Massacre*." *Wide Angle* 3, no. 2 (1979): 5−11.

———. "Beauty Bests the Beast." *American Film* 8, no. 10 (1983): 63−65.

———. "Burying the Undead: The Use and Obsolescence of Count Dracula." *Mosaic* 16, nos. 1−2 (1983): 175−187.

———. "Return of the Repressed." *Film Comment* 14, no. 4 (July−August 1978): 25−32. Reprinted in *Planks of Reason: Essays on the Horror Film*, edited by Barry K. Grant, pp. 164−200. Metuchen, N.J.: Scarecrow Press, 1984.

Wood, Robin, and Richard Lippe, eds. *The American Nightmare: Essays on the Horror Film*. Toronto: Festival of Festivals, 1979.

Zimmerman, Bonnie. "Lesbian Vampires." *Jump Cut*, nos. 24−25 (1981): 23−24. Reprinted in *Planks of Reason: Essays on the Horror Film*, edited by Barry K. Grant, pp. 153−163. Metuchen, N.J.: Scarecrow Press, 1984.

Melodrama

Aspinall, Sue, and Robert Murphy, eds. *Gainsborough Melodrama*. London: British Film Institute, 1983.

Bourget, Jean-Loup. "Romantic Drama of the Forties: An Analysis." *Film Comment* 10, no. 1 (January−February 1974): 46−51.

Creed, Barbara. "The Position of Women in Hollywood Melodrama." *Australian Journal of Screen Theory* 4 (1978): 27−31.

Cunningham, Stuart. "Stock Shock and Schlock." *Enclitic* 5, no. 2/6, no. 1 (Fall 1981/Spring 1982): 166–171.

Durgnat, Raymond. "Ways of Melodrama." *Sight and Sound* 21, no. 1 (August–September 1951): 34–40.

Earley, Steven C. *An Introduction to American Movies.* New York: Mentor, 1978.

Ehrenstein, David. "Melodrama and the New Woman." *Film Comment* 14, no. 5 (September–October 1978): 59–62.

Film Reader 3, ed. Valentin Almendarez et al. Evanston, Ill.: Northwestern University, 1978.

Haskell, Molly. "The Woman's Film." In *From Reverence to Rape: The Treatment of Women in the Movies.* Baltimore: Penguin, 1974.

Kaplan, Ann. "Theories of Melodrama: A Feminist Perspective." *Women and Performance: A Journal of Feminist Theory* 1, no. 1 (1983): 40–48.

Kehr, Dave. "The New Male Melodrama." *American Film* 8, no. 6 (1983): 42–47.

Klinger, Barbara. "'Cinema/Ideology/Criticism' Revisited: The Progressive Text." *Screen* 25, no. 1 (January–February 1984): 30–44.

Kuhn, Annette. "Women's Genres." *Screen* 25, no. 1 (January–February 1984): 18–28.

Lehman, Peter, ed. "Melodrama." *Wide Angle* 4, no. 2 (1980). Special issue.

Lippe, Richard. "Melodrama in the Seventies." *Movie,* nos. 29–30 (1982): 122–127.

Merritt, Russell. "Melodrama: Postmortem for a Phantom Genre." *Wide Angle* 5, no. 3 (1983): 24–31.

Modleski, Tania. "Time and Desire in the Woman's Film." *Cinema Journal* 23, no. 3 (Spring 1984): 19–30.

Morse, David. "Aspects of Melodrama." *Monogram,* no. 4 (1972): 16–17.

Mulvey, Laura. "Douglas Sirk and Melodrama." *Australian Journal of Screen Theory* 3 (1977): 26–30.

———. "Notes on Sirk and Melodrama." *Movie* 25 (Winter 1977/1978): 53–56.

Nowell-Smith, Geoffrey. "Minnelli and Melodrama." *Screen* 18, no. 2 (Summer 1977): 113–118.

Pollock, Griselda, et al. "Dossier on Melodrama." *Screen* 18, no. 2 (Summer 1977): 105–113.

Rodowick, D. N. "Madness, Authority, and Ideology in the Domestic Melodrama of the 1950s." *Velvet Light Trap,* no. 19 (1982): 40–45.

Schatz, Thomas. *Hollywood Genres: Formulas, Filmmaking, and the Studio System.* New York: Random House, 1981.

Seiter, Ellen. "Men, Sex, and Money in Recent Family Melodramas." *Journal of the University Film and Video Association* 35, no. 1 (1983): 17–37.

Thomson, David. "Women's Realm and Man's Castle." Chap. 7 in *America in the Dark: Hollywood and the Gift of Unreality.* New York: William Morrow, 1977.

Viviani, Christian. "Who Is without Sin? The Maternal Melodrama in American Film, 1930–39." *Wide Angle* 4, no. 2 (1980): 4–17.

Waldman, Diane. "'At Last I Can Tell It to Someone!': Feminine Point of View and

Subjectivity in the Gothic Romance Film of the 1940s." *Cinema Journal* 23, no. 2 (Winter 1984): 28–40.

Walker, Michael. "Melodrama and the American Cinema." *Movie*, nos. 29–30 (1982): 2–38.

Williams, Linda. "'Something Else beside a Mother': *Stella Dallas* and the Maternal Melodrama." *Cinema Journal* 24, no. 1 (Fall 1984): 2–27.

Musical Films

Altman, Charles F. "The American Film Musical: Paradigmatic Structure and Mediatory Function." *Wide Angle* 2, no. 2 (1978): 10–17. Reprinted in *Genre: The Musical*, edited by Rick Altman, pp. 197–207. London: Routledge and Kegan Paul, 1980.

Altman, Rick, ed. *Genre: The Musical*. London: Routledge and Kegan Paul, 1980.

Bach, Steven. "The Hollywood Idiom: Give Me That Old Soft Shoe." *Arts Magazine*, no. 42 (December 1967–January 1968): 15–16.

Belton, John. "The Backstage Musical." *Movie*, no. 24 (Spring 1977): 36–43.

Bergman, Andrew. *We're in the Money*. New York: Harper and Row, 1972.

Cohen, Daniel. *Musicals*. Greenwich, Conn.: Bison Books, 1984.

Croce, Arlene. *The Fred Astaire and Ginger Rogers Book*. New York: Vintage Books, 1972.

Cutts, John. "Bye-Bye Musicals." *Films and Filming* 10, no. 2 (November 1963): 42–45.

Delamater, Jerome. *Dance in the Hollywood Musical*. Ann Arbor: UMI Research Press, 1981.

———. "Performing Arts: The Musical." In Stuart Kaminsky, *American Film Genres: Approaches to a Critical Theory of Popular Film*. Dayton, Ohio: Pflaum, 1974.

Domarchi, Jean. "Evolution du film musical." *Cahiers du Cinéma* 9, no. 54 (1955): 34–39.

Dowdy, Andrew. *The Films of the Fifties: The American State of Mind*. New York: Morrow, 1975.

Dyer, Richard. "Entertainment and Utopia." *Movie*, no. 24 (Spring 1977): 36–43. Reprinted in *Genre: The Musical*, edited by Rick Altman, pp. 175–189. London: Routledge and Kegan Paul, 1980.

Earley, Steven C. *An Introduction to American Movies*. New York: Mentor, 1978.

Ehrenstein, David, and Bill Reed. *Rock on Film*. New York: Delilah Books, 1982.

Feuer, Jane. *The Hollywood Musical*. Bloomington: Indiana University Press, 1982.

———. "Hollywood Musicals: Mass Art as Folk Art." *Jump Cut*, no. 23 (1980): 23–25.

Giles, Dennis. "Show-Making." *Movie*, no. 24 (Spring 1977): 14–25. Reprinted in *Genre: The Musical*, edited by Rick Altman, pp. 85–101. London: Routledge and Kegan Paul, 1980.

Godfrey, Lionel. "A Heretic's Look at Musicals." *Films and Filming* 13, no. 6 (March 1967): 5–10.

Green, Stanley. *Encyclopedia of the Musical Film*. New York: Oxford, 1981.

Henderson, Brian. "Musical Comedy of Empire." *Film Quarterly* 35, no. 2 (Winter 1981–1982): 2–16.

Higham, Charles, and Joel Greenberg. *Hollywood in the Forties*. London: Zwemmer; New York: A. S. Barnes, 1968.

Hirschhorn, Clive. *The Hollywood Musical*. New York: Crown, 1981.

Jablonski, Edward. "Filmusicals." *Films in Review* 6, no. 2 (February 1955): 56–69.

Kehr, David. "Can't Stop the Musicals." *American Film* 9, no. 7 (1984): 32–37.

Kobol, John. *Gotta Sing Gotta Dance: A Pictorial History of Film Musicals*. London: Hamlyn, 1972.

Licata, Sal. "From Plymouth Rock to Hollywood in Song and Dance: Yankee Mythology in the Film Musical." *Film and History* 4, no. 1 (February 1974): 1–3.

Lockhart, Freda Bruce. "The Seven Ages of the Musical." In *International Film Annual*, no. 1, edited by Campbell Dixon, pp. 107–115. London: John Calder, 1957.

Marcus, Greil. "Rock Films." In *The Rolling Stone Illustrated History of Rock & Roll*, edited by Jim Miller, pp. 390–400. New York: Random House/Rolling Stone Press, 1980.

Marsh, Dave. "Schlock around the Rock." *Film Comment* 14, no. 4 (July–August 1978): 7–13.

McVay, Douglas. *The Musical Film*. New York: A. S. Barnes, 1967.

Mueller, John. "Fred Astaire and the Integrated Musical." *Cinema Journal* 24, no. 1 (Fall 1984): 28–40.

Mordden, Ethan. *The Hollywood Musical*. New York: St. Martin's Press, 1980.

Newton, Douglas. "Poetry in Fast and Musical Motion." *Sight and Sound* 22, no. 1 (July–September 1952): 35–37.

Pally, Marcia. "Dancing for Their Lives." *Film Comment* 20, no. 6 (November–December 1984): 51–55.

Pantasios, Anastasia J. "Rock Music and Film." *Mise-en-Scène*, no. 1 (n.d.): 42–47.

Patrick, Robert, and William Haislip. "'Thank Heaven for Little Girls': An Examination of the Male Chauvinist Musical." *Cinéaste* 6, no. 1 (1973): 22–25.

Pechter, William S. "Movie Musicals." *Commentary* 53, no. 5 (May 1972): 77–81.

Ray, Robert B. *A Certain Tendency of the Hollywood Cinema, 1930–1980*. Princeton: Princeton University Press, 1985.

Rickey, Carrie. "Let Yourself Go!" *Film Comment* 18, no. 2 (1982): 43–47.

Roth, Mark. "Some Warners Musicals and the Spirit of the New Deal." *Velvet Light Trap*, no. 17 (Winter 1977): 1–7. Reprinted in *Genre: The Musical*, edited by Rick Altman, pp. 57–69. London: Routledge and Kegan Paul, 1980.

Schatz, Thomas. *Hollywood Genres: Formula, Filmmaking and the Studio System*. New York: Random House, 1981.

Scheurer, Timothy E. "The Aesthetics of Form and Convention in the Movie Musical." *Journal of Popular Film* 3, no. 4 (Fall 1974): 307–324. Reprinted in

Film Genre: Theory and Criticism, edited by Barry K. Grant, pp. 145–159. Metuchen, N.J.: Scarecrow Press, 1977.

———. "I'll Sing You a Thousand Love Songs: A Selected Filmography of the Musical Film." *Journal of Popular Film and Television* 8, no. 1 (Spring 1980): 61–67.

Sennett, Ted. *Hollywood Musicals.* New York: Abrams, 1981.

Shout, John D. "The Film Musical and the Legacy of Show Business." *Journal of Popular Film and Television* 10, no. 1 (1982): 23–26.

Sidney, George. "The Three Ages of the Musical." *Films and Filming* 14, no. 9 (June 1986): 4–9.

Solomon, Stanley J. *Beyond Formula: American Film Genres.* New York: Harcourt Brace Jovanovich, 1976.

Speigel, Ellen. "Fred and Ginger Meet Van Nest Polglase." *Velvet Light Trap,* no. 10 (Fall 1973): 17–22.

Springer, John. *All Talking! All Singing! All Dancing! A Pictorial History of the Movie Musical.* New York: Citadel Press, 1966.

Stern, Lee Edward. *The Movie Musical.* New York: Pyramid, 1974.

Taylor, John Russell, and Arthur Jackson. *The Hollywood Musical.* New York: McGraw-Hill, 1971.

Telotte, J. P. "A 'Golddigger' Aesthetic: The Depression Musical." *Post Script* 1, no. 1 (Fall 1981): 18–24.

———. "Ideology and the Kelly-Donen Musicals." *Film Criticism* 8, no. 3 (Spring 1984): 36–46.

———. "The Movie Musical and What We 'Ain't Heard' Yet." *Genre* 14 (1981): 505–520.

———. "Narrative Strategy in the Astaire-Rogers Films." *Journal of Popular Film and Television* 8, no. 3 (Fall 1980): 15–24.

———. "Scorsese's *Last Waltz* and the Concert Genre." *Film Criticism* 4, no.2 (Winter 1980): 9–20.

———. "Self and Society: Vincente Minnelli and Musical Formula." *Journal of Popular Film and Television* 9, no. 4 (1982): 181–193.

———. "A Sober Celebration: Song and Dance in the 'New' Musical." *Journal of Popular Film and Television* 8, no. 1 (Spring 1980): 2–14.

Vaughan, David. "Dance in the Cinema." *Sequence,* no. 6 (Winter 1948–1949): 6–13.

Wiener, Thomas. "The Rise and Fall of the Rock Film." 2 pts. *American Film* 1, no. 2 (November 1975): 25–29; no. 3 (December 1975): 58–63.

Woll, Allen L. *The Hollywood Musical Goes to War.* Chicago: Nelson-Hall, 1983.

———. *Songs from the Hollywood Musical Comedies, 1927 to the Present.* New York: Garland, 1975.

Wood, Michael. "Darkness in the Dance." Chap. 7 in *America in the Movies.* New York: Delta, 1975.

Wood, Robin. "Never Never Change, Always Gonna Dance." *Film Comment* 15, no. 5 (September–October 1979): 29–31.

Science Fiction Films

Amelio, Ralph J., ed. *Hal in the Classroom: Science Fiction Films.* Dayton, Ohio: Pflaum, 1974.

Anderson, Craig. *Science Fiction Films of the Seventies.* Jefferson City, N.C.: McFarland, 1985.

Arnold, Francis. "Cut of This World." *Films and Filming* 9, no. 9 (June 1963): 14–18.

Atkins, Thomas, ed. *Science Fiction Films.* New York: Monarch Press, 1976.

Baxter, John. *Science Fiction in the Cinema.* New York: Paperback Library, 1970.

Benson, Michael. *Vintage Science Fiction Films: The Pioneers, 1896–1949.* Jefferson City, N.C.: McFarland, 1985.

Biskind, Peter. "War of the Worlds." *American Film* 9, no. 3 (1983): 36–42.

Bouyxou, J. P. *La Science Fiction au cinéma.* Paris: Union Génerale d'Editions, 1971.

Brosnan, John. *Future Tense: The Cinema of Science Fiction.* New York: St. Martin's Press, 1978.

Brustein, Robert. "Reflections on Horror Movies." *Partisan Review* 25, no. 2 (Spring 1958): 288–296.

Chappell, Fred. "The Science Fiction Film Image." *Film Journal* 2, no. 3 (1974): 8–13.

Dean, Joan F. "Between *2001* and *Star Wars.*" *Journal of Popular Film and Television* 7, no. 1 (1978): 32–41.

Denne, John D. "Society and the Monster." *December* 9, nos. 2–3 (1967): 180–183.

Dowdy, Andrew. *The Film of the Fifties: The American State of Mind.* New York: Morrow, 1975.

Earley, Steven C. *An Introduction to American Movies.* New York: Mentor, 1978.

Edelson, Edward. *Visions of Tomorrow: Great Science Fiction from the Movies.* New York: Doubleday, 1975.

Evans, Walter. "Monster Movies: A Sexual Theory." *Journal of Popular Film* 3, no. 1 (Winter 1974): 31–38. Reprinted in *Planks of Reason: Essays on the Horror Film,* edited by Barry K. Grant, pp. 53–64. Metuchen, N.J.: Scarecrow Press, 1984.

Frank, Alan. *The Science Fiction and Fantasy Film Handbook.* Totowa, N.J.: Barnes and Noble, 1983.

Franklin, H. Bruce. "Don't Look Where We're Going: Visions of the Future in Science Fiction Films, 1970–82." *Science Fiction Studies,* no. 29 (March 1983): 70–80.

———. "Future Imperfect." *American Film* 8, no. 5 (1983): 46–49, 75–76.

Geduld, Harry M. "Return to Méliès: Reflections on the Science Fiction Film." *The Humanist* 27, no. 6 (November–December 1968): 23–24, 28.

Gifford, Denis. *Movie Monsters.* New York: Dutton, 1969.

———. *Science Fiction Films.* New York: Dutton, 1971.

Glut, Donald F. *Classic Movie Monsters.* Metuchen, N.J.: Scarecrow Press, 1978.

———. *The Frankenstein Catalog.* Jefferson City, N.C.: McFarland, 1984.

Gow, Gordon. "The Non Humans." *Films and Filming* 20, no. 12 (September 1974): 59–62.

Grant, Barry K. "From Film Genre to Film Experience." *Paunch*, nos. 42–43 (December 1975): 123–137.

Greenberg, Harvey R. *The Movies on Your Mind.* New York: Saturday Review Press/Dutton, 1975.

Hardy, Phil. *Science Fiction: The Complete Film Sourcebook.* New York: Morrow, 1984.

Hauser, Frank. "Science Fiction Films." *International Film Annual,* edited by William Whitebait, pp. 87–90. New York: Doubleday, 1958.

Hodgens, Richard. "A Brief and Tragical History of the Science Fiction Film." *Film Quarterly* 13, no. 2 (Winter 1959): 30–39.

Houston, Penelope. "Glimpses of the Moon." *Sight and Sound* 22, no. 2 (April–June 1953): 185–188.

Hurley, Neil P. "A Cinematic Theology of the Future." Chap. 10 in *Towards a Film Humanism.* New York: Delta, 1970.

Huss, Roy, and T. J. Ross, eds. *Focus on the Horror Film.* Englewood Cliffs, N.J.: Prentice-Hall, 1972.

Hutchinson, Tom. *Horror and Fantasy in the Cinema.* London: Studio Vista, 1974.

Johnson, William, ed. *Focus on the Science Fiction Film.* Englewood Cliffs, N.J.: Prentice-Hall, 1972.

Jurkiewicz, Kenneth. "Technology in the Void: Politics and Science in Four Contemporary Space Movies." *New Orleans Review* 9, no. 1 (1982): 16–20.

Kaminsky, Stuart M. "Psychological Considerations: Horror and Science Fiction." Chap. 7 in *American Film Genres: Approaches to a Critical Theory of Popular Film.* Dayton, Ohio: Pflaum, 1974.

Kane, Joe. "Nuclear Films." *Take One* 2, no. 6 (1969): 9–11.

Landrum, Larry. "A Checklist of Materials about Science Fiction Films of the 1950's: A Bibliography." *Journal of Popular Film* 1, no. 1 (Winter 1972): 61–63.

Lee, Walt. *Reference Guide to Fantastic Films: Science Fiction, Fantasy and Horror.* 3 vols. Los Angeles: Chelsea-Lee Books, 1972.

Lenne, Gérard. *Le Cinéma "fantastique" et ses mythologies.* Paris: Editions du Cerf, 1970.

Lentz, Harris M., III. *Science Fiction, Horror and Fantasy Film and Television Credits.* 2 vols. Jefferson City, N.C.: McFarland, 1983.

Menville, Douglas. *A Historical and Critical Survey of the Science Fiction Film.* New York: Arno Press, 1975.

Murphy, Brian. "Monster Movies: They Came from beneath the Fifties." *Journal of Popular Film* 1, no. 1 (Winter 1972): 31–44.

Nagl, Manfred. "The Science Fiction Film in Historical Perspective." *Science Fiction Studies,* no. 31 (November 1983): 262–277.

Naha, Ed. *Horror from Screen to Scream.* New York: Avon, 1975.

Parish, James Robert, and Michael R. Pitts. *The Great Science Fiction Pictures.* Metuchen, N.J.: Scarecrow Press, 1977.

Peary, Danny, ed. *Screen Flights/Screen Fantasies: The Future According to Science Fiction Cinema*. Garden City: Doubleday, 1984.

Rogers, Ivor A. "Extrapolative Cinema." *Arts in Society* 6 (Summer–Fall 1969): 287–291.

Roth, Lane. "The Rejection of Rationalism in Recent Science Fiction Films." *Philosophy in Context* 2 (1981): 42–55.

Rovin, Jeff. *A Pictorial History of Science Fiction Films*. Secaucus, N.J.: Citadel Press, 1975.

Samuel, S. "The Age of Conspiracy and Conformity." *American History/American Film*, edited by J. E. O'Connor and M. Jackson, pp. 203–217. New York: Ungar, 1979.

Siclier, Jacques, and André S. Labarthe. *Images de la science fiction*. Paris: Editions du Cerf, 1958.

Slusser, George E., and Eric S. Rabkin, eds. *Shadows of the Magic Lamp: Fantasy and Science Fiction in Film*. Carbondale: Southern Illinois University Press, 1985.

Sobchack, Vivian C. "The Alien Landscape of the Planet Earth." *Film Journal* 2, no. 3 (1974): 16–21.

———. *The Limits of Infinity: The American Science Fiction Film*. South Brunswick, N.J., and London: Barnes/Yoseloff, 1980.

Solomon, Stanley J. *Beyond Formula: American Film Genres*. New York: Harcourt Brace Jovanovich, 1976.

Sontag, Susan. "The Imagination of Disaster." In *Against Interpretation*, pp. 209–225. New York: Delta, 1966.

Stanbury, C. M. "Monsters in the Movies: A Mythology of the Absurd." *December* 10, no. 1 (1968): 74–76.

Steinbrunner, Chris, and Bert Goldblatt. *Cinema of the Fantastic*. New York: Saturday Review Press, 1972.

Telotte, J. P. "Human Artifice and the Science Fiction Film." *Film Quarterly* 36, no. 3 (Spring 1983): 44–51.

Warren, Bill. *Keep Watching the Skies! American Science Fiction Movies of the Fifties*, vol. 1, *1950–1957*; vol. 2, *1958–1962*. Jefferson, N.C.: McFarland, 1982, 1985.

Wharton, Lewis. "Godzilla to Latitude Zero: The Cycle of the Technological Monster." *Journal of Popular Film* 3, no. 1 (Winter 1974): 31–38.

Williams, Tony. "Close Encounters of the Authoritarian Kind." *Wide Angle* 5, no. 4 (1983): 22–29.

Willis, Don. *Horror and Science Fiction Films: A Checklist*. Metuchen, N.J.: Scarecrow Press, 1972.

———. *Horror and Science Fiction Films II*. Metuchen, N.J.: Scarecrow Press, 1977.

Sports Films

Farber, Manny. "The Fight Films." In *Movies*, pp. 64–67. New York: Stonehill, 1976. Originally published as *Negative Space*. London: Studio Vista, 1971.

Jahiel, Edwin. "The Ring and the Lens: Films on Boxing." *Film Society Review,* September 1966, pp. 26–28.

Sayre, Nora. "'Win This One for the Gipper!' And Other Reasons Why Sports Movies Miss the Point." *Village Voice,* December 1, 1975, pp. 30–32, 35, 37. Reprinted in *Film Genre: Theory and Criticism,* edited by Barry K. Grant, pp. 182–194. Metuchen, N.J.: Scarecrow Press, 1977.

Spears, Jack. "Baseball on the Screen." *Films in Review* 19, no. 4 (April 1968): 198–217.

War Films

Adair, Gilbert. *Hollywood's Vietnam: From "The Green Berets" to "Apocalypse Now."* New York: Proteus, 1981.

Auster, Al, and Leonard Quart. "Hollywood and Vietnam: The Triumph of the Will." *Cineaste* 9, no. 3 (Spring 1979): 4–9.

Belmans, Jacques. "Cinema and Man at War." *Film Society Review* 7, no. 6 (February 1972): 22–37.

Boehringer, Kathe. "Banality Now." *Australian Journal of Screen Theory,* no. 8 (1980): 89–95.

Butler, Ivan. *The War Film.* New York: A. S. Barnes, 1974.

Deming, Barbara. *Running Away from Myself.* New York: Grossman, 1969.

Dick, Bernard F. *The Star-Spangled Screen: The American World War Two Film.* Lexington: University Press of Kentucky, 1985.

Dowling, John. "Nuclear War and Disarmament—Selected Film/Video List." *Sightlines* 15, no. 3 (1982): 19–21.

Dworkin, Martin S. "Clean Germans and Dirty Politics." *Film Comment* 3, no. 1 (Winter 1965): 36–41.

Earley, Steven C. *An Introduction to American Movies.* New York: Mentor, 1978.

Fyne, Robert. "The Unsung Heroes of World War II." *Literature/Film Quarterly* 7, no. 2 (1979): 148–154.

Gillett, John. "Westfront 1957." *Sight and Sound* 27, no. 3 (Winter 1957–1958): 122–127.

Grossman, Edward. "Bloody Popcorn." *Harper's,* December 1970, pp. 32–40.

Guy, Rory. "Hollywood Goes to War." *Cinema* (U.S.) 3, no. 2 (March 1966): 22–29.

Higham, Charles, and Joel Greenberg. *Hollywood in the Forties.* London: Zwemmer; New York: Barnes, 1968.

Hughes, Robert, ed. *Film, Book 2: Films of Peace and War.* New York: Grove Press, 1962.

Isaacs, Hermine Rich. "Shadows of War on the Silver Screen." *Theatre Arts* 26, no. 11 (November 1942): 689–696.

Isenberg, Michael T. "An Ambiguous Pacifism: A Retrospective on World War I Films, 1930–38." *Journal of Popular Film* 4 (1975): 98–115.

———. *War on Film: The American Cinema and World War I.* Rutherford, N.J.: Fairleigh Dickenson University Press, 1981.

Jacobs, Lewis. "World War II and the American Film." *Cinema Journal* 7 (Winter

1967–1968): 1–21. Reprinted in *Film Culture,* no. 47 (Summer 1969): 28–42.

Jeavons, Clyde. *A Pictorial History of War Films.* Secaucus, N.J.: Citadel Press, 1974.

———. "Why They Fought." *The Movie* (U.K.), no. 22 (1980): 438–440.

Jones, Dorothy B. "War Films Made in Hollywood, 1942–1944." *Hollywood Quarterly* 1, no. 1 (October 1945): 1–19.

Jones, Ken D., and Arthur F. McClure. *Hollywood at War: The American Motion Picture and World War II.* New York: A. S. Barnes; London: Thomas Yoseloff, 1973.

Kagan, Norman. *The War Film.* New York: Pyramid, 1974.

Kane, Kathryn. *Visions of War: The Hollywood Combat Films of WW II.* Ann Arbor: UMI Research Press, 1982.

King, Larry. "The Battle of Popcorn Bay." *Harper's,* May 1967, pp. 50–54.

Kozloff, Max, William Johnson, and Richard Corliss. "Shooting at Wars: Three Views." *Film Quarterly* 21, no. 2 (Winter 1967–68): 27–36.

Kuiper, John B. "Civil War Films: A Quantitative Description of a Genre." *Journal of the Society of Cinematologists* 5 (1965): 81–89.

Landrum, Larry M., and Christine Eynon. "World War II in the Movies: A Selected Bibliography of Sources." *Journal of Popular Film* 1, no. 2 (Spring 1972): 147–153.

Lewis, Leon, and William David Sherman. "War Movies." In *The Landscape of Contemporary Cinema,* pp. 49–55. Buffalo: Buffalo Spectrum Press, 1967.

Lingeman, Richard R. "Will This Picture Help Win the War?" In *Don't You Know There's a War On? The American Home Front, 1941–1945.* New York: Putnam, 1970.

Lundquist, Arthur Joseph. "Only a Push-Button Away." *Midnight Marquee,* no. 30 (Fall 1981): 10–13.

McClure, Arthur F. "Hollywood at War: The American Motion Picture and World War II, 1939–1945." *Journal of Popular Film* 1, no. 2 (Spring 1972): 123–135.

Madsen, Alex. "Vietnam and the Movies." *Cinema* (U.S.) 4, no. 1 (Spring 1968): 10–13.

Manchel, Frank. "A Representative Genre of the Film." Chap. 2 in *Film Study: A Resource Guide.* Rutherford, N.J.: Fairleigh Dickinson University Press, 1973.

Mann, Klauss. "What's Wrong with Anti-Nazi Films?" *Decision* 2, no. 2 (August 1941): 27–35.

Manville, Roger. *Films and the Second World War.* New York: Delta, 1976.

Mariani, John. "Let's Not Be Beastly to the Nazis." *Film Comment* 15, no. 1 (January–February 1979): 49–53.

Mast, Gerald, ed. "The War Abroad, a War at Home (1941–1952)." Part 6 in *The Movies in Our Midst.* Chicago: University of Chicago Press, 1982.

Morella, Joe, et al. *The Films of World War II.* Secaucus, N.J.: Citadel Press, 1975.

Parish, Robert. "The Battle of Midway." *The Movie* (U.K.), no. 22 (1980): 430–431.

Pym, John. "A Bullet in the Head: Vietnam Remembered." *Sight and Sound* 48, no. 2 (Spring 1979): 82–83, 115.

Ray, Robert B. *A Certain Tendency of the Hollywood Cinema, 1930–1980.* Princeton: Princeton University Press, 1985.

Rubin, Steven Jay. *Combat Films: American Realism, 1945–1970.* Jefferson, N.C.: McFarland, 1981.

Skogsberg, Bertil. *Wings on the Screen: A Pictorial History of Air Movies.* San Diego: A. S. Barnes, 1981.

Smith, Julian. *Looking Away: Hollywood and Vietnam.* New York: Charles Scribner's Sons, 1975.

Soderbergh, Peter A. *"Aux Armes!* The Rise of the Hollywood War Film, 1916–1930." *South Atlantic Quarterly* 65, no. 4 (Autumn 1966): 509–522.

Solomon, Stanley J. *Beyond Formula: American Film Genres.* New York: Harcourt Brace Jovanovich, 1976.

Spears, Jack. "World War I on the Screen." 2 pts. *Films in Review* 17, no. 5 (May 1966): 274–292; no. 6 (June–July 1966): 347–365.

———. *The Civil War on the Screen and Other Essays.* South Brunswick, N.J., and London: Barnes/Yoseloff, 1972.

Suid, Lawrence. *Guts and Glory: Great American War Movies.* Reading, Mass.: Addison-Wesley, 1978.

———. "Hollywood and Vietnam." *Film Comment* 15, no. 5 (September–October 1979): 20–25.

———. "The Pentagon and Hollywood." In *American History/American Film,* edited by J. E. O'Connor and M. Jackson, pp. 219–236. New York: Ungar, 1979.

Tyler, Parker. "The Waxworks of War." In *Magic and Myth in the Movies,* pp. 132–147. New York: Simon and Schuster, 1947.

Whitehall, Richard. "One . . . Two . . . Three." *Films and Filming* 10, no. 11 (August 1964): 7–12.

Zinser, William. *Seen Any Good Movies Lately?* Chap. 13. New York: Doubleday, 1958.

Western Films

Adams, Lee, and Buck Rainey. *Shoot 'Em Up: The Complete Reference Guide to Westerns of the Sound Era.* New Rochelle, N.Y.: Arlington House, 1978.

Agel, Henri, ed. *The Western. Etudes Cinématographiques* 12–13, vol. 2. Paris: Lettres Modernes, 1961.

Alloway, Lawrence. *Violent America: The Movies, 1946–1964.* New York: Museum of Modern Art, 1971.

Amelio, Ralph J. "Bonanzaland Revisited: Reality and Myth in the Western Film." *See* 4, no. 1 (1970): 24–28.

Anderson, Robert. "The Role of the Western Film Genre in Industry Competition, 1907–1911." *Journal of the University Film Association* 31, no. 2 (Spring 1979): 19–26.

Armes, Roy. "The Western as a Film Genre." In *Film and Reality*. Baltimore: Penguin, 1975.

Austen, David. "Continental Westerns." *Films and Filming* 17, no. 10 (July 1971): 36–42.

Baker, Bob, et al. "ABC of the Western." *Kinema*, no. 3 (August 1971): 20–34.

Bataille, Gretchen M., and Charles L. P. Silet. "Bibliography: Additions to the Indian in American Film." *Journal of Popular Film and Television* 8, no. 1 (Spring 1980): 50–53.

———. "A Checklist of Published Materials on Popular Images of the Indian in American Film." *Journal of Popular Film* 5 (1976): 171–182.

———. *The Pretend Indians: Images of Native Americans in the Movies*. Ames: University of Iowa Press, 1980.

Bazin, André. "The Western, or the American Film *par excellence*," and "The Evolution of the Western." In *What Is Cinema?* 2: 140–148, 149–157. Berkeley: University of California Press, 1971.

Beale, L. "The American Way West." *Films and Filming* 28, no. 7 (April 1972): 24–30.

Bellour, Raymond, and Patrick Brion, eds. *Le Western: Sources, thèmes, mythologies, auteurs, acteurs, filmographies*. Paris: Union General d'Editions, 1966.

Blount, Trevor. "Violence in the Western." *Kinema*, no. 3 (August 1971): 14–19.

Bluestone, George. "The Changing Cowboy: From Dime Novel to Dollar Film." *Western Humanities Review* 14 (Summer 1960): 331–337.

Blumenberg, Richard. "The Evolution and Shape of the American Western." *Wide Angle* 1, no. 1 (Spring 1976): 39–49.

Boatright, Mody C. "The Formula in Cowboy Fiction and Drama." *Western Folklore* 28, no. 2 (April 1969): 136–145.

Brauer, Ralph. "Who Are Those Guys? The Movie Western during the TV Era." *Journal of Popular Film* 2, no. 4 (Fall 1973): 389–404.

Brauer, Ralph, and Donna Brauer. *The Horse, the Gun, and the Piece of Property: Changing Images of the TV Western*. Bowling Green: Bowling Green University Popular Press, 1975.

Buscombe, Edward. "Painting the Legend: Frederic Remington and the Western." *Cinema Journal* 23, no. 4 (Summer 1984): 12–27.

Calder, Jenni. *There Must Be a Lone Ranger*. London: Hamish Hamilton, 1974.

Cawelti, John G. *Adventure, Mystery and Romance: Formula Stories as Art and Popular Culture*. Chicago: University of Chicago Press, 1976.

———. "Cowboys, Indians, Outlaws: The West in Myth and Fantasy." *American West* 1 (Spring 1964): 28–35, 77–79.

———. "The Gunfighter and Society: Good Guys, Bad Guys, Deviates, and Compulsives—A View of the Adult Western." *American West* 5, no. 2 (March 1968): 30–35, 76–78.

———. "Prolegomena to the Western." *Studies in Public Communication*, no. 4 (Autumn 1962): 57–70.

———. "Reflections on the New Western Films." *University of Chicago Magazine*, January–February 1973, pp. 25–32.

————. *The Six-Gun Mystique*. Bowling Green, Ohio: Bowling Green University Popular Press, [1970]. Rev. ed., 1985.

————. "Zane Grey and W. S. Hart: The Romantic Western of the 1920's." *Velvet Light Trap*, no. 12 (Spring 1974): 6–10.

Clapham, Walter C. *Western Movies*. London: Octopus, 1974.

Collins, Richard. "Genre: A Reply to Ed Buscombe." *Screen* 11, nos. 4–5 (August–September 1970): 66–75.

Cowie, Peter. "The Growth of the Western." In *International Film Guide, 1966*, edited by Peter Cowie, pp. 39–43. London: Tantivy; New York: Barnes, 1966.

Durer, C. S., et al., eds. *American Renaissance and American West*, Part 4. Laramie: University of Wyoming, 1982.

Durgnat, Raymond, and Scott Simmon. "Six Creeds That Won the West." *Film Comment* 16, no. 5 (September–October 1980): 61–70.

Earley, Steven C. *An Introduction to American Movies*. New York: Mentor, 1978.

Elkin, Frederick. "The Psychological Appeal of the Hollywood Western." *Journal of Educational Sociology* 24, no. 2 (October 1950): 72–86.

Essleman, Kathryn C. "When the Cowboy Stopped Kissing His Horse." *Journal of Popular Culture* 6, no. 2 (Fall 1972): 337–349.

Etulain, Richard W., and Michael T. Marsden, eds. "The Popular Western." *Journal of Popular Culture* 7, no. 3 (Winter 1973): 645–751.

Everson, William K. *A Pictorial History of the Western Film*. New York: Citadel Press, 1967.

Eyles, Allen. *The Western: An Illustrated Guide*. New York: A. S. Barnes, 1967.

Fenin, George N. "The Western—Old and New." *Film Culture* 2, no. 2 (1956): 7–10.

————, and William K. Everson. *The Western from Silents to Cinerama*. New York: Orion Press, 1962.

————. *The Western: From Silents to the Seventies*. New York: Bonanza Books, 1973.

Fiedler, Leslie A. *The Return of the Vanishing American*. New York: Stein and Day, 1960.

Folsom, James K. "'Western' Themes and Western Films." *Western American Literature* 2, no. 3 (Fall 1967): 195–203.

Ford, Charles. *Histoire du western*. Paris: Editions Pierre Horay, 1964.

Franklin, Eliza. "Westerns, First and Lasting." *Quarterly of Film, Television and Radio* 7, no. 2 (Winter 1952): 109–115.

Frayling, Christopher. *Spaghetti Westerns*. London: Routledge and Kegan Paul, 1981.

French, Philip. "The Indian in the Western Movie." *Arts in America* 60, no. 4 (July–August 1972): 32–39.

————. *Westerns*. New York: Viking, 1974.

Friar, Ralph, and Natasha Friar. *The Only Good Indian . . . : The Hollywood Gospel*. New York: Drama Book Specialists, 1972.

Garfield, Brian. *Western Films: A Complete Guide*. New York: Rawson Associates, 1982.

Godfrey, Lionel. "A Heretic's View of Westerns." *Films and Filming* 13, no. 8 (May 1967): 14–20.

Hardy, Phil. *The Western.* New York: Morrow, 1983.

Homans, Peter. "Puritanism Revisited: An Analysis of the Contemporary Screen-Image Western." *Studies in Public Communication,* no. 3 (Summer 1961): 73–84.

Horwitz, James. *They Went Thataway.* New York: Dutton, 1976.

Jones, Daryl E. "The Earliest Western Films." *Journal of Popular Film and Television* 8, no. 2 (1980): 42–46.

Kaminsky, Stuart M. "Comparative Forms: The Samurai Film and the Western" and "The Genre Director: Character Types in the Films of John Ford." Chaps. 3 and 11 in *American Film Genres: Approaches to a Critical Theory of Popular Film.* Dayton, Ohio: Pflaum, 1974.

———. "Once Upon a Time in Italy: The Italian Western beyond Leone." *Velvet Light Trap,* no. 12 (Spring 1974): 31–33. Reprinted in *Graphic Violence on the Screen,* edited by Thomas R. Atkins, pp. 47–67. New York: Monarch Press, 1976.

Kitchen, Lawrence. "Decline of the Western." *The Listener* 14 (July 1966): 54–57.

Kitses, Jim. *Horizons West.* Bloomington and London: Indiana University Press, 1970.

Knies, Donald V. "The Aging Hero in the Changing West." *West Virginia University Philological Papers* 26 (August 1980): 66–73.

Larkins, Robert. "Hollywood and the Indian." *Focus on Film,* no. 2 (March–April 1970): 44–53.

Lenihan, John H. *Showdown: Confronting Modern America in the Western Film.* Chicago: University of Chicago Press, 1980.

Lovell, Alan. "The Western." *Screen Education,* no. 41 (September–October 1967): 92–103.

MacArthur, Colin. "The Roots of the Western." *Cinema* (U.K.), no. 4 (October 1969): 11–13.

McMurtry, Larry. "Cowboys, Movies, Myths, and Cadillacs: Realism in the Western." In *Man and the Movies,* edited by W. R. Robinson. Baltimore: Penguin, 1967.

Markfield, Wallace. "The Inauthentic Western." *American Mercury* 75 (September 1952): 82–86.

Maynard, Richard A., ed. *The American West on Film: Myth and Reality.* Rochelle Park, N.J.: Hayden Book Co., 1974.

Mitchell, Charles Reed, and Frank Scheide. "The Reformation of the Good Badman." *Velvet Light Trap,* no. 12 (Spring 1974): 11–14.

Nachbar, Jack. "A Checklist of Published Materials on Western Movies." *Journal of Popular Film* 2, no. 4 (Fall 1973): 411–428.

———, ed. *Focus on the Western.* Englewood Cliffs, N.J.: Prentice-Hall, 1974.

———. "Seventy Years on the Trail: A Selected Chronology of the Western Movie." *Journal of Popular Film* 2, no. 1 (Winter 1973): 75–83.

————. *Western Films: An Annotated Critical Bibliography.* New York: Garland Publishing Co., 1975.

Nussbaum, Martin. "Sociological Symbolism of the 'Adult Western.'" *Social Forces* 39, no. 1 (October 1960): 25–28.

O'Connor, John E. *The Hollywood Indian: Stereotypes of Native Americans in Films.* Trenton: New Jersey State Museum, 1980.

Palmer, R. Barton. "A Masculinist Reading of Two Western Films: *High Noon* and *Rio Grande.*" *Journal of Popular Film and Television* 12, no. 4 (Winter 1984–1985): 156–162.

Parish, James Robert, and Michael R. Pitts. *The Great Western Pictures.* Metuchen, N.J.: Scarecrow Press, 1976.

Park, William. "The Losing of the West." *Velvet Light Trap,* no. 12 (Spring 1974): 2–5.

Parkinson, Michael, and Clyde Jeavons. *A Pictorial History of Westerns.* London: Hamlyn, 1972.

Parks, Rita. *The Western Hero in Film and Television: Mass Media Mythology.* Ann Arbor: UMI Research Press, 1982.

Peary, Gerald. "Selected Sound Westerns and Their Novel Sources." *Velvet Light Trap,* no. 12 (Spring 1974): 11–14.

Pilkington, William T., and Don Graham, eds. *Western Movies.* Albuquerque: University of New Mexico Press, 1979.

Podheiser, Linda. "Pep on the Range or Douglas Fairbanks and the World War I Era Western." *Journal of Popular Film and Television* 11, no. 3 (Fall 1983): 122–130.

Pye, Douglas. "Genre and Movies." *Movie,* no. 20 (Spring 1975): 29–43.

————. "Genre and History: *Fort Apache* and *The Man Who Shot Liberty Valance.*" *Movie* 25 (Winter 1977–1978): 1–11.

Rainey, Buck. *Saddle Aces of the Cinema.* San Diego: A. S. Barnes, 1980.

Ray, Robert B. *A Certain Tendency of the Hollywood Cinema, 1930–1980.* Princeton: Princeton University Press, 1985.

Rieupeyrout, Jean Louis. "The Western: A Historical Genre." *Quarterly of Film, Radio and Television* 7, no. 2 (1952): 116–128.

————. *Le Western, ou le cinéma américain par excellence.* Paris: Editions du Cerf, 1953.

Ross, T. J. "Fantasy and Form in the Western: From Hart to Peckinpah." *December* 12, no. 1 (Fall 1970): 158–169.

Rothel, David. *The Singing Cowboys.* South Brunswick, N.J., and New York: A. S. Barnes, 1978.

Ryall, Tom. "The Notion of Genre." *Screen* 11, no. 2 (March–April 1970): 22–32.

Sarf, Wayne Michael. *God Bless You, Buffalo Bill: A Layman's Guide to History and the Western Film.* Rutherford, N.J.: Fairleigh Dickinson University Press, 1983.

Sarris, Andrew. "Death of the Gunfighters." *Film Comment* 18, no. 2 (1982): 40–42.

Schatz, Thomas. *Hollywood Genres: Formulas, Filmmaking and the Studio System*. New York: Random House, 1981.

Schein, Harry. "The Olympian Cowboy." *American Scholar* 24 (Summer 1955): 309–320.

Self, Robert T. "Ritual Patterns in Western Film and Fiction." In *Narrative Strategies: Original Essays in Film and Prose Fiction*, edited by Syndy M. Conger and Janice R. Welsch, pp. 105–114. Macombe: Western Illinois University Press, 1980.

Silet, Charles L. P., and Gretchen M. Bataille. "The Indian in the Film: A Critical Survey." *Quarterly Review of Film Studies* 2 (February 1977): 56–74.

Smith, Henry Nash. *Virgin Land: The American West as Symbol and Myth*. New York: Vintage, 1950.

Solomon, Stanley J. *Beyond Formula: American Film Genres*. New York: Harcourt Brace Jovanovich, 1976.

Spears, Jack. "The Indian on the Screen." *Films in Review* 10 (January 1959): 18–35.

Staig, Lawrence, and Tony Williams. *Italian Westerns: The Opera of Violence*. London: Lorrimer, 1975.

Tatum, Stephen. "The Western Film Critic as 'Shootist.'" *Journal of Popular Film and Television* 11, no. 3 (Fall 1983): 114–121.

Tudor, Andrew. *Image and Influence: Studies in the Sociology of Film*. London: George Allen and Unwin, 1974.

Tuska, Jon, and Nicki Pierarski. *The Frontier Experience: A Reader's Guide to the Life and Literature of the American West*. Jefferson, N.C.: McFarland, 1984.

Vallance, Tom (also credited to Eric Warman). *Westerns: A Preview Special*. London: Golden Pleasure Books, 1964.

Wallington, Mike. "The Italian Western: A Concordance." *Cinema* (U.K.), nos. 6–7 (August 1970): 31–34.

Warshow, Robert. "Movie Chronicle: The Westerner." In *The Immediate Experience*, pp. 35–54. New York: Atheneum, 1971.

Willett, Ralph. "The American Western: Myth and Anti-Myth." *Journal of Popular Culture* 4, no. 2 (Fall 1970): 455–463.

Williams, John. "The 'Western': Definition of the Myth." In *The Popular Arts: A Critical Reader*, edited by Irving and Harriet A. Deer, pp. 98–111. New York: Scribner's, 1967.

Wright, Will. *Sixguns and Society: A Structural Study of the Western*. Berkeley: University of California Press, 1976.

Miscellaneous

Anderson, J. L. "Japanese Swordfighters and American Gunfighters." *Cinema Journal* 12, no. 2 (Spring 1973): 1–21.

Cawelti, John G. *Adventure, Mystery and Romance: Formula Stories as Art and Popular Culture*. Chicago: University of Chicago Press, 1976.

Cheatwood, Derral. "The Tarzan Films: An Analysis of Determinants of Maintenance and Change in Conventions." *Journal of Popular Culture* 16, no. 2 (Fall 1982): 143–153.

Cripps, Thomas. *Black Film as Genre*. Bloomington and London: Indiana University Press, 1979.

Crozier, Ralph C. "Beyond East and West: The American Western and the Rise of the Chinese Swordplay Movie." *Journal of Popular Film* 1, no. 3 (Summer 1972): 229–243.

Davis, John. "Warner's Genres of the 30's and 40's." *Velvet Light Trap*, no. 15 (Fall 1975): 56–60.

Desser, David. "Toward a Structural Analysis of the Postwar Samurai Film." *Quarterly Review of Film Studies* 8, no. 1 (Winter 1983): 25–41.

Dorfman, Richard. "Conspiracy City" (on paranoia films). *Journal of Popular Film and Television* 7, no. 4 (1980): 434–456.

Durgnat, Raymond. "Genre: Populism and Social Realism." *Film Comment* 11, no. 4 (July–August 1975): 20–29, 63.

Flanigan, B. P. "Kung Fu Krazy, or the Invasion of the 'Chop Suey Easterners.'" *Cinéaste* 7, no. 3 (n.d.): 8–11.

Genelli, Tom, and Lyn Davis. "Between Two Worlds: Some Thoughts beyond the 'Film Blanc.'" *Journal of Popular Film and Television* 12, no. 3 (Fall 1984): 100–111.

Goodwin, Michael. "Velvet Vampires and Hot Mamas: Why Exploitation Films Get to Us." *Village Voice*, July 7, 1975, pp. 65–67.

Horton, Andrew. "Hot Car Films and Cool Individualism." *Cinéaste* 8, no. 4 (Summer 1978): 12–15.

Kaminsky, Stuart M. "Kung Fu as Ghetto Myth." *Journal of Popular Film* 3, no. 2 (Spring 1974): 129–138. Reprinted in *Graphic Violence on the Screen*, edited by Thomas R. Atkins, pp. 57–67. New York: Monarch Press, 1976.

Marsden, Michael T., John G. Nachbar, and Sam L. Grogg, eds. *Movies as Artifacts: Cultural Criticism of Popular Film*. Chicago: Nelson-Hall, 1982.

Mayer, Geoff. "Formula and Genre, Myths and Patterns" (on prison films). *Australian Journal of Screen Theory* 4 (1978): 59–65.

Meyers, Richard. *For One Week Only: The World of Exploitation Films*. Piscataway, N.J.: New Century Publishers, 1983.

O'Connor, John E., and Martin Jackson, eds. *American History/American Film: Interpreting the Hollywood Image*. New York: Ungar, 1979.

Palmer, James W., and Michael M. Riley. "America's Conspiracy Syndrome: From Capra to Pakula." *Studies in the Humanities* 8, no. 2 (1981): 21–27.

Querry, Ronald B. "Prison Movies: An Annotated Filmography, 1921–Present." *Journal of Popular Film* 2, no. 2 (Spring 1973): 181–197.

Ransom, James. "Beach Blanket Babies." *Esquire* 64, no. 1 (July 1965): 90–94, 108.

Reimer, Robert C. "Nazi-Retro Films: Experiencing the Mistakes of the Ordinary Citizen." *Journal of Popular Film and Television* 12, no. 3 (Fall 1984): 112–117.

Richie, Donald. *Japanese Cinema: Film Style and National Character*. New York: Doubleday, 1971.

Sing-hon, Lau, ed. *A Study of the Hong Kong Swordplay Film (1945–1980)*. Hong Kong: Urban Council, 1981.

Staehling, Richard. "From *Rock around the Clock* to *The Trip*: The Truth about Teen Movies." In *Kings of the B's,* edited by Todd McCarthy and Charles Flynn, pp. 220–251. New York: Dutton, 1975.

Thrower, Rayner. *The Pirate Picture*. Totowa, N.J.: Barnes and Noble, 1980.

Valenti, Peter L. "The Film Blanc: Suggestions for a Variety of Fantasy, 1940–1945." *Journal of Popular Film* 6, no. 4 (1978): 295–303.

Wead, George. "Toward a Definition of Filmnoia." *Velvet Light Trap*, no. 13 (Fall 1974): 2–6.

White, Armond. "Kidpix." *Film Comment* 21, no. 4 (August 1985): 9–15.

Notes on Contributors

ANDREW TUDOR has taught sociology at the University of Essex and York in England. He is the author of *Theories of Film* (1973) and *Image and Influence: Studies in the Sociology of Film* (1974).

EDWARD BUSCOMBE is general editor in the Publishing Department of the British Film Institute. He has written widely on film and television in such journals as *Screen, Cinema Journal, Film Reader*, and *Quarterly Review of Film Studies*.

RICK ALTMAN is Associate Professor of Film, French, and Comparative Literature at the University of Iowa. He has published numerous articles on film and is the editor of *Cinema/Sound* (1980) and *Genre: The Musical* (1981).

JUDITH HESS WRIGHT has taught literature, film, and folklore at Sonoma State University in California and is currently Professor of Marketing in the School of Business there. She has published two books on computer selection.

JEAN-LOUP BOURGET has published several books on American film, the most recent being a genre study of the romantic drama, *Le Mélodrame Hollywoodien* (1985). From 1973 to 1981 he was French cultural attaché in London, Chicago, New York, and Barcelona. At present he teaches English and film at the University of Toulouse.

ROBIN WOOD is a prolific writer of film criticism. His early work was classically auteurist: *Hitchcock's Films* (1965), *Howard Hawks* (1968), *Ingmar Bergman* (1969), and *Claude Chabrol* (with Michael Walker, 1970). During the seventies his work became increasingly politicized, as in *Personal Views* (1976). Currently he teaches film at Atkinson College, York University, Toronto, and his latest book is *Hollywood from Vietnam to Reagan* (1985).

BARBARA KLINGER teaches film in the comparative literature program at Indiana University at Bloomington. She has published previously in *Screen, Camera Obscura*, and *Wide Angle*.

THOMAS SCHATZ teaches film at the University of Texas at Austin. He is the author of *Hollywood Genres: Formulas, Filmmaking, and the Studio System* (1981).

THOMAS SOBCHACK is Associate Professor of English and Film at the University of Utah. He is the co-author (with Vivian C. Sobchack) of *An Introduction to Film* (1980) and has published in such journals as *Literature/Film Quarterly* and *Journal of Popular Film and Television*.

RICHARD DE CORDOVA teaches film and television studies at DePaul University in Chicago. His work has appeared in *Ciné-tracts, Quarterly Review of Film Studies, Wide Angle,* and *Planks of Reason: Essays on the Horror Film* (1984).

DOUGLAS PYE teaches film studies at Bulmershe College of Higher Education in Earley Reading, England, where he is currently Principal Lecturer in Film Studies, Head of the Division of Film and Drama, and course leader of the B.A. major in film and drama. He is a member of the editorial board of *Movie.*

EDWARD MITCHELL has taught English at the University of Ohio in Athens, Ohio. He is currently district agent for Northwestern Mutual Life Insurance in Illinois.

PAUL SCHRADER is the former editor of *Cinema* (U.S.) and the author of *Transcendental Style in Film: Ozu, Bresson, Dreyer* (1972). He is also a noted screenwriter (*The Yakuza,* 1974; *Taxi Driver,* 1976; *Rolling Thunder,* 1977) and director (*Blue Collar,* 1978; *Hard Core,* 1980; *American Gigolo,* 1980; *Cat People,* 1982; *Mishima,* 1985).

JOHN G. CAWELTI is Professor of English at the University of Kentucky at Lexington. A noted scholar of popular culture and film, he is the author of *Apostles of the Self-Made Man* (1968), *The Six-Gun Mystique* (1970, rev. ed. 1985), and *Adventure, Mystery and Romance: Formula Stories in Art and Popular Culture* (1976).

TAG GALLAGHER is the author of *John Ford: The Man and His Films* and numerous articles on film. He is currently preparing a biographical study of Roberto Rossellini.

MAURICE YACOWAR is Professor of Film and Dean of Humanities at Brock University, St. Catharines, Ontario. He is the author of *Hitchcock's British Films* (1977), *Tennessee Williams and Film* (1977), *Loser Take All: The Comic Art of Woody Allen* (1979), and *Method in Madness: The Comic Art of Mel Brooks* (1981).

BRUCE KAWIN is Professor of English and Film Studies at the University of Colorado at Boulder. His books include *Telling It Again and Again: Repetition in Literature and Film* (1972), *Faulkner and Film* (1977), *Mindscreen: Bergman, Godard and First-Person Film* (1978), *The Mind of the Novel: Reflexive Fiction and the Ineffable* (1982), and *Faulkner's MGM Screenplays* (1982).

MARGARET TARRATT has served on the lecture panel of the British Film Institute. Her essay on Luchino Visconti's *The Damned* appeared in *Screen.*

THOMAS ELSAESSER teaches film and English at the University of East Anglia, Norwich, England. Formerly editor of the British film journal *Monogram,* he has published in *Screen, Sight and Sound, Framework, Wide Angle, October, American Film,* and other journals.

BRIAN HENDERSON is Professor of Film at the State University of New York at Buffalo. He is the author of *A Critique of Film Theory* (1980) and editor of *Five Screenplays of Preston Sturges* (1985).

JANE FEUER teaches film and popular culture at the University of Pittsburgh. She is the author of *The Hollywood Musical* (1982) and co-author (with Paul Kerr and Tise Vahimagi) of *MTM: Quality Television* (1984).

SETH FELDMAN teaches film studies at York University in Toronto. He is the author of *Dziga Vertov: A Guide to References and Resources* (1979), co-editor (with Joyce Nelson) of *Canadian Film Reader* (1977), and editor of *Take Two: A Tribute to Film in Canada* (1984). He has also produced a number of radio documentaries for the Canadian Broadcasting Corporation, including studies of the film and video documentary.

JIM LEACH teaches film and dramatic literature at Brock University, St. Catharines, Ontario. He is the author of *A Possible Cinema: The Films of Alain Tanner* (1984) and has published in such journals as *Wide Angle, Literature/Film Quarterly,* and *Cinema Canada.*

Index

Boldface page numbers indicate photographs.

A bout de souffle (*Breathless*),
115–116, 170
Ace in the Hole, 179
Act of Violence, 178
Adorno, Theodore, 41, 286
Air Force, 110
Air Mail, 212
Airport, 219, 224
Airport 75, 219, 224–225, 230–231
Akins, Claude, 152
Al Capone, 162
Aldrich, Robert, 179, 180
Alger, Horatio, Jr., 160–162, 171,
181
Alien, **244,** 245, 248
All I Desire, 290, 298, 305, 306
All in the Family (TV series), 350
All That Heaven Allows, 51, 81,
295–296
All the King's Men, 295
All the President's Men, 116
All through the Night, 35
Aloha Bobby and Rose, 116
Althusser, Louis, xiii, 75–76, 86
Altman, Rick, 244–245
Altman, Robert, 199, 208, 359
Alton, John, 173–174
Amazing Colossal Man, The, 218
American in Paris, An, 343 n
American Werewolf in London, An,
239
Ami des lois, L', 282

Amis, Kingsley, 262
Anderson, Bronco Billy, 206–207
Andromeda Strain, The, 230
Andy Hardy films, 62
Angel, 326
Anthony Adverse, 51, 55
Antonioni, Michelangelo, 9
Arcand, Denys, 364–366
Aristophanes, 192
Aristotle, 11, 102, 106, 108–109,
113, 309, 312, 327 n
Arnheim, Rudolf, 114
Arnold, Francis, 258
Arzner, Dorothy, 80
Astaire, Fred, 55, 98, 121, 129, 225,
330, 331, 333, 340
Astor, Mary, 135
Astounding Science Fiction, 242
Atlantis, 219
Atomic Kid, The, 218
Attack of the Crab Monsters, 221
Atwood, Margaret, 357, 367
auteurism, xi–xiii, 3, 8, 19–20, 22,
51, 59–73, 75, 79–80, 126
Avventura, L', 9
Awful Truth, The, 313, 318, 322,
323–326

Bacall, Lauren, 177, 187, 287
Bacchae, The (Euripides), 242
Back Street (1932), 51; (1961), 57 n
Bacon, Lloyd, 288

Bacon, Roger, 262
Bad and the Beautiful, The, 298
Badlands, 116, 322
Balazs, Bela, 103
ballet, 291, 314
Balzac, Honoré de, 75–76, 284–285
Band Wagon, The, 55, 131, 330–343
Barkleys of Broadway, The, 330–342
Barry, Philip, 317
Barthes, Roland, xii, xiii, 150–152, 349
Bates, Harry, 249
Battle in the Clouds, 219
Battle of Algiers, The, 347
Bazin, André, xi, xiv, 4, 59, 93
Beast from 20,000 Fathoms, The, 218, 243
Beauty and the Beast, 240
Beauvoir, Simone de, 320
Bed-Sitting Room, The, 222–223
Beginning of the End, The, 218
Bellamy, Ralph, 313
Bells of St. Mary's, The, 80–81
Ben, 217
Bend of the River, 291
Benson, Sally, 67
Benveniste, Emile, 130, 133, 322–323
Beowulf, 246
Berger, John, xiii
Berger, Thomas, 196
Bergman, Ingmar, 9
Bergson, Henri, 309
Berkeley, Busby, 55, 104, 288
Bernhardt, Curtis, 173
Berrigan brothers, 347
Bettelheim, Bruno, 349
Between Friends, 361, 362, 362, 365–366
Beyond the Forest, 290
B films, 75, 78, 79, 181, 294
Bidney, David, 95
Big Bus, The, 223–225, 223, 227–229, 231
Big Carnival, The. See Ace in the Hole
Big Clock, The, 178
Big Combo, The, 173, 174, 175–176, 179

Big Flame, The, 352
Bigger than Life, 137, 298, 305
Big Heat, The, 64, 162–64, 163, 166, 174, 179
Big Sky, The, 153–154
Big Sleep, The (1946), 172, 174, 178, 183, 185, 187, 188
Bingo, 363
Bird of Paradise, 51–52
Birds, The, 217–218, 225–226, 228–229, 232
Birth of a Nation, 207, 282, 346
Black Bird, The, 190
black humor, 191
Black Mask, 183
Blair, Linda, 225
Blazing Saddles, 190–193
Blob, The, 221
Blood Wedding, 253
Blow Out, 253, 255
Blow-Up, 255
Blue Dahlia, The, 172
Boetticher, Budd, 18
Bogart, Humphrey, 19–20, 177, 183, 187
Bogdanovich, Peter, 35, 198, 199
Bonnie and Clyde, 116, 190, 195, 197–198
Boomerang!, 178
Born for Hell, 363
Born to be Bad, 307n
Borzage, Frank, 58n
Boy and His Dog, A, 223, 228
Boys from the Blackstuff, 347
Bracken, Eddie, 313
Bradley, A. C., 309
Brahm, John, 173, 180
Brainstorm, 256
Braudy, Leo, 29, 202–203, 207, 213, 215n
Breaking Away, 211
Breathless. See A bout de souffle
Brecht, Bertolt, xiii, 279
Bride of Frankenstein, The, 239, 250, 269–271
Brigadoon, 54
Bringing Up Baby, 62, 64, 127, 310,

311, **312**, 318, 323
Britton, Andrew, 61
Broken Arrow, 52
Broken Blossoms, 282
Bronson, Charles, 5
Brooks, Mel, 190, 192–193, 199
Brute Force, 178
Buchanan, R., 279
Buffalo Bill and the Indians, 208
Bujold, Genevieve, 225
Bullitt, 114, 225
Buñuel, Luis, 115, 307n
Burch, Noel, xiii
Burke, Kenneth, 93, 311
Burn!, 56
Byron, Lord, 279

Cabaret, 343n
Cabinet of Dr. Caligari, The, 251, 254
Cabiria, 222
Caged Heat, 84
Cagney, James, **165, 167,** 178, 295
Cahiers du Cinéma, 29, 35, 74
Cain, James M., 174
Cain and Mable, 335
Call Northside 777, 172, 178
Campbell, John, Jr., 242–243, 250
Camus, Albert, 174
Capote, Truman, 344
Capra, Frank, 62–73
Captain Blood, 56
Carey, Harry, 206–207
Carné, Marcel, 170
Carrie, 237
Cars That Ate Paris, The, 219
Casablanca, 19–20, 178
Cassidy, Hopalong, 62–63
Cassirer, Ernst, 95
Catastrophe of the Balloon "Le Pax," 217
Cat Ballou, 5–6, 192
Cather, Willa, 307n
Cathy Come Home, 347
Cat People (1942), 60, 62, 64
Caughie, John, 351, 354–355
Caught, 179

Cawelti, John G., 29, 31, 94–97, 100n, 109, 202
CBC (Canadian Broadcasting Company), 344–345, 354
Chabrol, Claude, 67, 114
Chamberlain, Richard, 225
Chandler, Raymond, 174–176, 177–178, 183, 184, 186
Chang, 252
Changeling, The, 359
Channing, Stockard, 231
Chapman Report, The, 304
Charlie Varrick, 112
Chat dans le sac, Le, 358, 368n
Cheyenne Autumn, 8, 126, 198, 212, 215n
Chicago Deadline, 177
China Syndrome, The, 347
Chinatown, 183–192, **189,** 194, 199
Chisum, 204
Christie, Agatha, 185
cinéma vérité, 346
Cinétique, 86
Cité foudroyée, La, 219
Citizen Kane, 105
City of Angels (TV series), 193
Clansman, The (Dixon), 346
Clarissa (Richardson), 280–281
Clarke, Arthur C., 242
classical narrative film, xiii, 60, 74–90, 294
Cliff, Jimmy, 163
Clock, The, 297
Close Encounters of the Third Kind, 244, 247
Cobweb, The, 288, 290, 297, 300–301, 304
Cocteau, Jean, 115
Colbert, Claudette, 19
Coleridge, Samuel Taylor, 242
Collins, Jim, 130
Collins, Wilkie, 284
Collision and Shipwreck at Sea, 217
Colossus: The Forbin Project, 221, 231
Comden, Betty, 330–331
comedy, 62, 190, 309–328

Comolli, Jean-Louis, 74, 76–77, 120, 132–133
Conquest of Space, 262, 271
Constant, Benjamin, 54
Conte, Richard, 178
contextualism, 114–128
Conversation, The, 255
Conway, Jack, 55–56
Cook, Pam, 78
Cooper, Gary, 16
Cooper, James Fenimore, 147–148, 155–156, 183, 193
Cooper, Merian C., 252
Coppola, Francis Ford, 198
Corman, Roger, 123
Cornered, 172
Corti, Maria, 87–88
Covered Wagon, The, 104
Coward, Noel, 314, 318
Cowboys, The, 103
Craven, Wes, 80
Crawford, Joan, 58n
Creature from the Black Lagoon, The, 218
Cremonini, Cesare, 75–76
crime films, 38, 87, 169–172, 178–179, 180, 359
Criminal, The, 292
Cromwell, John, 180
Cronenberg, David, 80, 233–235, 364
Crosby, Bing, 222
Cruze, James, 24
Cry of the City, 178
Cukor, George, 54–55, 287, 302, 304, 317, 320
Culloden, 347, 352
Curtiz, Michael, 19–20, 56, 80, 177
Cyclops, The, 218

D.O.A., 174, 179
Dain Curse, The (Hammett), 183
Daisy Kenyon, 305
Dames, 329–330, 339
Darby, Kim, 193
Dark Mirror, The, 178
Dark Passage, 178

Dark Past, The, 177
Dark Victory, 133
Dark Waters, 178
Darwin, Charles, 160
Dassin, Jules, 172, 178, 180
Daves, Delmer, 51–52, 156–157
Davis, Bette, 78, 133
Davis, Peter, 348
Dawn of the Dead, 250
Day After, The, 349–352
Day at the Races, A, 61
Day of the Triffids, The, 220
Days of Wine and Roses, 303
Day the Earth Caught Fire, The, 222, 276
Day the Earth Stood Still, The, 47, 220, 222, **245–247**, 249, 268–269
Day the Sky Exploded, The, 222
Day the World Ended, The, 222
Dead Reckoning, 172, 178
Dead Zone, The, 359
Death Line, 219
Death Weekend, 361, 364
de Antonio, Emile, 348
Demarest, William, 313
DeMille, Cecil B., 52, 222
Demons of the Swamp, 231
de Rochemont, Louis, 172
Deserto Rosso, Il, 9
Design for Living, 314–315; (Coward), 318
Designing Woman, 297
Destination Moon, 242, 244, 276
detective fiction, 183, 185
detective films, 105, 110–111, 135, 183–190, 194
Detective Story, 179
de Toth, André, 180
Detour, 292
Dewey, John, 117, 119
Dickens, Charles, 284–285
Dickinson, Angie, 16, 17
Dickstein, Morris, 119
Dieterle, William, 119
Dietrich, Marlene, 53, 58n, 288
disaster films, 38, 116, 217–235, 359
Disher, Maurice Wilson, 307n

Dishonored, 53
Dixon, Thomas, Jr., 346
Dmytryk, Edward, 180
Dr. Jekyll and Mr. Hyde (1931), 258, 269; (Stevenson), 37
docudrama, 344–356
Dolce Vita, La, 9
Donovan's Reef, 52
Don't Look Now, 250
Dostoyevsky, Feodor, 286
Double Indemnity, 133, 174, 176, 178, **292**
Douglas, Gordon, 180
Douglas, Kirk, 16
Doulos, Le, 170
Dracula (1930), 44–**46**, 79, 104–105, 221, 254; (1979), 239
Dragnet (TV series), 180
Drake, Francis, 251
Dreamworks, 245
Dreyer, Carl Theodore, 214
Drums along the Mohawk, 31, 33, 60
Dunaway, Faye, 187
Durgnat, Raymond, 169–170, 177
Duvivier, Julien, 170
Dwan, Allan, 51–52
Dyer, Richard, 40
Dylan, Bob, 116

Earp, Wyatt, 215n
Earth Dies Screaming, The, 221
Earthquake, 116, 218–219, 224, 228–231
Earth vs. the Flying Saucers, 46
Easter Parade, 55
East of Eden, 293
Eastwood, Clint, 5
Easy Rider, 169
Edison, Thomas A., 345
8½, 9
Eisenhower, Dwight D., 180
Eisenstein, Sergei, 114, 121
Eisler, Hanns, 286
Elam, Jack, 5
Elephant Walk, 217
Eliot, T. S., 126
Elsaesser, Thomas, 81, 82–83, 342

Emilia Galotti (Lessing), 280
Enchanted Island, 51
Enforcer, The, 175, 177
epic films, 55
Eruption of Mt. Pelee, The, 217
Every Day except Christmas, 352
Every Man Out of His Humor (Johnson), 310
Everything You Always Wanted to Know about Sex, 223
Executive Action, 116
Exhibitor's Trade Review, 206, 207
Exorcist, The, 221
Experiment Perilous, 296
exploitation films, 75, 78, 79
Exterminating Angel, The, 224

Face-Off, 363–364
Fade to Black, 116
Fail-Safe, 242
Fallen Angel, 178
Fantastic Voyage, 232
Farewell, My Lovely, 186
"Farewell to the Master" (Bates), 249
Fassbinder, Rainer Werner, 114
Fell, John, 94
Fellini, Federico, 9, 115
Feuer, Jane, 40, 130, 132
Fiedler, Leslie, 156
Fighting Seabees, The, 121
film noir, 20, 36, 62, 75, 79, 81, 82–88, 116, 133–135, 167–182, 184, 323
Filon, Pierre Marie Augustin, 306–307n
Fires Were Started, 222, 352
Fiske, John, 350–351
Five, 225
5,000 Fingers of Dr. T., The, 253
Five Women, 352
Flaherty, Robert, 345
Fleischer, Richard, 180
Fleming, Victor, 204
Flight of the Phoenix, The, 221
Fly, The, 248
Flynn, Errol, 57, 110
Focillon, Henri, 202–203

Fonda, Henry, 5, 121, 313
Fonda, Jane, 116
Food of the Gods, 225, 228, 230, 232
Foolish Wives, 286
Forbidden Planet, 221, 244, 248, 259–262, 260, 261, 269
Forbin Project, The, 221, 231
Force of Evil, 178
Ford, Francis, 207
Ford, John, 18, 24, 35, 52, 62, 63, 121, 126, 150–151, 153, 175, 198–199, 200, 207, 209–213, 214, 215n, 318, 362
formalism, 87
For the Record (TV series), 347, 354
Forty-Second Street, 294, 329, 330
Four Horsemen of the Apocalypse, The, 288–289
Frankenstein (1931), 44–45, 220, 239, 243, 245, 248–250, 259, 269–270; (Shelley), 37, 239, 250
Frankfurt School, 29
Free Cinema, 352
Freed Unit, 330, 342
French, Philip, 202
Freud, Sigmund, 109, 135, 190, 239–241, 251, 259, 265, 273, 284, 296–297, 304, 309–310, 324, 326, 328n
Freund, Karl, 173, 174, 239
Friday the 13th, 237, 241, 244, 253
Frogs, 217, 225, 228, 231–232
Frye, Northrop, xv, 27, 94–95, 100n, 111, 127, 144–147
Fulford, Robert, 362
Fuller, Samuel, 180
Funhouse, The, 241
Fun in Acapulco, 27
Furthman, Jules, 319, 320

Gable, Clark, 18
Gammick, La, 361, 365–366, 368n
Gandhi, 347
gangster films, xi–xii, 4, 13, 18–19, 35, 42–43, 48–49, 62, 99, 116, 158–168, 181–182, 294
Gardner, Ava, 225

Garland, Judy, 55
Garnet, Tony, 352
Garnett, Tay, 177
Gaslight, 178, 296
Geduld, Harry M., 102
genre: and acting, 19–20, 129–139; and audience, 29, 35–36, 93, 97, 102–113, 114–128; and auteur, xi–xiii, 3, 8, 19–20, 22, 59–73, 126; and characterization, 107–108, 121–122; and contextualism, 114–128; and conventions, xii, 5, 13–25, 57, 93, 98–99, 102; and criticism, xi–xiii, 11–13, 25–39, 59–62, 74–90, 91–101, 114–128, 129–139, 158, 202–216; and culture, 6–9, 40, 95–97, 109; definitions of, 3–10, 11–24, 26–39; evolution of, 33–35, 39, 183–201, 202–216; and expectations, 8, 18, 115; and experience, 38, 114–128; and feminism, 74–76, 86; and formalism, 87; iconography, 21, 105–106; ideology, xii–xiii, xv, 29, 30, 35–36, 41–49, 50–57, 59–73, 74–90, 109–111, 120–121, 127; and language, 96, 322–333; and literature, 11–13, 26–39, 87–88, 103–104, 190–193; and Marxism, xiii, 74–77, 86; and myth, xii, xiii, 29, 30, 35–36, 93–97, 115–117, 184, 198–199, 331; and narrative, 26–40, 82, 83, 92, 98–99, 102–106, 111–113, 143–158; and national cinema, xv, 9, 357–369; parody, 5, 190–193; and popular culture, 93–94, 99, 191; and psychoanalysis, 20, 74–77, 239–241; and semiology, xiii, 27–28, 33, 74–77, 87; and spectating subject, xii, 35, 114–128; and star system, 22–23, 98, 121–122, 225; and structuralism, xii–xiii, 28, 74–77, 99–101. *See also individual genres*
German expressionism, 46, 87, 170, 172–174, 175, 184, 287
Gestalt psychology, 239–241

Ghost Story, 241; (Straub), 236–237
Giant Gila Monster, The, 218, 237
Giant Leeches, The, 231
Gigi, 53
Gilda, 178
Gina, 365–366, 368n
Glass Key, The, 171, 178, 183
Gledhill, Christine, 82
G-Men, 35
Godard, Jean-Luc, 114, 342
Godbout, Jacques, 366
Godfather, The, 49, 126, 190, 198
Godfather II, 164
Godzilla, 218
Gojira, 243
Golem, Der, 220
Gombrich, E. H., 143, 146
Gone with the Wind, 222
Good Guys and the Bad Guys, The, 5
Gordon, Ruth, 225, 320
Gorgo, 218
Gortner, Marjoe, 225
Gottesman, Ronald, 102
Graduate, The, 319–320
Graham, Billy, 46
Grant, Cary, 16
Grapes of Wrath, The, 210, 212
Great Day in the Morning, 291
Great Train Robbery, The (1902),
  xi–xii, 103, 204, 205
Green, Adolph, 330–331
Greenberg, Joel, 20, 170
Greene, Graham, 177
Green Slime, The, 221
Grey Gardens, 346
Grierson, John, 345, 349, 352–353,
  358
Griffi, Giuseppi Patroni, 9
Griffith, D. W., 50, 126, 175, 282,
  346
Grizzly, 227, 229
Gun Crazy, 84, 85, 178–179, 182
Gunfighter, The, 204
*Guns in the Afternoon. See Ride the
  High Country*

Halloween, 237
Halloween II, 253
Hammer Studios, 123
Hammett, Dashiell, 174, 177, 183,
  184, 186
Hangover Square, 53
Harcourt, Peter, 362
Harder They Come, The, 163, 164
Hardy, Oliver, 222
Harold and Maude, 225
Harrison, Rex, 55
Hart, William S., 206–207
Harte, Bret, 193
Hartley, John, 350–351
Harvey, Sylvia, 81, 83
Hathaway, Henry, 172, 178, 180
Hawks, Howard, 121, 126, 152–154,
  180, 200, 242, 250, 287, 295,
  311–312, 318–319, 320
Hayden, Tom, 116
Hay Fever (Coward), 314
Hays Code, 18, 71
Hays Office, 178
Heart of Darkness (Conrad), 238,
  250
Heath, Stephen, 88
Hecht, Ben, 314–315
Hegel, G. W. F., 309, 320
Heidi, 52–53
Heine, Heinrich, 279
Heisler, Stuart, 180
He Knows You're Alone, 253
Hell Bent, 206
Hellinger, Mark, 172
Hellstrom Chronicle, The, 232
Hemingway, Ernest, 174
Hepburn, Audrey, 54
Hepburn, Katharine, 78
Hernadi, Paul, 30
Heston, Charlton, 225, 229–230
High, Wide and Handsome, 31
Higham, Charles, 20, 170
High and the Mighty, The, 219
High Anxiety, 190
High Noon, 10, 15, 193, 204
High Sierra, 162–163
Highway Patrol (TV series), 180

Hilda Crane, 61, 290, 299, 303
Hills Have Eyes, The, 79, 82
Hill Street Blues (TV series), 350
Hindenberg, The, 219, 224–225, 227, 230–232
Hiroshima Mon Amour, 9
His Girl Friday, 295, 313, 318, 322, 325
historical films, 56
Hitchcock, Alfred, 18, 20, 36, 62–73, 106, 114, 180, 280, 287, 296, 305
H-Man, The, 221
Hobbes, Thomas, 234
Hoda, F., 258, 268
Hodgens, Richard, 258
Hoffer, Tom W., 346–348, 352–353
Hoffman, Dustin, 196
Holiday, 313, 318, 323, 325
Holliday, Judy, 55
Holocaust, 349–352
Hombre, 219
Home from the Hill, 81, 84, 288, 291, 300–302
Homer, 103, 106
Hooper, Tobe, 241
Hope, Bob, 222
horror films, xiii, 4, 19, 34, 35, 37, 42–43, 46, 62, 75, 78–80, 81, 82–84, 111, 119, 122–123, 221, 236–257
Hour of the Gun, 204, 209
House of Wax, 253
House on Haunted Hill, The, 253
House on 92nd Street, The, 172, 178
Houston, Penelope, 258
Hoveyda, Fereydoun, 258
How Green Was My Valley, 211, 212
Howling, The, 239, 250
Hugo, Victor, 279, 284–285
Hunt, Albert, 351
Hurricane, The (1937), 52, 212, 218
Huston, John, 180, 286

I, the Jury (1953), 174, 179; (Spillane), 186
I am Legend (Matheson), 249–250
Iliad, The (Homer), 106

Imitation of Life (1959), 51, 82, 298, 306
In a Lonely Place, 179
Ince, Thomas, 207
Incident, The, 219
In Cold Blood, 344
Incredible Shrinking Man, The, 218–220, 271–274
Incredibly Strange Creatures Who Stopped Living and Became Zombies, The, 221
Informer, The, 212
In Name Only, 58n
Interlude, 296
Interrupted Honeymoon, The, 217
In the King of Prussia, 347, 348
Intolerance, 217, 282
Invasion of the Body Snatchers (1956), 46, 47, 221, 253, 274–275
Invasion USA, 220
Iron Horse, The, 104
It Came from beneath the Sea, 218
It Came from Outer Space, 268–269, 274
It Conquered the World, 221
It Happened One Night, 18, 325
It's Alive, 68, 81
It's Always Fair Weather, 343n
It's a Mad, Mad, Mad, Mad World, 222
It's a Wonderful Life, 60–73, 66, 67, 82

Jackson County Jail, 81
Jakobson, Roman, 87, 96
James, Henry, 242
Jameson, Frederic, 30, 40
Jaws, 217, 227–230
Jazz Singer, The (1927), 329
Jenkins, Dan, 315
Jesse James, 207
Jetée, La, 249
Joffe, Roland, 353
Johnny O'Clock, 178
Johnson, Samuel, 11, 103
Jones, James, 288
Jones, Jennifer, 225

Jonson, Ben, 310
Juggernaut, 227
Juliet of the Spirits, 9
Jump Cut, 29
Jung, Carl G., 239–241

Kabale und Liebe (Schiller), 280
Kafka, Franz, 286
Kaminsky, Stuart, 91–92
Kanin, Garson, 320
Kaplan, Abraham, 119
Kaplan, E. Ann, 77–78
Karlson, Phil, 180
Kawin, Bruce, 119
Kazan, Elia, 178, 180
Keaton, Buster, 129, 251, 309–310
Kelly, Gene, 57, 331
Killers, The (1946), 172, 174, 177, 178
Killing, The, 177
King, Stephen, 242, 249–250
King Kong (1933), 79, 218, 251–252, 254
Kinsey, Alfred Charles, 269
Kiss Me Deadly, 81, 169, 179, 182
Kiss of Death, 172, 178
Kiss Tomorrow Goodbye, 169, 174, 178–179, 182
Kitses, Jim, 4, 16, 17–19, 23, 31, 92–93, 95
Knight, Arthur, 92, 170
Kracauer, Siegfried, 259
Krakatoa, East of Java, 218
Kronos, 218
Kubrick, Stanley, 180
Kwaidan, 253

La Cava, Gregory, 311
Ladd, Alan, 5, 6, 177
Lady from Shanghai, The, 176, 280
Lake, Veronica, 177
Lancaster, Burt, 178
Lanchester, Elsa, 271
Lang, Fritz, 115, 121, 173, 180, 287
Langer, Suzanne, 115
Last Days of Pompeii, The, 218–219, 222

Last Hurrah, The, 3
Last Laugh, The, 251
Last Wave, The, 241, 250, 254
Laura, 171, 176, 178
Laurel, Stan, 222
Lawrence, D. H., 125
Laya, Jean-Louis, 282
Leach, Edmund, 96–97
Lee, Christopher, 105
Lefebvre, Jean-Pierre, 368–369n
Lefèvre, Raymond, 258
Left-Handed Gun, The, 195, 291
Leo the Last, 222
LeRoy, Mervyn, 56
Lessing, Gotthold Ephraim, 280
Letter from an Unknown Woman, 53
Levenc, Sam, 347
Leviathan (Hobbes), 234
Lévi-Strauss, Claude, 27–29, 38, 93, 96–97, 115, 312, 331, 335, 342, 343n
Lewis, Joseph H., 180
Lewton, Val, 55, 122
Lifeboat, 221, 225–226
Lineup (TV series), 180
Lion in the Streets, A, 295
Little Big Man, 52, 194–197, 196
Little Caesar, 48–49, 104, 121, 122, 164, 165, 182, 295
Litvak, Anatole, 173
Lloyd, Peter, 291
Loach, Ken, 352
Locket, The, 82
Lodger, The (1926), 286; (1944), 178
Lombard, Carole, 58n
Loneliness of the Long Distance Runner, The, 352
Lonely Are the Brave, 13
Lone Ranger, The, 154–155
Long, Long Trailer, The, 290
Long Goodbye, The, 190, 194, 199
Long Wait, The, 179
Lorre, Peter, 108
Losey, Joseph, 180, 287, 300
Lost Weekend, The, 178
Lost World, The, 218
Loth, Jean, 258

Lovecraft, H. P., 242
Lubitsch, Ernst, 287, 311, 314, 318, 326–327
Lugosi, Bela, 45, 105, 108
Lumière, Auguste and Louis, 345
Lump, The, 352

M*A*S*H, 190
Mabuse films, 170
McArthur, Colin, 92–93
McCabe and Mrs. Miller, 194, 199, 208
McCarey, Leo, 313
McConnell, Frank, 29, 202, 215–216n
McCoy, Horace, 174
McCrea, Joel, 313
Macdonald, John D., 184
Macdonald, Ross, 184, 186
McGraw, Charles, 178
MacLaine, Shirley, 54
McLean, Albert F., 331
MacMurray, Fred, 178
Madame Bovary (Flaubert), 307n
Mad Love, 238–240, 250–251, 254
Made for Each Other, 58n
Magnificent Obsession (1954), 83, 254
Magnificent Seven, The, 10
Mahagonny (Brecht), 279
Major Dundee, 8
Malinowski, Bronislav, 95, 115
Maltese Falcon, The (1931), 183; (1941), 103–104, 105, 135, 136, 170, 171, 178, 183, 185, 188; (Hammett), 183, 186
Mankiewicz, Joseph H., 80
Mann, Anthony, 18, 180, 295
Man Who Shot Liberty Valance, The, 3, 126, 198, 204, 210–211
Mare, Il, 9
Margie, 298
Marie Antoinette, 56
Marnie, 62
Marooned, 221, 276
Marriage Circle, The, 326
Marseillaise, La, 133

Marsh, Ngaio, 185
martial arts films, 108
Martin, Dean, 152
Marvin, Lee, 6, 7, 178
Marxism, 75–77, 86
Mask of Dimitrios, The, 172, 178
Massey, Raymond, 52
Mast, Gerald, 92
Maté, Rudolph, 173, 180
Matheson, Richard, 249–250
Maudite Galette, La, 365, 366, 368n
Mayerling, 53
Mean Streets, 165–166
Medea (Euripides), 242
Medium Cool, 169
Meeker, Ralph, 179
Meet Me in St. Louis, 53, 298
Méliès, Georges, 217, 345
melodrama, 34, 36, 53, 54, 58n, 75, 79–80, 81, 82–84, 86, 119, 135–137, 169, 172, 278–308
Menander, 312
Metropolis, 219, 259
Metz, Christian, 33, 127, 133, 202, 207
MGM Studios, 330–331, 340–342
Mildred Pierce, 81, 174, 177, 178
Milne, Tom, 258
Minnelli, Vincente, 34, 36, 54–55, 80, 287–290, 294, 297, 300–302, 304
Minow, Newton, 352
Miracle of Merriford, The, 212
Misérables, Les (Hugo), 284–285
Misfortunes of an Explorer, The, 217
Mr. Smith Goes to Washington, 210
Mitchum, Robert, 193
Mitry, Jean, 30–31
Mix, Tom, 206
Mizoguchi, Kenji, 287, 307n
Moby Dick (Melville), 156
Monthly Film Bulletin, 258
Monvel, J. M. Boutet de, 282
Morgan!, 319
Morocco, 319
Mothra, 218
M-Squad (TV series), 180

Mummy, The, 44–46, 239, 254
Mummy's Ghost, The, 237, 241, 253
Murder, My Sweet, 178
Murnau, F. W., 287
musical films, 18–19, 34, 35–36, 38,
   53, 54, 58n, 88, 116, 130–132,
   294, 329–344
Musketeers of Pig Alley, The, xii
My Bloody Valentine, 241
My Darling Clementine, 10, 63, 64,
   150–154, **152, 153,** 156, 204,
   209–210, 215n
My Fair Lady, 53, 54–55
Mystères de Paris (Sue), 284
myth, 85–97. *See also* genre: and
   myth

Nachbar, Jack, 202–203, 209
Naked City, The, 178
Naked Jungle, The, 217
Naked Prey, The, 221
Nanook of the North, 345
Narboni, Jean, 74, 76–77, 120
narrative, 26–40, 82–83, 92, 98–99,
   143–147
Nashville, 190, 199
National Film Board of Canada, 353–
   354, 358
Neale, Stephen, 88, 354–355
Nelson, Richard Alan, 346–348,
   352–353
Neo-Aristotelians, 12
Neptune Factor, The, 219, 230
New Criticism, 12
New Journalism, 344
Nicholson, Jack, 187, **188**
Nietzsche, Friedrich, 109, 306
Night Moves, 195
Night of the Blood Beast, 221
Night of the Living Dead, 79, 122–
   126, **125,** 221, 224, 226, 229,
   236–237, 250
Night to Remember, A, 219
1984 (1955), 228
Nixon, Richard, 46, 116
No Blade of Grass, 224, 228, 231
Nobody Waved Goodbye, 358

No Highway in the Sky, 219
Nosferatu (1922), 104–105, 221,
   236, 239, 242
Not of This Earth, 221
Notorious, 296
Nôtre-Dame de Paris (Hugo), 284
Nouvelle Héloïse, La (Rousseau), 280
Nowell-Smith, Geoffrey, 135
Nyby, Christian, 242, 250

Odyssey, The (Homer), 106
O'Hara, John, 174
O Haru, 307n
Oliver Twist (Dickens), 284
Olsen-Johnson films, 222
Omega Man, The, 230
Once Upon a Time in the West, 5,
   121, 207
On Dangerous Ground, 179, 307n
One Hour with You, 326
On est au coton, 365, 368n
On est loin du soleil, 365, 368n
Only Angels Have Wings, 219, 223,
   295, 319
*On n'engraisse pas les cochons a l'eau
   claire. See Pigs Are Seldom Clean*
On the Beach, 221
opera, 279, 291, 314
Ophuls, Max, 54, 173, 180, 214, 287
Oppenheimer, 347
Orphans of the Storm, 51, 282, 283
Our Hospitality, 309
Out of the Past, 62, 176–177, 179,
   292
Ox-Bow Incident, The, 204

Pal, George, 258
Palance, Jack, 5
Panic in the Streets, 179
Panic in the Year Zero, 221
Panofsky, Erwin, 287
Panorama du film noir (Borde and
   Chaumeton), 181
Paperback Hero, 361, 362, 363
Parallax View, The, 116
Paramount Studios, 178
Parasite Murders, The. See Shivers

parody, 5, 190–193
Partisan Review, xi, 181
Partners, 361
Pascal, Blaise, 322
Peckinpah, Sam, 10, 18, 22–24, 126,
    199, 359
Peeping Tom, 250, 253–255
Penn, Arthur, 195–198, 199
Pennies from Heaven, 126
Pepper, Stephen C., 119–120, 126–
    127
Perls, Fritz, 239–241
Perrault, Pierre, 358
Pet Sematary (King), 256
Petulia, 225
Phantom of the Opera (1925), 251;
    (Leroux), 238
Phase IV, 217
Philadelphia Story, The, 318
Pickup on South Street, 180
Picture of Dorian Gray, The, 53
Pigs Are Seldom Clean, 365–366,
    368–369n
Pilgrimage, 212
Pirate, The, 55, 57, 341, 343n
Pitfall, The, 178
Plague of the Zombies, 221
Planet of the Apes, 221, 222
Plan 9 from Outer Space, 221
Poe, Edgar Allan, 242
Polanski, Roman, 184, 187, 189, 191,
    194, 198
political conspiracy films, 116
Poltergeist, 241
Pontecorvo, Gillo, 56
Pope, Alexander, 103
popular culture, 119–120. *See also*
    genre: and popular culture
Poseidon Adventure, The, 116, 227,
    229–230, 232
Possessed, 137
Postman Always Rings Twice, The
    (1946), 176, 178
Prairie, The (Cooper), 147
Preminger, Otto, 173, 180, 287
Presley, Elvis, 27
Price, Vincent, 108

Prisoner of Shark Island, The, 56, 212
Projected Man, The, 275–276
Prologue, 361
Propp, Vladimir, 27–28, 93, 131, 349
Psycho, 20, 79, 80, 84, 117–119,
    122, 251, 253
psychoanalytical criticism, 20, 238–
    241, 258–277, 301
Public Enemy, The, 48, 104, 162–
    164, 182
Pynchon, Thomas, 191
Pyx, The, 359–361, 360, 362

Quatermass Experiment, The, 221
Quebec: Duplessis and After, 365
Quemada, 56
Quiet Man, The, 212

Racine, Jean Baptiste, 103
Raging Bull, 347
Rainer, Yvonne, 319
Rains Came, The, 218
Rains of Ranchipur, The, 218
Rampage, 62
Rango, 252
Raw Deal, 174, 178, 323
Raw Meat, 219
Ray, Nicholas, 179, 180, 287, 294,
    296, 298, 300, 302, 305, 307n
Reade, Charles, 284
realism, 54, 58n, 78, 104, 172–174
Real People, 344
Rear Window, 253
Rebecca, 66, 296
Rebel without a Cause, 294
Recherche de l'absolu, La (Balzac), 37
Red Badge of Courage, The, 286
Red Harvest (Hammett), 183
Red Planet Mars, 220
Red River, 32, 121, 126, 153–154
Reinhard, Gottfried, 286
Reinhardt, Max, 287
Réjeanne Padovani, 365–366
Remington, Frederic, 149, 206
Renoir, Jean, 115, 180, 287
reporter films, 38
Reptilicus, 218

Repulsion, 254
Resnais, Alain, 9
Richards, Dick, 193
Richardson, Samuel, 280–281
Ricoeur, Paul, 343 n
Ride the High Country, 8, 10, 22–24, 23, 192, 193
Ride the Pink Horse, 172, 178
Rio Bravo, 16, 17, 152–154, 206, 319
"Rip Van Winkle" (Irving), 156
Rise and Fall of Legs Diamond, The, 295
Ritchie, Michael, 315
RKO Studios, 330
Roaring Twenties, The, 167, 171, 295
Robinson, Edward G., 121, 122, 123, 124, 166
Rodan, 218
Rogers, Ginger, 330, 340
Rogers, Roy, 3, 62
Rohmer, Eric, 67
romantic comedy, 18, 309–328
Romero, George, 122, 236–237, 247, 250
Roots, 347, 349–351
Rose, Ruth, 252
Ross, Lillian, 286
Rossellini, Roberto, 214
Rossen, Robert, 180
Rothman, Stephanie, 80
Rousseau, Jean-Jacques, 280
Ruby Gentry, 280
Run of the Arrow, 291
Russ, Joanna, 237, 248
Ruthless, 178
Ryan, Robert, 178

Sade, Marquis de, 282
Salem's Lot (King), 249–250
Salesman, 346
Samson and Delilah, 222
Sands of the Kalahari, 221, 225, 228
San Francisco, 222, 232
Sarris, Andrew, xi, 19, 35
Saturday Night and Sunday Morning, 352

Saussure, Ferdinand de, 27–28, 96
Savage Is Loose, The, 221, 225, 228, 231
Sayers, Dorothy, 185
Scandal in Paris, A, 280
Scarface (1932), 48, 162, 164, 176, 182, 295
Scarlet Drop, The, 206
Scarlet Street, 121, 122, 123, 124, 178
Schaefer, Jack, 5
Schatz, Thomas, 29, 35, 202–207, 209–213
Schiller, Friedrich, 280
Schoedsack, Ernest B., 252
science fiction films, 35, 42–43, 46– 48, 79, 111, 117, 217, 221, 241– 250, 258–277
Scorsese, Martin, 165
Scott, Randolph, 16, 22–23
Scott, Walter, 279
Screen, 59
screwball comedy, 55, 62, 127, 312– 313
Sea Hawk, The, 56
Searchers, The, 60, 62, 65, 154–156, 198–199, 207, 210
Second Wind, 361, 364
Secret beyond the Door, 296
semiology, xiii, 27. *See also* genre: and semiology
Semi-Tough, 315–328
Sennett, Mack, 222
Senso, 284
Set-Up, The, 175, 178
Seventh Heaven, 58 n
Seventh Seal, The, 9, 224
Seven Women, 212
Shadow of a Doubt, 60–73, 69, 70, 81–82
Shakespeare, William, 120
Shall We Dance, 330, 340
Shane, 5, 6, 8, 62, 193, 204, 207
Shanghai Express, 319
Shary, Dore, 286
Shaw, Irwin, 288
Shebib, Don, 366

Sheen, Martin, 348
Shelley, Mary Wollstonecraft, 242
Sherlock, Jr., 251
Sherlock Holmes and the Voice of
    Terror, 35
She Wore a Yellow Ribbon, 212
Shinheike Monogatari, 307n
Shivers, 220–221, 233–235, 361,
    364
Shuster, Nat, 362
Siegel, Don, 180
Sign of the Pagan, 295
Silence, The, 9
Silkwood, 347
Sims, G. R., 279
Since You Went Away, 296, 299–300
Singin' in the Rain, 27, 55, 330–343
Siodmak, Curt, 259
Siodmak, Robert, 173, 180
Sirk, Douglas, 34, 36, 51, 57, 61, 80,
    83, 173, 278, 280, 287–289, 293–
    296, 298, 300, 302, 305–306
Sklar, Robert, 91–92
Slaughterhouse Five, 222
Sleep, My Love, 296
Sobchack, Thomas, 94–96
So Dark the Night, 178
Solomon, Stanley J., 91–92
Some Came Running, 280, 288–289
Sontag, Susan, xiv, 217
Soylent Green, 221
Spellbound, 61, 178
Spencer, Herbert, 160
Spider Woman, 269
Spillane, Mickey, 184, 186
Splendor in the Grass, 137, 291
Squawman, The (1913), 52; (1918),
    52; (1931), 52
Stack, Robert, 288
Stagecoach (1939), 4, 121, 126, 194,
    204, 207–212, 211, 215–216n,
    219
Stage Fright, 280
Stahl, John, 57n
Star Is Born, A (1954), 343n
Star Trek, 248
Star Trek II: The Wrath of Khan, 249

Star Trek III: In Search of Spock, 249
Star Trek (TV series), 249
Star Wars, 35, 208
Steiner, Max, 173
Stella Dallas, 305
Sternberg, Josef von, 50, 170, 214,
    287, 288, 319
Stevens, George, 5, 8
Stewart, James, 16, 295
Storch, Larry, 231
Strachey, James, 310
Straight Shootin' (1925), 207
Straight Shooting (1917), 207
Strange Love of Martha Ivers, The,
    178
Stranger, The (1946), 280; (Camus),
    174
Strangers on a Train, 280
Straub, Peter, 237
Stroheim, Erich von, 53
structural film, 114
structuralism, xiii, 27–28, 74–77,
    99–101
Student Nurses, 78
Sturges, Preston, 56–57, 313
Sue, Eugène, 284
Sugarland Express, The, 116
Sullivan's Travels, 56–57
Sumner, William Graham, 160
Sunset Boulevard, 134, 176, 179
Support Your Local Sheriff, 5
Surfacing (Atwood), 357, 367
Suspicion, 66, 296
Sutherland, Ronald, 357
Swanson, Gloria, 225
swashbucklers, 110

Take Me to Town, 280
Taking of Pelham One Two Three,
    The, 219
Tale of Two Cities, A, 55; (Dickens),
    284
Tarantula, 218
Targets, 224, 253
Tarnished Angels, The, 280, 294, 300
Tar Sands, The, 344, 356n
Taylor, Elizabeth, 231

Teenage Caveman, 222
television, 180, 184, 346–354
Tempest, The (Shakespeare), 221, 262
Temple, Shirley, 52
Ten Commandments, The (1923), 222; (1956), 222
Terminal Island, 82
Terror Strikes, The, 218
Tessier, Max, 307–308n
Texas Chainsaw Massacre, The, 79, 81, 241
That's Entertainment, 342
That's Entertainment, Part 2, 342
Them!, 217–218, 229, 254, 271, 275
Theophrastus, 312
Theory of Literature (Wellek and Warren), 12–13
There's Always Tomorrow, 306
There's No Business like Show Business, 62
They Came from Within. See Shivers
They Died with Their Boots On, 292
They Live by Night, 174, 175, 179
Thieves Highway, 178
Thieves like Us, 116, 199
Thin Man, The, 183
Thing, The (1951), 46, 220, 226, 228, 230, 242–248, 250, 256, 262–268, 263, 264, 271
Thing, The (1982), 250
Things to Come, 222
Third Man, The, 170
This Gun for Hire, 171, 178
This Island Earth, 247–248
This Sporting Life, 352
Three Bad Men, 210
Three Godfathers, 210
Three Mounted Men, 207
Threepenny Opera, The (Brecht), 279
3:10 to Yuma, 156–157
Three Women, 322
thrillers, 4, 18, 36, 62, 85
Tingler, The, 253
Titanic, 219
T-Men, 174, 175, 176, 178
To Be or Not to Be (1942), 51
Todorov, Tzvetan, 27–28, 30

To Have and Have Not, 178, 287–288, 319
Tom Sawyer (Twain), 316
Top Hat, 340
Tora! Tora! Tora!, 219
Touch of Evil, 170, 179
Tourneur, Jacques, 55–56
Towering Inferno, The, 116, 219, 225–226, 228–229, 231
Towne, Robert, 187
tragedy, 54, 119, 190, 192, 242
Treasure of the Golden Condor, 51–52
Trodd, Kenith, 352–353
Trouble in Paradise, 50
True Grit, 103, 193–194, 195
True Heart Susie, 286
Truffaut, François, 114
Tudor, Andrew, 115, 348
Turn of the Screw, The (James), 238, 250
Twain, Mark, 193
Twentieth Century, 295, 318
20 Million Miles to Earth, 47, 220, 258, 266–271
Twenty Million Sweethearts, 329
Two Rode Together, 8, 215n
2001: A Space Odyssey, 244, 249, 276
Two Weeks in Another Town, 288–289
Tyjanov, Jurij, 87
Typee (Melville), 51–52

Ulmer, Edgar G., 173
Unconquered, 31
Undead, The, 221
Undercurrent, 296
Underworld, 295
Underworld USA, 176
Union Station, 174, 178
United Kingdom, 353
Universal Studios, 122, 206
Unmarried Woman, An, 78

Vampyr, 242, 253–255, 254
Van Cleef, Lee, 5

Van Vogt, A. E., 243, 245
Vaughan, Robert, 225
Verdi, Giuseppi, 284
Vernet, Marc, 30–31
Vertigo, 253, 255
Victimes clôitrées, Les (Monvel), 282
Vidor, King, 180
Virginian, The, 43, 204
Volcano, 218

Wagner, Fritz, 174
Wagon Master, 126, 210, 212
Waking Up the Town, 219
Wallach, Eli, 5
Walsh, Raoul, 179, 180, 291, 295
Warner Brothers Studios, 56, 170, 175
war films, 110, 118, 227, 311
War Game, The, 221, 222, 228, 352
War o' Dreams, 219
War of the Colossal Beast, 218
War of the Worlds, 222, 224, 229, 258
Warren, Austin, 12–13
Warshow, Robert, xi–xii, xiv, 42, 43, 48–49, 62, 98, 109, 164, 181–182, 202–203, 213
Wasp Woman, 269
Waste Land, The (Eliot), 189–190
Watkins, Peter, 352
Waxman, Franz, 173
Way Down East, 282
Wayne, John, 16, 17, 98, 107–108, 121, 133, 152, 193, **194, 195**
We Are the Lambeth Boys, 352
Weekend, 219
Welch, Raquel, 232
Wellek, René, 12–13
Welles, Orson, 180, 280, 287
Wells, H. G., 242
western films, xi–xii, 3–10, 13–18, 30–31, 34, 35, 38, 40, 42–44, 62, 98–99, 111, 148–158, 183, 202–216
Westworld, 221
When Worlds Collide, 222
Where's Poppa?, 225

Where the Sidewalk Ends, 174, 179, 292
Whirlpool, 296
White, D. L., 119
White Heat, 18, 162, 164, **165**, 174, 179, 292, 295
"Who Goes There?" (Campbell), 250
Whole Town's Talking, The, 121, 212
Wichita, 291
Wild Bunch, The, 8, 10, 22, 190, 199, 204
Wilde, Cornell, 230
Wilder, Billy, 173
Wilder, Thornton, 67
Wild Strawberries, 9
Willard, 217–218, 221
Williams, Raymond, 22
Winchester 73, 15, 291
Winslow Boy, The, 35
Winston, Brian, 347–348
Winter Light, 9
Wise, Robert, 180
Wiseman, Frederick, 356n
Wittgenstein, Ludwig, 314
Wizard of Oz, The, 211, 240–241
Wolf Man, The, 44–46, 239, 250, 254
Wollen, Peter, xiii, 62
Woman in the Window, The, 178
Woman of the Ganges, 319
Woman on the Beach, The, 296
Woman's Secret, A, 307n
women's films, 75, 79–80, 296
Wood, Michael, 29, 91–92, 97, 99
Wood, Robin, 20, 78–79, 81–83, 117–118, 120, 241
World, the Flesh and the Devil, The, 221, 225
Wow, 361
Wright, Will, 29, 33, 35, 91–93, 99, 101n
Written on the Wind, 51, 81, 93, 94, 278, 289–290, 294, 297–298, 300, 302–305

X from Outer Space, 220
X the Unknown, 221

Yacowar, Maurice, 121
Young Frankenstein, 190, 191, 192
Young Mr. Lincoln, 35, 212
You Only Live Once, 171

Zabriskie Point, 222
Zanuck, Darryl F., Jr., 304
Zardoz, 228

Zeppelin, 219
Zero Population Growth, 222, 226
Ziegfield Girl, 335
Zinnemann, Fred, 83, 173
Zombies of the Stratosphere, 221
Zoo in Budapest, 53, 58n
Zu neuen Ufern, 280, 306